# THE EUROPEAN UNION AND INTERNATIONAL INVESTMENT LAW REFORM

In order to understand the reform of international investment law envisioned by the European Union (EU), the author provides a comprehensive but concise analysis of the EU reform approaches, its constitutional and legal framework, the concepts of the rule of law and legitimacy and the reasons for the reform. In particular, the book exposes tensions between the EU aspiration to enhance the rule of law in international investment law, as a means of legitimising this legal discipline, and the challenges of its reform approaches in practice. The analysis combines substantive and procedural aspects of the EU reform of international investment law in the intra-EU context and EU external relations. This book critically evaluates the EU vision of the rule of law in international law and its contribution to the development of international law in the field of investment.

IVANA DAMJANOVIC is an interdisciplinary researcher and legal scholar. Her research areas include international investment law, EU law and EU external trade and investment relations. She has a PhD from the Australian National University and master's degrees from the University College Dublin and the University of Zagreb. She is a qualified Australian lawyer and since 2016 has taught law at the University of Canberra, where she is a full-time faculty member. From 2004 to 2013 she was a member of the Croatian diplomatic service.

CAMBRIDGE INTERNATIONAL TRADE AND ECONOMIC LAW



Processes of economic regionalisation and globalisation have intensified over the last decades, accompanied by increases in the regulation of international trade and economics at the levels of international, regional and national laws. At the same time, significant challenges have arisen with respect to economic liberalization, rule-based systems of trade and investment, and their political and social impacts. The subject matter of this series is international economic law, in this contemporary context. Its core is the regulation of international trade, investment, finance and cognate areas such as intellectual property and competition policy. The series publishes books on related regulatory areas, in particular human rights, labour, environment and culture, as well as sustainable development. These areas are horizontally interconnected and vertically linked at the international, regional and national levels. The series also includes works on governance, dealing with the structure and operation of international organisations related to the field of international economic law, and the way they interact with other subjects of international and national law. The series aims to include excellent legal doctrinal treatises, as well as cutting-edge interdisciplinary works that engage law and the social sciences and humanities.

*Books in the Series*

*Capital Controls and International Economic Law*
Bryan Mercurio

*The Law and Practice of Global ICT Standardization*
Olia Kanevskaia Whitaker

*Between Market Economy and State Capitalism: China's State-Owned Enterprises and the World Trading System*
Henry S. Gao and Weihuan Zhou

*New Asian Regionalism in International Economic Law*
Pasha L. Hsieh

*Essential Interoperability Standards: Interfacing Intellectual Property and Competition in International Economic Law*
Simon Brinsmead

*Digital Services in International Trade Law*
Ines Willemyns

*Law and Politics on Export Restrictions: WTO and Beyond*
Chien-Huei Wu

*Energy in International Trade Law: Concepts, Regulation and Changing Markets*
Anna-Alexandra Marhold

*Shareholders' Claims for Reflective Loss in International Investment Law*
Lukas Vanhonnaeker

*Transparency in the WTO SPS and TBT Agreements: The Real Jewel in the Crown*
Marianna B. Karttunen

*Preferential Services Liberalization: The Case of the European Union and Federal States*
Johanna Jacobsson

*Emerging Powers in International Economic Law: Cooperation, Competition and Transformation*
Sonia E. Rolland and David M. Trubek

*Commitments and Flexibilities in the WTO Agreement on Subsidies and Countervailing Measures*
José Guilherme Moreno Caiado

*The Return of the Home State to Investor-State Disputes: Bringing Back Diplomatic Protection?*
Rodrigo Polanco

*Industrial Policy and the World Trade Organization: Between Legal Constraints and Flexibilities*
Sherzod Shadikhodjaev

*The Public International Law of Trade in Legal Services*
David Collins

*The Prudential Carve-Out for Financial Services: Rationale and Practice in the GATS and Preferential Trade Agreements*
Carlo Maria Cantore

*Preferential Services Liberalization: The Case of the European Union and Federal States*
Johanna Jacobsson

*Judicial Acts and Investment Treaty Arbitration*
Berk Demirkol

*Distributive Justice and World Trade Law: A Political Theory of International Trade Regulation*

Oisin Suttle

*Freedom of Transit and Access to Gas Pipeline Networks under WTO Law*

Vitaliy Pogoretskyy

*Reclaiming Development in the World Trading System, 2nd edition*

Yong-Shik Lee

*Developing Countries and Preferential Services Trade*

Charlotte Sieber-Gasser

*Establishing Judicial Authority in International Economic Law*

Edited by Joanna Jemielniak, Laura Nielsen and Henrik Palmer Olsen

*WTO Dispute Settlement and the TRIPS Agreement: Applying Intellectual Property Standards in a Trade Law Framework*

Matthew Kennedy

*Trade, Investment, Innovation and their Impact on Access to Medicines: An Asian Perspective*

Locknie Hsu

*The WTO and International Investment Law: Converging Systems*

Jürgen Kurtz

*The Law, Economics and Politics of International Standardisation,*

Edited by Panagiotis Delimatsis

*Export Restrictions on Critical Minerals and Metals: Testing the Adequacy of WTO Disciplines*

Ilaria Espa

*Optimal Regulation and the Law of International Trade: The Interface between the Right to Regulate and WTO Law*

Boris Rigod

*The Social Foundations of World Trade: Norms, Community, and Constitution*

Sungjoon Cho

*Public Participation and Legitimacy in the WTO*

Yves Bonzon

*The Challenge of Safeguards in the WTO*

Fernando Piérola

*General Interests of Host States in International Investment Law*

Edited by Giorgio Sacerdoti, with Pia Acconci, Mara Valenti and Anna De Luca

*WTO Disciplines on Subsidies and Countervailing Measures: Balancing Policy Space and Legal Constraints*

Dominic Coppens

*The Law of Development Cooperation: A Comparative Analysis of the World Bank, the EU and Germany*
Philipp Dann

*Liberalizing International Trade after Doha: Multilateral, Plurilateral, Regional, and Unilateral Initiatives*
David A. Gantz

*Domestic Judicial Review of Trade Remedies: Experiences of the Most Active WTO Members,*
Edited by Müslüm Yilmaz

*The Relevant Market in International Economic Law: A Comparative Antitrust and GATT Analysis*
Christian A. Melischek

*International Organizations in WTO Dispute Settlement: How Much Institutional Sensitivity?*
Marina Foltea

*Public Services and International Trade Liberalization: Human Rights and Gender Implications*
Barnali Choudhury

*The Law and Politics of WTO Waivers: Stability and Flexibility in Public International Law*
Isabel Feichtner

*African Regional Trade Agreements as Legal Regimes*
James Thuo Gathii

*Processes and Production Methods (PPMs) in WTO Law: Interfacing Trade and Social Goals*
Christiane R. Conrad

*Non-Discrimination in International Trade in Services: 'Likeness' in WTO/GATS*
Nicolas F. Diebold

*The Law, Economics and Politics of Retaliation in WTO Dispute Settlement*
Edited by Chad P. Bown and Joost Pauwelyn

*The Multilateralization of International Investment Law*
Stephan W. Schill

*Trade Policy Flexibility and Enforcement in the WTO: A Law and Economics Analysis*
Simon A. B. Schropp

# THE EUROPEAN UNION AND INTERNATIONAL INVESTMENT LAW REFORM

## Between Aspirations and Reality

IVANA DAMJANOVIC
*Lecturer, University of Canberra*
*Visiting Fellow, Australian National University*

CAMBRIDGE
UNIVERSITY PRESS

CAMBRIDGE
UNIVERSITY PRESS

Shaftesbury Road, Cambridge CB2 8EA, United Kingdom

One Liberty Plaza, 20th Floor, New York, NY 10006, USA

477 Williamstown Road, Port Melbourne, VIC 3207, Australia

314–321, 3rd Floor, Plot 3, Splendor Forum, Jasola District Centre, New Delhi – 110025, India

103 Penang Road, #05–06/07, Visioncrest Commercial, Singapore 238467

Cambridge University Press is part of Cambridge University Press & Assessment, a department of the University of Cambridge.

We share the University's mission to contribute to society through the pursuit of education, learning and research at the highest international levels of excellence.

www.cambridge.org
Information on this title: www.cambridge.org/9781009345392

DOI: 10.1017/9781009345422



First published 2023

*A catalogue record for this publication is available from the British Library.*

*A Cataloging-in-Publication data record for this book is available from the Library of Congress*

ISBN 978-1-009-34539-2 Hardback

# CONTENTS

# FIGURES

# TABLES

# FOREWORD

International investment law in the form of bilateral investment treaties (BITs) witnessed a boost in the 1960s. What gradually emerged was a web of bilateral commitments involving so-called investor-state dispute settlement (ISDS). A multilateral framework for the settlement of such investment disputes was created above all with the establishment of the International Centre for Settlement of Investment Disputes (ICSID) in 1966.

This development, of course, was enhanced by the decolonisation process, with a considerable number of new States emerging in Africa in particular. The developed world, fearing nationalisations and other measures affecting its investments in the developing countries, sought better guarantees in the form of obligatory and binding ISDS. Many of the developing countries on the other hand were suspicious of investment protection mechanisms that could undermine their ability to control their own natural and other resources.

Thus, the international investment protection system was already in these early days characterised by political discord. Yet, BITs continued to be concluded and the number of arbitral awards continued to rise. Some further multilateral contexts and treaties emerged, such as the UNCITRAL Arbitration Rules (which cover ISDS as well) initially of 1976 and the Energy Charter Treaty (which includes rules on investment protection), signed in 1994.

The international investment protection system has become even more multifaceted with the increased involvement of the European Union (EU) in the conclusion of bilateral agreements with third countries providing for State-to-State arbitration as well as ISDS. As the Lisbon Treaty of 2007 provides for an exclusive Union competence in the field of foreign direct investment and a competence shared with its Member States in the field of so-called portfolio investment, the Union is in the process of partly overtaking the role traditionally held by its Member States in the creation and application of international investment rules. The European Court of Justice (ECJ) has been called upon to rule on various aspects of international investment law and the Court has established a clear distinction between internal (the relations between the Member States) and external investment dispute settlement, only the latter being covered by the international ISDS rules.

Alongside these developments, public opinion, this time mainly in the developed world, and in Europe in particular, has expressed concerns about ISDS, fearing that arbitration procedures result in a bias in favour of protection of foreign investment, at the expense of societal values such as health and the environment and without due regard to procedural fairness. The EU has tried to take these concerns into account by, inter alia, advocating the establishment of investment courts providing for substantive, institutional and procedural guarantees that exceed those offered by ad hoc arbitration.

There is no shortage of literature on international investment law. Much of it focusses on specific topics rather than a holistic analysis. The present book by Ivana Damjanovic adds to the existing literature above all by providing a well-written and interesting discussion on the overall role of the EU in the development of investment law, taking into account both the internal and external dimensions and focussing on investment law reform, with a view to strengthening the rule of law. It can be highly recommended both to those who wish to improve their knowledge of international investment law and to experts in the field who seek to deepen their understanding of the reform process as driven by the EU in particular.

**Allan Rosas**

# ACKNOWLEDGEMENTS

This book evolved from my doctoral research, which I successfully completed at the Australian National University (ANU) in November 2020. It has been updated in view of new developments in this fast-moving field and takes account of the state of law and events up to 31 December 2022. In many ways, this book is my journey of becoming an academic. The ideas expressed here are the result of many research trips, discussions, conferences, seminars, lectures and debates across four continents: Europe, Asia, Australia and North America. They have also developed thanks to my fascination with different legal systems and perspectives, which stems from my legal education in Europe and Australia, and my diplomatic experience. During this journey, I have met many inspiring scholars and practitioners whose perspectives have fostered my interest in the relationship between international investment and EU law. Therefore, I should really thank all of them.

My warmest gratitude goes to Professor Murray Raff, who was my doctoral research mentor and has continued to be a wise and kind-hearted source of advice and insight, both academically and personally. I am also indebted to Professor Nicolas de Sadeleer, whose comments, reviews and advice have helped me to understand the intricacies of EU law. I have benefited tremendously from our seminars in Brussels and cooperation through joint research projects.

Conversations with many professionals and scholars have informed my approach and improved my understanding of the field. I thank officials in the EU and Member States' institutions in Brussels, including my former fellow diplomats, as well as the Client Earth team, all of whom generously provided opportunities to share their policy insights with me. I am grateful to the EU Delegation in Canberra for the opportunity to work with their trade team, which, albeit short, provided many insights into the internal workings of the EU and its trade policy. I thank the reviewers of this work, whose constructive suggestions have helped me to improve it. I am particularly grateful to Professor Allan Rosas and

Professor Martti Koskenniemi for their endorsements. I also thank Professor Nicolas Angelet for his support and our many conversations in Brussels. All omissions and mistakes in this work remain mine.

I am thankful to my colleagues at the ANU's Centre for European Studies, which has been my intellectual 'home' in Canberra during my PhD research. In particular, I would like to thank Professor Jacqueline Lo, Dr Annmarie Elijah, Anne McNaughton, Dr Ottavio Quirico and Dr Kasia Williams. My doctoral thesis benefited from a scholarship from the Australian government. I am grateful to the ANU for financial support for my various research trips. The update, research, production and promotion activities for this book have been supported by the EU Erasmus+ 620168-EPP-1-2020-1-AU-EPPJMO-PROJECT 'EU Climate Change Agenda and External Trade and Investment' and the University of Canberra. I also thank my two Heads of Canberra Law School, Professor Alison Gerard and Professor Benedict Sheehy, and other colleagues at the Law School of the University of Canberra for their support and for accommodating my obligations in a way that has assisted me to see first my PhD and then this book through to its completion.

The editorial team at Cambridge University Press has provided valuable support in the preparation of the manuscript and at various stages of the book's production.

I am grateful to my many friends in Canberra and Brussels who have provided moral support, food and welcome distractions over the years. Most of all, I am grateful to my parents and my sister Ana, who remain my bastion of support, regardless of distance between the continents and my too many missed calls during this project. I dedicate this book to my father Filip and mother Danica, whose remarkable professional journeys have inspired my own development and instilled my spark for law.

Pieter van der Borcht's allegory on the difficulty of governing, which I discovered at the Prints in the Age of Bruegel exhibition at Bozar in Brussels in February 2019, could be interpreted as depicting the dynamics between the two legal regimes that I have aimed to explain in this book. It is somewhere between divergent interests and legal considerations of the EU's reform (the aspiration, symbolised by the fantasy animal) and the established practice of arbitration (the reality, symbolised by the secular and ecclesiastical princes in the background) that the international investment regime will evolve into its future shape.

# TABLE OF CASES

## European Court of Justice

Case 10/61 *Commission v Italy* [1962] ECR 1
Case 6/64 *Flaminio Costa v E.N.E.L.* [1964] ECR 1141
Case 22/70 *AETR* [1971] ECR 263
Case 22-70 *Commission v Council* (European Road Transport Agreement) [1971] ECR 263
Case 48/71 *Commission v Italy* [1972] ECR 529
Case 2/74 *Reyners* [1974] ECR 631
Case C-41/74 *Yvonne van Duyn v Home Office* [1974] ECR 1337
Case 45/76 *Comet BV v Produktschap voor Siergewassen* [1976] ECR 2043
Case 111/75 *Mazzalai v Ferrovia del Renon* [1976] ECR 657
Case 33/76 *Rewe-Zentralfinanz* [1976] ECR 1998
Case 120/78 *Cassis de Dijon* [1979] ECR 649
Case 175/78 *Saunders* [1979] ECR 1129
Opinion 1/78 [1979] ECR 2871
Case 812/79 *Burgoa* [1980] ECR 2787
Case 203/80 *Casati* [1981] ECR 2595
Case 66/80 *International Chemical Corporation v Administrazione delle Finanze dello Stato* [1981] ECR 1191
Joined Cases 55/80 and 57/80 *Musik-Vertrieb Membran GmbH v GEMA* [1981] ECR 147
Case 222/84 *Johnston v Chief Constable of the Royal Ulster Constabulary* [1986] ECR 1651
C-294/83 *Parti écologiste 'Les Verts' v European Parliament* [1986] ECR 1339
Case 222/86 *Heylens and Others* [1987] ECR 4097
C-235/87 *Matteucci* [1988] ECR 5589
C-38/89 *Blanguernon* [1990] ECR I-83
C-213/89 *The Queen v Secretary of State for Transport, ex parte: Factorame* [1990] ECR I-2433
C-159/90 *Grogan* [1991] ECR I-4605
C-300/89 *'Titanium Dioxide'* [1991] ECR I-2867
Joined Cases C-6/90 and C-9/90 *Francovich* [1991] ECR I-5357

C-97/91 *Borelli* [1992] ECR-I 6313
Case 3/91 *Exportur SA v Lor SA and Confiserie du Tech SA* [1992] ECR 1-5529
C-19/92 *Kraus v Land Baden-Wuerttemberg* [1993] ECR I-1663
Opinion 2/91 [1993] ECR I-1061
Opinion 1/94 [1994] ECR I-5267
C-55/94 *Gebhard* [1995] ECR I-4165
C-312/93 *Peterbroeck, Van Campenhout & Cie SCS v Belgian State* [1995] ECR I-4599
C-80/94 *Wielockx* [1995] ECR I-2493
Joined Cases C-163/94, C-165/94 and C-250/94 *Sanz de Lera and Others* [1995] ECR I-4821
C-61/94 *Commission v Germany* [1996] ECR I-3989
C-72/95 *Kraaijeveld and Others* [1996] ECR I-5403
C-180/96 *United Kingdom v Commission* [1996] ECR I-3903
Joined Cases C-46/93 and C-48/93 *Brasserie du Pêcheur and Factorame III* [1996] ECR I-1029
Opinion 2/94 [1996] ECR I-1759
C-183/95 *Affish* [1997] ECR I-4315
C-373/95 *Maso* [1997] ECR I-4051
C-169/95 *Spain v Commission* [1997] ECR I-135
C-212/97 *Centros* [1999] ECR I-1459
C-126/97 *Eco Swiss China Time Ltd v Benetton International NV* [1999] ECR I-3055
C-302/97 *Konle* [1999] ECR I-3099
C-222/97 *Trummer and Mayer* [1999] ECR I-1671
C-435/97 *World Wildlife Fund (WWF) and Others* [1999]
C-478/98 *Commission v Belgium* [2000] ECR I-7587
C-269/97 *Commission v Council* [2000] ECRI-2257
C-62/98 *Commission v Portugal* [2000] ERC I-5171
C-84/98 *Commission v Portugal* [2000] ERC I-5215
Joined Cases C-300/98 and C-392/98 *Dior* [2000] ECR I-11307
C-54/99 *Église de Scientologie* [2000] ECR I-1335
C-287/98 *Grand Duchy of Luxemburg v Berthe Linster, Aloyse Linster and Yvonne Linster* [2000] ECR I-6917
C-473/98 *Kemikalieinspektionen v Toolex Alpha* [2000] ECR I-5681
C-35/98 *Verkooijen* [2000] ECR I-4071
C-424/99 *Commission v Austria* [2001] ECR I-9285
C-453/99 *Courage v Crehan* [2001] ECR I-6297
C-123/00 *Criminal Proceedings Against Bellamy and English Shop Wholesale* [2001] ECR I-2795
Opinion 2/00 [2001] ECR I-9713
C-163/99 *Portugal v Commission* [2001] ECR I-2613
C-471/98 *Commission v Belgium* ("Open Skies") [2002] ECR I-9681
C-503/99 *Commission v Belgium* [2002] ECR I-4809

C-467/98 *Commission v Denmark* ('Open Skies' Agreement) [2002] ECR I-9519
C-483/99 *Commission v France* [2002] ECR I-4781
C-367/98 *Commission v Portugal* [2002] ECR I-4731
Joined Cases C-515/99, C-519/99 to C-524/99 and C-526/99 to C-540/99 *Reisch and Others* [2002] ECR I-2157
C-50/00 P *Unión de Pequeños Agricultores v Council* [2002] ECR I-6677
C-114/01 *AvestaPolarit Chrome Oy* [2003] ECR I-8725
C-364/01 *Barbier* [2003] ECR I-15013
C-216/01 *Budějovický Budvar* [2003] ECR I-13617
C-211/01 *Commission v Council* [2003] ECR I-3651
C-463/00 *Commission v Spain* [2003] ECR I-45
C-467/01 *Eribrand* [2003] ECR I-6471
C-112/00 *Eugen Schmidberger, Internationale Transporte und Planzüge v Republik Österreich* [2003] ECR I-5659
C-224/01 *Köbler* [2003] ECR I-10239
C-13/01 *Safalero* [2003] ECR I-8679
C-338/01 *Commission v Council* [2004] ECR I-4829
C-334/02 *Commission v France* [2004] ECR I-2229
C-95/01 *Greenham and Abel* [2004] ECR I-1333
Joined Cases C-37/02 and C-38/02 *Di Lenardo and Dilexport* [2004] ECR I-6911
C-36/02 *Omega* [2004] ECR I-9609
C-242/03 *Weidert and Paulus* [2004] ECR I-7379
C-512/03 *Blanckaert* [2005] ECR I-7685
C-147/03 *Commission v Austria* [2005] ECR I-5969
C-376/03 *D* [2005] ECR I-5821
C-196/04 *Cadbury Schweppes and Cadbury Schweppes Overseas* [2006] ECR I-7995
C-386/04 *Centro di Musicologia Walter Stauffer* [2006] ECR I-8203
C-94/03 *Commission v Council* [2006] ECR I-1
C-459/03 *Commission v Ireland* [2006] ECR I-4635
Joined Cases C-282/04 and C-283/04 *Commission v Netherlands* [2006] ECR I-9141
C-178/03 *Commission v Parliament and Council* [2006] ECR I-107
C-452/04 *Fidium Finanz AG* [2006] ECR I-9521
C-265/04 *Margaretha Bouanich v Skatteverket* [2006] ECR I-923
C-470/04 *N* [2006] ECR I-7409
Opinion 1/03 (New Lugano Convention) [2006] ECR I-1145
C-310/04 *Spain v Council* [2006] ECR I-7285
C-446/04 *Test Claimants in the FII Group Litigation* [2006] ECR I-11753
C-506/04 *Wilson* [2006] ECR I-8613
C-513/03 *Van Hilten-van der Heijden* [2006] ECR I-1957
C-101/05 *A* [2007] ECR I-11531
C-112/05 *Commission v Germany* [2007] ECR I-8995
C-260/04 *Commission of the European Communities v Italian Republic* [2007] ECR I-7083

C-370/05 *Festersen* [2007] ECR I-1129
C-341/05 *Laval un Partneri Ltd v Svenska* [2007] ECR I-11767
C-231/05 *Oy AA* [2007] ECR I-6373
Joined Cases C-338/04, C-359/04 and C-360/04 *Placanica and Others* [2007] ECR I-1891
C-432/05 *Unibet* [2007] ECR I-2271
C-438/05 *The International Transport Workers' Federation and The Finnish Seamen's Union* [2007] ECR I-10779
C-127/07 *Arcelor* [2008] ECR I-9895
C-120/06 *FIAMM v Council and Commission* [2008] ECR I-6513
C-308/06 *Intertanko and Others v Secretary of State for Transport* [2008] ECR I-4057
Joined Cases C-402/05 P and C-415/05 P *Kadi* [2008] ECR I-6351
C-105/07 *Lammers and Van Cleeff* [2008] ECR I-173
C-478/07 *Budějovický Budvar* [2009] ECR I-772
C-35/08 *Busley et Cibrian Fernandez* [2009] ECR I-9807
C-205/06 *Commission v Austria* [2009] ECR I-1301
C-13/07 *Commission v Council*, Opinion of AG Kokott ECLI:EU:2009:190
C-370/07 *Commission v Council* [2009] ECR I-8917
C-118/07 *Commission v Finland* [2009] ECR I-10889
C-249/06 *Commission v Sweden* [2009] ECR I-1335
C-110/05 *Commission of the European Communities v Italian Republic* [2009] ECR I-519
C-301/08 *Irène Bogiatzi, married name Ventouras v Deutscher Luftpool and Others* [2009] ECR I-10185
Opinion 1/08 [2009] ECR I-11129
C-201/08 *Plantanol* [2009] ECR I-8343
C-567/07 *Woningstichting Sint Servatius* [2009] ECR I-9021
Joined Cases C-317/08 to C-320/08 *Alassini* [2010] ECR I-2213
C-246/07 *Commission v Sweden* ECLI:EU:C:2010:203
C-173/09 *Elchinov* [2010] ECR I-8889
C-208/09 *Ilonka Sayn Wittgenstein v Landeshauptmann von Wien* [2010] ECR I-13693
C-108/09 *Ker-Optika* [2010] ECR I-12213
C-510/08 *Mattner* [2010] ECR I-3553
C-548/09 P *Bank Melli Iran v Council* [2011] ECR I-11381
C-10/10 *Commission v Austria* [2011] ECR I-5389
C-155/09 *Commission v Greece* [2011] ECR I-65
C-264/09 *Commission v Slovakia*, Opinion of AG Jääskinen ECLI:EU:2011:150
C-264/09 *Commission v Slovakia* [2011] ECR I-8065
C-347/11 *Santander Asset Management SGIIC* ECLI:EU:C:2012:286
C-370/12 *Pringle* ECLI:EU:C:2012:756
C-123/11 *A* ECLI:EU:C:2013:84
C -93/12 *Agrokonsulting-04* ECLI:EU:C:2013:432

C-617/10 *Åklagaren v Hans Åkerberg Fransson* ECLI:EU:C:2013:105
C-176/12 *Association de médiation sociale*, Opinion of AG Cruz Villalon ECLI:EU:C:2013:491
C-414/11 *Daiichi Sankyo Co. Ltd and Sanofi-Aventis Deutschland* ECLI:EU:C:2013:520
C-583/11 P *Inuit Tapiriit Kanatami and Others v Parliament and Council* ECLI:EU:C:2013:625
C-322/11 *K* ECLI:EU:C:2013:716
C-420/11 *Leth* ECLI:EU:C:2013:166
C-101/12 *Schaible* ECLI:EU:C:2013:661
C-399/11 *Stefano Melloni v Ministerio Fiscal* ECLI:EU:C:2013:107
C-418/11 *Texdata Softwarer* ECLI:EU:C:2013:588
C-181/12 *Welte* ECLI:EU:C:2013:662
C-562/13 *Centre Public d'Action Sociale d'Ottignies-Louvain-la-Neuve v Abdida* ECLI:EU:C:2014:2453
C-114/12 *Commission v Council* ECLI:EU:C:2014:2151
C-658/11 *European Parliament v Council* ECLI:EU:C:2014:2025
C-356/12 *Glatzel* ECLI:EU:C:2014:350
C-580/12 P *Guardian Industries and Guardian Europe v Commission* EU:C:2014:2363
Opinion 1/13 ECLI:EU:C:2014:2303
Opinion 2/13 ECLI:EU:C:2014:2454
C-222/13 *TDC* ECLI:EU:C:2014:2265
C-425/13 *Commission v Council* ECLI:EU:C:2015:483
C-160/14 *Ferreira da Silva e Birto and Others* ECLI:EU:C:2015:565
C-62/14 *Peter Gauweiler and Others v Deutscher Bundestag*, ECLI:EU:C:2015:400
C-358/15 P *Bank of Industry and Mine v Council* EU:C:2016:338
C-244/15 *Commission v Greece* ECLI:EU:C:2016:359
C-526/14 *Kotnik and Others* ECLI:EU:C:2016:570
Joined Cases C-8/15 P to C-10/15 P *Ledra Advertising v Commission and ECB* ECLI:EU:C:2016:701
C-566/14 P *Marchiani v Parliament* ECLI:EU:C:2016:437
Opinion 2/15, Opinion of AG Sharpston ECLI:EU:C:2016:992
C-252/14 *Pensioenfonds Metaal en Techniek* ECLI:EU:C:2016:402
C-477/14 *Pillbox 38* ECLI:EU:C:2016:324
C-689/13 *Puligienica Facility Esco SpA* ECLI:EU:C:2016:199
C-464/14 *SECIL* ECLI:EU:C:2016:896
C-168/15 *Tomášová* ECLI:EU:C:2016:602
C-332/14 *Wolfgang und Wilfried Rey Grundstücksgemeinschaft GbR* ECLI:EU:C:2016:417
C-284/16 *Achmea*, Opinion of AG Wathelet ECLI:EU:C:2017:699
C-682/15 *Berlioz Investment Fund* ECLI:EU:C:2017:313
C-687/15 *Commission v Council* ECLI:EU:C:2017:803
Joint Cases C-504/16 and C-613/16 *Deister Holding and Juhler Holding* EU:C:2017:1009

C-600/14 *Germany v Council*, ECLI:EU:C:2017:935
C-503/15 *Margarit Panicello* ECLI:EU:C:2017:126
C-106/16 *POLBUD – WYKONAWSTWO* ECLI:EU:C:2017:804
Opinion 1/15 ECLI:EU:C:2017:592
Opinion 2/15 ECLI:EU:C:2017:376
C-284/16 *Achmea* ECLI:EU:C:2018:158
C-64/16 *Associação Sindical dos Juízes Portugueses* ECLI:EU:C:2018:117
C-685/16 *EV* ECLI:EU:C:2018:743
C-679/17 *Huijbrechts* ECLI:EU:C:2018:940
C-45/17 *Jahin* ECLI:EU:C:2018:18
Joined Cases C-52/16 and C-113/16 *SEGRO and Horváth* ECLI:EU:C:2018:157
C-540/16 *Spika and Others* ECLI:EU:C:2018:565
C-493/17 *Weiss and Others* ECLI:EU:C:2018:1000
C-266/16 *Western Sahara Campaign UK* ECLI:EU:C:2018:118
C-621/18 *Whitgman* ECLI:EU:C:2018:999
Joined Cases C-360/15 and C-31/16 *Visser Vastgoed Beleggingen* [2018] OJ C 112/2
C-625/18 *AK (Independence of the Disciplinary Chamber of the Supreme Court)* ECLI:EU:C:2019:982
C-619/18 *Commission v Poland* ECLI:EU:C:2019:531
C-620/17 *Hochtief Solutions AG* ECLI:EU:C:2019:630
Opinion 1/17, Opinion of AG Bot ECLI:EU:C:2019:72
Opinion 1/17 ECLI:EU:C:2019:341
C-457/18 *Slovenia v Croatia* ECLI:EU:C:2020:65
Joined Cases C-798/18 and C-799/18 *Anie and Others* ECLI:EU:C:2021:280
Opinion 1/19, Opinion of AG Hogan ECLI:EU:C:2021:198
Opinion 1/19 (not yet reported)
C-109/20 *PL Holdings* ECLI:EU:C:2021:875
Joined Cases C-748/19 to C-754/19 *Prokuratura Rejonowa w Minsku Mazowieckim* ECLI:EU:C:2021:931
C-741/19 *République de Moldavie* Case C-741/19 *v Komstroy* ECLI:EU:C:2021:655
C-487/19 *WZ* ECLI:EU:C:2021:798
C-638/19 P *Commission v European Food and Others* ECLI:EU:C:2022:50
Joined Cases C-306/19, C-512/19, C-595/19 and C-608/20 to C-610/20 *Milis Energy SpA and Others* ECLI:EU:C:2022:164
Opinion 1/20 ECLI:EU:C:2022:485
C-333/19 *Romatsa and Others* ECLI:EU:C:2022:749

## General Court

T-76/96 *Pfizer* [1996] ECR II-815
T-199/99 *Sgaravatti Mediterranea Srl v Commission of the European Communities* [2002] ECR II-3731

Joined Cases T-50/06 RENV II and T-69/06 RENV II *Ireland v Commission* ECLI:EU:T:2016:227
T-754/14 *Efler and Others v Commission* ECLI:EU:T:2017:323
T-624/15 *European Food and Others v Commission* ECLI:EU:T:2019:423

## EFTA Court

E-2/06 *EFTA Surveillance Authority v The Kingdom of Norway* [2007] OJ C301/18

## European Court of Human Rights

*Campbell and Fell v the UK* App nos 7819/77 and 7878/77 (ECtHR, 28 June 2014)
*De Cubber v Belgium* App no 9186/80 (ECtHR, 26 October 1984)
*James and Others v United Kingdom* App no 8793/79 (ECtHR, 21 February 1986)
*Mellacher and Others v Austria* App nos 10522/83; 11011/84; 11070/84 (ECtHR, 19 December 1989)
*Micallef v Malta* App no 17056/06 (ECtHR, 15 October 2009)
*Oleksandr Volkov v Ukraine* App no 21722/11 (ECtHR, 9 January 2013)
*Piersack v Belgium* App no 8692/79 (ECtHR, 1 October 1982)

## European Commission

Case SA.40348 (2015/NN) Commission Decision C (2017) 7384 final
Case SA.54155 (2021/NN) Commission Decision C (2021) 5405 final

## International Court of Justice

*Barcelona Traction Case, Light and Power Company Limited, Case concerning (New Application, 1962)* (Belgium v Spain) (Second Phase) [1970] ICJ Rep 3
*Case Concerning the Factory at Chorzów* (Germany v Poland) (Indemnity) [1928] PCIJ Rep Series A No 17
*Elettronica Sicula S.p.A. (ELSI)* (United States of America v Italy) (Judgment) [1989] ICJ Rep 15

## Arbitration Decisions and Awards

*Achmea B.V. v The Slovak Republic (formerly Eureko B.V. v Slovak Republic)*, PCA Case No. 2008-13, Award on Jurisdiction, Arbitrability and Suspension (26 October 2010), Final Award (7 December 2012)
*ADC Affiliate Limited and ADC & ADMC Management Limited v The Republic of Hungary*, ICSID Case No. ARB/03/16, Award (2 October 2006)

*Addiko Bank AG and Addiko Bank d.d. v Republic of Croatia*, ICSID Case No. ARB/17/37, Decision on Croatia's Jurisdictional Objection Related to the Alleged Incompatibility of the BIT with EU Acquis (12 June 2020)

*AIG v Islamic Republic of Iran* (1983) 4 Iran–USCTR 96

*Aguas del Tunari, S.A. v Republic of Bolivia*, ICSID Case No. ARB/02/3, Decision on Respondent's Objections to Jurisdiction (21 October 2005)

*Amco v Indonesia*, ICSID Case No. ARB/81/1, Award (5 June 1990)

*AMF Aircraftleasing Meier & Fischer GmbH & Co. KG v Czech Republic*, PCA Case No. 2017-15, Final Award (11 May 2020)

*Apotex Holdings Inc. and Apotex Inc. v United States of America*, ICSID Case No. ARB (AF)/12/1, Award (25 August 2014)

*Autopista Concesionada de Venezuela, C.A. v Bolivarian Republic of Venezuela*, ICSID Case No. ARB/00/5, Decision on Jurisdiction (27 September 2001)

*Bernhard von Pezold and Others v Republic of Zimbabwe*, ICSID Case No. ARB/10/15, Procedural Order No. 2 (26 June 2012)

*Bilcon of Delaware et al v Government of Canada*, PCA Case No. 2009-04, Award on Jurisdiction and Liability (17 March 2015), Dissenting Opinion of Professor Donald McRae (10 March 2015)

*Biwater Gauff (Tanzania) Ltd. v United Republic of Tanzania*, ICSID Case No. ARB/05/22, Award (24 July 2008)

*Blusun S.A., Jean-Pierre Lecorcier and Michael Stein v Italian Republic*, ICSID Case No. ARB/14/3, Final Award (27 December 2017)

*Burlington Resources Inc. v Republic of Ecuador*, ICSID Case No. ARB/08/5, Decision on Ecuador's Counterclaims (7 February 2017)

*CEF Energia BV v Italian Republic*, SCC Case No. 158/2015, Award (16 January 2019)

*Charanne B.V. v Spain* SCC Arb. No. 062/2012, Final Award (21 January 2016)

*Chemtura Corporation v Government of Canada* (formerly *Crompton Corporation v Government of Canada*), Award (2 August 2010)

*Chevron Corporation and Texaco Petroleum Corporation v The Republic of Ecuador*, UNCITRAL, PCA Case No. 2009-23, Second Partial Award on Track II (30 August 2018)

*CMS Gas Transmission Company v The Republic of Argentina*, ICSID Case No. ARB/01/8, Decision of the Tribunal on Objections to Jurisdiction (17 July 2003), Award (12 May 2005); Decision on Annulment (25 September 2007).

*Compañía del Desarrollo de Santa Elena S.A. v Republic of Costa Rica*, ICSID Case No. ARB/96/1, Award (17 February 2000)

*Compañia de Aguas del Aconquija SA and Vivendi Universal v Argentine Republic*, ICSID Case No. ARB/97/3, Decision on Annulment (3 July 2002); Award (20 August 2007)

*Continental Casualty Company v The Argentine Republic*, ISCID Case No. ARB/03/9, Award (5 September 2008)

*Cortec Mining Kenya Limited, Cortec (Pty) Limited and Stirling Capital Limited v Republic of Kenya*, ICSID Case No. ARB/15/29, Award (22 October 2018)

*Dan Cake (Portugal) S.A. v Hungary*, ICSID Case No. ARB/12/9

*Eastern Sugar BV (Netherlands) v The Czech Republic*, UNCITRAL arbitration SCC No. 088/2004, Partial Award (27 March 2007)

*Eco Oro Minerals Corp. v Republic of Colombia*, ICSID Case No. ARB/16/41, Decision on Jurisdiction, Liability and Directions on Quantum (9 September 2021)

*EDF (Services) Limited v Romania*, ICSID Case No. ARB/05/13, Award (8 October 2009)

*Eiser Infrastructure v Spain*, ICSID Case No. ARB/13/36, Final Award (4 May 2017)

*El Paso Energy International Company v Argentine Republic*, ICSID Case No. ARB/03/15, Decision on Jurisdiction (27 April 2006), Award (31 October 2011)

*Electrabel S.A. v Hungary*, ICSID No. ARB/07/19, Decision on Jurisdiction, Applicable Law and Liability (30 November 2012)

*Eli Lilly and Company v The Government of Canada*, UNCITRAL, ICSID Case No. UNCT/14/2, Final Award (16 March 2017)

*Emilio Agustín Maffezini v The Kingdom of Spain*, ICSID Case No. ARB/97/7, Decision of the Tribunal on Objections to Jurisdiction (28 October 1999), Award (13 November 2000)

*Enron Corporation and Ponderosa Assets, L.P. v Argentine Republic*, ICSID Case No. ARB/01/3, Award (22 May 2007)

*Enron Corporation and Ponderosa Assets, L.P. v Argentine Republic*, ICSID Case No. ARB/01/3, Decision on Annulment (20 July 2010).

*Eskosol S.P.A. in liquidazione v Italian Republic*, ICSID Case No. ARB/15/50, Decision on Termination Request and Intra-EU Objection (7 May 2019)

*Eureko B.V. v Republic of Poland*, Partial Award (19 August 2005)

*European American Investment Bank AG v The Slovak Republic*, PCA Case No. 2010-17, Award on Jurisdiction (22 October 2012)

*Fireman's Fund Insurance Company v The United Mexican States*, ICSID Case No. ARB (AF)/02/1, Award (17 July 2006)

*Gas Natural SDG S.A. v Argentine Republic* (ICSID Case No. ARB/03/10) Decision of the Tribunal on Preliminary Questions on Jurisdiction (17 June 2005)

*GBM Global et al. v Kingdom of Spain*, ICSID Case No. ARB/18/33

*Generation Ukraine, Inc. v Ukraine*, ICSID Case No. ARB/00/9, Award (16 September 2003)

*Global Trading Resource Corp. and Globex International, Inc. v Ukraine*, ICSID Case No. ARB/09/11, Award (1 December 2010)

*GPF GP S.à.r.l v Republic of Poland*, SCC Case No. V 2014/168, Award (29 April 2020)

*Green Power K/S and Obton A/S v Spain*, SCC Case No. 2016/135, Award (22 June 2022)

*Greentech Energy Systems A/S, et al v Italian Republic*, SCC Case No. V 2015/095, Final Award (23 December 2018)

*Hesham T. M. Al Warraq v Republic of Indonesi*a, UNCITRAL, Final Award (15 December 2014)

*H&H Enterprises Investments, Inc. v Arab Republic of Egypt*, ICSID Case No. ARB 09/15, Award (6 May 2014)

*Infracapital F1 S.à r.l. and Infracapital Solar B.V. v Kingdom of Spain*, ICSID Case No. ARB/16/18, Decision on Respondent Request for Reconsideration regarding the Intra-EU Objection and the Merits (1 February 2022)

*Infrastructure Services Luxembourg S.à.r.l. and Energia Termosolar B.V. (formerly Antin) v Spain*, ICSID Case No. ARB/13/31, Award (15 June 2018)

*International Thunderbird Gaming Corporation v The United Mexican States*, UNCITRAL, Arbitral Award (26 January 2006)

*Ioan Micula, Viorel Micula, S.C. European Food S.A, S.C. Starmill S.R.L. and S.C. Multipack S.R.L. v Romania*, ICSID Case No. ARB/05/20, Decision on Jurisdiction and Admissibility (24 September 2008), Final Award (11 December 2013)

*Joy Mining Machinery Limited v Arab Republic of Egypt*, ICSID Case No. ARB/03/11, Award on Jurisdiction (6 August 2004)

*LG&E Energy Corp. v Argentine Republic*, ICSID Case No. ARB/02/1, Award (25 July 2007)

*Loewen Group, Inc. and Raymond L. Loewen v United States of America*, ICSID Case No. ARB(AF)/98/3, Award (26 June 2003)

*Magyar Farming Company Ltd, Kintyre Kft, & Anicia Zrt v Hungary*, ICSID Case No. ARB/17/27

*Malaysian Historical Salvors, SDN, BHD v The Government of Malaysia*, ICSID Case No. ARB/05/10, Decision on the Application for Annulment (16 April 2009)

*Marfin Investment Group Holdings S.A., Alexandros Bakatselos and Others v Republic of Cyprus*, ICSID Case No. ARB/13/27, Award (27 July 2018)

*Marvin Roy Feldman Karpa v United Mexican States*, ICSID Case No. ARB(AF)/99/1, Award (16 December 2002)

*Masdar Solar & Wind Cooperatief U.A. v Kingdom of Spain*, ICSID Case No. ARB/14/1, Award (16 May 2018)

*Merrill and Ring Forestry L.P. v Canada*, ICSID Case No. UNCT/07/1, Award (31 March 2010)

*Metalclad Corp v United Mexican States*, ICSID Case No. ARB (AF)/97/1, Award (30 August 2000)

*Methanex Corporation v United States of America*, Final Award of the Tribunal on Jurisdiction and Merits (3 August 2005)

*Metalpar S.A. and Buen Aire S.A. v The Argentine Republic*, ICSID Case No. ARB/03/5, Award (6 June 2008)

*Mondev International Ltd. v United States of America*, ICSID Case No. ARB(AF)/99/2, Award (11 October 2002)

*Mr. Franck Charles Arif v Republic of Moldova*, ICSID Case No. ARB/11/23, Award (8 April 2013)

*Muszynianka v Slovakia*, PCA Case No. 2017-08, Award (7 October 2020)

*Noble Ventures, Inc. v Romania*, ICSID Case No. ARB/01/11, Award (12 October 2005)

*Nord Stream 2 AG v the European Union*, PCA Case No. 2020-07, Procedural Order No. 7 (16 March 2022)

*Novenergia II – Energy & Environment (SCA) (Grand Duchy of Luxembourg), SICAR v The Kingdom of Spain*, SCC Case No. 2015/063, Award (15 February 2018)

*Nykomb Synergistics Technology Holding AB v Latvia*, Arbitral Award (16 December 2003)

*Occidental Exploration and Production Company v The Republic of Ecuador*, LCIA Case No. UN3467, Final Award (1 July 2004)

*Occidental Petroleum Corporation and Occidental Exploration and Production Company v The Republic of Ecuador*, ICSID Case No. ARB/06/11, Award (5 October 2012)

*Pac Rim Cayman LLC v Republic of El Salvador*, ICSID Case No. ARB/09/12, Decision on Respondent's Jurisdictional Objections (1 June 2012)

*Pantechniki S.A. Contractors & Engineers (Greece) v The Republic of Albania*, ICSID Case No. ARB/07/21, Award (30 July 2009)

*Parkerings-Compagniet AS v Republic of Lithuania*, ICSID Case No. ARB/05/8, Award (11 September 2007)

*Philip Morris Asia Limited v The Commonwealth of Australia*, UNCITRAL, PCA Case No. 2012-12, Award on Jurisdiction and Admissibility (17 December 2015)

*Philip Morris Brands Sàrl, Philip Morris Products SA and Abal Hermanos SA Oriental v Republic of Uruguay*, ICSID Case No. Arb/10/7, Award (8 July 2016)

*PL Holdings S.à.r.l. v Republic of Poland*, SCC Case No. V 2014/163

*Plama Consortium Limited v Republic of Bulgaria*, ICSID Case No. ARB/03/24, Decision on Jurisdiction (8 February 2005)

*Pope & Talbot Inc. v The Government of Canada*, UNCITRAL, Interim Award (26 June 2000), Award on the Merits of Phase 2 (10 April 2001), Award in Respect of Damages (31 May 2002)

*Poštová Banka, a.s. and Istrokapital SE v The Hellenic Republic*, ICSID Case No. ARB/13/8

*PSEG Global, Inc., The North American Coal Corporation, and Konya Ingin Electrik Üretim ve Ticaret Limited Sirketi v Republic of Turkey*, ICSID Case No. ARB/02/5, Award (19 January 2007)

*Quiborax S.A., Non Metallic Minerals S.A. and Allan Fosk Kaplún v Plurinational State of Bolivia*, ICSID Case No. ARB/06/2, Decision on Jurisdiction (27 September 2012)

*Raiffeisen Bank International AG and Raiffeisenbank Austria d.d. v Republic of Croatia (I)*, ICSID Case No. ARB/17/34, Decision on Respondent's Jurisdictional Objections (30 September 2020)

*Ronald S. Lauder v The Czech Republic*, UNCITRAL, Final Award (3 September 2001)

*Romak S.A. (Switzerland) v The Republic of Uzbekistan*, UNCITRAL, PCA Case No. AA280, Award (26 November 2009)

*RREEF Infrastructure (G.P.) Limited and RREEF Pan-European Infrastructure Two Lux S.à r.l. v Kingdom of Spain*, ICSID Case No. ARB/13/30, Decision on Jurisdiction (6 June 2016)

*Rupert Joseph Binder v Czech Republic*, UNCITRAL, Award on Jurisdiction (6 June 2007)

*RWE AG and RWE Eemshaven Holding II BV v Kingdom of the Netherlands*, ICSID Case No. ARB/21/4

*Saluka Investments B.V. v The Czech Republic*, UNCITRAL, Partial Award (17 March 2006)

*Salini Costruttori S.p.A. and Italstrade S.p.A. v The Hashemite Kingdom of Jordan*, ICSID Case No. ARB/02/13, Decision on Jurisdiction (9 November 2004)

*Salini Costruttori S.p.A. and Italstrade S.p.A. v Kingdom of Morocco*, ICSID Case No. ARB/00/4, Decision on Jurisdiction (31 July 2001)

*S. D. Myers, Inc. v Government of Canada*, Partial Award (13 November 2000)

*Sempra Energy International v The Argentine Republic*, ICSID Case No. ARB/02/16, Award (28 September 2007)

*Sempra Energy International v The Argentine Republic*, ICSID Case No. ARB/02/16, Decision on Annulment (29 June 2010)

*Sevilla Beheer and Others v Kingdom of Spain*, ICSID Case No. ARB/16/27, Decision on Jurisdiction, Liability and the Principles of Quantum (11 February 2022)

*SGS Société Générale de Surveillance S.A. v Islamic Republic of Pakistan*, ICSID Case No. ARB/01/13, Decision of the Tribunal on Objections to Jurisdiction (6 August 2003)

*SGS Société Générale de Surveillance S.A. v Republic of the Philippines*, Decision of the Tribunal on Objections to Jurisdiction, (29 January 2004)

*Siemens A.G. v The Argentine Republic*, ICSID Case No. ARB/02/8, Decision on Jurisdiction (3 August 2004), Award (17 January 2007)

*Sodexo Pass International SAS v Hungary*, ICSID Case No. ARB/14/20

*Spyridon Roussalis v Romania*, ICSID Case No. ARB/06/1, Award (7 December 2011)

*Stadtwerke München GmbH, RWE Innogy GmbH, and Others v Kingdom of Spain*, ICSID Case No. ARB/15/1, Award (2 December 2019)

*Strabag et al v Poland*, ICSID Case No. ADHOC/15/1, Partial Award on Jurisdiction (4 March 2020)

*Suez, Sociedad General de Aguas de Barcelona SA, and InterAguas Servicios Integrales del Agua SA v The Argentine Republic*, ICSID Case No. ARB/03/17, Decision on Jurisdiction (16 May 2006)

*Técnicas Medioambientales Tecmed, S.A. v The United Mexican States*, ICSID Case No. ARB (AF)/00/2, Award (29 May 2003)

*Theodoros Adamakopoulos, Ilektra Adamantidou, Vasileios Adamopoulos and Others v Republic of Cyprus*, ICSID Case No. ARB/15/49, Statement of Dissent of Professor Marcelo G. Kohen (3 February 2020)

*Tidewater Inc., Tidewater Investment SRL, Tidewater Caribe, C.A., et al. v The Bolivarian Republic of Venezuela*, ICSID Case No. ARB/10/5, Decision on Jurisdiction (8 February 2013)

*Tippetts v Iran* (1986) 6 Iran-US Cl Trib Rep 219

*The Rompetrol Group N.V. v Romania*, ICSID Case No. ARB/06/3, Decision on Jurisdiction and Admissibility (18 April 2008)

*Tokios Tokelés v Ukraine*, ICSID Case No. ARB/02/18, Decision on Jurisdiction (29 April 2004)

*Tokios Tokelés v Ukraine*, ICSID Case No. ARB/02/18, Dissenting Opinion (Chairman Professor Weil) (29 April 2004)

*Transglobal Green Energy, LLC and Transglobal Green Energy de Panama, S.A. v The Republic of Panama*, ICSID Case No. ARB/13/28, Award (2 June 2016)

*TSA Spectrum de Argentina S.A. v Argentine Republic*, ICSID Case No. ARB/05/5, Award (19 December 2008)

*UAB E energija (Lithuania) v Republic of Latvia*, ICSID Case No. ARB/12/33

*Uniper SE, Uniper Benelux Holding B.V. and Uniper Benelux N.V. v Kingdom of the Netherlands*, ICSID Case No. ARB/21/22

*UP (formerly Le Chèque Déjeuner) and C.D Holding Internationale v Hungary*, Award (9 October 2018)

*Urbaser S.A. and Consorcio de Aguas Bilbao Biskaia Ur Partzuergoa v Argentine Republic*, ICSID Case No. ARB/07/26, Award (8 December 2016)

*Vacuum Salt Products Ltd. v Republic of Ghana*, ICSID Case No. ARB/92/1, Award (16 February 1994)

*Vattenfall AB, Vattenfall Europe AG, Vattenfall Europe Generation AG v Federal Republic of Germany (I)*, ICSID Case No. ARB/09/6

*Vattenfall AB and Others v Federal Republic of Germany (II)*, ICSID Case No. ARB/12/12, Decision on *Achmea* issue (31 August 2018)

*Waste Management, Inc. v United Mexican States ("Number 2")*, ICSID Case No. ARB (AF)/00/3, Award (30 April 2004)

*Wena Hotels Ltd v Arab Republic of Egypt*, ICSID Case No. ARB/98/4, Decision on Annulment (5 February 2002)

## Other Jurisdictions

*AWG Group Ltd. & Anor v Morrison & Anor* [2006] EWCA Civ 6

BGH (German Federal Court of Justice), Judgment of 31 October 2018, I ZB 2/15

BHB (German Federal Court of Justice), Judgment of 17 November 2021, I ZB 16/21.

BVerfG, *The Vattenfall Case*, Judgment of the First Senate of 6 December 2016, 1 BvR 2821/11

*Cooper v Board of Works for the Wandsworth District* (1863) 143 ER 414

*Henn & Darby v DPP* [1981] AC 850

*Howell & Ors v Lees Millais & Ors* [2007] EWCA Civ 720

*Infrastructure Services Luxembourg S.A.R.L v Kingdom of Spain* [2021] FCAFC 112

*Ioan Micula et al v Romania*, Case No. Ä 2550-17, Nacka District Court, Decision (23 January 2019)

*Kingdom of Spain v Infrastructure Services Luxembourg S.à.r.l.* [2021] FCAFC 3

Luxembourg, Court of Cassation, Case No. 116/2022, CAS-2021-00061 (14 July 2022)

*Micula v Gov't of Rom.*, 404 F. Supp. 3d 265 (D.D.C. 2019)

*Micula v Gov't of Romania*, 2022 WL 18356669 (D.D.C. 22 December 2022)

*Micula and Others v Romania* [2020] UKSC 5

*Infrared Environmental Infrastructure GP Limited and Others v Kingdom of Spain*, Civil Action No. 1:20-cv-00817 (D.D.C., 29 June 2021).

*MSC v Poland*, PCA Case No. 2015-18, Brussels Court of First Instance, Judgment (19/3390/A, 18 February 2022)

*Novenergia II – Energy & Environment (SCA(Grand Duchy of Luxembourg), SICAR v The Kingdom of Spain*, Civil Action No. 18-cv-01148 (TSC) (D.D.C., 27 January 2020)

*Novenergia II v Spain*, SCC Case No. 2015/063, Decision from the Sea Court of Appeal (13 December 2022)

*RREEF Infrastructure (G.P.) Limited and RREEF Pan-European Infrastructure Two Lux S.à r.l. v Kingdom of Spain*, Civil Action No. 1:19-cv-03783 (D.D.C., 31 March 2021)

Panel of Expert Proceedings Constituted under Art. 13.15 of the EU-Korea FTA, Report (20 January 2021)

*PL Holdings S.a.r.l. v Poland*, Judgment of the Supreme Court of Sweden, No. V 2014/163 (14 December 2022)

*R v Sussex Justices, Ex Parte McCarty* [1924] 1 KB 256

*Slot v Poland*, PCA Case No. 2017-10, Judgment of the Paris Court of Appeal (19 April 2022)

*Strabag et al v Poland*, Judgment of the Paris Court of Appeal (19 April 2022)

Tribunal fédéral [TF], 23 February 2021, 4A_187/2020

# TABLE OF LEGISLATION

## EU Treaties and Acts of Accession

Treaty Establishing the European Coal and Steel Community (signed 18 April 1951, entered into force 22 July 1952, by its terms expired 23 July 2002) 261 UNTS 140

Treaty Establishing the European Economic Community (signed 25 March 1957, entered into force 1 January 1958) 298 UNTS 3, 4 Eur YB 412

Treaty Establishing the European Atomic Energy Community (signed 25 March 1957, entered into force 1 January 1958) 298 UNTS 259, 5 Eur YB 454

Treaty on the European Union (signed 7 February 1992, entered into force 1 November 1993) [1992] OJ C191/1, 31 ILM 253

Act of Accession of the Czech Republic, Estonia, Cyprus, Latvia, Lithuania, Hungary, Malta, Poland, Slovenia, and the Slovak Republic [2003] OJ L236/33

Act of Accession of Bulgaria and Romania [2005] OJ L157/203

Treaty on the Functioning of the European Union – Declarations annexed to the Final Act of the Intergovernmental Conference which adopted the Treaty of Lisbon, signed on 13 December 2007 – A. Declarations concerning provisions of the treaties – 17. Declaration concerning primacy [2008] OJ C 115/344

Treaty on the European Union (consolidated) [2010] OJ C83/13

Treaty on the Functioning of the European Union (consolidated) [2010] OJ C83/47

Act of Accession of the Republic of Croatia [2012] OJ L112/21

Charter of Fundamental Rights of the European Union [2012] OJ C 326/391

European Agreement establishing an association between the European Economic Communities and their Member States, of the one part, and Romania, of the other part [1994] OJ L357/2

Agreement for the termination of Bilateral Investment Treaties between the Member States of the European Union [2020] OJ L 169/1

## EU External Agreements

Agreement on the Withdrawal of the United Kingdom of Great Britain and Northern Ireland from the European Union and the European Atomic Energy Community, 2020 OJ (L 29) 7

General Agreement on Trade in Services (WTO) – Annex 1 – Annex 1B – WTO [1994] OJ L336/191

Stabilisation and Association Agreement between the European Communities and their Member States, of the one part, and the Republic of Croatia, of the other part [2005] OJ L26/3

Stabilisation and Association Agreement between the European Communities and their Member States of the one part, and the Republic of Montenegro, of the other part [2010] OJ L108/3

Free Trade Agreement between the European Union and its Member States, of the one part, and the Republic of Korea [2011] OJ L127/6

Comprehensive Economic and Trade Agreement between Canada, of the one part, and the European Union and its Member States, of the other part [2017] OJ L11/23

Agreement between the European Union and Japan for an Economic Partnership [2018] OJ L330/3

Investment Protection Agreement between the European Union and its Member States, of the one part, and the Republic of Singapore, of the other part (signed 15 October 2018)

Investment Protection Agreement between the European Union and its Member States on the one part, and the Socialist Republic of Viet Nam, of the other part (signed 30 June 2019)

## EU Secondary Legislation and Acts

Council Directive 88/361/EEC of 24 June 1988 for the implementation of Article 67 of the Treaty [1988] OJ L178/5

Decision 001/2021 of the CETA Joint Committee of 29 January 2021 setting out the administrative and organisational matters regarding the functioning of the Appellate Tribunal

Decision 002/2021 of the CETA Joint Committee of 29 January 2021 adopting a procedure for the adoption of interpretations in accordance with Articles 8.31.3 and 8.44.3(a) of CETA as an Annex to its Rules of Procedure (2021/265)

Decision No. 1/2021 of the Committee on Services and Investment of 29 January 2021 adopting a code of conduct for Members of the Tribunal, Members of the Appellate Tribunal and mediators

Statement submitted by the European Communities to the Secretariat of the Energy Charter pursuant to Article 26(3)(b)(ii) of the ECT [1998] OJ L69/115

Services Directive 2006/123 [2006] OJ L376/36

European Parliament and Council Directive (EC) 2019/944 concerning common rules for the internal market in electricity and amending Directive 2012/27/EU [2019] OJ L158/125

European Parliament and Council Directive (EC) 2009/73 concerning common rules for the internal market in natural gas and repealing Directive 2003/55/EC [2009] OJ L211/94

Framework agreement on the relationship between the European Parliament and the European Commission [2010] OJ L 304/47

European Parliament Resolution 2010/2203 (INI) of 4 April 2011 on the future of European international investment policy [2012] OJ C 296E/34

Regulation (EU) 1219/2012 of the European Parliament and of the Council of 12 December 2012 establishing transitional arrangements for bilateral investment agreements between Member States and third countries [2013] OJ C131/2

Regulation (EU) 912/2014 of the European Parliament and of the Council of 23 July 2014 establishing a framework for managing financial responsibility linked to investor-to-state dispute settlement tribunals established by international agreements to which the European Union is party [2014] OJ L257/121

Council Decision (EU) 2017/38 of 28 October 2016 on the provisional application of the Comprehensive Economic and Trade Agreement (CETA) between Canada, of the one part, and the European Union and its Member States, of the other part [2017] OJ L 11/1080

Council Decision (EU) 2022/438 of 14 March 2022 on the position to be adopted on behalf of the EU within the Administrative Council of the ICSID, ST/6125/2022/ INIT, OJ L 89

European Parliament Resolution 2014/2228(INI) of 8 July 2015 containing the European Parliament's recommendations to the European Commission on the negotiations for the Transatlantic Trade and Investment Partnership (TTIP) [2017] OJ C 265/35

European Parliament Resolution 2017/2192(INI) of 26 October 2017 containing the Parliament's recommendation to the Council on the proposed negotiating mandate for trade negotiations with Australia [2018] OJ C 346/212

European Parliament Resolution 2021/2176(INI) of 23 June 2022 on the future of EU international investment policy

European Parliament Resolution 2022/2934(RSP) of 23 November 2022 on the outcome of the modernisation of the Energy Charter Treaty

Statement submitted to the Energy Charter Treaty (ECT) Secretariat pursuant to Article 26(3)(b)(ii) of the ECT replacing the statement made on 17 November 1997 on behalf of the European Communities [2019] OJ L115/1

## International Agreements

Agreement between the Republic of Austria and the Republic of Croatia for the Promotion and Protection of Investments (signed 19 February 1997, entered into force 1 November 1999)

Agreement between Japan and the Republic of Colombia for the Liberalisation, Promotion and Protection of Investment (signed 12 September 2011, entered into force 11 September 2015)

Agreement for the Reciprocal Promotion and Protection of Investments between Columbia and France (signed 10 July 2014)

Agreement between Hungary and the Kingdom of Cambodia for the Promotion and Reciprocal Protection of Investments (signed 14 January 2016, entered into force 30 August 2017)

Agreement between the Slovak Republic and the Islamic Republic of Iran for the Promotion and Reciprocal Protection of Investments (signed 19 January 2016, entered into force 30 August 2017)

Agreement for the Promotion and Protection of Investment between the Government of the Republic of Austria and the Government of the Kyrgyz Republic (signed 22 April 2016)

Agreement between the Slovak Republic and the United Arab Emirates for the Promotion and Protection of Investments (signed 22 September 2016, entered into force 5 February 2018)

Agreement between the Government of Hungary and the Government of Cabo Verde for the Promotion and Reciprocal Protection of Investments (signed 28 March 2019)

Amending Agreements to the Canada–Chile Free Trade Agreement (entered into force 5 February 2019)

Australia-India Economic Cooperation and Trade Agreement (signed 2 April 2022)

Convention on the Recognition and Enforcement of Foreign Arbitral Awards (adopted 10 June 1958, entered into force 7 June 1959) 330 UNTS 3

Convention on the Settlement of International Investment Disputes between States and Nationals of Other States (adopted 18 March 1965, entered into force 14 October 1966) 575 UNTS 159

Convention on Transparency in Treaty-based Investor–State Arbitration (adopted on 10 December 2014, entered into force 18 October 2017)

Comprehensive and Progressive Agreement for Trans-Pacific Partnership (signed 8 March 2018, entered into force 30 December 2018)

The Energy Charter Treaty (adopted 17 December 1994, entered into force 16 April 1998) 2080 UNTS 95

European Convention on Human Rights (adopted 4 November 1950, entered into force 3 September 1953) 213 UNTS 221

General Agreement on Tariffs and Trade (adopted 30 October 1947, entered into force 1 January 1948) 55 UNTS 194

General Agreement on Trade in Services, Marrakesh Agreement Establishing the World Trade Organization, Annex 1B (signed 15 April 1994, entered into force 1 January 1995) 1869 UNTS 183, 33 ILM 1167

Germany and Pakistan Treaty for the Promotion and Protection of Investments (with Protocol and exchange of notes) between (signed 25 November 1959, entered into force 28 November 1962) 457 UNTS 24

North American Free Trade Agreement (adopted 17 September 1992, entered into force 1 January 1994)

Netherlands and Indonesia Agreement on economic cooperation (with protocol and exchanges of letters dates on 17 June 1968) (signed 7 July 1968, entered into force 17 July 1971)

Reciprocal Investment Promotion and Protection Agreement between the Government of the Kingdom of Morocco and the Government of the Republic of Nigeria (signed 3 December 2016)

Statute of the International Court of Justice (signed 26 June 1945, entered into force 24 October 1945)

Treaty between the Government of the United States of America and the Government of Croatia Concerning the Encouragement and Reciprocal Protection of Investment (signed 13 July 1996, entered into force 20 June 2001)

US–Mexico–Canada Trade Agreement (signed 30 November 2018, entered into force 1 July 2020)

Vienna Convention on the Law of the Treaties (concluded 23 May 1969, entered into force 27 January 1980) 1155 UNTS 331

# ABBREVIATIONS

| | |
|---|---|
| AG | Advocate General |
| AIIB | Asian Infrastructure and Investment Bank |
| APEC | Asia-Pacific Economic Cooperation |
| BIT(s) | bilateral investment treaties |
| BRI | Belt and Road Initiative |
| BRIC(S) | Brazil, Russia, India, China (and South Africa) |
| CAJAC | China-Africa Joint Arbitration Centre |
| CARIFORUM | Caribbean Forum |
| CCIAG | Corporate Counsel International Arbitration Group |
| CCP | Common Commercial Policy |
| CCSI | Columbia Center on Sustainable Investment |
| CEE | Central and Eastern Europe |
| CEO | chief executive officer |
| CETA | Comprehensive Economic and Trade Agreement (EU–Canada) |
| CFR | Charter of Fundamental Rights of the European Union |
| CFSP | Common Foreign and Security Policy |
| CIDS | Center for International Dispute Settlement |
| CIETAC | China International Economic and Trade Arbitration Commission |
| CIL | customary international law |
| CJEU | Court of Justice of the European Union |
| CPTPP | Comprehensive and Progressive Agreement for Trans-Pacific Partnership |
| CUP | Cambridge University Press |
| EAC | East African Community |
| EC | European Commission |
| ECHR | European Convention on Human Rights |
| ECT | Energy Charter Treaty |
| ECtHR | European Court of Human Rights |
| ECR | European Court Reports |
| EEA | European Economic Area |
| EEC | European Economic Community |

| | |
|---|---|
| EFTA | European Free Trade Association |
| EP | European Parliament |
| EPA | Economic Partnership Agreement |
| ESA | Eastern and Southern Africa |
| EU | European Union |
| EU IIP | EU international investment policy |
| EUSFTA | EU–Singapore Free Trade Agreement |
| EUSIPA | EU–Singapore Investment Protection Agreement |
| EUVIPA | EU–Vietnam Investment Protection Agreement |
| FCN | treaty of friendship, commerce and navigation |
| FDI | foreign direct investment |
| FET | fair and equitable treatment |
| FMV | fair market value |
| FTA(s) | free trade agreement(s) |
| GATS | General Agreement on Trade in Services |
| GATT | General Agreement on Tariffs and Trade |
| GFC | Global Financial Crisis |
| GSP | Generalised Scheme of Preferences |
| HKIAC | Hong Kong International Arbitration Centre |
| IBA | International Bar Association |
| ICC | International Chamber of Commerce |
| ICJ | International Court of Justice |
| ICS | Investment Court System |
| ICSID | International Centre for the Settlement of Investment Disputes |
| IIA(s) | international investment agreement(s) |
| IIED | International Institute for Environment and Development |
| IIL | international investment law |
| IIR | international investment regulation |
| IISD | International Institute for Sustainable Development |
| ILC | International Law Commission |
| ILO | International Labour Organization |
| IMF | International Monetary Fund |
| INTA | The Committee on International Trade of the European Parliament |
| IPA | Investment Protection Agreement |
| IPCC | Intergovernmental Panel on Climate Change |
| IPR | intellectual property rights |
| ISDS | investor-State dispute settlement |
| ITA | investment treaty arbitration |
| MAI | Multilateral Agreement on Investment |
| MFN | most favoured nation |
| MIA | Multilateral Investment Agreement |

| | |
|---|---|
| MIC | Multilateral Investment Court |
| MIRA | Multilateral Investment Reform Agreement |
| MLI | Multilateral Convention to Implement Tax Treaty Related Measures to Prevent Base Erosion and Profit Sharing |
| MNE(s) | multinational enterprise(s) |
| MST | minimum standard of treatment |
| NAFTA | North America Free Trade Agreement |
| NGO(s) | non-governmental organisation(s) |
| NIEO | New International Economic Order |
| NT | national treatment |
| OBOR | One Belt One Road |
| OECD | Organization for Economic Cooperation and Development |
| OJ | Official Journal |
| OUP | Oxford University Press |
| PCA | Permanent Court of Arbitration |
| PCIJ | Permanent Court of International Justice (replaced by ICJ) |
| PNG | Papua New Guinea |
| QMV | qualified majority voting |
| SAA | Stabilisation and Association Agreements |
| SADC | Southern African Development Community |
| SCC | Stockholm Chamber of Commerce |
| SME(s) | small and medium size enterprise(s) |
| SRF | Silk Road Fund |
| TEU | Treaty on European Union |
| TFEU | Treaty on the Functioning of the European Union |
| TPP | Trans-Pacific Partnership |
| TRIPS | Agreement on Trade-Related Aspects of Intellectual Property Rights |
| TSD | trade and sustainable development |
| TTIP | Transatlantic Trade and Investment Partnership (EU–US) |
| UNCITRAL | United Nations Commission on International Trade Law |
| UNCLOS | United Nations Convention on the Law of the Sea |
| UNCTAD | United Nations Conference on Trade and Development |
| UNGA | United Nations General Assembly |
| UNTS | United Nations Treaty Series |
| UK | United Kingdom |
| US | United States |
| USMCA | United States–Mexico–Canada Agreement |
| VCLT | Vienna Convention on the Law of Treaties |
| WG | Working Group |
| WTO | World Trade Organization |
| WWII | World War II |

# General Introduction

Public and political controversies over investor-state dispute settlement (ISDS) have prompted reform processes at international and regional levels. As an emerging actor in this field, the European Union (EU) has been particularly active in shaping new developments, within and outside the EU, and proposing the establishment of a Multilateral Investment Court (MIC). This research examines the underlying reasons and ways in which the EU has been shaping the field of international investment law (IIL) in order to address its own and global ISDS problems. The analysis of EU law and policy solutions envisioned to reform investment law in this book is undertaken in light of the IIL controversies, the EU constitutional and legal framework and the rule of law and legitimacy, as the normative goals of the ISDS reforms. In doing so, this book evaluates the contribution of the EU to the development of international law in the field of foreign investment.

## Fundamental Issues and the Objectives of This Book

### *The Reform Problem: International Investment Law between Law and Politics*

International investment law sets standards according to which States must treat foreign investors. These standards include substantive and procedural rights, and most notably an option for foreign investors to sue their host State before a tribunal independent from that State. The flaws of this system have crystalised over the last twenty years, leading States to address them through a legal reform, which should improve international investment governance. However, this multilateral reform faces a number of challenges, stemming from the legal design and operation of IIL, tensions within and outside the system and its intersections between legitimacy and the rule of law. The analysis of these key features and reform challenges (Part I) lays ground for the treatment of the EU reform in this book.

International investment law lacks a multilateral legal basis and a central authority. Over 2,500 different international investment agreements (IIAs) in force are interpreted by hundreds of *ad hoc* tribunals, with no appellate mechanism nor competent international court to give authentic interpretations. Due to the factual and legal diversity of investment claims, jurisprudence lacks consistency in painting the full picture of standards of protection. Despite this fragmentation, the field functions effectively according to strikingly similar rules and principles. The private law background of the system and its narrow legal specialisation have created a distinct and uniform culture within the broader system of public international law.

The principled idea behind IIL was to establish a parallel legal system in international law with a new set of rights and procedures, unilaterally and exclusively open to foreign investors. The system was created on a rather simple assumption that it would protect 'good' (Western) investors from the hands of 'bad' (decolonised) States, revengeful for the colonial past. It was meant to provide a neutral forum, which could detach the present from the past, and law from politics. In fact, however, it largely institutionalised the application of foreign (Western) law in the new sovereign States. The colonial origins and its transnational private justice nature did not pose a problem until the system turned against its creators. In the new narrative of globalisation, capital has become the 'good', and regulatory activity of any State, which can negatively affect the interests of capital, the 'bad'. High-profile cases against developed States,[1] opened the debate: is this legal system needed alongside the functioning domestic legal systems? On the other hand, could the abolition of ISDS pose a threat for foreign investors in the countries with 'bad' legal systems? Could the system be reformed without returning it to its binary colonial origins while sufficiently protecting globalised capital?

The complexity of this essentially legal reform is further compounded by the new constellation of international relations in the post–Cold War world. Instead of reaching the 'end of history' as predicted by Francis Fukuyama in 1989,[2] a brave new multipolar world has been created,[3]

[1] *Vattenfall AB, Vattenfall Europe AG, Vattenfall Europe Generation AG v Federal Republic of Germany (I)*, ICSID Case No. ARB/09/6 and *(II)*, ICSID Case No. ARB/12/12; *Philip Morris Asia Limited v The Commonwealth of Australia*, UNCITRAL, PCA Case No. 2012-12.

[2] F. Fukuyama, 'The End of History?' (1989) 16 *The National Interest* 3.

[3] See L. C. Thurow, *The Future of Capitalism: How the Today's Economic Forces Will Shape Tomorrow's World* (William Morrow and Company 1996).

resulting in a regulatory competition between the United States, the EU, China and 'the others'.[4] Globalisation has led to economic decline in the West, with domestic populism influencing foreign trade and investment policies. Contemporary IIL is accordingly shaped around the divergent interests of States, their domestic constituencies and transnational elites. International investment law, like much of international economic law, has failed to keep pace with these rapid global changes.

This legal and political complexity of international investment regulation explains the fragmentation of the system, the need for its reform and the challenges of this reform at a multilateral level.

### *The Normative Problem: International Investment Law between Perceptions and Law*

International investment law has become perceived as a 'privatised justice system for global corporations'[5] and a 'Trojan Horse'[6] that undermines democracy, the public good and the sustainable development agenda of national public policies. Critics also emphasise the arbitration industry, 'the elite club of lawyers behind the scenes',[7] that promotes ISDS for its own interests. The perceived flaws of the system are both substantive and procedural, and intertwined. While the critics would like to see the system abolished, most States have opted for a reform, which has its normative dimension in the rule of law, as primarily a legal concept, and legitimacy, as primarily a political concept.

However, the reform debate has been caught between 'perceptions' as a subjective concept and 'law' as an objective concept. On one side of the spectrum are those within the system, who insist that most issues are only matters of perception and politics. They approach IIL purely from the perspective of technical legal rules, which are always objective, and are in principle working well. On the other side are those who perceive

[4] Depending on the context, the constellation of the big players also involves Russia. However, instead through IIL, Russia has found other ways to retain its influence in the countries of the former Soviet Union.

[5] T. McDonagh, 'Unfair, Unsustainable, and Under the Radar: How Corporations Use Global Investment Rules to Undermine a Sustainable Future' (*The Democracy Center* 2013) 8.

[6] M. Rimmer, 'Trojan Horse Clauses: Investor-State Dispute Settlement', Trade and Foreign Investment (Protecting the Public Interest) Bill 2014, Submission 104 – Supplementary Submission to the Australian Parliament.

[7] McDonagh (n 5) 8.

the system as unfair, for both political and legal reasons. In their view, any reform must fix the systemic problems of IIL; otherwise the system should be dissolved. Most States that participate in the reform are touting the middle ground between these two positions.

This book aims to provide a different perspective on the reform by examining how these issues, which in their essence concern the rule of law and legitimacy in IIL, intersect. In analysing these concepts as the reform's normative goals, the focus is placed on both their formal and their substantive aspects. Rather than excluding legitimacy as political, the aim is to determine the normative dimension of legitimacy and aspects in which it overlaps with the rule of law. At the same time, the aim is also to elucidate the aspects of IIL's legitimacy that are difficult to resolve through traditional international law. The rule of law is examined not only as an instrument of formal and procedural equality but also as a concept with an important substantive dimension, which questions the assumed neutrality of IIL and the perceived bias of arbitration as its dispute settlement mechanism.

In considering the substantive issues of legitimacy and the rule of law, the technical legal aspects of IIL are placed in the broader perspective of general international law. In this respect we will consider how the developments in IIL relate to the transition of international law to a fragmented positivism, in which technical rules and narrow expertise dominate different fields of international law to the exclusion of others.[8] How will the EU reform affect the issues of control and fragmentation in IIL and international law more broadly? The analysis in this book thus aims at transcending the technicalities of international law and exploring its normative core in order to derive new perspectives on the link between the two.

### *The Aspiration: The EU as an Emerging Actor in the Field of Investment*

The aspirations of the EU as a normative power are defined in its founding treaties. The Lisbon Treaty of 2009 confirmed the EU's commitment to multilateralism, development of international law and good global governance when developing and implementing foreign policy.[9]

[8] M. Koskenniemi, *The Politics of International Law* (Hart 2011).

[9] Arts. 3(5) and 21(1)(h) Treaty on the European Union (consolidated) [2010] OJ C83/13 (TEU).

These principles equally apply to its Common Commercial Policy (CCP). The Lisbon Treaty has extended the scope of the CCP to foreign direct investment (FDI).[10] This change introduced the EU to the field of investment, traditionally occupied by its Member States, and opened a new chapter of international investment policy (IIP) in Europe. The Lisbon Treaty changes have set the platform for the EU to become an international player in the field of foreign investment, as part of the EU's broader external trade agenda.

At the time of these changes, IIL had already been facing a legitimacy crisis. Protests against ISDS took place in the broader context of globalisation fatigue. Mega trade agreements, such as the Trans-Pacific Partnership (TPP) for Pacific nations (excluding China) and the Transatlantic Trade and Investment Partnership (TTIP) for Atlantic nations (United States and the EU), were strongly opposed on the basis that they included ISDS and promoted capital interests. On the other hand, in the aftermath of the Global Financial Crisis (GFC), global capital was seen by States as a condition of economic recovery, and IIL as a tool for attracting foreign capital.

In developing an IIP, the EU must comply with international law and support an international system based on multilateralism and good global governance. In addition, it must comply with its own constitutional requirements. Moreover, the EU is called upon to 'promote multilateral solutions to common problems, in particular in the framework of the United Nations'.[11] To what extent does the EU achieve this objective in its reform of IIL? In what ways does its reform develop the system of international law? The EU reform strives to resolve the ISDS crisis in the EU by enhancing the rule of law in IIL, which is also its core constitutional value. This book explores how these EU aspirations are challenged by a range of internal limitations (shared competence for international investment) and external realities (complexity of IIL and its reform).

### *The Reality: The EU Approach to International Investment Law*

The relationship between the EU and IIL in this book is examined at the level of the EU (Part II) and internationally (Part III), exposing the

[10] Art. 207 Treaty on the Functioning of the European Union (consolidated) [2010] OJ C83/47 (TFEU).

[11] Art. 21(1) TEU, second sentence.

complexity and contradictions of EU approaches to IIL. Multilateralism remains the EU's preferred option, at least in theory. In practice, however, the approaches incorporate 'pragmatic-lateralism' (multi-, pluri-, bi-, or uni-), with different solutions for the settlement of disputes between investors and States depending on the issue at hand.

Multilateral cooperation is taking place through the ISDS reform in the United Nations Commission on International Trade Law (UNCITRAL), while supporting other multilateral reform initiatives, for example, in the International Centre for the Settlement of Investment Disputes (ICSID). At the plurilateral level, the EU has lead the modernisation of the controversial Energy Charter Treaty (ECT). Bilaterally, the situation is particularly complex, due to a range of instruments: Member States' pre- and post-Lisbon BITs with third States, new EU IIAs (so far with only five countries – Canada, Singapore, Vietnam, Mexico and Chile), as well as a range of new EU bilateral trade agreements with no ISDS (e.g. Japan, New Zealand). The elimination of intra-EU BITs, which are in essence reminiscent of pre-enlargement West-East divisions, and the replacement of ISDS by the EU judicial system demonstrate the unilateral approach in situations when IIL clashes with the EU legal order.

The EU reform of IIL is piecemeal, long-term and ongoing. While it builds around the idea of a new Investment Court System (ICS) and the establishment of an MIC, in its essence it does not call the ISDS as a system into question. It does not even exclude traditional ISDS in its practice. The dispute settlement mechanism has been the core feature of the EU approach, however, the reform has also introduced new substantive standards of protection. Competence in the field of investment, shared between the EU and its Member States, further compounds the complexity of the EU approach.

The analysis of the reform in this book thus interrelates the different pieces of the EU approach and correlates them to the EU constitutional and legal framework (competences, principles, procedures), while considering both substantive and procedural aspects of the EU reform (within the EU, and in EU and Member States' IIAs). The aim of the book is to connect internal and external dimensions of the EU and to explain how the EU seeks to influence the reform of IIL and the development of international law.

Further, this analysis is placed in the normative framework of the rule of law and legitimacy, which form the red thread of the book. The rule of law is the central concern of the EU reform, and is also one of its core values. The improvement of rule of law qualities of IIL, in particular with respect to the independence of adjudicators, should then also increase the legitimacy of the new system.[12] The focus is on the mode in which the EU incorporates its own vision of the rule of law, replacing traditional ISDS within the EU and externally. In the intra-EU dimension, the emphasis is placed on the role of EU law and its incompatibilities with IIL, the CJEU and the EU judicial system; in the external dimension on the independence of the ICS/MIC judges, and compatibilities with the EU constitutional framework. Ultimately, and in the long run, coherence in the external dimension is to be achieved through the institution of a court, subject to the EU requirements of independence and access to justice (constitutionalism). In its essence, an MIC is thus also a unilateral EU solution for its own investment policy within a multilateral forum, with a hope to achieve a 'Brussels effect'[13] in IIL. This book analyses the limitations of this EU approach in the specific legal and political context of IIL.

## The Scope and Methodology of This Book

Because of the complexity of the topic and its related fundamental issues, the following methodological choices were made in undertaking this research.

### *The Scope of Investment*

In this research it is the broad scope of investment that is considered. Investment encompasses a variety of economic operations and overlaps with broad areas of private and public law (property law, contract law, administrative law, etc.). Investment further overlaps with other concepts which can have legal as well as political meaning, such as public health, the environment, human rights or sustainable development. In economic and legal terms, a distinction can be made between different forms of investment (FDI, portfolio). The analysis in this book illustrates a variety of investment issues, taking into account its interdisciplinary character. The primary focus of this research is international and the EU context,

[12] See EC, 'Multilateral Reform of Investment Dispute Resolution, Impact Assessment' SWD (2017) 302 final.

[13] The process of *de facto* externalisation of EU regulation outside its borders through market mechanisms. The scholarly authority on the topic is A. Bradford, *The Brussels Effect: How the European Union Rules the World* (OUP 2020).

however, where relevant, we also consider the effects of investment regulation in domestic law.

### *Systemic Comparative Analysis*

The emphasis of this research is on the analysis of IIL and EU law as two separate legal orders with their own rules and logic, which overlap in the field of investment. Because they have different objectives, they are only partially comparable. However, comparative systemic analysis serves to explain why and how they produce different legal effects on private and public rights in international and domestic legal spheres.

Most studies focus on some aspects of the interaction between IIL and EU law through the lens of one or the other system. However, this book attempts to explain this interaction in light of the distinct systemic features and legal postulates according to which each system operates. This approach should provide a more global understanding of investment regulation in each legal system and across them, and present the system-specific insights which can better explain their normative relationships. It will enhance the understanding of the relevant features of EU law among international investment lawyers, and *vice versa*, in dealing with legal issues that involve both legal systems.

The first part of the book examines IIL. The focus is placed on the macro legal questions in order to determine the international investment mechanisms in which IIL functions as a legal system, despite its fragmented nature. In the remaining parts, the emphasis is placed on the main features of the EU legal order and its interaction with IIL, in the internal and external dimensions of the EU regulation of investment. While examining the core substantive and procedural rules relating to investment in each legal order, the analysis is largely comparative. On one hand, it aims to explain systemic conflicts between IIL and EU law in the relations between the Member States. On the other hand, when considering EU and Member States' relations with third States, comparative analysis is utilised to determine the extent of cross-fertilisation between international investment and EU rules. In this regard, the analysis examines how the two legal orders interact when developing new rules in IIL.

### *Law in Context*

This research takes into account relevant aspects of political economy and international relations as these contexts inevitably shape international investment governance. On one hand, the aim is to explore the rationale of the EU investment agenda and enquire how this agenda relates to the broader EU objectives, both internally (EU integration) and externally (pragmatic-lateralism, free and fair trade). In this context, the research examines whether law serves as an instrument of politics. On the other hand, the work aims to place the EU investment agenda in the broader context of international investment governance in order to illustrate the external challenges that the EU reform faces, in UNCITRAL and beyond, as the EU needs to gather broad political support for its proposal.

The law in context issues in IIL, including the early developments of the new EU international investment policy, have been explored in the literature in a rather one-dimensional way (within the IIL context or within the EU context). Through the examination of international and EU legal rules, this book aims to provide a comprehensive global understanding of the implementation of EU investment policy internally, in relations between the Member States, and externally, in bilateral and plurilateral relations between the EU/Member States and third States, and multilaterally in UNCITRAL. These different dimensions have their distinct law and policy perspectives, where law serves both to facilitate and to complicate the political process.

This book thus aims to interrelate different dimensions and perspectives (internal, external, bilateral, multilateral, legal, political) and correlate them to the broader framework of EU integration and the international relations context.

### *From Positive Law to Legal Scholarship and Policy Considerations*

This research is based on rules found in the primary legal sources (treaties, investment awards, court decisions, formal statements, proposals), which are critically considered through a variety of secondary sources (legal and political scholarship). In light of the fragmented nature of the field, in the selection of the treaties, importance has been placed on those of the Western States that have had a defining role in the development of the rules (the United States, European States in the pre-Lisbon era). In the selection of investment awards importance was given to those awards that have set important principles for the subsequent awards, dealt with important broader public policy issues or have provided relevant opinions supporting the development of legal scholarship. The focus of the analysis is placed on the main components of the system and their controversial aspects in the legal literature. When examining the legal nature and methods of interpretation and application of international investment rules, parallels have been drawn with other international rules (general international law, trade law, EU law) and legal families (common law, civil law). In this sense, the analysis should be of interest to a broader legal audience.

It follows from the historical and contemporary political context of IIL that analysis of the legal rules must also question the politics behind the law. International investment law as a system and its rules are evaluated normatively against their legitimacy and the rule of law. In defining and assessing the rule of law, the relevance is given to legal scholarship, soft law sources and case law (the CJEU and the European Court of Human Rights), therefore acknowledging different understandings of the rule of law in a variety of contexts (domestic, international, European). In assessing legitimacy, the approach combines theoretical concepts of political science with legal scholarship on the legitimacy of international courts. The theoretical framework of legitimacy and the rule of law guides the analysis and the proposed EU solutions for the reform of IIL throughout the book.

When examining EU law, importance has been placed on CJEU judgments that are landmarks in shaping the EU legal order, and its normative relationships with domestic (Member States' legal orders) and international law. When examining the role of law and the CJEU in defining and shaping EU investment regulation, the analysis unfolds around three core CJEU decisions in the field of investment: the *Achmea* judgment[14] (defining internal EU aspects of investment regulation), Opinion 2/15[15] (defining the EU's investment sovereignty) and Opinion 1/17[16] (defining external EU aspects of investment regulation, both bilaterally and multilaterally). Policy implications of these legal decisions are explained in order to relate the CJEU's legal reasoning to the broader policy context (law as a limitation of policy and law as an instrument of policy). They serve to support the integrationist judicial approach in the intra-EU dimension and a more politically pragmatic approach to EU international relations. The examination of EU rules is inspired by legal scholarship on the international rule of law in the EU context and constitutionalism.

[14] Case C-284/16 *Achmea* ECLI:EU:C:2018:158. See Chapter 5.
[15] Opinion 2/15 ECLI:EU:C:2017:376. See Chapter 6.
[16] Opinion 1/17 ECLI:EU:C:2019:341. See Chapters 8 and 9.

Since this research examines two international legal systems in their political contexts, it has also been inspired by general international legal theory on politics and fragmentation in international law. This book challenges legalistic approaches to IIL and its reform, and confronts the many problems they encounter with the realism of international law and international relations. Consequently, this work will be of interest to lawyers and also to political scientists in the field of international law, as well as to policy practitioners working on IIL reform.

### *Boundaries of This Research*

The reader should bear in mind that IIL is a fast-changing field of law and is highly influenced by political developments. Some findings thus might need to be revisited as new developments occur in the coming years: new awards, particularly in the intra-EU context, and their climate change jurisprudence; the CJEU and domestic courts jurisprudence, particularly on the enforcement of intra-EU awards, within the EU and in third States; the legal text and political developments in relation to the ECT modernisation; and the outcomes of the ongoing UNCITRAL reform process. The EU ICS is not yet functional so its practical implementation could not inform the analysis of the new system. However, the contours of the EU approach to the field have been delineated in light of the landmark judgments of the CJEU, and new solutions considered in light of the existing mechanisms and jurisprudence on which they build. The book strives to emphasise the long-term vision of EU investment law and policy, outline the major trends and give indications whether the envisaged outcomes could constitute a workable compromise, while fulfilling the ideals of the normative framework.

This book does not offer a comprehensive analysis of all IIL issues, nor is it intended to compile a digest of those IIL issues with which it deals. In the same manner, the purpose is not to cover comprehensively all intricacies of EU law, in particular in those parts that deal with substantive EU law. Rather, the book strives to provide a critical overview of different complexities (substantive, procedural, legal, political) involved in the reform of IIL by examining a sufficiently representative selection of issues and jurisprudence. In the part dealing with EU law, it focuses on the institutional and constitutional framework of the EU legal order and its methods (for example, its approach to public interest assessment) and procedures (for example, the relationship with domestic courts). The emphasis is on structural issues and a bird's-eye perspective. At the same time, the analysis of selected issues provides sufficient detail through extensive reference to case law and thus will also be of interest to legal practitioners in both fields. A reader might find a disbalance between approaches in the analysis of IIL and EU law, with the analysis of the former focusing more significantly on controversies. However, this approach is necessary as it outlines the critical position from which the analysis of the EU reform is pursued.

While great effort has been put into presenting different perspectives, some generalisations could not be avoided in the course of providing a general understanding of investment issues across the board. The aim of the book has, however, always remained the same: to provide an objective analysis in a highly polarised legal field. Ultimately, this research is a story about a clash between private and public justice paradigms, a clash which continues without discussion of the concept of justice appropriate to the issues in dispute, thus inviting the reader to reach their own conclusions about what justice in IIL should be.

## How to Read This Book

This book is divided into ten chapters, which are organised into three distinctive parts. In Part I we explore the regulation of international investment – the global problem that the EU aims to resolve. In Part II we consider the ways in which the EU has developed solutions to address the IIL crisis in its internal relations between the Member States, and in Part III in its external relations with third States, bilaterally and multilaterally. Each part of the book provides separate introductory and concluding remarks, which the reader might find useful in understanding the main findings of the analysis. A general conclusion at the end of the book, drawing upon this research as a whole, outlines its essential messages.

A busy reader might choose to focus their attention on specific parts or chapters. Those less familiar with IIL should start with Part I, which outlines its evolution and the main legal features (Chapter 1). Chapter 2 considers the main tensions within the regime of international investment from an interdisciplinary perspective, and thus will be of interest to readers interested in understanding the main challenges of the ISDS reform. Chapter 3 provides a theoretical framework for the analysis and the search for objectivity of IIL through lenses of legitimacy and the rule of law.

Those interested in the interaction between IIL and the EU legal order should focus on Part II. Chapter 4 provides a systemic overview of the EU legal order and analyses the fundamental nature of its clash with IIL, through its internal market and investment regulation. This chapter will be of particular interest for those less familiar with the EU legal order. Chapter 5 then moves to explain the clash between IIL and the EU legal order in the intra-EU dimension. This chapter provides an extensive analysis of legal and policy aspects of this clash, with separate focus on the ECT, enforcement of intra-EU awards, termination of intra-EU BITs and implications of Brexit. It will thus also be of interest to legal and policy practitioners working in this field. Chapter 6, as the final chapter in Part II, turns to analysis of the EU institutional framework in international investment. This chapter combines both internal (competence) and external (treaty-making) aspects of the EU constitutional arrangements in which law functions as a limitation for a more efficient external investment policy. It will be of particular interest to those interested in understanding the rules and procedures for concluding EU trade and investment agreements.

Part III of the book is the longest, reflecting the aim to provide a thorough analysis of the EU approach to the reform of IIL in its external relations. First, the EU international investment policy is assessed in the broader political context of the EU external trade agenda (Chapter 7). As a policy chapter, it will be of particular interest to those seeking to understand the politics behind the evolution of EU international investment policy and its relationship with trade policy. The following two chapters then comprehensively explain the substantive, procedural and dispute settlement aspects of the EU external investment regulatory framework. In Chapter 8 new standards in the post-Lisbon world, in EU IIAs, Member States' extra-EU BITs and the ECT are analysed and discussed in light of the long-term perspective of the EU international investment policy. Those interested in the EU's investment court system should read Chapter 9, which explains and critiques the new mechanism against the rule of law criteria. Finally, Chapter 10 focuses on the UNCITRAL reform process and debates, explaining the EU proposal for a new investment court (MIC) in the context of this reform and its normative goals. This chapter also reconnects the ongoing ISDS reform discussions with the analysis of IIL in Part I. As the reform process is ongoing and its outcomes – including an MIC – uncertain, this is one of the shortest chapters of this book. Its brevity is also an indication of a process that will likely result in many more books to come.

# PART I

# International Investment Regulation

# Introduction to Part I

## International Investment Regulation

> International law is at its strongest when developed in politically and intellectually interesting, but financially mostly irrelevant, directions. When international law meets the cruel external world of private financial interests, it is on much more precarious ground[1]

International investment law (IIL) and its dispute settlement mechanism is a rare model in international law that allows foreign investors to bring claims for monetary awards directly against States in an international forum, on the basis of international law. Traditionally, individuals have not been subjects of public international law, while State sovereignty has been the main tenet of public international law. How then could individuals, let alone foreign private entities, compel States to engage in dispute resolution with far-reaching consequences? Born out in the 1960s of necessity to protect cross-border investment flows, this area of international law has developed into an extensive and yet fragmented system of instruments for protection of foreign investments and liberalisation of international markets. The development of IIL in a relatively short period of time has been stimulated by an increase in the number of international investment agreements (IIAs) and driven by the rise of investment treaty arbitration (ITA) and jurisprudence. Consequently, the institutional design for investment disputes has become the focus of intense criticism. Debate has evolved around questions of the legitimacy of the international investment regime and its compliance with the rule of law.

In order to contextualise the investor-State dispute settlement (ISDS) reform trends, Part I of this study provides an overview of international investment regulation (IIR), focusing on its legal, political and economic characteristics. Chapter 1 explains the emergence of IIR and discusses its complexities through legal analysis of select substantive and procedural issues. Chapter 2 identifies different tensions within the field as

[1] M. Parish, *Mirages of International Justice* (Edward Elgar 2011) 153.

challenges of the ISDS reform. In Chapter 3 these challenges are linked to the conceptual framework of the legitimacy and the rule of law. Part I thus sets the stage for the analysis of investment issues within the EU in Part II, and the consideration of EU external investment dimension, in particular the proposed Multilateral Investment Court (MIC) as a response to ISDS challenges, in Part III.

# 1

# International Investment Law

## History, Rules and Procedures

The legal foundation of international investment regulation (IIR) is vast, complex and varied, across numerous substantive and procedural rules. It is laid down in close to 3,000 different international investment agreements (IIAs).[1] This network of investment treaties is complemented by two key arbitration treaties: the 1958 New York Convention for the enforcement of arbitral awards,[2] and the 1965 International Centre for the Settlement of Investment Disputes (ICSID) Convention,[3] which provides a forum and procedural rules for investment treaty arbitration (ITA). This complex landscape thus legitimately begs the question: how have we come to this network of legal instruments, and what do they entail?

## 1.1 Historical Development of International Investment Law

International investment law (IIL) is a rather new subfield of international law; however, the need for foreign investment protection is not a modern phenomenon. The historical development of IIL can be followed through several stages, spanning the colonial period to modern-day globalisation.

### *1.1.1 Early Development of International Protection of Foreign Investors*

Before World War II, investment was an ancillary of various commerce agreements and a feature of customary international law (CIL), while the

[1] Detailed overview of IIAs and investment dispute settlement is available at UNCTAD, *Investment Policy Hub* <https://investmentpolicy.unctad.org>.

[2] Convention on the Recognition and Enforcement of Foreign Arbitral Awards (adopted 10 June 1958, entered into force 7 June 1959) 330 UNTS 3 (New York Convention).

[3] Convention on the Settlement of International Investment Disputes between States and Nationals of Other States (adopted 18 March 1965, entered into force 14 October 1966) 575 UNTS 159 (ICSID Convention).

enforcement of property protections for foreign subjects was left to gunboat diplomacy.

During the period of colonisation, Western commercial interests in colonised territories were protected under imperial laws and enforced through political and military control in the colonies. Outside colonised territories, mostly in Asia and the Far East, foreign commercial interests were guaranteed through extraterritorial application of European or American laws, ensured through treaties.[4] Among the Western powers, the predecessors of today's investment agreements were bilateral 'treaties of friendship, commerce and navigation' (FCNs), which governed commerce relations between the United States and its trading partners. The focus of FCNs, however, was trading rights and protection of property, rather than investment protections as such. Therefore, the principal mechanisms for protection of foreign commercial interests in this era were non-legal. Protection was granted through foreigners' home State diplomatic protection, supported if necessary by military means, which were at the time recognised as legitimate in cases of breaches of international law.[5] According to the then-dominant theory, under CIL, the property of foreign subjects was entitled to a minimum standard of treatment (MST), but the content of this standard was vague and unclear.[6]

The main opponent of the Western interpretations of CIL and the MST principles were Latin American States, which adhered to national treatment according to the Calvo doctrine. The compromise between the two opposing theories was found in the mechanism of espousal, whereby the home State would espouse the investor's claim, but only after all local remedies of the host country had been exhausted. The disagreement between the United States and Latin American countries over the MST received an additional dimension in view of the Hull Rule, which demanded 'adequate, effective and prompt' compensation for expropriation of property as an international law standard, and emerged as a response to Mexican expropriations of American oil interests in 1938.[7]

[4] H. H. A. Van Harten, 'The Emerging System of International Investment Arbitration' (DPhil thesis, London School of Economics 2005) 31–32.

[5] See K. J. Vandevelde, 'A Brief History of International Investment Agreements' (2005) 12 *UC Davis Journal of International Law and Policy* 157, 158–161.

[6] A. Newcombe and L. Paradell, *Law and Practice of Investment Treaties: Standards of Treatment* (Kluwer 2009) 11–12.

[7] ibid 18.

While IIL hardly had relevance for investors in the colonial period as they relied on diplomatic protection, the contours of the divide between capital-importing and capital-exporting States started to appear. The Soviet nationalisation of private property in Russia in 1917 introduced ideological divisions that would dominate the next period.

### *1.1.2 Post-colonial Development in International Investment Law*

Following World War II and until the end of the Cold War in 1989, the development of IIL was shaped by decolonisation and the establishment of a multilateral economic framework.[8]

The decolonisation of Africa and Asia reformulated the balance of power in international relations. Former colonies, now newly independent States, believed that economic independence was an integral part of their political self-determination and were determined to gain greater control of their resources. Many embraced a socialist economic agenda, which allowed them to nationalise key sectors of their economy, expropriating existing foreign investment.[9] Foreign capital and foreign ownership and control over the means of production were seen as a new form of colonisation, which could lead to foreign interference in domestic affairs.[10] With the balance of power in the UN General Assembly, and supported by the Eastern Bloc, developing States pressed for the Declaration on the New International Economic Order (NIEO) in 1974,[11] which proclaimed the entitlement of each State to exercise effective control over their natural resources and all economic activities, 'including the right to nationalisation or transfer of ownership to its nationals', without specifying any obligation to pay compensation.[12] Although by nature political, these UN instruments denounced the Hull Rule as a rule of CIL, leaving the status of foreign investment in the former colonies uncertain.

While developing States embraced a State-controlled economy with the premise of nationalism, the West was heading towards economic liberalisation. International consensus on trade liberalisation was reached

[8] Vandevelde (n 5) 161.

[9] Newcombe and Paradell (n 6) 19.

[10] Vandevelde (n 5) 166.

[11] Declaration on the Establishment of a New International Economic Order, UNGA Res 3201 (S-VI) (1 May 1974) UN Doc A/RES/320 (S-VI).

[12] ibid 4(e).

in the General Agreement on Tariffs and Trade (GATT).[13] However, investment liberalisation posed more difficulties. The failed Havana Charter,[14] which attempted to provide a legal framework for both trade and investment, indicated that IIL would be developed separately from trade. Other non-governmental initiatives that emerged at the time were equally unable to mount a consensus on a multilateral legal framework for investment.[15] In the absence of a multilateral investment agreement and with uncertain CIL on investment, a new bilateral mechanism was progressively introduced to allow protection of foreign investment under international law in the volatile political and economic environments of newly formed States.

The first bilateral investment treaty (BIT) was signed between West Germany and Pakistan in 1959.[16] Failing to induce a multilateral agreement, Germany introduced its own BIT programme, with other European countries soon to follow this practice. The BIT with Pakistan set out a series of rights for investors with an objective to create favourable investment conditions for the promotion of investment and encouragement of private industrial and financial prosperity. The underlying consideration was nevertheless political. Pakistan's internal instability prompted Germany to gain reassurance that its economic interests in Pakistan would be protected, while Pakistan differentiated itself from its rival India.[17] The United States kept FCNs with improved investment focus until it established its own BIT programme in 1977.[18]

In this initial period, BITs were signed exclusively between developed and developing countries. In theory, they had reciprocal obligations and could be considered symmetrical in their legal effects. In practice, they were asymmetrical in their political and economic effects with a one-sided flow of foreign capital from developed to developing countries. This led to *de facto* asymmetrical legal effects with obligations borne by the developing countries. Bilateral investment treaties formalised the Hull

[13] General Agreement on Tariffs and Trade (adopted 30 October 1947, entered into force 1 January 1948) 55 UNTS 194 (GATT 1947).

[14] Havana Charter for an International Trade Organisation (1948) UN Doc E/CONF.2/78.

[15] See Section 10.1 in Chapter 10.

[16] Germany–Pakistan BIT, Treaty between the Federal Republic of Germany and Pakistan for the Promotion and Protection of Investments (with Protocol and exchange of notes) (signed 25 November 1959, entered into force 28 November 1962) 457 UNTS 24.

[17] M. Parish, *Mirages of International Justice* (Edward Edgar 2011) 128.

[18] A. T. Guzman, 'Why LDCs Sign Treaties That Hurt Them: Explaining the Popularity of Bilateral Investment Treaties' (1998) 38 *Virginia Journal of International Law* 639, 654.

Rule, undermining the economic independence that developing countries so fiercely and collectively promoted. However, developing countries were willing to enter into BITs individually to better compete for Western foreign investment with other developing countries. At the same time, they were unwilling to enter into a multilateral investment treaty, which would undermine their comparative advantage in attracting foreign investment obtained by signing a BIT.[19]

The first BITs did not provide for investor-state dispute settlement (ISDS). A conditional ISDS provision was introduced in the Netherlands–Indonesia BIT in 1968.[20] A year later, the Italy–Chad BIT incorporated the first unconditional ISDS clause. Investor-state dispute settlement provisions started to be included in BITs following the establishment of the International Centre for Settlement of Investment Disputes (ICSID) in 1965–1968.[21] Under the auspices of the World Bank, ICSID was created with a view to providing a neutral forum for the settlement of disputes between investors and States, outside the ambit of influence of national laws. It was seen as an important step in placing investment protection 'in the realm of law rather than politics'.[22] However, ICSID was primarily envisaged as a forum for disputes arising from large contracts between States and foreign investors. Its focus shifted from arbitration under State contracts to treaty-based arbitration only because State contracts did not generate a sufficient number of disputes – until 1990 ICSID had only twenty-six registered cases.[23]

Bilateral investment treaties provided a credible commitment to consent to private arbitration and were an important development in IIL. However, in this early period BITs were still weak instruments with imperfect dispute settlement provisions.[24] Their number remained modest with less than 400 agreements concluded between 1959 and

[19] ibid 679.

[20] The operation of ISDS was conditional upon the host State giving consent to arbitration to ICSID: see Art. 11 Netherlands–Indonesia BIT, Netherlands and Indonesia Agreement on economic cooperation (with protocol and exchanges of letters dates on 17 June 1968) (signed 7 July 1968, entered into force 17 July 1971).

[21] For a history of ICSID, see C. Baltag, 'The ICSID Convention: A Successful Story – The Origins and History of the ICSID' in C. Baltag (ed), *ICSID Convention after 50 Years: Unsettled Issues* (Kluwer 2017) 1–24.

[22] Vandevelde (n 5) 175.

[23] V. Heiskanen, 'Forbidding Dépeçage: Law Governing Investment Treaty Arbitration' (2009) 32 *Suffolk Transnational Law Review* 367.

[24] See J. W. Yackee, 'Conceptual Differences in the Empirical Study of Bilateral Investment Treaties' (2008) 33 *Brooklyn Journal of International Law* 405.

1989. It is only the next period in the history of IIL that brought a proliferation of different instruments.

### *1.1.3 International Investment Law in the Post–Cold War Period: Towards International Investment Regulation*

The end of the Cold War opened a new chapter in the development of IIL. With the dissolution of the Soviet Bloc, the new global political and economic order was to be based on democracy and market capitalism, as neoliberalism became the dominant creed. International investment law was to be developed on the same ideological foundation.

In the new order, the old differences – capital-exporting versus capital-importing and free market versus State-controlled economies – would diminish. The triumph of the Western political and economic idea suggested that we might have reached 'the end of history' – with liberal democracy and free market capitalism as the final form of human government.[25] The role of the State was to fundamentally change, from ownership of business enterprises to regulator with little involvement in the market. There was a dramatic rise in the number of BITs concluded because they signalled a country's openness to foreign investment. The World Bank promoted this practice, as the access to development funds was made conditional upon signing BITs.

In parallel, a new generation of comprehensive bilateral and regional trade agreements started to emerge, encompassing trade and investment provisions to better reflect new economic realities, shaped by the economic activity of multinational and transnational companies. These global enterprises rose in numbers and size, but also in power, with the ability to influence trade by controlling foreign direct investment (FDI) flows. Their economic activity had significant impact on production, sales, services and employment in many different locations.[26] Their effect, however, transcends a purely economic sphere. The concept of globalisation advances the idea of a global system in which transnational corporations are dominant forces. Ultimately, they necessitate legal instruments to facilitate their cross-border operations.

[25] F. Fukuyama, 'The End of History?' (1989) 16 *The National Interest* 3.

[26] J. M. Kline and R. D. Ludema, 'Building a Multilateral Framework for Investment: Comparing the Development of Trade and Investment Accords' (1997) 6 *Transnational Corporations* 1, 20–21.

New global economic governance meant closer economic integration between countries with differing economic development. In North America, this integration was to happen in 1994 through the North American Free Trade Agreement (NAFTA), a new regional trade agreement between Canada, the United States and Mexico, while in Europe it was through the enlargement of the EU. In this global era of IIL, the distinctions of the previous era seemed to disappear, with investment agreements being concluded at all levels (bilateral, regional and plurilateral) and between any States, regardless of their economic development or geographic position. States were willing to enter into these agreements in the expectation of increased levels of investment capital inflows.[27] This era marked a shift from nation-State-centred IIL towards the implementation of treaties through specialised bodies and their international investment regulation.[28]

However, while seen as instruments for attracting foreign capital, States were not fully aware of the policy implications of IIAs.[29] Arbitral proceedings under BITs were rare and there was no jurisprudence to indicate their practical effects. Since then, ITA has risen to over 1,200 cases as per mid-2022.[30]

### *1.1.4 (Re)Politicisation of Investor-State Dispute Settlement?*

The rise of ITA brought to States awareness of possible negative implications of IIAs, not only because of large monetary compensations[31] but also increased limitations on government regulatory powers, prompting the change in the approach to investment treaties.[32] The change of mood

[27] UNCTAD, 'Trade and Development Report 2014: Global Governance and Policy Space for Development' (2014), UNCTAD/TDR/2014, 141.

[28] See M. Koskenniemi, *The Politics of International Law* (Hart 2011) 318–324.

[29] See L. N. Skovgaard Poulsen and E. Aisbett, 'When the Claim Hits: Bilateral Investment Treaties and Bounded Rational Learning' (2013) 65 *World Politics* 273, and C. Côté, 'Is Chilling Out There? International Investment Agreements and Government Regulatory Autonomy' (2016) 16 *Academy of International Business Insights* 14.

[30] UNCTAD, 'International Investment Dispute Settlement Navigator' (*Investment Policy Hub*).

[31] See, for example, *Occidental Petroleum Corporation and Occidental Exploration and Production Company v The Republic of Ecuador*, ICSID Case No. ARB/06/11, Award (5 October 2012). Ecuador was compelled to pay US$1.8 billion (US$2.3 billion with interest) for terminating the contract with the oil company, which was later reduced to US$1 billion plus interest.

[32] UNCTAD 2014 (n 27) 141. Other factors are also mixed results from studies on the impact of BITs on investment flows: see Section 2.1.2 in Chapter 2.

can also be linked to the Global Financial Crisis (GFC) of 2007–2008. In the age of 'guarded globalisation',[33] countries have become aware of the risks that come with opening markets to foreign competition, showing signs of reversion towards economic protectionism. This trend was exacerbated by American policy under the Trump administration and accelerated during the Covid-19 pandemic. Countries have been moving away from unconstrained cross-border cooperation, prioritising economic sovereignty over mutual interdependence. Russia's invasion of Ukraine in February 2022 might well be the end of the unfettered globalisation of the last three decades.

Investment treaty arbitration was promoted as a tool for the depoliticisation of disputes involving a foreign investor and a sovereign State. It built upon instruments of international commercial arbitration, with the same aim of removing business conflicts involving States from Cold War politics.[34] However, while the credibility of commercial arbitration remains largely intact, there is a growing distrust in the arbitration system for matters involving public interest. Commercial diplomacy remains an important aspect of investment dispute settlement and in some cases is even more desirable than law. On the other hand, legal disputes in investment arbitration are now seen as instruments of politics in the hands of foreign investors and specialised legal experts.

Accordingly, in the age of increasing politicisation, ISDS suffers from the same ills. Heated political debate has prompted States to react, through bilateral and multilateral ISDS reforms. Next, we explain substantive and procedural rules to provide a legal framework of contemporary IIR against which the reform process will be considered. The aim is to demonstrate that issues of relevance for IIR are not exclusively matters of politics and public perception but also matters of law.

## 1.2 Substantive Rules of International Investment Law

International investment agreements provide a legal framework for foreign investment in the host States by including specific substantive and procedural guarantees for foreign investors. While IIL lacks a multilateral legal basis, substantive protections provided in numerous treaties are

[33] I. Bremmer, 'The New Rules of Globalization' (2014) 92 *Harvard Business Review* 103.
[34] Y. Dezalay and B. G. Garth, *Dealing in Virtue* (University of Chicago Press 1996) 311.

considerably similar.[35] Given the complexity of substantive protections, we limit this discussion to key guarantees provided to foreign investors in IIAs and their interpretation by investment tribunals. Recent trends of States in improving substantive protection provisions are also noted. The discussion is not meant to be exhaustive but rather functional to the examination of relevant legal issues, with focus placed on the most contentious and systemic issues.

### *1.2.1 Protection against Expropriation*

International law duly protects foreign property against expropriation. However, this concept has always been the subject of controversy. On the one hand, expropriation of private property is an exercise of State sovereignty. On the other hand, private property is an inalienable individual right.[36] As discussed, in the second half of the twentieth century, the debate was centred on divergent views between developed and developing countries regarding the standard of compensation for 'direct' expropriation of property that was nationalised. With the proliferation of IIAs at the end of twentieth century, full compensation for expropriation has become an accepted standard. The debate has since shifted toward the issue of what constitutes expropriation, especially in situations other than the classical category of nationalisation, and the impact of the concept of expropriation on regulatory powers of the State for the protection of health, safety, environment and other legitimate public policy goals.

There are two types of expropriation. 'Direct' or *de iure* expropriation results in the transfer of title to foreign property or its physical possession, with permanent deprivation of property. 'Indirect' or *de facto* expropriation refers to government measures without formal transfer of title, which interfere with exercise of property rights, leading to effective loss of control or significant depreciation of property value.[37] Such measures are also described as measures 'tantamount' or 'equivalent' to

[35] See M. F. Houde and K. Yannaca-Small, 'Relationships between International Investment Agreements' (OECD Publishing 2004) Annex III.

[36] M. Raff, *Private Property and Environmental Responsibility: A Comparative Study of German Real Property Law* (Kluwer 2003) 165–166.

[37] UNCTAD, 'International Investment Agreements: Key Issues' (2004), UNCTAD/ITE/IIT/2004/10 (Vol. I) 236.

expropriation or nationalisation.[38] While the first category, well recognised and prohibited in international law, has become more rare, the significance of the second category has greatly increased through jurisprudence of investment tribunals.[39]

States generally have a right to expropriate, but this right is limited by fulfilment of certain conditions in order for the expropriation to be legal. These conditions include: the public interest purpose of the measure; absence of discrimination; due process of law; and payment of *prompt, adequate and effective* compensation.[40] German BITs refer only to public purpose and compensation requirements but require that the legality of a measure and the amount of compensation be subject to review by due process of law.[41] Therefore, even in the cases when expropriation is legal, treaties require the payment of compensation, usually in the amount of 'fair market value'. Only exceptionally can compensation be excluded, and that is in cases which fall within the police powers doctrine.[42] In practice, this leads to an unsatisfactory 'all or nothing approach', where the essential question becomes not whether expropriation was lawful or unlawful but whether or not it has occurred.[43] If expropriation happened, it will trigger the liability of the State to pay full indemnification to the affected investor.[44] If the expropriation did not happen, the investor

[38] *Técnicas Medioambientales Tecmed, S.A. v The United Mexican States*, ICSID Case No. ARB (AF)/00/2, Award (29 May 2003) para. 114.

[39] M. W. Reisman and R. D. Sloane, 'Indirect Expropriation and Its Valuation in the BIT' (2004) *Yale Law School Faculty Scholarship Series*, Paper 1002, 118–119.

[40] See, for example, Art. 13(1) Energy Charter Treaty (adopted 17 December 1994, entered into force 16 April 1998) 2080 UNTS 100 (ECT); Art. 6 US Model BIT (2012); Art. 1110 North American Free Trade Agreement (adopted 17 September 1992, entered into force 1 January 1994) (NAFTA); Art. 8.12 Comprehensive Economic and Trade Agreement between Canada, of the one part, and the European Union and its Member States, of the other part [2014] OJ L11/23 (CETA) (emphasis added).

[41] R. Dolzer and Y. Kim, 'Germany' in C. Brown (ed), *Commentaries on Selected Model Investment Treaties* (OUP 2013) 309–310.

[42] *Philip Morris Brands Sàrl, Philip Morris Products SA and Abal Hermanos SA Oriental v Republic of Uruguay*, ICSID Case No. Arb/10/7, Award (8 July 2016) paras. 188, 295.

[43] U. Kriebaum, 'Regulatory Takings: Balancing the Interests of the Investor and the State' (2007) 8 *The Journal of World Investment and Trade* 717, 719–720.

[44] The difference between lawful and unlawful expropriation is in the payment of compensation or damages, with unlawful expropriation requiring *restitutio in integrum*: *Case Concerning the Factory at Chorzów (Germany v Poland)*, (Indemnity) [1928] PCIJ Rep Series A No. 17; *ADC Affiliate Limited and ADC & ADMC Management Limited v The Republic of Hungary*, ICSID Case No. ARB/03/16, Award (2 October 2006) paras. 484–494 and cases cited within.

alone will bear the full economic damage to his investment caused by a regulatory measure.

The greatest difficulty in the context of protection against expropriation is, thus, determining the line between a non-compensable regulatory measure and compensable indirect expropriation. While the majority of treaties offer limited guidance in this regard, arbitral tribunals have developed a number of criteria relevant for the determination of expropriation on a case-by-case basis, but offering only limited predictability, as their positions in regard to the relevance of facts in the exercise of tribunals' judgment vary from case to case.[45] In general, tribunals have focused on the extent, severity and duration of the impact of a regulatory measure on the investment as decisive elements in determining whether expropriation took place.

For expropriation to be found, the effect of the measure must result in 'substantial deprivation' of the investor's property interests: of relevance is whether the particular interference with business activities was 'sufficiently restrictive to support the conclusion that the property has been "taken" from the owner';[46] that is, 'ousting the investor from full ownership and control of [the] investment'.[47] Tribunals also examine the effect of the measure on the economic value of investment – for expropriation to be established, the effects of the measure must result in 'depriving the owner in whole or in significant part of the use or reasonably-to-be-expected economic benefit of the property';[48] in other words, depriving the investor in whole or in part of its investment where 'the loss of value is such that it can be considered equivalent to a deprivation of property'.[49] Depending on the context and circumstances, deprivation can amount to an expropriation even if it was 'partial and temporary', but it will usually have to amount to 'a lasting removal of the ability of an owner to make use of its economic rights'.[50] The difficulty lies in

45 The challenge of predictability was expressed by the Tribunal in *Generation Ukraine, Inc. v Ukraine*, ICSID Case No. ARB/00/9, Award (16 September 2003) para. 20.29.

46 *Pope & Talbot Inc. v The Government of Canada*, UNCITRAL, Interim Award (26 June 2000) para. 102.

47 ibid para. 100.

48 *Metalclad Corp v United Mexican States*, ICSID Case No. ARB (AF)/97/1, Award (30 August 2000) para. 103. See also *CME Czech Republic B.V. v The Czech Republic*, Final Award (14 March 2003) paras. 591, 604–608.

49 *Charanne B.V. v Spain*, SCC Arb. No. 062/2012, Final Award (21 January 2016) para. 465.

50 *S. D. Myers, Inc. v Government of Canada*, Partial Award (13 November 2000) para. 283. In this case the Tribunal did not find that the Canadian government measure, which

determining what constitutes 'substantial deprivation', which is a 'fact-sensitive assessment' and 'cannot be conducted on the basis of rigid binary rules', thus indicating that the assessment is qualitative rather than quantitative.[51]

While there is no doubt that the gravity of the effects of a government measure on an investment should be a significant factor in determining expropriation, it is more controversial whether it should be the *only* relevant criterion, which is the approach reflecting the 'sole effect' doctrine. Such an approach disregards the purpose of the government measure, which can entail an important public interest. In some cases where the sole effect doctrine has been applied, tribunals have explicitly stated that motivations behind the State measure play no role in determining expropriation.[52] The diametrically opposite approach is the one that applies the 'police powers' doctrine: the principle that the State's reasonable *bona fide* exercise of police powers in matters of public order, health or morality excludes compensation even when it causes economic damage to an investor, and thus as it is not considered expropriation, does not give rise to *any* compensation.[53]

The criteria for determining when a government measure will not be considered expropriation include 'non-discriminatory regulation', made for a 'public purpose', which is 'enacted with due process' and does not involve any 'specific commitments' that the government would refrain from such regulation given by the government to the putative investor.[54] Such regulation must be made in good faith and in the 'normal exercise' of the State's regulatory powers.[55] However, the mentioned criteria for determining whether an expropriation occurred significantly overlap with the criteria for determining lawful expropriation when expropriation has occurred, and which requires payment of compensation.

consisted in a temporary closure of the border for a duration of eighteen months, amounted to expropriation.

51 *Chemtura Corporation v Government of Canada* (formerly *Crompton Corporation v Government of Canada*), Award (2 August 2010) para. 249.

52 For example, in *Metalclad* (n 48) para. 111; *Tippetts v Iran* (1986) 6 Iran-US Cl Trib Rep 219, 225–226.

53 *Philip Morris* (n 42) paras. 188, 295 (emphasis added). However, it is also significant to note that, in coming to this conclusion, the Tribunal first examined the effects of the challenged legislation on the value of investment, establishing that 'sufficient value' remained after the measures have been implemented: para. 286.

54 *Methanex Corporation v United States of America*, Final Award of the Tribunal on Jurisdiction and Merits (3 August 2005) part IV, ch. D, para. 7.

55 *Saluka Investments B.V. v The Czech Republic*, Partial Award (17 March 2006) para. 255.

In addition, it remains unclear what regulations would be permissible as falling within the police powers doctrine, effectively leaving to investment tribunals in each particular case to answer the question '*when, how and at what point*' a regulation becomes, '*in fact and effect*', an (un)lawful expropriation, which requires the payment of compensation or damages.[56] In some cases, when characterising a measure as within a State's police power, tribunals have shown a willingness to accept 'scientific consensus on public health issues' and a State's international obligations in regard to a particular measure, while allowing for 'substantial deference' to decision-making of specialised national authorities in assessing the necessity of the measure.[57]

Seeking a middle way between the sole effect and police powers doctrines, tribunals attempted to apply a more balanced approach by taking into consideration the effects of the measure on the investor as well as the purpose of the measure. However, although recognising that it is appropriate for tribunals to examine the 'purpose and effect of a government measure', the tribunals effectively still focus on the measure's effect, and not its purpose.[58] In the equation, a relevant factor in determining expropriation is also the investor's reasonable 'investment-backed expectations', involving consideration of the governmental interference 'in light of the investor's chosen business model, the nature of the enterprise, the regulatory regime in place at the time of investment, and associated expectations'.[59] However, this approach also proceeds from examination, first, of the effects of the measure before considering the balancing process.

In some cases, tribunals resorted to the proportionality test to establish whether expropriation took place, examining the measure undertaken by government in light of the protected public interest and the legally granted investment protection. However, in this exercise the tribunals also prioritised the significance of a measure's impact on investment as a key element for assessing proportionality.[60] While the proportionality approach in this context has been inspired by the jurisprudence of the

[56] This quote is adopted from *Saluka* (ibid) paras. 263–264.

[57] *Philip Morris* (n 42) paras. 95, 418–419; *Chemtura* (n 51) paras. 134–138.

[58] *S. D. Myers* (n 50) paras. 281–282; *Marvin Roy Feldman Karpa v United Mexican States*, ICSID Case No. ARB(AF)/99/1, Award (16 December 2002) paras. 110–111.

[59] *Fireman's Fund Insurance Company v The United Mexican States*, ICSID Case No. ARB (AF)/02/1, Award (17 July 2006) para. 176.

[60] *Tecmed* (n 38) para. 122.

European Court of Human Rights (ECtHR),[61] it has been applied differently; it is used for determining whether expropriation occurred, and not whether it achieved a fair balance between protection of private and public rights after establishing that lawful expropriation occurred, which can lead to compensation below market value.[62]

Based on the controversies noted in the jurisprudence, more recent IIAs have attempted to strike a balance between compensable and non-compensable regulatory measures by providing a clarification of what constitutes indirect expropriation, or by providing guidance in regard to criteria which should be used when assessing indirect expropriation.[63] While giving more clarity in defining the concept of indirect expropriation, this approach mainly codifies the middle way already adopted by arbitral tribunals.[64]

### *1.2.2 Fair and Equitable Treatment*

Another key substantive protection afforded in IIAs is the right to fair and equitable treatment (FET). Due to its divergent formulation and breadth, FET has been widely used by investors as a catch-all provision. Investors have relied upon it in cases when their claims have not been covered by more specific protection clauses.[65] While difficult to be defined precisely, FET is understood as

> [g]overnment according to the rule of law that establishes basic substantive and procedural rights concerning the stability and predictability of the legal framework; consistency of the host State's decision making; the protection of investor confidence or "legitimate expectations"; procedural

[61] ibid para. 122.

[62] Kriebaum (n 43) 730.

[63] See for example, the US Model BIT 2012 in Annex B, Arts. 4(b) and 4(a) respectively. See also Section 8.2.1.2 in Chapter 8 for EU practice.

[64] The new US–Mexico–Canada Trade Agreement (signed 30 November 2018, entered into force 1 July 2020) (USMCA) limits the scope of ISDS clauses to direct expropriation only: Art. 14.D.3(1), with the exception of covered government contracts in Annex 15-E, whereby ISDS remains available for both direct and indirect expropriation: see Annex 14-E, Arts. 2(a)(i) and (b)(i).

[65] *PSEG Global, Inc., The North American Coal Corporation, and Konya Ingin Electrik Üretim ve Ticaret Limited Sirketi v Republic of Turkey*, ICSID Case No. ARB/02/5, Award (19 January 2007) para. 238. Comparison could be made with civil law codes, which include a number of specific clauses, but also a general clause of duty to act in good faith, as a catch-all provision.

due process and the prohibition of denial-of-justice; protection against discrimination and arbitrariness; and the requirement of transparency.[66]

International investment agreements refer to these elements differently in their formulation of the FET standard. For example, German BITs include the FET standard as an autonomous obligation, stipulating that investors will be accorded the 'fair and equitable standard and full protection', without specifying the content of the standard, and without reference to international law. The Energy Charter Treaty (ECT) clarifies that FET treatment in any case shall not be 'less favourable than the treatment required under international law'.[67] US BITs identify FET standard as a standard of protection in accordance with international law.[68] These different formulations have thus raised the issue of how the standard is to be measured: as an MST of aliens under CIL or as an unqualified concept. The difference is significant as the former position sets a much higher threshold of liability for States than the latter one, which is thus more favourable to investors.

Depending on the treaty in question, tribunals have approached this issue differently, with many observing that the FET standard is not the same as an MST but it is still a standard which has to be determined by reference to international law, part of which is CIL.[69] The issue has been most prominent in the context of NAFTA, where the Contracting States, being dissatisfied with tribunals' interpretations of the FET standard beyond the MST, issued a binding interpretation.[70] Despite the initial resistance,[71] tribunals have generally accepted that the NAFTA FET standard reflects the MST under CIL, which has nevertheless evolved over time,[72] protecting 'against all such acts or behaviour that might infringe a sense of fairness, equity and reasonableness'.[73] It has been

66 C. N. Brower and S. W. Schill, 'Is Arbitration a Threat or a Boon to the Legitimacy of International Investment Law' (2009) 9 *Chicago Journal of International Law* 471, 487.

67 Moreover, the FET standard of treatment in the ECT is higher than under CIL: see Art. 10(1) ECT.

68 Art. 5 US Model BIT 2012.

69 *Philip Morris* (n 42) paras. 316–317; *Tecmed* (n 38) para. 155; *Saluka* (n 55) para. 294.

70 Provision B, NAFTA Free Trade Commission, 'Notes of Interpretation of Certain Chapter 11 Provisions (31 July 2001).

71 See *Pope & Talbot* (n 46) Award in Respect of Damages (31 May 2002) para. 47; Award on the Merits of Phase 2 (10 April 2001) para. 110.

72 *Mondev International Ltd. v United States of America*, ICSID Case No. ARB(AF)/99/2, Award (11 October 2002) para. 116; *Chemtura* (n 51) paras. 121–122.

73 *Merrill and Ring Forestry L.P. v Canada*, ICSID Case No. UNCT/07/1, Award (31 March 2010) para. 210.

argued that in the NAFTA context tribunals have generally interpreted the FET standard as being comprised of a limited number of defined elements (e.g. denial of justice, failure to protect full protection and security, etc.),[74] which have been interpreted by tribunals in 'greatly varying ways' but have not been equated with more abstract notions of justice or the rule of law.[75] Importantly, the MST under CIL is a general obligation under international law, which applies to inter-State relations regardless of a treaty. Tribunals' divergent approaches to the interpretation of MST can lead to fragmentation of international law, and arguably are contrary to *opinio iuris*.[76]

The duty to accord FET treatment expands to the overall treatment of investors by the host State, whereby all kinds of government actions, whether legislative, administrative or judicial, can potentially be in breach of the FET standard.[77] The FET standard entails an obligation to provide stability and predictability of the legal and business framework in which the investment has been made.[78] This obligation corresponds to an investor's legitimate expectations, which is one of the most important concepts of the FET standard. However, legal stability is not absolute and does not exclude the State's sovereign authority to legislate and to adapt its legal system to changing circumstances.[79] Such 'virtual freezing of the legal regulation of economic activities' would be contrary to 'the State's normal regulatory power and the evolutionary character of economic life' and would not be 'legitimate nor reasonable'.[80]

Accordingly, some tribunals have claimed that unless the State made *specific* promises or representations to the investor, the investor cannot treat a BIT as an 'insurance policy against the risk of any changes in the

[74] See Chapter 8 for influence of NAFTA jurisprudence on the EU's FET standard.

[75] See, for example, *Apotex Holdings Inc. and Apotex Inc. v United States of America*, ICSID Case No. ARB(AF)/12/1, Award (25 August 2014) paras. 9.41–9.47.

[76] Accordingly, the *Mondev* tribunal applied the NAFTA Free Trade Commission statement on the basis that the MST now incorporates heightened MST: *Mondev* (n 72) para. 125. Such an approach is basically in contradiction with the NAFTA Free Trade Commission Notes of Interpretation.

[77] UNCTAD, 'Fair and Equitable Treatment' (2012) Issues in International Investment Agreements (Second series), UNCTAD/DIAE/IA/2011/5, 12.

[78] *Occidental Exploration and Production Company v The Republic of Ecuador*, LCIA Case No. UN3467, Final Award (1 July 2004) para. 191; *EDF (Services) Limited v Romania*, ICSID Case No. ARB/05/13, Award (8 October 2009) para. 217.

[79] *Philip Morris* (n 42) para. 422; *BG Group v Argentina*, UNCITRAL, Final Award (24 December 2007) paras. 292–310.

[80] *EDF* (n 78) para. 217.

host State's legal and economic framework'.[81] However, in the exercise of its legislative power, a State cannot act 'unfairly, unreasonably or inequitably'.[82] In other words, regulatory change cannot be arbitrary, which includes 'wilful disregard of due process of law, an act which shocks, or at least surprises, a sense of judicial propriety' and which is therefore 'opposed to the rule of law'.[83] A foreign investor whose interests are protected under an investment treaty is entitled to expect that the State will not act in a way that is 'manifestly inconsistent' and 'unreasonable'.[84] Closely related to the arbitrariness is also the obligation of the host State to act in good faith,[85] which includes the duty not to act for 'purely arbitrary reasons' related to domestic politics and 'nationalistic reasons of a discriminatory character'.[86] Ultimately, the FET standard requires weighing of the investor's legitimate and reasonable expectations on the one hand and the State's legitimate regulatory interests on the other.[87] However, reasonableness rather than proportionality is still the more commonly applied principle in review of government conduct under the FET standard.[88]

The minimalist wording of FET clauses, indeterminacy of the State's liability threshold and the lack of clear legal test for the standard leaves for arbitrators a wide discretion in the interpretation of FET provisions, resulting in inconsistent application and allowing tribunals to review a range of government actions which were previously seen as outside of the scope of international law.[89] In practice, this has led to the establishment

[81] ibid.

[82] *Parkerings-Compagniet AS v Republic of Lithuania,* ICSID Case No. ARB/05/8, Award (11 September 2007) para. 332.

[83] *Elettronica Sicula S.p.A. (ELSI)* (*United States of America v Italy*) (Judgment) [1989] ICJ Rep 15, para. 128.

[84] *Saluka* (n 55) para. 309.

[85] *Waste Management, Inc. v United Mexican States ("Number 2"),* ICSID Case No. ARB (AF)/00/3, Award (30 April 2004) para. 138.

[86] *Eureko B.V. v Republic of Poland,* Partial Award (19 August 2005) para. 233.

[87] *Saluka* (n 55) para. 306.

[88] J. Bonnitcha, *Substantive Protection under Investment Treaties: A Legal and Economic Analysis* (CUP 2014) 224. To add to rich divergent practice, the Tribunal in *Blusun v Italy* concluded that legality of regulatory changes in the absence of specific representation must be assessed on the basis of proportionality and not 'unreasonableness', which can be criticised as 'an open-ended mandate to second-guess the host State's policies'. On the contrary, 'disproportionality carries in-built limitations and is more determinate': *Blusun S.A., Jean-Pierre Lecorcier and Michael Stein v Italian Republic,* ICSID Case No. ARB/14/3, Final Award (27 December 2017) para. 318.

[89] UNCTAD 2012 (n 77) 11–13, 22.

of breaches in very broad categories of State regulatory actions, such as tariff regulations, conduct of negotiations, organisation of tenders and communication between State and investor. Therefore, FET raises the same issues of balancing investment protections with the State's right to regulate in the public interest as indirect expropriation. Additionally, different approaches to the FET standard pose a significant challenge for States in the practical implementation of the standard domestically – between different branches and different levels of government – as it becomes difficult to predict what kind of specific conduct could lead to breach of the FET standard.

In order to overcome some of the problems noted to arise from this jurisprudence, the US Model BIT 2012 provides explanations of concepts of FET and 'full protection and security',[90] while also defining CIL.[91] The US–Mexico–Canada (USMCA) Trade Agreement goes even further in limiting FET.[92] European Union agreements also provide more detailed FET language.[93] However, it remains to be seen whether more clarity in the expression of the FET standard results in more certainty.

### *1.2.3 Protection against Discrimination*

Protection against discrimination in IIL is provided through national treatment (NT) and most-favoured-nation treatment (MFN) and it is also included in the concept of FET.[94] Unlike FET, which is an absolute standard, NT and MFN are relative standards, whose meaning is defined by reference to the treatment afforded to other investments. While the principle of NT aims to accord to foreign investors the same treatment as that granted to domestic investors, the MFN standard affords foreign investors the treatment comparable to other foreign investors operating in the host country.

90 Art. 5(2) US Model BIT 2012.

91 ibid Annex A.

92 In Art. 14.6 the USMCA prescribes the obligation of treatment in accordance with CIL, including FET (limited to denial of justice in criminal, civil or administrative proceedings and due process) and full protection and security (the level of police protection under CIL). The mere fact that an investor's expectations have not been met does not constitute the breach, even if there is consequent loss or damage to the covered investment. Breach of FET treatment is excluded from the scope of ISDS clauses in Annex 14-D but not from the ISDS scope of covered government contracts in limited sectors, in accordance with Annex 14-E.

93 See Section 8.2.1.3 in Chapter 8.

94 *Saluka* (n 55) para. 309; *Waste Management* (n 85) para. 98.

International investment agreements offer different formulations of NT and MFN in one combined or separate clauses, most commonly requiring treatment 'no less favourable' than that accorded to national[95] or other foreign investors[96] respectively, with or without qualification 'in like circumstances'.[97] In the European type of BITs, NT and MFN are guaranteed only in the post-establishment stage of investment, while in the US BITs and regional agreements these treatments are also extended to the pre-entry stage.[98] Additionally, the application of the NT and MFN clauses can be limited by providing a list of categories of investment or activities to which these standards apply (positive list approach) or from the application of which they are excluded (negative list approach). Further, treaties can offer a number of more general exceptions relating to public health, order and national security, which apply not only to NT and MFN but the whole of the treaty.[99] In the case of a conflict between NT and MFN standards, treaties sometimes prescribe that the standard most favourable to investors applies.[100]

Another notable issue is the application of NT and MFN standards in regard to subnational authorities which can accord preferential treatment to businesses at local level, and especially when such authorities have a constitutional power to make investment policy. In the case of the United States, such treatment would not extend to domestic investors outside of a particular local subdivision, thus also preventing foreign investors from invoking it.[101] Under Comprehensive Economic and Trade Agreement (CETA), full NT and MFN standards apply to all levels, sub-federal in Canada, and EU Member States and sub-EU Member States levels in the

95 Art. 3(1) German Model BIT (2008); Art. 3 US Model BIT 2012; Art. 8.6 CETA.

96 Art. 3(2) German Model BIT 2008; Art. 4 US Model BIT 2012; Art. 8.7 CETA.

97 Although this is found in NAFTA and the US Model BIT 2012, as well as CETA, there is no such formulation in German BITs, which thus arguably offer the widest scope for comparison.

98 See Section 2.1.2 in Chapter 2 for further discussion. CETA is an exception in this regard as it follows the North American model.

99 See, for example, Art. 24 ECT; Art. 18(2) US Model BIT 2012; Art. 28.3 CETA. In German BITs, such general exception is given in the context of Art. 3 which defines NT and MFN standards.

100 Art. 10(7) ECT.

101 See, for example, USA–Croatia BIT (signed 13 July 1996, entered into force 20 June 2001).

EU.[102] The ECT provides for similar broad extension of specific subnational treatment to foreign investors.[103]

In the practice of arbitral tribunals regarding NT, the most prominent issue is the scope of comparable activities between national and foreign investors, and, in this regard, the relevance of World Trade Organization (WTO) jurisprudence in the interpretation of BITs. In some cases, tribunals take into consideration the same economic or business sector,[104] while in others the examination can be broader, outside the particular sector.[105] Some tribunals accepted the WTO jurisprudence of 'like products' for interpretation of BITs,[106] while others explicitly rejected the notion of NT under WTO law, which interprets 'like products' in light of the objective of avoiding the distortion of competition.[107] These tribunals embraced the view that BITs address 'like situations' with a different aim, which is to avoid exporters being placed at a disadvantage in foreign markets.[108]

In assessing 'like circumstances', tribunals take into account 'circumstances that would justify governmental regulations that treat [domestic and foreign investors] differently in order to protect the public interest'.[109] Differences in treatment will not violate the NT standard if they have 'a reasonable nexus to rational policies' that do not distinguish between domestic and foreign investors, and do not otherwise unduly undermine 'the investment liberalising objectives', focusing on the regulatory context.[110] In assessing the measure, tribunals examine both *de iure*[111] and *de facto*[112] discrimination, whereby the protectionist intent of the host State is less relevant than the practical effect of the measure.[113] The latter line of reasoning corresponds with the WTO approach.

102 Arts. 8.6.2 and 8.7.2 CETA. In practice, this application of NT could lead to a potentially more advantageous treatment of Canadian investors than domestic investors in a particular EU Member State: see Section 8.2.1.4 in Chapter 8.

103 Art. 23(1) ECT.

104 *Marvin Feldman* (n 58) para. 172; *S. D. Myers* (n 50) para. 248.

105 *Occidental* (n 78) para. 173.

106 *S. D. Myers* (n 50) paras. 244–247; *Marvin Feldman* (n 58) para. 165.

107 Report of the Appellate Body of 18 January 1999, Korea – Taxes on Alcoholic Beverages, WT/DS75/AB/R, para. 118, referenced in *Occidental* (n 78) para. 174.

108 ibid para. 176.

109 *S. D. Myers* (n 50) para. 249.

110 *Pope & Talbot* (n 46) Award on the Merits of Phase 2, para. 78.

111 *S. D. Myers* (n 50) para. 252.

112 ibid; *Marvin Feldman* (n 58) para. 173.

113 *S. D. Myers* (n 50) para. 254; *Marvin Feldman* (n 58) para. 183; *Pope & Talbot* (n 46) Award on the Merits of Phase 2, para. 78; *Siemens A.G. v The Argentine Republic*, ICSID

However, the 'rational nexus' test adopted by investment tribunals differs from the WTO closed list of policy objectives in GATT Article XX, which applies a stricter 'necessity test' between the measure and the policy purpose.[114] This dual approach to the same standard in trade and investment law contributes to further fragmentation of international law. Different aims of trade and investment law are moreover less justified in cases of IIAs which have investment liberalisation at the forefront of their objectives.[115]

Similarly, MFN clauses also leave wide scope for competing interpretations. Usually, foreign investors use such clauses to import certain standards of protection, whether substantive or procedural, from other IIAs (third party treaties), which are unavailable in the basic treaty directly applicable in their case. The International Law Commission (ILC) adopted the *ejusdem generis* principle in the application of the MFN clause, whereby MFN from a third party treaty can apply to a basic treaty only in relation to the same subject matter of the same category (*idem genus*).[116] While this rule seems straightforward, its practical application in tribunals' jurisprudence has proved to be challenging. Some tribunals have resorted to a broader interpretation of the clause, allowing for incorporation of both substantive and procedural protections non-existent in the basic treaty,[117] while others have restricted such incorporation to substantive protections only.[118] In order to avoid uncertainties, recent IIAs contain MFN clauses which expressly exclude from their application substantive and procedural obligations provided for under other IIAs.[119]

Case No. ARB/02/8, Award (17 January 2007) para. 320. However, discriminatory intent was required by the *Methanex* (n 54) Tribunal: part IV, ch. B, para. 12.

114 N. DiMascio and J. Pauwelyn, 'Nondiscrimination in Trade and Investment Treaties: Worlds Apart or Two Sides of the Same Coin?' (2008) 102 *The American Journal of International Law* 48, 76–77.

115 See Section 2.1.2 in Chapter 2.

116 ILC Draft Arts. 9 and 10 with Commentary, ILC, 'Report of the International Law Commission to the General Assembly on the Work of Its Thirtieth Session' (1978) UN Doc A/33/10.

117 For example, *Siemens* (n 113), Decision on Jurisdiction (3 August 2004) para. 103; *Emilio Agustín Maffezini v The Kingdom of Spain*, ICSID Case No. ARB/97/7, Decision of the Tribunal on Objections to Jurisdiction (28 October 1999) para. 56.

118 *Plama Consortium Limited v Republic of Bulgaria*, ICSID Case No. ARB/03/24, Decision on Jurisdiction (8 February 2005) para. 218.

119 For example, Art. 8.7.4 CETA; Art. 14.D.3(1)(a)(i)(A) fn 22 USMCA.

The standards of NT and MFN together serve to maintain a level playing field between foreign and domestic investors in a host State's investment market. However, special protections that can be given to foreign companies through IIAs, as opposed to domestic companies, can reverse the principle of national treatment by discriminating against domestic companies. Additionally, foreign investors may, depending on the circumstances, resort to a more favourable treatment accorded to other foreign investors, which might be contrary to the original intentions of the host State. Ultimately, whether and what kind of a level playing field is achieved in a particular market will depend on the interpretation and application of the relevant NT and MFN provisions in each individual case.

### *1.2.4 Free Transfer of Capital*

International investment agreements generally provide for free transfer of capital in a separate, usually very specific clause.[120] Free transfer provisions usually contain a broad guarantee for free transfer of payments related to an investment, often listing in a non-exhaustive manner types of funds which can be transferred,[121] the currency and exchange rate for the transfer[122] and the time period in which free transfer is guaranteed to investors.[123] Usually, free transfer clauses will be restricted by a number of exceptions, which allow States 'equitable, non-discriminatory, and good faith application of its laws and regulations' generally aimed at prevention of abuses of justice.[124]

Provisions concerning the free transfer of capital have not had great relevance in the practice of investment tribunals.[125] The recent more restrictive trend in drafting these clauses recognises the need of States to adopt extraordinary regimes for extraordinary times, which is certainly a well-learnt lesson of the GFC and the Euro crisis.[126]

[120] Art. 5 German Model BIT 2008; Art. 7 US Model BIT 2012; Art. 14 ECT; Art. 8.13 CETA.

[121] Art. 7(1) US Model BIT 2012; Similarly, see Art. 14.9(1) USMCA.

[122] Art. 14.9(2) USMCA.

[123] Art. 5(2) German Model BIT 2008.

[124] Art. 14(4) ECT; Art. 8.13.4 CETA; Art. 14.9(5) USMCA. German BITs are an exception in this regard as they guarantee free transfer without any restrictions.

[125] For current practice, see for example *Metalpar S.A. and Buen Aire S.A. v The Argentine Republic*, ICSID Case No. ARB/03/5, Award (6 June 2008).

[126] For EU IIA practice, see Section 8.1.1.1 in Chapter 8.

## 1.3 Procedural Rules of International Investment Law

Most commonly, modern IIAs offer to investors the choice of ITA, granting them specific procedural rights and remedies as the most important component of IIAs.[127] In international law the participation of sovereign States in dispute resolution generally depends on their consent, which in IIL is given through IIAs.[128] Investment treaties incorporate in their ISDS clauses an offer to arbitrate, extended by the host State to an undefined number of current and future investors of the other Contracting Party for all future disputes arising out of investments made in its territory. It is for the eligible investor to accept this standing offer by correctly initiating the proceedings against the host State in accordance with the requirements defined in the treaty's ISDS clause, at which stage the arbitration contract is perfected. Through offer and acceptance both parties express their mutual consent to arbitration,[129] which is the precondition for jurisdiction of the arbitral tribunal.[130] This unusual arbitration contract in investment disputes, commissioned through an international treaty, gives IIL its public-private nature.

However, ISDS is a rather generic term which encompasses a number of different mechanisms.[131] It is exactly with regard to the regulation of the dispute settlement clauses that IIAs differ most. The following sections provide an overview of procedural issues stemming from IIAs and practice.[132] The aim is to explain the procedural framework in which

[127] This has been recognised both in scholarly literature and in the practice of international tribunals. See, for example, *Emilio Maffezini* (n 117) Decision of the Tribunal on Objections to Jurisdiction, para. 55; *Gas Natural SDG S.A. v Argentine Republic* (ICSID Case No. ARB/03/10) Decision of the Tribunal on Preliminary Questions on Jurisdiction (17 June 2005) para. 29.

[128] See, for example, Art. 26(3)(a) ECT; Art. 10(2) German Model BIT 2008; Art. 24 US Model BIT 2012; Art. 8.18.1 CETA.

[129] *El Paso Energy International Company v Argentine Republic*, ICSID Case No. ARB/03/15, Decision on Jurisdiction (27 April 2006) para. 25.

[130] The mutual consent takes place only *after* the dispute has arisen. It was said that this 'contract' lacks privity between the host State and an individual foreign investor as the offer to arbitrate in an IIA is extended to all foreign investors: J. Paulsson, 'Arbitration without Privity' (1995) 10 ICSID *Review – Foreign Investment Law Journal* 232.

[131] See J. Pohl, K. Mashigo and A. Nohen, 'Dispute Settlement Provisions in International Investment Agreements: A Large Sample Survey' (OECD Publishing 2012).

[132] This includes cases of contract-based relationships between the foreign investor and State, which have come under the protection of an IIA (due, for example, to the umbrella clause).

ITA takes place and to indicate relevant systemic issues, rather than being exhaustive.

### *1.3.1 Access to ISDS: 'Investment' and 'Investor'*

International investment agreements allow for a broad scope of claims that can be subject to investment arbitration, sometimes expressly defining the scope of disputes to breaches of substantive protections under the treaty,[133] and linking the claim to the loss or damage caused to the investor by the breach.[134] The disputed investment must be within the definition of 'investment' provided in the IIA, which is usually set out in broad terms, and sufficiently broad to include both direct and non-direct types of foreign investment (portfolio investment).[135] In some cases, the scope of investment disputes can be limited by the scope of the treaty in question,[136] or IIAs can expressly limit the scope of ISDS clauses in regard to the subject matter of claims.[137] The German Model BIT and EU investment agreements, unlike the US Model BIT, limit the jurisdiction of arbitral tribunals to breaches of substantive protections in regard to *established* investments, thus excluding the pre-establishment phase of investment from the scope of ISDS clauses. The USMCA is an exception from the previous US practice, which now provides for limited ISDS in the post-establishment phase.[138]

Under the ICSID Convention, for a dispute to fall within the ICSID jurisdiction, the dispute must be 'legal' and 'arising directly out of an investment', which is decided on the facts of each particular case.[139] The definition of 'investment' in the particular IIA and the views of the

[133] For example, Art. 26(1) ECT, Arts. 24(1)(a)(i)(A) and 24(1)(b)(i)(A) US Model BIT 2012; Art. 3.1.1 EUSIPA. The US BITs also include investment authorisation and investment contracts: US Model BIT 2012 Arts. 24(1)(a)(i)(B), 24(1)(b)(i)(B), 24(1)(a)(i)(C) and 24(1)(b)(i)(C) respectively.

[134] For example, Arts. 24(1)(a)(ii) and 24(1)(b)(ii) US Model BIT 2012; Art. 3.1.1 EUSIPA; Art. 8.18.1 CETA.

[135] See Art. 1(1) German Model BIT 2008); Art. 1(6) ECT; Art. 1 US Model BIT 2012); Art. 1.2 EUSIPA. The general definition usually includes a list of illustrative but non-exclusive categories of investments.

[136] For example, the ECT is limited to energy sector related disputes: Arts. 1(6) and 2 ECT.

[137] For example, Art. 14.D.3(1) USMCA limits ISDS to direct expropriation and discrimination (breaches of NT and MFN) in the post-establishment phase, with the exception of government contracts in the 'covered sectors'.

[138] See ibid Art. 14.D.3(1).

[139] Art. 25(1) ICSID Convention.

parties on the subject matter of the dispute are not binding or decisive.[140] The ICSID jurisdiction, although widely interpreted, is not available for any kind of activity that parties might regard as an investment if such activity does not fall within the ICSID set of criteria for investment,[141] and even if the activity in question is defined as investment under the particular IIA.[142] Latter situations include purely commercial transactions arising out of contracts for international sale of goods,[143] which could alternatively be submitted to an *ad hoc* United Nations Commission on International Trade Law (UNCITRAL) arbitration if the specific IIA's definition of investment covers these commercial transactions and offers the option of an *ad hoc* arbitration.[144]

In essence, the particular set of criteria developed by ICSID tribunals set the objective 'outer limits' of investment beyond which parties' consent is ineffective.[145] They indicate ICSID's public law character, reflected in the ICSID Convention Preamble, which balances 'the need for international cooperation for economic development' and the role that private investment has for that development.[146] However, in light of tribunals' inconsistent jurisprudence, such conclusions cannot be categorical.[147] On the other hand, the UNCITRAL Rules, originally

140 *Aguas del Tunari, S.A. v Republic of Bolivia*, ICSID Case No. ARB/02/3, Decision on Respondent's Objections to Jurisdiction (21 October 2005) para. 278.

141 Although the ICSID Convention does not define 'investment', ICSID arbitral tribunals have developed an objective definition of investment in their practice, based on a set of criteria, which include: (i) a substantial contribution of money and resources, (ii) a certain duration, (iii) risk and (iv) the contribution to the economic development of the host State: *Salini Costruttori S.p.A. and Italstrade S.p.A. v Kingdom of Morocco*, ICSID Case No. ARB/00/4, Decision on Jurisdiction (31 July 2001) para. 52 (so-called 'Salini test'). The 'Salini test' is often cited as an authority for determining investment under ICSID Convention: see, for example, *Joy Mining Machinery Limited v Arab Republic of Egypt*, ICSID Case No. ARB/03/11, Award on Jurisdiction (6 August 2004) para. 53.

142 *Joy Mining* (ibid) para. 50.

143 *Joy Mining* (n 141) para. 52; *Global Trading Resource Corp. and Globex International, Inc. v Ukraine*, ICSID Case No. ARB/09/11, Award (1 December 2010) paras. 56–57.

144 The definition of investment in some IIAs expressly excludes claims to money solely from commercial contracts for the sale of goods and services and domestic financing of such contracts: see, for example, Art. 14.1 (j) USMCA; Arts. 8.1(i) and (ii) CETA.

145 *The Rompetrol Group N.V. v Romania*, ICSID Case No. ARB/06/3, Decision on Jurisdiction and Admissibility (18 April 2008) para. 80.

146 ICSID Convention, Preamble and *Salini* (n 141) para. 52.

147 Some ICSID decisions have rejected the contribution to the development of the host State as an element of the objective definition of investment: see *Quiborax S.A., Non Metallic Minerals S.A. and Allan Fosk Kaplún v Plurinational State of Bolivia*, ICSID Case No. ARB/06/2, Decision on Jurisdiction (27 September 2012) paras. 219–225.

intended and commonly involved in international commercial arbitration, reflect the principle of freedom of contract of private parties, whereby any kind of asset, even a '"pure" one-off sales contract' may constitute an investment if such was the intention of the parties.[148] Additionally, UNCITRAL tribunals in their approach to investment also reflect the commercial character of investment, which does not necessarily involve any element of contribution to the economic development of the host State.[149] This leads to two observations.

First, different approaches to the characterisation of investment reflect conceptual differences that underpin the international regulation of investments. If IIL serves to promote economic liberalisation and the free flow of capital, any kind of activity, even that for purely private commercial purposes, should be regarded as investment. However, if IIL primarily seeks to facilitate global economic cooperation and development through special protections given to foreign investment, recognition should be given to genuine investments, which necessarily also have a potential to contribute to the economic development of the host State. In the latter case, the need to balance private interests of foreign investors and public interests of host States would be an essential principle.

Second, the difference in tribunals' approaches to the characterisation of investment also reflects the need for a more consistent doctrinal development of IIL, as opposed to the currently prevailing fragmented approach in which the doctrine is used according to the needs of a particular case. In this context, the difference reflects divergent doctrinal approaches to the characterisation of ICSID within IIL. If ICSID is procedurally an autonomous system, it necessarily supersedes party autonomy reflected in the particular IIAs. However, if the question of

Others have emphasised the need to take into account the definition of investment in particular IIA even if all of the *Salini* criteria are not satisfied: see *Biwater Gauff (Tanzania) Ltd. v United Republic of Tanzania*, ICSID Case No. ARB/05/22, Award (24 July 2008) para. 314–318; *Malaysian Historical Salvors, SDN, BHD v The Government of Malaysia*, ICSID Case No. ARB/05/10, Decision on the Application for Annulment (16 April 2009) para. 80; *RREEF Infrastructure (G.P.) Limited and RREEF Pan-European Infrastructure Two Lux S.à r.l. v Kingdom of Spain*, ICSID Case No. ARB/13/30, Decision on Jurisdiction (6 June 2016) para. 158.

148 Such intention must be undoubtedly ascertained from the particular IIA: *Romak S.A. (Switzerland) v The Republic of Uzbekistan*, UNCITRAL, PCA Case No. AA280, Award (26 November 2009) para. 205. Similarly, see *Vacuum Salt Products Ltd. v Republic of Ghana*, ICSID Case No. ARB/92/1, Award (16 February 1994) fn 14 on p. 90.

149 To that effect, see *Romak* (ibid) para. 207.

the autonomy of ICSID is answered in the negative, a particular IIA would be given preference as *lex specialis*. Accordingly, the definition of investment in a particular IIA would supersede the *lex generalis* ICSID provision on investment.

Similar to the definition of investment, foreign investors must meet the requirements of a particular IIA and the ICSID Convention in order to bring a claim to an ICSID tribunal. Under IIAs the definition of 'investor' usually includes natural and legal persons, which must have the nationality of one of the Contracting Parties to the IIA; the requirements of nationality are determined with reference to the law of the Contracting Party whose nationality is claimed.[150] The ICSID Convention requires that the investor must be a national of a Contracting State,[151] which includes both 'natural' and 'juridical' persons with 'the nationality of a Contracting State other than the State party to the dispute'.[152] The requirement of nationality in regard to natural persons is arguably easier to establish[153] and the nationality of legal persons is more controversial. Especially contentious is the criterion for establishing the link between a legal person submitting a claim under an IIA and the Contracting State to that IIA.

IIAs use objective criteria to determine the nationality of a legal person,[154] usually combining: the place of incorporation as the place where the legal person is constituted or organised in accordance with the laws of the country,[155] the place of the seat of the corporation (with

150 For example, Art. 1(7)(a) ECT; Art. 1(3) German BIT 2008; Art. 1 US Model BIT 2012; Art. 1.2.3 EUSIPA; Art. 8.1 CETA.

151 Art. 25(1) ICSID Convention.

152 ibid Art. 25(2).

153 The requirement is formal and does not apply a test of dominant or effective nationality: *Ioan Micula, Viorel Micula, S.C. European Food S.A., S.C. Starmill S.R.L. and S.C. Multipack S.R.L. v Romania*, ICSID Case No. ARB/05/20, Decision on Jurisdiction and Admissibility (24 September 2008) para. 100.

154 In this respect, IIAs cover a range of different legal entities: with or without legal personality (the definition of juridical person under Art. 1(3)(a) German Model BIT 2008); for profit or non-profit (Art. 1(3)(a) German Model BIT 2008; Art. 1 US Model BIT 2012), privately or government owned (definition of an enterprise under Art. 1 US Model BIT 2012, which has a non-exhaustive list of entities considered to be enterprises); including (US Model BIT 2012) or excluding a branch (Art. 8.1 CETA, also expressly excluding a representative office).

155 Most IIAs use this criterion. For example, Art. 1(7)(a)(ii) ECT; Art. 1.2.5 EUSIPA; Art. 1 US Model BIT 2012.

respect to the effective management of the legal person) and less frequently the criterion of the State which controls the operations of the legal person.[156] The German Model BIT 2008 abandons the earlier prevailing criterion of the seat and adopts, in line with its domestic and EU law, the principle of constitution and incorporation, recognising also the EU freedom of establishment under TFEU Articles 49 and 54.[157] Unlike the US Model BIT, the German BIT does not require that the legal person must have substantial business activity in the host State through its denial of benefits clause.[158]

Under CIL a subsidiary has the nationality of the host State,[159] so the ICSID Convention in its definition of a juridical person in Article 25(1) allows a local subsidiary under the control of a foreign person to be granted ICSID jurisdiction, if the host State agrees, expressly or impliedly, to treat the subsidiary as a foreign national. However, tribunals have approached the foreign control test differently in cases where the host State treats a subsidiary as a foreign national. Some have argued that the criteria are objectively determined to restrict the jurisdiction of ICSID tribunals to cases of real control, regardless of parties' intent.[160] Others have decided in favour of extending this jurisdiction by challenging the inference of jurisdictional restrictions in the text of the ICSID Convention.[161] In its essence, this dilemma reflects the dilemma discussed above about the jurisdictional autonomy of the ICSID in the determination of whether the dispute concerns 'investment'.

[156] There are also examples of IIAs which incorporate all criteria: see definition of 'enterprise of a Party' in Art. 8.1 CETA.

[157] Art. 1(3)(a) German Model BIT 2008. EUSIPA also contains reference to Art. 54 TFEU in defining the concept of 'substantive business operations': Art. 1.2(5) fn 2. On freedom of establishment, see Section 4.5.1 in Chapter 4.

[158] Art. 17 US Model BIT 2012. Similarly, Art. 17 ECT.

[159] *Barcelona Traction Case, Light and Power Company Limited, Case concerning (New Application, 1962)* (*Belgium v Spain*) (Second Phase) [1970] ICJ Rep 3.

[160] *Vacuum Salt Products* (n 148) para. 36. See also *TSA Spectrum de Argentina S.A. v Argentine Republic*, ICSID Case No. ARB/05/5, Award (19 December 2008) paras. 152–153.

[161] *Tokios Tokelės v Ukraine*, ICSID Case No. ARB/02/18, Decision on Jurisdiction (29 April 2004) para. 46, also referring to cases *Wena Hotels Ltd. v Arab Republic of Egypt*, ICSID Case No. ARB/98/4, Summary Minutes of the Session of the Tribunal held in Paris (25 May 1999) and *Autopista Concesionada de Venezuela, C.A. v Bolivarian Republic of Venezuela*, ICSID Case No. ARB/00/5, Decision on Jurisdiction (27 September 2001) paras. 110–114. Also *The Rompetrol Group* (n 145) para. 93.

### 1.3.2 'Shopping' in Investment Treaty Arbitration

Definitions of investors in IIAs, which in most cases focus on the formal nationality criteria of incorporation in accordance with local laws, and arbitral tribunals' interpretations of such definitions, allow for the practice of *treaty* shopping. This involves investors structuring investments through intermediate holding companies in order to take advantage of a particular IIA which otherwise would not have been available to these investors. Treaty shopping can take place in several ways, which include:[162] structuring an investment in the host State (subsidiary) through an intermediate company established in the home State by an investor (parent company) from a third country;[163] structuring an investment in the host State (subsidiary) through an intermediate company in the home State, which is effectively owned and controlled by an investor (parent company) from the host State;[164] and structuring an investment in the host State (subsidiary) through an intermediate company in a third country which is owned by an investor (parent company) from the home State.[165] The practice of treaty shopping can further be encouraged through broadly worded MFN clauses.[166]

While treaty shopping disregards the origin of capital when determining the nationality of the claimant,[167] and thus supports the neoliberal vision of flow of capital, it raises a number of policy issues.[168] In particular, the concerns include uncertainty of host States about the extent of their legal obligations under IIAs, because a particular IIA, instead of being a treaty with a particular Contracting Party becomes in practice a treaty with an undefined number of non-Contracting Parties. Additionally, treaty shopping opens doors for domestic investors to access investment arbitration, which otherwise would not be available

[162] For detailed analysis, see UNCTAD, 'Scope and Definition (A sequel) – UNCTAD Series on Issues in International Investment Agreements II' (2011), UNCTAD/DIAE/IA/2010/2, 86–92.

[163] For example, *ADC v Hungary* (n 44) paras. 352–362.

[164] *Tokios Tokelés* (n 161) para. 52.

[165] *Waste Management* (n 85) para. 80–85.

[166] See Section 1.2.3.

[167] *Tokios Tokelés* (n 161) paras. 80–81. See the Dissenting Opinion of Professor Weil, who considered such an approach to be contrary to the object and purpose of the ICSID Convention: Dissenting Opinion (Chairman Professor Weil) (29 April 2004) paras. 19–20.

[168] D. Gaukrodger and K. Gordon, 'Investor–State Dispute Settlement: A Scoping Paper for the Investment Policy Community' (OECD Publishing 2012) 56–57.

to them, thus effectively undermining the purpose of IIAs.[169] In order to distinguish 'legitimate' recourse to international arbitration from 'illegitimate' which constitutes abuse of rights, tribunals engage in analysis of all the circumstances of a particular case, including the timing of the investment and of the claim, the substance of the transaction, the true nature of the operation and the degree of foreseeability of the governmental action at the time of restructuring.[170] However, in light of broader policy concerns, treaty shopping beyond cases which bluntly include shell companies should also be addressed. Treaty regimes for claims by shareholders for reflective loss, which are usually available under typical BITs but unavailable under domestic corporate law, have attracted insufficient attention in policy discussions.[171]

In addition to treaty shopping, the heterogeneity of dispute settlement options and applicable substantive and procedural rules, which can lead to different outcomes, creates an incentive for *forum* shopping.[172] In most cases, access to international arbitration is provided in addition to domestic judicial review proceedings, with States adopting different approaches in coordinating such access. Some IIAs give investors a choice between domestic or international fora; this choice can be final

169 ibid.

170 *Transglobal Green Energy, LLC and Transglobal Green Energy de Panama, S.A. v The Republic of Panama*, ICSID Case No. ARB/13/28, Award (2 June 2016) para. 103. *Philip Morris Asia Limited v The Commonwealth of Australia*, UNCITRAL, PCA Case No. 2012-12, Award on Jurisdiction and Admissibility (17 December 2015) para. 540; *Tidewater Inc., Tidewater Investment SRL, Tidewater Caribe, C.A., et al. v The Bolivarian Republic of Venezuela*, ICSID Case No. ARB/10/5, Decision on Jurisdiction (8 February 2013) paras. 145–146, 184; *Pac Rim Cayman LLC v Republic of El Salvador*, ICSID Case No. ARB/09/12, Decision on Respondent's Jurisdictional Objections (1 June 2012) para. 2.99.

171 See D. Gaukrodger, 'Investment Treaties as Corporate Law: Shareholder Claims and Issues of Consistency' (OECD Publishing 2013) and 'Investment Treaties and Shareholder Claims: Analysis of Treaty Practice' (OECD Publishing 2014). For shareholders' claims under CETA, see Section 8.2.1.1 in Chapter 8.

172 See, for example, *Vattenfall II* case in which the Swedish investor in Germany challenged the constitutionality of the legislation phasing out nuclear energy before German courts, while also bringing a claim against Germany before the ICSID for financial compensation for the breaches of investor's rights under the ECT: BVerfG, *The Vattenfall Case*, Judgment of the First Senate of 6 December 2016, 1 BvR 2821/11; *Vattenfall AB and others v Federal Republic of Germany (II)*, ICSID Case No. ARB/12/12. For analysis of this case under domestic, EU and international law, see I. Damjanovic and O. Quirico, 'Intra-EU Investment Dispute Settlement in Light of *Vattenfall* and *Achmea*: A Matter of Priority' (2019) 26 *Columbia Journal of European Law* 102.

and exclusive by inclusion of a fork-in-the-road provision.[173] In some cases, waiver of domestic remedies,[174] or more recently, exhaustion of local remedies,[175] is a condition precedent to bringing a case to international arbitration. The aim of these provisions is to disallow parallel proceedings. The new generation of EU IIAs contain more detailed provisions, which disallow parallel proceedings[176] but allow return to domestic proceedings after investment arbitration in certain circumstances.[177] In many cases, the possibility of multiple proceedings will depend on the wording of the particular IIA but also on the arbitral tribunals' characterisation of the dispute.[178]

Forum shopping is also encouraged by umbrella clauses, found in some IIAs such as German Model BIT, which may bring under the protection of the IIA 'any other obligations' between the foreign investor and the host State. This can include contractual obligations, such as concession contracts, and unilateral commitments of the host State regarding investments in its territory.[179] These clauses have potential to extend the jurisdiction *ratione materiae* of international investment arbitration to commercial breaches of contract committed at the level of domestic law in the State's function as a merchant.[180] They may encourage the claimant to bring the same claim under domestic law, through a dispute settlement mechanism envisaged in the contract for breach of contractual obligation, and under international law, through a dispute settlement mechanism in the particular IIA for breach of treaty

[173] See C. Schreuer, 'Travelling the BIT Route of Waiting Periods, Umbrella Clauses and Forks in the Road' (2004) 5 *The Journal of World Investment and Trade* 231, 239–249.

[174] See Art. 26(2)(b) US Model BIT 2012.

[175] Art. 5, Annex 14-D USMCA; Art. 15 Indian Model BIT 2016.

[176] Arts. 8.22.1(f) and (g) CETA; Art. 3.7(f) EUSIPA.

[177] Art. 8.22.5 CETA.

[178] In arbitral jurisprudence, the triple identity test (the same parties, the same object and the same cause of action) has been developed when determining whether the claims in the domestic proceedings are the same as those in the international proceedings. See for example, *CMS Gas Transmission Company v The Republic of Argentina*, ICSID Case No. ARB/01/8, Decision of the Tribunal on Objections to Jurisdiction (17 July 2003) para. 80; *H&H Enterprises Investments, Inc. v Arab Republic of Egypt*, ICSID Case No. ARB 09/15, Award (6 May 2014) paras. 368–369; *Pantechniki S.A. Contractors & Engineers (Greece) v The Republic of Albania*, ICSID Case No. ARB/07/21, Award (30 July 2009) para. 67.

[179] Art. 7(2) German Model BIT 2008.

[180] *SGS Société Générale de Surveillance S.A. v Republic of the Philippines*, Decision of the Tribunal on Objections to Jurisdiction (29 January 2004) paras. 127–128. Cf. *SGS Société Générale de Surveillance S.A. v Islamic Republic of Pakistan*, ICSID Case No. ARB/01/13, Decision of the Tribunal on Objections to Jurisdiction (6 August 2003).

obligation.[181] Accordingly, the same set of facts can give rise to different causes of action before different dispute settlement bodies. The controversy created by arbitral tribunals' inconsistent interpretation of this clause has led to the tendency to eliminate these clauses in the new generation of IIAs;[182] however, they are still present in around 40 per cent of IIAs.[183]

International investment agreements also offer to foreign investors the choice of an international forum.[184] The issue of forum shopping becomes particularly problematic when competing forums have strong incentives to retain their jurisdiction, which is more prevalent for international investment forums than for domestic courts.[185] Unlike domestic courts, arbitral tribunals are not permanent; they are constituted for the particular investment dispute, under the auspices of an arbitration administering institution or as *ad hoc* tribunals. The arbitration rules of the chosen forum govern arbitration, unless the applicable IIA has specific procedural provisions which then apply as *lex specialis*.[186] In most cases, IIAs do not have particularly detailed rules and therefore issues such as the appointment of arbitrators, applicable law, allocation of costs, transparency and remedies are addressed in detail in arbitration rules.

The ICSID and UNCITRAL, as the most prominent sets of arbitration rules,[187] have their advantages but they are also prone to specific

[181] The Tribunal in *SGS v Pakistan* found that the contractual obligation did not elevate to a treaty obligation; however, it found that it had jurisdiction for BIT breaches arising from the same host State's conduct: paras. 185–189.

[182] P. Pereire de Souza Fleury, 'Umbrella Clauses: A Trend towards Its Elimination' (2015) 31 *Arbitration International* 679. For example, CETA has no umbrella clause. EUSIPA limits the scope of the umbrella clause: Art. 2.4.6 EUSIPA. Unlike NAFTA, USMCA contains an umbrella clause for 'covered government contracts', which may give rise to treaty arbitration under Annex 14-D.

[183] UNCTAD, 'Mapping of IIA Project' (*Investment Policy Hub*).

[184] Art. 24(3) US Model BIT 2012; Art. 26(4) ECT; CETA, as it moves from the traditional ISDS model, leaves the parties the choice of rules instead of the choice of forum: Art. 8.23.2. Similarly see Art. 3.6 EUSIPA.

[185] See G. Van Harten, 'Pro-Investor or Pro-State Bias in Investment-Treaty Arbitration? Forthcoming Study Gives Cause for Concern' (2012) *Editorials and Commentaries* 136. See also Section 3.2 in Chapter 3.

[186] Art. 24(5) US Model BIT 2012.

[187] For comparison of ICSID and UNCITRAL Rules, see A. Hyder Ali and others, *The International Arbitration Rulebook: A Guide to Arbitral Regimes* (Kluwer 2019). ICSID Rules have been amended four times, with most recent amendments entering into force on 1 July 2022. UNCITRAL Arbitration Rules, approved in 1976 and updated in 2010,

criticisms. The ICSID has been criticised for its close connections with the World Bank and the United States, and for generally favouring the role of foreign investors through its loans programme by making loans conditional on structural adjustments imposed on governments.[188] United Nations Commission on International Trade Law is prone to criticism for the 'privatisation' of disputes that involve States and significant public interest.[189] The lack of a coordinating mechanism between different international arbitral proceedings can lead to parallel proceedings stemming from the same investment event being pursued under different BITs.[190]

### *1.3.3 The Tip of the Iceberg: Arbitration as a Dispute Resolution Method*

The non-permanent arbitration panel format and arbitrators who sit on these panels are among the most contentious elements of the ISDS regime.[191] In practice, law firms that represent the parties propose to their clients potential arbitrators, effectively giving law firms that specialise in international investment arbitration considerable influence over people who sit on arbitration panels. The mechanism currently in place does not include appellate proceedings, which would allow for corrections of errors of law and/or fact and consistency with arbitral jurisprudence.[192]

were further amended in 2013 to include UNCITRAL Rules on Transparency and in 2021 to incorporate Expedited Arbitration Rules.

188 This criticism is voiced particularly strongly by Latin American countries. See S. K. Fiezzoni, 'The Challenge of UNASUR Member Countries to Replace ICSID Arbitration' (2011) 2 *Beijing Law Review* 134.

189 G. Sacerdoti, 'Investment Arbitration under ICSID and UNCITRAL Rules: Prerequisites, Applicable Law, Review of Awards' (2004) 19 *ICSID Review – Foreign Investment Law Journal* 1, 47.

190 See *Ronald S. Lauder v The Czech Republic*, UNCITRAL, Final Award (3 September 2001) and *CME Czech Republic B.V. v The Czech Republic*, UNCITRAL, Final Award (14 March 2003).

191 C. A. Rogers, 'The Politics of International Investment Arbitrators' (2013) 12 *Santa Clara International Law Review* 223, 226–228.

192 In this respect CETA departs from the old system by creating an Appellate Tribunal: Art. 8.28 CETA. Some more recent IIAs leave the possibility of introducing an appeal through a future multilateral appellate mechanism: see, for example, Art. 28 US Model BIT 2012; Art. 9.23(11) CPTPP. There is no reference to appellate mechanism in the USMCA.

With parties actively participating in the process of selection, the impartiality of arbitrators remains questionable as some empirical studies indicate that arbitrators might be inclined to render compromised judgments which maximise their chances to be selected for future disputes.[193] In this way, arbitrators become party advocates within the system that expects their objectivity.[194] Moreover, revolving-door practice, with an established practice of 'double hatting' and the exchange of different roles (arbitrators, counsels, expert witnesses, tribunal secretaries) between a very small pool of 'power broker' investment lawyers is common.[195] Legal rules on the appointment of arbitrators, their qualifications and conflict of interest serve to eliminate these biases, but they fail to address the perceptions of systemic bias.[196]

## 1.4 Conclusion

Looking at the past, the development of IIR can be described as a one-way street. It was a mechanism developed by the need to protect the interests of the capital-exporting countries in their capital-importing counterparts. In the beginning it was the relationship between colonisers and the either *de iure* or *de facto* colonised, which in the period after decolonisation metamorphosed into the relationship between developed and developing countries. The States, not fully aware of the real economic, political and legal implications, were the main players in the development of instruments of IIL, acting individually rather than collectively.

In the meantime, the one-way street has turned into a road with many directions. In the multipolar economic order, the clear differentiation between capital-exporting and capital-importing States has disappeared. The power has diversified between economically powerful States acting

[193] J. Dammann and H. Hansmann, 'Globalising Commercial Litigation' (2008) 94 *Cornell Law Review* 1, 34–35.

[194] H. Smit, 'The Pernicious Institution of the Party-Appointed Arbitrator' (2010) 33 *Columbia FDI Perspectives*.

[195] M. Langford, D. Behn, and R. Hilleren Lie, 'The Revolving Door in International Investment Arbitration' (2017) 20 *Journal of International Economic Law* 301.

[196] The ICSID Convention prescribes competence for arbitrators in Art. 14(1) and warrants disqualification on the basis of Art. 57. See also amended ICSID Arbitration Rules 22 and 23, and UNCITRAL Rules 6-12. These rules are less strict compared to the requirements of judicial independence: see Chapters 3 and 9. A comprehensive Code of Conduct for adjudicators is envisaged as part of the UNCITRAL ISDS reform: see Chapter 10.

alone and others formed in different regional economic interest blocks or supranational entities. Transnational private capital interests have diversified from the interests of their home States. Regulation of investment, domestically and internationally, has been shaped by investment claims and jurisprudence emanating from arbitral tribunals. The global economic world order has introduced 'transnational' players into the arena: multinational enterprises (MNEs), legal practitioners, arbitrators, academics, civil society. All of them, one way or another, participate in defining the – modern, global and 'managerial' – international investment governance.[197]

[197] Koskenniemi (n 28) 324.

# 2

# Mapping the Challenges of ISDS Reform

Building upon issues identified in the preceding chapter, this chapter delves into tensions in the field of international investment regulation (IIR) stemming from divergent political ideologies, economic objectives and legal methods that come into play in the interpretation and implementation of international investment agreements (IIAs). Tensions between different actors and their perspectives on these issues are also considered. The aim is to provide reflection on issues that occupy the current debate on IIR and challenges encountered when addressing them.

## 2.1 Political, Economic and Legal Tensions

### *2.1.1 Tensions between Ideologies*

History demonstrates how the development of IIR has been a contentious issue from its very beginning. The different bodies of opinion have had underlying ideological and geopolitical divisions. The earliest period was dominated by conflict about the minimum standard of treatment (MST) of foreign investments under customary international law (CIL) and it emerged as a reaction to the US attempts for economic dominance in Latin America. In the aftermath of decolonisation, the conflict about this same issue – in essence concerning the level of appropriate protection standards – continued to dominate the debate, now within a more global context. In line with the Cold War divisions between State-controlled and capitalist economies, capital-importing developing countries sided with the political economy of the former, and capital-exporting developed countries with the latter. The inability to find a compromise ultimately led to the failure of a multilateral investment framework. As an alternative, a network of bilateral investment treaties (BITs) between capital-importing and capital-exporting countries emerged, and the International Centre for the Settlement of Investment Disputes (ICSID) in Washington was established to provide a neutral and depoliticised forum for the resolution of potential investment disputes. These underlying conflicts in essence embraced the efforts of politically weaker developing countries to protect newly gained independence, which was under threat from politically and economically dominant developed countries. Developing countries feared that Western States, through the economic activities of their investors, would exercise political dominance, ultimately undermining their State sovereignty.

The deeply rooted ideological divisions within the international community apparently disappeared with the fall of communism, bringing victory for the liberal capitalist political and economic agenda. The era of 'a new world order'[1] began, which prompted the idea of global governance, driven by economic globalisation. The General Agreement on Tariffs and Trade (GATT), which allowed the proliferation of trade liberalisation through a multilateral framework, was successful in reducing traditional tariff barriers in the trade of manufactured goods. GATT was then upgraded to the World Trade Organization (WTO) in 1995, encompassing a broader range of issues: trade in services, intellectual property rights and trade-related investment measures. This new agenda reflected the new global commerce supported by the development of information technologies, which transformed trade from traditional physical exchange of goods towards complex exchange of goods and services, facilitated through the global operations of multinational enterprises (MNEs).[2] However, economic globalisation produced winners and losers, creating, instead of a bipolar Cold War world, the contemporary multipolar world.

Unlike trade, investment did not manage to stimulate negotiation of a multilateral framework. By creating enhanced protection rights, BITs served as a mechanism for promoting economic nationalism of developed countries rather than economic liberalism.[3] While the more closely aligned interests of developed countries in the area of trade allowed for a common framework, their more diversified interests in relation to investment led to fragmentation of investment instruments. The United States and the United Kingdom, the two countries that led the initiative for a multilateral trade framework, were sceptical or

[1] G. Bush, 41st President of the USA, 'Address before a Joint Session of the Congress of the State of the Union' (Washington DC 29 January 1991).

[2] J. M. Kline and R. D. Ludema, 'Building a Multilateral Framework for Investment: Comparing the Development of Trade and Investment Accords' (1997) 6 *Transnational Corporations* 1, 19.

[3] K. J. Vandevelde, 'The Political Economy of a Bilateral Investment Treaty' (1998) 92 *The American Journal of International Law* 621, 633.

negative about the desirability of a multilateral treaty approach regarding investment; on the other hand, Germany strongly supported it. The United States believed that the standard of protection for investors would be lowered in a multilateral setting; Germany believed that its interests would be better protected multilaterally since in the post-WWII period Germany lacked both political power and colonial ties through which it could afford protection for its investors in third countries.[4] Additionally, the failed Havana Charter,[5] which aimed to provide a multilateral framework for trade and investment, attempted to incorporate different economic doctrines.[6] With the success of the German BIT programme, the United States introduced its own programme, which followed a protectionist agenda.[7] The early US model BITs of the 1980s were the most protective investment instruments.[8] Similarly, other BITs, the majority of which were developed following the German or the early US model, embraced the same tendency towards economic nationalism.

This economic approach was in contradiction to the rhetoric of newly emergent economic globalisation and free trade, which embraced a neoliberal narrative. Yet, the vast majority of BITs were signed in the 1990s, containing elements of the past times that did not match contemporary political economy and economic realities of the present. Developed countries continued to sign these treaties to retain preferential protections for their investors abroad. Developing and transitional economies used them to demonstrate their new economic policies and to continue receiving credit ratings from international rating agencies, which allowed them to borrow money on international financial markets at lower interest rates.[9] At the same time, the realisation of the intrinsic links between trade and investment in the times of economic globalisation led to the emergence of new preferential trade *and* investment agreements, such as the North America Free Trade Agreement

[4] R. Dolzer and Y. Kim, 'Germany' in Chester Brown (ed), *Commentaries on Selected Model Investment Treaties* (OUP 2013) 293–295.

[5] Havana Charter for an International Trade Organisation (1948) UN Doc E/CONF.2/78.

[6] Kline and Ludema (n 2) 7.

[7] J. E. Pattison, 'The United States-Egypt Bilateral Investment Treaty: A Prototype for Future Negotiation' (1983) 16 *Cornell International Law Journal* 305, 307–310.

[8] J. E. Alvarez, 'The Return of the State' (2011) 20 *Minnesota Journal of International Law* 223, 231–232.

[9] EP, DG for External Policies, 'Investor–State Dispute Settlement provisions in the EU's international investment agreements: Volume 2-Studies' (September 2014) EXPO/B/INTA/2014/08-09-10, 10.

(NAFTA) and the Energy Charter Treaty (ECT). These agreements had economic liberalisation at the forefront of their agenda, prominently influencing evolution of IIR in the years to come.

With the stagnation and ultimate failure of the WTO negotiations in 2006, it became obvious that the future of world trade and investment would be fragmented and that new free trade agreements (FTAs) had gained an increasing geopolitical importance. Fragmentation has ultimately exacerbated the different forms of the contemporary multipolar world. With the rise of BRIC(S) countries (Brazil, Russia, India, China, South Africa), the traditional contours of developed versus developing countries (also known as the North–South divide) have been lost. Additionally, the competition between the developing countries has increased, leading to a South–South divide.

With the start of the new millennium, IIAs became more complex. They gradually expanded their content and scope with the new generation of BITs following the trends of standards set in preferential trade and investment agreements and the new North American BIT model.[10] The new approach to drafting investment treaties narrowed the scope of investor rights to some extent. This change can be explained by the pursuit of economic liberalisation on the one hand, and the move towards protection of States' sovereign policy space on the other.[11]

Finally, the Global Financial Crisis (GFC) of 2008 demonstrated that economic globalisation brought about divisions within the multipolar world but, even more so, divisions within society. Business elites, in both developing and developed countries, profited from globalisation, which in turn left many workers and poorer elements of society worse off. These elites, in the literature described as the transnational capitalist class, encompass business elites affiliated with MNEs, but also globalising bureaucrats, politicians, professionals, merchants and media. Altogether they form a dominant force in the political sphere of the contemporary global system.[12] Their private interests extend beyond nation States and they dominate the discourse of globalisation. As strong market players, MNEs have the strongest capacity to survive different types of crises

[10] UNCTAD, 'Recent Developments in International Investment Agreements' (2005) IIA Monitor No. 2, UNCTAD/WEB/ITE/IIT/2005/1, 4–6. See also discussion on the North American model in Section 2.1.2.

[11] Cf. Alvarez (n 8).

[12] L. Sklair, 'The Transnational Capitalist Class and the Discourse of Globalisation' (2000) 14 *Cambridge Review of International Affairs* 67.

because their global operations allow them to shift from a troubled country or region towards more robust foreign markets.[13]

Recent political events, such as Brexit, demonstrate citizens' concerns in the West over globalisation and neoliberal discourse, suggesting that we have not yet reached the 'end of history'.[14] Given the global reach of private capital operating in world markets according to opportunities, incentives and disincentives determined through transnational neoliberal discourse, contrasted with the reach of States' policies limited by territorial boundaries, neoliberalism has reached the point of no return.[15] States' domestic economic policies, especially since the GFC, demonstrate forms of return to State intervention in economies, which conflicts with the neoliberal discourse promoted through IIAs. The number of investment arbitration claims has risen, resulting in the rise of States' scepticism towards investor-State dispute settlement (ISDS). Contemporary threats to State sovereignty in the area of investment do not come from other States as in the past, but from private capital. In the words of Nobel Prize–winning economist Joseph Stiglitz: 'Companies can sue governments for full compensation for any reduction in their future expected profits resulting from regulatory changes'.[16] Modern IIAs are accordingly an attempt to align legal institutions with political and economic realities of contemporary international trade and investment, in which States are both exporters and importers of capital. While sets of standards developed in Washington or Brussels still drive the rules of global governance, new investment governance is increasingly shaped by divergent policies of the West, emerging players like China and underlying scepticism towards ISDS, in particular in the global South.

The US approach under the former administration of President Trump has been more hostile towards ISDS, significantly limiting its scope in the United States–Mexico–Canada Agreement (USMCA). However, ISDS remains the preferred option with few limitations for government contracts in sectors such as oil and gas, turning ISDS back to its beginnings when contract-based rather than treaty-based arbitration

[13] See empirical research conducted in the study by D. Dikova and others, 'Immediate Responses to Financial Crises: A Focus on U.S. MNE Subsidiaries' (2013) 22 *International Business Review* 202.

[14] F. Fukuyama, 'The End of History?' (1989) 16 *The National Interest* 3.

[15] H. Patomaki, 'Neoliberalism and Global Financial Crisis' (2009) 31 *New Political Science* 431, suggesting that return of national social democracy is unlikely but might be replaced by 'green global Keynesianism'.

[16] J. Stiglitz, 'The Secret Corporate Takeover' (*Project Syndicate* 17 May 2015).

was prevalent.[17] In addition, the USMCA brings back into the fray some unresolved issues of the past – by excluding non-market economies as potential claimants[18] and as treaty partners of the USMCA partners.[19] More specifically, even post-Trump, the US concerns are focused on containing China, while still being more generally related to the impact of international rules on US sovereignty, both in trade (WTO) and investment. The United States remains committed to ISDS and the regulation of investment relations at a bilateral level, and has been critical of the EU's proposal for a permanent multilateral institution.[20]

China is increasingly emerging as a rule-maker, in particular in the sphere of its own commercial interests. While concluding many IIAs, China's experience with ISDS has been limited.[21] More recently, China has advanced its own investment initiatives, most notably the Belt and Road Initiative (BRI),[22] and is developing more effective domestic and investment regulation for these new investments.[23] It has expanded the jurisdiction of its own arbitral institutions to include foreign investment claims.[24] It established a new court for BRI commercial disputes.[25] In Africa it started the China–Africa Joint Arbitration Centre (CAJAC), with five regional centres.[26] While these institutions remain embedded in the existing international system of arbitration,[27] China has taken a

[17] See Chapter 1.

[18] Art. 14.D.1 USMCA.

[19] Art. 32.10 USMCA.

[20] See Chapter 10.

[21] This might be due to China's reservations on the applicability of the ICSID Convention (limited to compensation arising from expropriation cases) and New York Convention (limited to commercial and not ISDS cases, which must be enforced before Chinese courts): see D. J. Lewis and D. Moise, 'One Belt One Road ("OBOR") Roadmaps: The Legal and Policy Frameworks' in J. Chaisse and J. Gorski (eds), *The Belt and Road Initiative: Law, Economics and Politics* (Brill 2018) 55–58.

[22] See A. Chuwen Dai, 'The International Investment Agreement Network under the "Belt and Road" Initiative' in Chaisse and Gorski (n 21) 220–224.

[23] See W. Zhu, 'Some Considerations on the Civil, Commercial and Investment Dispute Settlement Mechanism between China and the Other Belt and Road Countries' in Chaisse and Gorski (n 21) 607–620.

[24] In particular, the Shenzhen Court of International Arbitration (SCIA) and China International Economic Trade Arbitration Commission (CIETAC). This is in addition to the Hong Kong International Arbitration Centre (HKIAC), which has also been designated for the BRI ISDS cases.

[25] China International Commercial Court in Xi'an and Shenzhen, known as the BRI Court.

[26] In Shanghai, Beijing, Shenzhen, Nairobi, Johannesburg.

[27] The notable exception is the BRI Court, which has been established by the Supreme People's Court of China.

proactive approach in developing new rules with 'Chinese' characteristics. *Inter alia,* focus has been on promoting mediation-arbitration techniques, expedient proceedings and lowering costs.[28] The EU, as a newcomer to the IIR field, is counting on China's cooperation in developing its own set of institutions, despite the policy gap between them.[29] In its efforts to reform the system, the EU is proposing flexible plurilateral solutions that fit all – and a Multilateral Investment Court (MIC) that can accommodate China's preference for an appellate mechanism in ISDS.[30] Given their overlapping interests in certain regions (Africa, European neighbourhood, Western Balkans), this approach seems sensible.

In light of political controversies around ISDS in the countries of the global North, investment dispute settlement is excluded altogether in some notable recent North–North IIAs given that the risk for investors in these countries generally remains low.[31] In North–South relations, in addition to issues with China, the design of rules is more complicated in relations with strong South players.[32] With negative experience of investment treaty arbitration (ITA) on a much larger scale, a number of these countries have decided to denounce the ICSID Convention and/or BITs, or alternatively have developed their own model BITs.[33] Treaties between South countries display a more balanced development-oriented standard[34] and in some cases orientate towards domestic measures and dispute prevention rather than dispute resolution.[35]

The contemporary political and economic world divided between North and South is more complex than the developed–developing divisions of the past. Between a neoliberal and restrictive ISDS agenda, and specific agendas of big players, the task of addressing political tensions in IIR remains as challenging as ever.

[28] H. Chen, 'China's Innovative ISDS Mechanisms and Their Implications' (2018) 112 *American Journal of International Law* 207.

[29] For a comprehensive overview, see J. Chaisse (ed), *China–European Union Investment Relationships: Towards a New Leadership in Global Investment Governance?* (Edward Elgar 2018).

[30] See Chapter 10.

[31] For example, in the USMCA between the United States and Canada.

[32] One such example is provided by India's stalled negotiations with the United States, Canada and the EU respectively. Australia-India Economic Cooperation and Trade Agreement 2022 does not include ISDS.

[33] For example, see the Indian Model BIT 2016, which retains ISDS but introduces exhaustion of local remedies.

[34] See, for example, the Nigeria–Morocco BIT (signed 3 December 2016). Among other provisions directed towards 'sustainable development', this BIT also envisaged the possibility for the developing States to establish new standards: see Art. 19.

[35] For example, Brazil has developed its own Cooperation and Investment Facilitation Agreements in 2015 with dispute prevention mechanisms and state-to-state arbitration.

### 2.1.2 Tensions between Economic Objectives

Given the divergent political visions, the next relevant issue for ISDS reform embraces the objectives and purposes that IIAs aim to achieve. Are they supposed to favour investors or provide a more balanced approach? In the broader context, are they supposed to provide benefits to private investors or increase the prosperity of Contracting States through protections that encourage investment activity? Or both? And in the context of the twenty-first century and global climate change concerns, how do they relate to sustainable development?

In general terms, BITs developed around two basic models, which still form the basis for the majority of claims. With respect to both types, their general purpose is 'promotion and protection' of investment, as often stated in their titles. The differences between the two models can be linked to their different philosophical postulates. The first is the 'European model', based on the German model BIT, while the second is the 'North American model', based on the US Model BIT developed in 2004.[36] While before the 1990s both models had protectionist interests at their cores, the two models later differentiated with respect to the regulation of the access of foreign investors to the host State.

In the European model, the investment treatment provisions apply to an investment after establishment, leaving the regulation of access, entry and establishment of foreign investment to the control and competence of each State.[37] The main aim is the protection of property and the promotion of development of the host State (as an ancillary aim), and not investment liberalisation through liberalisation of the legal regime of the counterpart State. Based on the German concept, the dominant European BIT approach generally does not include clauses advancing non-investment aims, and can be characterised as 'investment-focused, traditional, short, not definition-prone, and embodying relatively high standards'.[38]

In the North American model, the treatment provisions apply to investment after it has been established in the host State but also in the pre-establishment phase; there is prohibition of imposing performance

[36] The German model is based on the failed Draft International Convention on Investments Abroad (Abs-Shawcross Draft Convention) model, endorsed by OECD ministers in 1962. The North American model is characteristic for the United States and Canada.

[37] This model is also called the 'admission model' and 'investment-control model', and it is usually easier to agree upon as it does not influence existing legislation. The majority of BITs today are still based on this model.

[38] Dolzer and Kim (n 4) 301. This approach is also suitable to German economic and investment policy, which is characterised as a 'social market economy', which is outward-oriented and strongly based on capital export.

requirements on investors or their investment,[39] and the model generally contains more detailed provisions in certain aspects, such as right of entry and the sojourn of aliens.[40] Although the European model is still more prevalent, the North American model seems to dominate the outline of the modern IIAs by considerably extending their length and by combining trade and investment, which is a move away from investment-only focused agreements.[41] In this regard, the old European BIT model can be considered an expression of a more economic nationalist policy, while the North American model, with its commitment to investment neutrality and market facilitation, is a tool for constructing a more liberal investment regime.[42] CETA provides a compromise between the old European and the North American model.[43] However, provisions on pre-investment remain outside the scope of the dispute settlement.[44]

The preamble of an investment agreement, although not imposing binding obligations, provides some reflections about the object and purpose of IIAs. The traditional European model, based on the German model, places an emphasis on the encouragement and protection of investment as a means of development. The North American model reflects key aspects of the US liberal economic policy with a view to stimulating flow of private capital, which is interrelated with economic development. In both cases, it is envisaged that both States will profit from the arrangement – the home State by encouraging overseas investment and the host State by receiving that investment. However, reliance on the preamble to determine object and purpose requires caution in treaty interpretation.

39 See Art. 8 US Model BIT 2012.

40 However, exceptions are allowed through a Non-Conforming Measures clause in Art. 14 US Model BIT 2012.

41 This is also in line with the US investment policy, which is both inward and outward FDI oriented. See L. M. Caplan and J. K. Sharpe, 'United States' in C. Brown (n 4) 758–760. See, for example, the investment chapter in Comprehensive and Progressive Agreement for Trans-Pacific Partnership (signed 8 March 2018, entered into force 30 December 2018) (CPTPP), which follows the North American model.

42 Vandevelde (n 3) 629–633. The US model imposes investment neutrality obligations on both home and host States by creating pre-establishment commitments, thus disallowing discrimination among investments for political reasons, grounded in the local laws.

43 See Arts. 8.6 and 8.7 CETA. CETA also precludes limitations on market access (Art. 8.4) and performance requirements (Art. 8.5) and includes a provision to ensure the neutrality of senior management and boards of directors (Art. 8.8).

44 Arts. 8.2.4, 8.18.1, 8.18.2, and 8.18.5 CETA. The same approach is followed in the new USMCA: See Arts. 14.4 (NT), 14.5 (MFN), and 14.D.3(1) (Submission of a Claim to Arbitration).

Many IIAs have imported the standard language developed for the first BITs when these treaties were meant to serve political purposes. They were not meant to provide greater rights to foreign investors but to provide guarantees that foreign investors would not be treated worse in the host States' domestic legal systems because of deficiencies of these systems.[45] Only with the development of arbitral jurisprudence post-1990s have the implications of IIAs clarified, including their object and purpose as seen by those who interpret them. Tribunals have referred to the treaty preamble and treaty purpose to infer a favourable disposition to foreign investment as justification for their 'effective' interpretation.[46] The object and purpose of IIAs so understood – to favour investment protection – ignores the 'idea of enhancing development' as a rationale for protecting foreign investment.[47] Additionally, even if greater protection of foreign investors was the main rationale, it would only be the reflection of political preferences of the developed nations at the time when the BITs were created. In recent times, developing States' IIAs in particular emphasise the development purpose of the investment, clearly stating such purpose as the main rationale of investment in the preamble of their treaties. Table 2.1 provides an illustration of different objectives in the preambles of the dominant IIA models.[48]

Some tribunals have understood present realities better than the others, with some recent awards achieving more balanced investor–State outcomes. A significant degree of deference to States' regulatory powers has been exemplified in the full dismissal of Phillip Morris' claims, thus recognising Uruguay's right to regulate a 'major' public

[45] See Chapter 1. Also, see the similar approach of the CJEU in Opinion 1/17 ECLI:EU:C:2019:341, in Chapter 9.

[46] See, for example, *SGS v Philippines*, ICSID Case No. ARB/02/6, Decision of the Tribunal on Objections to Jurisdiction (29 January 2004) para. 116; *Siemens A.G. v The Argentine Republic*, ICSID Case No. ARB/02/8, Decision on Jurisdiction (3 August 2004) para. 81; *Noble Ventures, Inc. v Romania*, ICSID Case No. ARB/01/11, Award (12 October 2005) para. 52; *Salini Costruttori S.p.A and Italstrade S.p.A. v The Hashemite Kingdom of Jordan*, ICSID Case No. ARB/02/13, Decision on Jurisdiction (9 November 2004) para. 95. On the other hand, there were also tribunals that, in the absence of specific treaty language, invoked the *dubio mitius* principle in favour of State sovereignty: see, for example, *SGS v Pakistan*, ICSID Case No. ARB/01/13, Decision of the Tribunal on Objections to Jurisdiction (6 August 2003) para. 171.

[47] J. Kleinheisterkamp, 'Investment Treaty Law and the Fear for Sovereignty: Transnational Challenges and Solutions' (2015) 78 *The Modern law Review* 793, 810.

[48] Emphasis added in the table.

Table 2.1 *Comparison of preambles extracted from international investment agreements*

| | |
|---|---|
| OLD EUROPEAN MODEL | GERMAN MODEL BIT 2008<br>Desiring to intensify **economic co-operation** between the two States,<br>Intending to **create favourable conditions for investments** by investors of either State in the territory of the other State,<br>Recognizing that **the encouragement and contractual protection of such investments are apt to stimulate private business initiative** and to **increase the prosperity of both nations** |
| NORTH AMERICAN MODEL<br>BIT 2012 | Desiring to promote greater **economic cooperation** between them with respect to investment by nationals and enterprises of one Party in the territory of the other Party;<br>Recognizing that agreement on the treatment to be accorded such investment will **stimulate the flow of private capital and the economic development of the Parties;**<br>Agreeing that a stable framework for investment will **maximize effective utilization of economic resources and improve living standards;**<br>Recognizing the importance of providing effective means of **asserting claims and enforcing rights** with respect to investment under national law as well as through international arbitration;<br>Desiring to achieve these objectives **in a manner consistent with the protection of health, safety, and the environment, and the promotion of internationally recognized labor rights;** |
| THE EUROPEAN UNION<br>EU-SINGAPORE INVESTMENT PROTECTION AGREEMENT | Desiring to further strengthen their relationship as part of and in a manner coherent with their overall relations, and convinced that this Agreement will create **a new climate for further development of investment** between the Parties;<br>Recognising that this Agreement will complement and promote **regional economic integration efforts;**<br>Determined to strengthen their economic, trade, and investment relations **in accordance with the** |

Table 2.1 (*cont.*)

| | |
|---|---|
| | **objective of sustainable development**, in its economic, social and environmental dimensions, and to **promote investment in a manner mindful of high levels of environmental and labour protection and relevant internationally-recognised standards and agreements to which they are parties**;<br>Reaffirming their commitment to the **principles of sustainable development and transparency** as reflected in the EUSFTA;<br>Reaffirming each Party's **right to adopt and enforce measures necessary to pursue legitimate policy objectives** such as social, environmental, security, public health and safety, promotion and protection of cultural diversity;<br>Reaffirming their **commitment to the Charter of the United Nations** signed in San Francisco on 26 June 1945 and having regard to the principles articulated in **The Universal Declaration of Human Rights** adopted by the General Assembly of the United Nations on 10 December 1948;<br>Recognising the importance of **transparency** in international trade and investment to the **benefit of all stakeholders**;<br>Building on their respective **rights and obligations under the WTO Agreement and other multilateral, regional and bilateral agreements and arrangements** to which they are party, in particular, the EUSFTA |

health issue ('lethal effects of tobacco'),[49] and in the acceptance of Argentina's necessity defence for emergency measures following the 2001 financial crisis.[50] States have made efforts to recalibrate the normative framework of investment protection, including more explicit

[49] *Philip Morris Brand Sarl, Philip Morris Products S.A. and Abal Hermanos S.A. v Oriental Republic of Uruguay*, ICSID Case No. ARB/10/7, Award (8 July 2016) para. 418.

[50] *Urbaser S.A. and Consorcio de Aguas Bilbao Biskaia Ur Partzuergoa v Argentine Republic*, ICSID Case No. ARB/07/26, Award (8 December 2016) para. 622.

language about the objects and purpose of the new generation of IIAs. These attempts to bring into line policy and law in IIR might well reflect the new realities of a contemporary multipolar world where States exercise the roles of both exporters and importers of capital.

### 2.1.3 *Tensions between Legal Methods and Cultures*

While negotiating IIAs is a political process of bargaining and consolidating different economic visions, interpretation and practical application of IIAs through dispute settlement is part of a more technical legal domain. The contemporary ISDS debate has brought into focus the legal reasoning and practice of international investment tribunals and exposed a number of issues pertinent to the character of international investment law (IIL) and the legal culture of its professional community.[51] The mixed character of IIL is due, on the one hand, to its international law basis (international treaties) and, on the other, to the commercial law character of its dispute settlement mechanism (method of interpretation and application).[52] The main challenge for ISDS reform thus lies in reconciling the private law practice of IIL with its intended international public law character. But in the sphere of legal methodology, these tensions have significant consequences for the legitimacy of ISDS; it is therefore important that any reform of ISDS appropriately addresses them.

International investment law has developed from private international commercial law, encompassing substantive contract law elements and arbitration between private parties as a procedural mechanism. To understand treaty-based investment arbitration, it is important to look at ways in which commercial arbitration, and in particular contract-based investment arbitration, developed as transnational law.[53] These developments can be traced back to North–South disputes and nationalisations of large oil and mega-construction projects in the 1970s and 1980s. Arbitration was successful as it was seen as a way to separate business from Cold War politics. The State-centred arbitration institutions, such as the Iran–United States Claims Tribunal (IUSCT) and ICSID, were established with this rationale. Importantly, developing

[51] See A. Roberts, 'Clash of Paradigms; Actors and Analogies Shaping the Investment Treaty System' (2013) 107 *American Journal of International Law* 45.

[52] See Chapter 1.

[53] See seminal work by Y. Dezalay and B. G. Garth, *Dealing in Virtue* (University of Chicago Press 1996).

States were more willing to accept arbitration for the resolution of their disputes with Western companies. They perceived it as independent because of arbitration's neutral setting, detached from the political conflict, and legal methods, which involved American-style adversarial tactics. Professional networks of lawyers with close personal relations played an important role in the development of the system, both in exacerbating conflicts and in taking the role of neutral intermediaries.[54]

Apart from the need to separate State contracts from domestic *courts* through arbitration, Western investors also needed ways to separate themselves from risks of recourse to developing countries' *laws.* Lawyers played an important role in developing *lex mercatoria* as 'general principles of international commerce' in substantive law as a way of compromise that avoided reference to either developed or developing States' laws.[55] *Lex mercatoria* was thus meant to serve as an internationalised law in arbitration, characterised by party autonomy and broad principles that ensured flexibility.[56] Through Article 42(1) of the ICSID Convention, internationalisation of disputes found its way into the treaty-based arbitration. However, the history of the ICSID Convention demonstrates that this was not the intention of the developing States, which were concerned about losing sovereignty as a consequence of the internationalisation of State contracts.[57]

With the increased dominance of Anglo-American law firms in the field of arbitration over time, the importance of *lex mercatoria* also diminished. General principles, more suitable for brief civil law contracts, did not have a place in more technical and specific common law contracts.[58] The dominance of common law practices is also noted in procedural aspects, combined with some civil law elements, allowing for procedural flexibility.[59] The ongoing cooperation between academics and practitioners has promoted acceptance and recognition of the system

[54] ibid 71–85.

[55] ibid 86.

[56] R. Howarth, 'Lex Mercatoria: Can General Principles of Law Govern International Commercial Contracts?' (2004) 10 *Canterbury Law Review* 36.

[57] See N. Nassar, 'Internalization of State Contracts: ICSID, The Last Citadel' (1997) 14 *Journal of International Arbitration* 185, 203–206. For argument on the internationalised nature of ICSID, see H. E. Kjos, *Applicable Law in Investor-State Arbitration: The Interplay between National and International Law* (OUP 2013) 53–59.

[58] Dezalay and Garth (n 53) 89–90.

[59] See, for example, S. H. Elsing and J. M. Townsend, 'Bridging the Common Law Civil Law Divide in Arbitration' (2002) 18 *Arbitration International* 1.

through reputational capital.[60] Others have claimed that uniform rules and standards ('international arbitration culture') have been created to highlight expertise and to capture the network benefits between a limited number of participants.[61]

The *modus operandi* in treaty-based arbitration has followed the patterns of its contract-based counterpart. Available empirical research shows that arbitrators mostly come from private law backgrounds, the majority of them from Western European or North American countries; they are either practitioners or academics (or both, with their time allocated in different proportions), and make an average of US$200,000 per case.[62] Appointments are made on the basis of their performance and reputation, which are key factors for their advancement in the field.[63] They are more likely to make decisions in favour of the party that has appointed them but this is also due to their policy preferences and background.[64] Importantly, arbitration functions like a small club in which different roles (arbitrator, legal counsel, expert witness, tribunal secretary) are interchangeable – sequentially or even simultaneously – between a small pool of highly influential and powerful individuals.[65] While a majority of arbitrators comes from the global North, the majority of respondent States are from the global South, or transition economies in the European context. The field lacks the cultural diversity necessary to properly appreciate cultural subtleties of legal facts.[66] This includes appreciation of domestic laws, when treated either as a fact, or in rare circumstances, as applicable law in ITA.

The cooperation between practitioners (more akin to common law tradition) and academics (more akin to civil law tradition) in arbitral tribunals' practice is evident in the reference to case law and scholarship.

[60] See empirical findings of S. Puig, 'Social Capital in the Arbitration Market' (2014) 25 *The European Journal of International Law* 387.

[61] T. Ginsburg, 'The Culture of Arbitration' (2003) 36 *Vanderbilt Journal of Transnational Law* 1335.

[62] J. A. Fontoura Costa, 'Comparing WTO Panelists and ICSID Arbitrators: The Creation of International Legal Fields' (2011) 4 *Oñati Socio-Legal Series* 1; J. Pauwelyn, 'The Rule of Law without the Rule of Lawyers? Why Investment Arbitrators Are from Mars, Trade Adjudicators from Venus' (2015) 109 *American Journal of International Law* 761; For similar findings in the context of ICSID appointments, see Puig (n 60) 403–407.

[63] Pauwelyn ibid 781.

[64] M. Waibel and Y. Wu, 'Are Arbitrators Political? Evidence from International Investment Arbitration' (2017).

[65] M. Langford, D. Behn, and R. Hilleren Lie, 'The Revolving Door in International Investment Arbitration' (2017) 20 *Journal of International Economic Law* 301. Similarly, see Puig (n 60).

[66] V. L. Kidane, *The Culture of International Arbitration* (OUP 2017).

Consistent with their role, arbitrators are more 'dispute-oriented' than 'legislator-oriented'.[67] Nevertheless, their jurisprudence has effectively created rules due to vaguely defined provisions of old BITs (akin to the flexibility of the *lex mercatoria*). As a response to such jurisprudence, the new generation of IIAs is much more detailed – akin also to detailed contracts favoured by common law tradition and the prevailing Anglo-American culture in arbitration. New treaty standards are still developed from the existing standards emerging from tribunals' jurisprudence.[68]

The methods of contract interpretation, flexibility and business rationale have all found their way into ITA. Generally speaking, in contract disputes, the main task of the adjudicator is to ascertain the intention of the parties.[69] This approach results in narrow interpretation, focused exclusively on the text, independent of broader public policy context and implications. Commercial contracts are thus drafted in great detail, exactly to avoid different interpretations that could arise from a different context (values and backgrounds of parties).[70] Applied to treaty-based arbitration, in some cases, the text of the treaties has been taken literally to justify some – from the policy perspective – doubtful interpretations; for example, parallel proceedings or treaty shopping. In other cases, broad treaty provisions have allowed the importation of contract law standards, such as 'stabilisation clauses'.[71] This approach has enabled claimants to argue that States have given up their right to expropriate and regulate, and must provide 'prompt, adequate and effective compensation' whenever regulation affects their legitimate expectations of a stable business environment. These claims have in particular been grounded in treaty provisions guaranteeing protection against regulatory takings (indirect expropriations) or fair and equitable treatment (FET).[72] When specific representations are made to an investor, parallels have been

[67] O. K. Fauchald, 'The Legal Reasoning of ICSID Tribunals – An Empirical Analysis' (2008) 19 *European Journal of International Law* 301, 357.

[68] See Chapters 1 and 8.

[69] The same applies in English and US common law traditions. However, this is always done objectively by also taking into account the factual matrix.

[70] T. W. Wälde, 'Interpreting Investment Treaties: Experiences and Examples' in *International Investment Law for 21st Century: Essays in Honour of Christoph Schreuer* (OUP 2009) 726–728.

[71] See J. Arato, 'The Logic of Contract in the World of Investment Treaties' (2016) 58 *William & Mary Law Review* 351. Accordingly, some more recent IIAs explicitly exclude stabilisation obligations: see Art. 4 Columbia–France BIT (signed 10 July 2014); Art. 4(2) Japan–Colombia BIT (signed 12 September 2011, entered into force 11 September 2015).

[72] See Section 1.2.2 in Chapter 1.

drawn with a common law doctrine of estoppel.[73] With the dominant contract law approach,[74] arbitral tribunals have in many cases failed to appreciate that the rights of private parties in contract law are absolute, while in public law (e.g. in administrative law) they become relative to other public interest goals.[75]

Interpretation of international agreements is governed by the Vienna Convention on the Law of Treaties (VCLT).[76] The Vienna Convention requires interpretation of the terms in good faith by giving them 'ordinary' meaning in their context and 'in the light of their object and purpose', where context also includes 'any agreement relating to the treaty between the parties'.[77] Arbitral tribunals, although they now regularly make reference to this general rule of treaty interpretation, do not properly nor systemically apply this interpretative method in determining State parties' intention.[78] The arbitrators' typical style of reasoning and argumentation focuses rather on procedural aspects, facts, particularities and winning,[79] and less on proper application of law, reasoning and soundness of argument in general, and with little understanding of international public law implications.[80]

The lack of a more proactive role of tribunals in establishing consistent jurisprudence and applying appropriate techniques of reasoning is an important reason why the confidence in the system has been undermined.

[73] While no tribunal made an explicit reference to estoppel, which is in international law applicable only between States, language resembling the doctrine of estoppel has been employed in practice through the reference to the investor's expectations when making an investment.

[74] Contracts of common law countries have more influenced the law of foreign investment given the driving role of the common law countries in utilising the system: see J. Chaisse and Y. Renouf, 'Investor–State Dispute Settlement' in J. Drake-Brockman and P. Messerlin (eds), *Potential Benefits of an Australia–EU Free Trade Agreement: Key Issues and Options* (Adelaide University Press 2018) 304.

[75] Naturally, there are limits to what parties can legally agree and contracts can be illegal for offending public policy. However, public policy in this narrow sense concerns basic community standards (e.g. contracts to commit crime or tort, or which prejudice the administration of justice would be illegal for being contrary to public policy).

[76] Vienna Convention on the Law of the Treaties (concluded 23 May 1969, entered into force 27 January 1980) 1155 UNTS 331 (VCLT).

[77] Art. 31 VCLT.

[78] Wälde (n 70) 730.

[79] Again, this style is more characteristic of common law adversarial systems of administration of justice.

[80] J. Paulsson, 'Avoiding Unintended Consequences' in K. P. Sauvant and M. Chiswick-Patterson (eds), *Appeals Mechanism in International Investment Disputes* (OUP 2008) 262–263.

## 2.2 Tensions between Actors and Their Perspectives

The peculiar mixed nature of IIL, which combines private and public roles of the State (contractual freedom and regulation), draws a number of civil society actors into the field. The perspectives of these actors have been in particular exposed in the main reform debate in the United Nations Commission on International Trade Law (UNCITRAL). These perspectives are divided along the lines of the business community that supports ISDS, and the non-governmental organization (NGO) sector in the sphere of 'public interest' (environmental, human rights, trade NGOs and think tanks) that opposes it, either in its current form or entirely. These views transcend States' borders into transnational activism. States thus have a challenging role when seeking to satisfy divergent civil society perspectives. This is further compounded by States' need to both export their own capital and attract foreign capital in order to create positive macroeconomic growth within their borders. The way in which today's global economy works places private capital in a strong position against States. Unlike in the area of trade law, where agreed rules affect foreign investment but do not give individuals instruments with which to act, the direct standing against States enjoyed in ISDS gives foreign investors a more influential role in the development of investment law standards.[81]

From the investors' perspective, typical discussion of ISDS is based on a simple reasoning. First, States need foreign direct investment (FDI) to develop their economies and create jobs. While FDI does not necessarily guarantee prosperity at a microeconomic level, it is a *conditio sine qua non* of the macroeconomic growth. Second, FDI needs a stable investment climate, which can only be guaranteed by ISDS. States therefore need ISDS if they wish to attract FDI. This logical conclusion is further supported by economic data about FDI flows expressed in gross terms. The investor's perception is thus based on the assumption that without ISDS there would not be FDI flows into the State and that States necessarily discriminate against foreign investment. Reform should

[81] Foreign investors' influence on the development of IIL could be examined through the lenses of Marc Galanter's seminal work 'Why the "Haves" Come out Ahead: Speculations on the Limits of Social Change' (1974) 9 *Law and Society Review* 95. Galanter argued that parties with more money, power and experience (repeat players – RPs) enjoy strategic advantage in the legal process and use that advantage to shape the development of the legal system. While foreign investors are rarely RPs, they have the resources to use the RP's legal advice (arbitration legal industry). On the analysis of the relationship between RP lawyers and ITA outcomes, see S. D. Franck and L. E. Wylie, 'Predicting Outcomes in Investment Treaty Arbitration' (2015) 65 *Duke Law Journal* 459, which confirms Galanter's thesis that a counsel's experience predicts dispute outcomes.

therefore take place within the current system of arbitration institutions and rules to improve it 'for all *users*'.[82]

On the other side of the ISDS discourse, a number of environmental NGOs, trade unions and labour groups, human rights and other sustainable development-oriented think tanks and research institutes have been vocal about different ISDS concerns. While many participate in the debate on the reform of ISDS, there is no comprehensive coordinative mechanism between their activities. Among them, there are those that categorically reject ISDS and advocate for its abolishment;[83] and those that recognise the political realities and advocate for a broader reform agenda within the limited UNCITRAL procedural mandate, or more holistic reform outside UNCITRAL.[84] Given their broader social agenda, they emphasise the importance of aligning ISDS with other State obligations, such as climate change and balancing business enterprises' rights with responsibilities towards local communities.[85] Same as investors, they reject the idea of a MIC but for different reasons; they see it as a mechanism for 'effectively lock[ing]-in the investment treaty regime'.[86]

Finally, lawyers have the most prominent role in the current ISDS debate, mostly in their advisory role, as members of government or observer delegations, or two informal groups that have been formed to support the work of UNCITRAL: the Practitioner Group and the Academic Forum.[87] The former gathers lawyers active in the field of ISDS as counsels or arbitrators. The latter is broader and gathers academics active in the field of ISDS, a number of whom are engaged in

[82] See Corporate Counsel International Arbitration Group (CCIAG), 'ISDS Reform, Submission by the CCIAG to UNCITRAL Working Group III' (18 December 2019) and European Federation for Investment Law and Arbitration (EFILA), 'EFILA's Written Comments Made at the UNCITRAL Working Group on ISDS Reform' (June 2018).

[83] See, for example, submission to UNCITRAL by Public Citizen, 'Recommendations for UNCITRAL ISDS Discussions' (15 July 2019).

[84] These are primarily research institutes and think tanks. See for example, the joint submission to UNCITRAL by Columbia Center on Sustainable Development (CCSI), International Institute for Environment and Development (IIED) and International Institute for Sustainable Development (IISD), 'UNCITRAL Working Group III on ISDS Reform: How Cross-Cutting Issues Reshape Reform Options' (15 July 2019).

[85] See for example, Client Earth, 'Potential Solutions for Phase 3: Aligning the Objectives of UNCITRAL Working Group III with States' International Obligations to Combat Climate Change'.

[86] '300+ Civil Society Organisations from 73 Countries Urge Real Reform at United Nations Discussions on Corporate Investor Rights' (*Center for International Environmental Law*, 30 October 2018).

[87] See B. Jaap-Verbeek, 'A Social Mapping of the UNCITRAL Process on ISDS Reform' (2020).

some capacity with ISDS. Divisions between academics follow the general division in ISDS discourse: between the investment lawyers who are interested in different degrees of reform in UNCITRAL[88] and academics who advocate for a broader reform agenda, within or outside the UNCITRAL process.[89] The latter remain a minority in UNCITRAL.

In addition to these actors, different international organisations and arbitral institutions take part in the UNCITRAL reform as observers, while in parallel undertaking their own reforms.[90] For example, ICSID reform includes modernisation and simplification of its procedural rules.[91] The work of United Nations Conference on Trade and Development (UNCTAD) is supporting States in their bilateral treaties and investment policy reforms.[92] The Organization for Economic Cooperation and Development (OECD) has undertaken work on business-related human rights,[93] which States refer to in an attempt to recalibrate the normative framework of IIL.

While many actors are interested in the outcomes of the ISDS reforms, States have a difficult task in balancing different interests and perspectives. As a multilateral forum UNCITRAL offers an opportunity for interested actors to voice their concerns and proposals; however, while inclusive, the reform process remains State-led,[94] whereas lobbying takes place in the background.

88 Some of the early considerations of the potential reform proposals came from prominent members of the Academic Forum: see G. Kaufmann-Kohler and M. Potestà, 'Can the Mauritius Convention Serve as a Model for the Reform of Investor–State Arbitration in Connection with the Introduction of a Permanent Investment Tribunal or an Appeal Mechanism? – Analysis and Roadmap' (3 June 2016), CIDS-Geneva Center for International Dispute Settlement, and 'The Composition of a Multilateral Investment Court and of an Appeal Mechanism for Investment Awards' (15 November 2017), CIDS Supplemental Report.

89 See 'An Open Letter to the Chair of UNCITRAL Working Group III and to all Participating States concerning the Reform of the ISDS: Addressing the Asymmetry of ISDS' (*Erasmus University Rotterdam*, 13 February 2019).

90 See UNCITRAL, 'ISDS Reform: On-line Resources' (*Working Group III: ISDS Reform*).

91 See amended ICSID Rules (entered into force 1 July 2022).

92 See UNCTAD, 'UNCTAD's Reform Package for the International Investment Regime (2018 edition)' (2018).

93 See OECD, 'OECD Guidelines for Multinational Enterprises' (OECD 2018).

94 See UNGA, 'Report of the United Nations Commission on International Trade Law Fiftieth Session' (July 2017) UN Doc A/72/17, paras. 250–251.

# 3

# Intersections of Law and Politics

## Legitimacy and the Rule of Law

This final chapter of Part I provides a conceptual framework for identified issues within the international investment regulation (IIR). The analysis in the preceding chapter has referred to a number of tensions existing within the field to paint the picture of reform challenges. In this chapter, these aspects are placed into the conceptual framework of legitimacy and the rule of law, with an aim of conceptualising systemic problems of investor-State dispute settlement (ISDS) relevant to its reform.

### 3.1 Legitimacy of International Investment Regulation

As a preliminary remark, it must be said that the concept of legitimacy varies across disciplines and includes divergent standards for different categories of institutions.[1] Many scholars have approached legitimacy from two perspectives: as a normative (philosophical concept) and as descriptive or sociological legitimacy (empirical concept).

From a normative perspective, legitimacy relates to the recognition of an institution's right to rule or govern, relying on moral arguments informed by political theory[2] and not coercion by the State.[3] It is assessed against the objective criteria, which focus on qualities of the institution that justify its authority to rule. In a domestic system that is democracy, while in an international setting it is State consent, although the latter has

[1] For overview of legitimacy standards with respect to international courts, see H. G. Cohen and others, 'Legitimacy and International Courts – A Framework' in N. Grossman and others (eds), *Legitimacy and International Courts* (CUP 2018).

[2] J. H. H. Weiler, 'Europe in Crisis – On "Political Messianism", "Legitimacy" and "the Rule of Law"' (2012) *Singapore Journal of Legal Studies* 248, 248.

[3] R. O. Keohane, 'Global Governance and Legitimacy' (2011) 18 *Review of International Political Economy* 99, 99–100.

been rejected as a sufficient basis of normative legitimacy.[4] A number of substantive and procedural factors, classified as input- and output-based legitimacy, related to the process by which decisions are made, and the effectiveness of the results of governance, have been identified as relevant in assessing normative legitimacy.[5]

*Input-based legitimacy* places emphasis on the issue of participation in the decision-making process and it can be referred to as 'government of the people', while *output-based* legitimacy relates to the efficiency of these decisions to provide solutions for 'common' problems, and can be referred to as 'government for the people'. Together they form the basis of democratic legitimacy, which can be summed up as 'trust in institutional arrangements'.[6] An additional element of normative legitimacy, which sits between input and output-based legitimacy, is *throughput legitimacy*. Its focus is the quality of the processes by which decisions are made, with reference to the efficacy of the form of government, the accountability and transparency of the processes and the processes' inclusiveness and openness to interest intermediation with the people, through civil society access to the process and information.[7] With the three elements put together, normative legitimacy is about input legitimacy, which is focused on politics (the 'who' of the decision-making); throughput legitimacy, which is focused on processes (the 'how' of the decision-making); and output legitimacy, concerned with policies (the 'what' of the decision-making).[8]

Sociological or descriptive legitimacy on the other hand relates to ways in which subjects of the State perceive the institution's right to govern.[9] In other words, sociological legitimacy concerns ways in which society and its different actors see and accept the institutions, which inevitably relates to the issue of how the institutions in question meet the interests of different actors within society. With respect to international institutions, this involves the perceptions of both States and civil society,

[4] D. Bodansky, 'Legitimacy in International Law and International Relations' (2011) APSA 2011 Annual Meeting Paper, 11–12.

[5] F. Scharpf, 'Economic Integration, Democracy and the Welfare State' (1997) 4 *Journal of European Policy* 18, 19.

[6] F. Scharpf, 'Problem-Solving Effectiveness and Democratic Accountability in the EU' (2003) Max Planck Institute for the Study of Societies Working Paper 03/1.

[7] V. A. Schmidt, 'Democracy and Legitimacy in the European Union Revisited: Input, Output and "Throughput"' (2013) 61 *Political Studies* 2, 5–7.

[8] ibid 8.

[9] B. R. Roth, *Governmental Illegitimacy in International Law* (OUP 2000) 9.

and their willingness to defer even to an institution's unpopular decisions.[10] While assessing normative legitimacy is subject to political, legal, philosophical and other standards, sociological legitimacy is assessed empirically.[11]

In IIR context, normative input-based legitimacy belongs to States as masters of international investment agreements (IIAs) and procedural rules (ICSID and UNCITRAL). Unlike in the World Trade Organization (WTO) or the EU, there are no international institutions with lawmaking powers.[12] Accordingly, input legitimacy relates primarily to the legitimacy of treaties laying down substantive standards and procedural rules for dispute settlement. Importantly, legality under international law (State consent) is not sufficient to ensure legitimacy.[13] The legitimacy of IIAs depends on the extent to which they reflect constituency preferences; thus they will be considered legitimate if they either do not violate dominant political interests, or if those who agreed to enter these agreements are subject to unlimited electoral accountability.[14] Generally speaking, it is more difficult for citizens to exercise democratic control over States' decisions in foreign relations.[15] In light of the historical development of IIR, it is difficult to assess the legitimacy of the early treaties, given that States, and even more so, their political subjects, were unaware of the real impact of these instruments. A more cautious approach of States in modern treaties demonstrates enhanced awareness of the impacts of IIR domestically. Ensuring legitimacy requires appropriate consultation processes before and during negotiations and, accordingly, implementing into new IIAs input from a broad range of stakeholders. Accordingly, input-based legitimacy in IIR is a matter for the domestic phases of treaty-making processes.[16]

10 D. Bodanski, 'Legitimacy in International Law and International Relations' in J. Dunoff and M. A. Pollack (eds), *Interdisciplinary Perspectives on International Law and International Relations: The State of the Art* (CUP 2013) 324.

11 Cohen and others (n 1) 4. Where relevant, reference is made to public perception (based on secondary sources), but this is a doctrinal study and empirical assessment of sociological legitimacy is outside its scope.

12 One exception would be arbitral institutions, which have powers to adopt their own arbitration rules in accordance with their own governance mechanisms.

13 Bodansky (n 4) 11–12.

14 Scharpf (n 6).

15 R. A. Dahl, 'Can International Organisations Be Democratic? A Sceptic's View' in I. Shapiro and C. Hacker-Cordon (eds), *Democracy's Edges* (CUP 2009) 19–36.

16 See Chapters 6 and 7 on the EU's approach towards increasing input legitimacy.

The core of the legitimacy of IIR, however, lies in the jurisprudence of arbitral tribunals, which primarily concerns procedural issues (throughput legitimacy) and substantive outcomes of these processes – tribunals' decisions (output-based legitimacy). Given the adjudicative character of arbitral tribunals, these criteria can be further broken down using a template for assessing the legitimacy standards of international courts. Of relevance are fairness and bias, and openness and transparency as elements pertinent to throughput legitimacy, and politically acceptable and legally sound decisions as elements pertinent to output-based legitimacy.[17] Throughput legitimacy overlaps with the procedural elements of the rule of law and will be considered in that context.[18]

Substantive elements of output-based legitimacy concern the 'normative currency' of tribunals' decisions in relation to the normative regime as envisaged by international actors.[19] In the case of international investment law (IIL), such a normative regime is defined in applicable IIAs. The legitimacy of tribunals depends on the extent to which tribunals' decisions coincide with the values and interests of international actors and are thus politically acceptable, and the extent to which they are legally sound.[20]

Before turning to the analysis of particular elements of legitimacy and the rule of law, Figure 3.1 depicts the relationship between the two concepts and applies it to the specific context of IIR.

### 3.1.1 *Output-Based Legitimacy through Politically Acceptable Norms*

The authority of international tribunals depends on whether their decisions are consistent with the views of international actors about what the law is or should be. In the context of investment treaty arbitration (ITA),

[17] This theoretical framework is taken and adjusted from N. Grossman, 'Legitimacy and International Adjudicative Bodies' (2009) 14 *The George Washington International Law Review* 107. While Grossman uses these criteria for sociological legitimacy, they also have a normative dimension. The sociological approach analyses whether judicial institutions are regarded as authoritative, while the normative approach explores whether they should be regarded as authoritative. But both categories have an external perspective (how relevant constituencies perceive or should perceive the authority of a court) and a normative component (whether the exercise of power is normatively justified): Y. Shany, 'Stronger Together? Legitimacy and Effectiveness of International Courts as Mutually Reinforcing or Undermining Notions' in N. Grossman and others (n 1) 355–356.

[18] See Section 3.2.2.

[19] Grossman (n 17) 143.

[20] ibid 143–144.

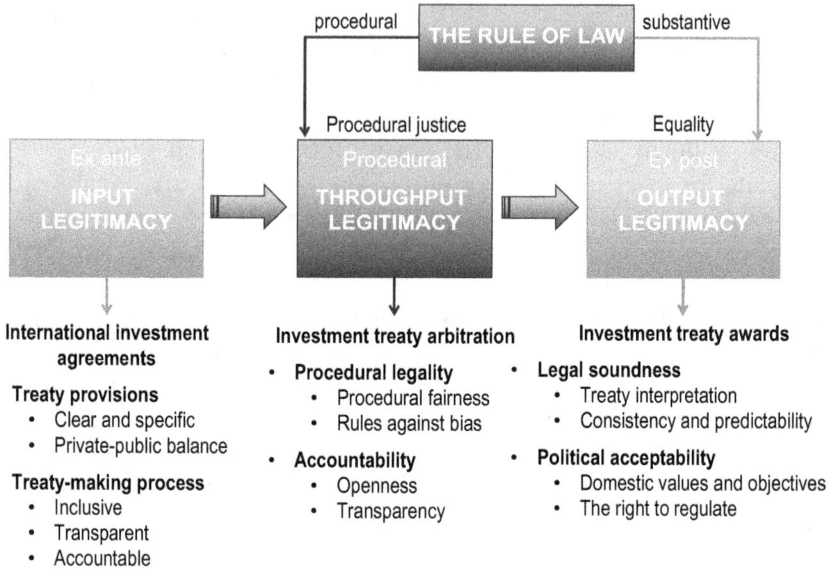


**Figure 3.1** The relationship between legitimacy and the rule of law in international investment regulation

political acceptability is related to the *de facto* lawmaking activity of arbitral tribunals or judicial activism. The focus is placed on the impact of tribunals' decisions on regulatory powers of the State and its sovereignty. Given the political dimension, consistency of tribunals' decisions with community values and interests enshrined in domestic law is particularly important for the adjudicators' authority among domestic constituencies.[21]

Arbitral tribunals are adjudicators and not lawmakers. Their decisions are not precedents and thus are not legally binding *erga omnes*.[22] Nevertheless, in practice, broad wording of IIAs has amplified the need for tribunals' interpretations in order to apply imprecise IIA provisions to specific factual situations. In this exercise, previous awards are regularly consulted and cited, contributing to the creation of case law or jurisprudence.[23] In the absence of more specific provisions, tribunals

[21] ibid 149.

[22] See Arts. 38(1)(d) and 59, Statute of the International Court of Justice.

[23] A. Bjorklund, 'Investment Treaty Arbitral Decisions as Jurisprudence Constante' (2008) UC Davis Legal Studies Research Paper No. 158.

have wide discretion in interpretation, which has led to a shift of interpretative power from States to tribunals, resulting in jurisprudence 'unconstrained by the discipline of the treaty parties' practice or expectations'.[24] Through expansive interpretations, tribunals have engaged in lawmaking beyond their mandates, extending States' obligations beyond those envisaged and agreed by the State signatories to the treaties.[25] While formally not lawmakers, their jurisprudence has *effectively* become the core of IIL.

When adjudicating, arbitral tribunals perform an assessment of State measures at different levels (legislative, executive, judicial). They can condemn States for illegal measures exclusively through monetary compensation and cannot require that the State remove unlawful measures. In that sense, investment tribunals differ from national courts and *formally* speaking do not question a State's sovereignty to adopt domestic measures. However, through their claims, investors have challenged a wide variety of State measures: less contentious State actions, such as direct expropriation of investments and breaches of investment contracts; but also some more dubious measures, such as changes in domestic regulation, withdrawal of subsidies, tax measures, revocation of licences and irregularities in public procurement.

Cases against Argentina, brought on the basis of a number of State measures adopted in response to a major financial crisis which affected this country in late 2001 and 2002,[26] illustrate investment tribunals' assessments of States' responses in protecting the public order. Foreign investors challenged the legality of Argentina's measures in a number of investment arbitration cases, while Argentina defended its right to impose the measures as a response to a severe economic, political and social crisis that was threatening the very existence of the State. First, Argentina argued the non-justiciability of the imposed measures.[27]

[24] A. Roberts, 'Power and Persuasion in Investment Treaty Arbitration: The Dual Role of States' (2010) 104 *American Journal of International Law* 179, 189–190.

[25] See Chapter 1.

[26] Most of the total of over sixty cases against Argentina have originated from measures adopted to stabilise the economy in response to the 2001 financial crisis: see *Continental Casualty Company v The Argentine Republic*, ISCID Case No. ARB/03/9, Award (5 September 2008) paras. 100–159.

[27] See for example, *Suez, Sociedad General de Aguas de Barcelona SA, and InterAguas Servicios Integrales del Agua SA v The Argentine Republic*, ICSID Case No. ARB/03/17, Decision on Jurisdiction (16 May 2006) para. 27; *El Paso Energy International Company v The Republic of Argentina*, ICSID Case No. ARB/02/17, Award (31 October 2011)

Tribunals nevertheless considered that measures of general economic policy, as long as they have a direct bearing on investment, do fall within their jurisdiction.[28] Second, Argentina argued that the measures were undertaken out of necessity and that the emergency measures were self-judging. The tribunals found that, in the absence of any clauses that explicitly established the self-judging nature of the non-precluded investment treaty provisions, they had the authority to *objectively* review the imposed emergency measures.[29]

The first three Argentine cases[30] applied an inflexible standard for reviewing Argentina's response to the financial crisis, by importing the narrow customary international law (CIL) concept of necessity defence, as defined in Article 25 of the Draft Articles on the Responsibility of States for Internationally Wrongful Acts,[31] and conflating it with the broader concept of non-precluded provisions of the US–Argentina BIT. In this way, the tribunals essentially denied Argentina any policy choices in response to the crisis, as Argentina was not able to demonstrate that the actions undertaken were the only measures available to address the critical events.[32] Given the noted errors in the tribunals' reasoning,[33] in other cases tribunals recognised the need for deference to State regulatory

para. 216; *Daimler Financial Services AG v Argentine Republic*, ICSID Case No. ARB/05/1, Award (22 August 2012) paras. 94–96.

28 *CMS Gas Transmission Co. v Argentine Republic*, ICSID Case No. ARB/01/8, Decision on Jurisdiction (17 July 2003) para. 27.

29 ibid para. 370. Thus, the tribunal effectively decided that Argentina did not have sole discretion to adopt emergency measures under Art. XI of the US–Argentina BIT.

30 ibid; *Enron Corporation and Ponderosa Assets, L.P. v Argentine Republic*, ICSID Case No. ARB/01/3; *Sempra Energy International v The Argentine Republic*, ICSID Case No. ARB/02/16. These cases are, together with *LG&E Energy Corp. v Argentine Republic*, ICSID Case No. ARB/02/1, known in the literature as the Argentine Gas Cases, and were brought on the basis of the US–Argentina BIT. Only the *LG&E* Tribunal accepted the necessity defence.

31 ILC, 'Report of the International Law Commission on the work of its Fifty-third Session' (November 2001) UN Doc Supp No. 10 (A/56/10).

32 See *CMS* (n 28) paras. 323–324; *Enron* (n 30) paras. 308–309; *Sempra* (n 30) paras. 350–351.

33 The ICSID Annulment Committee in the *CMS* case (n 28) found this legal reasoning a 'manifest error of law' but it was beyond its mandate to change the decision: see Decision on Annulment in *CMS* case (n 28) (25 September 2007) paras. 95–97, 125, 130, 136, 146, 158. Cf. Decision on Annulment in *Sempra* (29 June 2010) paras. 208–209 and Decision on Annulment in *Enron* (20 July 2010) paras. 373–377, where it constituted a manifest excess of the Tribunal's powers, resulting in the annulment of the award.

powers when assessing the necessity of emergency measures.[34] The Argentinean cases, *inter alia*, demonstrate the tendency of arbitral tribunals to 'second-guess' politically sensitive actions taken by sovereign States.[35]

More recent examples confirm that legitimacy problems persist, particularly in cases dealing with domestic law and policy, emphasising the thin line between law (presumably always objective when exercised by arbitral tribunals) and politics (presumably mainly subjective as exercised by national authorities). Decisions of tribunals in cases such as *Bilcon v Canada* exemplify the potential impact of tribunals' decisions on domestic administrative law, even in States with robust judicial review.[36] Canada was condemned for rejecting the operation of a quarry based on an environmental impact assessment (EIA) that found the project would have an adverse impact on the 'core community values', a new standard not recognised in Canadian law.[37] However, there was a disagreement whether this was indeed a new standard created by the Joint Review Panel (JRP), the body that conducted the EIA, or rather a different expression for 'human environment effects', mandated as a relevant standard under Canadian law.[38] Additionally, even if this had been a new standard, the assessment would have been overturned in the domestic judicial review process.[39]

While the Bilcon Tribunal's decision challenged the way in which Canadian laws have been implemented rather than the laws themselves, it has significant implications for the domestic regulatory space. First, the decision creates additional control mechanisms over domestic environmental review panels with significant implications for their work and the

[34] See *LG&E* (n 30) Award (25 July 2007) paras. 239–242 and *Continental Casualty* (n 26) paras. 192–195. However, there is no agreement of the two tribunals on what constitutes the requirements of a non-precluded measures provision.

[35] J. E. Alvarez and K. Khamsi, 'The Argentine Crisis and Foreign Investors: A Glimpse into the Heart of the Investment Regime' in K. P. Sauvant (ed), *The Yearbook on International Investment Law and Policy 2008/2009* (OUP 2009) 383.

[36] *Bilcon of Delaware et al v Government of Canada*, PCA Case No. 2009-04, Award on Jurisdiction and Liability (17 March 2015).

[37] ibid paras. 505, 590–591.

[38] Professor McRae, the dissenting arbitrator, disagreed with the majority, concluding that the JRP did not act *ultra vires* and there was no breach of due process: Dissenting Opinion of Professor Donald McRae (10 March 2015) paras. 15–27.

[39] In any case, Professor McRae noted that the Canadian conduct would not meet a high threshold of *Waste Management* standard of treatment ('grossly unfair, unjust or idiosyncratic' and 'involving a lack of due process leading to an outcome which offends judicial propriety'): ibid para. 40.

application of environmental laws. Human environmental concerns will be subjugated to the 'scientific and technical feasibility of the project', thus intruding 'not only into the way an environmental review process is conducted' but also 'the environmental public policy of the State'.[40] Put in the context of legitimacy, one could ask, what more could undermine the legitimacy of a quasi-judicial international institution than condemnation of the State for 'the community's own expression of its interests and values'?[41] Second, the Tribunal's decision allows the investors to bypass domestic judicial mechanisms of executive action (judicial review) and obtain damages in investment arbitration, which otherwise would not be available under domestic law. The dissenting arbitrator called this 'a significant intrusion into domestic jurisdiction', which will 'create a chill on the operation of environmental review panels'.[42] It could be added that it also more generally undermines the domestic rule of law. Domestic legal protection under a robust legal system such as Canada's should thus suffice.[43]

In light of the above examples, several conclusions can be made about tribunals' normative legitimacy. First, under the treaties, tribunals lack lawmaking legitimacy or input-based legitimacy. However, a *de facto* lawmaking role has been assumed through treaty interpretations and adjudication. The quality of such lawmaking has become an issue of output-based legitimacy. In this regard, and as a second point, the tribunals' legitimacy is questioned because of the impact that tribunals' decisions could have on the State regulatory powers and dominant community values and interests, enshrined in domestic law. Judicial activism in decisions of arbitral tribunals has the potential to *de facto*, if not *de iure*, restrain democratic majority rule expressed in the decisions made by the national authorities. This is particularly emphasised in cases in which tribunals bring into question States' capacities to make fundamental socio-economic and political choices.

The issue is what strategies could States employ to address this problem. One such approach would be to require clearer and more detailed drafting of the provisions of the new treaties and the introduction of provisions which can provide more space for States to regulate.[44] In other

[40] ibid para. 49.
[41] ibid.
[42] ibid para. 48.
[43] To that effect see also ibid paras. 46–47.
[44] On the EU strategies to secure the right to regulate, see Chapter 8.

words, addressing the *ex post* problem with *ex ante* strategies. However, these strategies seem not to be effective given the ways in which the system operates.[45] New studies demonstrate that arbitral tribunals interpret new IIAs like old ones, rendering State treaty innovations for rebalancing investment protection and State sovereignty futile in practice.[46] For example, public policy carve-outs in new generation bilateral investment treaties (BITs) are proving insufficient for excluding States' liability for compensation.[47]

Another possible strategy could be to develop an *ex post* mechanism to correct tribunals' interpretations that stray from States' intentions, values and objectives. However, the effectiveness of this approach could be questioned from the perspective of international law imperatives. On the one hand, the problem could be the willingness of dispute settlement bodies to accept States' interpretations over their own understanding of norms.[48] On the other, and at the level of States, some values and objectives will always prevail over others, which brings back into the fray the power play between the States – exactly the problem that the creation of ISDS attempted to avoid.

The current normative regime of IIL that has developed over time lacks congruence with interests and values enshrined in domestic law – both Western and developing States' laws. While this is a relevant issue from the legitimacy point of view, its potential to demonstrate doctrinal bias against domestic law or values *per se* is limited given the existence of other cases in which the tribunals were willing to adopt a deferential approach.[49] More generally, the issue of domestic law and values remains a challenge for any system of international law and for IIL in particular given its broad potential to affect domestic policies.

As new values constantly emerge, their clash with IIL is likely to continue. Most recently, as States take action to address climate change,

[45] See Section 3.2.

[46] W. Alschner, *Investment Arbitration and State-Driven Reform* (OUP 2022).

[47] See the arbitral tribunal's interpretation of the GATT-style environmental carve-out in Art. 2201(3) of Canada-Columbia FTA (also in contradiction with interpretations of Art. XX GATT), in *Eco Oro Minerals Corp. v Republic of Colombia*, ICSID Case No. ARB/16/41, Decision on Jurisdiction, Liability and Directions on Quantum (9 September 2021).

[48] In the same case, Canada's interpretation of the carve-out was dismissed: see ibid para. 836.

[49] See C. Henckels, 'Balancing Investment Protection and the Public Interest: The Role of the Standard of Review and the Importance of Deference in Investor–State Arbitration' (2013) 4 *Journal of International Dispute Settlement* 197.

IIL has come under increased scrutiny for its incompatibility with State climate policies, in particular in developed countries. The Energy Charter Treaty (ECT), as currently the most litigated IIA in the world, which protects around 345 billion euro worth of fossil fuel infrastructure in the EU,[50] is particularly problematic for the EU's climate objectives. It exposes Member States to expensive fossil fuel ISDS claims for implementing new climate policies.[51] These concerns are particularly shared by other developed States. It is the pressure of international law (the 2015 Paris Agreement),[52] the objective of climate neutrality and the cost for developed States that might eventually turn the tide against IIL.[53]

### 3.1.2 *Output-Based Legitimacy through Legally Sound Norms*

In addition to political acceptability, decisions of international tribunals have authority when considered legally sound and in accord with a commonly accepted legal discourse. This element is important for tribunals' authority as it prevents decisions from appearing political, arbitrary or biased.[54] Standards such as coherence (with previously applied rules and principles), adherence (to the organised normative hierarchy of rules) and determinacy (clarification of rules through interpretation) are used for assessing legal soundness of norms in international law.[55] Investment treaty arbitration underperforms with respect to all three elements.

First, wide discretion left to arbitrators in ITA has resulted in divergent interpretations of similar treaty provisions. While these discrepancies have been justified by the specifics of each case, tribunals' practice of

[50] See O. Moldenhauer and N. Schmidt, 'ECT Data Analysis: Results and Methods', *Investigate Europe* (23 February 2021).

[51] See *RWE AG and RWE Eemshaven Holding II BV v Kingdom of the Netherlands*, ICSID Case No. ARB/21/4 and *Uniper SE, Uniper Benelux Holding B.V. and Uniper Benelux N.V. v Kingdom of the Netherlands*, ICSID Case No. ARB/21/22. These are intra-EU cases, which are illegal under EU law: see Chapter 5. Uniper agreed to withdraw its claim as part of its agreement on stabilisation measures with the German Federal Government reached on 22 July 2022.

[52] See IPCC, 'Climate Change 2022, Mitigation of Climate Change', Working Group III contribution to the IPCC Sixth Assessment Report (4 April 2022) 2433, 2442, 2582.

[53] See also OECD, 'Investment Treaties and Climate Change', Public Consultation, Compilation of Submissions (13 April 2022).

[54] Grossman (n 17) 149.

[55] T. M. Franck, *The Power of Legitimacy Among Nations* (OUP 1990); Grossman (n 17) 149–151.

referring to previous decisions is rather unpredictable and the reference to case law insufficiently scrutinised.[56] In the system of numerous treaties and *ad hoc* tribunals, there is no clear hierarchy of rules.[57] Some commentators compare the state of precedent in ITA to precedent in England prior to adopting the doctrine of *stare decisis*, with no hierarchy of courts nor reporting of cases but with judges seeking the guidance of other courts' decisions in similar cases.[58] A pertinent question is whether jurisprudence, in its current form as developed by *ad hoc* tribunals, should be followed. While arbitrators themselves speak about proper consideration of earlier cases as their 'moral duty' in fostering a predictable normative environment,[59] practice has not ensured legal certainty – on the contrary.

Second, due to the specific character of treaty-based arbitration, mixed methods of interpretation, flexibility and business rationale, as dominant features of contract-based arbitration, have found their way into ITA.[60] At the same time, the system is embedded in public international law. As a consequence, the method of interpretation in IIL, which favours protection of the rights of private parties in the absolute, is in disagreement with the interpretative principles dominant in the field of public law, which require private rights to be balanced with other public policy goals.[61] The jurisprudence is thus discordant with what is normatively expected of a public law system.

Third, the jurisprudence of arbitral tribunals can be so diverse that it is difficult to settle on what is the dominant rule and what are the exceptions. This is further compounded by the doctrine, which is a decisive factor in distinguishing facts from *perception*, given the practical experience and *technical* expertise of those who develop the doctrine and

[56] Z. Douglas, 'Nothing If Not Critical for Investment Treaty Arbitration: Occidental, Eureko and Methanex' (2006) 22 *Arbitration International* 27. Douglas particularly emphasises the failure of tribunals to distinguish between *ratio decidendi* (legal rule) and *obiter dictum* (legal opinion) of previous decisions when using *obiter* as a rule in subsequent decisions.

[57] Conflicts of laws in international law are resolved with reference to general conflict rules under international law in Art. 30 VCLT, but the tribunals have also been inconsistent in applying these rules.

[58] J. P. Commission, 'Precedent in Investment Treaty Arbitration: A Citation Analysis of a Developing Jurisprudence' (2007) 24 *Journal of International Arbitration* 129, 158.

[59] G. Kaufmann-Kohler, 'Arbitral Precedent: Dream, Necessity or Excuse?' (2007) 23 *Arbitration International* 357, 374.

[60] See Section 2.1.3.

[61] See also the comparison of IIL with the EU legal order in Chapter 4.

also participate in adjudication. Others outside the system, it is claimed, lack knowledge to properly understand the complex rules and procedures, and to appreciate how the system works more generally. Given the diversity of interpretations, awards – containing (objective) facts and rules – defend the system from publicly perceived – subjective and inherently political – criticism. The mystique of legal expertise cloaks the system. For legal professionals in the field, the legitimacy of the system strictly relates to its legality. This *legal* legitimacy stems from specialisation that ensures the *correctness* of the decisions in the totality of the specific circumstances of each case.[62] Any other legitimacy is seen as political. This also includes normative assessment of the legal soundness of jurisprudence by those who are outside of the system, regardless of whether they are lawyers, States or the public.[63]

However, it would be wrong to say that the legal profession in the arbitration field has not noted the problems of the system's legitimacy.[64] This problem has primarily been attributed to the *ad hoc* nature of adjudication and the lack of a mechanism that could correct inconsistent decisions. For these reasons, the profession has been generally supportive of an appellate mechanism as a reform proposal for ISDS. While this solution could improve the legal soundness of the system, it will not resolve the issue of the quality of decisions and their alignment with interests and values enshrined in domestic law (political acceptability).

To achieve a substantive reform, the system needs more radical change of the *principles* underpinning its normative framework that will ensure more balanced outcomes. This includes opening the professional network to a greater gender, regional and legal diversity and also cutting the umbilical cord with the ISDS narrative about the methods of interpretation and in the application of law. The field must be opened to those

[62] Parallels could be drawn here with Max Weber's understanding of legal-rational authority, derived from legal norms that define the scope of jurisdiction of the authority. Importantly, the authority rests upon norms the legitimacy of which stem from the fact that they have been established in a manner which is recognised to be legal: see M. E. Spencer, 'Weber on Legitimate Norms and Authority' (1970) 21 *The British Journal of Sociology* 123, 125. Indeed, the legality of ISDS is not the issue as it stems from international law.

[63] Normative assessment of the quality of arbitral tribunals' decisions tends to be seen as an issue of perception and thus attributed to sociological rather than normative legitimacy: see, for example, Bjorklund (n 23) 234–283.

[64] See, for example, S. D. Franck, 'The Legitimacy Crisis in Investment Treaty Arbitration: Privatizing Public International Law through Inconsistent Decisions' (2005) 73 *Fordham Law Review* 1521.

who understand how a public law system works – especially at the level of domestic law. Addressing only the former (enhancing diversity in formal terms) without the latter (addressing diversity in substantive terms) will result in the newcomers adjusting to the dominant culture and principles of the system. This will expand the pool of lawyers but not change the nature of the system. Enhancing legal legitimacy, which remains embedded in the current profession's legal specialisation, will be insufficient to ensure legitimacy and stability of the system over time. The risk of the system's encroachment on the political authority of States and the lack of value-rational authority of arbitral tribunals in the eyes of the States and/or their domestic constituencies will thus remain.[65] The ongoing risk of ISDS reform is that reform solutions remain captured by the profession and its dominant ISDS culture.

The analysis so far has addressed the issues related to arbitral decisions (political acceptability and legal soundness) that are pertinent to their output-based legitimacy. The other set of legitimacy criteria – those primarily related to the procedural aspects of ISDS as a dispute settlement mechanism and throughput-based legitimacy – overlap with the principles that are subsumed under the umbrella of the rule of law.

## 3.2 The Rule of Law in International Investment Regulation

Similar to legitimacy, the rule of law is a concept with many meanings across disciplines and legal and political systems.[66] As an expression of liberal democracy, in a domestic context the rule of law places restrictions on the exercise of regulatory powers rather than duties on citizens.

[65] This is the fourth type of authority which Spencer adds to Max Weber's authority types in order to explain patterns of legitimacy of democratic political institutions, which is lacking in Weber's articulation of legality. According to Spencer, 'formal legality, without a substantive principle (or value norms, where laws and authority are accepted because of their congruence with extra-legal values) is not sufficient to justify supreme authority and ensure the stability of institutions': Spencer (n 62).

[66] For example, there are differences in how the rule of law is understood in the context of Western liberal democracies (supremacy of law over arbitrary power; separation of powers and checks and balances; independence of courts; authority of law stemming from the Constitution and democratic political institutions and processes) and in China (authority of law based on its legality, stemming from the authority of the lawmaking institutions and processes). In common law legal systems, the rule of law includes the uniformity of law through the system of precedent – and thus its predictability. In civil law legal systems, the concept is more abstract, and the predictability is ensured by general consistency between norms and principles of the legal system.

Although subject to different interpretations, the concept is mostly focused on formal characteristics of laws. Accordingly, laws should be known and internally consistent and applied equally to all by an independent judiciary. The rule of law is thus necessarily concerned with formal equality and procedural justice, rather than substantive justice.

In international law, the mere existence of a mechanism through which international rules can be enforced contributes to an *international* rule of law. For example, the Court of Justice of the European Union (CJEU) has emphasised that 'the very existence of effective judicial review designed to ensure compliance with EU law is of the essence of the rule of law'.[67] The broader notion of this concept necessarily involves the independence of courts as one of the requirements essential to 'effective judicial protection'.[68] Accordingly, it could be argued that the very existence of ISDS as a mechanism to enforce protections guaranteed in IIAs enhances the rule of law in IIL. Moreover, enforceable awards are the 'essential' feature of the current ISDS system.[69] In addition, adherence to international investment rules is also meant to enhance the rule of law in host States as it ensures protection of the private rights of foreigners against arbitrary and undue interference by the State. In this way, ISDS ensures supremacy of law over the arbitrary power of host States.

On the other hand, the very existence of ISDS limits the reach of domestic courts and thus undermines their authority. Investor-State dispute settlement could be considered a method of alternative dispute resolution (ADR). Alternative dispute resolution itself challenges the rule of law as it takes disputes away from transparent public courts into the sphere of the private and confidential. Importantly, however, ADR does not function as a parallel judicial mechanism in domestic legal systems. The control of the domestic courts over arbitration is ensured through legislation. In this way, independent domestic courts perform an oversight over private justice and its compliance with public policy. Unlike arbitration in the domestic context, ITA – in particular in the context of International Centre for the Settlement of Investment Disputes (ICSID) – functions more like an internationalised system, outside of control by

[67] Case C-64/16 *Associação Sindical dos Juízes Portugueses* ECLI:EU:C:2018:117, para. 36.

[68] In the EU such protection is guaranteed under Art. 19(1) TEU and Art. 47 CFR.

[69] Corporate Counsel International Arbitration Group (CCIAG), 'ISDS Reform, Submission by the CCIAG to UNCITRAL Working Group III' (18 December 2019) 4.

domestic courts.[70] The issue is then: what ensures the accountability of ISDS and its compliance with public policy, or more broadly, the rule of law?

In theory, the concept of the rule of law is understood as a formal (narrow) and substantive (broader) concept. Formal conceptions of the rule of law focus on formal legality of laws in constraining arbitrary government power.[71] In accordance with liberal rational thought, the aim of formal legality is to ensure law's neutrality. Translated into the domestic legal system, the rule of law is meant to ensure a proper system of checks and balances between the different branches of government, and more broadly between law and politics. In this system, political questions – what law *should be* – are for the democratically accountable legislatures, while matters of law – what law *is* – are for the courts. Accordingly, the courts' discretion in applying the law should be minimal.[72] In addition, neutrality of law is ensured through the legality of the procedures by which laws are put into operation. Procedural legality presupposes adjudication conducted by independent and unbiased courts that can hear both sides of the case and whose processes and reasoning are subject to public scrutiny. The rule of law is thus meant to be normatively neutral and fully objective. Its *ideal* is to be autonomous from politics and economics, and their goals.

Unlike the formal rule of law, which is neutral on political questions, such as what the appropriate government limits on private rights are, substantive rule of law focuses on the broader issue of the rules' values. Building upon formal characteristics, substantive rule of law considers the content of legal norms and their compliance with concepts such as human rights and justice.[73] Importantly, there is no universal consensus on substantive *standards* that rules should embrace, which makes this broader conceptualisation of the rule of law rather political. For example, depending on their legal and political systems, States do disagree on the scope and content of property rights or individual liberties.[74]

70 An exception to this is arbitration under UNCITRAL rules, which provide the possibility to challenge the awards on public policy grounds in the State of the seat of the arbitration: Art. V(2) New York Convention.

71 See Lon L. Fuller, *The Morality of Law* (Yale University Press 1969) 41–42.

72 See, for example, T. D. Campbell, *The Legal Theory of Ethical Positivism* (Routledge 1996).

73 M. H. Kramer, *Objectivity and the Rule of Law* (CUP 2007) 142–144.

74 See J. Raz, *The Authority of Law: Essays on Law and Morality* (Oxford Scholarship Online 2012) 210.

Importantly, the formal conception of the rule of law that ensures the functionality of the legal system is a necessary condition of the broader substantive conception.[75]

The international standard of the rule of law combines both formal and substantive characteristics. For example, the Commission of Venice of the Council of Europe identifies the core components of the rule of law as: legality, legal certainty, the prohibition of arbitrariness, access to justice before an independent and impartial court, non-discrimination and equality before the law and respect for human rights.[76] The assessment of the rule of law in IIL requires the consideration of IIL as a system with substantive rules outlined in IIAs and enforced through ISDS as its procedural mechanism. The rule of law would therefore require, first, that IIAs comply with formal legality as a minimum, which can ensure the neutrality of laws and limit arbitrariness of decision-makers in the implementation of IIAs; and, second, that ISDS procedures comply with the principles of procedural legality.

We have already considered that IIAs containing vague substantive provisions and tribunals' jurisprudence that implements these provisions do not comply with the formal requirements of the rule of law.[77] We have also considered that in substantive terms tribunals' jurisprudence does not produce politically acceptable norms from the States' domestic perspectives.[78] What we have not yet considered is (i) whether in substantive terms tribunals' jurisprudence is neutral and apolitical or instead promotes a certain normative agenda, and (ii) whether procedures before arbitral tribunals, through which IIAs are put into operation, comply with the principles of procedural legality. Both of these aspects are considered next, the first as substantive (normative) and the second as procedural (formal) attributes of the rule of law.

### 3.2.1 *Substantive Rule of Law: Neutrality or Normativity?*

The logic of law's neutrality is transposed into the international context only with difficulty. The normative character of IIL more broadly

[75] Kramer (n 73) 183–184.

[76] Commission of Venice, 'The Rule of Law Checklist' (Council of Europe 2016) 33.

[77] See Section 3.1.2. In light of Fuller's principles (n 71), the jurisprudence fails beside several criteria, as a minimum on predictability but arguably also on logical consistency, stability and enforceability in practice. The discussed criteria of determinacy concerns interpretative proficiency in public law, which could be considered a substantive rather than a formal characteristic of legality: Kramer (n 73) 181–183.

[78] See Section 3.1.1.

concerns the role of international law in international politics, and *vice versa*. International law seeks to provide a flexible framework for cooperation; its purpose is not to determine legal standards but provide a framework for substantive resolution elsewhere in the international system.[79] Law must thus ensure that 'correctness' and 'normativity' be seen as neutral.[80] Correctness guarantees the distance of law from natural justice theories (what law should be); while normativity guarantees the distance between the law and actual State behaviour or its interests and ensures that law is applied, regardless of the political preferences of its subjects. However, the two elements cannot exist simultaneously as they 'cancel each other out'. Correctness implies 'closeness' of law to State practice. However, if correctness is too close to State practice, it seems to be 'just another apology for existing power'; that is, the power of those States that have set the rule of correctness. On the other hand, the more the rule is 'normatively' distanced from State practice, the more political it seems, because it cannot be related to the States' social context.[81]

Applied to the realm of IIL, it has to be recalled that BITs have been introduced with an intention to depoliticise disputes between investors and States.[82] Accordingly, the concept of 'correctness' refers to procedural correctness – the neutral forum in which ITA takes place, detached from politics of States involved in each particular case. 'Normativity' refers to the *standard* of applicable rules in this process, which determines the substantive outcomes of their application – a tribunal's decision in each case. Correctness disguises normativity by applying the 'correct' standard of review to a State's behaviour. It has therefore been claimed that investment arbitration has been transformed into an 'adjudicative mechanism to control the exercise of public authority', comparable to a system of administrative law.[83]

Because it is taking place before a neutral international forum, it is presumed that the process and applied standard of review are detached

[79] M. Koskenniemi, *The Politics of International Law* (Hart 2011) 58–59. For more on legal indeterminacy in international law, consider the example of the Libyan arbitrations: see A. A. Shalakany, 'Arbitration and the Third World: A Plea for Reassessing Bias under the Specter of Neoliberalism' (2000) 41 *Harvard International Law Review* 419, 448–451.

[80] Koskenniemi ibid 38.

[81] ibid 38–39.

[82] See Section 1.1 in Chapter 1.

[83] G. Van Harten and M. Loughlin, 'Investment Treaty Arbitration as a Species of Global Administrative Law' (2006) 17 *European Journal of International Law* 121, 143. This logic of procedural correctness, leading to substantive correctness, is fully acceptable to a procedurally oriented common law lawyer but is more difficult in civil law systems, which are less procedural in their pursuit of neutrality.

from politics. However, if this arbitration review *process* produces *outcomes* detached from the State's social context, the whole process will seem political from the perspective of that State and its domestic constituencies. Those who conduct the review will be seen as political in determining the standard of review. This can be seen as bias, either in favour of more powerful State players (Western States), or in favour of private rights, interests or capital (MNEs, the legal profession). In other words, to speak of *correctness*, even if limited to procedural correctness, means taking a *normative* stance on what 'correct' is – and that is inherently political.

What is therefore a 'correct' normative standard in IIL? And who should set such a standard? For economists of law, the appropriate standard is determined with reference to the State's interference in the functioning of the market. The State is not supposed to intervene by planning the market. The market itself is better placed to reach distributional outcomes due to its non-coercive character, competition which allows freedom of individual choice, and the price mechanism that renders decisions based on the best possible information filtered by the market itself. In line with this, formal law ensures the rule of law by providing a stable framework in which individuals can plan their actions, and in that sense it is meant to be instrumental in allowing individuals to realise their choices rather than making choices on their behalf. On the other hand, according to the same economic argument, government policy aimed at substantive justice is inevitably a form of arbitrary government. Accordingly, the substantive ideal of distributive justice expressed in the concept of social welfare is incompatible with formal laws enshrined in the rule of law.[84]

More broadly, this neoliberal notion of the rule of law has been promoted in the policies of the World Bank following the end of the Cold War, emphasising the link between the rule of law and the market economy.[85] The rule of law implies 'good governance', which serves to determine the proper delineation between the public sector and its interference with the private sector.[86] Good governance further prefers 'private sector development', conditioned upon laws which create a

[84] F. Hayek, *The Road to Serfdom* (first published 1944, University Chicago Press 1994).

[85] S. Humphreys, *Theatre of the Rule of Law: Transnational Legal Intervention in Theory and Practice* (CUP 2010) 132–147.

[86] ibid 133–135.

'stable and supportive business climate, both for domestic and foreign investors'.[87] A 'sound legal and institutional framework' includes 'a comprehensive, well-defined body of laws and regulations' but also 'a court system to enforce property and contractual rights'.[88] The rule of law so understood becomes the basic prerequisite of development strategy, leading to economic growth and the reduction of poverty.[89] Private sector investors ultimately serve the public interest. Their capital effectively *is* the public good.[90]

While the rule of law presupposes neutral law, a similar neoliberal narrative is present in IIL. The logic of economics and dichotomies between the normative notion of the rule of law, which implies 'procedural' or 'formal justice', 'private law', 'civil and political rights', 'negative freedom and government constraint' as opposed to 'substantive justice', 'public law', 'social and economic rights', 'positive freedom' through government intervention and 'administrative discretion',[91] can be recognised in the manner in which IIL operates. The State is to provide a stable framework in which investors can plan their investments and know with certainty how the State will use its coercive powers. Rules should be long-term and should not change with changing circumstances. Private rights of the individuals (property and freedom of contract) should be protected against State action and given preference over public goals. International investment agreements serve to ensure such a stable legal framework for foreign investors, in the absence of which they would be hesitant to invest. International investment agreements recognise a State's 'right to regulate' (negative freedom), which defies a State's *duty* to regulate (positive freedom), even when such duty is recognised as an obligation in the State's Constitution.[92] Investment treaty arbitration serves to ensure 'neutral' enforcement of foreign investors' rights, while the

[87] D. Gustafson, E. Jimenez, and J. F. Linn, 'Developing the Private Sector: A Challenge for the World Bank Group' (World Bank Group 1989); Humphreys (n 85) 136.

[88] I. Shihata, 'The World Bank and Private Sector Development – A Legal Perspective' in F. Tschofen and Antonio R. Parra, *The World Bank in a Changing World*, vol 1 (Brill 1991).

[89] Humphreys (n 85) 139.

[90] See also N. M. Perrone and D. Schneiderman, 'International Economic Law's Wreckage: Depolitization, Inequality, Precarity' in E. Christodoulidis, R. Dukes and M. Goldoni, *Research Handbook on Critical Legal Theory* (Edward Elgar 2019).

[91] Humphreys (n 85) 59–62.

[92] See for example, *Vattenfall AB and others v Federal Republic of Germany (II)*, ICSID Case No. ARB/12/12.

system's close alliance with the World Bank through ICSID ensures its effectiveness.[93]

Further, the neutrality of law is important for law's equality, which is one of the fundamental principles of the rule of law. Differences in treatment, as exceptions from the principle of formal equality (reverse discrimination), must be justified. International investment law offers in any case greater procedural rights for foreign investors, and, depending on the specific circumstances, it can provide greater substantive rights. This inherent bias of the system in favour of foreign investors is nevertheless justified in the service of good governance and in order to achieve economic growth *for all*. Promotion of such rule of law is 'not political' because it addresses the 'application of rules rather than their substance'.[94] Nevertheless, such 'governance' replaces formal 'government' – which presupposes some form of (democratic) accountability – with more ambivalent delegation of formal authority to international structures.[95] Yet, the effects of foreign capital on development remain inconclusive,[96] and consequently also the justifiability of favouring private rights as a precondition of economic development,[97] and economic growth over other pillars of sustainable development.

In light of arbitral jurisprudence, States are making an effort to introduce provisions with the aim of ensuring better balance between investment protection and public interest. Apart from the right-to-regulate type of clause,[98] some new IIAs introduce the duty of foreign

[93] States can face serious financial consequences for non-compliance with ICSID awards. See World Bank, 'Disputes over Defaults on External Debt, Expropriation, and Breach of Contract' (July 2001) Operational Manual OP 7.40, para. 5.

[94] I. Shihata, as cited in Humphreys (n 85) 138.

[95] See Koskenniemi (n 79) 321; W. E. Scheuerman, 'Economic Globalization and the Rule of Law' (1999) 6 *Constellations* 3, 5.

[96] C. Bellak, 'Economic Impact of Investment Agreements' (2015) Vienna University Department of Economics Working Paper Series 200; S. I. Akhtar and M. A. Weiss, 'U.S. International Investment Agreements: Issues for Congress' (2013) Congressional Research Service, 16–17; L. N. Skovgaard Poulsen, 'The Importance of BITs for Foreign Direct Investment and Political Risk Insurance' in K. Sauvant (ed), *Yearbook on International Investment Law and Policy 2009–2010* (OUP 2010).

[97] See D. W. Kennedy, 'Some Caution About Property Rights as a Recipe for Economic Development' (2011) 1 *Accounting Economics and Law* 1.

[98] On the right to regulate in CETA and new EU IIAs, see Chapter 8. See, Arts. G-14 (environmental measures) and G-15 (energy regulatory measures) modernised Canada–Chile FTA; Art. 32.1 Indian Model BIT 2016; Art. 23 Nigeria–Morocco BIT; Arts. 21 and 22 SADC Model BIT 2012.

investors to comply with the host State's laws,[99] include a reference to Corporate Social Responsibility (CSR) soft law commitments[100] and the possibility that the investor's failure to comply with these instruments could be taken into account when deciding claims.[101] These efforts are directed at increasing State's opportunities for utilising defences and counterclaims,[102] but they still leave affected third parties without a procedural remedy under international law.[103] Some treaties include an explicit possibility of counterclaims.[104] In an attempt to limit the availability of the system to genuine foreign investment disputes, some new treaties also exclude from the jurisdiction of investment tribunals frivolous claims, corruption or other process abuses.[105]

[99] Art. 7(1), Dutch Model BIT 2019; Arts. 10 (Common Obligation against Corruption) and 11 (Compliance with Domestic Law), SADC Model BIT 2012.

[100] See, for example, Art. G-14 *bis* on CSR, modernised Canada–Chile FTA; Art. 9.17 CPTPP; Art. 7 Dutch Model BIT 2019. However, in most treaties that include reference to sustainable development and CSR, State parties (and not investors) commit to best-effort obligations ('shall encourage' 'voluntarily incorporate'). See also Arts. 14–16 SADC Model BIT.

[101] Art. 23, Dutch Model BIT 2019; Art. 19.1 SADC Model BIT 2012.

[102] Although often in State practice wrongly conflated with defence, a counterclaim is an autonomous claim of the respondent State against the investor for the breach of obligations it owes to the State, which must be sufficiently connected with the investor's primary claim. Counterclaims have mostly been unsuccessful due to the lack of reciprocal obligations for investors in IIAs (as opposed to such obligations in investment contracts or domestic law, when incorporated into an IIA): see *Burlington Resources Inc. v Republic of Ecuador*, ICSID Case No. ARB/08/5, Decision on Ecuador's Counterclaims (7 February 2017). Counterclaims will be dismissed if obligations fall on States rather than investors: see *Urbaser S.A. and Consorcio de Aguas Bilbao Bizkaia, Bilbao Biskaia Ur Partzuergoa v The Argentine Republic*, ICSID Case No. ARB/07/26, Award (8 December 2016).

[103] Claims by third parties against investors must be pursued in domestic legal systems under domestic law and cannot qualify as counterclaims: see *Hesham T. M. Al Warraq v Republic of Indonesia*, UNCITRAL, Final Award (15 December 2014).

[104] See for example, Art. 19.2 SADC Model BIT 2012. For a tribunal to consider a counterclaim, the jurisdiction of the tribunal in IIA should not be limited to alleged breaches of international treaty obligations, and governing law should not be limited to international law, without reference to domestic law. See also Art. 46 ICSID Convention.

[105] For example, Art. 8.18.3 CETA and Art. 16(2) Dutch Model BIT 2019 introduce the 'clean hands' doctrine. Similarly, the Indian Model BIT 2016 in Art. 13.4. See also Art. 8.32 CETA for frivolous claims. The Dutch Model BIT 2019 in Art. 16(3) denies the jurisdiction of the tribunal in the case of corporate restructuring for the main purpose of gaining the protection of the agreement: see Art. 16(3).

### *3.2.2 Procedural Rule of Law: Procedural Justice, Openness and Transparency*

International investment law has developed on the presumption that ITA provides a *neutral forum* for the settlement of investment disputes. From a procedural perspective, neutrality requires procedural legality. Judicial bodies must comply with the requirements of procedural justice, which encompass the right to a fair hearing (*audi alteram partem*) and the rule against bias (*nemo iudex in causa sua*). These standards are considered fundamental rules of domestic administrative law, rooted in common law tradition.[106] The fair and unbiased nature of international tribunals is equally important for ensuring their legitimacy although some studies demonstrate that the element of bias carries greater weight.[107]

Procedural rules in ITA depend on whether arbitration is *ad hoc* or institutional, and in the latter case the rules of that institution apply.[108] The content of these rules is beyond the scope of this study but all of them aim to find an appropriate balance between procedural fairness and efficiency.[109] Importantly, failure to accord due process in arbitration proceedings is a ground for later challenge of the award before a national court or a ground for annulment of an ICSID award before the ICSID annulment committee.[110] Procedural justice in the ISDS context is particularly concerned with the issue of bias. In this sense, bias can be seen as institutional, stemming from the *modus operandi* of the arbitration and related conflicts of interest; and disciplinary, stemming from the attitudes of the arbitrators.

Institutional bias concerns the interpretation of treaty provisions related to a tribunal's jurisdiction (parallel proceedings, treaty shopping, forum shopping).[111] Arbitrators, who are appointed on a case-by-case basis, have an inherent financial interest in adopting a more expansive interpretation of treaties, which can stimulate the ISDS industry.[112]

[106] *Cooper v Board of Works for the Wandsworth District* (1863) 143 ER 414.
[107] Grossman (n 17) 123, 128–129.
[108] See Section 1.3.3.
[109] See A. H. Ali and others, *The International Arbitration Rulebook: A Guide to Arbitral Regimes* (Kluwer 2019).
[110] Art. 52(1) ICSID Convention.
[111] See Section 1.3.2 in Chapter 1.
[112] G. Van Harten, 'Leaders in the Expansive and Restrictive Interpretation of Investment Treaties: A Descriptive Study of ISDS Awards to 2010' (2018) 29 *European Journal of International Law* 507.

Default appointing authorities might also have a role by favouring individual arbitrators who adopt such practices.[113] Additionally, some studies indicate the possibility of a bias towards investors from Western capital-exporting States.[114] While empirical evidence remains inconclusive, from a normative perspective there are characteristics of the system which bring into question its institutional independence: asymmetrical claims structure allowing only investors to initiate proceedings, party autonomy in arbitral appointments and related conflict of interest. Legal rules on the appointment of arbitrators, their qualifications and conflict of interest serve to eliminate these biases but fail to address the perceptions of systemic bias.[115] Importantly, for ensuring procedural justice, the rule against bias is infringed when bias would be *reasonably perceived*, even if not real[116] – justice must also be seen to be done.

Disciplinary bias concerns attitudes of the legal discipline in the practice of ITA. The 'resolutely private law sensibility' of ITA is where 'the fundamentally apolitical stance of neoliberalism finds its legal manifestation'.[117] The bias of arbitration is not anymore in favour of the economic interests of the North, as was perceived in the past, but in favour of private rights and restriction of State intervention into the market. This change of approach coincides with globalisation and the move from State-centred international law towards fragmentation, with increasing normative and jurisdictional conflicts between different international law subdisciplines or 'regimes' (trade law, investment law, environmental law, European law, etc.). It gives an impression of a metamorphosis of international law from political into apparently apolitical and technical law.[118]

Given the open-ended rules in each subfield of modern international law, it is now the discipline, or rather the legal and technical experts appointed to the field's supervisory institutions, that determines their scope and substance – United Nations Commission on International

113 ibid.

114 G. Van Harten, 'Arbitrator Behaviour in Asymmetrical Adjudication: An Empirical Study of Investment Treaty Arbitration' (2012) 50 *Osgoode Hall Law Journal* 211.

115 See Section 1.3.3 in Chapter 1.

116 Impartiality should be examined from a subjective as well as from an objective perspective since bias can be either manifest or apparent: International Commission of Jurists, 'International Principles on the Independence and Accountability of Judges, Lawyers and Prosecutors' (2007) Practitioner Guide No. 1, 28. For instance, a manifest bias would be a case of identity between a party and the arbitrator. In contrast, an apparent bias would occur if the arbitrator has been previously advising the party.

117 Shalakany (n 79) 425.

118 See Koskenniemi (n 79) 318–330, 358.

Trade Law (UNCITRAL), ICSID and the different arbitration centres in the case of IIL. In this way international rules in a particular subfield have become the instrument of the discipline itself, determined by the manner in which the relevant institution understands its mission.[119] Accordingly, reference to international law in IIAs, as understood by arbitral tribunals, does not 'incorporate the universe of international law' but only the body of law relevant to the protection and promotion of foreign investment.[120] If the mission of IIL is to *protect* private investors from host States' regulatory actions, the discipline interprets the rules through lenses that favour private interests rather than a State's regulatory action, even when the issue at hand concerns the public interest. In IIL so understood, the protection of foreign investment is a precondition of development and not a tool for development. International investment law so perceived necessarily *favours* the economy, conventionally understood, above the other two pillars of sustainable development – society and environment.

The recent trend in the evolution of treaties sees the *disciplinary* bias of arbitrators addressed by provisions requiring that they have *additional* expertise in 'public international law', with a *dominant* specialisation in investment or trade law.[121] On the other hand, some treaties empower arbitral institutions to appoint arbitrators, which effectively endorses disciplinary bias.[122] So far, the lack of disciplinary diversity among investment adjudicators has received insufficient attention in the current UNCITRAL reform.[123]

Finally, openness and transparency play an important role for the rule of law and legitimacy. Within the rule of law framework these principles are important for ensuring the scrutiny and accountability of the system to the public. They allow for the assessment of whether a tribunal's application of rules is fair and unbiased. They also ensure that the voices of otherwise excluded stakeholders are heard. In the framework of

[119] ibid 334–336.

[120] See, for example, *Bernhard von Pezold and Others v Republic of Zimbabwe*, ICSID Case No. ARB/10/15, Procedural Order No. 2 (26 June 2012) para. 57.

[121] See, for example, Art. 8.27.4 CETA; Art. 20(5) Dutch Model BIT 2019.

[122] See Art. 20 of the Dutch Model BIT 2019. Also, while CETA introduces new tribunals, ICSID remains the Secretariat for its First Instance Tribunal: see UNCITRAL, 'Possible Reform of ISDS: Submissions from International Organisations' (13 October 2017) UN Doc A/CN.9/WG.III/WP.1432. One way to overcome investment bias could be by establishing a special roster of arbitrators for environmental issues (as the Permanent Court of Arbitration did) or human rights issues.

[123] See UNCITRAL, 'Report of Working Group III (ISDS Reform) on the Work of Its Resumed Thirty-Eighth Session' (28 January 2020) UN Doc A/CN/9/1004/Add.1, 16. Moreover, some reform proposals advocate for even greater specialisation in ISDS, which necessarily excludes broader understanding of different cross-sectoral policies.

legitimacy, openness and transparency are important prerequisites for evaluating a system's normative regime; that is, its dominant values and legal soundness.[124]

Investment treaty arbitration has traditionally been rather closed to the public;[125] however, in recent times a trend has emerged towards greater openness and transparency, at the level of procedural rules and in the new IIAs.[126] With the UNCITRAL Rules on Transparency in Treaty-based Investor–State Arbitration, transparency has replaced confidentiality as a default rule for UNCITRAL arbitrations, albeit still with limited reach.[127] The amended ICSID Rules are, *inter alia*, aimed at enhancing transparency. Reforms include 'deemed' consent of the parties to publication of the awards,[128] publishing written submissions or supporting documents with the consent of the parties,[129] more detailed rules on non-disputing party participation[130] and a possibility of open hearings unless either party objects.[131] Amendments also envisage broader mandatory third-party funding disclosures.[132] These rules improve the openness and transparency of the proceedings. However, the process still remains controlled by the parties and dependant on the tribunals' discretion, which places the interests of the disputing parties before the interest of the public participation in the process.[133] Access to justice in the ISDS context is primarily focused on enabling greater use of the system by small and medium enterprises (SMEs).[134]

124 Grossman (n 17) 152.

125 One exception has been the participation of non-disputing parties through *amici curiae* briefs. See L. Crema, 'Testing *Amici Curiae* in International Law: Rules and Practice' (2012) *The Italian Yearbook of International Law* 91, 108–117.

126 See, for example, Art. 8.38.2 CETA; Art. 25 Indian Model BIT 2016.

127 The UNCITRAL Rules apply only to UNCITRAL arbitrations and to treaties concluded on or after 1 April 2014, unless the parties agree otherwise. The UN Convention on Transparency in Treaty-based Investor–State Arbitration (adopted on 10 December 2014, entered into force 18 October 2017) (Mauritius Convention) allows the application of UNCITRAL Transparency Rules to treaties concluded before 1 April 2014, regardless of the arbitration rules. Many new IIAs include provisions on the application of the UNCITRAL Rules in their transparency clause: see, for example, Art. 8.36 CETA, Art. G-29 Canada–Chile FTA; or have an autonomous transparency clause: see, for example, Art. 9.24 CPTPP.

128 Amended ICSID Rules (entered into force 1 July 2022), Rule 62(3).

129 ibid Rule 64.

130 ibid Rule 67.

131 ibid Rule 65.

132 ibid Rule 14.

133 See ibid Rule 66.

134 See, for example, Art. 8.39.6 CETA and the EU commitment in the Statement No. 36, Council of the EU, 'CETA – Statements to the Council minutes' (27 October 2016) 13463/1/16. In the framework of UNCITRAL, discussions about the possible Advisory

Incremental reform proposals to improve the rule of law in respect of ITA – both procedurally and normatively – are many and ongoing. While investment dispute settlement contributes to the rule of law in international law, its effects on improving the domestic rule of law remain inconclusive[135] and arguably limited. Investment tribunals cannot mandate the removal of illegal domestic measures but only condemn the States for their non-compliance with IIL. On the one hand, this can potentially encourage States to abandon illegal practices with respect to foreign investors. On the other hand, this can also have counterproductive effects by discouraging States from regulating in the public interest when such regulation could have a negative impact on investors' private rights. Some BITs take a novel approach by imposing additional duties on States in an effort to encourage them to enhance the domestic rule of law – albeit these efforts remain limited to business-related human rights abuses.[136] In the EU, elimination of the ISDS mechanism in intra-Member States relations and providing for the supremacy of EU mechanisms, while envisaged for different purposes, could in the long run have positive effects on the rule of law beyond the narrow scope of foreign investors' protections.[137]

Drawing on the discussion about legitimacy and the rule of law in this chapter, Table 3.1 summarises the key aspects of both concepts in the context of IIR.

## 3.3 Beyond Legitimacy and the Rule of Law: The *Sui Generis* Character of Arbitration

The evaluation of IIL beside legitimacy and the rule of law criteria does not take into account the specific character of arbitration as a dispute settlement mechanism in the sphere of business disputes. Of importance here are the criteria usually applied to ADR mechanisms, such as efficiency, cost and duration of proceedings, party autonomy, confidentiality and continuous relationships between subjects. In this context, legitimacy occupies a different dimension, measured by business correlations. It has been argued by scholars that the efficacy of ICSID and investment

Centre have also been inspired with a view to benefiting SMEs: see UNCITRAL, 'Possible Reform of ISDS: Advisory Centre' (25 July 2019) UN Doc A/CN.9/WG.III/WP.168.

135 See B. K. Guthrie, 'Beyond Investment Protection: An Examination of the Potential Influence of Investment Treaties on Domestic Rule of Law' (2013) 45 *New York University Journal of International Law and Politics* 1151.

136 For example, Art. 5, Dutch Model BIT 2019.

137 See Chapter 5.

Table 3.1 *International investment regulation in the framework of legitimacy and the rule of law*

<table>
<tr><th></th><th>Investment treaty arbitration</th><th>International investment agreements</th></tr>
<tr><td>Legitimacy</td><td>Throughput-based legitimacy<br>• Fairness and non-bias (institutional and disciplinary)<br>• Openness and transparency: accountability of tribunals to the public (public proceedings)<br>Output-based legitimacy<br>• Politically acceptable decisions<br>- Interests and values enshrined in domestic law<br>- Public-private balance<br>• Legal soundness of decisions<br>- Coherence<br>- Adherence<br>- Determinacy</td><td>Input-based legitimacy<br>Substantive provisions of treaties:<br>• The right to regulate and State sovereignty<br>• No greater rights for foreign investors<br>Treaty-making process:<br>• Transparent<br>• Accountable<br>• Inclusive<br>• Democratic</td></tr>
<tr><td>The rule of law</td><td>Procedural legality<br>• Procedural fairness:<br>- Fair hearing before investment tribunals<br>- The rule against bias: independence from external pressures and impartiality (actual or perceived)<br>• Possibility of an appeal<br>• Access to justice: opportunity for third parties to participate (submissions)<br>• Public accessibility: open hearings, public pleadings and awards<br>Formal characteristics of jurisprudence<br>• Consistency and coherence</td><td>Formal characteristics of treaties<br>• Clear and specific substantive provisions to limit the discretion of arbitral tribunals in the application of IIAs<br>• Compliance of State authorities with international obligations through effective enforcement mechanism<br>• Equality before the law: differentiations objectively justified on the basis of a reasonable aim and in conformity with the principle of proportionality<br>- Special regime for foreign investors should not provide greater rights<br>- Public–private balance</td></tr>
</table>

Table 3.1 (*cont.*)

| Investment treaty arbitration | International investment agreements |
|---|---|
| • Predictability and legal certainty<br>**Substantive characteristics of jurisprudence**<br>• Interpretative proficiency in public law | • Effective remedy in international law<br>- Special remedies for foreign investors should not circumvent the applicability of effective domestic remedies |

arbitration have bolstered the system's normative legitimacy but undermined its sociological legitimacy.[138]

The main incentives to engage in international arbitration are also some of the main points of contemporary criticism of it: party appointment of adjudicators with an expectation that the designated arbitrator will be sympathetic to the party's view, supra-national neutrality and the promise of its simplicity, speed and economy. It has therefore been argued that the types of control mechanisms used in domestic contexts are not appropriate for international arbitration and, instead, international arbitration should develop its own mechanisms of control. Such mechanisms would preferably involve other international institutions rather than domestic courts.[139]

For investors, it is important that arbitration should retain its private law character. Accordingly, party autonomy, efficiency and effectiveness of enforcement play a more important role than proper mechanisms of public control.[140] Abandoning party autonomy in the selection of arbitrators in favour of a permanent court would not only disturb this balance in favour of States but it would also eliminate the diversity of adjudicators. While control mechanisms remain important, it has been stressed that 'consistency' in jurisprudence must be balanced against 'correctness', which in turn must be balanced against 'the need for

[138] Bjorklund (n 23) 234–283.

[139] See M. Reisman, 'The Breakdown of the Control Mechanism in ICSID Arbitration' (1989) 4 *Duke Law Journal* 739.

[140] CCIAG submission to UNCITRAL (n 69) provides an excellent overview of investors' views on ISDS reform.

finality'.[141] An appellate mechanism would disturb such balance, in favour of consistency and against correctness and finality. Instead, effective control could be ensured by the parties themselves, for example, by parties' prior scrutiny of awards which could better achieve 'correctness'.[142] The investor's vision of ISDS therefore endorses its private law character which directly contradicts the conceptualisation of ISDS as a public law system.

For States, the challenge remains in balancing their commercial with their public hat in the dispute settlement context. Under the commercial hat, States will prefer dispute settlement mechanisms that are more efficient and favourable in continuing business relationships with investors.[143] In such relationships, there is an expectation of mutually beneficial control on both sides.[144] In these situations, conflicts are about interests and they are more likely to be settled or resolved through a private system of dispute settlement. However, under States' public law hat, the nature of the disputes moves from conflicts about interests (who gets what) to conflicts about value differences (who is right). In such situations, there is little incentive for the State to settle or resolve a dispute through a private dispute settlement mechanism and will prefer courts in order to obtain authoritative interpretations of public policy.[145] Accordingly, the dispute settlement mechanism that the State will prefer depends on the State's perception of its functions in a given situation.

In the broader context of legal dispute resolution, which generally exhibits a trend of shifting from courts (public) to ADR (private), the current developments in the ISDS sphere move in different directions. Some proposals aim at formalising justice in an institution that is a (quasi-)court.[146] Some other examples (USMCA) show a tendency to limit arbitration to its commercial beginnings. Various multilateral

[141] It is claimed that precedent and *absolute* consistency would undermine correctness, implying flexibility is required for a tribunal to reach a correct decision in each particular case: ibid 4.

[142] ibid 18. In support, the reference is made to Art. 9.23(10) CPTPP, which allows parties to provide written comments on the draft award to the tribunal.

[143] See UNCITRAL, 'Possible Reform of ISDS: Cost and Duration' (31 August 2018) UN Doc A/CN.9/WG.III/WP.153.

[144] M. Galanter, 'Why the "Haves" Come Out Ahead: Speculations on the Limits of Social Change' (1974) 9 *Law and Society Review* 95, 110–111. These controls depend on the availability of sanctions, such as withdrawal and refusal to continue beneficial relations, which are more likely in the case of larger investors (MNEs), with more resources and power.

[145] ibid 112.

[146] See Chapter 9.

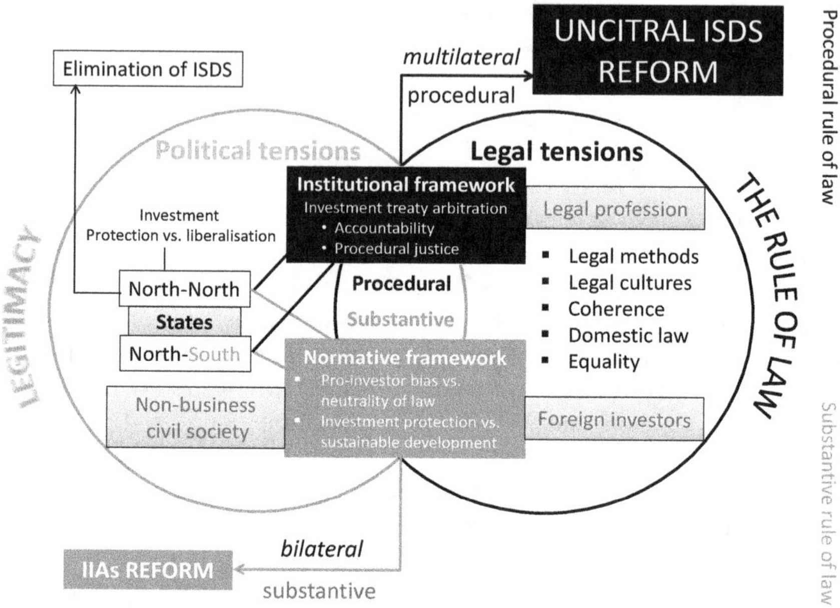


**Figure 3.2** Challenges and reforms of international investment regulation

proposals differently strike the balance between the private nature of ISDS and the need for public oversight – from improving the current mechanism to creating new institutions.[147] The guiding principles of ADR mechanisms – dispute prevention and resolution through an advisory centre, flexibility through expedited procedures and case management and access to justice for SMEs – are also gaining strong ground in the reform of the system.

In light of different proposals and State practices, ISDS is likely to continue its existence between different degrees of informal (private) and formal (public) justice. Despite the different visions of ISDS, consensus is achieved on at least one element of the rule of law: any future mechanism must produce enforceable decisions. Effective enforcement puts the supporters of the existing arbitration system in a strong position, while posing complex difficulties for a more systemic reform of ISDS.

As a final point, Figure 3.2 depicts the discussed political and legal challenges of the reforms in the international investment realm.

[147] See Chapter 10.

# Conclusion to Part I

## Towards International Investment Regulation Reforms

In Part I of this study we undertook a historical overview of IIL and its institutions and examined the core substantive and procedural rules (Chapter 1), mapped tensions (Chapter 2) and normatively conceptualised the reform challenges (Chapter 3). The complexity of this field of international law is magnified by its internal fragmentation – the large number of different legal instruments and their mixed private–public nature. The manner in which the field operates autonomously from other areas of international law supports the wider phenomenon of fragmentation in international law. Finally, the high financial stakes involved in investment have led to further politicisation of this already politicised field of international law.

The reform process in IIL is as fragmented as the field itself. The reform is ongoing and is taking place at different levels – bilateral, regional, multilateral, substantive, procedural – and in the framework of different institutions. While a detailed account of the reform processes is beyond the scope of this study, several remarks that indicate reform trends can be made.

At bilateral and regional levels, States are making efforts to update their old BITs, introduce 'modern' model BITs and conclude new generation IIAs. While aiming to improve procedural elements of dispute settlement, the main focus of bilateral reform is on substantive provisions. On the one hand, changes include clearer and more detailed investment protection standards, while on the other explicit provisions to guarantee a State's 'right to regulate' in the public interest. While these efforts serve to limit the discretion of investment tribunals in the application of IIAs, they largely codify the existing jurisprudence in IIL. Importantly, the new generation IIAs endorse the imperfect obligations of the old treaties. There are no obligations for investors under the new treaties beyond the already existing obligation to comply with the host States' (domestic) laws – now stated explicitly, best effort clauses and voluntary CSR. There are no procedural remedies for those affected by the investors' activities, with the exception of the very limited scope of still rare counterclaims. Some treaties have endeavoured to address normative asymmetry by limiting the jurisdiction of ITA through mechanisms such as the 'clean hands' doctrine.

At the multilateral level in UNCITRAL, the reform process is focused on investment dispute settlement. The reform does not question the desirability of a special adjudication mechanism for foreign investors over State adjudication. It proceeds on the premise that such adjudication has technocratic advantages – cheaper, faster, specialised – and thus focuses on its improvements. The reform questions are thus relocated to the technical sphere of policy considerations (the scope of appeal, appointments of adjudicators, enforcement, etc.). More broadly, the focus is on reforming the system in ways which will revive the classical advantages of a mechanism for the settlement of investment disputes; in other words, keeping it specialised but also making it cheaper, faster, more consistent and adjusted to new circumstances and public scrutiny. The UNCITRAL reform is thus broader than adjudication and involves the creation of an advisory centre and advancement of different methods of dispute prevention and resolution (mediation, conciliation). A variety of actors take part in this reform as observers, while the reform process remains State-led.

Developments in IIL are more generally symptomatic of the fragmentation in international law, which leads to competition for 'institutional hegemony'. Given the cross-cutting nature of investment within the range of domestic policy areas (health, environment, public safety, human rights, taxation), the question is – which discipline should have the authoritative voice in deciding particular issues? As Martti Koskenniemi well notes, 'If there are no regime-independent ways of describing an issue, the door is open to the unilateral assumption of jurisdiction by experts who feel themselves powerful enough to have the last word'.[1]

Accordingly, the institutional reform should provide clarity on jurisdictional issues – who and on what basis decides whether a dispute should be adjudicated by the investment dispute settlement body. Issues of substance and related balance between private and public interest considerably depend on these preliminary jurisdictional issues.

[1] M. Koskenniemi, *The Politics of International Law* (Hart 2011) 338.

In order to ensure the accountability of investment dispute settlement bodies it is important to further develop cooperation mechanisms between States through which interpretative standards for treaty provisions can be agreed. While joint interpretative statements already exist in international law, they have been under-utilised in the area of investment. Given the fragmented nature of the field, their reach is also limited. More structured 'interpretative dialogue' can ensure the proper delegation of interpretative authority from States to tribunals;[2] however, it is important not to compromise the independence of the process and the institutions. While such a mechanism can recalibrate the power balance between the States and tribunals, it cannot avoid power play between the States in setting the dominant interpretative standards.

Finally, in light of systemic bias – institutional, disciplinary and ultimately normative – formal legality, procedural correctness and efficiency do not suffice in enhancing the rule of law or ensuring the normative legitimacy of ITA. While multilateral procedural reform aims at avoiding difficult issues of substance, which is a politically cunning approach, limiting the scope of reform to formal procedural issues diverts the reform process from its core rationale – addressing substantive *injustices* of the current system. A genuinely systemic reform is unlikely if the issues of the system's objectives – what is international investment law for? – remain unsettled. This, however, opens an even more difficult but fundamental question about any legal system – justice for whom? So far, the reform has avoided dealing with these questions.

Against this background, while not attempting to answer these fundamental questions, and on the premise that political reality, at least for the moment, renders the elimination of ISDS unviable, in the remaining parts of this study we will turn to analyse the EU solutions for investment regulation, in intra- (Part II) and extra-EU contexts, including multilaterally (Part III). In this analysis, we will consider the umbrella concepts of legitimacy and the rule of law, as the guiding principles of legally functional and politically acceptable regulatory systems.

[2] See A. Roberts, 'Power and Persuasion in Investment Treaty Arbitration: The Dual Role of States' (2010) 104 *American Journal of International Law* 179.

# PART II

# The Internal Investment System of the EU

# Introduction to Part II

## The Internal Investment System of the EU

> To read the debate about fragmentation as if it had to do only with coherence in the abstract is to be mistaken about what is actually at stake. Special regimes and new organs are parts of an attempt to advance beyond the political present that in one way or another has been revealed unsatisfactory. The jurisdictional tensions express deviating preferences held by influential players in the international arena. Each institution speaks its own professional language and seeks to translate that into a global Esperanto, to have its special interests appear as the natural interests of everybody.[1]

As analysed in Part I, international investment law (IIL) and its tribunals have been established with a view to overcoming distrust of investors in national courts, providing investors from developed States with protections against political risks in unpredictable markets of host, usually developing, States. In the EU context, a *mutatis mutandi* constellation of these relations was evident in the period after the fall of communism and before the accession of Central and Eastern European (CEE) States to the EU. In the post-enlargement context that emerged, investor mistrust in the courts of the (Eastern) Member States and the recourse to private arbitrators through investment treaty arbitration (ITA) has become politically inappropriate and contrary to the principles on which the EU is founded.

In Part II we will place and examine the internal investment relations between the Member States within the framework of the EU legal order, which has been an important defining factor of EU investment policy, both internally and externally.[2] The focus of the analysis is on systemic differences and normative conflicts between the EU legal order and IIL. The EU legal framework serves as a catalyst for EU integration in the

[1] M. Koskenniemi and P. Leino, 'Fragmentation of International Law? Postmodern Anxieties' (2002) 15 *Leiden Journal of International Law* 553, 578.

[2] For external aspects, see Part III.

field of investment, a field which was traditionally the privilege of Member States. The elimination of investor-State dispute settlement (ISDS) in intra-EU dimension aims not only at achieving the objectives of internal market and closer EU integration; it is also meant to enhance the rule of law within the EU through the implementation of EU law by national authorities and State courts, despite distrust of investors in such outcomes. Ultimately, this clash between the two legal orders is also a tale about fragmentation in international law.

Our analysis proceeds as follows. First, in Chapter 4 we will examine the key features of the EU legal order, aiming to uncover the roots of systemic conflicts and incompatibilities between EU law and IIL. This chapter thus provides a legal framework for the analysis that follows in the remaining chapters of Part II. Chapter 5 analyses particularities of normative conflicts in the intra-EU dimension, in light of the jurisprudence of international investment tribunals and the Court of Justice of the EU (CJEU). Chapter 6 provides an analysis of the institutional framework for investment treaty-making, in order to explain internal EU dynamics and limitations on investment policy efficiency imposed by EU law. The analysis in Part II thus examines and uncovers ways in which law serves as a catalyst for political processes, with the key role of the CJEU and its case law in the development of EU investment policy.

# 4

# The EU Legal Order, Internal Market and Investment in the EU

In this introductory chapter to Part II, we will examine the key specifics of the EU legal order and investment protection mechanisms under EU law, with a view to expose *systemic* similarities and differences between the EU legal order and international investment law (IIL). First, we will explain the basic features of the EU legal order. Second, we will expose the *modus operandi* of the EU judicial system and the Court of Justice of the European Union (CJEU) as its integral part. Finally, we will explain the scope of investment issues in the EU legal order to understand the reasons which render IIL more attractive to intra-EU investors than EU law. This chapter thus provides the context to the discussion on intra-EU dispute settlement in the next chapter. The divergent approaches to intra-EU investor-State dispute settlement (ISDS) between investment tribunals and the CJEU epitomise the fundamental differences of the two legal orders discussed in this chapter. The tensions between these two legal orders can only be understood in light of the constitutionalisation of the EU legal order, the process in which the CJEU plays the key role.

## 4.1 The Autonomy of the EU Legal Order within the International Legal Order

The EU legal order, like the EU itself, is a legal order *sui generis*, and combines elements of international and supranational law. Since it is based on international treaties, EU law forms part of international law. However, unlike 'ordinary' international treaties, the EU founding treaties have created its 'own legal system' with its own set of institutions and capacity of representation on the international plane.[1] EU law has been transformed and developed into an autonomous legal order with quasi-federal features through the process of 'constitutionalisation'. In this

[1] Case 6/64 *Flaminio Costa v E.N.E.L.* [1964] ECR 1141.

process, the EU founding treaties have evolved from international law instruments, which horizontally bind sovereign Member States into a 'vertically integrated legal order' which confers enforceable rights and obligations on Member States, their sub-components, citizens and other entities, both private and public, in the territory of the EU as a whole.[2]

The EU has legal personality[3] under international law and it is a party to different international agreements, including international investment agreements (IIAs). In theory, the EU takes a monist view on the status of international agreements to which the EU is a party within its legal order. These international agreements form its integral part,[4] are binding on the EU institutions and the Member States[5] and prevail over EU secondary law and the national legal orders of Member States.[6] The EU must respect international law in the exercise of its powers and EU measures adopted by virtue of those powers must be interpreted in light of the relevant rules of international law.[7]

However, international agreements should always be compatible with primary EU law.[8] Obligations imposed by an international agreement cannot have the effect of prejudicing the constitutional principles of the EU founding treaties.[9] Consequently, EU international agreements are applicable to the extent that they are compatible with primary EU law. Although the CJEU does not have the power to declare international agreements invalid in the case of their substantive inconsistency, it is competent to *disapply* incompatible provisions of such agreements.[10]

The relationship between EU law and international law is therefore, in practical terms, determined by the internal effects of international agreements in the EU legal order, arguably rendering EU law dualist.[11] Accordingly, provisions of international agreements concluded by the EU do not necessarily have direct effect in the EU legal order and in

[2] A. Stone Sweet, *Governing with Judges: Constitutional Politics in Europe* (OUP 2010) 160.
[3] Art. 47 TFEU.
[4] Case C-301/08 *Irène Bogiatzi, married name Ventouras v Deutscher Luftpool and Others* [2009] ECR I-10185, para. 23.
[5] Art. 216(2) TFEU.
[6] Case C-61/94 *Commission v Germany* [1996] ECR I-3989, para. 52.
[7] Joined Cases C-402/05 P and C-415/05 P *Kadi* [2008] ECR I-6351, para. 291.
[8] ibid.
[9] ibid para. 285.
[10] Case C-266/16 *Western Sahara Campaign UK* ECLI:EU:C:2018:11, paras. 45–48.
[11] See F. Martines, 'Direct Effect of International Agreements of the European Union' (2014) 25 *European Journal of International Law* 129.

national legal orders of the Member States.[12] The preclusion of direct effect of some international agreements serves to shield the autonomy of the EU legal order, which is more in danger in cases of international agreements that confer rights on individuals and also establish their own dispute settlement mechanisms. It can be assumed that for such reasons the new generation of EU free trade agreements (FTAs) explicitly exclude their direct effect.[13]

The EU legal order is thus only conditionally open towards international law.[14] The CJEU, as the supreme guardian of the EU legal order, considers EU law as specific international law to which other international law instruments should conform, when it is necessary to achieve the objectives of the EU founding treaties. In symbolic terms, 'the entire EU enterprise is about the son (EU law) "killing" the father (international law)'.[15] In any case, the CJEU's conditional openness to international law is always justified by the international character of EU law, as an autonomous legal order based on international treaties, which cannot be trumped by other international agreements.[16]

## 4.2 Nature of the EU Legal Order and Legal Obligations

Although both EU law and IIL form part of the international legal order, the systemic nature of EU law, reinforced by its constitutional features, stands in contrast to fragmented IIL within the fragmented international law.[17]

The EU legal order reveals its monist supranational character in its relationship with national laws and nationals of Member States. In the complex web of different national and supranational legal instruments,

[12] Case C-308/06 *Intertanko and Others v Secretary of State for Transport* [2008] ECR I-4057, para. 64.

[13] See, for example, Art. 30.6 CETA.

[14] B. de Witte, 'Direct Effect, Primacy and the Nature of the Legal Order' in P. Craig and G. de Búrca (eds), *The Evolution of EU Law* (2nd ed., OUP 2011) 334, 337.

[15] P. d'Argent, 'Sources and the Legality and Validity of International Law: What Makes Law "International"?' in S. Besson and J. d'Aspremont (eds), *The Oxford Handbook on the Sources of International Law* (OUP 2017) 560.

[16] *Kadi* (n 7) paras. 281, 316; Case C-284/16 *Achmea* ECLI:EU:C:2018:158, para. 33.

[17] ILC, 'Fragmentation of International Law: Difficulties Arising From the Diversification and Expansion of International Law' (2006) Report of the Study Group, UN Doc A/CN.4/L682, 11; D. Schneiderman, 'Global Constitutionalism and Its Legitimacy Problems: Human Rights, Proportionality and International Investment Law' (2017) 12 *Journal of Law and Ethics of Human Rights* 251, 274–275.

their relationship is clearly defined and vertically integrated. The implementation of EU law by the Member States cannot be made subject to reciprocity; the founding treaties and the CJEU case law provide remedies in cases when Member States fail to fulfil their obligations.[18] In comparison, IIL also prevails over national legal orders under the customary international rule of *pacta sunt servanda*[19] and the Vienna Convention on the Law of Treaties (VCLT).[20] However, in the complex web of different IIAs, the relationship between these different agreements is rather horizontal and agreements produce vertical effects only in relation to foreign investors. The effective dispute settlement and enforcement mechanisms ensure the compliance of States with their obligations stemming from IIAs.

Rights of individuals under EU law, in comparison to IIL, are not absolute private rights but rights that stem from the EU's exercise of its public law prerogatives. Economic freedoms institutionalised in the founding treaties are not unfettered. The capacity of EU law to produce effects within the legal systems of Member States extends beyond individual interests, to include also the protection of a range of general public interests, such as the environment.[21] The CJEU has repeatedly ruled that protection of the health and life of humans 'rank foremost' among the assets and interests protected by the Treaty[22] and that public health protection 'must take precedence over economic considerations' even in situations where legitimate expectations have been created.[23] In comparison, while IIAs impose obligations on States, they confer private law rights on a specific category of individuals – foreign investors in the host State. They thus create discriminatory effects towards other categories of

[18] Case C-38/89 *Blanguernon* [1990] ECR I-83, para. 7; Case C-163/99 *Portugal v Commission* [2001] ECR I-2613, para. 22; C-118/07 *Commission v Finland* ECLI:EU:C:2009:715, para. 48.

[19] This rule is also enshrined in Art. 26 VCLT.

[20] Art. 27 VCLT precludes a party to an international treaty to rely on the provisions of domestic law as an excuse for its failure to perform a treaty obligation.

[21] See, for example, Case C-72/95 *Kraaijeveld and Others* [1996] ECR I-5403; Case C-435/97 *World Wildlife Fund (WWF) and Others* [1999]; Case C-287/98 *Grand Duchy of Luxemburg v Berthe Linster, Aloyse Linster and Yvonne Linster* [2000] ECR I-6917.

[22] See, for example, Case C-473/98 *Kemikalieinspektionen v Toolex Alpha* [2000] ECR I-5681, para. 38; Case C-108/09 *Ker-Optika* [2010] ECR I-12213, para. 58.

[23] Case C-183/95 *Affish* [1997] ECR I-4315, paras. 43 and 57. This judgment confirms the case law of *United Kingdom v Commission* concerning export prohibitions of beef and veal due to contamination by bovine spongiform encephalopathy (BSE): see Case C-180/96 *United Kingdom v Commission* [1996] ECR I-3903; Case T-76/96 *Pfizer* [1996] ECR II-815.

economic actors, including domestic investors.[24] Therefore, compared to IIL, on a general level EU law allows for a wider scope of guarantees for both private and public interests.

## 4.3 The Role of the CJEU

Similar to the role of investment tribunals in IIL, the CJEU plays a central role in the development of the EU legal order through interpretation of its legal instruments. At the same time, in normative terms the CJEU enjoys relatively higher authority compared to numerous investment tribunals because of its more inclusive relationship with domestic law and courts. The authority and legitimacy of the CJEU explain why the EU envisaged the IIL reform through the institution of a court.

### *4.3.1 Interpretation of EU Law*

The CJEU, as the only authority for interpretation of EU law under the founding treaties, ensures the development of consistent and systematic EU jurisprudence.[25] This contrasts with the inconsistent and often conflicting jurisprudence of investment tribunals, which lack an analogous central point for interpretation. Additionally, even with an appellate mechanism and the system of precedent, which is atypical in international law, investment tribunals would retain one important point of difference with respect to EU law: the method of interpretation of legal instruments. This difference is well described in the words of Lord Diplock:

> The European Court, in contrast to English courts, applies teleological rather than historical methods to the interpretation of Treaties and other Community legislation. It seeks to give effect to what it conceives to be the spirit rather than the letter of the Treaties: sometimes, indeed, to an English judge, it may seem to the exclusion of the letter. It views the Communities as living and expanding organisms and the interpretation of the provisions of the Treaties as changing to match their growth.[26]

Teleological interpretation of the founding treaties stems from the CJEU's federalist vision of the EU, where founding treaties have had

24 Cf. Opinion 1/17 ECLI:EU:C:2019:341. See Chapter 9 on the issue of equality under CETA.

25 This includes powers under Arts. 258, 259, 260 and 263 TFEU.

26 *Henn & Darby v DPP* [1981] AC 850, at 905 (per Lord Diplock).

'the nature of a real constitution', in the absence of a formal constitution.[27] The CJEU's interpretation method can thus be compared to interpretations of a constitutional court, with the similar mission of protecting the fundamental values of the legal order in which it operates. This constitutional character of the CJEU has particularly been demonstrated in decisions concerning the relationship between the EU legal order and international law and its courts.[28]

The CJEU operates on a level of abstraction which is unknown to common law courts, which focus strongly on the facts of each case.[29] Therefore, the case law of the CJEU sits more easily with the French notion of *jurisprudence*, which means the body of law developed through the decisions of the courts,[30] than with common law approaches. Its rulings and opinions can be applied regardless of the specific case scenario where the relevant case law principle is part of the body of law relevant to the case. For this reason, the CJEU uses the exact wording of a particular principle from its past judgments.[31]

International investment tribunals lack such focus and such clear objectives when developing their jurisprudence. They largely rely on textual interpretation of an international agreement in question, and at times on the spirit of the agreement. They are guided by the prevailing letter of IIAs, understood in light of a spirit of unreserved protection of the investors' interests of the time when the relevant agreements were created. A broader range of involved interests in the spirit of the present times is of lesser importance, even when such focus could be supported by the letter of the treaty. In contrast, the CJEU seeks 'to strike the balance imposed by the rule of law among the different interests at stake in [the EU's] multilayered system of governance'.[32]

Despite this difference in hermeneutic approach, the CJEU and investment tribunals engage in creating law through their interpretations. Just as arbitral tribunals have clarified through their jurisprudence the meaning of IIAs' vague substantive investment protections, the CJEU has

[27] *Costa v E.N.E.L.* (n 1), Opinion of AG Lagrange.
[28] See, for example, judgments in *Kadi* (n 7) and *Achmea* (n 16) and Opinions 1/09 [2011] ECR I-1137; 2/13 ECLI:EU:C:2014:2454; and 1/17 (n 24).
[29] K. Schiemann, 'From Common Law Judge to European Judge' (2005) 13 *Zeitschrift für Europäisches Privatrecht* 741 (as cited in K. Lenaerts, 'How the ECJ Thinks: A Study on Judicial Legitimacy' (2013) 36 *Fordham International Law Journal* 1302, 1303).
[30] I. McDeod, *Legal Theory* (2nd ed., Palgrave 2003) 3.
[31] Schiemann (n 29).
[32] Lenaerts (n 29) 1303.

fleshed out in its case law the meaning of legal obligations under the EU founding treaties. In both cases, the interpretations arrived at have departed from the initial intentions of the respective Contracting Parties. However, the CJEU has never rivalled the same level of criticism attracted by international investment tribunals. Despite some predictions made by both legal and political scholars in the 1990s,[33] the CJEU remains 'the most trusted governmental institution' among the EU and national institutions.[34]

The literature has sought to explain this phenomenon by examining the rationale of Member States' governments, including their national courts, for accepting the CJEU's jurisprudence. Of importance is the role of the CJEU in 'constitutionalising' the EU, which can also be defined as 'judicialisation of EU governance'. According to this theory, through its case law the CJEU produces new rules, unintended by the Member States, which are implemented in subsequent policymaking and institutionalised as governance arrangements.[35] This leads to both deepening and widening of EU integration. General geopolitical context of EU integration, including the efforts for stronger integration and the need to overcome political fragmentation of power in decentralised EU governance, has contributed to this judicialised mode of governance in the EU, leading to its acceptance.[36]

Arguably, IIL has also been drawn into a process of 'judicialisation', at least with respect to the International Centre for the Settlement of Investment Disputes (ICSID) system, evidenced by the application by investment tribunals of reasoning methods developed by courts.[37] However, 'constitutionalisation' in the case of IIL is rather fragmented and uncoordinated given the fragmented nature of international investment regulation (IIR). In addition, it exposes a number of methodological problems on the side of investment tribunals in applying relevant

[33] See, for example U. Haltern, 'Integration through Law' in A. Wiener and T. Diez (eds), *European Integration Theory* (OUP 2005) 191–195.

[34] R. D. Kelemen, 'The Court of Justice of the European Union in the Twenty First Century' (2016) 79 *Law and Contemporary Problems* 117, 123. Cf. M. A. Pollack, 'The Legitimacy of the European Court of Justice' in N. Grossman and others (eds), *Legitimacy and International Courts* (CUP 2018), who challenges the legitimacy of the CJEU on normative grounds.

[35] A. Stone Sweet, 'The European Court of Justice and the Judicialization of EU Governance' (2010) Yale Law School Faculty Scholarship Series Paper No. 70, 28–29. This article provides a comprehensive review of literature on this topic.

[36] Kelemen (n 34) 120–123.

[37] A Stone Sweet, 'Arbitration and Judicialisation' (2011) 1 *Onati Socio-Legal Series* 1.

reasoning methods that are usually applied by courts.[38] As a result, consistency, coherence and predictability of arbitral decisions by ISDS tribunals have been at the core of the concerns of States participating in the global reform of ISDS.[39] A number of States have been reforming their investment policies to address these issues. Undoubtedly, new rules produced through the jurisprudence of international investment tribunals, unintended by State parties to IIAs, have influenced policymaking in the area of international investment and its global reform. However, different to judicialisation at EU level which led to strengthening of the CJEU's authority, rethinking of the IIR is aimed at restraining the activism of international investment tribunals and possibly institutional redesign of investment dispute settlement.

### *4.3.2 Judicial Review*

Parallels between EU law and IIL can also be found with respect to the power of judicial review, exercised by their dispute settlement bodies. The EU legal system is envisaged as a complete system of remedies and procedures in which neither EU institutions nor the Member States can avoid judicial review of the legality of their measures under the founding treaties.[40] Individual parties have the right to challenge before the courts the legality of any decision or other national measures relating to the application of an EU act to them.[41] Effective judicial control is a general principle of EU law, stemming from the constitutional traditions common to the Member States, enshrined in Articles 6 and 13 of the European Convention on Human Rights (ECHR) and Article 47 of the EU Charter of Fundamental Rights (CFR).[42] The expression of this

[38] N. J. Calamita, 'The Principle of Proportionality and the Problem of Indeterminacy in International Investment Treaties' (2014) *Yearbook on International Investment Law and Policy* 157.

[39] See UNCITRAL Secretariat, 'Possible Reform of ISDS: Consistency and Related Matters' (28 August 2018) UN Doc A/CN.9/WG.III/WP.150.

[40] Case C-294/83 *Parti écologiste "Les Verts" v European Parliament* [1986] ECR 1339, para. 23.

[41] Case C-583/11 P *Inuit Tapiriit Kanatami and Others v Parliament and Council* ECLI:EU:C:2013:625, paras. 91, 94; Case C-64/16 *Associação Sindical dos Juízes Portugueses* ECLI:EU:C:2018:117, para. 31.

[42] Charter of Fundamental Rights of the European Union [2012] OJ C 326/391; Case 222/84 *Johnston v Chief Constable of the Royal Ulster Constabulary* [1986] ECR 1651, paras. 18–19; Case 222/86 *Heylens and Others* [1987] ECR 4097, para. 14; Case C-424/99 *Commission v Austria* [2001] ECR I-9285, para. 45; Case C-50/00 P *Unión de Pequeños*

principle is in Article 19 of the Treaty on European Union (TEU), which entrusts the exercise of judicial review in the EU legal order to the CJEU and all national courts of the Member States. In this symbiosis, the work is mostly done by national courts because private individuals are primarily invited to enforce their rights under EU law before the national courts.

When reviewing compliance of national legislation with EU law, Member States are endowed with procedural autonomy.[43] It is for domestic legal systems of Member States to determine the jurisdiction and procedural rules of their courts that govern actions for the protection of individual rights under EU law, including an individual's standing and legal interest in bringing procedures.[44] Accordingly, EU law is intended to create new substantive *rights* for individuals but not new *remedies*, except for the cases where no legal remedy exists in national law.[45] Nevertheless, national law cannot in any case undermine the right to effective judicial protection.[46]

Deference to national law is also evident in the CJEU's review of Member States' legislation against public policy grounds which justify Member States' restrictions on free movement. These grounds are either explicitly stated in the founding treaties[47] or can be subsumed under the umbrella concept of 'public interest'.[48] The assessment of public policy exceptions is carried out in light of EU obligations. While its *scope* cannot be determined unilaterally by each Member State without the control by the EU institutions,[49] the *meaning* of public policy accommodates the

*Agricultores v Council* [2002] ECR I-6677, para. 39; Case C-467/01 *Eribrand* [2003] ECR I-6471, para. 61; Case 432/05 *Unibet* [2007] ECR I-2271, para. 37; *Associação Sindical dos Juízes Portugueses* (n 41) para. 35.

43 A. Rosas and L. Armati, *EU Constitutional Law: An Introduction* (Hart 2010) 231–232.

44 *Unibet* (n 42) paras. 39, 42.

45 ibid para. 40–41. However, examples of new remedies grounded in EU law are interim relief: Case C-213/89 *The Queen v Secretary of State for Transport, ex parte: Factorame* [1990] ECR I-2433, and state liability in damages: Joined Cases C-6/90 and C-9/90 *Francovich* [1991] ECR I-5357; Joined Cases C-46/93 and C-48/93 *Brasserie du Pêcheur and Factorame III* [1996] ECR I-1029.

46 Case 33/76 *Rewe-Zentralfinanz* [1976] ECR 1998, para. 5; Case 45/76 *Comet BV v Produktschap voor Siergewassen* [1976] ECR 2043, paras. 13–16; Case C-312/93 *Peterbroeck, Van Campenhout & Cie SCS v Belgian State* [1995] ECR I-4599, para. 12; Case C-453/99 *Courage v Crehan* [2001] ECR I-6297, para. 29; Case C-13/01 *Safalero* [2003] ECR I-8679, para. 49; *Unibet* (n 42) para. 43.

47 For example, Arts. 36, 45(3), 52(1), 62 and 65(1) TFEU.

48 See, for example, Case C-123/00 *Criminal Proceedings Against Bellamy and English Shop Wholesale* [2001] ECR I-2795, para. 18.

49 Case C-36/02 *Omega* [2004] ECR I-9609, para. 30 (emphasis added).

diverse legal interpretations made by national authorities,[50] described by the CJEU as a 'margin of discretion'[51] or 'margin of appreciation'.[52] However, Member States must comply with the principle of proportionality, meaning that their choice must be confined to what is necessary for safeguarding the particular public good, and that the measure must be proportionate to the objective pursued, which could not have been otherwise attained by measures less restrictive of intra-EU trade.[53] The CJEU will be willing to allow the Member States discretion in the level of protection of their constitutional principles of fundamental importance, as long as such principles do not conflict with core values and principles of the EU[54] and pass the proportionality test.[55]

In a similar manner, international investment tribunals exercise the power to review national measures by assessing the effects of the challenged measures on foreign investors, operating as a constitution-like transnational regime[56] or global administrative law regime.[57] Arguably, however, in carrying out such review they lack the legitimacy that the CJEU and national courts enjoy, at least in relative terms.[58] An inability to appropriately accommodate the national rule of law in investment tribunals' review has led to criticism of ISDS, which is seen as a limitation

[50] Case C-41/74 *Yvonne Van Duyn v Home Office* [1974] ECR 1337 para. 18.

[51] Case C-112/00 *Eugen Schmidberger, Internationale Transporte und Planzüge v Republik Österreich* [2003] ECR I-5659.

[52] Case C-110/05 *Commission of the European Communities v Italian Republic* [2009] ECR I-519, para. 65.

[53] Case C-95/01 *Greenham and Abel* [2004] ECR I-1333, para. 39. Additionally, Member States' justifications for public policy exceptions must be consistent with the national legislation as a whole aimed at protecting that particular public interest: see, for example, Joined Cases C-338/04, C-359/04 and C-360/04 *Placanica and Others* [2007] ECR I-1891.

[54] Case C-399/11 *Stefano Melloni v Ministerio Fiscal* ECLI:EU:C:2013:107, para. 60; Case C-617/10 *Åklagaren v Hans Åkerberg Fransson* ECLI:EU:C:2013:105, para. 29.

[55] Case C-208/09 *Ilonka Sayn Wittgenstein v Landeshauptmann von Wien* [2010] ECR I-13693.

[56] Schneiderman (n 17).

[57] G. Van Harten and M. Loughlin, 'Investment Treaty Arbitration as a Species of Global Administrative Law' (2006) 17 *European Journal of International Law* 121.

[58] However, legitimacy of national courts is a complex topic. New Member States still face the challenges of their legacy and transition to democracy. For example, the controversial reform of the Polish judiciary, which has been ongoing since 2015 and which has been heavily criticised by the EU for its non-compliance with the rule of law, has been justified by the Polish Government by reference to low public trust in the judiciary: see Polish Government, White Paper on the Reform of Polish Judiciary (7 March 2018).

to state sovereignty in domestic policymaking, and has triggered its legitimacy crisis.[59]

### 4.3.3 *The Relationship with Domestic Courts*

The authority of the CJEU has been established through an innovative approach in the interpretation of EU law, which respects the national rule of law as an integrative part, and also by an innovative mechanism of cooperation between the CJEU and national courts.

The process of 'constitutionalisation' of the EU Treaty system has been possible due to the procedure prescribed in Treaty on the Functioning of the European Union (TFEU) Article 267 and it has been driven by private litigants, national courts and the CJEU.[60] The preliminary ruling procedure allows 'direct cooperation' between the CJEU and national courts. However, this cooperation embodies 'a clear separation of functions' between the two, and thanks to which the CJEU remains the ultimate authority for all issues of EU law.[61] This judicial dialogue is the 'cogwheel' of the mechanism which enables the CJEU to centrally integrate national and supranational legal orders, but which would not be possible without national courts and private litigants.[62] The rationale of this cooperation is not only the effectiveness of EU law but also the necessity of its very existence.[63]

This process has led to judicial empowerment at the level of EU courts and in the national courts, regarding their mutual links but also their relationships with other branches of government.[64] European Union law has empowered national courts with the judicial review of national measures, regardless of whether they had such power under their national legal systems, therefore giving the national courts greater powers

[59] S. W. Schill, 'Enhancing International Investment Law's Legitimacy: Conceptual and Methodological Foundations of a New Public Law Approach' (2011) 52 *Virginia Journal of International Law* 57; Schneiderman (n 17). See also Chapter 3.

[60] Stone Sweet (n 2) 160–163.

[61] Case C-62/14 *Peter Gauweiler and Others v Deutscher Bundestag* ECLI:EU:C:2015:400 para. 15.

[62] Stone Sweet (n 2) 165.

[63] M. Claes, 'The Validity and Primacy of EU Law and the "Cooperative Relationship" between National Constitutional Courts and the Court of the Justice of the European Union' (2016) 23 *Maastricht Journal of European and Comparative Law* 151, 154.

[64] J. H. H. Weiler, 'The Transformation of Europe' (1991) 100 *Yale Law Journal* 2403, 2419.

to control State acts and other branches of government.[65] Private litigants also have their own interests in raising legal challenges against non-compliance by Member States with their EU law obligations, fuelling the system with a number of cases. Gradually, through incremental decision-making of the CJEU, enforced by national courts, EU law has expanded its reach while influencing the Member States' behaviour and policymaking in the direction of their compliance with EU law.[66] The preliminary ruling mechanism, with individual litigants as decentralised agents, the CJEU as central authority in respect of interpretation of EU law, and national courts who render final decisions, has ensured the effectiveness of the Member State compliance with the rule of law in the EU.[67]

While EU law works to empower the role of the national courts, IIL in its essence undermines their role. International investment tribunals have been established with the principal reason of operating outside the judicial system of States.[68] On a more general level, investment tribunals have been established with a view to overcoming investors' distrust of national courts and indeed in some cases such distrust remains justified.[69] However, investment tribunals challenge national courts in a number of ways. Depending on the investment agreement in question, parallel proceedings before national courts and investment tribunals are possible and can lead to diverging outcomes.[70] Arbitral tribunals have the power to review the decisions of national courts, even in States with developed legal systems.[71] They can find breaches of IIAs even when the conduct of the court has complied with the national requirements of due process, thus challenging the domestic rule of law.[72] Their decisions can

[65] K. J. Alter, 'The European Court's Political Power' (1996) 19 *West European Politics* 458, 466–467.

[66] K. J. Alter, *Establishing the Supremacy of European Law: The Making of an international Rule of Law in Europe* (OUP 2001) 218–221.

[67] ibid 217–221; Weiler (n 64).

[68] Opinion 2/15 ECLI:EU:C:2017:376, para. 292; *Achmea* (n 16) para. 45.

[69] See *Chevron Corporation and Texaco Petroleum Corporation v The Republic of Ecuador*, UNCITRAL, PCA Case No. 2009-23, Second Partial Award on Track II (30 August 2018).

[70] See Section 1.3.2 in Chapter 1.

[71] See, for example, *Loewen v USA*, ICSID Case No. ARB(AF)/98/3, Award (26 June 2003); *Eli Lilly and Company v The Government of Canada*, UNCITRAL, ICSID Case No. UNCT/14/2, Final Award (16 March 2017).

[72] For example, in *Mr. Franck Charles Arif v Republic of Moldova*, ICSID Case No. ARB/11/23, Award (8 April 2013) paras. 415–416, 447–453.

lead to conflicts between international law and domestic law and to internal tensions between different branches of government, challenging also the principle of the separation of power.[73]

## 4.4 Summary of Systemic Differences and Parallels between the EU Legal Order and International Investment Regulation

The autonomy of the EU legal order and its specific relationship with international law shape the uneasy relationship between EU law and IIL in intra-EU relations.[74] Nevertheless, the two legal orders display a number of parallels, which explains how the EU legal order has shaped the EU's external investment regulation.[75] Table 4.1 summarises the key features, parallels and differences between the legal orders of the EU and international investment.

The judicial 'dialogue' between the CJEU and national courts has ensured the relative respect for the rule of law in the EU and the relative success of EU law compared to other regimes of international law. While in a number of aspects similar to IIL, the EU legal order has generally been accepted by national actors, including courts. Proportionality, balancing economic and other fundamental rights, deference to national laws through respect for Member States' procedural autonomy and diversity of their constitutional and legal traditions in interpretation and implementation of EU rules have played a role, with the CJEU as the main pillar of EU legitimacy. It is therefore not a surprise that the establishment of a court for IIL reform came from the EU as a solution for its legitimacy problems.

However, the CJEU, as an international court, is a unique example. In the EU, law has become 'a convenient expedient for politics' with the key role played by the CJEU in this process.[76] The development of EU investment regulatory framework, as explained in the following chapters, supports this thesis. The CJEU has been well aware that it sits within the complex political processes of the EU. Judges are not politically accountable but they are conscious of the need to secure the acceptability of their

[73] For example, in *Chevron* (n 69) para. 10.13, the Tribunal effectively called upon the executive government to take responsibility and remedy the actions of its judicial branch.

[74] See Chapter 5.

[75] See Chapters 8 and 9.

[76] A. Cohen, 'The European Court of Justice in the Emergent European Field of Power: Transnational Judicial Institutions and National Career Paths' in Y. Dezaley and B. Garth (eds), *Lawyers and the Construction of Transnational Justice* (Routledge 2012) 243.

Table 4.1 *Comparisons between EU law and international investment law*

| | EU | IIR | Parallels and differences |
|---|---|---|---|
| **Sources** | • International treaties (EU founding treaties)<br>• EU secondary law | • International treaties (IIAs) – bilateral (BITs) and plurilateral (PTIAs) | No secondary laws in IIR but State parties to IIAs can make binding interpretations under international law. |
| **Hierarchy of rules** | • Vertical and structured<br>• The doctrine of primacy of EU law | • Horizontal and fragmented<br>• Conflict rules in international law for determining the primacy of rules | In both cases domestic law is subordinate but EU law prevails over the international agreements of Member States and primary EU law prevails over international agreements to which the EU is a party. |
| **Enforcement of rights** | • Through domestic courts and the CJEU<br>• Appeals mechanism<br>• The CJEU is the supreme authority for the interpretation of EU law | • Through *ad hoc* investment tribunals<br>• No appellate mechanism<br>• No supreme authority for the interpretation of rules | In both cases private individuals can directly invoke international treaties (the doctrine of direct effect in EU law and offer to arbitrate in ISDS clause in IIR).<br>In the case of IIR, domestic courts have no role and their decisions can be challenged by investors. |
| **Scope** | • Internal market<br>• Four freedoms<br>• Charter of Fundamental Rights<br>• Compliance mechanisms through the CJEU | • Substantive protections and a dispute resolution mechanism for foreign investors | The EU is a more comprehensive system with access to justice for a broader range of economic and non-economic actors. |

| | | | |
|---|---|---|---|
| **Objectives** | • Trade liberalisation and level playing field in the EU<br>• Regulatory approximation/ harmonisation<br>• EU integration | • Protection of foreign investors and their legitimate expectations | The EU objectives are much broader in scope and include both trade and non-trade objectives.<br>While protection of investment arguably contributes to an increase in investment flows, in essence it is a protectionist measure not aimed at achieving investment liberalisation or a level playing field.[a] |
| **Nature of the system** | • Public international and supranational law<br>• Constitutional system | • Public international law with private law elements | Although based on public international law, EU law resembles domestic constitutional systems.<br>Although based on public international law (IIAs), IIR has been developed on a private law model of arbitration, which is at its core. |
| **Applicable law in the proceedings** | • Founding treaties (primary EU law)<br>• International law that binds the EU<br>• Secondary EU law | • IIAs (BITs and PTIAs)<br>• General principles of international law<br>• Domestic law<br>• Procedural rules: UNCITRAL and ICSID | Both interpret rules of international law but the scope of applicable EU rules is wider and includes EU secondary rules.<br>Depending on the legal instrument, IIR tribunals can interpret domestic law. |
| **Remedies** | • Substantive protections for private individuals under primary and secondary EU law | • Substantive protections under individual IIAs<br>• Specific procedural rights available to foreign investors only (offer to arbitrate) | Both offer protections to private individuals but the scope of protection and available remedies in IIR are limited to foreign investors only.<br>Under EU law rights are harmonised across the EU while the remedies differentiate |

Table 4.1 (*cont.*)

| | EU | IIR | Parallels and differences |
|---|---|---|---|
| | • Remedies against unlawful EU measures defined in EU law<br>• Remedies against unlawful national measures defined in domestic law | • Remedies against unlawful host State measures defined in IIAs (limited to monetary compensation) | across different Member States. In IIR both rights and remedies are defined in an individual IIA but they are largely harmonised across the different treaties. |
| **Principles of interpretation** | • Consistent interpretation<br>• Proportionality in balancing public-private interests<br>• Teleological interpretation in view of EU policy objectives | • No precedent and inconsistent decisions possible<br>• VCLT but inconsistently applied<br>• Focus on textual interpretation<br>• Interpretation in favour of protection of investors | Both apply genuinely different methods of interpretation, in particular in balancing public–private interests, resulting in different outcomes and impact on domestic measures:<br>• Elimination of illegal measures under EU law;<br>• Possible 'regulatory chill' under investment law. |
| **Applicability of decisions** | • *Erga omnes*<br>• *Ex tunc* | • *Inter partes*<br>• *Ex nunc* | Decisions of the CJEU are legally binding on the courts of all Member States and in that sense have lawmaking effect. |

| | | | |
|---|---|---|---|
| | | | IIR tribunals' decisions apply only to the case in point but are often referred to by subsequent tribunals. |
| **Scope of proceedings** | • Judicial review of the legality of EU acts<br>• The assessment of national rules that conflict with EU law through preliminary ruling procedure | • The assessment of the effects of national rules against international investment law (IIAs, ICSID) takes *de facto* a form of judicial review | In both cases, functionally at least, judicial review of national measures and new rules are produced through case law, often unintended by the States. |
| **Relationship with domestic courts and institutions/ domestic law** | • Judicial dialogue through preliminary ruling procedure<br>• Procedural autonomy of the Member States<br>• Mutual trust and sincere cooperation<br>• Deference to domestic law | • No involvement of domestic courts<br>• Genuine mistrust in domestic institutions<br>• Usually no margin of appreciation nor deference to domestic law | Domestic courts are part of the EU judicial system while IIR operates as a parallel system to domestic courts.<br>EU law more deferential towards domestic institutions and political imperatives of Member States in defending public interest. |

[a] See the analysis in Section 2.1.2 in Chapter 2.

decisions. Since the EU judicial system relies on the willingness of cooperation between central and peripheral courts, it can at times come into question.

However, reference by the CJEU to internal law in developing its case law, which brought the EU law closer to the national laws of the Member States than to international law, serves to legitimise the CJEU's approach in constitutionalising Europe without a formal constitution.[77] On the other hand, IIL lacks clear objectives and any centralised institution could hardly consolidate the competing and fragmented interests of States in international investment.

With the EU legal order as the framework for EU investment policy, the remaining part of this chapter focuses more specifically on EU internal market and investment protection mechanisms under EU law.

## 4.5 The Internal Market and Investment in the EU

Investment primarily concerns domestic law measures and spreads across a number of areas which fall within either shared[78] or exclusive Member States'[79] competence. The purpose of this section is therefore to explain *mechanisms* of protection for investors under EU law rather than an exhaustive presentation of the substantive law.[80] These mechanisms are explained with respect to (1) free movement provisions in the Treaty law; (2) private rights; and (3) enforcement mechanism and remedies. We conclude this section with observations about the reasons which render IIL more attractive to intra-EU investors than EU law.

[77] A. Cohen, 'Constitutionalism without Constitution: Transnational Elites between Political Mobilisation and Legal Expertise in the Making of a Constitution for Europe (1940s–1960s)' (2007) 32 *Law and Social Inquiry* 109.

[78] For example, internal market, financial services, energy, transport, telecommunications, intellectual property, etc.

[79] For example, direct taxation. Nevertheless, Member States must exercise that competence consistently with EU law: Case C-334/02 *Commission v France* [2004] ECR I-2229, para. 21; Case C-155/09 *Commission v Greece* [2011] ECR I-65, para. 39; Case C-10/10 *Commission v Austria* [2011] ECR I-5389, para. 23. Property ownership also falls within Member States' exclusive competence under Art. 345 TFEU, but in exercising their competences regarding property law Member States must comply with the fundamental principles of EU law, as prescribed by the CFR and the founding treaties: Opinion 2/15 (n 68) para. 107.

[80] The essential reading on internal market is C. Barnard, *The Substantive Law of the EU: The Four Freedoms* (6th ed., OUP 2019).

### 4.5.1 *Free Movement in the EU and Investment*

The creation of the internal market has had an important role in enhancing intra-EU investment conditions. Its basic objective is the creation of 'an area without internal frontiers in which the free movement of goods, persons, services and capital is ensured',[81] popularly known as 'four freedoms'. With an aim of removing barriers to economic activity within the EU, the focus is primarily on eliminating divergences in Member States' national legal systems which could be perceived as obstacles to fundamental economic freedoms. This includes elimination of all national measures that serve as economic restrictions; those that are discriminatory (applied only to other EU nationals, including investors) and that are non-discriminatory (applied to both Member State and EU nationals). These Member State measures can be challenged under primary EU law (negative integration) or secondary EU law which seeks to achieve a more or less complete harmonisation (positive integration). The EU's approach is thus functional towards achieving 'free movement'.

These economic freedoms could be considered 'economic free movement rights'[82] although they differ from private law rights in domestic legal systems.[83] In the context of intra-EU investment, of primary importance are the Treaty provisions on the rights of establishment and free movement of capital. While the former applies only to the 'establishment of nationals of a Member State in the territory of another Member State',[84] free movement of capital involves both intra- (between the Member States) and extra-EU (between the Member States and third countries) dimensions.[85] In the context of trans-border intra-EU investment liberalisation, the freedom to provide services within the EU is also of relevance.[86]

Freedom of establishment guarantees *access* to the market, via primary (setting up a company) and secondary (setting up a branch, agency or a subsidiary) establishment, and *operating* on the market. However, this freedom applies only to actual establishments of the investor in the host State through a fixed establishment for an indefinite period and in the

81 Art. 26 TFEU.
82 Rosas and Armati (n 43) 181.
83 See Section 4.5.2.
84 Art. 49 TFEU. Nationals include private individuals and legal persons. Legal persons must be incorporated in accordance with the law of the Member State: Art. 54 TFEU.
85 Art. 63 TFEU.
86 Arts. 56 and 57 TFEU.

pursuit of genuine economic activity.[87] These conditions include only foreign direct investment (FDI) types of investments which give investors 'a definite influence over the company's decisions', allowing them 'to determine [their] activities'.[88] These limitations are understandable given the objective of the freedom of establishment, which is 'assisting economic and social interpenetration' of EU nationals within the EU[89] and allowing them 'to participate, on a stable and continuing basis, in the economic life of a Member State other than his State of origin and to profit therefrom'.[90] Investments that do not satisfy freedom of establishment criteria, such as portfolio investments, are capital movements subject to the freedom of capital provisions.

Freedom of capital guarantees free movement of capital investments, which include both FDI and portfolio investment.[91] A *capital movement* is defined in the secondary EU law[92] and the CJEU's case law. With respect to their scope, capital movements in EU law are a wider concept than the definition of investment in IIL. They include investments such as 'direct investment in the form of participation in an undertaking by means of a shareholding or the acquisition of securities on the capital market',[93] 'granting credit on a commercial basis',[94] 'the acquisition of shares on the capital market solely with the intention of making a

[87] Case C-196/04 *Cadbury Schweppes and Cadbury Schweppes Overseas* [2006] ECR I-7995, para. 54.

[88] Case C-231/05 *Oy AA* [2007] ECR I-6373, para. 20; Case C-464/14 *SECIL* ECLI:EU:C:2016:896. In a situation when a company holds a 15 per cent share in a subsidiary, it should not be implied that such a company exercises a definite influence over the decisions of the company distributing the dividends. Accordingly, the free movement of capital would prevail. See Joint Cases C-504/16 and C-613/16 *Deister Holding and Juhler Holding* EU:C:2017:1009, paras. 79–80; Case C-685/16 *EV* ECLI:EU:C:2018:743, para. 40.

[89] Case 2/74 *Reyners* [1974] ECR 631, para. 21.

[90] Case C-55/94 *Gebhard* [1995] ECR I-4165, para. 25; Case C-470/04 *N* [2006] ECR I-7409, para. 26. See also Section 8.2.1.1 in Chapter 8 on 'malibox' companies.

[91] Joined Cases C-282/04 and C-283/04 *Commission v Netherlands* [2006] ECR I-9141, para. 19.

[92] Council Directive 88/361/EEC of 24 June 1988 for the implementation of Article 67 of the Treaty [1988] OJ L178/5; Case C-222/97 *Trummer and Mayer* [1999] ECR I-1671, para. 21; Case C-452/04 *Fidium Finanz AG* [2006] ECR I-9521, para. 41; Joined Cases C-515/99, C-519/99 to C-524/99 and C-526/99 to C-540/99 *Reisch and Others* [2002] ECR I-2157, para. 30; Case C-513/03 *Van Hilten-van der Heijden* [2006] ECR I-1957, para. 39.

[93] Case C-367/98 *Commission v Portugal* [2002] ECR I-4731, para. 38.

[94] *Fidium Finanz AG* (n 92) paras. 42–43. This is also considered a provision of services and it is covered by Art. 49 TFEU (freedom of establishment).

financial investment'[95] or 'a resale of shares to the issuing company'.[96] But capital can also take the form of a mortgage,[97] or other investment in real estate on the territory of a Member State by non-residents,[98] both in the form of ownership and administration of such property;[99] usufruct over agricultural land;[100] and even an inheritance can be investment.[101] Unlike *establishment*, there is no requirement that the capital movement must be an economic activity. Importantly, the list of capital movements in the secondary law is not exhaustive and transactions that are linked to the listed measures can constitute capital movement.[102]

There is a close proximity between the freedom of establishment and free movement of capital and a potential overlap of these two freedoms.[103] Generally speaking, freedom of capital is a precondition for the exercise of other freedoms.[104] The approach of the CJEU in applying relevant Treaty provisions has been to identify the principal purpose of national restrictions (whether to regulate establishment or capital), and, when both apply, the emphasis is placed on whether the measures allow a 'definite influence over [the] company's decision'.[105] The distinction between FDI and portfolio investment therefore is of relevance. The distinction between freedom of establishment and capital is significant with respect to the territorial scope of their application,[106] but also with respect to the Treaty derogations from these freedoms, which are more extensive in the case of capital movements.[107] Of similar importance is

[95] *Commission v Netherlands* (n 91) para. 19.

[96] Case C-265/04 *Margaretha Bouanich v Skatteverket* [2006] ECR I-923, para. 29.

[97] *Trummer and Meyer* (n 92) paras. 23–24.

[98] See Case C-364/01 *Barbier* ECLI:EU:C:2003:665, paras. 58–59; Case C-512/03 *Blanckaert* [2005] ECR I-7685, para. 35; Case C-567/07 *Woningstichting Sint Servatius* ECLI:EU:C:2009:593, para. 20; Case C-45/17 *Jahin* ECLI:EU:C:2018:18, para. 22.

[99] Case C-386/04 *Centro di Musicologia Walter Stauffer* [2006] ECR I-8203, para. 24.

[100] Joined Cases C-52/16 and C-113/16 *SEGRO and Horváth* [2016] ECLI:EU:C:2018:157, para. 57.

[101] *Van Hilten-van der Heijden* (n 93); Case C-35/08 *Busley et Cibrian Fernandez* ECLI:EU:C:2009:625; Case C-510/08 *Mattner* [2010] ECR I-3553; Case C-244/15 *Commission v Greece* ECLI:EU:C:2016:359; Case C-679/17 *Huijbrechts* ECLI:EU:C:2018:940.

[102] For example, see Case C-35/98 *Verkooijen* [2000] ECR I-4071, paras. 28–30.

[103] See Art. 65(2) TFEU.

[104] Case 203/80 *Casati* [1981] ECR 2595, para. 8.

[105] Barnard (n 80) 527–529.

[106] Freedom of establishment applies intra-EU only, while free movement of capital both intra- and extra-EU, albeit not to the same extent in both dimensions.

[107] See Art. 65(1) TFEU (freedom of capital) cf. Art. 52(1) TFEU (freedom of establishment).

the distinction between free movement of capital and services in the aspect of liberalisation of capital.

Given that Member States are more sensitive to the impact of capital exports on national economies, liberalisation of capital generally took longer than liberalisation of other freedoms.[108] Early in its case law the CJEU noted the close connection between capital movements and economic and monetary policies of the Member States. The Court thus recognised that 'complete freedom of movement of capital may undermine the economic policy of one of the Member States or create an imbalance in its balance of payments, thereby impairing the proper functioning of the Common Market'.[109] The Court thus found a valid justification even to limit the EU fundamental freedom. Importantly, the reasons were found in the potential for the complete liberalisation of capital to undermine the internal market as the ultimate goal of EU integration, rather than in protecting the interests of Member States *per se*. For this reason, the Court concluded that free movement of capital differs from other freedoms of goods, persons and services, and the obligation to liberalise exists only 'to the extent necessary to ensure the *proper functioning of the internal market*'.[110]

In the meantime, capital movements have been liberalised, at least in the intra-EU context, due to the establishment of the economic and monetary union (EMU). However, additional Treaty restrictions continue to apply,[111] in particular with respect to extra-EU movements of capital.[112] The Council has been given extra powers to adopt restrictive measures on these movements.[113] The objectives of the EU and its internal market, rather than Member States' interests, serve as justifications for these additional extra-EU restrictions.

The main rationale of the free movement guarantees in the EU is the elimination of national measures which have, directly or indirectly, a discriminatory effect within the internal market or obstruct free circulation of investment even if non-discriminatory.[114] This is in line with the principle of the internal market as a competitive playing field that

[108] Barnard (n 80) 519.
[109] *Casati* (n 104) para. 9.
[110] ibid para. 10 (emphasis added).
[111] Art. 65 TFEU.
[112] Art. 64 TFEU.
[113] Arts. 64(3), 65(4) and 66 TFEU. See also Section 8.1.1.1 in Chapter 8.
[114] S. Hindelang, *The Free Movement of Capital and Foreign Direct Investment* (OUP 2009) 166 and seq.

underpins the founding treaties. It is an EU version of the national treatment in IIAs, which goes beyond the equal treatment of nationals and non-nationals.[115] The CJEU emphasises 'national measures liable to hinder or make less attractive the exercise of fundamental freedoms guaranteed by the Treaty',[116] demonstrating the Court's 'obstacle' rather than 'discrimination approach'.[117]

#### 4.5.1.1 Derogations in the Treaty Law

The CJEU has developed extensive case law regarding national measures that are prohibited under freedom of establishment (and closely related to that, freedom to provide and receive services) and freedom of capital provisions. Additionally, the CJEU has developed a number of public interest justifications, which supplement general Treaty derogations invoked by the Member States to justify discriminatory measures or other conduct which impedes access to or the exercise of the freedoms.

While it is beyond the scope of this chapter to delve into the very complex CJEU case law, some examples are given to illustrate the discernible approach of the CJEU in assessing the prohibited measures and striking a balance between the objectives of EU integration and Member States' public interest with respect to freedom of establishment and capital.

Regarding free movement of capital, the CJEU has identified three types of Member State measures as restrictions that are prohibited under Article 63 TFEU.[118] First, measures that deter investment in other Member States, which are primarily discriminatory against transnational activities.[119] Further, measures which restrict investment in a Member State, for example, through prior administrative authorisation schemes.[120] Finally, measures which limit control over the investment,

[115] In addition, the general non-discrimination clause in Art. 18 TFEU prohibits any discrimination on grounds of nationality. Further, Art. 21 CFR prohibits 'any discrimination on any ground'.

[116] *Gebhard* (n 90) para. 37.

[117] P. Craig and G. de Búrca, *EU Law, Text, Cases and Materials* (6th ed., OUP 2015) 806. Cf. Jukka Snell, 'Non-Discriminatory Tax Obstacles in Community Law' (2007) 56 *The International and Comparative Law Quarterly* 339, 349. See Section 4.5.1.2 on taxation issues.

[118] D. Chalmers, G. Davies and G. Monti, *European Union Law* (2nd ed., CUP 2010) 725–726.

[119] *Van Hilten-van der Heijden* (n 92) para. 44; Case C-101/05 *A* [2007] ECR I-11531, para. 40; Case C-370/05 *Festersen* [2007] ECR I-1129, para. 24.

[120] Case C-302/97 *Konle* [1999] ECR I-3099.

given the potential of such measures to undermine the decision-making authority of the undertaking and thus affect the quality and predictability of public intervention into the market.[121] The effects of any Member States' restrictions will be reviewed against their impact on the *functioning of the internal market* (through their impact on investment), and not against their impact on *investors*, although the two in many cases overlap.

Nevertheless, national restrictive measures in an intra-EU setting will be lawful if they can be justified by the pursuit of a legitimate public interest, subject to proportionality. If the measure is directly discriminatory, the Member State can rely only on the express derogations in the founding treaties,[122] whereby more extensive derogations apply to the free movement of capital.[123] A critical distinction must be made between unequal treatment, which is permitted under Article 65(1)(a) TFEU, and arbitrary discrimination which is prohibited by Article 65(3) TFEU.[124] Importantly, although Article 65(1) gives Member States more leeway in their regulatory activity, measures which are arbitrarily discriminatory are absolutely prohibited in virtue of Article 65(3) TFEU. As a derogation from the fundamental principle of the free movement of capital, Article 65(1) TFEU derogation must be strictly interpreted.[125] In order to fall within the scope of Article 65(1)(a) TFEU, 'the difference in treatment must concern situations not objectively comparable or be justified by an overriding reason in the public interest'.[126]

[121] Case C-112/05 *Commission v Germany* [2007] ECR I-8995 and other 'golden shares' case law.

[122] Art. 52(1) TFEU, which includes grounds of public policy, security and health. Of relevance is also Treaty exclusion of the applicability of freedom of establishment provisions to Member States' activities connected, even occasionally, with the exercise of official authority: Art. 51(1) TFEU. These provisions *mutatis mutandi* apply to the freedom to provide services: Art. 62 TFEU.

[123] Art. 65(1)(a) and (b) TFEU. First, this provides specific derogation in relation to a tax regime, while providing second, a more general derogation in relation to regulatory supervision of the taxation and financial institutions and grounds of public policy or public security.

[124] See also Case C-252/14 *Pensioenfonds Metaal en Techniek* ECLI:EU:C:2016:402, para. 47.

[125] Case C-181/12 *Welte* ECLI:EU:C:2013:662, para. 42; Case C-322/11 *K* ECLI:EU:C:2013:716, para. 34; *Jahin* (n 98) para. 32.

[126] Case C-347/11 *Santander Asset Management SGIIC* ECLI:EU:C:2012:286, para. 23 and the case law cited. By way of illustration, the social security fees to be paid by a French citizen who is a non-resident in France and contributes to a private social security scheme in a third State would fall within the scope of exception on the grounds that his situation is not comparable with the one of EU residents: *Jahin* (n 98) para. 41.

When national restrictions on free movement are not arbitrarily discriminatory, the scope of public interest grounds referred to as 'imperative requirements' is wider and open ended.[127] For example, ensuring energy supply or the protection of the environment can be such a legitimate goal, and acquiring public control over hydropower resources and related installations can be a means of attaining these goals.[128] With many derogations, internal market case law in this aspect does not provide clear dividing lines between these categories.[129] The CJEU emphasised that any derogations must be interpreted strictly, that they cannot serve purely economic ends and that any affected individual must be granted access to a legal redress.[130] Importantly, 'general financial interests of a Member State' or 'economic policy objectives' are not adequate justifications.[131]

In the context of investment, of relevance is also the requirement of legal certainty. Accordingly, any prior authorisation for FDI must be precise regarding the specific conditions in which the authorisation is required in order to indicate to investors the extent of their rights and obligations guaranteed by Article 63 TFEU.[132] Any reference formulated in general terms, such as 'the protection of national interest', gives 'a wide discretionary power' to the executive in granting prior authorisation and 'constitutes a serious interference with the free movement of capital, and may have the effect of excluding it altogether'.[133] The criteria must be objective and subject to judicial review in order to satisfy the requirements of legal certainty.[134] Such a restricted approach of the CJEU in assessing Member States' measures, which prohibits any arbitrary decisions based on uncertain or political criteria, can provide confidence to investors that their rights will be guaranteed.

In light of the above discussion on free movement provisions in the Treaty law and their derogations, Table 4.2 summarises the main features of the two fundamental freedoms.

[127] Case C-19/92 *Kraus v Land Baden-Wuerttemberg* [1993] ECR I-1663, para. 32; *Gebhard* (n 90) para. 37.

[128] E-2/06 *EFTA Surveillance Authority v The Kingdom of Norway* [2007] OJ C301/18, paras. 84–88. However, Member States have the burden of proof in demonstrating an *essential interest*: Case C-260/04 *Commission of the European Communities v Italian Republic* [2007] ECR I-7083, para. 33.

[129] Craig and de Búrca (n 117) 807.

[130] Case C-54/99 *Église de Scientologie* [2000] ECR I-1335, para. 17.

[131] *Commission v Portugal* (n 93) para. 52.

[132] *Église de Scientologie* (n 130) paras. 21–22.

[133] Case C-483/99 *Commission v France* [2002] ECR I-4781, paras. 50–52.

[134] Case C-503/99 *Commission v Belgium* [2002] ECR I-4809, para. 52.

Table 4.2 *Comparison between freedom of establishment and free movement of capital in EU law*

<table>
<tr><th>Category</th><th>Freedom of establishment<br>(Article 49 TFEU)</th><th>Free movement of capital<br>(Article 63 TFEU)</th></tr>
<tr><td>Type of investment</td><td>• Economic activity<br>• FDI</td><td>• Financial investment<br>• FDI + portfolio investment</td></tr>
<tr><td>Territorial scope</td><td>Intra-EU</td><td>Intra- and extra-EU</td></tr>
<tr><td rowspan="2">Derogations</td><td>• General<br>- public policy, public security, public health;<br>- exercise of official authority</td><td>• General<br>- regulatory supervision of taxation and financial institutions;<br>- public policy or public security<br>• Specific: taxation<br>- discrimination between place of residence vs. place of capital invested</td></tr>
<tr><td colspan="2">• Imperative requirements in the general interest + non-discrimination + proportionality</td></tr>
<tr><td>Direct effect</td><td>• Vertical (individual–State)<br>• Limited horizontal applicability (individual–private parties)</td><td>• Vertical (individual–State)</td></tr>
</table>

#### 4.5.1.2 The Specific Case of Bilateral Taxation

A large number of cases in the area of freedom of establishment and capital relate to national taxation. While direct taxation falls within the competence of Member States, the exercise of power of taxation must comply with EU law and the principle of national treatment of nationals and non-nationals within the EU.[135] However, the prohibition of differences in treatment is not absolute. A national measure will be considered legal where the difference in treatment relates 'to situations which are not

[135] Case C-80/94 *Wielockx* [1995] ECR I-2493, para. 16; *Verkooijen* (n 102) para. 32; *Commission v France* (n 79) para. 21; C-242/03 *Weidert and Paulus* [2004] ECR I-7379, para. 12.

objectively comparable'[136] or can be 'justified by an overriding reason in the public interest', subject to the usual proportionality test.[137] Taxpayers' residence is a factor that may justify differences of treatment between resident and non-resident taxpayers,[138] and additionally, in the case of capital movements, the place where the capital is invested.[139] While the prevention of tax evasion or tax abuse is a legitimate objective,[140] the CJEU strictly scrutinises national laws, whereby *general* presumptions of tax evasion or abusive practices do not *per se* justify restrictions on freedom of establishment[141] or capital.[142]

Double taxation international agreements between the Member States constitute one specific example. While they provide a special tax treatment only to the nationals of some Member States (those that are parties to a specific bilateral agreement), they are not considered to be discriminatory under EU law.[143] They also demonstrate that EU founding treaties, unlike IIAs, do not recognise MFN treatment, which would extend favourable tax treatment to other non-nationals.[144] Moreover, international double taxation more generally is not an obstacle to the free movement provisions and thus is also not illegal under EU law.[145] Reasoning by analogy, the Opinion of AG Wathelet in *Achmea* suggested that the same conclusion could be reached regarding intra-EU BITs.[146]

However, there are important differences between treatment of taxation and investment in the EU context, in particular with respect to different interactions of investment law with the internal market. Tax law

[136] This in line with the more general principle of equal treatment, which requires that 'comparable situations must not be treated differently and different situations must not be treated in the same way unless such treatment is objectively justified': Case C-580/12 P *Guardian Industries and Guardian Europe v Commission* EU:C:2014:2363, para. 51; Case C-477/14 *Pillbox 38* ECLI:EU:C:2016:324, para. 35.

[137] Case C-123/11 *A* ECLI:EU:C:2013:84, para. 33 (for freedom of establishment), Case C-446/04 *Test Claimants in the FII Group Litigation* [2006] ECR I-11753, para. 167 (for free movement of capital).

[138] *A* (n 137) para. 33.

[139] Arts. 65(1)(a) and 65(3) TFEU.

[140] Art. 65(1)(b) TFEU.

[141] Case C-105/07 *Lammers and Van Cleeff* [2008] ECR I-173, paras. 27–28.

[142] Case C-478/98 *Commission v Belgium* [2000] ECR I-7587, para. 45.

[143] Case C-376/03 *D* [2005] ECR I-5821.

[144] *Achmea* (n 16), Opinion of AG Wathelet ECLI:EU:C:2017:699, para. 71.

[145] For detailed analysis of the CJEU's approach, see Snell (n 117) 358–366.

[146] See *Achmea*, Opinion of AG Wathelet (n 144) paras. 73–80.

is at the core of national sovereignty and has been accordingly recognised in the allocation of powers between the EU and the Member States. The CJEU has readily applied the territoriality principle in this area of law. However, the principle was rejected in some other areas; for example, in intellectual property, where it held that

> the essential purpose of the Treaty, which is to unite national markets into a single market, could not be attained if, under the various legal systems of the Member States, nationals of those Member States were able to *partition the market* and bring about *arbitrary discrimination* or *disguised restrictions* on trade between Member States.[147]

*Mutatis mutandi*, the same could be applied to investment law given the proprietary nature of investment. Equally fundamental to State sovereignty, tax issues are arguably also more politically sensitive for *all* Member States, unlike investment issues which seem to concern different Member States differently.[148]

### *4.5.2 Private Rights and Investment in the EU*

While the free movement provisions imply guarantees of access to the market in intra-EU relations (and extra-EU in the case of capital), EU law continues to apply to the established investments throughout their lifetime, alongside the national law of the Member State in which the investor has been established.[149] In this sense, the scope of EU law is much wider as it implies both investment liberalisation (market access) and investment protection (post-establishment). As discussed, IIL is mostly focused on post-establishment protections for investors.[150] Nevertheless, the scope and mechanisms of these protections under the two regimes are different. In light of the private nature of *rights* conferred on investors under IIL, it could be argued that EU law with respect to these rights plays the same role as it plays more generally regarding private law in national legal systems. The EU's power to regulate private law stems from the variety of different competences under EU

[147] Joined Cases 55/80 and 57/80 *Musik-Vertrieb Membran GmbH v GEMA* [1981] ECR 147, para. 14 (emphasis added). Following the Lisbon Treaty, Art. 118 TFEU provides an explicit legal basis for EU-wide intellectual property rights (IPR).

[148] See Chapter 5.

[149] See, for example, *SEGRO and Horváth* (n 100).

[150] See Section 2.1.2 in Chapter 2.

treaties,[151] leading to fragmentation of EU regulation in the area of private law.[152]

Rights of investors under EU law are not absolute private law rights but rights that stem from the EU's exercise of its public law prerogatives. Accordingly, investors have only limited rights under EU law, derived from the obligation of Member States to comply with the fundamental freedoms.[153] For example, with respect to property rights, while Member States do have exclusive competence over property ownership,[154] their own system of property ownership is not a valid justification for obstacles to the exercise of freedoms guaranteed under the founding treaties.[155]

In addition, EU law attempts to harmonise substantive national rules on the functioning of the internal market across the EU. Harmonisation through secondary legislation is aimed at complementing the four freedoms and extending the reach of EU law to 'purely internal' situations to which free movement provisions otherwise do not apply.[156] Of particular importance for investors is the Services Directive that provides for specific obligations related to both services and establishment.[157] In interpreting this Directive, the CJEU has extended the freedom of establishment to internal situations, allowing domestic investors to challenge public law measures that are likely to hinder their establishment in intra-State situations.[158] In this regard, EU law aims at eliminating reverse discrimination between domestic and foreign investors, which is inherent to IIL.

Finally, the EU legal order is a constitutional order underpinned by fundamental rights, derived from the general principles of EU law and the EU Charter of Fundamental Rights (CFR). These rights are applicable whenever EU institutions act and Member States take national measures

[151] Arts. 114 and 115 TFEU (harmonisation of national rules affecting the internal market); Art. 153 TFEU (harmonisation of labour law); Art. 118 TFEU (IPR); Art. 50 TFEU (EU company law); Arts. 67 and 81 TFEU (judicial cooperation in civil matters); Art. 352 TFEU (the flexibility clause).

[152] European Parliamentary Research Service, 'EU Competence in Private Law' (2015) 14.

[153] P. Strik, *Shaping the Single European Market in the Field of Foreign Direct Investment* (CUP 2014) 197.

[154] Art. 345 TFEU.

[155] Case C-463/00 *Commission v Spain* [2003] ECR I-45, para. 67.

[156] Case 175/78 *Saunders* [1979] ECR 1129.

[157] Services Directive 2006/123 [2006] OJ L376/36. See recitals 43, 45, 47, and 48.

[158] Joined Cases C-360/15 and C-31/16 *Visser Vastgoed Beleggingen* [2018] OJ C 112/2, para. 115.

that fall within the scope of EU law.[159] Rights are therefore justiciable and can be invoked by litigants before EU courts and domestic courts, provided that the subject matter *is covered by EU law*.[160] However, these rights are not absolute and may be subject to restrictions.

#### 4.5.2.1 The Right to Property under EU Law

The CJEU has long recognised that the right to property under EU law is a general principle of EU law, which does not constitute an 'absolute prerogative' but must be viewed in relation to its social function.[161] Under EU law, the right to property is under Article 17 CFR a right to protection of lawfully acquired possessions. Dispossession is possible only in the public interest under conditions prescribed by law, and with the payment of fair compensation.[162] The Charter also recognises that the use of property may be regulated if it is necessary for the general interest,[163] thus also recognising the possibility of 'indirect' expropriation. The meaning and scope of the right to property in the CFR must be read consistently with Article 1, Protocol 1 of the ECHR.[164] The ECHR similarly recognises that deprivation of possession can only be in the public interest and subject to conditions provided for by law,[165] where States also retain the right to control the use of property in accordance with the general interest.[166] Thus, the right to property in the ECHR intends to achieve 'a fair balance between the demands of the general interests of the community and the requirements of the protection of the individual's fundamental rights'.[167]

The standard of compensation depends on the assessment of proportionality, so the ECHR does not guarantee a right to full compensation in all circumstances. Legitimate objectives of public interest designed to achieve greater social justice may lead to compensation below the full

[159] Case C-159/90 *Grogan* [1991] ECR I-4605, para. 31.

[160] Cf. CFR principles, which are obligations of the EU and Member States when implementing EU law. They cannot by themselves confer on individuals a subjective right which they may invoke as such: Case C-176/12 *Association de médiation sociale* ECLI:EU:C:2014:2, para. 45; Case C-356/12 *Glatzel* ECLI:EU:C:2014:350, para. 78.

[161] Case C-120/06 *FIAMM v Council and Commission* [2008] ECR I-6513, para. 183.

[162] Second sentence Art. 17(1) CFR.

[163] Third sentence Art. 17(1) CFR.

[164] Art. 52 CFR.

[165] Art. 1(1) Protocol 1 ECHR.

[166] Art. 1(2) Protocol 1 ECHR.

[167] *Mellacher and Others v Austria* App no 10522/83; 11011/84; 11070/84 (ECtHR, 19 December 1989) para. 48.

market value, where the Court's review is limited to 'ascertaining whether the choice of compensation terms falls outside the State's *wide* margin of appreciation'.[168] In the practice of the CJEU, the exercise of the right to property may be restricted, particularly in the context of the internal market, if restrictions correspond to 'objectives of general interest pursued by the EU' and they do not constitute with respect to their aim 'a disproportionate and intolerable interference which infringes upon the *very substance* of the rights guaranteed'.[169] Not providing compensation or a remedy in the legislation that does not fulfil these requirements and thus limits the property right can in itself constitute an infringement and gives rise to non-contractual liability.[170] However, only 'a sufficiently serious breach of the appellants' right to property, within the meaning of Article 17(1) CFR, can lead to such liability.[171]

Direct (*de iure*) expropriation fundamentally entails compensation, which can nevertheless be below market value. By contrast, indirect (*de facto*) expropriation can lead to either (below market value) compensation, or no compensation.[172] This is an important difference for investors who under IIL can claim the (fair) market value of their expropriated investment,[173] except in rare cases when the police powers doctrine applies, resulting in no compensation.[174] Therefore, while EU law is

168 *James and Others v United Kingdom* App no 8793/79 (ECtHR 21 February 1986) para. 54 (emphasis added).

169 C-548/09 P *Bank Melli Iran v Council* EU:C:2011:735, para. 114; Joined Cases C-8/15 P to C-10/15 P *Ledra Advertising v Commission and ECB* ECLI:EU:C:2016:701, para. 70; C-358/15 P *Bank of Industry and Mine v Council* EU:C:2016:338, para. 56. See Art. 52 (1) CFR.

170 *FIAMM* (n 161) para. 183.

171 *Ledra* (n 169) para. 68.

172 See, for instance, *James and Others v United Kingdom* (n 168) para. 54. For a scholarly opinion, see S. Kirchner and K. Geler-Noch, 'Compensation under the European Convention on Human Rights for Expropriations Enforced Prior to the Applicability of the Convention' (2012) 19 *Jurisprudence* 21, 25.

173 In cases of unlawful expropriation, States have a duty of full reparation to re-establish the situation which would have existed if the unlawful act had not been committed: *Case Concerning the Factory at Chorzów* (Germany v Poland) (Indemnity) [1928] PCIJ Rep Series A No 17; *Amco v Indonesia*, ICSID Case No. ARB/81/1, Award (5 June 1990). For methods of calculating damages, see H. Wöss and A. San Román, 'Full Compensation, Full Reparation and the But-For Premise' (*Global Arbitration Review* 29 November 2018). In essence, tribunals will award either market or fair market value (FMV). FMV does not consider the reduction in the value of the property due to distress, threat and economic crisis and thus leads to a higher compensation.

174 *Philip Morris v Uruguay*, ICSID Case No. ARB/10/7, Award (8 July 2016) para. 293.

more favourable to States in examining permissible limitations to private property, IIL mostly reflects the interests of the investors.[175]

For investors, interference with their property rights by national measures for economic governance across the EU is of particular importance, in particular with respect to instruments adopted under the European Stability Mechanism (ESM). Some intra-EU cases specifically deal with measures adopted by the Greek and Cypriot governments during their banking crises, which resulted in significant losses for investors.[176] Most of these measures have been adopted under the relevant Memorandum of Understanding (MoU) between the Troika and the Member State in need of financial assistance, and thus fall within exclusive Member State competence. Accordingly, acts of the ESM fall outside the EU legal order.[177] While measures adopted within the ESM framework would thus not be subject to review by the CJEU, the CJEU found that the *conduct* of EU institutions (the Commission and the ECB) linked to the adoption of an MoU on behalf of the ESM must be consistent with EU law. Consequently, the CJEU held that it has jurisdiction to review such conduct of EU institutions and to consider an action for compensation based on its unlawfulness under EU law.[178]

In the case of Cyprus, in its *Ledra* judgment the CJEU did not find that the measures imposed on investors under the MoU were illegal. The Court found that restrictions on investors' property rights were made in the pursuit of the legitimate EU objective. The measures aimed at ensuring stability of the banking system in the Eurozone, which could otherwise produce negative spill-over effects in other sectors of the economy.[179] The CJEU found that the measures satisfied the requirements of proportionality and did not constitute an 'intolerable interference impairing the very substance of the appellants' right to property'.[180] Accordingly, there was no breach of the CFR right to property due to the

[175] See Section 1.2.1 in Chapter 1.

[176] For example, *Theodoros Adamakopoulos, Ilektra Adamantidou, Vasileios Adamopoulos and Others v Republic of Cyprus*, ICSID Case No. ARB/15/49; *Poštová Banka, a.s. and Istrokapital SE v The Hellenic Republic*, ICSID Case No. ARB/13/8; and *Marfin Investment Group Holdings S.A., Alexandros Bakatselos and Others v Republic of Cyprus*, ICSID Case No. ARB/13/27.

[177] Case C-370/12 *Pringle* ECLI:EU:C:2012:756; *Ledra* (n 169) para. 54.

[178] In particular under Arts. 268 and 340(2) and (3) TFEU: *Ledra* (n 169) para. 55. Moreover, the Commission, as the guardian of the treaties, has a duty to refrain from signing an MoU when it doubts its consistency with EU law: ibid paras. 57–59.

[179] ibid para. 72.

[180] ibid para. 74.

MoU measures, no liability of EU institutions for any unlawful conduct and no right to compensation for investors.

While IIL arguably provides investors with more protections,[181] it does not guarantee their absolute protection against restrictive stabilisation measures.[182] The judgment in *Ledra* demonstrates that even measures falling within exclusive Member States' competence can be indirectly reviewed by the CJEU. The judgment is thus an important testament for the rule of law in the EU. However, intra-EU investors might be less enthusiastic about the practical effects of the judgment (the lack of compensation) and the CJEU's approach to private property restrictions that 'genuinely meet the objectives of general interest'.[183] It cannot be excluded that in the future the CJEU might not repurpose such interest to other legitimate objectives pursued by the EU (e.g. the fight against climate change)[184] as the Court finds fit.

#### 4.5.2.2 The Principle of Legitimate Expectations under EU Law

European Union law protects the legitimate expectations of investors. State acts must not violate the legitimate expectations of investors and must carefully balance them against the public interest. The CJEU has recognised that legitimate expectations are a basic principle of EU law, whose breach gives rise to actions for damages for non-contractual State or EU liability.[185] This principle is rooted in the principle of legal certainty. Legitimate expectations arise when the investor receives precise, unconditional and consistent assurances from the State.[186] Therefore, national legislation breaches legal certainty and protection of legitimate expectations when it suddenly and unexpectedly withdraws existing rights, without allowing the rights-holders the necessary time to adjust.[187]

[181] See *Achmea*, Opinion of AG Wathelet (n 144) paras. 185–190.

[182] In the cases of *Poštová Banka* and *Marfin* (n 176) tribunals decided in favour of the State.

[183] *Ledra* (n 169) para. 70.

[184] See discussion on EU values and objectives in Section 7.1 in Chapter 7.

[185] Case T-199/99 *Sgaravatti Mediterranea Srl v Commission of the European Communities* [2002] ECR II-3731, paras. 111–117. The case law on legitimate expectations in EU law is extensive and beyond the scope of this section.

[186] Case C-566/14 P *Marchiani v Parliament* ECLI:EU:C:2016:437, para. 77; Joined Cases T-50/06 RENV II and T-69/06 RENV II *Ireland v Commission* ECLI:EU:T:2016:227, para. 213.

[187] Case C-332/14 *Wolfgang und Wilfried Rey Grundstücksgemeinschaft GbR* ECLI:EU:C:2016:417, paras. 56–58.

However, this does not entail that legal positions cannot be absolutely altered, particularly in the field of investment, where there is a need for constant legal adjustment to economic reality.[188] On the other hand, investors can rely on their legitimate expectations when they act in a 'prudent and circumspect' manner.[189] The principle of legitimate expectations under EU law also requires the legality of national measures. When a diligent investor knew or should reasonably have known that the rules on which they relied were contrary to EU law, the protection cannot be invoked.[190] In the same manner, when a Member State grants State aid to investors contrary to its obligations under EU law in Articles 107 and 108 TFEU, legitimate expectations that the aid is lawful and will be paid cannot be entertained. Additionally, any award of compensation by an arbitral tribunal, on the basis that legitimate expectations (FET standard) have been breached due to State's modification of an illegal State aid scheme, could constitute State aid in itself.[191]

The circumstances in which investors can rely on legitimate expectations under EU law are thus more restrictive than under the fair and equitable treatment (FET) standard in IIL. The Energy Charter Treaty (ECT) renewable energy cases against Spain but also Italy have served as a prime example of differences between the concept of legitimate expectations under EU law and IIL. The CJEU established that under secondary EU law Member States are free to adopt, alter or withdraw their support schemes as long as they do not breach freedom to conduct a business and the right to property guaranteed in Articles 16 and 17 of the CFR, respectively.[192] Moreover, Member States retain their discretionary powers and economic operators cannot justifiably

[188] Case C-526/14 *Kotnik and Others* ECLI:EU:C:2016:570, paras. 66 and 68; Joined Cases C-37/02 and C-38/02 *Di Lenardo and Dilexport* [2004] ECR I-6911, para. 70; Case C-310/04 *Spain v Council* [2006] ECR I-7285, para. 81; Case C-201/08 *Plantanol* [2009] ECR I-8343, para. 53.

[189] *Plantanol* paras. 53–57.

[190] Case C-169/95 *Spain v Commission* [1997] ECR I-135, para. 51.

[191] See Case SA.40348 (2015/NN) Commission Decision C (2017) 7384 final, paras. 158, 164–165. See also Case SA.54155 (2021/NN) Commission Decision C (2021) 5405 final. Cf. *Infrastructure Services Luxembourg S.à.r.l. and Energia Termosolar B.V. (formerly Antin) v Spain*, ICSID Case No. ARB/13/31, Award (15 June 2018).

[192] See Joined Cases C-798/18 and C-799/18 *Anie and Others* ECLI:EU:C:2021:280; Joined Cases C-306/19, C-512/19, C-595/19 and C-608/20 to C-610/20 *Milis Energy SpA and Others* ECLI:EU:C:2022:164.

claim legitimate expectations that an existing situation which may be altered in the exercise of such powers will be maintained.[193] The manner in which the Italian legislation was drafted indicated to a 'prudent and circumspect economic operator' that the incentives at issue were not guaranteed, could be altered or withdrawn, and were thus foreseeable.[194] In light of the principles of legal certainty and the protection of legitimate expectations under EU law, these incentives, which were not yet due, thus did not fall within the scope of property rights nor did they limit the freedom to conduct a business, as guaranteed under the CFR.[195] In addition to a more restrictive concept of legal certainty and legitimate expectations, the level of compensation is also less lucrative under EU law, as it usually amounts to reasonable costs that the investor incurred due to its reliance on government assurances, without taking into account the investor's interest in the future performance.[196]

### 4.5.3 *Enforcement and Remedies*

European Union law establishes relevant enforcement mechanisms to ensure its full effectiveness. While EU law creates new substantive *rights*, national laws provide procedural *remedies* for the enforcement of these rights.

The Treaty provisions on the prohibition of restrictions of free establishment and the free movement of capital have direct effect.[197] Accordingly, they can be relied upon by individuals and invoked before the national and EU courts. While vertically binding on States, it is less clear when these Treaty provisions are also horizontally applicable in relations between private parties. With respect to freedom of services and

[193] *Anie* (n 192) para. 42 and case law cited.

[194] ibid paras. 46, 53.

[195] ibid paras. 54, 61, 64–65. The CJEU thus also confirmed the conclusions of the Italian Constitutional Court, Decision No. 16/2017 (24 January 2017), which upheld the legality of the provisions under the Italian Constitution. Cf. *Greentech Energy Systems A/S, et al v Italian Republic*, SCC Case No. V 2015/095, Final Award (23 December 2018); *CEF Energia BV v Italian Republic*, SCC Case No. 158/2015, Award (16 January 2019).

[196] Strik (n 153) 197; *Anie* (n 192) para. 39.

[197] Joined Cases C-163/94, C-165/94 and C-250/94 *Sanz de Lera* [1995] ECR I-4821, para. 43.

establishment, the CJEU has confirmed their horizontal effect in very specific situations.[198] However, the horizontal effect of free movement of capital is less likely.[199]

With respect to private parties, Member States must ensure the full effectiveness of EU rules within their respective jurisdictions, including the availability of appropriate legal remedies for the protection of individuals' rights guaranteed under EU law and the access to domestic courts for their enforcement. Member States can be held liable for the loss or damage caused to individuals as a result of breaches of EU law and be ordered to pay compensation.[200] State liability extends to liability for all violations of EU law, even those that follow from legislative acts[201] or national court rulings.[202] However, in principle national courts assess whether a breach of EU law is sufficiently serious for a Member State to incur non-contractual liability vis-à-vis an individual.

In their mutual relations Member States are bound by the principle of mutual trust.[203] This includes trust that the courts and tribunals of each Member State guarantee the right to an effective remedy before an independent tribunal, as outlined in Article 47 CFR.[204] Accordingly, the level of justice across different EU Member States should be the same. The CJEU takes seriously any attempts that could undermine the independence of judiciary in the EU, even in politically sensitive issues,[205] albeit investors might be less convinced about their level of protection before domestic courts in the EU.

Before turning to concluding remarks for this chapter, Table 4.3 summarises and compares the facets of investment under IIL and EU law.

[198] Case C-341/05 *Laval un Partneri* [2007] ECR I-11767 (freedom of services) and Case C-438/05 *The International Transport Workers' Federation and The Finnish Seamen's Union* [2007] ECR I-10779 (freedom of establishment). Both cases included actions of companies against trade unions. See Craig and de Búrca (n 117) 798–799.

[199] Barnard (n 80) 526.

[200] *Francovich* (n 45) paras. 31–35. This is also called the doctrine of governmental liability.

[201] *Brasserie du Pêcheur and Factorame III* (n 45).

[202] Case C-224/01 *Köbler* [2003] ECR I-10239; Case C-160/14 *Ferreira da Silva e Birto and Others* ECLI:EU:C:2015:565; Case C-168/15 *Tomášová* ECLI:EU:C:2016:602; Case C-620/17 *Hochtief Solutions AG* ECLI:EU:C:2019:630.

[203] Art. 19(1) TEU.

[204] Opinion 1/17 (n 24) para. 128.

[205] See, for example, C-619/18 *Commission v Poland* ECLI:EU:C:2019:615.

Table 4.3 *Investment protections under international investment law and EU law*

| Category | International investment law | Investment in EU law (internal market rules) |
|---|---|---|
| **Definition of investment** | • Treaty specific definition of investment<br>- Usually broad definition<br>- Can include contractual obligations (umbrella clauses)<br>- Includes FDI + portfolio<br>• Additional criteria for ICSID jurisdiction: (i) a substantial contribution of money and resources, (ii) a certain duration, (iii) risk and (iv) the contribution to the economic development of the host State | • Definition of capital and establishment<br>• *Capital*: capital movement rules apply intra-EU and extra-EU (Arts. 63–66 TFEU)<br>- All types of economic assets which involve border crossing<br>- Financial operations essentially concerned with the investment of funds<br>- Includes FDI + portfolio<br>• *Establishment*: freedom of intra-EU establishment of companies/firms and agencies/branches/ subsidiaries (Arts. 49–55 TFEU)<br>- Characteristics:<br>(i) managerial control over the establishment;<br>(ii) profit-making;<br>(iii) permanent link with the host Member State<br>- Presupposes economic activity<br>- Includes FDI only |
| **Definition of foreign investor** | • Applies to **all investments**<br>• Natural persons: nationality (law of the home State)<br>• Corporate nationality: **place of incorporation; effective seat; managerial control** | • Not relevant for free movement of goods and capital<br>• Applies to **freedom of establishment and services** only<br>- For natural persons: nationality (law of the Member States)<br>- Corporate nationality: **place of incorporation and effective seat** |

Table 4.3 (*cont.*)

| Category | International investment law | Investment in EU law (internal market rules) |
| --- | --- | --- |
| **Phase of investment** | • Focus on treatment of investment in post-establishment phase<br>• Pre-establishment costs usually excluded from definition of investment | • Pre-establishment (market access) and post-admission treatment: subject to intra-EU liberalisation and NT (non-discrimination) under EU law = free movement and four freedoms apply<br>• Post-establishment: subject to domestic law and EU law protections = internal market negative and positive harmonisation |
| **Mechanisms and level of protection** | • Rather similar substantive and procedural standards of investors' protection across different IIAs<br>• No annulment of illegal measure as a remedy<br>• Relevance of the effect of the measure on economic value of investment (no threshold)<br>• Compensation based on market value<br>• Enforcement under ICSID and New York Convention (applies worldwide in States signatories) | • Twenty-seven different substantive and procedural law mechanisms for protection of investors across the EU<br>• Breach leads to annulment of illegal measure<br>• Only 'sufficiently serious' breach of EU law warrants compensation<br>• 'Fair' compensation (can be below market value)<br>• EU rules (Brussels I Regulation) and national rules and procedures of the Member State of enforcement (limited to the EU) |

## 4.6 Conclusion

Investment protection mechanisms in the EU legal order appear less attractive to intra-EU investors than protections under IIL for several reasons.

*First*, the logic underlying EU law and IIL is fundamentally different. While *prima facie* both legal orders demonstrate interest in economic activity, EU law has essentially developed around the objective of EU integration. Its main paradigm has been market liberalisation, although since the Lisbon Treaty and in particular its CFR, there is more emphasis on private rights. The fragmented nature of EU competences to regulate rights and the tendency to address rights from an economic-functionalist perspective[206] renders EU law very different to IIL. The main objective of IIL has been the creation of private rights for investors. International investment law's logic thus endorses the private law perspective of regulating the relationship between foreign investors as private parties and the State, which is different to regulating the internal market. While the former aims at creating protections for a certain category of private parties, the latter's focus is on creating a level playing field for the purposes of fair competition. The logic of the two legal orders is thus not only divergent but also in contradiction.

*Second*, investment protection mechanisms under EU law are scattered between EU and national laws. The numerous exceptions from fundamental freedoms under national laws compound the complexity of investors' protections in the EU. While protections under IIL are far from coherent, they are nevertheless more uniform, having their source in a particular bilateral treaty. National law primarily serves as a matter of fact which has to be proved in the investment treaty arbitration (ITA) proceedings, and it is not a source of rights for investors.[207]

*Third*, investment protections under EU law display a diversity of standards across the EU, which still largely depend on national laws of Member States, in particular when harmonisation has been achieved through directives. Available remedies remain the prerogative of the Member States. There are no common EU rules on damages or lost profit. There is an assumption that all national courts are equally effective

[206] European Parliamentary Research Service (n 152) 20.

[207] In particular, ICSID tribunals are fully internationalised as they do not apply national law despite provision of the ICSID Convention in Art. 42(1), second sentence. See H. E. Kjos, *Applicable Law in Investor–State Arbitration: The Interplay between National and International Law* (OUP 2013) 62.

in providing judicial protection. On the contrary, IIL displays more uniformity while providing similar substantive and procedural standards of protection, despite the diversity of IIAs.

Accordingly, it remains arguable whether EU Treaties and intra-EU IIAs cover the 'same subject matter'.[208] Investment tribunals have dismissed this argument.[209] Nevertheless, it is undisputable that EU law and IIL overlap, with EU law being broader in its general scope. Investors' rights, such as the (in)famous FET standard, are still guaranteed under EU law albeit being differently framed.

While investors can be certain that the CJEU's stringent approach to free movement derogations and the general principles of EU law, such as legal certainty, non-discrimination, proportionality and protection of legitimate expectations, will protect them from arbitrary economic policy measures of Member States, they can be less certain that their protection will be equally unqualified when the CJEU pursues the attainment of EU policy objectives. In this regard, the CJEU's approach is not different from any other State supreme court protecting its own constitutional order. Tensions between EU law and IIL turned problematic only when intra-EU BITs became an impediment to the internal market and the objectives of EU integration. These tensions are discussed in more detail in the next chapter.

[208] This has proven to be of relevance in the context of the application of Arts. 30 (Application of successive treaties related to the same subject matter) and 59 (Termination or suspension of the operation of a treaty implied by conclusion of a later treaty) VCLT.

[209] See Section 5.2.1.2 in Chapter 5.

# 5

# 'International' Investment in the EU

## Intra-EU Investment Agreements and Dispute Settlement

In this chapter we examine how international investment law (IIL) in relations between the Member States poses a challenge to EU law and its autonomy, hindering internal market integration as one of the core EU objectives, and the rule of law in the EU as its core value. We analyse tensions between IIL and EU law, focusing first on intra-EU international investment agreements (IIAs) and the objectives of EU integration, and second on intra-EU investment treaty arbitration (ITA) and the autonomy of the EU legal order. The *Achmea* judgment of the Court of Justice of the European Union (CJEU) is the apotheosis of these tensions, and it has been endorsed in subsequent CJEU judgments. In the final part of this chapter, we analyse legal and policy implications of this jurisprudence, in the broader context of EU integration and the rule of law in the EU.

## 5.1 Tensions between Intra-EU IIAs and the Objectives of EU Integration

### *5.1.1 Intra-EU BITs and Their Political Dimension*

Intra-EU bilateral investment treaties (BITs) have become a political and a legal problem in the EU following the 2004 accession of Central and Eastern European (CEE) States to the EU. Before joining the EU, these prospective Member States were encouraged to conclude BITs with the Member States.[1] Embracing the traditional investor-State dispute settlement (ISDS) narrative, BITs were intended to establish 'a favourable climate for private investment, both domestic and foreign' in the

[1] See, for example, Art. 64 of the European Agreement establishing an association between the European Economic Communities and their Member States, of the one part, and Romania, of the other part [1994] OJ L357/2.

candidate countries.[2] The accession to the EU did not imply a duty to terminate BITs. Only in the case of Croatia, which joined the EU in 2013, the termination of intra-EU BITs was raised as a legal obligation; however, due to political reasons it was enforced as an obligation of means. Austria explicitly rejected the mutual termination of its BIT with Croatia as it held that they were not in contradiction with EU law, and similar positions were taken by Germany, France and the United Kingdom.[3]

Political sensitivity of intra-EU BITs and divergent positions of Member States first emerged in EU policy documents.[4] In 2006, the European Commission (EC) noted that 'arbitration risks and discriminatory treatment of investors' stem from intra-EU BITs, the content of which was partly 'superseded by Community law upon accession'. It invited Member States to review the need for these agreements 'in order to avoid legal uncertainties'.[5] As noted in 2007 and 2008, 'most Member States' did not share the EC's concerns, with a 'clear majority' preferring to maintain intra-EU BITs.[6] At that stage, it was also an accepted view that any concerns should be addressed through bilateral actions, rather than more coordinated action at the EU level.[7]

With the conferral of competence for foreign investment on the EU in the Lisbon Treaty,[8] the EC took a more proactive stance in 'monitoring developments' and 'tak[ing] the appropriate action'.[9] The EC's concerns were raised in all subsequent Economic and Financial Committee of the Council of the EU (EFC) reports but this had limited effects.[10] The split

[2] Art. 85 Stabilisation and Association Agreement between the European Communities and their Member States, of the one part, and the Republic of Croatia, of the other part [2005] OJ L26/3.

[3] Government of the Republic of Croatia, Answer to the written question posed by MP Goran Aleksic in relation to a proceeding before ICSID in Washington (October 2017) (in Croatian).

[4] The annual reports of the Economic and Financial Committee of the Council of the EU (EFC) provide a historical overview of the Commission's concerns and Member States' responses in relation to intra-EU BITs.

[5] 2007 EFC Report to the Commission and the Council on the Movement of Capital and the Freedom of Payments (8 January 2008) 5123/08, para. 14.

[6] ibid para. 15; 2008 EFC Report to the Commission and the Council on the Movement of Capital and the Freedom of Payments (17 December 2008) 17363/08, para. 16.

[7] 2007 EFC Report (n 5) para. 15; 2008 EFC Report (n 6) para. 17.

[8] See Chapter 6.

[9] 2009 EFC Report to the Commission and the Council on the Movement of Capital and the Freedom of Payments (10 December 2009) 17446/09, para. 18.

[10] Some Member States unilaterally denounced their intra-EU BITs in an earlier stage, notably Ireland and Italy in 2012 and 2013, respectively.

between the Member States was along political lines, between those Member States that are investors' countries of origin and those that regularly appear as respondent States.[11] The Commission used its legal powers to compel some Member States to terminate their BITs but its actions were suspended in light of the pending *Achmea* proceedings before the CJEU. The CJEU's judgment facilitated the achievement of political consensus on the termination of intra-EU BITs.[12]

### 5.1.2 Intra-EU BITs and Their Legal Status under EU Law

Intra-EU BITs are international agreements of Member States, which are valid under international law and form part of the national legal orders of Member States. Primacy of EU law over the national laws of Member States, and thus also over Member States' international agreements, is enshrined in the case law of the CJEU[13] and is codified in Declaration 17 of the Treaty of Lisbon.[14] Accordingly, Member States cannot enter into international agreements which would contain commitments capable of jeopardising the attainment of the EU objectives or affecting EU rules.[15] The principle of primacy equally applies to international treaties concluded between a Member State and a non-Member State that after the conclusion of the agreement acceded to the EU.[16] While EU law cannot invalidate international agreements, it imposes a number of obligations on Member States, regarding both their *inter se* as well as agreements concluded with third States.

Primary EU law does not affect the duties of the Member States towards third parties under their international agreements, preserving the general principle *pacta sunt servanda*.[17] However, Member States still have the obligation to take all necessary steps to eliminate any incompatibilities between their pre-accession international obligations and EU

[11] See Case C-284/16 *Achmea*, Opinion of AG Wathelet ECLI:EU:C:2017:699, paras. 34–38.

[12] See Section 5.2.2.

[13] See Chapter 4.

[14] Consolidated version of the Treaty on the Functioning of the European Union – Declarations annexed to the Final Act of the Intergovernmental Conference which adopted the Treaty of Lisbon, signed on 13 December 2007 – A. Declarations concerning provisions of the treaties – 17. Declaration concerning primacy [2008] OJ C 115/344.

[15] Case 22/70 *AETR* [1971] ECR 263, paras. 17, 22; Opinion 2/91 [1993] ECR I–1061, paras. 10–11.

[16] Case C-478/07 *Budějovický Budvar* [2009] ECR I-7721, paras. 97–99.

[17] Art. 351(1) TFEU.

law,[18] and where this is not possible, an obligation to denounce such international agreements is not excluded.[19] Regarding Member States' *inter se* agreements, the position is the same as with Member States' national laws:[20] EU law takes unconditional precedence. The provisions of these agreements cannot affect EU law, nor could a private party rely on such an agreement to justify a breach of EU law.[21] In the same manner as a conflicting national norm, a norm of a Member State's *inter se* international agreement that conflicts with EU law does not become invalid but *inapplicable*; accordingly, it must be 'disapplied' by the national judge. Importantly, the foreign interests of Member States cannot override their obligation to align their international agreements with EU law.[22]

From the perspective of EU law, Member States' BITs cannot be applied whenever they conflict with EU law. This is a logical consequence of the modus in which the EU legal order operates as a whole. Member States could not be permitted to diverge from internal market rules by an international treaty any more than they could by domestic legislation.[23] With this in view, some intra-EU BITs have an explicit clause recognising the primacy of EU law over the BIT in question.[24]

### *5.1.3 The Energy Charter Treaty and EU Law*

The Energy Charter Treaty (ECT) is a multilateral IIA to which twenty-six Member States (all except Italy), as well as the EU, are parties.[25] Concluded in the 1990s,[26] at the time it was a geopolitically important mechanism aimed at facilitating the political and economic transition of energy markets after the fall of communism in Eastern Europe. The EU,

[18] Art. 351(2) TFEU.

[19] Case C-62/98 *Commission v Portugal* [2000] ERC I-5171, paras. 44, 49–50; Case C-84/98 *Commission v Portugal* [2000] ERC I-5215, paras. 53, 58–59.

[20] See, for example, Case C-235/87 *Matteucci* [1988] ECR 5589, para. 22; Case 3/91 *Exportur SA v Lor SA and Confiserie du Tech SA* [1992] ECR 1-5529, para. 8; Case 10/61 *Commission v Italy* [1962] ECR 1, para. 23.

[21] Case T-70/89 *BBC v Commission* [1991] ECR II-335, para. 77.

[22] P. Eeckhout, *External Relations of the European Union, Legal and Constitutional Foundations* (OUP 2004) 342.

[23] See, for example, *Matteucci* (n 20) paras. 19–22.

[24] For example, Art. 11(2) Austria–Croatia BIT 1997.

[25] See J. Kleinheisterkamp, 'Investment Protection and EU Law: The Intra- and Extra-EU Dimension of the Energy Charter Treaty' (2012) 15 *Journal of International Economic Law* 85.

[26] 2080 UNTS 95 (adopted 17 December 1994, entered into force 16 April 1998). In late 2022, a number of Member States announced their decisions to withdraw from the ECT.

which then had twelve Member States and none of which the former communist CEE States, played a 'major role' in facilitating the conclusion of the ECT. Its intra-EU economic interests were aligned: while ensuring Member States' expansion into new markets, the ECT was intended to guarantee sustainable supply of energy in Europe.[27]

The ECT was concluded as an EU external agreement but effectively it was also an intra-EU agreement concluded between all EU Member States.[28] As the EU is its Contracting Party, the ECT is a source of EU law,[29] and prevails over secondary EU law and national legislation of Member States. Accordingly, EU secondary legislation in the area of energy must be interpreted in a manner that is consistent with the ECT.[30] The ECT binds Member States as a matter of EU law and international law but it cannot override the primacy of the EU founding treaties under EU law.

Since the conclusion of the ECT, EU secondary law acts have profoundly changed the EU internal energy market, transforming it into a single market.[31] While arguably still relevant for global energy markets, the added value of the ECT in the intra-EU context has thus significantly diminished.[32] However, the ECT remains an effective tool of intra-EU investors, with most of the ITA cases under the ECT being intra-EU ITAs.[33]

## 5.2 Tensions between Intra-EU Investment Treaty Arbitration and the Autonomy of the EU Legal Order

### *5.2.1 The International Investment Law Perspective: Concurrent Intra-EU Jurisdiction of Arbitral Tribunals*

Since the first United Nations Commission on International Trade Law (UNCITRAL) arbitration of *Eastern Sugar v Czech Republic*[34] under the

[27] EC, 'ECT, Background Note' (16 December 1994) MEMO/94/75.

[28] *Achmea*, Opinion of AG Wathelet (n 11) 43. Italy withdrew from the ECT in 2016.

[29] See Case C-264/09 *Commission v Slovakia*, Opinion of AG Jääskinen ECLI:EU:2011:150, paras. 60–63.

[30] Case C-61/94 *Commission v Germany* [1996] ECR I-3989, para. 52.

[31] See L. Hancher and P. Larouche, 'The Coming of Age of EU Regulation of Network Industries and Services of General Economic Interest' in P. Craig and G. de Búrca (eds), *The Evolution of EU Law* (2nd ed., OUP 2011) 752–756.

[32] The success of the ECT inevitably must be assessed in the context of Russia, a major signatory of the ECT, which never ratified it and withdrew from the ECT in 2009. For external aspects of the ECT, see Section 8.3 in Chapter 8.

[33] The Secretariat of the ECT, 'Statistics of the ECT Cases' (10 January 2023).

[34] *Eastern Sugar BV (Netherlands) v The Czech Republic*, UNCITRAL arbitration SCC No. 088/2004, Partial Award (27 March 2007).

Netherlands–Czech Republic BIT in 2004, Member States, supported by the EC as *amicus curiae*, have been challenging the jurisdiction of arbitral tribunals in intra-EU ITAs under both intra-EU BITs and the ECT. They have claimed that intra-EU IIAs have been superseded by EU law under the general Vienna Convention on the Law of Treaties (VCLT) rules[35] or special conflict clauses in EU law or IIAs.[36] Three main issues have been considered in decisions on intra-EU jurisdiction of arbitral tribunals in order to determine the applicability of intra-EU BITs and the ECT: (i) whether Member States intended that in *inter se* relations EU law supersedes intra-EU IIAs; (ii) whether intra-EU IIAs and EU law deal with the same subject matter; and (iii) whether intra-EU IIAs are inconsistent with the EU legal order. In all but one intra-EU ECT case seated in Stockholm, investment tribunals confirmed their jurisdiction for intra-EU disputes under both intra-EU BITs and the ECT.[37]

#### 5.2.1.1 The Application of Intra-EU IIAs or EU Treaties in *Inter Se* Relations of Member States

Tribunals rejected the argument of Member States that the application of EU law instead of the BITs was intended in their mutual relations from the date of their accession to the EU,[38] thus terminating intra-EU BITs in accordance with Article 59 VCLT. Tribunals relied on the *explicit* provisions of the Accession Treaty, in which they found no provisions terminating the intra-EU BITs.[39] In addition, parties gave no notice to terminate the intra-EU BITs,[40] nor was there a *common* intention between them[41] or a consensus within the EU on the status of these agreements, as required under Article 59 VCLT.[42] Even if intra-EU BITs were terminated under

35 Arts. 30 and 59 VCLT.

36 Art. 351 TFEU.

37 *Green Power K/S and Obton A/S v Spain*, SCC Case No. 2016/135, Award (22 June 2022) and analysis in Section 5.3.3. See also *Theodoros Adamakopoulos and Others v Republic of Cyprus*, ICSID Case No. ARB/15/49, Statement of Dissent of Professor Marcelo G. Kohen (3 February 2020) under an intra-EU BIT.

38 See Arts. 2 and 6 of the Act of Accession (which is part of the Treaty of Accession) of the Czech Republic, Estonia, Cyprus, Latvia, Lithuania, Hungary, Malta, Poland, Slovenia and the Slovak Republic [2003] OJ L236/33; Arts. 2 and 6 of the Act of Accession of Bulgaria and Romania [2005] OJ L157/203; Arts. 2 and 6 of the Act of Accession of the Republic of Croatia [2012] OJ L112/21.

39 *Eastern Sugar* (n 34) paras. 147–148.

40 ibid para. 153.

41 ibid para. 167 (emphasis in the original).

42 *Rupert Joseph Binder v Czech Republic*, UNCITRAL, Award on Jurisdiction (6 June 2007) para. 64.

Article 59 VCLT, it was considered that sunset clauses could have continued to apply under Article 70(1) VCLT[43] for another ten, fifteen or twenty years from 2004, depending on the particular BIT.

In the context of the ECT, the respondent Member States and the EC claimed that only relations between the Member States and third States (extra-EU) were intended to be governed by the ECT. The possibility of an intra-EU claim under the ECT was accordingly *ab initio* excluded,[44] in particular in the fields that were harmonised by EU law.[45] In addition, the EU as a Regional Economic Integration Organisation (REIO) should be seen as a 'single investment area' and accordingly, the offer to arbitrate made by the Member States in the ECT ISDS clause must be interpreted as if that offer is made *only* to third State investors.[46] However, intra-EU ECT tribunals have rejected this interpretation relying on the interpretative rules in Articles 31 and 32 VCLT.[47] First, they reasoned that the ECT language does not support the exclusion of intra-EU claims and that no limitation on the Member States' competence was communicated at the time when the ECT was signed.[48] In addition, such interpretation would also be contrary to Article 46 VCLT.[49] Second, EU Member States, while being members of the REIO, have not lost their national Member

[43] *Eastern Sugar* (n 34) paras. 175–177.

[44] *Eskosol S.P.A. in liquidazione v Italian Republic*, ICSID Case No. ARB/15/50, Decision on Termination Request and Intra-EU Objection (7 May 2019) para. 65, citing the EC's submission.

[45] This is because, in accordance with the AETR-ERTA doctrine, Member States have transferred their external competence in the field of energy to the EU through internal regulation: see Section 6.1.2 in Chapter 6. From an international law perspective, an explicit disconnection clause in this case would have added transparency towards third parties although it would not be necessary from an EU law perspective. See M. Cremona, 'Disconnection Clauses in EU Law and Practice' in C. Hillion and P. Koutrakos (eds), *Mixed Agreements Revisited, the EU and Its Member States in the World* (Hart 2010) 179–181.

[46] *Eskosol* (n 44) para. 62, citing the EC's submission.

[47] Only the main arguments are briefly summarised here. For detailed reasoning, see for example, *Vattenfall AB and Others v Federal Republic of Germany (II)*, ICSID Case No. ARB/12/12, Decision on *Achmea* issue (31 August 2018) and *Eskosol* (n 44).

[48] *Blusun S.A., Jean-Pierre Lecorcier and Michael Stein v Italian Republic*, ICSID Case No. ARB/14/3, Final Award (27 December 2016) para. 283. Cf. *Green Power* (n 37) paras. 358, 362.

[49] See *Eskosol* (n 44) para. 89. However, the division of competence between the EU and Member States could be considered 'a rule of fundamental importance', given the powers of the CJEU to invalidate acts based on an improper legal basis: see Chapter 6.

State character.[50] Finally, in the absence of an explicit disconnection clause, inapplicability of the ECT in the relations between Member States cannot be implied and would be contrary to the purpose of the ECT, which was intended to apply unconditionally and integrally.[51]

The next issue is whether the successive EU Treaties (Treaty of Amsterdam, Treaty of Nice, Treaty of Lisbon and all Member States' accession treaties) have superseded intra-EU BITs and the ECT in accordance with the general (Article 30 VCLT) and special conflict rules[52] in international law. Under EU law, the special conflict rule is primacy,[53] enshrined in Article 351 of Treaty on the Functioning of the European Union (TFEU). According to the interpretation of the CJEU, *a contrario* reasoning of Article 351(1) renders inapplicable the *pacta sunt servanda* guarantee otherwise applicable to international treaties concluded between EU Member States and third States.[54] The International Law Commission (ILC) has sided with this interpretation, acknowledging that the EU Treaty takes 'absolute precedence over agreements that Member States have concluded between themselves'.[55] However, in the intra-EU context, in particular under the ECT, only two tribunals found this reasoning convincing,[56] while others ruled in favour of the 'clearer'

[50] *Vattenfall II* (n 47) para. 181; *Eiser Infrastructure v Spain*, ICSID Case No. ARB/13/36, Final Award (4 May 2017). Indeed, Member States are Parties to the ECT in their own right.

[51] See Arts. 46 and 26 ECT and *RREEF Infrastructure (G.P.) Limited and RREEF Pan-European Infrastructure Two Lux S.a.r.l. v Kingdom of Spain*, ICSID ARB/13/30, Decision on jurisdiction (6 June 2016) para. 85. For remarks on the EU's 1998 statement made to the ECT Secretariat, see *Eskosol* (n 44) paras. 92–93. The *travaux préparatoires* reveal that the EU had proposed the insertion of a disconnection clause, which was ultimately dropped from the draft ECT: *Vattenfall II* (n 47) para. 205. Cf. *Green Power* (n 37) para. 409.

[52] Art. 351 TFEU, Art. 16 ECT and conflict rules in individual intra-EU BITs. See for example, Art. 3(5) Netherlands–Czech Republic BIT (signed 29 April 1991, entered into force 1 October 1992) and Art. 11(2) Austria–Croatia BIT (signed 19 February 1997, entered into force 1 November 1999).

[53] See Chapter 4.

[54] See Case C-264/09 *Commission v Slovakia* ECLI:EU:C:2011:580, para. 41; Case C-147/03 *Commission v Austria* ECLI:EU:C:2005:427, para. 58.

[55] ILC, 'Fragmentation of International Law: Difficulties Arising from the Diversification and Expansion of International Law' (2006) Report of the Study Group, UN Doc A/CN.4/L682, para. 283 and seq.

[56] See *Electrabel S.A. v Republic of Hungary*, ICSID Case No. ARB/07/19, Decision on Jurisdiction, Applicable Law and Liability (30 November 2012) para. 4.183; *Green Power* (n 37) para. 496.

ECT conflict rule in Article 16 ECT,[57] which prohibits the terms of another agreement being *construed* so as to derogate from the investors' rights under the ECT.[58] Given that the ECT is more favourable to investors, tribunals have concluded that Article 16 poses 'an insurmountable obstacle' to supremacy of EU law over the ECT.[59]

In most cases, tribunals have relied on the general conflict rule in Article 30 VCLT to determine the primacy between different treaties. This provision was interpreted as requiring two cumulative criteria: 'sameness' of the subject matter; and incompatibility. They held that either the subject matter of the intra-EU IIAs and the EU Treaties is not the same, or there is no conflict between their provisions, or both. These criteria are discussed next.

#### 5.2.1.2 Intra-EU BITs and EU Treaties Dealing with the Same Subject-Matter

International investment law and EU law overlap in many aspects. Substantive protections in intra-EU IIAs overlap with EU law provisions on freedom of establishment, free movement of capital and the Charter of Fundamental Rights (CFR) provisions.[60] In the specific ECT context, secondary EU legislation has harmonised energy and gas markets within the EU, replacing a much less integrated regime under the ECT.[61] The CJEU jurisprudence on renewable energy support schemes also demonstrates that the subject matter considered before the ECT arbitral

[57] See, for example, the reasoning of the *Vattenfall II* Tribunal: *Vattenfall II* (n 47) paras. 225–229.

[58] However, given its reference to 'construing' rights, Art. 16 could be understood as an interpretative rather than a conflict rule.

[59] *Vattenfall II* (n 47) para. 229. The Tribunal applied Art. 16 ECT as both a rule of treaty interpretation (to support the Tribunal's jurisdiction under Art. 26 ECT: see para. 194) and a conflict rule (to establish the supremacy of the ECT over EU law and to assert the supremacy of Art. 16 as a conflict rule in the ECT over Art. 351 TFEU). Accordingly, any later treaty (*lex posterior* rule under Art. 30 VCLT) or any modifications of the ECT by a later treaty would not be allowed in light of Art. 16 ECT: paras. 217, 221. Cf. *Green Power* (n 37) para. 470.

[60] See Chapter 4.

[61] Of importance is the Electricity Market Design (part of the Clean Energy for all Europeans Package), in particular: EP and Council Directive (EC) 2019/944 concerning common rules for the internal market in electricity and amending Directive 2012/27/EU; and regarding gas, the Third Energy Package: EP and Council Directive (EC) 2009/73 concerning common rules for the internal market in natural gas and repealing Directive 2003/55/EC [2009] OJ L211/94.

tribunals, particularly in cases against Italy and Spain, has been covered by EU law.[62] In addition, awards can concern EU State aid rules in Articles 107 and 108(2) TFEU, which fall under the exclusive EU competence.[63] In procedural terms, EU law has its own enforcement and dispute settlement mechanisms.[64]

In analysing the applicability of EU law in intra-EU ITA under Article 30 VCLT, tribunals have mostly agreed that the two legal orders do not cover the same subject matter.[65] In doing so, the emphasis has been placed on the *strict* interpretation of the requirement of sameness. For example, the *Eastern Sugar* Tribunal understood sameness as providing equal rights to investors. It therefore concluded that the mere fact that 'the EU does not provide for a possibility for an investor *to sue a host state directly*, and that *in international BIT arbitration* this is an essential feature of most [BITs]' was sufficient to reject the argument of *equal* rights.[66] On the contrary, intra-EU BITs and EU Treaties deal with the same subject matter on not only substantive but also procedural issues related to the treatment of investors.[67] The rights stemming from the participation in the single European market are larger and offer to EU investors more substantive rights than to non-EU investors, even when the latter have the benefit of protection under BITs.[68] At the same time, EU investors already enjoy international protection under EU law, including the protection of a permanent international Court – the

[62] See Joined Cases C-798/18 and C-799/18 *Anie and Others* ECLI:EU:C:2021:280; Joined Cases C-306/19, C-512/19, C-595/19 and C-608/20 to C-610/20 *Milis Energy SpA and Others* ECLI:EU:C:2022:164. See also Section 4.5.2 in Chapter 4.

[63] *Green Power* (n 37) paras. 448–455.

[64] See Section 4.5.3 in Chapter 4.

[65] *Vattenfall II* (n 47) para. 212; *Eastern Sugar* (n 34) para. 159; *Achmea B.V. v The Slovak Republic (formerly Eureko B.V. v Slovak Republic)*, PCA Case No. 2008-13, Award on Jurisdiction, Arbitrability and Suspension (26 October 2010) para. 258; *European American Investment Bank AG v The Slovak Republic*, PCA Case No. 2010-17, Award on Jurisdiction (22 October 2012) para. 184; *Novenergia II – Energy & Environment (SCA) (Grand Duchy of Luxembourg), SICAR v The Kingdom of Spain*, SCC Case No. 2015/063, Award (15 February 2018) para. 439.

[66] *Eastern Sugar* (n 34) para. 180 (emphasis in the original). This conclusion comes after Art. 30 VCLT was cited in the preceding paragraph (para. 179) so it can be inferred that it is directly related to the requirements of Art. 30 VCLT.

[67] See *Green Power* (n 37) para. 393, where the Tribunal asserted that it is only relevant whether both EU law and the ECT address the applicability of the unilateral offer to arbitrate ISDS disputes, concluding that they do and hence considering EU law as 'relevant' under Art. 31(3)(c) VCLT.

[68] Statement of Dissent of Marcelo Kohen (n 37) paras. 25–30.

CJEU.[69] Therefore, if the ISDS clause were essential for the protection of foreign investors, the dispute resolution *body* would become more important for such protection than substantive *law* itself.[70]

From a public international law perspective, a formalistic and narrow interpretation of the 'same subject-matter' requirement is 'neither necessary nor reasonable'.[71] As noted by the ILC, 'terms such as "human rights law", "trade law" or "environmental law" and so on are arbitrary labels of professional specialisation'.[72] The focus should thus be placed on the 'assessment of whether the fulfilment of the obligation under one treaty affects the fulfilment of the obligation of another'. The assessment of the effects depends on whether the pre-existing agreement 'strictly prevent[s] the fulfilment of the other obligation or undermining its object and purpose'.[73]

Accordingly, the conflict between State obligations in two successive treaties rather than the formalistic criterion of sameness should be taken as a relevant criterion under Article 30 VCLT. Applied to intra-EU ITAs, of issue is whether the fulfilment of the Member State obligations under an intra-EU BIT/the ECT affects their obligations under the EU Treaties. Tribunals have answered this question in the negative, while the CJEU has answered it in the positive.[74]

#### 5.2.1.3 Compatibility of Intra-EU IIAs with the EU Legal Order

All tribunals, except one,[75] found no actual or potential conflict between substantive and procedural provisions of intra-EU BITs/the ECT and the founding EU Treaties. They reasoned that the two legal orders are complementary and, in any case, consistent,[76] and thus can co-exist.[77]

With respect to substantive issues, it has been noted that free movement of capital under EU law and protection of investment under IIL are

69 ibid para. 34.
70 ibid para. 32 (emphasis added).
71 ILC (n 55) para. 253.
72 ibid para. 254.
73 ibid.
74 See Section 5.2.2.
75 See analysis in Section 5.3.3.
76 See for example, *Achmea* PCA Case (n 65) para. 245; *Electrabel* (n 56) para. 4.172.
77 See, for example, *Electrabel* (n 56) para. 4.146; *Charanne B.V. v Spain*, SCC Arb. No. 062/2012, Final Award (21 January 2016) para. 438; *RREEF* (n 51) para. 79; *Eiser* (n 50) para. 199; *Novenergia II* (n 65) paras. 438–442.

'different but complementary'.[78] Free movement of capital guarantees capital flows in the pre-establishment stage of investment,[79] while BITs provide protections in the post-establishment stage – 'during the investor's investment in the host country'.[80] That BITs give to investors from some Member States more rights than to other EU investors – the fundamental problem of intra-EU BITs for the EU legal order – has been recognised but also justified. As noted by the tribunal in *Eastern Sugar*, 'the fact that these rights are unequal does not make them incompatible'.[81] Although a State measure might be non-discriminatory under EU law, it can be qualified as unfair and inequitable under IIL.[82] With respect to procedural rights, tribunals did not find inconsistency between the ISDS mechanism and the dispute settlement provisions of the EU founding treaties, in particular Articles 267 and 344 TFEU.[83] They reasoned that Article 344 applies to inter-Member State disputes and not investor–State disputes involving intra-EU investors and Member States.[84]

While finding no conflict between intra-EU BITs/the ECT, some tribunals delved into a hypothetical analysis of primacy between the two legal orders in case of such a conflict. The tribunal in *Electrabel* found that EU law would prevail over international law, both under the special conflict rule of Article 351 TFEU and the general conflict rule in Article 30 VCLT.[85] Other tribunals downplayed the relevance of the *Electrabel* tribunal's reasoning, given the *hypothetical* character of its analysis; the *ratio* of its decision confirmed tribunals' jurisdiction for intra-EU disputes.[86] They were adamant that in the case of inconsistency, absent the possibility that such inconsistency can be reconciled through interpretation, an 'unqualified obligation' of any arbitral tribunal constituted under an IIA would be to apply public international law. This

[78] *Eastern Sugar* (n 34) para. 169.

[79] ibid paras. 161–163.

[80] ibid para. 164.

[81] ibid para. 170. Cf. Statement of Dissent of Marcelo Kohen (n 37) para. 46, who found intra-EU BITs to be 'an elementary infringement of Art. 18 TFEU' and thus a 'major incompatibility' with EU Treaties.

[82] *Achmea* PCA Case (n 65) paras. 250–251, where the imposition of a flat-rate corporate tax, as a legally protected right or a legal duty under EU law, is given as an example.

[83] See, for example, *Electrabel* (n 56) para. 4.175; *Blusun* (n 48) para. 303.

[84] *Charanne* (n 77) paras. 441–447.

[85] *Electrabel* (n 56) paras. 4.178–4.191.

[86] See, for example, *Blusun* (n 48) para. 298.

applies to all cases, even when it undermines EU law, since 'EU law does not and cannot "trump" public international law'.[87]

On the other hand, the primacy of EU law was confirmed by the *Green Power* tribunal, which – unlike the *Electrabel* tribunal– found that the material conflict between EU law and the ECT existed with respect to arbitration clauses and Articles 267 and 344 TFEU.[88] This incompatibility could be seen even more broadly as incompatibility with the whole EU legal system. That EU law prevails in all cases of inconsistent international obligations of Member States concerning matters covered by EU law is long and consistent practice of the Member States, based on such interpretation of the CJEU since the early days of the European Communities.[89] It is not for EU investors to decide which of the two adjudicative mechanisms is most favourable,[90] and to 'rely on EU advantages while ignoring the entire EU system'.[91]

Indeed, EU law provides that investors must sue States before *domestic* courts to seek remedies under *EU* law. This key feature of EU law is accordingly in *direct contradiction* with the rationale of ITA, which is envisaged to bypass domestic courts. While the inconsistencies between IIL and EU law are both substantive and procedural, the CJEU focused exclusively on the compatibility of the ISDS mechanism with EU law, and both *actual and hypothetical* conflicts between the two legal orders.

### *5.2.2 The EU Law Perspective: Exclusive Intra-EU Jurisdiction of the EU Courts System*

In its landmark *Achmea* judgment delivered on 6 March 2018, the CJEU ruled that ISDS clauses in intra-EU BITs, such as the one in Article 8 of the Netherlands–Slovakia BIT, *contravene* Articles 267 and 344 TFEU.[92] The same reasoning was applied in *Komstroy* in 2021, when the CJEU

[87] *RREEF* (n 51) para. 87.
[88] *Green Power* (n 37) paras. 423–425.
[89] Statement of Dissent of Marcelo Kohen (n 37) paras. 60, 63, 67–68. Similarly, the dissenting view of arbitrator Tomov in *Raiffeisen Bank International AG and Raiffeisenbank Austria d.d. v Republic of Croat*ia *(I)*, ICSID Case No. ARB/17/34, Decision on Respondent's Jurisdictional Objections (30 September 2020) para. 258.
[90] ibid para. 51.
[91] ibid para. 69.
[92] Case C-284/16 *Slovakische Republik v Achmea* ECLI:EU:C:2018:15 (emphasis added). The CJEU did not answer the question on the compatibility of the ISDS clause with the principle of non-discrimination enshrined in Art. 18 TFEU.

ruled on the inapplicability of the ISDS clause in Article 26 of the ECT in intra-EU disputes.[93] The CJEU's reasoning is based on classification of EU law as both part of domestic law of Member States as well as international law.[94] It considers different aspects of the EU legal order (i-ii) and the effects of the ISDS mechanism on the EU legal order (iii-v). Accordingly, the CJEU concluded that intra-EU ITA under both intra-EU BITs and the ECT is incompatible with EU law, with express analogies between the two.[95] In its ruling in *PL Holdings*,[96] the CJEU clarified that Member States' obligations under the EU founding treaties, as interpreted in *Achmea*, cannot be circumvented through an implicit *ad hoc* arbitration agreement of the same content as an intra-EU BIT (vi). Different aspects of these CJEU's judgments are discussed below.

### (i) The EU Constitutional Aspect: The Autonomy of EU Law, Mutual Trust and Sincere Cooperation

The CJEU emphasised the 'constitutional structure of the EU' and the autonomous character of EU law.[97] The autonomy flows from the unique EU constitutional framework.[98] It is especially enshrined in Article 344 TFEU, which precludes Member States from submitting *any dispute* concerning the *interpretation and application* of the Treaties to any dispute settlement other than the one provided for in the Treaties.[99] Observance of the autonomy is strictly ensured by the CJEU through Article 344 TFEU, ensuring that the Court is the *only* authority for the interpretation and application of EU law.[100]

In addition, EU law is based on the set of common values on which the EU is founded and which are shared among the Member States.[101] This implies the existence of mutual trust between the Member States that these values will be recognised and that law that implements them will be respected. Mutual trust and the principle of sincere cooperation between the Member States, enshrined in Article 4(3) TEU, ensure that Member States provide in their respective territories appropriate measures, which

[93] Case C-741/19 *Republic of Moldova v Komstroy* ECLI:EU:C:2021:655.
[94] *Achmea* (n 92) para. 33.
[95] *Komstroy* (n 93) para. 64.
[96] Case C-109/20 *PL Holdings* ECLI:EU:C:2021:875.
[97] *Achmea* (n 92) para. 33; *Komstroy* (n 93) para. 43.
[98] *Komstroy* (n 93) para. 43.
[99] *Achmea* (n 92) para. 32 (emphasis added); *Komstroy* (n 93) para. 42.
[100] See also Section 4.1 in Chapter 4.
[101] Art. 2 TEU.

serve as assurance to other Member States that EU law is respected and properly applied.[102]

#### (ii) The EU Judicial Aspect: The Preliminary Ruling Procedure as the 'Keystone' of the EU Judicial System

The autonomy of the EU legal order is preserved through the EU judicial system.[103] Mutual trust also includes trust in the Member States' courts, which, in accordance with Article 19 TEU, ensures the full application of EU law and judicial protection of individuals under EU law.[104] The 'keystone' of the EU judicial system is the preliminary ruling procedure in Article 267 TFEU, which establishes a 'dialogue' between the national courts and the CJEU. It accordingly secures the uniform interpretation of EU law and thus ensures its consistency and effectiveness.[105]

After reiterating the core elements of the EU legal order, the CJEU considered how the ISDS mechanism affects EU law and its autonomy.

#### (iii) EU Substantive Law Interference: Investment Tribunals May Interpret or Apply EU Law

First, the CJEU considered whether an ISDS tribunal can interpret and apply EU law.[106] In the intra-EU BIT context in *Achmea*, in analysing the applicable law provision of the Netherlands–Slovakia BIT, the Court ascertained that a tribunal is called on to rule on possible infringements of the BIT[107] by also taking into account 'the law in force of the contracting party concerned and other relevant agreements between the contracting parties'.[108] Accordingly, given the constitutional character of EU law,[109] whereby EU law forms part of the national laws of Member States, an ISDS tribunal '*may* be called on to interpret or indeed apply EU law', and *in particular* the EU founding treaties' provisions on fundamental freedoms, including freedom of establishment and free movement of capital.[110]

[102] *Achmea* (n 92) para. 34. See also Section 4.5.3 in Chapter 4.
[103] *Achmea* (n 92) para. 35.
[104] ibid para. 36.
[105] *Komstroy* (n 93) para. 46.
[106] *Achmea* (n 92) para. 39.
[107] Art. 8(1) of the Netherlands–Slovakia BIT.
[108] *Achmea* (n 92) para. 40, referring to Art. 8(6) of the Netherlands–Slovakia BIT.
[109] ibid para. 41, with reference to para. 33.
[110] ibid para. 42 (emphasis added). Cf. *Achmea*, Opinion of AG Wathelet (n 11) para. 173.

In the ECT context, the applicable law clause limits the jurisdiction of investment tribunals to the application of the ECT and international law, without reference to domestic law of the Contracting Parties.[111] Nevertheless, the ECT is an international agreement to which the EU is a party and thus forms part of EU law.[112] Accordingly, the CJEU concluded that investment tribunals are required to interpret and 'even apply' EU law.[113] It found it 'clearly in the interest of the EU' that the same ECT provisions are interpreted uniformly in situations falling directly within the scope of EU law to 'forestall' differences of interpretation of EU law.[114] The Court is not concerned that this could lead to diverging interpretations of the ECT under international law and EU law, but it rather assumes its core duty to protect the EU legal order.

#### (iv) The Procedural Interference: ISDS Tribunals Cannot Refer Questions for Preliminary Ruling to the CJEU

Second, since ISDS tribunals *could* interpret or apply EU law, the CJEU had to establish whether they could, in the same manner as national courts, refer questions of EU law for preliminary ruling to the CJEU, in order to secure uniform interpretation of EU law, and hence its consistency and effectiveness.[115] Only national courts or tribunals can refer questions to the CJEU in accordance with the procedure in Article 267 TFEU. The CJEU concluded that ISDS tribunals are *not* part of the national judicial system, and hence are also not part of the EU judicial system.[116] Tribunals' jurisdiction *outside* of the national judicial systems is at the very core of ISDS.[117] The CJEU comes to the same conclusion in the intra-EU BITs and the ECT context, drawing clear analogies between the two.[118]

#### (v) The Judicial Review Interference: The CJEU and National Courts Do Not Have Control over Investment Arbitral Awards

Third, given that ISDS tribunals are outside the EU judicial system, the CJEU had to ascertain whether an award issued by these tribunals could

[111] Art. 26(6) ECT.
[112] *Komstroy* (n 93) para. 23.
[113] ibid paras. 49–50.
[114] ibid para. 29. In particular, this could be the case when proceedings are brought before domestic courts of Member States in accordance with Art. 26(2)(a) ECT.
[115] ibid para. 43.
[116] ibid para. 46.
[117] ibid para. 45. Cf. Opinion of AG Wathelet in *Achmea* (n 11) para. 127.
[118] *Komstroy* (n 93) paras. 52–53.

be reviewed by national courts. This would ensure the correct application of EU law, including through the preliminary ruling mechanism.[119] The CJEU noted that ISDS awards are final and that their review depends on the choice of arbitration procedure, their seat and the applicable law.[120] Accordingly, the possibility of judicial review and control by national courts and the CJEU over ISDS awards is limited.

The CJEU, however, made a distinction between investment and commercial arbitration, reaffirming that the latter is compatible with EU law. Two reasons were provided to support this distinction. First, commercial arbitration originates in 'the freely expressed wishes of the parties' stated in an arbitration agreement. On the other hand, ITA originates in an IIA between two Member States, which is in direct contradiction with the Member States' EU obligations.[121] Second and more importantly, the review of commercial awards regarding their compatibility with EU law is possible in the enforcement stage.[122] National courts can review the validity of arbitration agreements under the applicable law and the consistency of the awards with public policy. Although limited in its scope, this review allows for examination of the compatibility of commercial awards with the fundamental provisions of EU law,[123] and allows national courts to refer any questions of EU law for a preliminary ruling.[124] Accordingly, national courts can review and control the compatibility of commercial awards with EU law, and thus ensure the full application of EU law in accordance with Member States' obligations under Article 19(1) TEU.

Finally, in its ruling in *PL Holdings*, the CJEU clarified the scope of Member States' obligations regarding intra-EU *investment* arbitrations.

### (vi) Member States' Obligations: Prevalence of EU Law

The participation of Member States in intra-EU arbitral proceedings is contrary to the fundamental principles of EU law, irrespective of the legal basis – an intra-EU BIT or an implicit *ad hoc* agreement of the same content – as they produce the same legal effects, that is the breach of

[119] *Achmea* (n 92) para. 50; *Komstroy* (n 93) para. 54.

[120] *Achmea* (n 92) para. 51; *Komstroy* (n 93) para. 55.

[121] *Achmea* (n 92) para. 55; *Komstroy* (n 93) para. 59.

[122] *Achmea* (n 92) para. 54; *Komstroy* (n 93) para. 58.

[123] Case C-126/97 *Eco Swiss China Time Ltd v Benetton International NV* [1999] ECR I-3055, paras. 35–36.

[124] ibid para. 40.

Articles 267 and 344 TFEU and Articles 19(1) and 4(3) TEU.[125] While under domestic law, an implicit arbitration agreement can be concluded as a result of an implied declaration of intent by not objecting to joining the proceedings within the time limit (commercial arbitration), this does not apply when an intra-EU BIT constitutes a formal ground for the initial proceedings (investment arbitration). Recognising the validity of the offer to arbitrate under such agreement would maintain the legal effects of an invalid offer under the BIT, and such validity cannot depend on the conduct of the Member State.[126] Moreover, any attempt of a Member State to remedy such an invalid offer by a contract with an investor from another Member State would be contrary to its *obligation* to challenge the validity of the arbitration clause, in an intra-EU BIT or an *ad hoc* arbitration agreement.[127]

### 5.2.3 *Interim Conclusion*

Based on these judgments, several inferences can be made in relation to intra-EU arbitration under EU law.

*First*, the emphasis of the CJEU reasoning is placed on the principles of mutual trust and sincere cooperation in relations between the Member States enshrined in Articles 19(1) and 4(3) TEU, which are called into question in any intra-EU ITA. The principle of mutual trust implies that there is no second-class justice in the EU and that investors can expect the same level of protection before the courts of any Member State. Even if it were established that there is a lacuna in the protection of investors' rights within the EU legal system, such lacuna must be filled within that system, and in any case cannot justify the breach of fundamental principles of EU law.[128] Accordingly, the CJEU clearly rejected the argument that EU law should be complemented by an international investment law regime in order to provide sufficient protections for intra-EU investors.

*Second*, the jurisdiction of an intra-EU ISDS tribunal, which is outside the EU judicial system, adversely affects the autonomy of the EU legal order. Tribunals could interpret and apply EU law without pre- or post-award recourse to the CJEU, which would ensure the correct interpretation of EU law. Awards of intra-EU tribunals can therefore affect the

[125] *PL Holdings* (n 96) paras. 44–48. The CJEU draws clear analogy with *Achmea*.
[126] ibid paras. 50–51.
[127] ibid paras. 52, 54.
[128] ibid para. 68.

allocation of powers between the EU and its Member States and consequently affect the autonomy of the EU legal system. Accordingly, Member States have an *obligation* to submit *all* intra-EU disputes to the judicial mechanism of the EU Treaties.

*Third*, even potential conflicts between the interpretation of EU law by an investment tribunal and the CJEU pose a risk for the autonomy of EU law. Indeed, in most cases, domestic law and thus also EU law will be taken as a matter of fact. Tribunals have also not hesitated to interpret EU law. They have held that there is no EU rule preventing an arbitral tribunal from applying EU law to an intra-EU dispute,[129] which is an interpretation of EU law in itself, albeit not an authoritative one. The incompatibility of intra-EU ISDS with the EU legal order is not dependent on the proof that an issue involving EU law will actually arise in a particular case; the possibility of it is sufficient.

*Fourth*, the analogies between *Achmea* and *Komstroy* and the same outcome with respect to incompatibility of intra-EU ITA with EU law should not surprise, despite the different nature of the international agreements that these judgments considered. The possibility of conflicts between intra-EU investment awards and EU law that could affect the allocation of powers fixed in the founding treaties is even higher in the ECT than intra-EU BITs context. As a matter of EU law, the ECT has direct effect in Member States.[130] Therefore, a private EU investor could rely on the ECT to challenge an act of an EU institution before EU courts, or the CJEU could examine the ECT on the basis of a request for a preliminary ruling from a national court of a Member State.[131] In this case, an award issued by an arbitral tribunal under the ECT could provide an authoritative interpretation of the obligations of the ECT Contracting Parties, possibly in conflict with the authoritative interpretation of the ECT as a source of EU law provided by the CJEU. Hence, the application of the ECT in intra-EU disputes could lead to different outcomes under the same legal instrument, depending on the body adjudicating such disputes, thus resulting in legal uncertainty.[132]

[129] *Charanne* (n 77) para. 438; *Novenergia II* (n 65) para. 440.

[130] *Komstroy* (n 93) para. 31.

[131] Statement submitted by the European Communities to the Secretariat of the Energy Charter pursuant to Article 26(3)(b)(ii) of the ECT [1998] OJ L69/115, [5].

[132] Case C-471/98 *Commission v Belgium* ("Open Skies") ECLI:EU:C:2002:628, paras. 137 to 142; and Opinion 2/13 ECLI:EU:C:2014:2454, paras. 198–199 and 208.

*Fifth*, for all these reasons, extra-EU situations, which include Member States' extra-EU BITs, extra-EU ITA under the ECT or bilateral agreements concluded by the EU and Member States with third States (e.g. CETA) should be distinguished from the intra-EU context.[133] While there is still a possibility of a conflict between ISDS awards under such agreements and EU law, these inconsistencies are less likely to affect the autonomy of EU law in the same manner as agreements *between* the Member States. The conflict in extra-EU relations must be *actual*, therefore depending on the demonstration that a conflict exists in each particular case. Indeed, in some cases the post-award control of the CJEU would be fully excluded; for example, for International Centre for the Settlement of Investment Disputes (ICSID) awards or those arbitrations that have their seat outside the EU. However, the possibility for these awards to affect the allocation of powers fixed in the EU Treaties, while not inconceivable, is rather remote.[134] The risk of adversely affecting the autonomy of the EU legal order is accordingly low and certainly superseded by political benefits of such agreements.[135]

*Sixth*, the CJEU provides an authoritative interpretation of EU Treaties and determination of legal rights and obligations of Member States under EU law. This jurisdiction is granted to the Court under public international law, that is, EU founding treaties.[136] *Rationae personae*, the judgment of the CJEU provided through the preliminary ruling procedure is directed to the national court that initiated the procedure, but it is legally binding for all national courts in the EU.[137] The national court thus must set aside an intra-EU arbitration award infringing Articles 267 and 344 TFEU and the principles of mutual trust, sincere cooperation and autonomy of EU law.[138] The rationale is to ensure that EU law applies uniformly in the EU, thus guaranteeing legal certainty.[139] *Ratione temporis,* since the CJEU did not provide any temporal limitation of the

[133] To that effect, see also *Komstroy* (n 93) para. 65.

[134] Cf. N. de Sadeleer, 'The End of the Game: The Autonomy of the EU Legal Order Opposes Arbitral Tribunals under Bilateral Investment Treaties Concluded between Two Member States' (2018) 9 *European Journal of Risk Regulation* 355.

[135] See Section 8.1.1.2 in Chapter 8.

[136] Art. 19(1) TEU; Art. 263 TFEU.

[137] Case C-173/09 *Elchinov* ECLI:EU:C:2010:581, para. 29; Case C-689/13 *Puligienica Facility Esco SpA* ECLI:EU:C:2016:199, para. 38.

[138] *PL Holdings* (n 96) para. 55.

[139] Case 66/80 *International Chemical Corporation v Administrazione delle Finanze dello Stato* [1981] ECR 1191, paras. 11–13.

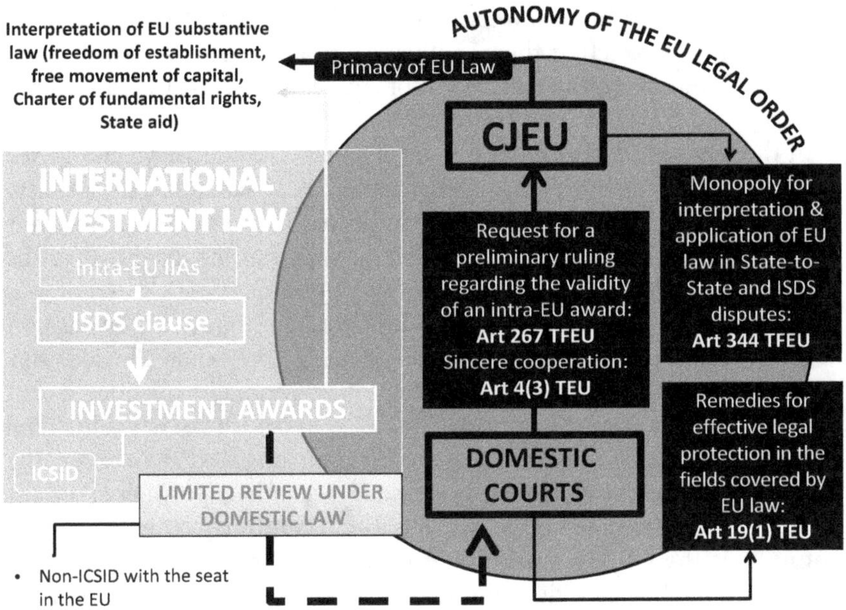


**Figure 5.1** The relationship between intra-EU BITs and the EU legal order

effects of its rulings, all EU Member States are bound *ex tunc.*[140] However, the principles of *res judicata* and legal certainty preclude questioning the legality of final awards in intra-EU ITAs where final awards have been issued prior to the *Achmea* ruling.[141]

In light of the preceding discussion, Figure 5.1 depicts the overlap and conflict between intra-EU arbitration and the EU legal order.

## 5.3 Intra-EU Investment Post-*Achmea*: Legal and Policy Implications

### 5.3.1 *Intra-EU Jurisdiction of Investment Tribunals*

In the aftermath of *Achmea*, the judgment has become a new ground for Member States in raising intra-EU jurisdictional objection. However,

[140] In this context, from the entry into force of the founding treaties: M. Broberg and N. Fenger, *Preliminary References to the European Court of Justice* (OUP 2010) 445. See *PL Holdings* (n 96) para. 64. This is different to a precedent of a common law court, which applies *ex nunc*.

[141] *Eco Swiss* (n 123) para. 43.

intra-EU arbitral tribunals, whether established under a BIT or the ECT, have continued rejecting them, with the exception of the *Green Power* tribunal.[142] Similarly, the annulment of awards on intra-EU grounds has been rejected by ICSID committees.[143]

In the intra-EU BITs context, in some cases tribunals have confirmed that *Achmea* covers different subject matter, thus excluding the priority of EU law under Article 30 VCLT.[144] In others, it was found that it refers to the 'national or regional context' and thus has no bearing on the 'multilateral public international treaty' context of ICSID.[145] Or it was found that a particular intra-EU BIT does not incorporate EU law as part of its applicable law in the same manner as the Netherlands–Slovakia BIT does in *Achmea*.[146] In the ECT context, it was initially considered that *Achmea* has 'no bearing' due to the ECT's nature as a multilateral external agreement of the EU,[147] confirming *no conflict* between the ECT and EU law, and *if there were* such a conflict, prevalence of the ECT.[148] Such tribunals' approach has been continued after *Komstroy*, noting that the CJEU's reasoning on intra-EU disputes in *Komstroy* is *obiter dictum*,[149] which does not reflect the correct interpretation of the ECT from the perspective of international law.[150] The tribunals have thus considered *Komstroy* to be 'irrelevant' to the question of their

142 See analysis in Section 5.3.3.

143 See, for example, *UAB E energija (Lithuania) v Republic of Latvia*, ICSID Case No. ARB/12/33; *Blusun* (n 48); *Sodexo Pass International SAS v Hungary*, ICSID Case No. ARB/14/20; *Dan Cake (Portugal) S.A. v Hungary*, ICSID Case No. ARB/12/9; *Infrastructure Services Luxembourg S.à.r.l. and Energia Termosolar B.V. (formerly Antin Infrastructure Services Luxembourg S.à.r.l. and Antin Energia Termosolar B.V.) v Kingdom of Spain*, ICSID Case No. ARB/13/31; *UP and C.D. (formerly Le Cheque Dejeuner) v Hungary*, ICSID Case No. ARB/13/35; *Magyar Farming Company Ltd, Kintyre Kft, & Anicia Zrt v Hungary*, ICSID Case No. ARB/17/27.

144 See, for example, *Marfin Investment Group Holdings S.A., Alexandros Bakatselos and Others v Republic of Cyprus*, ICSID Case No. ARB/13/27, Award (27 July 2018) para. 595.

145 *UP* (n 143) Award (9 October 2018) para. 253.

146 *Addiko Bank AG and Addiko Bank d.d. v Republic of Croatia*, ICSID Case No. ARB/17/37, Decision on Croatia's Jurisdictional Objection Related to the Alleged Incompatibility of the BIT with EU Acquis (12 June 2020) para. 267. Cf. Dissenting view of arbitrator Tomov in *Raiffeisen Bank* (n 89) paras. 255–258.

147 See, for example, *Masdar Solar & Wind Cooperatief U.A. v Kingdom of Spain*, ICSID Case No. ARB/14/1, Award (16 May 2018) paras. 340–341.

148 *Vattenfall II* (n 47) paras. 212, 214, 229.

149 The case concerns two non-EU parties, with the seat of arbitration in the EU.

150 *Sevilla Beheer and Others v Kingdom of Spain*, ICSID Case No. ARB/16/27, Decision on Jurisdiction, Liability and the Principles of Quantum (11 February 2022) paras. 267–269.

jurisdiction, which has to be decided on international law, and not 'principles of sub-systems of international law such as EU treaties'.[151]

Ultimately, the differences in reasoning between investment lawyers and EU lawyers reflect the different interpretative approaches of these two legal orders.[152] While both approaches endorse 'systemic integration' in international law, they attach different meanings to this concept. Systemic interpretation under EU law means interpretation of the ECT (as a source of EU law) and Member States' intra-EU BITs (as integral part of the EU legal order) in conformity with the EU founding treaties,[153] which precludes intra-EU ITA. For investment tribunals, systemic interpretation means that intra-EU IIAs and EU Treaties belong to different orders of international law, which excludes material conflict between the two and allows them to co-exist.[154]

In *Achmea* and *Komstroy*, the CJEU provided an authoritative interpretation of EU law, in accordance with its jurisdiction under public international law. While recognising that EU law forms part of international law, investment tribunals have simply disagreed with the CJEU's interpretations and accordingly have proceeded with intra-EU arbitration. In other fields, the CJEU held that it is beyond its jurisdiction to decide matters under a bilateral arbitration agreement between two Member States governed by international law, the subject of which does not fall within the areas of EU competence referred to in Articles 3 to 6 TFEU and to which the EU is not a party.[155] However, given the broad scope of investment, it is inevitable that intra-EU IIAs encroach on EU competence and adversely affect the allocation of powers between the EU and its Member States.[156]

While investment tribunals are not bound by the CJEU's decisions, EU Member States are. This was particularly highlighted in *PL Holdings*, where the CJEU emphasised the Member States' obligation to comply

[151] *Infracapital F1 S.à r.l. and Infracapital Solar B.V. v Kingdom of Spain*, ICSID Case No. ARB/16/18, Decision on Respondent Request for Reconsideration regarding the Intra-EU Objection and the Merits (1 February 2022) paras. 107, 116.

[152] See Section 4.3.1 in Chapter 4.

[153] See C-266/16 *Western Sahara* EU:C:2018:118, paras. 42–51.

[154] See, for example *Electrabel* (n 56) para. 4.130; *RREEF* (n 51) para. 76; *Ioan Micula, Viorel Micula, S.C. European Food S.A, S.C. Starmill S.R.L. and S.C. Multipack S.R.L. v Romania [I]*, ICSID Case No. ARB/05/20, Final Award (11 December 2013) paras. 326–327.

[155] Case C-457/18 *Slovenia v Croatia* ECLI:EU:C:2020:65, para. 102.

[156] See Chapter 6.

with EU Treaties, which cannot be circumvented via an *ad hoc* arbitration agreement producing the same legal effects as an intra-EU BIT.[157] While such an agreement could have been a practical solution for many pending intra-EU arbitral proceedings, it was clearly established by the CJEU as unacceptable. It would constitute a precedent for a 'multiple disputes which may concern the application and interpretation of EU law', thus potentially repeatedly undermining the autonomy of EU law.[158] Ultimately, disregard of the CJEU's rulings by arbitral tribunals places EU Member States in a precarious position of choosing between their competing obligations.

The present situation compounds the problem of fragmentation of international law and the competition for 'institutional hegemony'.[159] The clash of these two international legal orders would be of interest only to legal scholars if it did not also have practical legal consequences for the adjudication of pending intra-EU investment disputes and the enforcement of intra-EU arbitral awards. There are also implications for the rule of law in the EU and the attainment of the EU integration objectives. These issues are discussed in the remaining sections of this chapter.

### 5.3.2 *Termination Agreement and Adjudication of Pending and New Intra-EU Disputes under BITs*

In January 2019, twenty-two EU Member States adopted a Declaration on Investment Protection in the EU,[160] sending a clear signal to the investment community that 'no new intra-EU investment proceedings should be initiated',[161] either under intra-EU BITs or under the ECT.[162] On 5 May 2020, twenty-three Member States signed the Agreement for the termination of BITs between the Member States of the EU (TA),[163] which implements the CJEU's *Achmea* judgment and the January

[157] *PL Holdings* (n 96) paras. 47, 52, 54.
[158] ibid para. 49.
[159] M. Koskenniemi, *The Politics of International Law* (Hart 2011) 338; ILC (n 55).
[160] Declaration of the Representatives of the Governments of the Member States of 15 January 2019 on the Legal Consequences of the Judgment of the Court of Justice in *Achmea* and on Investment Protection in the European Union.
[161] ibid para. 3.
[162] ibid para. 1.
[163] Agreement for the termination of Bilateral Investment Treaties between the Member States of the European Union [2020] OJ L 169/1 (TA).

Declaration.[164] It entered into force on 29 August 2020 following its ratification by Denmark and Hungary.[165]

The TA terminates all intra-EU BITs and their sunset clauses (listed in Annex A) and the sunset clauses of already terminated BITs (listed in Annex B).[166] It also clarifies that ISDS arbitration clauses in intra-EU BITs are inapplicable as of the date of the EU accession of the last of the parties to the BIT,[167] and cannot serve as a legal basis for any 'new arbitration proceedings'[168] – initiated on or after 6 March 2018 (*Achmea* judgment).[169] However, the TA does not affect proceedings *concluded* before that date.[170] Member States have a duty to inform tribunals in all pending and new arbitration proceedings about the legal consequences of *Achmea*.[171]

Pending disputes – initiated but not concluded prior to the *Achmea* judgment – can be resolved through a 'structured dialogue' between the investor and the Member State, which is to be overseen by the commonly agreed 'impartial facilitator'.[172] The initiative for this procedure is placed on the investor and it can be initiated only within six months from the termination of the relevant BIT under which the arbitration proceedings have been established.[173] However, several provisions mandate that the settlement procedure will be conditioned upon the established actual or potential violations of EU law[174] and be guided by EU law.[175] Unlike the arbitrator, whose role is to adjudicate, the facilitator is focused on the *process* of negotiations, through which the parties should reach a settlement.[176]

As an alternative to the 'structured dialogue' for pending cases, including cases where the settlement has not been reached through the structured dialogue, the investor is entitled to access national courts, even if

[164] Termination Agreement (TA) constitutes a special agreement between the Member States in accordance with Art. 273 TFEU: Art. 14(3) TA.

[165] OJ L 281/1; Art. 16 TA.

[166] Arts. 2, 3 and 4(2) TA.

[167] ibid Art. 4(1).

[168] ibid Art. 5.

[169] ibid Art. 1(6).

[170] ibid Art. 6.

[171] See ibid Art. 7(a) and Annex C; *PL Holdings* (n 96) para. 53.

[172] Art. 9 TA.

[173] ibid Arts. 9(1) and (2).

[174] See ibid Arts. 9(3), (4) and (6).

[175] The facilitator must have in-depth knowledge of EU law and take due account of it: see ibid Arts. 9(8)–(10).

[176] ibid Art. 9(7).

national time-limits for bringing actions have expired.[177] However, in such proceedings, the provisions of BITs will not be considered applicable law and no new judicial remedies, otherwise unavailable under national law, would be created.[178] In all other cases, including those where the cause of action involves measures challenged in arbitration proceedings started on or after 6 March 2018, the investor will be entitled only to the regular access to national courts. Different factual scenarios under the TA are summarised in Table 5.1.

Respondent Member States have attempted to draw legal consequences from the January Declaration and the TA, in accordance with Article 31 VCLT, as a means for the interpretation of intra-EU BITs. These arguments have been rejected by arbitral tribunals, either because the Declaration sets out the obligations under EU law and thus does not qualify as a subsequent interpretation of the BITs and a withdrawal of a consent to arbitrate,[179] or it was not 'a subsequent agreement' reached during negotiations of the BIT,[180] or such interpretation was not supported by the ordinary meaning of the ISDS clause in the BIT, whereby EU law cannot 'trump' or 'amend' the text of the clause.[181] However, instead of focusing on a narrow and formalistic interpretation of particular arbitration clauses, the tribunals should take into account the compatibility of the *relationship* between the two conventional arrangements – under intra-EU BITs and the EU Treaties – as a whole. It is the Member States' common understanding about such holistic incompatibility, which also includes individual arbitration clauses, that has been invoked in Member States' declarations and the TA.[182]

Similarly, in cases where respondent States raised the TA *before* its entry into force for the relevant intra-EU BIT parties, tribunals considered that the TA does not carry bearing on the dispute. In procedural terms, they found that their jurisdiction was determined at the time of the institution of the proceedings, regardless of the BIT's termination. In substantive terms, they concluded that protections that were in force and binding

[177] This is subject to time limits and conditions laid down in Art. 10(1) TA.
[178] ibid Art. 10(3) and (4).
[179] *Theodoros Adamakopoulos* (n 37) para. 179.
[180] *GPF GP S.à.r.l v Republic of Poland*, SCC Case No. V 2014/168, Award (29 April 2020) paras. 350–351.
[181] *Strabag et al v Poland*, ICSID Case No. ADHOC/15/1, Partial Award on Jurisdiction (4 March 2020) paras. 8.124–8.128.
[182] See Statement of Dissent of Marcelo Kohen (n 37) para. 56. On the relevance of declarations in the ECT context, see *Green Power* (n 37) paras. 372, 386.

Table 5.1 *The effects of the Termination Agreement on intra-EU arbitration under intra-EU BITs*

| The stage of intra-EU arbitration proceedings | Effects of the plurilateral agreement on the arbitration proceedings/awards |
|---|---|
| Arbitration proceedings concluded and awards/settlement agreements executed before 6 March 2018 | ***Res judicata* / no effect of the Termination Agreement** |
| Arbitration proceedings concluded (with no challenge to final award pending) before 6 March 2018 but award not executed | **Award can be executed under EU law before domestic courts of Member States** |
| Arbitration proceedings concluded (with no challenge to final award pending) before 6 March 2018 and the award set aside/annulled before the entry into force of the Termination Agreement | ***Res judicata* / no effect of the Termination Agreement** |
| Pending arbitration proceedings initiated but not concluded before 6 March 2018 (and no pending parallel domestic proceedings) | **Settlement in accordance with the 'structured dialogue' in Article 9 / access to national courts in the alternative in accordance with Article 10** |
| Arbitration proceedings initiated before 6 March 2018 and concluded before the entry into force of the Termination Agreement (and no pending parallel domestic proceedings) | **Settlement in accordance with the 'structured dialogue' in Article 9 / access to national courts in the alternative in accordance with Article 10** |
| New arbitration proceedings: initiated on or after 6 March 2018 (pending or concluded) | **Offer to arbitrate inapplicable / arbitration proceedings illegal under EU law /regular access to the competent national court** |

upon the respondent Member State at the time of the alleged breaches remain equally unaffected.[183] Accordingly, it is likely to expect that arbitrations that have been, or are to be, initiated before the date of the entry into force of the TA for the relevant intra-EU BIT parties will continue.

From an international law perspective, *after* the entry into force of the TA, there should be no doubt about the termination of intra-EU BITs in accordance with Article 54(b) VCLT, given the express and consensual intention of Member States in the TA.[184] The same should apply to sunset clauses given that the TA explicitly states that they shall not produce legal effects,[185] in accordance with Article 70 VCLT. Member States thus have the autonomy as masters of their treaties to mutually agree to terminate their treaties and decide what the consequences of terminations are.[186]

However, it cannot be excluded that investment tribunals might differently interpret the applicability of the TA and the legal effects of the sunset clauses. It has already been reasoned that the possibility of States to revoke the sunset clauses has been limited by the general principles of legal certainty and *res inter alios acta, aliis nec nocet nec prodest* doctrine, with a view to guarantee stability to investors.[187] However, such interpretation changes the inter-State nature of IIAs, denying that investors' rights depend on the will of the State parties and their continuous approval, which can be taken away without investors' consent.[188] In particular, in case of the mutual termination of a treaty, Article 70(1) VLCT does not support the view that any vested rights created through the execution of such treaty apply to individuals.[189] Similarly, investors' rights are not considered rights of third parties under Article 37(2) VCLT, which requires the consent of third *States* to revoke or modify a right which was intended not to be revocable or modified without such consent.

Notably, tribunals so far referred to acquired rights of investors regarding their right to arbitration in pending cases following the *Achmea* judgment, thus dismissing the relevance of Member States' declarations.[190] However, the acquired rights view argues that Member

183 *Muszynianka v Slovakia*, PCA Case No. 2017-08, Award (7 October 2020) paras. 263–264.
184 Art. 2(1) TA.
185 ibid Arts. 2(2) and 3.
186 ILC, Draft Articles on the Law of Treaties with commentaries (1966) 249, 265–266.
187 *Magyar* (n 143) Award (13 November 2019) paras. 222–223.
188 See Statement of Dissent of Marcelo Kohen (n 37) para. 59.
189 ILC, Draft Articles (n 186) 265.
190 *Eskosol* (n 44) para. 226; *AMF Aircraftleasing Meier & Fischer GmbH & Co. KG v Czech Republic*, PCA Case No. 2017-15, Final Award (11 May 2020) paras. 336–338; *Muszynianka* (n 183) paras. 263–264.

States, although being masters of their treaties, cannot consensually agree to retroactively terminate the perfected *consent* for any pending intra-EU arbitrations through the TA, whether initiated before or after *Achmea*.[191] On the other hand, subsequent Member States' interpretations of intra-EU BITs should not be ignored. By doing so, tribunals, whose jurisdiction stems from the will of the Contracting Parties expressed in the treaties, have assumed the role that belongs to the Parties – telling them that they 'misinterpreted their own Treaties'.[192] It is exactly in the aspect of the international treaties' State-centric approach and quasi-contractual rights of investors under these treaties where public and private nature of IIL clash.[193]

All signatories of the TA have ratified it, and it can be expected that the remaining non-signatories Member States will terminate their BITs on bilateral basis, under the threat of infringement proceedings under EU law.[194] The TA thus marks the end of intra-EU BITs, but not yet the end of intra-EU ITA, particularly in light of politically and legally more complex ECT.

### 5.3.3 *The Future of Intra-EU Arbitration under the ECT*

In addition to the majority's 15 January Declaration, there were two extra declarations from six Member States that expressed reservations about the applicability of the Declaration to intra-EU disputes under the ECT.[195] The TA thus excludes from its scope intra-EU disputes under Article 26 ECT, which is to be dealt at a later stage.[196]

[191] J. Tropper and A. Reinisch, 'The 2020 Termination Agreement of Intra-EU BITs and Its Effect on Investment Arbitration in the EU' (2022) 16 *The Austrian Yearbook on International Arbitration* 301.

[192] Statement of Dissent of Marcelo Kohen (n 37) para. 58.

[193] See also Section 2.1.3 in Chapter 2.

[194] See, for example, EC, 'December Infringements Package: Key Decisions' (2 December 2021).

[195] Declaration of the Representatives of the Governments of the Member States of 16 January 2019 on the Enforcement of the Judgment of the Court of Justice in *Achmea* and on Investment Protection in the European Union (signed by Sweden, Luxembourg, Malta, Finland and Slovenia), which stated that 'it would be inappropriate' to express views on the applicability of *Achmea* to the ECT in the absence of a specific judgment on the matter at the time; and Declaration of the Representative of the Government of Hungary of 16 January 2019 on the Legal Consequences of the Judgment of the Court of Justice in *Achmea* and on Investment Protection in the European Union, which explicitly stated that *Achmea* 'does not concern and pending or prospective arbitration proceedings initiated under the ECT': para. 8.

[196] Preamble, TA.

The CJEU ruling in *Komstroy* confirmed the incompatibility of intra-EU ITA with EU law, thus removing any legal doubts expressed in the separate Member States' declarations. The CJEU reaffirmed this ruling in its decision in Opinion 1/20, although it found that Belgium's request for an opinion on the compatibility of intra-EU arbitration in the ongoing ECT modernisation process, made in accordance with Article 218(11) TFEU, was premature and thus inadmissible.[197] The only arbitral tribunal that endorsed the CJEU reasoning in *Achmea* and *Komstroy*, thus accepting the intra-EU objection as jurisdictional objection *rationae voluntatis*, was the *Green Power* tribunal. Its award indicates that the exclusion of intra-EU arbitration could be construed based on the contextual interpretation of the unilateral offer to arbitrate in Article 26(3)(a) ECT, in accordance with Articles 31 and 32 VCLT.

The tribunal found that the relevance of EU law for matters governed by the ECT is expressly acknowledged and incorporated by the specific provisions in the ECT,[198] but also by contemporaneous legal instruments clarifying the application of the ECT provisions regarding *inter se* relations of Member States.[199] In addition, the Declaration of 15 January as a subsequent legal instrument signed by both home and host Member States, which confirms the legal effects of *Achmea* later endorsed by the *Komstroy* judgment, represents authentic interpretation of the ECT and therefore, does not retroactively modify the understanding of relations between the ECT and EU law.[200] Accordingly, it is relevant even when it post-dates the commencement of arbitral proceedings.[201] Finally, EU law

[197] Opinion 1/20 ECLI:EU:C:2022:485 of 16 June 2022, delivered several days before the conclusion of negotiations for the modernised ECT. See also Section 8.3.2 in Chapter 8.

[198] Arts. 1(2), (3) and (10) ECT, respectively containing definitions of the Contracting Party, REIO and Area of a Contracting Party, and Art. 25, which recognises that EU Member States may grant to each other special benefits arising from a special network of relations between them as parties to an Economic Integration Agreement: see *Green Power* (n 37) paras. 351–354.

[199] Declaration No. 5 clarifying the purpose of Art. 25 in the EU context, that is to safeguard the preferential treatment resulting from the wider process of the EU integration: ibid para. 358; and Statement submitted to the ECT Secretariat pursuant to Article 26(3)(b)(ii), clarifying the applicability of EU legal system as 'the natural means of dispute settlement of investor claims', thus withholding the unconditional consent to arbitrate: see ibid paras. 360–363.

[200] The Tribunal clarified that both the *Achmea* judgment and the Declaration are authentic interpretations, noting the CJEU case law but also referring to ILC Commentary to its Draft Articles on the Law of Treaties and NAFTA jurisprudence, which had only declaratory effect: see ibid paras. 379, 381–383.

[201] ibid para. 376.

must be taken into account in the interpretation of the ECT for systemic integration purposes under Article 31(3)(c) VCLT. The tribunal thus expanded the narrow operation of this provision in intra-EU relations adopted by other tribunals, while clarifying that consideration of EU law would be excluded in extra-EU relations.[202]

Accordingly, the *Green Power* tribunal reached the conclusion that the ECT ISDS clause must be interpreted in light of the wider body of legal relations between the home and host Member States – the relevant norms of EU law, which are applicable both as rules of international law and as part of *lex arbitri* given the seat of this arbitration in Sweden.[203] Such interpretation renders invalid the unilateral offer to arbitrate in Article 26 ECT given by an EU Member State to the investors of another EU Member State, which therefore must be 'disapplied' for its incompatibility with EU Treaties.[204] The award in *Green Power* thus fully endorses the legal effects of the *Achmea* and *Komstroy* judgments, dismissing the difference between BITs and the ECT in intra-EU arbitration.[205]

The award is relevant for future intra-EU arbitrations for several reasons. First, it confirms the relevance of EU law for the interpretation of the ECT in intra-EU relations as a matter of international *and* domestic law, thus confirming the findings of the *Electrabel* tribunal.[206] While the relevance of Sweden as the seat of arbitration has been emphasised throughout the award, the reasoning of this tribunal leaves sufficient scope to be applicable not only to non-ICSID but also ICSID awards.[207]

Second, the award endorses the underlying *rationale* of the *Achmea* judgment – the preservation of the autonomy of EU law guaranteed in Articles 267 and 344 TFEU.[208] The autonomy comes under threat not only when a tribunal must decide the merits of claims in matters under the exclusive EU competence, such as State aid, but also in cases when investment tribunals 'could affect' the interpretation of EU Treaties 'in a manner which is detrimental to the consistent and uniform

[202] ibid paras. 392–393. Cf. *Vattenfall II* (n 47) paras. 152–165.
[203] ibid paras. 166, 168–169, 172.
[204] ibid paras. 375, 445, 477.
[205] ibid para. 425.
[206] ibid para. 422.
[207] ibid para. 447. Cf. para. 439.
[208] Moreover, the award clarifies the applicability of Art. 344 TFEU to ISDS as per *Achmea*: ibid para. 423.

interpretation of EU law'.[209] The reference to *Achmea* as 'fully relevant' for jurisdictional objection *ratione voluntatis* thus leaves sufficient scope for it to be applicable to any intra-EU arbitration.[210]

Finally, the award recognised that there is a normative conflict between the ECT and EU law, which had been denied in previous awards, and reverses the conflict rule from *lex specialis* or *lex posterior* to *lex superior*, confirming the primacy of EU law which stems from the founding treaties.[211] Importantly, the tribunal dismissed the relevance of (in)famous Article 16 ECT as the pivotal conflict norm. Instead, primacy is to be determined with reference to international law beyond the ECT, whereby the ECT cannot present a limitation to the application of rules that are 'deemed to be overriding by the very States whose relations are at stake in the present arbitration'.[212] The tribunal thus adopted a broader holistic approach to the interpretation of intra-EU relations under international law, while recognising the central role of the States in determining their relations under public international law.

It remains to be seen to what extent will other ECT tribunals in pending intra-EU arbitrations follow this award, particularly in cases seated in the EU. Given the overwhelming ECT tribunals' jurisprudence in which intra-EU jurisdictional objection has been rejected, and for the purposes of legal certainty, the modernised ECT clarifies that Article 26 ECT does not apply between Contracting Parties which are members of the same REIO. Thus, if it ever sees its completion, the modernised ECT will explicitly exclude intra-EU ITA from the scope of the ECT ISDS clause.[213]

### 5.3.4 *Enforcement of Intra-EU Arbitral Awards*

Illegality of intra-EU investment awards under EU law poses a challenge to their enforcement in the EU and possibly also outside the EU. The success of the enforcement could also depend on whether the

209 ibid paras. 428, 454, 456.

210 See ibid para. 445. In demonstrating its reasoning, the tribunal makes great effort in distinguishing different arbitral tribunal and ICSID annulment committee decisions: see ibid paras. 437–441.

211 ibid para. 469.

212 ibid para. 470. The tribunal also recognises the primacy of EU law under *lex arbitri* in Swedish law: para. 475.

213 See EC, 'Agreement in Principle Reached on Modernised Energy Charter Treaty', 24 June 2022.

enforcement is sought based on the 1958 New York Convention (non-ICSID awards) or the challenged award has been rendered under the ICSID Convention. Finally, even when successfully enforced, payment of compensation under an intra-EU investment arbitral award can conflict with EU State aid rules.[214]

In intra-EU non-ICSID awards, Member States have been invoking Article V(2)(b) of the 1958 New York Convention, which allows the refusal of recognition or enforcement of a foreign award contrary to EU law and thus public policy.[215] States have also argued non-arbitrability of the intra-EU subject matter under Article V(2)(a) and illegality of the intra-EU arbitration agreements due to the lack of consent in accordance with Article V(1)(a). Since Member States' *lex fori* necessarily incorporates EU law, all intra-EU awards with a seat of arbitration in the EU are likely be set aside in a judicial review by the Member States' national courts as contrary to EU law on either of these grounds, given the priority of EU law over international law in the national legal orders of EU Member States. This duty of the national court has been explicitly stated by the CJEU.[216] In accordance with the CJEU's jurisprudence on intra-EU disputes in *Achmea*, *Komstroy* and *PL Holdings*, national courts have already started the practice of annulment of intra-EU investment awards based on intra-EU BITs due to arbitral tribunals' lack of jurisdiction.[217] Similar actions of national courts are taking place with respect to intra-EU awards rendered under the ECT.[218] Moreover, following *Komstroy*, EU law applies in the enforcement proceedings before the national courts whenever the non-EU parties have chosen a Member State as a seat of their ECT arbitration.[219] In addition to annulment of awards, these

[214] See observations of the arbitral tribunal in *Eskosol* (n 44) paras. 231–232.

[215] See *PL Holdings S.a.r.l. v Poland*, Judgment of the Supreme Court of Sweden No. V 2014/163 (14 December 2022). For comment on the concept of EU public policy, see G. A. Bermann, 'The Prospects of *Eco Swiss v Benetton* for International Commercial Arbitration: A Comment on *Eco Swiss v Benetton*' in P. Wautelet and others (eds), *The Practice of Arbitration: Essays in Honour of Hans van Houtte* (Hart 2012).

[216] *PL Holdings* (n 96) para. 55.

[217] *Slot v Poland*, PCA Case No. 2017-10, Judgment of the Paris Court of Appeal (19 April 2022); *Strabag et al v Poland*, Judgment of the Paris Court of Appeal (19 April 2022). On the same basis, the German Supreme court annulled the award in the *Achmea* intra-EU dispute: BGH, I ZB 2/15, 31.10.2018.

[218] See *Novenergia II v Spain*, SCC Case No. 2015/063, Decision from the Sea Court of Appeal (13 December 2022).

[219] In such cases, the CJEU can provide the interpretation of the ECT as EU law, but it is in discretion of national courts to refer any such questions: *Komstroy* (n 93) para. 35.

CJEU's decisions could also present a bar to arbitral *proceedings* based on intra-EU IIAs due to the lack of a valid arbitration agreement, especially for arbitrations seated in Germany.[220]

The situation is more complex in the cases of ICSID awards. Under Article 53 of the ICSID Convention, these awards are considered final and are not subject to domestic judicial review. Accordingly, States have an obligation to enforce pecuniary obligations imposed by an award as it were the final judgment of their national court.[221] However, in the EU, the ICSID Convention cannot trump EU law. As the ICSID Convention does not form part of EU law, but is an international agreement of Member States, it ranks below EU law in the hierarchy of rules in the EU legal order. Accordingly, if faced with an ICSID award,[222] the Member State national court must apply EU law and refuse to recognise that the award has legal consequences in that jurisdiction.[223] Furthermore, enforcement of an intra-EU ICSID award could be refused on the grounds that any other final judgment of national court which is in violation of EU law could also not be enforced.[224]

A further pending question is whether the reach of EU law could go as far as to present a bar on intra-EU arbitral proceedings initiated under the de-localised regime of ICSID.[225] The conflict between EU law and

[220] Based on Art. 1032(2) of the German Code of Civil Procedure, which allows a German court to assess the validity of the arbitration agreement pending the constitution of the arbitral tribunal, Croatia succeeded in obtaining a declaration of inadmissibility of arbitral proceedings initiated under an intra-EU BIT in *Raiffeisen Bank International AG and Raiffeisenbank Austria d.d. v Republic of Croatia (II)*, PCA Case No. 2020-15): BHB, I ZB 16/21, 17.11.2021.

[221] Art. 54(1) ICSID Convention.

[222] Art. 54(2) ICSID Convention involves two types of proceedings: recognition (that an award is binding) and enforcement (of the obligations imposed by the award).

[223] See Judgment of the Luxembourg Court of Cassation, Case No. 116/2022, CAS-2021-00061 (14 July 2022), regarding the *Micula* award (n 154). The Luxembourg Court found that Romania's consent to waive its sovereign immunity under the Sweden-Romania BIT was nullified when Romania joined the EU in 2007, as the BIT became contrary to Arts. 267 and 344 TFEU and the arbitration clause in the BIT devoid of any purpose. Accordingly, Romania had immunity from jurisdiction regarding the recognition of an award under Art. 54 ICSID Convention.

[224] See also *Ioan Micula et al v Romania*, Case No. Ä 2550-17, Nacka District Court, Decision (23 January 2019), concerning the incompatibility of a payment under the award with EU State aid rules.

[225] In 2021, the Netherlands submitted anti-arbitration injunctions based on Art. 1032(2) of the German Code of Civil Procedure against two intra-EU ICSID arbitrations under the ECT by German energy companies RWE and Uniper. See Ministry of Economic Affairs and Climate of the Netherlands, Letter to the Parliament (17 May 2021); T. M. Rusche,

intra-EU IIAs thus indirectly also challenges the ICSID regime and contributes to the debate about the autonomy of ICSID as a self-contained system, which decides its own jurisdiction[226] and is isolated from domestic courts,[227] albeit arguably not from substantive law which forms the basis of its jurisdiction. On the one hand, if there was no consent to arbitration under an intra-EU IIA in the first place, Article 26 of the ICSID Convention would not have effect. On the other hand, EU law is integrated into domestic law (e.g. German procedural law), which should not impede access to ICSID arbitration.[228]

Consequently, intra-EU awards can thus only be enforced in non-EU States. Non-EU courts have no obligation to comply with EU law but might stay enforcement or eventually uphold the intra-EU objection in cases of non-ICSID awards seated in the EU, which are challenged under the New York Convention – either for the lack of validity of the underlying arbitration agreement under the applicable EU law, or because an award which is illegal under EU law could also be considered contrary to domestic public policy of the State in which its enforcement is sought.[229] With respect to ICSID awards, EU law should not affect the jurisdiction of non-EU courts to recognise the binding nature of an intra-EU award 'as if it were a final judgment of a court' in the non-EU State where enforcement is sought.[230] In Australia, courts have found that an EU respondent State has waived its sovereign immunity by becoming a party to the ICSID Convention, thus authorising the Australian court to exercise subject matter jurisdiction in an action to enforce an ICSID award. Accordingly, Spain had no immunity from jurisdiction regarding the recognition of an award under Article 54(2) ICSID Convention.[231]

'Available Actions in the German Courts against the Abuse of Intra-EU Investor-State Arbitration Proceedings' (2021) 6 IPRax.

226 Art. 44 ICSID Convention.

227 ibid Art. 26.

228 See *SGS Société Générale de Surveillance S.A. v Islamic Republic of Pakistan*, ICSID Case No. ARB/01/13, Procedural Order No. 2 (16 October 2002). On the relationship of the ICSID Convention and IIAs regarding jurisdictional issues see also Section 1.3.1 in Chapter 1.

229 See, for example, Tribunal fédéral [TF], 23 February 2021, 4A_187/2020, where the Swiss court upheld the UNCITRAL award in *AES Solar and others (PV Investors) v Spain*, PCA Case No. 2012-14.

230 Art. 54(1) ICSID Convention.

231 *Kingdom of Spain v Infrastructure Services Luxembourg S.à.r.l.* [2021] FCAFC 3; *Infrastructure Services Luxembourg S.A.R.L v Kingdom of Spain* [2021] FCAFC 112. The case is pending before the High Court of Australia: [2022] HCATrans 39.

However, as in case of any award, investors still face the domestic sovereign immunity laws of the State in which enforcement is sought[232] and the practical problem of the availability of respondent States' assets to be seized in the State of enforcement.[233]

In the United Kingdom, with respect to an intra-EU award incompatible with EU law and rendered under the pre-Brexit regime, the court affirmed the priority of the UK's duties under Article 54 of the ICSID Convention over the duty of sincere cooperation under EU law. The UK Supreme Court reasoned that, in accordance with Article 351 TFEU, the UK's obligations under the ICSID Convention, owed to all ICSID Contracting Parties, precede the UK's accession to the EU, and are not subject to the overriding effect of EU law.[234] While this judgment appears to be in contradiction with the UK obligations under EU founding treaties in the transition period,[235] it is indicative of the post-Brexit approach of the UK courts regarding the recognition of intra-EU awards.

In the United States, courts have expressed reluctance 'to wade' into intra-EU territory unnecessarily, staying enforcement of intra-EU awards until the conclusion of set-aside proceedings in case of UNCITRAL awards[236] or the ICSID annulment proceedings.[237] In the (in)famous *Micula* case, a US federal district court enforced an intra-EU ICSID award which was considered an illegal State aid under EU law. However, the analysis of the US court in effect adopted the reasoning in the judgment of the General Court, which distinguished *Micula* from *Achmea*,[238] and

[232] In accordance with Arts. 54(3) and 55 ICSID Convention. For example, in Australia, *execution* of the award (process by which enforcement is carried out), as the next step following its recognition, remains subject to foreign sovereign immunity, and in further proceedings could still prevent investors from obtaining State assets located in Australia: see ibid.

[233] On (non)effectiveness of the ICSID regime in this regard, see E. Gaillard and I. M. Penushliski, 'State Compliance with Investment Awards' (2020) 35(3) *ICSID Review* 540.

[234] *Micula and others v Romania* [2020] UKSC 5, paras. 104–106, concerning the incompatibility of a payment under the award with EU State Aid rules.

[235] The EC accordingly launched the infringement proceedings against the United Kingdom in accordance with Art. 87 of the Withdrawal Agreement: see EC Press Release, 9 February 2022.

[236] *Novenergia II* (n 65) 18-cv-01148 (D.D.C. 27 January 2020).

[237] See for example, *RREEF* (n 51) 1:19-cv-03783 (D.D.C. 31 March 2021); *Infrared Environmental Infrastructure GP Limited and Others v Kingdom of Spain*, 1:20-cv-00817 (D.D.C. 29 June 2021). Subsequently, both awards were upheld by the ICSID Committee in June 2022.

[238] Case T-624/15 *European Food and Others v Commission* ECLI:EU:T:2019:423, which annulled the 2015 Decision of the Commission ordering Romania to recover partial

which was eventually set aside by the CJEU on the appeal.[239] First, as challenged measures occurred prior to the Member State's access to the EU, there was no breach of EU law and arbitration agreement applied; and second, as EU law did not apply in Romania, the arbitration did not relate to the interpretation and application of EU law. The US court thus concluded that 'the concern that animated *Achmea* – the un-reviewability of an arbitral tribunal's determination of EU law by an EU court' – was not present in the *Micula* case.[240] The US court's judgments confirm its pro-arbitration stance. However, its engagement with EU law in this ICSID case leaves some uncertainty about the relevance of *Achmea* for future enforcement proceedings of intra-EU awards before US courts.[241]

Finally, payment of compensation under an intra-EU investment arbitral award can be contrary to EU State aid rules. This issue has become prominent in the *Micula* context[242] and the ECT cases against Spain, many of which are still pending.[243] Thus, it could be argued that investors had no legitimate expectations of receiving protection under intra-EU IIAs, especially in all cases initiated after *Achmea*, and possibly also before, since *Achmea* applies to *Micula* regarding the lack of jurisdiction of arbitral tribunals after Romania's accession to the EU.[244] Accordingly, even if intra-EU awards are enforced and executed in non-EU States, any amounts so collected by an investor could be illegal State aid under EU law.

payment and suspend any further action regarding the execution of the 2013 Award in *Micula* (n 154) as unlawful state aid, finding that the Commission had no competence for the Decision.

239 Case C-638/19 P *Commission v European Food and Others* ECLI:EU:C:2022:50, finding that the right to compensation (i.e. the State aid) stems from the date of the award in 2013, which is thus the reference date for the EC competence.

240 See *Micula v Gov't of Rom.*, 404 F. Supp. 3d 265, 276–280 (D.D.C. 2019). This was confirmed in *Micula v Gov't of Rom.*, 2022 WL 18356669 (D.D.C. 22 December 2022).

241 Cf. Waiver theory adopted by the Australian court, which did not engage with questions of EU law.

242 *Micula* (n 154).

243 See Case SA.40348 (2015/NN) Commission Decision C (2017) 7384 final, para. 164, which explicitly refers to payment of the award compensation in *Eiser* (n 50), which was eventually annulled by the ICSID *ad hoc* committee on different grounds: see Decision on annulment (11 June 2020). The Commission has started State aid investigation, underlying Spain's obligation not to pay the compensation pending this investigation in *Infrastructure Services (formerly Antin)* (n 143), noting that this obligation applies irrespective of Arts. 53–55 of the ICSID Convention: Case SA.54155 (2021/NN) Commission Decision C (2021) 5405 final.

244 See *Commission v European Food* (n 239) para. 145. While the case is still pending before the General Court, the decision on the legality of payment of compensation in *Micula* under EU State aid rules will be decisive for other intra-EU ITAs.

The Commission could accordingly require the respondent Member States to recover the equivalent amounts from the investor in the EU, with only possibility to challenge the legality of State aid decisions before the General Court in first instance. The risks for investors associated with enforcement of intra-EU awards in violation of EU State aid rules are thus considerable, offering the Commission an effective option in ensuring compliance of intra-EU awards with EU law.[245]

While intra-EU awards enforcement is an evolving area of law, the number of intra-EU disputes will eventually decline, and EU investors will likely seek protections through (re)structuring of their investments through third countries covered with Member States' extra-EU BITs. After Brexit, the United Kingdom has become a third country, however, its pre-Brexit BITs with Member States provide uncertain prospects for investment protection.

### 5.3.5 *Formerly Intra-EU IIAs with the UK*

The United Kingdom signed the 15 January Declaration but not the TA and thus has not formally terminated its eleven BITs with Member States. However, the United Kingdom's obligation to remove its intra-EU BITs from its legal order applied during the transition period.[246] While now not bound by EU law, the United Kingdom remains responsible under international law for failure to fulfil obligations under EU Treaties before the end of the transition period. Accordingly, it can be subject to infringement proceedings before the CJEU within four years after the end of the transition period.[247]

Pending further EU action,[248] the validity of UK's BITs with Member States thus remains questionable. The United Kingdom's withdrawal from the EU has not changed the pre-Brexit legal effects of *Achmea* under EU law. While the EU-UK Trade and Cooperation Agreement (TCA) has no express termination clause like EU agreements with other

[245] See Case C-333/19 *Romatsa and Others* ECLI:EU:C:2022:749, in which the CJEU held that the ICSID award contrary to EU State aid rules cannot be enforced before national courts of Member States.

[246] Art. 127 Agreement on the Withdrawal of the United Kingdom of Great Britain and Northern Ireland from the European Union and the European Atomic Energy Community, 2020 OJ (L 29) 7.

[247] ibid Art. 87.

[248] The EC has initiated the infringement proceedings: see 'October infringements package: key decisions' (30 October 2020).

trading partners, the EU position will be that intra-EU BITs have become either impliedly terminated under Article 59 VCLT, or inapplicable under Article 30 VCLT, from the date of the accession of each Contracting Party to the EU. On the other hand, the United Kingdom's position could likely be that its BITs with Member States have not been impliedly nor expressly terminated and can now co-exist with the TCA given the substantially wider scope of the BITs.[249] Since similar arguments have already been considered by arbitral tribunals in intra-EU ITAs, relying on UK's BITs with Member States post-Brexit would likely involve all legal challenges already associated with intra-EU ITAs, as discussed in this chapter.

The situation would, however, be different with respect to the ECT, since there were no similar obligations for the United Kingdom to remove its intra-EU legal effects. While any pending pre-Brexit ECT arbitrations could still face intra-EU challenges for clashes with EU law, post-Brexit the ECT applies between the United Kingdom and Member States as any other extra-EU IIA.[250]

### 5.3.6 *The Rule of Law and the Future of Investment in the EU*

In the short- and medium-term, legal uncertainty created around the adjudication of intra-EU arbitration proceedings and the enforcement of intra-EU awards undermines the rule of law. However, in the long-term, the legal consequences of *Achmea* should lead to the strengthening of the rule of law in the EU.

The mechanism of judicial review carried out through judicial cooperation between the CJEU and national courts is designed to ensure compliance with EU law, which 'is of the essence of the rule of law'.[251] In the absence of ISDS, investors will be encouraged to seek protections under EU law, fuelling the EU judicial system with cases, which will allow for more expansive judicial review of the legality of national acts under EU law and rule-making by the CJEU, through the preliminary ruling procedure, to address any lacunae regarding protection of investor rights within the EU.[252] Judicial review should thus on one hand strengthen the

[249] The TCA includes only limited substantive protections (NT and MFN), and no ISDS clauses.

[250] See Chapter 8.

[251] Case C-64/16 *Associação Sindical dos Juízes Portugueses* ECLI:EU:C:2018:117, para. 36.

[252] To that effect, see *PL Holdings* (n 96) para. 68.

role of national courts, and, on the other hand, expand the reach of EU law.

Unlike ISDS arbitrators, whose powers are limited to monetary compensation for the adverse impact of the illegal measure on the investor, national judges are empowered to 'disapply' national measures inconsistent with EU law and award damages to investors in case of a breach of EU law. Ultimately, this should eliminate illegal national policies and influence the Member States' behaviour and policymaking towards their compliance with the rule of law in the EU.[253] The broader normative reach of EU law in striking the balance between private interests and public policy goals should also address the legitimacy concerns of ISDS. On the other hand, the rule of law in some Member States has been the subject of concern for investors.[254] However, the CJEU has defended national courts against the politics of Member States,[255] while national courts have rejected arguments about the denial of effective legal protection for investors before national courts of other Member States.[256]

Member States have pledged to enhance the mechanisms of protection of intra-EU investors under EU law, which would incentivise investments within the internal market.[257] The Commission has identified uneven level of investment protection, and difficulties in enforcing rights and obtaining effective remedies across Member States, as core problems affecting investors within the internal market. Among possible interventions at the EU level, it envisages a range of legal instruments to supplement the existing substantive rules, and even the creation of a specialised

[253] J. H. H. Weiler, 'The Transformation of Europe' (1991) 100 *Yale Law Journal* 2403, 2421; K. J. Alter, *Establishing the Supremacy of European Law: The Making of an international Rule of Law in Europe* (OUP 2001) 217–221; see also Section 4.3.3 in Chapter 4.

[254] See W. Sadowski, 'Protection of the Rule of Law in the European Union through Investment Treaty Arbitration: Is Judicial Monopolism the Right Response to Illiberal Tendencies in Europe?' (2018) 55 *Common Market Law Review* 1025.

[255] Case C-625/18 *AK (Independence of the Disciplinary Chamber of the Supreme Court)* ECLI:EU:C:2019:982; Case C-487/19 *WZ* ECLI:EU:C:2021:798; Joined Cases C-748/19 to C-754/19 *Prokuratura Rejonowa w Minsku Mazowieckim* ECLI:EU:C:2021:931.

[256] See, for example, BHB (n 220) para. 41. See also Judgment of the Brussels Court of First Instance (19/3390/A, 18 February 2022), setting aside the investment award under an extra-EU BIT in *MSC v Poland*, PCA Case No. 2015-18, that found Poland liable for denial of justice by the Polish Supreme Court. On the contrary, the Belgian Court found that arbitral tribunal failed to identify any malfunctioning in the Polish judicial system as a whole. Similarly, see Decision of the *Swedish Court in Novenergia II* (n 218).

[257] Preamble, TA. See also declarations to TA by Lithuania, Luxembourg and Portugal.

EU investment court, modelled on the Unified Patent Court.[258] While the intra-EU investment policy post-intra-EU IIAs is in the making, the prospects of a new court remain distant and legally and politically difficult.

## 5.4 Conclusion

Law has played an important role in overcoming Member States' political differences and fostering EU integration.[259] Developments in intra-EU investment confirm this thesis. While political disagreements between Member States about intra-EU BITs started some fifteen years ago, the CJEU's judgments opened the way for political consensus on termination of intra-EU IIAs. Law has thus been an important integrative *factor* and the CJEU an important *actor* in consolidating divergent Member States' interests in this field.

Termination of intra-EU BITs by Member States sends clear signals to investors and arbitral tribunals that intra-EU investment regime as a whole is incompatible with the EU legal order. Intra-EU ITAs, particularly under the ECT, are likely to continue based on complex legal formalism in reasoning of arbitral tribunals. However, disregard of the CJEU judgments places Member States in a difficult situation in which they must choose between fulfilling their obligations under international law or EU law. This can lead to diplomatic tensions, refuting the very depoliticising purpose of ISDS. At the same time, uncertainty regarding intra-EU awards enforcement could transform them into a lucrative investment for secondary financial investors, driving IIL away from its core objectives. Ongoing intra-EU arbitrations can thus only further undermine the legitimacy of ISDS.[260]

Intra-EU IIAs and ITAs fragment the internal market. If the internal market is the quintessence of EU integration, it is quite logical that anything that undermines this goal must accommodate to it, or otherwise be eliminated. *Prima facie*, it seems that the EU and international investment regulation (IIR) have much in common, at least regarding

[258] See EC, Inception Impact Assessment, Ares(2020)2716046, and the public consultation process 'Cross-border investment within the EU – clarifying and supplementing EU rules' (26 May 2020).

[259] A. Burley and W. Mattli, 'Europe before the Court: A Political Theory of Legal Integration' in M. Eilstrup-Sangiovanni (ed), *Debates on European Integration* (Palgrave 2006) ch. 9.

[260] For this conclusion see also Statement of Dissent of Marcelo Kohen (n 37) paras. 80–82.

economic goals; however, their differences are not only institutional but also normative. In its intra-EU investment judgments, the CJEU endorsed a federalist vision of the EU, which prevails over particular interests, whether Member States' or business. The CJEU's approach confirms that EU integration remains its ultimate goal, and any hostility towards IIL is exclusive to this context.

Finally, the core issue in the CJEU's judgments was not the protection of intra-EU investors but the autonomy of the EU legal order. These judgments favour the cooperation between national courts and the CJEU, allowing expansion of the reach of EU law and thus supporting the project of EU integration. The main objective of the autonomy is not to depart from international standards but to ensure that these standards do not impede EU integration. Without tools to defend its autonomy, the EU project would be seriously undermined.

The clash between IIL and EU law in intra-EU investment is in its essence a clash between two autonomous legal orders in a fragmented system of international law, which bounds States in a complex network of legal relations. The post-*Achmea* developments demonstrate that fragmentation in international law has serious implications for legal certainty. Therefore, full recognition of the relevance and legal effects of the principles affirmed by the CJEU jurisprudence regarding intra-EU arbitration is a welcome development. It goes beyond the 'binary logic' of IIAs and EU law as separate planes, and above the rigid choices between EU law or public international law as two mutually exclusive systems. Eventually, it should also translate into benefits for the rule of law in the EU legal order.

# 6

# EU Institutional Framework

## Legal Limitations to Policy Efficiency

In this final chapter of Part II, we analyse the key legal issues related to the allocation of international investment competence within the EU and examine their implications for policy efficiency and choices in external EU trade and investment relations. Following the Lisbon Treaty of 2009, the EU has gained competence for international investment treaty-making, which previously fell within the scope of the Member States' competence. Given the relevance of international investment for the EU, on the one hand, and the cross-cutting nature of investment within the range of domestic policy areas on the other, the exercise of competences relating to foreign investment has been surrounded by controversies. Importantly, treaty-making procedure in the EU is not a matter of political inter-institutional preference but it is defined by the delineation of competences, grounded in primary law. The focus of our analysis in this chapter is placed on the internal EU institutional framework regarding competences between the EU and its Member States for investment and the conclusion of EU international investment agreements (IIAs), and the role of the Court of Justice of the European Union (CJEU) in defining the scope of EU policy. The content of EU international investment policy is then analysed in Part III.

### 6.1 Power to Decide Investment Issues in the EU: A Question of Competence

It has always been a particular challenge to specify the exact division of competences between the EU and its Member States. Similar to a federal structure, the powers and competences of EU institutions in a particular policy area are defined by the founding treaties, and are clarified through the case law of the CJEU. Treaty provisions confer on the EU competence in order to achieve objectives particular to that policy area, which are interpreted in light of the general objectives of the EU.[1] Competence stems from a particular legal basis, which empowers the EU to exercise its competence in a given field. The choice of legal basis for a particular EU action determines which institution has competence to act, what procedure is to be followed, which objectives are to be achieved and what types of acts can be adopted. Competence and legal bases could therefore be described as two sides of the same coin, which define the institutional power within the EU in a certain policy area. The principle of conferred powers must be respected both in the internal (intra-EU) action and the external (international) action of the EU.[2] In the context of international investment, this has important consequences for the efficiency of the EU's international investment policy (IIP), its policy choices and accordingly also the EU's role in geopolitics of international trade.

European Union's international investment competence has been the subject of marked controversy, with Member States and the EU disagreeing on the matter. Divergent institutional opinions regarding the extent and nature of EU foreign investment powers led the European Commission (EC) to request from the CJEU the clarification of the competence of the EU to sign and conclude a free trade agreement (FTA) with Singapore (EUSFTA).[3] Such requests can be made pursuant to Article 218(11) Treaty on the Functioning of the European Union (TFEU) and may relate to the issue of competence (whether any institution of the EU has the power to conclude the agreement) or the issue of substance (whether the content of the agreement is compatible with EU law).[4] Request for Opinion 2/15 is related strictly to the issue of competence.[5]

In order to answer the question of who holds power to decide foreign investment issues in the EU, the CJEU examined EU competence with respect to the investment chapter of the EUSFTA,[6] clarifying two aspects:

[1] Arts. 5(1) and (2) TEU. Parts of this chapter have been published in I. Damjanovic, 'Investment and EU International Agreements' in X. Groussot and others (eds), *The EU Law of Investment: Past, Present and Future* (Hart 2023).

[2] Opinion 2/94 [1996] ECR I-1759, para. 24.

[3] EC, 'Decision Requesting an Opinion of the Court of Justice Pursuant to Article 218(11) TFEU on the Competence of the Union to Sign and Conclude a Free Trade Agreement with Singapore' C (2014) 8218 final.

[4] Opinion 2/15 ECLI:EU:C:2017:376, para. 9 and case law therein cited.

[5] The later request by the Kingdom of Belgium, which resulted in CJEU's Opinion 1/17 related to the issue of compatibility of CETA's investment chapter with EU law: see Chapter 9.

[6] Ch 9 EUSFTA containing provisions on investment protection and dispute settlement. Importantly, since Opinion 2/15, what is now referred as the EU–Singapore FTA differs from the EUSFTA examined by the CJEU in Opinion 2/15, and is incapsulated in the Investment Protection Agreement (IPA) with Singapore (EUSIPA).

(i) the scope of EU competence regarding foreign investment, both with respect to the type of investment (FDI vs portfolio investment) as well as the phases of investment (pre-establishment vs post-establishment), and (ii) the nature of EU investment competence (internal vs external; exclusive vs shared; express vs implied). The CJEU's conclusions are explained next through the prism of these intertwined elements.

### 6.1.1 *The Scope of EU Foreign Investment Competence*

In general terms, the scope of competence determines the aspects of a certain policy area for which Member States have conferred competence on the EU. Article 207(1) TFEU is the key provision for defining the scope of the EU's international investment competence:

> The common commercial policy shall be based on uniform principles, particularly with regard to changes in tariff rates, the conclusion of tariff and trade agreements relating to trade in goods and services, and the commercial aspects of intellectual property, *foreign direct investment*, the achievement of uniformity in measures of liberalisation, export policy and measures to protect trade such as those to be taken in the event of dumping or subsidies. The common commercial policy shall be conducted in the context of the principles and objectives of the Union's external action.[7]

The provision lists foreign direct investment (FDI) as one of the aspects of the Common Commercial Policy (CCP) and thus provides an explicit legal basis for the EU's competence over investment regulation, including the conclusion of international agreements.[8] However, the definition of investment in IIAs is broader than FDI, also including portfolio investment,[9] which led to divergent interpretations of the exact scope of the EU foreign investment power. In its Opinion 2/15, the CJEU distinguished between two types of foreign investment: 'direct' and 'non-direct' or 'portfolio', concluding that *only* FDI falls within the scope of CCP and Article 207(1) TFEU.[10]

Direct investment relates to those investments which 'establish or maintain *lasting and direct links* between the persons providing the capital and the undertakings to which that capital is made available in

[7] Art. 207(1) TFEU (emphasis added).
[8] Art. 207(3) and (4) TFEU.
[9] Art. 9.1 EUSFTA.
[10] See Opinion 2/15 (n 4) para. 83 (emphasis added).

order to carry out an economic activity', thus enabling the shareholder 'to participate effectively in the *management* of [the] company or in its *control*'.[11] Differently to that, 'non-direct foreign investment', also known as portfolio investment, is made 'with the intention of making a financial investment without *any* intention to influence the management and control of the undertaking', thus constituting free movement of capital for the purposes of Article 63 TFEU.[12] Importantly, free movement of capital applies between the Member States as well as between Member States and third countries.[13] As examples of portfolio investment the Court mentioned 'types of investment other than the acquisition of company securities, such as certain categories of real-estate investment or the use of loans'.[14]

Additionally, the CJEU clarified that EU competence under Article 207 (1) TFEU with respect to FDI includes acts related to *admission* as well as *protection* of FDI.[15] The former concerns the (pre-) establishment phase – admission and post-admission treatment of the investment – while the latter the post-establishment phase – protection of investment once the investment has been made.

Trade treaties of the EU with third States in pre-Lisbon times, building upon the General Agreement on Trade in Services (GATS) classification of services,[16] involved provisions on the admission of investment (investment liberalisation) and its related post-admission treatment, through provisions on establishment for supply of services and capital movements.[17] The main purpose of these provisions was to secure market access to third countries for EU investors while granting to third countries' foreign investors access to the EU market in the course of trade

[11] ibid para. 80 (emphasis added).

[12] Opinion 2/15 (n 4) para. 227. Free movement of capital is not defined in the treaties and its meaning is determined by reference to the nomenclature in Annex I to Council Directive 88/361/EEC of 24 June 1988 for the implementation of Article 67 of the Treaty [1988] OJ L178/5. The nomenclature is not exhaustive: see Case C-222/97 *Trummer and Mayer* [1999] ECR I-1671, paras. 7, 13.

[13] See Art. 63 TFEU. Free movement of capital is subject to limitations in Arts. 64 and 65 TFEU. See Section 4.5.1 in Chapter 4.

[14] Opinion 2/15 (n 4) para. 228.

[15] ibid paras. 87, 109.

[16] Art. I(2) General Agreement on Trade in Services, Marrakesh Agreement Establishing the World Trade Organization, Annex 1B (signed 15 April 1994, entered into force 1 January 1995) 1869 UNTS 183, 33 ILM 1167 (GATS). Most investments fall into mode 3 (commercial presence).

[17] See A. Dimopoulos, *EU Foreign Investment Law* (OUP 2011) 82.

exchange. Depending on the third country involved, they provided for different levels of investment liberalisation and reciprocity, by including diverse market access restrictions in specific sectors or providing different levels of accorded treatment (NT or MFN, or both). Establishment of legal persons under these pre-Lisbon GATS regulatory model treaties, although within the EU competence, did not fall within the scope of the CCP, or, to the extent that it fell under the CCP, it was subject to different qualifications and sectoral limitations.[18] In addition, some EU agreements were inspired by primary EU law and thus contain clauses on establishment, which mirror EU law provisions on freedom of establishment and free movement of capital.[19] Finally, provisions on post-establishment treatment of investments, both the narrower post-admission treatment in GATS-style agreements, as well as broader investment protection standards of traditional BITs,[20] equally did not exclusively fall within the pre-Lisbon CCP scope. This fragmentation required the EU to conclude international agreements concerning foreign investment jointly with the Member States.

With the explicit inclusion of FDI into the CCP in the Lisbon Treaty, all aspects of FDI – admission, post-admission treatment and protection – now fall within the CCP. On the contrary, portfolio investment in its entirety falls outside the CCP scope, but it is nevertheless within EU competence. This difference is pertinent to the nature of EU competence, which ultimately determines the extent of EU powers with respect to these two different types of investment, as explained next.

### 6.1.2 *The Nature of EU Foreign Investment Competence*

Once it is determined which aspects of a certain policy area fall within EU competence, the nature of competence determines the extent to

[18] Opinion 1/94 [1994] ECR I-5267, in which the CJEU assessed different GATS modes of supply of services and concluded that mode 3 was not covered by the CCP: see paras. 43–47. After the Treaty of Nice all four WTO modes of provision of services fall within the CCP, however subject to conditions laid down in Arts. 133(5) and (6) TEC (agreements in defined sectors to be concluded jointly by the Community and the Member States): Opinion 1/08 [2009] ECR I-11129.

[19] See Arts. 31–35 (ch. on Right of Establishment) and 40–45 (ch. on Capital), Agreement on European Economic Area and establishment clauses in Stabilisation and Associations Agreements with Western Balkans countries; for example, Art. 53 Stabilisation and Association Agreement between the European Communities and their Member States of the one part, and the Republic of Montenegro, of the other part [2010] OJ L108/3.

[20] The ECT is the only such agreement concluded by the EU pre-Lisbon.

which the EU may exercise its competence independently from the Member States, both internally and externally.[21] The internal dimension relates to the adoption of secondary legislation, while the external dimension includes the conclusion of international agreements (treaty-making competence). European Union competence can be either *exclusive* or *shared* with the Member States. Exclusive EU competence is either expressed in Article 3 TFEU (*express exclusive EU competence*) or can be implied with respect to external action (treaty-making) in the exercise of EU internal competence (*implied exclusive EU competence*). Therefore, to determine the exact nature of EU competence in shared policy areas, both internal and external dimensions of EU action have to be taken into consideration. The extent to which the EU can act independently from the Member States is not necessarily the same with respect to its internal and external action. Consequently, EU internal action can be a source of the EU's creeping international competence.

Generally speaking, in the areas of exclusive competence, the EU is authorised to act alone and Member States can neither legislate internally nor enter into international obligations externally, unless empowered by the EU.[22] In the areas of shared competence both the EU and Member States may act to exercise their competence.[23] However, Member States may exercise their competence to the extent that the EU does not exercise its own competence (principle of pre-emption).[24] Nevertheless, the EU action must be in accordance with the principles of subsidiarity[25] and proportionality,[26] both enshrined in Articles 5(3) and 5(4) TFEU, respectively. If the EU has not taken action, Member States maintain their competences but must act in accordance with EU law.[27] With EU

[21] Opinion 2/94 (n 2) para. 24 and Case C-370/07 *Commission v Council* [2009] ECR I-8917, para. 46.

[22] Art. 2(1) TFEU.

[23] Art. 2(2) first sentence TFEU.

[24] Art. 2(2) second sentence TFEU. These are known as shared pre-emptive competences. In some areas shared competences are parallel: see Arts. 4(3) and (4) TFEU.

[25] The aim is to determine whether the EU is the appropriate decision-maker in certain matters of shared competence, subject to sufficiency and value-added test, and *ex-ante* scrutiny by national parliaments and *ex-post* judicial control: see A. Rosas and L. Armati, *EU Constitutional Law: An Introduction* (Hart 2010) 24–25.

[26] The aim is to determine the appropriateness of EU action in certain matters of shared competence, with the choice of action confined to what is necessary to achieve the objectives of the treaties.

[27] Case C-114/01 *AvestaPolarit Chrome Oy* [2003] ECR I-8725, para. 57. Additionally, Member States are bound by the principle of sincere cooperation enshrined in Art. 4(3)

eagerness to harmonise different policy areas falling into the scope of shared competences, through the adoption of secondary legislation (regulations, directives and framework decisions), national competences have been constantly shrinking, both internally and externally.

European Union treaty-making competence is defined in Article 216 TFEU, which should be read in conjunction with Article 3 TFEU. Exclusive EU competence for the conclusion of international agreements can be either: (a) explicit, where the treaties provide the EU with the power to conclude an international agreement, or (b) implicit, which includes three possible situations: (i) when conclusion of an international agreement is necessary to achieve one of the objectives of the EU's policies; (ii) when an EU legislative act requires the EU to conclude an international agreement; or (iii) when it is likely that the Member States' exercise of treaty-making powers could 'affect common [internal] rules or alter their scope'. This last scenario of implied exclusive EU competence is usually the result of internal harmonisation through EU legislation, developed in line with the CJEU case law, the so-called AETR-ERTA principle,[28] now enshrined in Article 3(2) TFEU.

Therefore, internal EU exercise of shared competence may lead to implied exclusive EU treaty-making competence. If the EU legislates internally the Member States lose competence to legislate and they may also lose competence to conclude international agreements in the same area, depending on the extent to which EU legislation and the international agreement coincide.[29] This loss of competence is justified whenever a Member State's international agreement 'is capable of undermining the uniform and consistent application of the EU rules and proper functioning of the system which they establish';[30] in other

TEU and should refrain from any measure which could jeopardise the attainment of the EU's objectives.

[28] Case 22–70 *Commission v Council* (European Road Transport Agreement) [1971] ECR 263, para. 17. See also Case C-467/98 *Commission v Denmark* ('Open Skies' Agreement) [2002] ECR I-9519, paras. 77–80.

[29] However, it is not necessary that they fully coincide but that the area to which international agreement relates has been 'covered to a large extent' by common EU rules. The analysis of the relationship between provisions of international agreement and EU rules has to take into account the scope, nature and content of provisions and rules, as well as foreseeable future development of EU rules in that area: Opinion 1/03 [2006] ECR I-1145, para. 126. Absence of contradiction between internal EU rules and the proposed agreement does not matter: ibid paras. 143 and 151. Post-Lisbon, this position has been reiterated rather liberally: Opinion 1/13 ECLI:EU:C:2014:2303.

[30] Opinion 1/13 (n 29) para. 74.

Table 6.1 *Overview of EU competences*

| EU competence | Exclusive Art 3 TFEU | Shared Art 4 TFEU | |
|---|---|---|---|
| Internal Power to legislate | Express:<br>- EU alone<br>- Includes CCP: Art. 3(1) (e) TFEU | Shared pre-emptive (EU has legislated):<br>- EU alone: Art. 2 (2) TFEU | • Shared non pre-emptive (EU has not legislated):<br>EU + Member States: Art. 2 (2) TFEU<br>• Shared parallel: EU + Member States: Art. 4(3) and (4) TFEU |
| External Treaty-making power | Express:<br>- EU alone<br>- Includes CCP: Art. 3(1)(e) TFEU/ancillary nature of institutional provisions | Implied exclusive EU treaty-making:<br>- EU alone: Art. 3 (2) TFEU (AETR-ERTA case law) | Shared treaty-making competence:<br>EU + Member States Includes 'Free movement of persons, services and capital' = internal market: Arts. 4(1) and 4(2)(a) |

words, any time when the objectives of EU integration *could* come under threat.

Applying these rules in the field of trade and investment, it becomes important that the CCP, as the key policy area for the exercise of EU international trade and investment competence,[31] is listed in Article 3(1)(e) among the express exclusive EU competences. The scope of the CCP therefore determines the scope of the exclusive EU treaty-making competence in the field of trade and investment. This issue was at the core of the CJEU Opinion 2/15. Table 6.1 summarises the key EU competences in the framework of the CCP.

In Opinion 2/15, the CJEU confirmed the exclusive EU competence with respect to all trade EUSFTA areas, clarifying that the EU alone is

[31] Case C-414/11 *Daiichi Sankyo Co. Ltd and Sanofi-Aventis Deutschland* ECLI:EU:C:2013:520, para. 50.

competent to conclude international agreements in these areas. The Court found that almost all trade issues fall with the scope of the CCP, and thus within express exclusive EU competence. The CJEU identified these components of the FTA by examining whether they display a 'specific link' with trade between the EU and Singapore, meaning that the commitments therein are (i) intended to promote, facilitate or govern trade *and* (ii) have direct and immediate effect on trade.[32] All trade-related chapters of the EUSFTA passed this test,[33] except trade in transport services, where they relate to public procurement for identified transport services and institutional provisions.[34]

With respect to trade in transport services and related public procurement for these services, the CJEU concluded that commitments in these EUSFTA areas fall within a field largely covered by common EU rules, thus being able to affect or alter their scope.[35] Consequently, the CJEU concluded that, in accordance with AETR-ERTA doctrine and Article 3(2) TFEU, these provisions fall within the implied exclusive EU competence. The Court further reiterated that institutional provisions of the EUSFTA, including those relating to transparency, because of their ancillary nature, fall within the same exclusive EU competence as substantive provisions which they accompany.[36]

With respect to investment provisions, while finding that FDI falls within the scope of the CCP and thus within express exclusive EU competence, the Court identified that the EU and Member States share competence with respect to non-FDI investment (portfolio investment) and investor-State dispute settlement (ISDS). In other words, the CJEU clarified that the EU is not exclusively competent for all investment issues. In coming to this conclusion, the CJEU rejected the Commission's argument that the AETR-ERTA doctrine could be applicable to portfolio investment commitments specified in Section A ('Investment Protection') of EUSFTA chapter 9. Since no secondary EU legislation has been adopted under Articles 63(1) and 64(2) TFEU relating to any type of investment

[32] Opinion 2/15 (n 4) paras. 36–38 and case law therein cited (emphasis added).
[33] See ibid paras. 40–55, 68, 74, 77, 130, 138, 167.
[34] ibid para. 62.
[35] For the analysis of relevant services, see: ibid paras. 182–193 (maritime), 197–202 (rail), 206–211 (road), 213–218 (internal waterway, however, implying exclusive EU competence in this aspect).
[36] ibid paras. 276–277, 282–283.

other than FDI,[37] the CJEU reasoned that primary EU law cannot be subsumed under 'common rules' within the meaning of Article 3(2) TFEU.[38]

Nevertheless, although not exclusively competent for portfolio investment commitments in the EUSFTA, the EU shares competence for these commitments with its Member States. This is because the conclusion of an international agreement such as the EUSFTA, which contributes to free movement of capital as one of the internal market freedoms, could be necessary for the achievement of the Treaty objectives related to the internal market (an area of shared competence).[39] Further, the EU also shares competence with the Member States for commitments in Section B ('Investor–State Dispute Settlement'). Contrary to the Advocate General's Opinion, the CJEU reasoned that ISDS, as a regime which 'removes disputes from the jurisdiction of the courts of the Member States', cannot be considered ancillary in nature to substantive provisions of the EUSFTA and consequently cannot be considered an exclusive EU competence. The CJEU emphasised that the EU must share competence with the Member States, given that the ISDS regime cannot be established without Member States' consent.[40] Finally, the Court also found that the institutional provisions relating to an area of shared competence in the investment chapter also fall within the competence shared between the EU and Member States.[41] The delineation of competences stemming from the CJEU's Opinion 2/15 is outlined in Table 6.2.

[37] See Opinion 2/15, Opinion of Advocate General Sharpston ECLI:EU:C:2016:992, para. 360.

[38] Opinion 2/15 (n 4) para. 235–238.

[39] In particular, the CJEU refers to the objectives of Title IV ('Free movement of persons, services and capital') of Part III ('Union policies and internal actions') of the TFEU. Given that Title IV relates to the internal market, it falls within the scope of Art. 4(2)(a) TFEU. Additionally, the EU and Member States also share objectives under Art. 216(1), in relation to Art. 4(1) TFEU, which provides that the EU and Member States share competence in areas which do not relate to Arts. 3 and 6 TFEU: ibid paras. 240–242.

[40] ibid paras. 292–293. Cf. Opinion of AG Sharpston (n 37) para. 535, where she asserted EU exclusive competence for ISDS, based on its ancillary nature: para. 529. Investor–State dispute settlement concerns the *manner* in which the competence is exercised, rather than the nature of the competence, which is determined by substantive provisions of the agreement (which she also asserted were within EU exclusive competence): paras. 525–527.

[41] Opinion 2/15 (n 4) paras. 278–279, 284. In particular, the areas of shared competence are the provisions of ch. 1 (Objectives and General Definitions), ch. 14 (Transparency), ch. 15 (Dispute Settlement between the Parties), ch. 16 (Mediation Mechanisms) and ch. 17 (Institutional, General and Final Provisions), insofar as they relate to provisions of ch. 9 that fall within shared competence.

Table 6.2 *EU competence for trade and investment in modern comprehensive FTAs*

| EU competence in EUSFTA (Opinion 2/15) | |
|---|---|
| **Exclusive EU competence** | |
| **Express:** CCP (Art. 3(1)(e) TFEU) or the ancillary nature of institutional provisions<br>. National Treatment and Market Access for Goods;<br>. Trade Remedies;<br>. Technical Barriers to Trade;<br>. Sanitary and Phytosanitary Measures;<br>. Customs and Trade Facilitation;<br>. Non-Tariff Barriers to Trade and Investment in Renewable Energy Generation;<br>. Services, Establishment and Electronic Commerce (except services relating to international maritime transport, rail transport, road transport, internal waterways transport);<br>. Government Procurement (except for international maritime transport services, rail transport services, road transport services, internal waterways transport services);<br>. Investment chapter (except non-direct investment and investment dispute settlement);<br>. Commercial aspects of intellectual property;<br>. Competition;<br>. Sustainable development;<br>. Provisions ancillary in nature to substantive provisions:<br>- Institutional framework (except for provisions relating to 'Investment Protection');<br>- Transparency (except for 'Investment Protection');<br>- Dispute settlement between the Parties to the agreement (except for 'Investment Protection') | **Implied:** Art. 3(2) TFEU or the ancillary nature of institutional provisions<br>. Services relating to international maritime transport, rail transport, road transport, internal waterways transport;<br>. Public procurement in the field of transport (international maritime transport services, rail transport services, road transport services, internal waterways transport services) |

Table 6.2 (*cont.*)

| EU competence in EUSFTA (Opinion 2/15) |
|---|
| **Shared EU (EU + Member States) competence: Arts. 4(1) and (2)(a) TFEU**<br>• Non-direct investment (portfolio investment)<br>• Investor–State dispute settlement<br>• Provisions ancillary in nature to substantive provisions:<br>- Dispute settlement between states parties to an agreement with respect to 'Investment Protection' |

The delineation of competences between the EU and Member States has important consequences for treaty-making. Member States cannot become parties to international agreements covering the areas of exclusive (express or implied) EU competence. Instead, the EU concludes such international agreements as EU-only agreements. In cases when international agreements cover the areas of shared competence, both the EU and Member States become a party to such treaties in order to assume international obligations in the area of their competence. Such agreements are thus concluded as 'mixed' agreements. Treaty will be mixed also if, in addition to areas of exclusive EU competence, it covers the areas of exclusive Member States competence. Accordingly, in cases of doubt, where the subject matter of an agreement does not follow a clear allocation in relation to the scope of the CCP, the agreement should be concluded as a mixed agreement. However, as long as the agreement does not cover any areas of exclusive Member State competences, the choice whether the agreement is an 'EU-only' or a 'mixed' is a matter of political discretion for the Council.[42]

The classification of international agreements has significant consequences for the EU's performance in international affairs. To cite AG Kokott: 'the more players there are on the European side at international level, the more difficult it will be to represent effectively the interests of the Community and its Member States outwardly, in particular vis-à-vis significant trading partners'.[43] On the other hand, the issue is important for the democratic legitimacy of EU treaty-making in the area of trade

[42] To that effect, see Case C-600/14 *Germany v Council*, ECLI:EU:C:2017:935, para. 68.
[43] Case C-13/07 *Commission v Council*, Opinion of AG Kokott ECLI:EU:2009:190, para. 72.

and investment, which is ensured through the ratification process. These implications are considered next.

## 6.2 EU Policymaking in International Investment: The Choice of a Legal Basis

Given the legal nature of EU integration, every EU action must be founded on one or more legal bases in the founding treaties. The legal basis determines the procedure to be followed for the adoption of a particular EU act, including the procedure for the conclusion of an international agreement. Importantly, the choice of legal basis, formally speaking, is not really a 'choice'. It 'does not follow from its author's conviction alone but must rest on objective factors', these being the aim and the content of the measure, rather than its effects.[44] This approach is also known as the 'centre of gravity theory'.

When a measure has more than one aim or more than one component, that measure should still be founded on a single legal basis – the basis required by the measure's predominant aim or component, if they can be established.[45] If, however, the measure 'simultaneously pursues several objectives which are inseparably linked without one being secondary and indirect in relation to the other', the measure can be founded on the corresponding bases,[46] unless multiple legal bases are procedurally incompatible or would undermine the role of the European Parliament.[47]

Given the fluidity of aims and objectives of the CCP, it is difficult to exactly delineate the scope of the areas covered by this policy area. As a matter of principle, the legal basis for the CCP in Article 207 TFEU, which involves exclusive EU competence to conclude an international agreement, cannot be used in combination with shared competences, except in rare circumstances. At the same time, given that international agreements could include a range of different commitments over different competence areas, their conclusion often involves multiple legal bases. Importantly thus, depending on the interpretation of the content and the aim of the measure, the issue of legal basis can lead to contradictory preferences between different EU institutions and Member States, as

[44] Opinion 2/00 [2001] ECR I-9713, para. 22 and case law cited therein.

[45] ibid para. 23 and case law cited therein.

[46] ibid. Such situations are considered exceptional, because, if the objectives can be separated, two separate legal acts on two different legal bases should be adopted.

[47] Case C-94/03 *Commission v Council* [2006] ECR I-1, para. 52.

the institutional powers of these actors vary considerably depending on the procedure used.[48]

While dual legal bases are an exception, in most cases involving complex subject matter, a distinction is drawn between provisions falling within the exclusive or shared competence. For example, the Council Decision to conclude the Rotterdam Convention on the Prior Informed Consent Procedure for Certain Hazardous Chemicals and Pesticides in International Trade[49] was based on both Articles 207 (CCP, exclusive competence) and 192 TFEU (environment, shared competence), given the 'indissociable' links between commercial and environmental components in the context of this Convention.[50] While the CJEU in this case combined two tests ('the centre of gravity' and the 'direct and immediate effects on trade'), its approach offers insufficient practical guidance on dealing with subject matter in an international treaty involving combined exclusive and shared competences.[51] Apart from a more complex procedure for the conclusion of mixed international agreements, shared competence in the matters of environment also allows the Member States to adopt more stringent measures,[52] which they would not be able to adopt under Article 207.

The choice of legal basis is of 'constitutional significance' and is subject to judicial review.[53] The CJEU has played an important role in shaping the CCP through review of the legal bases of different international agreements for compliance with the founding treaties.[54] European Union acts based on an inappropriate legal basis can be invalidated. In the case of international agreements signed on the basis of such acts, the

[48] R. Barents, 'The Internal Market Unlimited: Some Observations on the Legal Basis of EU Legislation' (1993) 30 *Common Market Law Review* 85; H. Cullen and H. Charlesworth, 'Diplomacy by Other Means: the Use of Legal Basis Litigation as a Political Strategy by the European Parliament and Member States' (1999) 36 *Common Market Law Review* 1243.

[49] Signed 10 September 1998.

[50] Case C-94/03 *Commission v Council* [2006] ECR I-1, para. 51; Case C-178/03 *Commission v Parliament and Council* [2006] ECR I-107, para. 44.

[51] N. de Sadeleer, *EU Environmental Law and the Internal Market* (OUP 2014) 164.

[52] See Art. 193 TFEU. This is however subject to the principle of sincere cooperation: Case C-246/07 *Commission v Sweden* ECLI:EU:C:2010:203.

[53] Opinion 1/08 (n 18) para. 110. See also, *inter alia*, Case C-300/89 *'Titanium Dioxide'* [1991] ECR I-2867, para. 10; Case C-269/97 *Commission v Council* [2000] ECRI-2257, para. 43; Case C-211/01 *Commission v Council* [2003] ECR I-3651, para. 38; Case C-338/01 *Commission v Council* [2004] ECR I-4829, para. 54.

[54] See P. Koutrakos, 'Legal Basis and Delimitation of Competence in EU External Relations' in M. Cremona (ed), *EU Foreign Relations Law* (Hart 2008) 171–198.

EU's consent to be bound by the agreement can be vitiated.[55] The CJEU has therefore emphasised the obligation to indicate the legal basis as part of the duty to state reasons. This serves to inform the Member States and third parties about the conditions that led to the adoption of a certain measure, thus also being the requirement of legal certainty.[56]

The choice of legal basis, as an issue of substantive law, albeit open to diverging interpretations, determines the decision-making process and political outcomes in certain policy areas. The rules determining the conclusion of EU international agreements differ according to the substantive legal basis of each agreement, requiring different procedures and levels of involvement by EU institutions and the Member States. Following Opinion 2/15 and the CJEU's generous application of the centre of gravity and AETR-ERTA doctrines, Articles 206 and 207 TFEU, which define the objectives and *rationae materiae* of the CCP, form the legal bases that empower the EU to conclude international agreements in trade and FDI.

The choice of the CCP as the legal basis simplifies the procedure for the conclusion of EU agreements. However, since not all investment issues fall within the scope of the CCP, international investment remains subject to additional legal bases and is included in different types of agreements, not limited only to traditional IIAs. General rules for the conclusion of all EU international agreements, including trade and investment, are outlined in Article 218 TFEU. In addition, Article 207 provides rules for negotiation and conclusion of international agreements in the areas of the CCP and is accordingly relevant in both substantive and procedural terms. Both Treaty articles must be considered in determining institutional equilibrium in EU international investment treaty-making. The procedure is governed by the principle of mutual sincere inter-institutional cooperation,[57] which includes duty of action or abstention, depending on circumstances.

While on the side of the EU the same procedure applies with respect to 'EU-only' and mixed agreements, in procedural terms the conclusion of mixed agreements additionally requires the ratification of the agreement by all Member States in accordance with their respective constitutional requirements.

[55] Opinion 1/08 (n 18) para. 110.

[56] *Commission v Council* (n 21) paras. 37–39.

[57] Art. 13(2) TEU.

### 6.2.1 *Conclusion of 'EU-Only' Agreements*

European Union international trade and investment agreements are negotiated, signed and concluded with the participation of all significant EU institutions: the EC, which has the leading role in the negotiation stage; the Council, with the leading role in authorising the Commission's actions at different stages of the procedure; and the European Parliament (EP), as the key institution for the ratification of EU agreements. Since the EC negotiates with third States, it can seem that the EC has the main role in the process of the agreements' conclusion. However, the EC's powers are confined by the roles played by the Council during the entire process, and by the EP, particularly at the end of the process.

The EC has the leading role in starting and negotiating EU trade and investment agreements. It proposes the opening of negotiations of an agreement with a specific country.[58] Once the Council authorises the opening of the negotiations, the Commission will conduct negotiations within the given mandate, propose the signature and the subsequent conclusion of the agreement.[59] During the negotiating process, the EC will be in *consultation* with the Council via the Trade Policy Committee of the Council (TPC), and it will also keep the Parliament *informed* via the EP's International Trade Committee (INTA).[60] In practical terms, the EC is the first point of contact with the third country negotiators, conducting negotiations 'on the ground'.

The Council acts as the first point of scrutiny of the Commission's actions and shares responsibility for compliance of the international agreement with the internal EU rules and policies.[61] It participates in the negotiations through the TPC.[62] However, the TPC or the Council itself cannot impose on the Commission as the negotiator detailed negotiating positions that would be binding, as this would go beyond the consultative function of Council enshrined in Article 218(4) TFEU.[63] The Council adopts decisions on opening of the negotiations, and signing and concluding the agreement, based on the EC's proposals.[64] These

[58] Arts. 218(3) TFEU; 207(3)(2) TFEU.
[59] Art. 218(4), (5), (6) TFEU.
[60] Art. 207(3)(3) TFEU.
[61] Art. 207(3)(2) TFEU.
[62] Arts. 218(4); 207(3)(3) TFEU.
[63] Case C-425/13 *Commission v Council* ECLI:EU:C:2015:483, paras. 88–90.
[64] Art. 218(2) TFEU.

decisions are adopted by qualified majority voting (QMV).[65] The Council can amend the Commission's proposals but only unanimously.[66] Unanimity is also required for the conclusion of association agreements,[67] which can, *inter alia*, include investment protection provisions.[68] Finally, unanimity is required for the negotiation and conclusion of international agreements in the field of FDI when such agreements include provisions which require unanimity for the adoption of internal rules.[69] While in practice most decisions regarding trade and investment agreements can be adopted by QMV, the Council has discretion to act via the process of common accord – the agreement of all Member States in order for the Council to approve the signature and conclusion of these agreements. However, the CJEU has emphasised that the practice of common accord cannot be an additional procedural step which would make the conclusion of the international agreement *contingent* on the prior establishment of a common accord.[70]

Every decision in this process is subject to judicial review by the CJEU, which can additionally be asked to provide binding opinions on the compatibility of the proposed international agreement with the treaties.[71] Measures adopted under Article 218 TFEU produce legal effects with respect to relations between the EU and its Member States, and between EU institutions and thus can be subject to an action for annulment.[72] Importantly, Article 218 TFEU constitutes 'an autonomous and general provision of constitutional scope' as it 'confers specific powers on EU institutions', intended at establishing inter-institutional balance.[73] Whenever this balance is disturbed, the CJEU will annul the contested measure.

[65] Arts. 218(8)(1); 207(4)(1) TFEU. This includes adopting restrictions under Art. 64(3) TFEU; internal market harmonising measures regarding non-direct investment under Arts. 115 and 352 TFEU; the establishment and treatment of FDI in international agreements concerning fields listed in Art. 207(4)(3) TFEU. See Dimopoulos (n 17) 131–133.

[66] Art. 293(1) TFEU.

[67] Art. 218(8)(2) TFEU.

[68] See, for example, chapter on Investment in the EU–Mexico Agreement in Principle (*European Commission*, 6 May 2020).

[69] Arts. 218(8)(2); 207(4)(2) TFEU.

[70] Opinion 1/19, paras. 249, 274.

[71] Art. 218(11) TFEU.

[72] Case C-114/12 *Commission v Council* ECLI:EU:C:2014:2151, para. 40.

[73] *Commission v Council* (n 63) para. 62.

Finally, the EP acts as the final point of scrutiny of the EC's and the Council's actions.[74] The consent of the Parliament is required for the conclusion of all trade and investment treaties given that the adoption of legislation in the area of the CCP involves ordinary legislative procedure.[75] The rationale of this provision is to ensure symmetry between the internal and external procedures and institutional balance of powers between the Council and the EP.[76] The consent of the EP is also required for the conclusion of the Association Agreements, which may include investment protection provisions.[77]

However, EP's input into the policy content is formally limited since the EP can only reject or accept the agreement as it is. During the negotiations the Parliament is only kept *informed* on the progress via its Committee on International Trade (INTA),[78] and in accordance with the framework agreement between the EC and the EP.[79] Nevertheless, given the EP's *de facto* veto powers at the very end of the treaty-making process, its input politically cannot be ignored and has changed the balance of power between the institutions.[80] In some other instances, the EP has used its power to reject an international treaty in order to enforce its role in the negotiating process.[81]

The consent of the EP, which is *de facto* the EU ratification of an international agreement, is meant to ensure the democratic legitimacy of the EU's CCP.[82] Since the EU is not a parliamentary democracy, the EP

[74] See Arts. 207(3), 218(6) and 218(10) TFEU.

[75] Art. 218(6)(a)(v) TFEU. See also Art. 218(6)(a)(iii) TFEU requiring the consent of the EP for agreements establishing a specific institutional framework by organising cooperation proceedings, and arguably such frameworks are established under each trade and investment treaty in the form of special committees for the implementation of agreements.

[76] Case C-658/11 *European Parliament v Council* ECLI:EU:C:2014:2025, paras. 57–58.

[77] Art. 218(6)(a)(i).

[78] Arts. 207(3)(3); 218(10) TFEU.

[79] Framework agreement on the relationship between the European Parliament and the European Commission, OJ 2010, L 304/47.

[80] For example, the EP has committed the EC to actions regarding the implementation of the EU-Korea FTA post its ratification, powers which the EP formally does not have under the founding treaties. See C. M. Brown, 'Changes in the Common Commercial Policy of the European Union after the Entry into Force of the Treaty of Lisbon: A Practitioner's Perspective' in M. Bungenberg and C. Herrmann (eds), *Common Commercial Policy after Lisbon* (Springer-Verlag Berlin Heidelberg 2013) 163–183.

[81] The SWIFT Agreement, the Anti-Counterfeiting Treaty (ACTA) and the EU-Morocco Fisheries Agreement.

[82] To that effect, see also a declaration signed by sixty academics from more than fifteen European countries: 'Trading Together – For strong and democratically legitimized EU international agreements' (25 January 2017).

can be politically more independent from the EC in exercising its power of consent, similarly to the role of the US Congress in the US presidential system.[83] However, it has been noted that the increased powers of the EP post-Lisbon, in combination with the diversity of the EU's external CCP objectives, have also increased the politicisation of the EU trade policy.[84] The EP's role was significant in defining the new EU IIP, exposing the traditional grudge between the EP and the Council in EU external trade policy.[85]

After receiving the consent from the Parliament, the Council will adopt the decision to conclude the agreement, which completes the procedure under Article 218 TFEU for 'EU-only' agreements.[86]

### 6.2.2 Conclusion of 'Mixed' Agreements

The conclusion of mixed agreements includes an additional layer of ratification by the Member States before the procedure under Article 218 TFEU can be completed. However, there are no special Treaty provisions on the negotiation and conclusion of these agreements. The Council will approve the conclusion of a mixed agreement only after all Member States have internally ratified it.

In legal terms, once a mixed agreement is concluded, both the EU and its Member States are a party to such agreement. The agreement is, in most cases, still bilateral – between the EU/Member States and the third State with which it is concluded. Until the ratification process in the Member States is concluded, the provisions of the mixed agreement that fall within the exclusive EU competence can enter into force in accordance with the Council's decision, on the recommendation from the EC[87] and after the EP has given its consent.[88] While the Treaty provision states

[83] M. Krajewski, 'New Functions and New Powers for the European Parliament: Assessing the Changes of the Common Commercial Policy from the Perspective of Democratic Legitimacy' in Bungenberg and Herrmann (n 80) 75–76.

[84] See A. R. Young, 'European Trade Policy in Interesting Times' (2017) 39 *Journal of European Integration* 909.

[85] See Chapter 7.

[86] Art. 218(6) TFEU. The EP gives its consent on the recommendation of its INTA Committee.

[87] Art. 218(5) TFEU. This decision can be adopted in the decision on the signing of the agreement (e.g. in the case of the EU-Korea FTA), or in a separate decision before the agreement's entry into force (e.g. in the case of CETA).

[88] While under the Treaties, the consent of the EP is not required for provisional application, this has generally been adopted as practice, and departed only in cases of technical

that this is done 'if necessary', provisional application of mixed agreements has rather become a rule, as the ratification process in the Member States can take a long time.[89] The provisional application of the agreement thus has positive effects on policy efficiency but on the other hand, it can place national parliaments before a *fait accompli*.

A related issue, is a situation in which the ratification of a bilaterally structured mixed agreement would be rejected in one or more Member States. Since the provisionally applied agreement must be approved by the EU in accordance with Article 218 TFEU procedures, its provisions form an integral part of the EU legal order.[90] It could therefore be argued that the rejection of the ratification, at least in cases when it is opposed by only one Member State, breaches the principle of sincere cooperation enshrined in Article 4(3) TEU. The importance of such agreement for the achievement of EU objectives would possibly have to be assessed on a case-by-case basis. On the other hand, there is a view that failure to ratify the agreement in any Member State would require the EU to terminate the provisional application of the agreement, as well as the agreement, unless some kind of remedial action to remove the impediment to ratification could be taken.[91] Indeed, Member States do not have an obligation to conclude a mixed agreement even when the Union intends to conclude such an agreement, as this approach would infringe the principle of division of competences in Article 4(1) TEU.[92]

measures or situations requiring urgency. For example, this was the case regarding EU-UK TCA.

[89] For example, while CETA provisionally entered into force in September 2017, the ratification of the agreement is still pending in ten Member States: European Commission, *Overview of FTA and other trade negotiations* (2022). See Council Decision (EU) 2017/38 of 28 October 2016 on the provisional application of the CETA between Canada, of the one part, and the European Union and its Member States, of the other part [2017] OJ L 11/1080.

[90] Case C-459/03 *Commission v Ireland* [2006] ECR I-4635, para. 82.

[91] See G. Van Der Loo and R. A. Wessel, 'The Non-Ratification of Mixed Agreements: Legal Consequences and Solutions' (2017) 54(3) *Common Market Law Review* 735, 760–761; A. Suse and J. Wouters, 'The Provisional Application of the EU's Mixed Trade and Investment Agreements' (Working Paper No. 201, 2018) 19–21, who remain sceptical to this argument. The impediments would need to be of the constitutional nature, while remedial action could take the form of a renegotiation to address the concerns of the Member State.

[92] Opinion 1/19, Opinion of AG Hogan ECLI:EU:C:2021:198, para. 203.

## 6.3 EU Treaty-Making in International Investment: Policy Implications

Opinion 2/15 of the CJEU proved important in setting the direction of the EU IIP. In light of the internal 'mixity' and in order to enhance the efficiency of the policy externally, the EC endorsed a new approach in trade negotiations. Trade and investment have been split in two parts: trade in an encompassing FTA concluded as an 'EU-only' agreement, and investment in a separate investment protection agreement (IPA), concluded as a mixed agreement. In principle both agreements are negotiated in parallel.[93]

Accordingly, EU FTAs still include FDI liberalisation issues (market access), while IPAs focus on the post-establishment protection of both FDI and portfolio investment, and provide for a reformed ISDS mechanism.[94] This approach seems pragmatic in light of the comprehensive definition of 'investment' in modern IIAs,[95] and it has also been supported by the EP.[96] At the same time, for the purposes of policy efficiency, the 'split' approach has not been endorsed with respect to all third States, particularly those with whom ISDS is not deemed necessary and would create additional negotiation hurdles due to divergent policy approaches of EU trading partners. In association agreements, which are usually concluded as mixed agreements as they pursue a number of political, economic and commercial objectives, investment protection and reformed ISDS have been included in some but excluded in other cases. In light of the preceding discussion, Table 6.3 explains the policy implementation of legal bases in main EU agreements with trade and investment provisions, providing for their classification.

As a final point, of importance is to emphasise the links between policy efficiency and policy legitimacy. Unlike trade agreements, EU IIAs remain mixed agreements. Mixed competence with respect to investment gives Member States more control over policy outcomes. In addition to their voice in the Council under Article 218 TFEU, mixed agreements require ratification in accordance with each Member States' specific

[93] Council of the European Union, 'Draft Council Conclusions on the Negotiation and Conclusion of EU Trade Agreements' (8 May 2018) 8622/18.

[94] See Chapter 9.

[95] See Section 1.3.1 in Chapter 1.

[96] For example, see EP Resolution 2017/2192(INI) of 26 October 2017 containing the Parliament's recommendation to the Council on the proposed negotiating mandate for trade negotiations with Australia [2018] OJ C 346/212.

Table 6.3 *Types of EU trade and investment agreements and corresponding legal bases*

| | Trade Agreements Main legal basis: Art. 207 TFEU (substantive); Art. 218(6)(a)(v) (procedural) | | | |
|---|---|---|---|---|
| Type | Free Trade Agreements (EU-only) | Trade Agreements (mixed) | Free Trade Agreement + Investment Protection Agreement | Investment Agreements (mixed) |
| **Features** | Comprehensive trade component and FDI liberalisation | Comprehensive trade component and FDI liberalisation<br>- Additional provisions in the sphere of shared competence (e.g. cultural cooperation; or ISDS) | Two separate agreements negotiated together:<br>- FTA: comprehensive trade component and FDI liberalisation (EU-only)<br>- IPA: comprehensive investment protection and investment dispute settlement (mixed) | FDI liberalisation and sustainable development issues (EU-only)<br>Comprehensive investment protection and investment dispute settlement provisions to follow (as mixed agreement) |
| **Countries** | - Japan<br>- Australia<br>- New Zealand | - Republic of Korea<br>- CETA<br>- Andean Community (Peru, Columbia, Ecuador) | - Vietnam<br>- Singapore | - CAI (**EU-only**)<br>- Myanmar |

| **Association Agreements (Mixed)** Main legal basis: Art. 217 TFEU (substantive); Arts. 218(6)(a)(i) and 218(8) (procedural) | | | | | |
|---|---|---|---|---|---|
| **Type** | **Stabilisation and Association Agreements (SAA)** | **Deep and Comprehensive Free Trade Agreements (DCFTA)** | **Modernised Association Agreements** | **Other Association Agreements** | |
| **Features** | EU *Acquis*, potential EU membership | EU *Acquis*, no future EU membership | Political dialogue, comprehensive trade and investment component | Political dialogue, comprehensive trade component | Trade, fisheries, law enforcement, level playing field, fundamental rights |
| **Countries** | Western Balkans | - Eastern Partnership (Ukraine, Georgia, Moldova)<br>- Mediterranean (Morocco, Tunisia) | - Mexico<br>- Chile | - Central America<br>- Mercosur | - The UK – 'exceptional and unique' character of the relationship<br>- **EU-only** |

| **Economic Partnership Agreements (Mixed)** Main legal basis: Art. 209 TFEU (substantive); Art. 218(6)(a)(iii) and (v) (procedural) | | |
|---|---|---|
| **Type** | **Economic Partnership Agreements (including interim and stepping stone EPAs)** | **Comprehensive enhanced Partnership Agreements** |
| **Features** | Trade preferential agreements, asymmetric liberalisation of investment, development cooperation | Political dialogue (CFSP), trade (CCP) and development cooperation<br>- Additional legal bases: Article 37 TEU, Article 207 TFEU |
| **Countries** | - Africa: SADC, West Africa, EAC, ESA, Central Africa (interim agreement), Ghana (stepping stone EPA)<br>- Caribbean: CARIFORUM<br>- Pacific States: PNG, Fiji, Papua New Guinea, Samoa | - Armenia<br>- Kazakhstan |

constitutional requirements, which can include not only national but also regional parliaments. Founding treaties require the active contribution of national parliaments to the good functioning of the Union.[97] It has been claimed that the expansion of the scope of the CCP has resulted in expansion of the EP's status at the expense of the marginalisation of the national parliaments.[98] Accordingly, in the field of investment, national parliaments' oversight over EU IIAs through the ratification process can provide greater legitimacy to EU policy.[99]

On the other hand, the ratification of mixed agreements further complicates the political process for the conclusion of the agreement on the EU side and dilutes its position with respect to its external counterparts. It has thus been argued that competence struggles between the EU and Member States, more than competing societal interests, have played a significant role in slowing down the development of the EU IIP.[100] Given the low number of concluded EU IIAs, none of which have yet entered into force, it can be deduced that the conclusion of investment agreements has not been a policy priority for the EU.[101] On the other hand, when political agreement could be reached in the Council, the Union and the Member States have acted jointly in the interest of the Union in the areas which fall within shared competence, while reiterating the Council's position that ISDS mechanisms cannot be established without the Member States' consent.[102]

Finally, policy legitimacy and policy efficiency should not be taken as mutually exclusive. Given the internal complexity of the EU treaty-making processes, the efficiency of its trade and investment policy largely depends on its legitimacy. The input of domestic constituencies in the

[97] Art. 12 TEU.

[98] Krajewski (n 83) 84–85.

[99] See letter to then EU Trade Commissioner Karel de Gucht, signed by fourteen national parliaments: Tweede Kamer der Staten-Generaal, 'The role of national parliaments in free trade agreements' (17 June 2014).

[100] R. Basedow, 'The EU's International Investment Policy Ten Years On: The Policy-Making Implications of Unintended Competence Transfers' (2021) 59(3) *Journal of Common Market Studies* 643, claiming that this struggle stems from pre-Lisbon resistance of Member States to empower the EU in international investment.

[101] Even the provisional application of provisions related to FDI protection (albeit not dispute settlement), which could enhance policy efficiency, has not been proposed by the Commission: see for example, Art. 4.15.4 EUSIPA.

[102] See Council Decision (EU) 2022/438 of 14 March 2022 on the position to be adopted on behalf of the EU within the Administrative Council of the ICSID, ST/6125/2022/INIT, OJ L 89, and its recital (3). The legal basis of this Decision are Arts. 207(4), first paragraph and 218(9) TFEU.

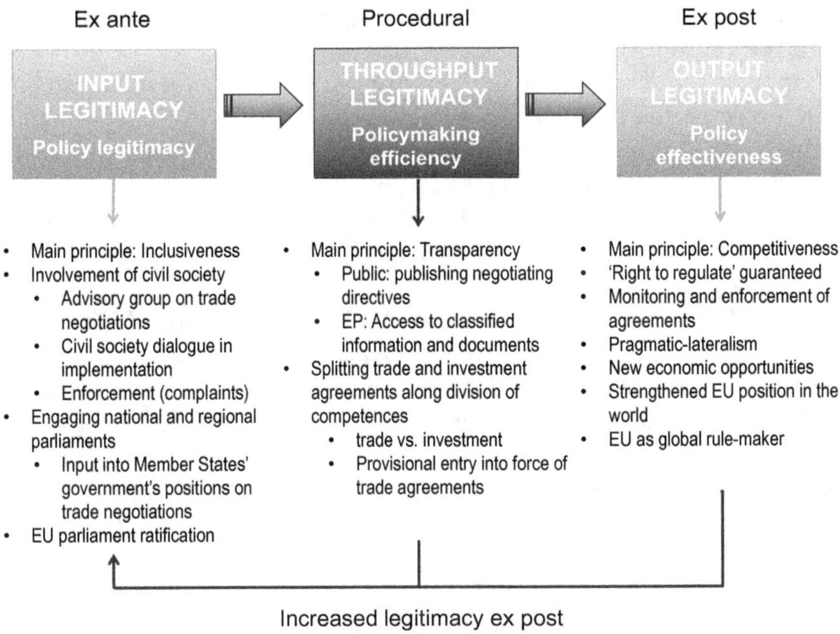


**Figure 6.1** Legitimacy of EU trade and investment policy

Member States' negotiating positions but also the policy results and the ability of the EC to deliver policy promises are important factors in balancing the demands of legitimacy and efficiency in the EU trade and investment context. Figure 6.1 depicts the relationship between legitimacy, efficiency and effectiveness of EU trade and investment policy.

## 6.4 Conclusion

The role of the CJEU in defining the EU's treaty-making powers in the field of trade and investment has been significant. In one of its early Opinions the CJEU emphasised that the CCP should be viewed as a progressive policy which should not form a barrier for the EU when developing a 'commercial policy aiming at a regulation of the world market' rather than striving for 'a mere liberalisation of trade'.[103] The scope of the CCP has been gradually expanding, culminating in the Lisbon Treaty changes. Opinion 2/15 follows this progressive

[103] Opinion 1/78 [1979] ECR 2871, paras. 44–45.

understanding of the CCP while still recognising remaining limitations with respect to investment.

Opinion 2/15 clarifies the EU's exclusive competence for all aspects of FDI; however, the competence of the EU and its Member States remains shared with respect to portfolio investment and ISDS. Given that conventional IIAs regulate both FDI and portfolio investment in addition to ISDS as their crucial element, EU IIAs must be concluded as mixed agreements, leaving the Member States with an essential role in the treaty-making process.

The CJEU ruling poses an important limitation on the EU's international investment power. The CJEU had a choice between, on one hand, the narrow reading of the CCP clause (portfolio investment as an exclusive competence of Member States) advocated by the Council and some Member States, particularly Germany and Belgium, and on the other hand, the broad reading of the CCP clause (portfolio investment as an exclusive competence of the EU) advocated by the EC. The CJEU chose the middle ground by defining portfolio investment as an area of shared competence. This reading allows for expansion of the EU's competence in the future through the EU exercise of internal powers by adopting secondary legislation, without the need to amend the founding treaties. However, since Article 63 TFEU does not provide a legal basis for EU internal legislative powers with respect to the liberalisation of portfolio investment, as opposed to its harmonisation, it is difficult to conceive how the EU internal action could pre-empt Member States' external action with respect to portfolio investment.[104]

As the CJEU clarified, the limited scope of EU investment competence is a consequence of 'unequivocal expression' of the intention of Member States, to which the Court refers to as 'framers of the TEU Treaty', not to include in the CCP types of foreign investment other than FDI.[105] Exclusive EU competence over all foreign investment would mean a significant loss of power for the Member States when creating their national investment protection policies.[106] More importantly, ISDS as a

[104] AG Sharpston in her Opinion (n 37) aligned with the EC arguments, suggesting that the legal basis for the EU's internal legislative powers regarding portfolio investment would be Article 114 TFEU, in so far as it concerns the approximation of laws governing internal markets, and Art. 352 TFEU: see para. 368.

[105] Opinion 2/15 (n 4) para. 83.

[106] This would particularly adversely affect the capital-exporting Member States (e.g. Germany), whose interest is to provide the best possible conditions for their investors in third countries through the conclusion of IIAs.

mechanism which directly affects the jurisdiction of domestic courts cannot be considered merely ancillary to investment protection provisions, and therefore, cannot be established without the Member States' consent.[107] Regardless of the shared competence, this leaves open the question whether it would be legally possible for any EU agreement containing ISDS to be concluded as an 'EU-only' agreement, even if such political agreement could be reached in the Council. The CJEU has thus impliedly recognised the profound implications of ISDS for the domestic rule of law. This view has been further endorsed in the CJEU's *Achmea* judgment.

Opinion 2/15 has important implications for the efficiency of the EU investment policy. Despite only a partial EU victory in Opinion 2/15, even limited investment sovereignty gives to the EU a considerable control in setting the direction of the EU IIP and in achieving a relative coherence between investment policies of the EU and its Member States.[108]

[107] Opinion 2/15 (n 4) para. 292.
[108] See Chapter 8.

# Conclusion to Part II

## The Rule of (EU) Law in Intra-EU Investment Relations

The key aspect of the EU investment policy – both internally and externally – has been the relationship between EU law and international law, and the protection of the autonomy of the EU legal order its key objective. Accordingly, law has been the key factor and the Court of Justice of the European Union (CJEU) the key actor in defining the policy scope. With every decision, the Court has allowed the institutions and the Member States to move forward, assisting them in legitimising the policy.

In the internal context, the *Achmea* judgment and its jurisprudence ascertained the incompatibility between EU law and international investment law (IIL). It has confirmed that Member States' sovereignty in international law ends where their sovereignty has a potential to undermine the objectives of EU integration, in particular the internal market. Between the Member States, investment is to be regulated and protected under EU law, replacing the existing network of intra-EU bilateral investment treaties (BITs). While it eliminates intra-EU investor-State dispute settlement (ISDS), *Achmea* ultimately demonstrates the CJEU's direction towards a stronger rule of EU law across all Member States. This serves several objectives.

First, *Achmea* has bridged the divide between political interests of Western and Eastern Member States regarding investment and has set the way forward in eliminating intra-EU BITs. Many controversial issues demonstrate the political sensitivity of investment law. Regardless, *Achmea* has started the final countdown for intra-EU ISDS, under both intra-EU BITs and the Energy Charter Treaty (ECT), despite the difference in their pace.

Second, *Achmea* has served to enhance the legitimacy of domestic courts over a 'parallel justice' of investment tribunals in the EU. While the investment community might not be convinced that domestic courts in each and every Member State can afford the full protection of their interests, *Achmea* is an important step towards enhancing the role of national courts in protection of investors within the EU. In addition, the findings of *Achmea* and subsequent CJEU judgments are being implemented by national courts of Member States, thus hampering the enforcement of intra-EU awards in the EU, but also demonstrating the power of EU law, which rests upon the cooperation between national courts and the CJEU.

Third, *Achmea* fosters the rule of law in the EU, which implies the control over governmental compliance with EU law through effective judicial review. Accordingly, EU law should not only guarantee that investors are compensated for breaches of their rights; more importantly, it should ensure that any national measures inconsistent with EU law are 'disapplied' and eventually eliminated from the EU legal order.

Finally, *Achmea* seeks to overcome the fragmentation of international law stemming from IIL and jurisprudence of international investment tribunals, as there is a single judicial authority, the CJEU. Investors under EU law still face another version of fragmentation – due to a diversity of standards and remedies in Member States' national legal orders. However, the elimination of IIL in intra-EU relations and its replacement by EU law has served the CJEU to underscore a conceptually systemic nature of EU law and its own central and sovereign role in the 'autonomous' EU legal order.[1]

Opinion 2/15 is another key decision relevant for both internal and external dimension of EU investment policy. It confirms that the CJEU does not see the EU as ready to take the treaty-making sovereignty away from the Member States in all aspects of investment. It thus indicates that investment dispute settlement concerns more deeply the issues of sovereignty than trade does; ISDS cannot be considered simply ancillary to the substantive provisions on investment.[2] Courts and tribunals, even those that stand outside the domestic legal systems (such as ISDS), remain an expression of the Member States' sovereignty. The lack of investment sovereignty complicates the political process and weakens the EU's power in global terms. However, the silver lining could be the improved internal democratic legitimacy for EU international investment policy (IIP), which should also safeguard the EU project more generally.

[1] See the quote at the beginning of Part II.

[2] Opinion 2/15 ECLI:EU:C:2017:376, paras. 292–293. Cf. Opinion 2/15, Opinion of AG Sharpston ECLI:EU:C:2016:992, paras. 529–535.

While the CJEU's reasoning has grounds in the founding treaties, these judgments provide an important insight into the CJEU's vision of the EU and its political objectives, which extend beyond the field of investment. This vision has further found its expression in the CJEU's affirmation of the external aspects of EU investment policy, whose analysis follows in Part III.

# PART III

# The External Investment System of the EU

# Introduction to Part III

## The External Investment System of the EU

> Following the recent public debate, the Juncker Commission has fundamentally reformed the existing system for settling investment-related disputes. A new system – called the Investment Court System, with judges appointed by the two parties to the FTA and public oversight – is the EU's agreed approach that it is pursuing from now on in its trade agreements. . . . Anything less ambitious, including coming back to the old Investor-to-State Dispute Settlement, is not acceptable. For the EU ISDS is dead.[1]

The EU proposal for investor-State dispute settlement (ISDS) reform introduces a shift from an *ad hoc* investment arbitration to a permanent court-type adjudication in order to address the legitimacy and rule of law concerns about the current international investment regulation (IIR). This paradigmatic shift at the EU level has been triggered by political controversies within the EU, emerging primarily from public reaction against ISDS. At the same time, the proposal has been shaped by the EU's own normative and institutional framework, based on the rule of law in which a court plays the central role. In Part III we will explore why old ISDS is 'dead' for the EU and what its envisaged replacement in EU external investment relations would be, both bilaterally and multilaterally.

In Part III we will proceed as follows. First, in Chapter 7, the EU external investment regulatory framework is placed within the broader agenda of EU external trade relations, providing a political context of EU international investment policy (IIP). The following two chapters turn to the implementation of EU IIP regarding substantive protections (Chapter 8) and the dispute settlement mechanism (Chapter 9) in bilateral relations. The focus is placed on the mode in which the EU incorporates its own institutional and normative ideas into international investment law (IIL) through new investment standards and the

[1] European Commission, 'A new EU trade agreement with Japan', Factsheet (July 2018) 6.

institution of a court, with a view to promote legitimacy and the rule of law, one of the core EU values. In the final chapter, we analyse the EU's plan and engagement in expanding its investment regulation from a micro (bilateral) to a macro (global) level through the establishment of a Multilateral Investment Court (MIC). As the reform process is ongoing and its outcomes – including an MIC – uncertain, this is one of the shortest chapters of this book. It reconnects the ongoing ISDS reform discussions with the analysis of IIR in Part I.

# 7

# Political Context of the EU International Investment Reform

In this introductory chapter to Part III, we examine the context of EU international investment regulation. We will analyse the objectives of EU trade and investment strategy, and shifts between multilateralism, bilateralism and unilateralism, effectively endorsing pragmatic-lateralism. First, EU values, objectives and principles are briefly introduced, to the extent to which they shape and define the EU's international action. This is followed by the examination of EU strategy for its integration with the wider world through trade and investment agreements, and the consideration of circumstances which led to the EU's international investment policy (IIP) reform. The aim of this chapter is to provide the political background of EU international investment regulatory framework, which is analysed in Chapters 8 and 9.

## 7.1 Values, Objectives and Principles of the EU as Defining Elements of Its International Identity

Values and objectives of the EU and its legal order, as defined in the EU Treaties, play a prominent role in shaping the EU's external action. The Lisbon Treaty has strengthened the constitutional nature of the EU by endorsing values and streamlining the objectives pursued by the EU.

The EU legal order is shaped by six core *values* outlined in Article 2 Treaty on European Union (TEU), ranging from human rights to the rule of law. They are a core internal component of the EU, common to all its Member States.[1] Importantly, values are not purely political aspirations, as they are binding upon EU institutions and Member States.[2] They cover any EU action, applying internally but also externally in EU

[1] Case C-64/16 *Associação Sindical dos Juízes Portugueses* ECLI:EU:C:2018:117, para. 30; Art. 2 TEU, second sentence.

[2] See Case C-621/18 *Whitgman* ECLI:EU:C:2018:999, para. 63, and Case C-619/18 *Commission v Poland* ECLI:EU:C:2019:531, para. 42.

relations with 'the wider world'.[3] Therefore, values must be implemented into secondary EU law and EU agreements concluded with international organisations and third States. A legal act that infringes EU values will be nullified by the Court of Justice of the European Union (CJEU).[4] The Common Commercial Policy (CCP) thus has to abide by EU values irrespective of its commercial nature.

Values are distinguished from objectives and principles, although the borderline between these different concepts is not clear even in Treaty law.[5] European Union acts may pursue an array of *objectives*, outlined in Article 3 TEU or in specific policy provisions. The Union is on the one hand obliged to 'promote its values and interests and contribute to the protection of its citizens' while, on the other, contribute to higher interests that surpass the narrower sphere of EU interests.[6] Article 21 (2) TEU outlines additional objectives in defining and pursuing EU policies and actions, which equally apply to the EU's external action,[7] ranging from safeguarding EU values to progressive trade liberalisation, sustainable development and promotion of a multilateral international system. While EU objectives have a more political nature than the values and the general principles of EU law,[8] they enter the legal arena whenever courts review the proportionality of EU and national measures.

European Union actions are further guided by a set of *principles* or must be consistent with general principles of EU law. The term 'principle' is ambiguous as it encompasses customary law principles, general principles of international law,[9] general principles of EU law,[10] the principles embodied in the EU Charter of Fundamental Rights (CFR), sectoral policy principles,[11] as well as policy implementation principles.[12] They may be the product of a purely judicial construction or enshrined in Treaty law and developed by the courts, like the general principle of

[3] Art. 3(5) TEU.

[4] Joined cases C-402/05 P and C-415/05 P *Kadi* [2008] ECR I-6351.

[5] For instance, under Art. 21(1) TEU, the rule of law is framed both as a 'value' and as a 'principle'. Judicial protection is defined as a general principle stemming from Member States' constitutional traditions and as a right for the purpose of Art. 47 CFR.

[6] Art. 3(5) TEU.

[7] Art. 21(3) TEU.

[8] See for example the Common Agriculture Policy objectives listed in Art. 43(1) TFEU.

[9] See the principle of reciprocity, mentioned by AG Bot in Opinion 1/17, Opinion of AG Bot ECLI:EU:C:2019:341.

[10] Art. 6 TEU.

[11] For instance, the environmental principles listed in Art. 191(2) TFEU.

[12] Arts. 35, 37 and 38 CFR.

judicial protection proclaimed in the European Convention on Human Rights (ECHR)[13] and the CFR. Principles can also be stated in soft law documents, such as the Council of Europe Magna Carta for Judges,[14] which although non-binding influence the interpretation of binding rules. The term 'principle' thus encompasses both rules that form the foundations of the meta-rules, such as the rule of law (for instance, the principles of equality, legal certainty, non-discrimination) and the rules of legal technique (for instance, the principle of proportionality).

The endorsement of values, objectives and principles in Treaty law has signalled a new phase towards their importance in EU's relations with 'the wider world'. Accordingly, EU trade and investment strategy implements EU values and objectives in its external relations.

## 7.2 EU Trade and Investment Strategy for a Globalised World

### *7.2.1 From Multilateralism to Bilateralism and Pragmatic-Lateralism in Trade Policy*

The Global Europe Strategy[15] of 2006 was a shift from the multilateral trade regime towards a new generation of bilateral and regional preferential trade agreements. These agreements expand beyond issues of tariff barriers and embrace a broad spectrum of regulatory areas, such as services, investment, intellectual property rights (IPR), public procurement, sustainable development and other areas impacting domestic regulatory standards ('deep' trade issues). The EU followed the suit of the United States, who embraced it in its bilateral trade relations in the 1990s. Trends towards regionalism emerged in the early 1990s with Asia-Pacific Economic Cooperation (APEC) and North America Free Trade Agreement (NAFTA).[16]

The EU's multilateral agenda was inspired by the EU's experience of the internal market, aimed at exporting its regulatory principles

[13] Convention for the Protection of Human Rights and Fundamental Freedoms (adopted 4 November 1950, entered into force 3 September 1953) 213 UNTS 221.

[14] Recommendation CM/Rec (2010)12 of the Committee of Ministers to member States on judges: independence, efficiency and responsibilities (adopted by the Committee of Ministers on 17 November 2010 at the 1098th meeting of the Ministers' Deputies).

[15] EC, 'Global Europe: Competing in the World – Contribution to the EU's Growth and Jobs Strategy', COM (2006) 567 final.

[16] World Trade Organisation, 'World Trade Report 2011, The WTO and Preferential Trade Agreements: From Co-existence to Coherence' (2011), 52.

worldwide to secure benefits for EU firms.[17] It incorporated the idea of 'managed globalisation', coined by Pascal Lamy in 1999, with the objective to codify the rules of globalisation and provide institutional structures for their compliance through organisations like the EU, World Trade Organization (WTO), International Monetary Fund (IMF) and Organization for Economic Cooperation and Development (OECD).[18] While aimed at trade liberalisation, 'managed globalisation' was supposed to promote non-trade objectives, such as social values, sustainable development and multilateralism, meant to appeal to a variety of social actors internally and to developing countries externally.[19] It was a tool to make liberalisation happen, combining different political ideologies: UK neoliberalism, German ordo-liberalism, French statist socialist economy, the European social model more generally, together with the realities of globalisation.[20] When this strategy did not gain fruitful ground at the multilateral level, it became the core of the EU's bilateral trade policy under different names: 'Trade, Growth and World Affairs',[21] 'Trade for All',[22] 'Harnessing Globalisation',[23] from 2006 onwards.

Therefore, unlike American-style neoliberalism, focused on eliminating barriers and reducing State intervention into the markets through regulation, European-style neoliberalism has been focused on promoting rules and regulations for free market operations. These rules for globalisation, however, are now meant to be made by international economic entities instead of States, preferably promoting EU standards and values. Nevertheless, there is a level of contradiction in the EU's approach given that preferential bilateralism and divergent regulatory structures have clear potential to undermine multilateral efforts.[24]

[17] B. A. Melo Araujo, *The EU Deep Trade Agenda* (OUP 2016) 30.

[18] R. Abdelal and S. Meunier, 'Managed Globalisation: Doctrine, Practice and Promise' (2010) 17 *Journal of European Public Policy* 350, 353.

[19] Araujo (n 17) 31–32.

[20] Abdelal and Meunier (n 18) 355.

[21] EC, 'Trade, Growth and World Affairs: Trade Policy as a Core Component of the EU's 2020 Strategy', COM (2010) 612.

[22] EC, 'Trade for All: Towards a More Responsible Trade and Investment Policy', COM (2015) 497.

[23] EC, 'Reflection Paper on Harnessing Globalisation', COM (2017) 240; EC, 'A Balanced and Progressive Trade Policy to Harness Globalisation', COM (2017) 492.

[24] EP, DG for External Policies, 'Comparing International Trade Policies: The EU, United States, EFTA and Japanese PTA Strategies' (2014), EXPO/B/INTA/FWC/2009-01/Lot7/36.

With a vision to complement the multilateral trading system, EU free trade agreements (FTAs) were envisaged as 'fully compatible with the WTO' and aimed at 'deep integration', especially in those areas where such integration has been difficult at a multilateral level.[25] However, 'deep integration' in trade affects also non-trade policy areas, such as labour standards, environment protection, food and product safety. On the one hand, States can lower their standards to attract trade and investment in a race to the bottom, while on the other, their attempts to increase standards can be undermined by trade and investment claims, leaving them reluctant to regulate – an effect known as 'regulatory chill'.

The constitutional changes made by the Lisbon Treaty have further enhanced EU trade policy aspirations, contributing to different levels of domestic politicisation of EU trade.[26] A broad range of actors, from civil society to national parliaments, has been actively engaged in EU trade policy. Given the public perception of higher EU standards,[27] the political debate has been focused on the perceived negative effects of trade agreements, in particular lowering regulatory standards beneficial for consumers and the environment while empowering corporations.[28] Citizens thus generally mistrust EU institutions when negotiating trade agreements on behalf of Member States.[29] To address these concerns, the Commission has promoted greater transparency in negotiations and early and 'appropriate' involvement of civil society and national parliaments.[30] However, their policy impact in decision-making remains questionable.[31]

The Commission has also become aware that international economic law has failed to keep pace with rapid global changes, and that trade has had divergent negative effects domestically, due to 'unfair trade

25 EC, 'Contribution to the EU's Growth and Jobs Strategy' (2006) SEC/2006/1230.

26 P. Leblond and C. Viju-Miljusevic, 'EU Trade Policy in the Twenty-First Century: Change, Continuity and Challenges' (2019) 26 *Journal of European Public Policy* 1836.

27 See Pew Research Center and Bertelsmann Foundation, 'Support in Principle for US–EU Trade Deal, But Some Americans and Germans Wary of TTIP Details' (*Pew Research Center*, 9 April 2014).

28 See A. R. Young, 'European Trade Policy in Interesting Times' (2017) 39 *Journal of European Integration* 909, 915.

29 Pew Research Center and Bertelsmann Foundation (n 27) 16.

30 EC, 'A Balanced and Progressive Trade Policy to Harness Globalisation' (n 23) 7–8.

31 See L. Drieghe, J. Orbie, D. Potjomkina and J. Shahin, 'Participation of Civil Society in EU Trade Policy Making: How Inclusive Is Inclusion' (2021) 27(4) *New Political Economy* 581.

practices', 'tax evasion' and, more generally, unfair competition.[32] In the post-COVID-19 reality, legal uncertainties in international trade and investment have only been further increased due to State intervention in the economy and political divisions. On the one hand, emergence of 'systemic rivals' as new regulatory powers has reduced the 'Brussels effect'[33] globally, while on the other, trends towards protectionism have increased pressures on the multilateral trading system. In a more hostile multipolar and less multilateral world, EU narrative has shifted towards 'strategic autonomy', geopolitics and assertiveness in order to promote EU values and objectives.[34]

The EU's geopolitical tools are envisaged at different levels – multilateral, bilateral and if necessary, autonomous – with a view to drive global change towards sustainability and climate neutrality enshrined in internal policies of the European Green Deal (EGD).[35] The new approach aims to address unfair trade practices and level up social, labour and environmental standards globally. At the same time, it seeks to ensure coherence between internal and external EU rule-making, as envisaged in the EU founding treaties. The narrative focuses on competitiveness and equality between the treatment internally and externally, thus serving to emphasise technical (i.e. economic and legal) rather than political aspects of the new strategy.

Whereas earlier 'trade for all' policy emphasised political persuasion, the new strategy reckons upon more assertive means, including autonomous measures and effective *enforcement*, in order to promote EU values *and interests*. While multilateral cooperation remains the EU's preferred option in theory, in practice the approach is shifting towards pragmatic-lateralism (multi-, pluri-, bi- or uni-), depending on the issue at hand. When faced with challenges in finding the common ground with 'like-minded' partners, the EU will be willing to go alone, if so necessary, in implementing its vision of 'progressive rules for global trade'.[36] Both the

[32] EC, 'Reflection Paper on Harnessing Globalisation' (n 23) 9.

[33] On Brussels effect, see A. Bradford, *The Brussels Effect: How the European Union Rules the World* (OUP 2020).

[34] EC, 'Trade Policy Review – An Open, Sustainable and Assertive Trade Policy', COM (2021) 66/2 final.

[35] EC, *A European Green Deal* (2019).

[36] See, for example, Proposal for a Regulation of the EP and of the Council establishing a carbon border adjustment mechanism, COM(2021) 564; and Proposal for a Directive of the EP and of the Council on Corporate Sustainability Due Diligence and amending Directive (EU) 2019/1937, COM(2022) 71.

'Brussels' effect of its internal market and its bilateral allegiances are to give the EU leverage in reforming the multilateral trading and investment system.

### *7.2.2 Post-Lisbon Generation of EU Trade and Investment Agreements*

Different EU trade agendas have been translated into the EU practice of concluding bilateral trade and investment agreements. Prior to the Global Europe Strategy, the so-called first-generation EU agreements primarily focused on the elimination of tariffs.[37] From 2006 onwards, EU agreements have extended to 'deep' trade issues. Depending on their legal basis,[38] new generation agreements embrace flexibility in considering the level of development of a trading partner and the desired relationship with the EU. The agreements range from more typical FTAs (South Korea, Canada, Japan, Singapore, Vietnam, Columbia, Peru and Ecuador, forthcoming agreements with Australia and New Zealand) to Association Agreements with modernised trade provisions (Central America, forthcoming agreements with Chile, Mexico, Mercosur), mostly without but some still with investment protection provisions in the same (Canada, Chile, Mexico) or a separate investment agreement (Singapore and Vietnam).

In addition, the EU has been concluding Deep and Comprehensive Free Trade Area agreements with countries in the EU neighbourhood, which aim at harmonising trading rules and transposing EU acquis (Ukraine, Georgia, Moldova, forthcoming agreements with Morocco and Tunisia), as well as Economic Partnership Agreements with African, Caribbean and Pacific countries, which focus on these countries' economic development. While the EU has forty-five trade agreements, they cover only around 33 per cent of total EU external trade.[39] Most of these are first-generation agreements and the EU does not yet have agreements with the biggest world economies (United States, China, India). Despite this, with the new trade policy, the EU's focus has been

[37] For example, Euro Mediterranean Association agreements, old Association agreements with Mexico and Chile.

[38] See Table 6.3 in Chapter 6.

[39] See Report from the Commission to the EP, the Council, the European Economic and Social Committee and the Committee of the Regions on Implementation and Enforcement of EU Trade Agreements, COM(2021) 654 final.

moving away from the conclusion of new agreements towards the implementation of the existing ones.

Most EU agreements build upon international standards in trade and investment, and include WTO-plus rules and improved investment protections.[40] Despite flexibility, there is a trend towards greater uniformity.[41] For example, post-Lisbon FTAs regularly include chapters on trade and sustainable development (TSD), whose objectives form 'an integral part' of the CCP.[42] Accordingly, the breach of the provisions related to social protection of workers and environmental protection in the TSD chapter could amount to a sufficiently serious breach which could give rise to the termination or suspension of trade treaty provisions.[43] A strong focus has been placed on 'the right to regulate' in the public interest, in both trade[44] and investment.[45] Therefore, regulatory cooperation in EU agreements cannot call into question the EU regulatory procedures.[46]

Whether trade and investment agreements serve as a tool for promoting high EU regulatory standards abroad remains doubtful. First, TSD chapters do not aim to create new substantive obligations but reaffirm certain existing international commitments. Their primary purpose is to ensure that conditions for trade and investment are not adversely affected because of different levels of protection.[47] The focus is on implementing the existing labour and environmental multilateral obligations,[48] and most recently, climate change objectives in accordance with the Paris Agreement.[49] Second, TSD obligations are still 'best endeavours' clauses concerning only the obligation of *means*, not results. The required standard is 'higher than undertaking merely minimal steps or none at all' but 'lower than a requirement to explore and mobilise all

[40] See Chapter 8.

[41] EP, DG for External Policies (n 24). The EC has however announced more tailored country-specific approach regarding the implementation of TSD chapters: see EC, 'The Power of Trade Partnerships: Together for Green and Just Economic Growth', COM (2022) 409 final, 6.

[42] Opinion 2/15 ECLI:EU:C:2017:376, para. 147.

[43] ibid para. 161.

[44] See, for example, Arts. 23.2 and 24.3 CETA.

[45] See Section 8.2.2 in Chapter 8.

[46] Opinion 1/17 ECLI:EU:C:2019:341.

[47] Opinion 2/15, Opinion of AG Sharpston ECLI:EU:C:2016:992, para. 471.

[48] For example, implementing in domestic legislation labour rights stemming from the eight core ILO Conventions. See for example, Art. 13.04 EU–Korea FTA.

[49] See for example, Art. 16.4.4 EU-Japan EPA and Art. 19.6 EU-New Zealand FTA.

measures available at all times'.[50] Therefore, in the 'absence of explicit targets' or 'at least any informal understanding' about the expected implementation milestones, they remain insufficiently effective. Finally, EU TSD chapters provide for a State-to-State consultation mechanism and a panel of experts but lack financial sanctions for non-compliance. However, a sanctions-based enforcement model is envisaged for future agreements, which will align TSD chapters with the general State-to-State dispute settlement under FTAs.[51]

Accordingly, the export of higher EU standards remains rather rhetorical, with the EU nevertheless achieving one of its objectives in external relations – the endorsement of the existing international law obligations. Given these limitations, a new approach envisages a range of tools to support the implementation of bilateral FTAs, in particular autonomous instruments.[52]

### 7.2.3 *The Making of the EU International Investment Policy*

While politicisation of EU trade policy has been a general trend, the EU IIP has attracted more significant public criticism, especially during the negotiations for the Transatlantic Trade and Investment Partnership (TTIP) with the United States and Comprehensive Economic and Trade Agreement (CETA) with Canada in 2014–2015. Additionally, framing of the new IIP led to inter-institutional disagreements within the EU, with an important role played by the European Parliament (EP) in setting the direction of the new policy.

Following the Lisbon Treaty changes,[53] a comprehensive European IIP was introduced in the Commission's 2010 Communication, with a view

[50] Panel of Expert Proceedings Constituted under Art. 13.15 of the EU-Korea FTA, Report (20 January 2021) para. 277. Most recent agreements introduce 'effective implementation' and broader commitments from partner countries (e.g. inclusion of occupational health and safety in labour standards; trade and gender equality), focusing also on regulatory cooperation framework (e.g. trade and climate change).

[51] In particular, trade sanctions would be applied in cases of failure to comply with obligations that 'materially defeat the object and purpose of the Paris Agreement' or 'in serious instances of non-compliance with the ILO fundamental principles and rights at work': see EC Communication (n 41) 11; See also TSD (ch. 19) and Dispute settlement (ch. 26) chapters of the agreed EU-New Zealand FTA (30 June 2022).

[52] See EC Communication (n 41) 3–4.

[53] See Section 6.1.1 in Chapter 6.

to integrating investment liberalisation and investment protection.[54] The policy was envisaged to ensure EU's external competitiveness and uniform treatment of all EU investors, while centralising comprehensive investment competence at the EU level. Internally, it envisaged coordination between EU institutions and Member States, while externally, it was intended to empower the EU's position in broader negotiations with trade partners, as investment would be part of such negotiations.[55] New EU agreements would gradually replace the existing network of over 1,000 Member States' bilateral investment treaties (BITs) with third States.

Then nascent policy already envisaged some of the principles that have become the guiding principles of EU international investment regulatory framework: the alignment with EU values and external action objectives; the right to regulate in pursuit of public policy objectives; transparency; consistency and predictability; quasi-permanent adjudicators; and the possible appellate mechanism.[56] While in favour of balancing the rights and responsibilities of investors, it planned retaining and improving the existing standards of investment protection and maintaining arbitration as the dispute settlement mechanism. The policy was therefore built upon the traditional investor-State dispute settlement (ISDS) narrative.

In line with the EU focus on multilateralism, the Commission also envisaged the possibility of a multilateral initiative in the long run.[57] The existing structures, particularly the International Centre for the Settlement of Investment Disputes (ICSID) Convention,[58] were, and remain, inadequate to accommodate the EU as a newcomer to the field and the Commission was aware that this could pose a significant challenge. The policy thus envisaged the possibility for the EU to embark on a different 'state-of-the art' dispute settlement mechanism. It also indicated that, where appropriate, EU law would be shaping investment protection provisions in EU international investment agreements (IIAs),

[54] EC, 'Towards a Comprehensive European International Investment Policy', COM (2010) 343, 5.

[55] ibid 4–5, 11.

[56] ibid 9–10.

[57] ibid 7.

[58] Signature and ratification of the ICSID Convention is open to Member States of the World Bank or a party to the Statute of the International Court of Justice, neither of which qualifies the EU to join the Convention. However, the ICSID Additional Facility Rules, as amended in 2022, now apply to disputes involving Regional Economic Integration Organisations, such as the EU.

considering established EU law concepts on freedom of establishment, free movement of capital, expropriation and adequate compensation.[59]

The response to the Commission's Communication was mixed. The Council, as the institution promoting interests of the Member States, took a more traditional ISDS stance, insisting on the widest possible protections and effective ISDS, along the lines of the Member States' BITs.[60] It stressed the 'crucial' importance of 'effective and ambitious investment protection and market access', including the right to 'prompt, adequate and effective compensation', and effective dispute settlement.[61] The Council also focused on retaining its power, by claiming the 'mixed competence' for the negotiation of new EU FTAs with an investment component, an issue on which it disagreed with the Commission, and which was resolved in Opinion 2/15 in favour of 'mixity'.[62] It emphasised that any future legal framework should still empower Member States to negotiate and conclude BITs with third States, when there is no interest for an EU IIA with those parties.[63] It believed that keeping with the practices of existing Member States' investment policies goes hand in hand with the principles and objectives of the EU external action and pursuit of public policy objectives.[64]

The EP had more reservations on the Commission's proposal. It emphasised some of the common concerns about ISDS, many of them shared by non-business civil society groups. While it did not discard the system, the EP's approach advocated for a more restrictive ISDS system, which will serve development goals of host States and reflect the EU's obligation to exercise coherence between its international investment and development policies.[65] The EP thus encouraged 'adequate'

[59] See EC (n 54) 8–10.

[60] See 'EU Negotiating Mandates on Investment (2011, EU–Canada/India/Singapore FTAs)'; Council of the EU, 'Directives for the Negotiation on the Transatlantic Trade and Investment Partnership between the European Union and the United States of America' (17 June 2013) 11103/13 DCL 1 (declassified) paras. 22–33.

[61] ibid paras. 14, 16, 18.

[62] See Section 6.1.2 in Chapter 6.

[63] Council of the EU, 'Conclusions on a Comprehensive European International Investment Policy', 3041st Foreign Affairs Council Meeting (25 October 2010) paras. 5, 10. Based on this, new provisional arrangements in the form of regulation were developed in 2012. See Section 8.1.2 in Chapter 8.

[64] ibid para. 17.

[65] EP Resolution 2010/2203 (INI) of 4 April 2011 on the future of European international investment policy [2012] OJ C 296E/34, paras. 6–7.

compensation[66] and the exclusion of 'speculative' forms of investment[67] on the one hand, and the inclusion of corporate social responsibility (CSR) and effective social and environmental clauses on the other.[68] It called on the Commission 'to produce clear definitions of investor protection standards' to limit the discretions of investment arbitrators.[69] The EP also emphasised transparency and the need for an appeal mechanism, along the lines of the EC's proposal, as well as the need to limit ISDS to a single place.[70] This latter suggestion indicated a possible policy direction away from conventional private arrangements towards a new public institutional setting. However, the EP called on the EC and the Member States, as 'major international players', to work towards necessary reforms of the ICSID and United Nations Commission on International Trade Law (UNCITRAL) rules which would allow membership of the EU in these organisations.[71] Accordingly, any new mechanisms were to be embedded in the existing international investment regulation (IIR).

The positions of the three institutions – the Commission, the Council and the EP – therefore emphasised their dissonant positions on investment standards. The Council favoured traditional standards that would be incorporated in new EU FTAs to leverage the negotiating power in relations with third States. The EP, considering public concerns, favoured a more significant move from 'old' ISDS standards, with no greater rights for foreign investors and more consideration for the public interest. The Commission was somewhere in between, referring to 'the best available standards', subject to the 'common understanding among experts in the field (lawyers, academics, arbitrators, judges)', and availing of the protection only genuine investors with substantive activities within the host State.[72] However, there was also a level of convergence about the future

[66] ibid para. 19.
[67] ibid para. 11. While alluding to portfolio investment as speculative, the EP does not provide further guidance on how to distinguish non-speculative from speculative investment.
[68] ibid paras. 27–28.
[69] ibid para. 24.
[70] ibid para. 31.
[71] ibid para. 33.
[72] EC, 'Follow up to the European Parliament Resolution on the Future European International Investment Policy' (5 July 2011).

institutional setting, with all three institutions favouring a possibility of an appellate mechanism.[73]

The strongest opposition to ISDS came from the public. The negotiations for the TTIP in 2014–2016 mobilised civil society in unpreceded ways. The petition by the self-organised European Citizen's Initiative 'Stop TTIP' was signed by more than 3.2 million people, requesting the termination of negotiations for the TTIP and non-ratification of CETA, due to a threat that ISDS and regulatory cooperation in these agreements pose to democracy and the rule of law. While the Commission refused to register the initiative on procedural grounds – the decision that was overturned by the CJEU in 2017,[74] it nevertheless launched an official public consultation on a possible EU approach to investment protection and ISDS in the TTIP. The consultation received an unpreceded number of answers, and a complete public rejection of the old ISDS was a clear outcome of this process.[75]

Public opposition in Germany prompted the then federal minister of economics, Social Democrat Sigmar Gabriel, to propose an alternative investment court with 'independent and professional judges',[76] submitted by the Socialists and Democrats (S&D group) to the EP in March 2015.[77] Along similar lines, the French government and its Foreign Trade Secretary of State Matthias Fekl had their list of demands for an acceptable dispute settlement mechanism: sanctions for business abuses, an appellate mechanism, more transparency and addressing conflicts of interest among arbitrators.[78] Similarly, the Dutch Parliament supported the idea of a 'Trade and Investment Court' with a permanent secretariat

[73] EC (n 54) 10; EP Resolution (n 65) para. 31; Council of the EU, TTIP Negotiation Directives (n 60) para. 23.

[74] Case T-754/14 *Efler and Others v Commission* ECLI:EU:T:2017:323.

[75] Nearly 150,000 responses, although 97 per cent pre-defined and channelled through online platforms in only several Member States, largely opposing ISDS in the TTIP or the TTIP generally. See EC, 'Online Public Consultation on Investment Protection and Investor-to-State Dispute Settlement (ISDS) in the Transatlantic Trade and Investment Partnership Agreement (TTIP)', SDW (2015) 3 final, 14; M. Bauer, 'Campaign-Triggered Mass Collaboration in the EU's Online Consultations: The ISDS-in-TTIP Case' (2015) 14 *European View* 121.

[76] S. Kinkartz, 'German Social Democrats Fear Free Trade' (*Deutsche Welle* 23 February 2015).

[77] Group of the Progressive Alliance of S&D in the EP, 'S&D Position Paper on Investor–State Dispute Settlement Mechanisms in Ongoing Trade Negotiations' (4 March 2015).

[78] C. Barbiere, 'France and Germany to Form United Front against ISDS' (*Euractiv* 15 January 2015).

and appeals mechanism.[79] Finally, Germany submitted its official proposal for a permanent international investment court in May 2015, tailored by Professor Markus Krajewski.[80] The French followed, endorsing the same idea.[81] Every element mentioned in these documents found its way into the later EU proposal for an Investment Court System (ICS).

### *7.2.4 From Bilateralism to Multilateralism and Pragmatic-Lateralism in International Investment Policy*

Following fierce debates at the national level, the European Commission (EC) proposed to replace ISDS with the ICS and an appellate mechanism.[82] This new adjudication mechanism was intended to 'transform' ISDS towards a system 'which functions more like traditional courts systems', by making adjudicators' appointments permanent, assimilating their qualifications to those of national judges and introducing an appeal system.[83] The proposal envisaged a two-pronged approach: bilateral and multilateral, to be developed in parallel.

The bilateral approach at that stage envisaged arbitration at first instance with a pre-established roster of arbitrators, who would be 'competent, independent, impartial' and 'trusted to decide in accordance with known and predictable legal principles'.[84] Eventually, the idea of a roster evolved into a permanent first-instance tribunal, as it became obvious that rosters could still lead to conflicts of interest. Additionally, the proposal envisaged a bilateral appellate mechanism, modelled largely on the institutional set-up of the WTO Appellate Body, with permanent members and similar qualifications.[85]

The multilateral approach envisaged the establishment of an international investment court and an appellate mechanism, which would be

[79] Tweede Kamer der Staten-Generaal, 'Improvements to CETA and beyond' (6 March 2015).

[80] M. Bungenberg, 'A History of Investment Arbitration and Investor–State Dispute Settlement in Germany' (2016), Centre for International Governance Innovation, Investor-State Arbitration Series Paper No. 12, 17.

[81] C. Barbiere, 'Mathias Fekl: The EU Should Have Its Own Arbitration Court' (*Euractiv* 3 June 2015).

[82] EC, 'Investment in TTIP and beyond – The Path for Reform. Enhancing the Right to Regulate and Moving from Current Ad Hoc Arbitration towards an Investment Court' (5 May 2015).

[83] ibid 4.

[84] ibid 7.

[85] ibid 9.

developed separately but would form part of a 'multilateral system'. First, a multilateral appellate mechanism would be developed from the bilateral TTIP mechanism, applying to 'multiple agreements and between different partners', based on an opt-in system. In any case, it would become a standard feature in all EU IIAs. Second, given the 'obvious technical and organisational challenges' of pursuing an individual investment court for each EU agreement, the EU should pursue the creation of *one* permanent court. The same as the appellate mechanism, such a court would allow for different membership on the opt-in basis, and it would be either a stand-alone international body or embedded into an existing multilateral organisation.[86] The proposal thus resonated with the German and French position of creating a permanent court in stages: initially as a European court, for all EU trade agreements, which would eventually evolve into a permanent international and multilateral court.[87]

The Commission's approach significantly reflected the desire of States to take control over the IIR and to reintroduce the rule of law, instead of the 'rule of lawyers'.[88] Thus, establishing a court as the new system's central element was to guarantee the rule of law. The EC proposal did not question the challenges for the rule of law stemming from the international context (inevitable politicisation of courts), as compared to the domestic context (possible independence of courts guaranteeing the rule of law). The new system projected an EU vision of the rule of law, combining best rule of law practice at the domestic (independence of courts) and international level (enforcement of international obligations). This approach would guarantee the regulatory sovereignty of States, as the first major public concern. On the investment protection side, the mechanism was to benefit small and medium size enterprises (SMEs) as opposed to multinational enterprises (MNEs), as the second major public concern.

Conceptually, the proposal did not question the desirability of ISDS as a mechanism that gives more rights to some (foreign investors) as compared to others (workers, the environment, consumers). The

86 ibid 11–12. For a comprehensive analysis about the influence of the WTO rules on the EU's ICS proposal, see J. Chaisse and Y. Renouf, 'Investor–State Dispute Settlement' in J. Drake-Brockman and P. Messerlin (eds), *Potential Benefits of an Australia–EU Free Trade Agreement: Key Issues and Options* (Adelaide University Press 2018) 290–294.

87 Barbiere (n 81).

88 C. Malmström, EU Commissioner for Trade, 'Discussion on Investment in TTIP at the Meeting of the International Trade Committee of the European Parliament' (Speech/15/4624, 18 March 2015).

Commission did not consider excluding investment dispute settlement altogether, even in relations with developed countries, such as the US. The reasons for this were explained as twofold. First, US law does not prohibit discrimination against foreign investors and guarantees under international law cannot be invoked in US courts.[89] This argument adopts a narrow understanding of the principle of non-discrimination, since the rule of law guarantees procedural justice and equality of parties in legal systems that adhere to the rule of law.[90] The US system generally adheres to the rule of law and provides effective mechanisms of judicial protection, and any imperfections apply to everyone, not foreign investors only.[91] It is a more convincing argument that the existing regulatory and institutional *systemic* differences could place foreign investors in a more detrimental position;[92] however, in the absence of illegal treatment, this could be considered as part of the investment risk. The second of the Commission's reasons for keeping ISDS is thus sounder: in the absence of an ISDS mechanism in the TTIP, the EU's main competitors in the US market – Canada and Japan – would have access to investment protection, while European investors would not.[93]

Instead of eliminating ISDS as a mechanism that favours private interests, a new mechanism was developed to provide an institutional setting (a court) that would strike the appropriate balance between the competing public and private interests. The right to regulate, as one of the basic principles of the new system, would provide guidance for the new court in striking that balance, similar to the approach of the CJEU in applying the principle of proportionality.[94] Clear drafting of investment protection standards, in many aspects largely inspired by the US Model

[89] ibid.

[90] See also 'Opinion of the Committee on Legal Affairs for the Committee on International Trade on recommendations to the Commission on the Negotiations for the Transatlantic Trade and Investment Partnership (TTIP)' (4 May 2015) 2014/2228(INI).

[91] However, for an opposite view, see the case *Loewen Group, Inc. and Raymond L. Loewen v United States of America* ICSID Case No. ARB(AF)/98/3, Award (26 June 2003), concerning the US judicial system (based on trial by jury and punitive damages). While this controversial case was eventually decided in favour of the State, the apologetic *obiter dictum* of the award recognises the possibility of the miscarriage of justice: ibid paras. 241–242. For a critique of the award, see N. Rubins, '*Loewen v United States*: The Burial of an Investor–State Arbitration Claim' (2005) 21 *Arbitration International* 1.

[92] See, for example, A. Auersperger Matic, 'Transatlantic Trade and the Case for Investment Protection' (2017), The German Marshall Fund of the United States, No. 20/2017, 14–15.

[93] Malmström (n 88).

[94] See Chapter 4 for the principle of proportionality and Chapter 8 for the right to regulate.

BIT 2012 and NAFTA case law, would significantly avoid expansive interpretations.[95] In rare cases when the new court 'strays' in its interpretations, States could correct such mistakes through binding interpretations.[96] The new institutional arrangement – with permanent, independent and impartial adjudicators, improved processes and an appeal – would ensure predictability, consistency and correctness of the awards. Taken together, these improvements would ensure that the issues of traditional ISDS are properly addressed and avoided.

The new adjudication mechanism, however, was not the end of the ISDS debate, which continued in the EP. The strongest opposition to ISDS came from the Committees on Legal Affairs and Constitutional Affairs, indicating that ISDS was not only a political but also significantly a legal problem in the EU context. While both committees opposed the inclusion of ISDS in the TTIP,[97] their remarks reflected wider EU legal concerns regarding international investment law (IIL): unequal treatment of local and foreign investors, inherent to ISDS;[98] 'serious' substantive and procedural weaknesses of the existing dispute settlement mechanisms;[99] tensions between different EU policy objectives and the need for regulatory coherence, both internally and externally;[100] conceptual differences between regulatory approaches;[101] the lack of efficient parliamentary oversight over the executive regulatory dialogue taking place in the framework of trade treaties;[102] and the potential of private arbitration to undermine the EU constitutional framework.[103]

Due to conceptual differences, the politicisation of ISDS continued. Criticism of the new mechanism also came from non-business civil society, which saw the ICS as disguised ISDS. Some legal experts – in

[95] For traditional ISDS standards, see Chapter 1. For ISDS standards in new EU IIAs, see Chapter 8.

[96] EC (n 82) 2.

[97] Committee on Legal Affairs (n 90) para. c; 'Opinion of the Committee on Constitutional Affairs for the Committee on International Trade on recommendations to the Commission on the Negotiations for the Transatlantic Trade and Investment Partnership (TTIP)' (16 May 2015) 2014/2228(INI) para. 1(d)(vi).

[98] Committee on Legal Affairs (n 90) para. b.

[99] ibid para. e.

[100] Committee on Constitutional Affairs (n 97) para. 1(d)(i)–(ii).

[101] For example, the EU precautionary principle: see Committee on Legal Affairs (n 90) para. k.

[102] Committee on Constitutional Affairs (n 97) para. 1(d)(iv).

[103] ibid para. 1(d)(vii). This issue was later addressed by the CJEU in Opinion 1/17 ECLI: EU:C:2019:341: see Chapter 8.

particular, domestic judges – saw no need to create special courts and pointed to a number of legal problems in the proposed adjudication mechanism. In particular, German judges stressed that the EU does not have a competence to create an investment court and the independence of the judges in this new mechanism would not be guaranteed.[104] Nevertheless, the new ICS softened opposition to ISDS in the EP, in particular among the S&D group, but led to internal disputes, with the radical left still strongly opposing any dispute settlement mechanism.[105] Despite mixed sentiments among thirteen EP parliamentary committees whose inputs informed the final report of the Committee on International Trade (INTA), it was recommended that 'a permanent solution' with 'independent professional judges in public hearings' and an appellate mechanism should be introduced, while in the medium term 'a public International Investment Court' would be the most appropriate for resolving investment disputes.[106] Accordingly, and in spite of a postponed vote and numerous amendments, in July 2015 the EP endorsed the new adjudication mechanism and voted in favour of replacing arbitration with the new system in the TTIP.[107] Effectively, at that point traditional arbitration-based ISDS was 'dead' for the EU.

The ICS was officially coined as such in the EC's proposal in September 2015, based on the Commission's concept paper, the EP's recommendations and input from Member States.[108] The final version for the TTIP was presented to the United States in November 2015.[109] Although negotiations with Canada and Singapore were then already closed, the ICS was included in the final version of agreements with both

[104] M. Juergen, 'German Association of Judges on the TTIP Proposal of the European Commission' (*Global Arbitration News* 21 March 2016). On the issue of independence, see Chapter 9.

[105] See D. Frantescu, 'How Will EU Parliamentarians Vote on TTIP?' (*VoteWatch Europe* 9 June 2015).

[106] Report containing the European Parliament's recommendations to the European Commission on the negotiations for the Transatlantic Trade and Investment Partnership (TTIP), 2014/2228(INI), 1 June 2015, para. 1(d)(xv).

[107] EP Resolution 2014/2228(INI) of 8 July 2015 containing the European Parliament's recommendations to the European Commission on the negotiations for the Transatlantic Trade and Investment Partnership (TTIP) [2017] OJ C 265/35, para. 2 (d)(xv).

[108] EC Press Release, 'Commission Proposes New Investment Court System for TTIP and Other EU Trade and Investment Negotiations' (16 September 2015).

[109] EC Press Release, 'EU Finalises Proposal for Investment Protection and Court System for TTIP' (12 November 2015).

countries.[110] The new anti-ICS sentiment culminated in October 2016 when the predominantly French-speaking Socialist-led Belgian region of Wallonia conditioned its consent to CETA on the CJEU's favourable ruling on the compatibility of the ICS with EU law. Consequently, the Belgian request for a CJEU's Opinion was made in accordance with Article 218(11) Treaty on the Functioning of the European Union (TFEU). The CETA was nevertheless signed and the later positive Opinion of the CJEU endorsed the ICS,[111] allowing the Commission to continue pursuing the ICS and the Multilateral Investment Court (MIC). Yet, this task has remained a challenge.

Negotiations with the United States on the TTIP eventually failed. However, there was an important geostrategic reason for the EU in using the TTIP to develop a new world-wide ISDS mechanism.[112] Both the EU and the United States have been the pillars of the ISDS regime, considering historical developments and the number of their BITs. Given the size of their economies, they are the main source of foreign direct investment (FDI) globally. Both have been focused on protecting regulatory sovereignty and promoting common values in international trade. As the United States made efforts over the years to improve its Model BIT and the EU endorsed such improvements in its own treaties, the EU procedural reform would bring further improvements, in addition to those already achieved by the United States. In particular, an appellate mechanism was seen as 'a realistic possibility' since the United States had already signalled the possibility of a future multilateral appellate mechanism in its agreements since 2002.[113] Reforms implemented in a common treaty between these two investment powers would prompt other EU partners to adopt similar reforms, giving the EU leverage in negotiations to upgrade the existing extra-EU BITs and conclude new bilateral EU IIAs.[114]

110 See 'Joint Statement: Canada–EU Comprehensive Economic and Trade Agreement (CETA)' (26 February 2016). Following the CJEU's Opinion 2/15 in 2017, the agreement with Singapore was split into two separate trade and investment agreements in 2018: see Chapter 6.

111 See Chapter 9.

112 For the broader geopolitical importance of TTIP, see 'Opinion of the Committee on Foreign Affairs for the Committee on International Trade on recommendations to the Commission on the negotiations for the Transatlantic Trade and Investment Partnership (TTIP)' (1 April 2015) 2014/2228(INI) para. 4.

113 See, for example, Art. 28 of the 2012 US Model BIT.

114 See Malmström (n 88).

At the same time, it was somewhat unreasonably optimistic to expect that the United States would ever accept any other investment dispute settlement than arbitration. The United States is generally sceptical of permanent international courts, and this would for investment disputes offer an inflexible bureaucratic apparatus, difficult to check on by the States and mistrusted by investors.[115] As a respondent, the United States has never lost an investment arbitration case. It has been the leader in developing investment standards and has successively argued correct interpretation of disputed standards, such as the fair and equitable treatment (FET).[116] More generally, US law firms have benefited from arbitration.[117] US businesses have been the most common individual State users of ISDS and their business organisations are strong supporters of ISDS.[118] Thus, ISDS has been developed in ways that benefit the United States and its investors. Moreover, the American vision of the rule of law in IIL is founded on the presumption that ISDS strengthens international law.[119]

The contours of the early EC proposal are clearly reflected in the current EU international investment strategy. The EU has aimed at building partnerships through bilateral agreements, which can support the multilateral efforts of the EU, or at least not undermine them. In CETA, investment protection agreements with Singapore and Vietnam, and other negotiations that followed (Mexico, Chile), a bilateral ICS is envisaged as an interim solution, to be replaced by a similarly conceived MIC at the multilateral level,[120] currently being negotiated in the framework of UNCITRAL.[121] Yet, just as in the case of the United States, there are EU partners which do not support the idea of a new court that would

[115] T. R. Bromund, J. M. Roberts and R. Dasgupta, 'The U.S. Should Reject the European Commission's Proposed Investment Court' (2015) 4485 *The Heritage Foundation.*

[116] See UK Government Department for International Trade, 'UK–US Trade & Investment Working Group' (2–7 November 2018) 32–33.

[117] Y. Dezaley and B. R. Garth, *Dealing in Virtue* (University of Chicago Press 1996).

[118] See American Chamber of Commerce to the EU, 'AmCham EU's Response to the European Commission's Public Consultation on Modalities for Investment Protection and ISDS in TTIP' (Consultation Response 11 July 2014). See also P. Chase and S. Heather, 'Investment Protection: If It Isn't Broken, Why "Fix" It?' (*US Chamber of Commerce* 1 October 2015).

[119] P. Chase, 'TTIP, Investor–State Dispute Settlement and the Rule of Law' (2015) 14 *European View* 217.

[120] See Art. 8.29 CETA. For the EU proposal of a MIC, see UNCITRAL, 'Possible Reform of ISDS, Submission from the EU and Its Member States' (24 January 2019) UN Doc A/CN.9/WG.III/WP.159/Add.1.

[121] See Chapter 10.

replace arbitration or oppose ISDS on conceptual grounds. The stalemate in developing trade agreements with these States (the CETA scenario) has been avoided by excluding investment protection and dispute settlement altogether from negotiations, or at least until the outcomes of the multilateral ISDS negotiations are known. The previous rule-of-law imperfections of the developed countries have thus become secondary to investment pragmatism.

With sustainability at the heart of the new EU trade strategy, the focus of the IIP is shifting towards substantive provisions and their compatibility with the EU's climate, environmental and human rights priorities. The EP has stressed the challenge of ensuring consistency between IIAs and the EGD, the Sustainable Development Goals and EU values.[122] On the one hand, Member States' environmental and climate measures can be undermined by their existing unreformed IIAs, which extend protections for fossil fuels.[123] On the other hand, the asymmetry enshrined in the IIR undermines the efforts for bringing investors to account in ways that are envisaged for accountability of economic operators in new trade policy.[124] The EP has thus called for a more substantive reform of EU IIP, which would entail the strict compliance of Member States' extra-EU BITs with EU law,[125] and the expansion of investor obligations and their enforcement in bilateral EU IIAs. Obligations for investors should also be implemented in separate international instruments and 'via domestic frameworks for human rights and environmental due diligence',[126] suggesting that autonomous measures should not be excluded as an option for EU IIP.

Beyond an MIC, modernisation of 'old' treaties with improved substantive and procedural provisions but 'old' ISDS approach of *ad hoc* arbitral tribunals has become an option not only for Member States' extra-EU BITs but even for EU IIAs, with the Energy Charter Treaty (ECT) as a case in point.[127] However, the ECT remains a bone of

122 See EP Resolution of 23 June 2022 on the future of EU international investment policy, 2021/2176(INI).

123 ibid paras. 20, 36.

124 See for example, Proposal for a Directive on Corporate Sustainability Due Diligence (n 36), to be applied across EU operators' value chains.

125 ibid para. 37.

126 ibid para. 27.

127 See Chapter 8. Cf. Modernisation of Association Agreements with Mexico (agreement in principle reached in April 2018) and Chile (negotiations concluded in December 2022), which include the ICS.

contention between the institutions and Member States, with uncertain prospects.[128] As outcomes of a structural ISDS reform remain uncertain and ISDS continues to 'chill' climate regulation, the focus of EU IIP is also shifting towards investment governance beyond ISDS, and aligning efforts in promoting sustainable development through both trade and investment. New bilateral agreements on investment facilitation with African countries with State-to-State measures and dispute settlement, which exclude portfolio investment and ISDS, seem to be a step in that direction, envisaged to be supported by the existing Member States' BITs and autonomous measures.[129]

The creation of an MIC remains the core aspect of the IIP and an important part of the Commission's multilateral agenda.[130] However, if the efforts to create an MIC fail, the future of EU IIP remains less clear, in light of the still dominant role of over a thousand Member States' extra-EU BITs with 'old'-type protections and traditional ISDS,[131] and shared investment competence within the EU. The existence of these agreements is inconsistent not only with the reformed approach of EU IIP, but also the EU's sustainability agenda. At the same time, the overwhelming focus of EU IIP reform on the ISDS mechanism indicates that the reform has not gone far enough to efficiently support the implementation of the EGD goals, demonstrating the challenges of achieving coherence between different EU policies and objectives.

## 7.3 Conclusion

The new generation of EU trade and investment agreements has been envisaged as a vehicle to export EU values, with a view to shaping global governance. The EU strategy in trade has thus shifted from multilateralism to bilateralism, and more recently even unilateralism, while in investment, the trend has been the opposite: from bilateralism towards envisaged multilateralism. In both aspects, the approach remains

[128] See EP Resolution (n 122) paras. 39–45. See also Section 8.3.2 in Chapter 8.

[129] See Council of the EU, 'Negotiating Directives for the Negotiation of an Agreement on Investment Facilitation with the Republic of Angola', 8441/21; the proposal for a revised EU Regulation on the Generalised Scheme of Preferences (COM(2021) 579), although related to trade preferences, focuses on the promotion of sustainable development, and includes a possibility for the EU to withdraw GSP benefits for serious and systemic violations of conventions on climate change and environmental protection.

[130] EC (n 34) 11.

[131] See Section 8.1 in Chapter 8.

sufficiently flexible to adopt pragmatic-lateralism the most suitable for the issue at hand. Historical developments clearly demonstrate that persisting dividing lines within EU IIP date back to the creation of the policy.

From its early days, the EU investment strategy has been characterised by attempts to strike the appropriate balance between policy legitimacy (public approval) and policy effectiveness (the protection of EU investors abroad), while policy efficiency (shared EU investment competence) remains the weakest link due to the lack of centralised authority at the EU level. As a consequence, EU IIP remains more exposed to politicisation due to the involvement of national and regional parliaments in the ratification of EU investment treaties.[132] Externally, the MIC is envisaged as a vehicle through which EU values, principles and objectives (the rule of law, strict observance of international law, protection of EU citizens (investors) abroad, free and fair trade, multilateral cooperation and good global governance) are translated into practice.

The early EU IIP outlined the contours of subsequent EU investment regulation for external relations: transitional arrangements retaining the important role of the Member States in international investment, enshrined in secondary law; the division of competences (Opinion 2/15) and the legality of the policy under EU law (Opinion 1/17). The CJEU played a crucial role in the consolidation of the policy, carefully balancing considerations of the EU legal order against the objectives and effectiveness of EU action externally (Opinions 2/15 and 1/17) and the objectives of EU integration internally (the *Achmea* judgment).

The following chapters turn to the implementation of EU IIP regarding substantive protections (Chapter 8) and the dispute settlement mechanism (Chapter 9) in bilateral relations, and multilateral engagement towards the creation of a new international investment court (Chapter 10).

132 See Chapter 6.

# 8

# EU Standards in International Investment Treaties

With the foreign investment competence in the Lisbon Treaty, the EU has set an objective to develop a coherent international investment policy (IIP). This policy is now being implemented through EU (mixed) international investment agreements (IIAs) and the Member States' extra-EU bilateral investment treaties (BITs) concluded with third countries in the post-Lisbon period. Both set of agreements serve to replace or supplement the existing extensive network of pre-Lisbon extra-EU BITs of Member States. As a matter of principle, a coherent EU IIP could ensure the same level of protection for all EU economic operators investing abroad, contributing to the uniformity of the Common Commercial Policy (CCP). Further, it supports the EU in the global reform of international investment governance. Ultimately, a coherent external approach of the EU and its Member States could improve consistency between the regulation of investment internally and externally, thus endorsing the EU vision of constitutionalism in international law.[1] In this chapter we examine the extent to which the EU has achieved coherence between EU's and Member States' IIAs. We analyse substantive and procedural provisions of pre- and post-Lisbon Member States' extra-EU BITs and EU IIAs in light of primary EU law, the existing transitional arrangements in EU secondary law and the Court of Justice of the European Union (CJEU) case law.

## 8.1 Member States' Extra-EU BITs

Before 2009 Member States led their independent international investment policies and concluded a large number of BITs with third non-EU States. In the postcolonial context, these agreements were particularly important for the Member States of the then European Economic

[1] See M. Koskenniemi, *The Politics of International Law* (Hart 2011) 345–350.

Community (EEC), guaranteeing protection for their investors in their former colonies.[2] The original six Member States developed an extensive network of extra-EU BITs following the entry into force of the EEC Treaty.[3] Subsequent Member States concluded BITs before and after their accession to the EU. Extra-EU BITs with the Central and East European States became intra-EU BITs following their accession to the EU.[4] However, Member States kept an additional 1,360 BITs with third non-EU States.[5] Unlike intra-EU BITs, they are less politically problematic for the EU.

Member States' extra-EU BITs remain valid under public international law; however, their status under EU law had to be clarified in light of the new EU competence. European Union Regulation 1219/2012 outlines transitional arrangements and prescribes procedures and requirements for amending the pre-Lisbon extra-EU BITs and concluding new Member States' BITs post-Lisbon. In addition to secondary legislation, the CJEU examined the compatibility of pre-Lisbon BITs with EU law in several of its judgments. It remains open to interpretation whether the CJEU's decisions in *Achmea* and Opinion 1/17 have relevance for Member States' extra-EU BITs. In any case, in light of the EU founding treaties, Member States have a duty to eliminate any inconsistencies between their extra-EU BITs and EU law and must comply with the principle of sincere cooperation in exercising their remaining investment competence. Eventually, Member States' extra-EU BITs should lose relevance as the EU concludes new IIAs with third countries.

### 8.1.1 *Pre-Lisbon Member States' Extra-EU BITs*

Regulation 1219/2012 'grandfathered' 1,360 Member State pre-Lisbon extra-EU BITs that were notified to the European Commission (EC) under the Regulation mechanism.[6] The majority of these BITs were concluded between 'old' Member States and developing States, while 'new' Member States concluded a number of agreements with

[2] See Section 1.1 in Chapter 1.

[3] See UNCTAD, 'Bilateral Investment Treaties 1959–1999' (2000) UNCTAD/ITE/IIA/2.

[4] See Section 5.1 in Chapter 5.

[5] List of the bilateral investment agreements referred to in Art. 4(1) of Regulation (EU) 1219/2012 of the EP and of the Council of 12 December 2012 establishing transitional arrangements for bilateral investment agreements between Member States and third countries [2013] OJ C131/2.

[6] Chapter II Arts. 2–6 Regulation 1219/2012.

Organization for Economic Cooperation and Development (OECD) countries during their transitions to market economies in the 1990s. Extra-EU BITs so notified remain in force; however, Member States still have a duty under primary EU law to bring all their agreements into conformity with EU law.

Article 351 Treaty on the Functioning of the European Union (TFEU) provides that EU founding treaties do not override treaties concluded by the EU Member States with third countries *prior* to the adoption of or the accession to the EU Treaties.[7] This provision enshrines international law principles, in particular the general *pacta tertiis nec nocent nec prosunt* rule, codified in Article 34 Vienna Convention on the Law of Treaties (VCLT), and the rule regarding the application of successive treaties in Article 30(4)(b) VCLT. Its purpose is merely to clarify that the application of the EU Treaties does not affect the *duty* of the Member State to respect the rights of third countries under a prior agreement.[8] The provision serves to protect third States. It does not allow Member States to exercise any rights that are conferred upon them under such agreement if that would result in the breach of EU law.[9] However, under EU law, Member States are obliged to bring any inconsistent pre-accession treaties into conformity with the EU Treaties.[10] This includes an obligation of a Member State to denounce an agreement with a third State if the Member State encounters difficulties which make the adjustment of the agreement impossible.[11] Importantly, foreign interests of Member States cannot override their obligation to align their international agreements with EU law.[12]

Article 351 TFEU refers explicitly to Member States' pre-accession agreements with third States with the effect of suspending the principle of primacy. This entails *a contrario* that EU law overrides treaties concluded by EU Member States and third countries *after* the adoption of or accession to the EU Treaties. As already mentioned, many of the

[7] Art. 351(1) TFEU.

[8] See Case 812/79 *Burgoa* [1980] ECR 2787, para. 8; Case C-84/98 *Commission v Portugal* [2000] ECR I-5215, para. 53; Case C-216/01 *Budějovický Budvar* [2003] ECR I-13617, paras. 144–145 (emphasis added).

[9] To that effect, see Case 10/61 *Commission v Italy* [1962] ECR 1, para. 10; Case C-158/91 *Levy* [1993] ECR I-4287, para. 12.

[10] Art. 351(2) TFEU.

[11] *Commission v Portugal* (n 8) para. 58.

[12] P. Eeckhout, *External Relations of the European Union, Legal and Constitutional Foundations* (OUP 2004) 342.

Member States' extra-EU BITs have been concluded with third States as their post-accession treaties. Given the principle of primacy of EU law, Member States' post-accession extra-EU BITs must also be brought into conformity with both EU Treaties and EU secondary legislation.[13] This obligation also stems from the principle of sincere cooperation enshrined in Article 4(3) Treaty on European Union (TEU).[14] Failure of a Member State to bring its post-accession international agreements into conformity with EU law could, in cases of incompatible obligations, effectively lead the Member States to a choice between incurring liability under EU law or under international law.[15]

Accordingly, Member States have the obligation under primary EU law to bring all their extra-EU BITs, concluded pre- and post-accession, into conformity with EU law. The same obligation is reiterated in Regulation 1219/2012 and the failure to do so can lead to infringement proceedings under Article 258 TFEU.[16] The compatibility of substantive provisions of extra-EU BITs was considered by the CJEU; however, following *Achmea* the compatibility of the investor-State dispute settlement (ISDS) mechanism in extra-EU BITs with EU law remains a controversy, which was to some extent clarified in *Komstroy*, with respect to the Energy Charter Treaty (ECT).

#### 8.1.1.1 Substantive Compatibility of Extra-EU BITs with Treaty Law

Free movement of capital in Article 63 TFEU prohibits all restrictions on the intra-EU movement of capital and, unlike other fundamental freedoms, guarantees that freedom between Member States and third countries.[17] However, additional restrictions apply with respect to extra-EU free movement of capital, and in particular regarding four types of capital movements: direct investment, establishment, the provision of financial services and the admission of securities to capital markets.[18] Further, the

[13] See P. Strik, *Shaping the Single European Market in the Field of Foreign Direct Investment* (CUP 2014) 163.

[14] A. Ali Ghouri, 'Resolving Incompatibilities of Bilateral Investment Treaties of the EU Member States with the EC Treaty: Individual and Collective Options' (2010) 16 *European Law Journal* 806, 830.

[15] Strik (n 13) 163–164.

[16] See Regulation 1219/2012, recital 11.

[17] See Section 4.5.1 in Chapter 4.

[18] Art. 64 TFEU.

Council is empowered to 'adopt measures which constitute a step backwards in Union law' regarding the liberalisation of extra-EU capital movements.[19] Finally, the Council can adopt safeguard measures when extra-EU movements of capital 'cause, or threaten to cause, serious difficulties' for the operation of the EU's Economic and Monetary Union (EMU). These measures can be taken in 'exceptional circumstances', if 'strictly necessary' and should not last longer than six months.[20]

In the infringement cases against Austria, Sweden and Finland, the CJEU assessed the compatibility of free transfer clauses in Member States' extra-EU BITs with primary EU law.[21] The CJEU found inconsistency with the Treaty provisions on capital movements in Articles 64, 66 and 215 TFEU, which are more restrictive than free transfer of capital guaranteed under international investment law (IIL).

The sued Member States claimed that the extra-EU BITs in question were not incompatible with the *existing* EU measures on free movement of capital. Since the Council had not adopted any specific measures, they claimed that incompatibility was purely *hypothetical*. According to them, *a potential future incompatibility* between their extra-EU BITs and secondary EU law does not fall within the scope of Article 351 TFEU and can, if at all, be confirmed only if the Council actually exercises its competence.[22] Moreover, they claimed that a wide interpretation of Article 351 TFEU would be an unwelcome precedent, which would challenge legal certainty and the distribution of powers between the EU and the Member States.[23]

The CJEU sided with the EC, reasoning that any potential Council measures would need to be applied *immediately*. Accordingly, neither the extra-EU BITs in question nor any other international law mechanism would allow the Member States to comply with their EU obligations at short notice.[24] Consequently, the CJEU condemned all three Member

[19] Art. 64(3) TFEU.

[20] Art. 66 TFEU.

[21] Case C-205/06 *Commission v Austria* ECLI:EU:C:2009:118; Case C-249/06 *Commission v Sweden* ECLI:EU:C:2009:119; Case C-118/07 *Commission v Finland* ECLI:EU:C:2009:715.

[22] *Commission v Austria* (n 21) paras. 18–23; *Commission v Sweden* (n 21) paras. 17–24 (emphasis added).

[23] *Commission v Sweden* (n 21) para. 19; *Commission v Finland* (n 21) para. 46.

[24] *Commission v Sweden* (n 21) paras. 38–41 (emphasis added).

States for the breaches of EU law and stated that 'the Member States must assist each other with a view to eliminating the incompatibilities established and must adopt, where appropriate, a common attitude'.[25] In other words, the CJEU reiterated the Member States' obligation in Article 351 (2) TFEU as an expression of the principle of sincere cooperation of Article 4(3) TEU.

In light of the CJEU's jurisprudence, the free transfer provisions of new EU IIAs reflect the limitations of the free capital provisions and are accordingly aligned with the Treaty law.[26] Many post-Lisbon Member States' extra-EU BITs do not in their transfer provisions explicitly refer to restrictive safeguard measures but contain a Regional Economic Integration Organisation (REIO) clause which aims to ensure that none of the BIT provisions prevent Member States from fulfilling their obligations resulting from their EU membership.[27] Some new extra-EU BITs, in addition to a REIO clause, include the possibility of measures that restrict transfers through a general exceptions clause.[28] The effectiveness of all these provisions remains to be tested in practice in the particular circumstances of each case.

While Member States have the obligation to bring extra-EU BITs in line with EU law, most BITs still retain broadly worded free transfer provisions. Any changes to free transfer of capital provisions depend on the willingness of third States and might be subject to reciprocity. In any case, third States remain protected under Article 351 TFEU.

[25] *Commission v Austria* (n 21) para. 44; *Commission v Sweden* (n 21) para. 44; *Commission v Finland* (n 21) para. 48.

[26] See Arts. 8.13, 13.16, 13.21 and Annex 13-B in CETA. Restrictions in case of serious balance of payment and external financial difficulties are also possible under general exceptions in Arts. 28.4 and 28.5 CETA. In EUSIPA the restrictive measures are included in the transfer provision of Art. 2.7 (cf. similar expression of Art. 66 TFEU).

[27] See, for example, Austria–Kyrgyzstan BIT (signed 22 April 2016), which contains the same transfer clause as Austria's pre-Lisbon BITs (Art. 9) but includes a REIO clause in Art. 3(4)(b). Similarly, see an REIO clause in Art. 2(5) of the Slovakia–UAE BIT (signed 22 September 2016, entered into force 5 February 2018); Art. 3(4) of the Slovakia–Iran BIT (signed 19 January 2016, entered into force 30 August 2017); Art. 2(5) Dutch Model BIT 2019.

[28] For example, Art. 13(2)(a) of the Hungary–Cambodia BIT (signed 14 January 2016, entered into force 30 August 2017). An REIO clause is included in Art. 13(5) and (6), which even clarifies that 'serious balance-of-payments difficulties, or the threat thereof' refer to the economic and monetary union of which a Contracting Party is a member. The drafting of this BIT is thus likely to be more effective than BITs which contain only a general REIO clause.

#### 8.1.1.2 Procedural Compatibility of Extra-EU BITs with Treaty Law

In its landmark *Achmea* judgment, the CJEU ruled that ISDS clauses in intra-EU BITs, such as the one in Article 8 of the Netherlands–Slovakia BIT, contravene Articles 267 and 344 TFEU.[29] According to the EC, *Achmea* applies exclusively to the intra-EU context.[30] The findings of *Achmea* were reiterated in *Komstroy*, which concerned a dispute between two non-EU parties (Ukraine and Moldova) with the seat of arbitration in the EU (Paris) under the ECT.[31] While the core of the *Komstroy* judgment focused on elaborating the inapplicability of the ECT to intra-EU disputes, it remains open to interpretation whether the implications of both *Achmea* and *Komstroy* could reach beyond Member States' *inter se* agreements.[32] The possible implications for Member States' extra-EU BITs depend on the manner in which the core aspects of these judgments are interpreted, in particular the *Achmea* judgment given its application in the BIT context.

**(i) The Applicable Law Clause Interpretation of *Achmea*** Although *Achmea* concerned a BIT between two Member States, reasoning by analogy, its findings could apply to a situation involving an international agreement between a Member State and a third non-EU State. As EU law forms part of the Member States' domestic legal orders, conflicts in the extra-EU context cannot be avoided. In fact, the ISDS mechanism in an extra-EU BIT could also violate Articles 267 and 344 TFEU when the arbitral jurisdiction concerns either the application or interpretation of EU law. For example, if under an extra-EU BIT an investor from a non-EU State challenges a measure which a host Member State adopted to comply with its EU obligations, an arbitral tribunal established under that extra-EU BIT could also interpret EU law, and thus potentially challenge its autonomy. Accordingly, in such cases the jurisdiction of arbitral tribunals to decide the case should be denied and foreign

[29] Case C-284/16 *Slovakische Republik v Achmea* ECLI:EU:C:2018:15. See Section 5.2.2 in Chapter 5.

[30] EC, 'Protection of intra-EU investment', COM (2018) 547 final, 3–4.

[31] Case C-741/19 *Republic of Moldova v Komstroy* ECLI:EU:C:2021:655.

[32] See, for example, S. Gáspár-Szilágyi, 'It Is Not Just About Investor-State Arbitration: A Look at Case C-284/16, Achmea BV' (2018) 3 *European Papers* 357; L. Ankersmit, '*Achmea*: The Beginning of the End for ISDS in and with Europe?' (*Investment Treaty News*, 24 April 2018).

investors should challenge the relevant Member State measure before the Member State's domestic courts.

It could be thus argued that the implications of *Achmea* depend on the applicable law clause in the BIT in question, since the applicable law clause of the Netherlands–Slovakia BIT was an important consideration for the CJEU in *Achmea*.[33] According to this argument, *Achmea* would apply and render inapplicable an ISDS clause in any extra-EU BIT, the applicable law clause of which explicitly contains reference to domestic law.[34] In addition, even extra-EU BITs that are silent on the applicable law could be contrary to EU law due to investment arbitration rules on the applicable law, which provide for a possibility of the domestic law application.[35] Moreover, given the level of abstraction applied by the CJEU, where all *potential* conflicts between intra-EU BITs and EU law were considered a threat to the autonomy of EU law, the same abstract concerns could apply to extra-EU BITs. Indeed, if one reads *Achmea* broadly, potentially any dispute settlement mechanism outside the EU judicial system might involve the interpretation or application of EU law.[36]

**(ii) The Mutual Trust Principle Interpretation of *Achmea*** On the other hand, *Achmea* could be read more narrowly. According to this interpretation, it would apply only to those cases that not only violate Articles 267 and 344 TFEU but also undermine the principles of mutual trust and sincere cooperation, enshrined in Articles 19(1) and 4(3) TEU. Indeed, these principles could be understood as the core elements of the *Achmea* judgment, which play an important role exclusively in the intra-EU context.[37] Since effective judicial protection must be guaranteed *within* the EU judicial system, there is no place for investment tribunals

[33] *Achmea* (n 29) paras. 40–42, 49. For this argument, see Q. Declève, '*Achmea*: Consequences on Applicable Law and ISDS Clauses in Extra-EU BITs and Future EU Trade and Investment Agreements' (2019) 4 *European Papers* 99.

[34] Declève (n 33) 104.

[35] In particular, Art. 42(1) ICSID Convention and Rule 35 of the 2010 UNCITRAL Arbitration Rules. See Declève (n 33) 105.

[36] N. de Sadeleer, 'The End of the Game: The Autonomy of the EU Legal Order Opposes Arbitral Tribunals under Bilateral Investment Treaties Concluded between Two Member States' (2018) 9 *European Journal of Risk Regulation* 355, 367.

[37] See, Opinion 1/17, Opinion of AG Bot ECLI:EU:C:2019:72, paras. 105, 112; Opinion 1/17 ECLI:EU:C:2019:341, paras. 126–129.

outside the EU judicial system, to protect rights of *EU* investors in the EU.[38]

In effect, Article 344 TFEU is an expression of the principle of sincere cooperation since it mandates the Member States not to submit a dispute concerning the interpretation or application of EU law to any dispute settlement mechanism *outside* the EU judicial system. The core rationale of this provision is to ensure consistent interpretation and thus *equal* application of EU law across different Member States. This Member State's obligation must be enforced *within* the EU judicial system, with an aim to enhance the rule of law across the EU.[39] In accordance with this reading of Article 344, two conditions must be satisfied for its application: (1) the dispute must concern the interpretation or application of EU law; *and* (2) the dispute must be submitted to a dispute settlement body placed outside the EU judicial system due to the lack of mutual trust in the institutions of the EU judicial system (the courts of other Member States). Arbitration under extra-EU BITs fulfils only the first criterion, and only in limited circumstances, when, depending on the applicable law clause, EU law could be interpreted or applied in the proceedings.

The principle of mutual trust does not apply in relations between the Member States and third States. In other words, there is no legal obligation of the Member States under EU law to trust courts or tribunals of third States, while this obligation exists with respect to Member States' courts. The jurisdiction of arbitral tribunals under Member States' extra-EU BITs, which are outside the EU judicial system, has been introduced *because* of the lack of trust in the courts of the third States. Given that effective judicial protection cannot be guaranteed before national courts and tribunals of third States, arbitral jurisdiction under extra-EU BITs could be justified in providing protection to Member States' investors abroad.[40]

Importantly, the emphasis in *Achmea* is placed on the integrationist rationale of the CJEU, which does not equally feature in intra- and extra-EU context. The attainment of EU objectives requires that EU law is 'fully

[38] Cf. commercial arbitral tribunals: see Section 5.2.2(v) in Chapter 5.

[39] S. Hindelang, 'Conceptualisation and Application of the Principle of Autonomy of EU Law – The CJEU's Judgement in *Achmea* Put in Perspective' (2019) 44 *European Law Review* 383.

[40] To that effect, see also Opinion 1/17 (n 37), in which the CJEU on these grounds found the justification for the ICS in CETA: see Chapter 9.

applicable at the same time and with identical effects over the whole territory of the Community without the Member States being able to place any obstacles in the way'.[41] Differentiation between the Member States due to international law mechanisms may be a disintegrating factor in the EU context.[42] However, a broad interpretation of *Achmea*, that applies to *all* intra-EU arbitrations, regardless of the applicable law clause in a particular intra-EU BIT, makes sense in light of the integrationist intra-EU considerations,[43] but it is of less relevance in the extra-EU context. In the former case, it is driven by the Court's practical consideration of effective and Union-wide uniform applicability of EU law.[44] However, these integrationist practical considerations have only limited relevance for the ISDS mechanism in the extra-EU context.

Politically speaking, an interpretation of *Achmea* that would render illegal under EU law all ISDS provisions in all Member States' extra-EU BITs could lead to problems in relations between the Member States and third countries. Such an interpretation would not be in the interests of the Member States whose investors would lose protection in third countries. On the other hand, the inapplicability of ISDS clauses in extra-EU BITs whenever they could concern interpretation or application of EU law would compound asymmetry with third countries. In other words, EU investors could avail themselves of protections under extra-EU BITs before arbitral tribunals while third country investors would not receive similar protection in the EU on the grounds that the tribunal could interpret and apply EU law. Such an investor would instead have to seek protections under the relevant Member State and EU law before the courts of that Member State.[45] It is difficult to imagine why any third State would accept such an arrangement.

**(iii) Implications of *Achmea* and Opinion 1/17 for Extra-EU BITs** A conflict between an ISDS clause in an extra-EU BIT and

41 Case 48/71 *Commission v Italy* [1972] ECR 529, para. 8.

42 B. de Witte, 'Variable Geometry and Differentiation as Structural Features of the EU Legal Order' in B. de Witte, A. Ott and E. Vos (eds), *Between Flexibility and Disintegration: The Trajectory of Differentiation in EU Law* (Edward Elgar 2017) 26.

43 See Opinion 1/17, Opinion of AG Bot (n 37) para. 105.

44 The same practical consideration is evident in the CJEU's reasoning that the Council's restrictive measures on capital movements could *potentially* conflict with free transfer provisions of extra-EU BITs and thus would not be uniformly applied across the EU once they are adopted. See discussion in Section 8.1.1.1.

45 See De Sadeleer (n 36) 368.

EU law, while not inconceivable, is rather exceptional. It would involve situations of non-EU foreign investors suing a host Member State under an extra-EU BIT for national measures that implement EU law where (1) the applicable law clause of the extra-EU BITs contains reference to domestic law or where procedural rules allow for such application, *and* (2) where the extra-EU arbitral tribunal applies or interprets EU law as a matter of *law*. In other words, an *actual* rather than a potential conflict between an extra-EU BIT and EU law is rare.

In most cases in practice, no questions of EU law arise under extra-EU BITs. This is because in most cases Member States' investors are more likely to bring claims against third States, and not *vice versa*; however, following *Achmea* such practice might change with intra-EU investors restructuring their investments through third countries. When third States' investors bring cases against Member States, in most such cases the claims will concern Member States' domestic policy measures and not EU measures.[46] Moreover, in most investment treaty arbitrations (ITAs), domestic law is treated as a matter of fact, and only exceptionally as a matter of law, even if a BIT in question allows for the application of domestic law as a matter of law. For example, domestic law will be relevant in determining whether covered investment has been made 'in accordance with host State law' as such reference is explicitly made in many IIAs. Domestic law can also be relevant in determining breaches of the substantive provisions of an IIA. The issue is, however, whether domestic law in such cases is taken as a fact or law, given that investment tribunals primarily apply international law.[47]

In rare cases when domestic law can be applied, international law prevails in the case of any conflicts between domestic and international

[46] A case would concern an EU measure only when a third State investor under an extra-EU BIT challenges either an EU measure which is directly applicable in the host Member State (e.g. a regulation), or a host Member State's measure that implements EU law (e.g. a directive).

[47] Some tribunals are more explicit about treating domestic law as a matter of fact: see, for example, *Nykomb Synergistics Technology Holding AB v Latvia*, Arbitral Award (16 December 2003) para. 3.7; *International Thunderbird Gaming Corporation v The United Mexican States*, UNCITRAL, Arbitral Award (26 January 2006) paras. 124–125; *Noble Ventures, Inc. v Romania*, Award (12 October 2005) para. 53; while others recognise that domestic law can be a source of rights and obligations, especially in cases related to expropriation: see, for example, *Enron Corporation and Ponderosa Assets, L.P. v Argentine Republic*, Award (22 May 2007) para. 206.

law.[48] Accordingly, while investment tribunals can apply domestic law as relevant law, they primarily apply international law as law applicable to the merits of investment disputes.[49] This is particularly the case in International Centre for the Settlement of Investment Disputes (ICSID) proceedings, where the prevailing view is that international law can be applied directly and without reference first to domestic law, and that arbitration is governed by international law.[50] In the case of non-ICSID awards, compatibility of extra-EU awards with EU law could be possible in the enforcement stage if the enforcement takes place in the EU.

Regulation 1219/2012 prescribes the obligation of Member States to notify the EC about their disputes under extra-EU BITs and to cooperate with the EC in ensuring the effective defence. This can include the participation of the EC in the arbitration proceedings[51] and the obligation of the Member State to take a particular position where the claim issue 'might affect the implementation of the Union's policies relating to investment, including in particular the CCP'.[52] So far, the EC has intervened or sought to intervene in small number of cases under extra-EU BITs, concerning different EU policies (State aid, the EU Single

[48] For example, the *Eastern* tribunal found that domestic law, and only its non-conflicting provisions, 'might be relevant' and 'could be taken into account' only where international law is silent. The tribunal thus applied domestic law (Czech law) with respect to statutory interest as these provisions did not conflict with international law: see *Eastern Sugar B.V. v Czech Republic*, SCC Case No. 088/2004, Partial Award (27 March 2007) paras. 196, 373.

[49] See *Achmea B.V. v The Slovak Republic* (formerly *Eureko B.V. v The Slovak Republic*) UNCITRAL, PCA Case No. 2008-13, Award on Jurisdiction, Arbitrability and Suspension (26 October 2010) para. 275. However, impliedly, the tribunal recognised that, if in the case there was an issue of EU law relevant for the proceedings, the tribunal would not have the authority to correctly apply EU law as the applicable law in the proceedings.

[50] Art. 42(1) ICSID Convention. See *Wena Hotels Ltd v Arab Republic of Egypt*, ICSID Case No. ARB/98/4, Decision on Annulment (5 February 2002); *Compañía del Desarrollo de Santa Elena SA v Republic of Costa Rica*, ICSID Case ARB/96/1, Award (17 February 2000) para. 65, confirmed in subsequent cases, in particular the Argentina cases: see, for example, *Compañia de Aguas del Aconquija SA and Vivendi Universal v Argentine Republic*, ICSID Case No. ARB/97/3, Decision on Annulment (3 July 2002) para. 60. See also D. Di Pietro, 'Applicable Law under Article 42 of the ICSID Convention' (*Transnational Notes,* 19 November 2011).

[51] Art. 13(b) Regulation 1219/2012.

[52] ibid Art. 13(a).

Resolution Mechanism and EU energy policy framework).[53] The objective of these interventions was 'to clarify the EU legal framework and procedures in connection with the facts of disputes'.[54] Decisions of arbitral tribunals in these extra-EU cases could have an indirect impact on EU policies and the EU's right to regulate although they do not bind the EU.[55] Hypothetically, they could influence the EU to abandon its legislation to spare Member States from paying damages for implementing EU law. The effect is more remote than in the cases involving the EU as a respondent but still possible.[56]

Therefore, it should not be assumed that ISDS clauses are compatible with EU law in all extra-EU BITs. This is confirmed by the CJEU's case law, which is strict regarding the legality of *any* measure – whether hypothetical[57] or actual – that is likely to breach EU law. In the absence of the CJEU's ruling on the matter of extra-EU BITs, the potential of arbitral tribunals to interpret EU law could still be sufficient to render the ISDS mechanism in extra-EU BITs incompatible, in line with the *Achmea* judgment.

Following Opinion 1/17, in which the CJEU ruled that the EU Investment Court System (ICS) in Comprehensive Economic and Trade Agreement (CETA) must comply with the Article 47 Charter of Fundamental Rights (CFR) criteria, the issue is whether its criteria of independence, impartiality and accessibility, equally apply to ISDS tribunals under Member States' extra-EU BITs. While extra-EU BITs do not bind the EU but the Member States that are parties to these agreements,[58] CFR applies every time when a Member State implements EU law.[59] Accordingly, the right to access an independent and impartial tribunal enshrined in Article 47 CFR would be applicable in all ITAs under extra-

[53] EC, 'Report from the Commission to the EP and the Council on the application of Regulation (EU) No 1219/2012 establishing transitional arrangements for bilateral investment agreements between Member States and third countries', COM (2020) 134 final, 7.

[54] ibid.

[55] For example, in the discontinued ICSID case *GBM Global et al. v Kingdom of Spain*, ICSID Case No. ARB/18/33 investors challenged the implementation of the EU's Single Resolution Mechanism in an EU regulation in Spain, in particular the way in which Spain implemented the EU mechanism (the sale of the bank as a response to the liquidity crisis) and not the mechanism itself.

[56] On the EU's right to regulate under CETA in Opinion 1/17, see Section 8.2.2.

[57] Case 120/78 *Cassis de Dijon* [1979] ECR 649; *Commission v Austria* (n 21); *Commission v Sweden* (n 21); *Commission v Finland* (n 21).

[58] Cf. Opinion 1/17 (n 37).

[59] Art. 52(5) CFR.

EU BITs involving EU or national measures implementing EU law. Proceedings before such extra-EU arbitral tribunals must comply with the requirements of Article 47 CFR.[60]

In light of *Achmea*, provisions in extra-EU BITs should be brought into conformity with EU law. In particular, applicable law clauses should exclude the application of domestic law as a matter of law.[61] In the meantime, ISDS provisions in extra-EU BITs remain applicable in accordance with the conflict of laws rules in Article 351 TFEU and Article 30 VCLT. The jurisdiction of an arbitral tribunal to decide a case under an extra-EU BIT should be challenged by a Member State whenever EU law prevails over international law under the conflict of laws rules and the tribunal interprets or applies EU law as a matter of law.[62] However, in such cases, arbitral tribunals would likely reason that ISDS cannot be excluded because EU law does not prevail over international law and/or the case in extra-EU context does not concern either the application or the interpretation of EU law.[63] Given the large numbers of extra-EU BITs concluded prior to Member States' accession to the EU, which would prevail over EU law under the conflict rules, their potential to affect the uniform application of EU law should not be ignored.[64]

60 On compliance of arbitral tribunals with Art. 47 CFR, see Section 8.3.2.

61 This is also the conclusion which is supported by the CJEU reasoning in Opinion 1/17: see Chapter 9. The modernised ECT adopts this approach: see Section 8.3.2.

62 The CJEU would have an opportunity to assess the compliance of an extra-EU BIT award with the right of access to an independent tribunal only if the award is challenged before the domestic court in the EU in the process of the enforcement. On the jurisdiction of the CJEU in extra-EU arbitration context of the ECT, see Section 8.3.1.

63 See for example, *Green Power K/S and Obton A/S v Spain*, SCC Case No. 2016/135, Award (22 June 2022) para. 392. *Mutatis mutandi*, the same argumentation as in intra-EU arbitrations could be applied. For reasoning of intra-EU arbitral tribunals, see Section 5.2.1 in Chapter 5.

64 See Case C-264/09 *Commission v Slovakia* EU:C:2011:580. While acknowledging that 'it is not for the Court to interpret the Investment Protection Agreement', the CJEU examined whether Slovakia was allowed to terminate the contract with a Swiss investor to align itself with obligations under the EU Directive 2003/54/EC concerning common rules for the internal market. The Court found that the contract 'may be regarded as investment protected by the Investment Protection Agreement' and that its termination would indirectly expropriate the investor's right to transmission, as established by the arbitral tribunal: paras. 50–51. The matter concerned a Member State's pre-accession obligation, which prevailed over Member State obligations under EU law. See also the discussion on the right to regulate in the EU in Section 8.2.2.

### *8.1.2 Post-Lisbon Member States' Extra-EU BITs*

Considering the changes brought by Article 207 TFEU in the Lisbon Treaty, Member States' extra-EU BITs should be abrogated as the EU concludes new IIAs with third countries.[65] EU IIAs will progressively replace them both as a matter of EU and international law.[66] Pre-Lisbon extra-EU BITs that were notified to the EC remain in force but cannot constitute an obstacle to the negotiation and conclusion of EU IIAs with third countries.[67] The EC publishes the list of all extra-EU BITs every twelve months and there are about 1,288 agreements in force.[68]

Until all extra-EU BITs are progressively replaced by EU IIAs, EU Regulation 1219/2012 re-empowers Member States to amend their existing pre-Lisbon BITs and even conclude new BITs, subject to procedural and substantive requirements outlined in chapter III of the Regulation.[69] Member States must seek and obtain the authorisation from the EC in order to, first, enter into negotiations with a third country[70] *and*, second, sign and conclude the new agreement.[71] The EC is kept informed throughout the negotiations,[72] while it informs other EU institutions about its decisions.[73] In substantive terms, the EC's authorisation to a Member State will be granted if the extra-EU BIT: (a) complies with EU law; (b) does not concern the third country with which the EU negotiates or plans to negotiate an IIA, and does not create a serious obstacle to the negotiation or conclusion of an EU's IIA with

65 Recital 5 Regulation 1219/2012.

66 Under Regulation 1219/2012: see Arts. 3, 11(4) and 12(6) and Art. 59 VCLT respectively. There are also provisions to that effect in new EU IIAs. See, for example, Art. 4.12.3 EUSIPA.

67 See Arts. 5 and 6 Regulation 1219/2012.

68 List of the bilateral investment agreements referred to in Art. 4(1) of Regulation 1219/2012, OJ C 142.

69 Since the EU competence for the regulation of FDI is exclusive (Art. 207 TFEU), Member States have no powers to regulate FDI unless they have been empowered by the EU. Accordingly, Member States can amend or conclude extra-EU BITs that concern FDI regulation only if so empowered by the EU: Art. 2(1) TFEU. On the division of competences, see Chapter 6.

70 Art. 8 Regulation 1219/2012.

71 ibid Art. 11.

72 ibid Art. 10.

73 ibid Arts. 9(4) and 11(7). In accordance with Art. 15, the EC has submitted its first report on the application of the Regulation in April 2020, recommending continuing the application of ch. III of the Regulation: EC (n 53).

that third country; and (c) is consistent with the principles and objectives of the EU external action and EU investment policy.[74]

The aim of the Regulation is to ensure the coherence between Member States' extra-EU BITs and EU law, and consistency of Member States' investment policy objectives with EU IIP. In accordance with their duty of sincere cooperation under Treaty law, which is also reflected in the duty to cooperate in Article 6 of the Regulation, Member States must take all appropriate measures to ensure the compliance of their existing and new extra-EU agreements with EU law and policy. Accordingly, the provisions in Member States' new extra-EU BITs must reflect the protection standards enshrined in EU IIAs.[75]

In the period of the first six years of the Regulation's implementation (2013–2019), the EC granted 322 authorisations, the majority being authorisations to open negotiations for new extra-EU BITs (164), of which only a small number have been concluded (24). Some Member States have been more active in seeking requests (Czech Republic, Hungary, Italy, Lithuania), while some requested authorisations for opening multiple negotiations for amending and concluding new agreements (Spain, Slovakia and the Netherlands).[76] In the same period, the EU has concluded three IIAs (with Canada, Singapore, Vietnam) but none have yet entered into force.[77] Upon their entry into force, these EU IIAs will replace all extra-EU BITs of Member States concluded with these three States. The third States for which Member States have submitted most requests for authorisation are Iran, Kazakhstan, Nigeria, Saudi Arabia, Qatar and United Arab Emirates.[78] Member States are precluded from entering negotiations with third States, with whom the EU is negotiating or planning to negotiate an agreement.

A high overall number of authorisations indicates that Member States remain active actors in the international investment sphere, in particular

[74] Art. 9(1) and (2) Regulation 1219/2012. The same criteria apply for the authorisation to sign and conclude the extra-EU BIT in accordance with Art. 11(4).

[75] The EC may request from the Member State the inclusion or removal of 'any clauses where necessary to ensure consistency with the Union's investment policy or compatibility with Union law': ibid Art. 9(2). The EC can always start infringement proceedings against disobedient Member States under Art. 258 TFEU.

[76] For the full statistics of all authorisations in this period and each year, see EC (n 53). However, the statistics do not indicate the number of requests by each Member State.

[77] On different types of EU agreements with investment protections, see Chapter 6.

[78] EC (n 53) 5–6.

in those regions in which the EU has limited investment interests (e.g. the Middle East). The EC's approach in granting authorisations is pragmatic but compounds the fragmentation in EU foreign investment regulatory framework, particularly considering the *relative* coherence between different new agreements, as discussed next.

## 8.2 EU Foreign Investment Provisions in Post-Lisbon IIAs

In the post-Lisbon period, EU external investment protection regulatory framework consists of: Member States' pre-Lisbon extra-EU BITs; their post-Lisbon BITs; and new EU IIAs. Pre-Lisbon extra-EU BITs have the classical features of 'old' IIAs, discussed in Part I. Of particular interest in the post-Lisbon period are new EU investment standards incorporated in EU IIAs and their coherence with standards of Member States' post-Lisbon extra-EU BITs.

In this section we will analyse new EU standards in CETA with reference to corresponding standards in other EU IIAs and Member States' post-Lisbon extra-EU BITs. First, we discuss substantive provisions, particularly focusing on the novelties introduced in EU IIAs. The discussion is limited to main issues and the purpose is to provide an overview rather than being exhaustive.[79] Second, in light of the CJEU's Opinion 1/17, we discuss how these standards of protection are balanced against the right to regulate in the EU. In the final part we focus on procedural novelties in new Member States' and EU IIAs,[80] with further analysis of the ICS in Chapter 9.

### *8.2.1 The Scope and Standards of Protection*

Investment standards in EU IIAs are largely based on the US Model BIT 2012, with some influences of EU law.[81] These standards are largely

[79] The analysis draws on the substantive standards discussed in Section 1.2 and definitions in Section 1.3.1 in Chapter 1. For free transfer of capital clauses see discussion in Section 8.1.1.1.

[80] See also Section 1.3 in Chapter 1, for procedural features of ITA.

[81] The focus of this analysis is placed on the CETA and the EU Investment Protection Agreement (IPA) with Singapore (EUSIPA). Where relevant, it will be complemented by the IPA with Viet Nam (EUVIPA) and the investment chapter of the EU–Mexico Association Agreement (FTA EU-MX).

adopted in the new extra-EU BITs, with different variations across BITs.[82] With a tedious drafting style, comprising the main text, footnotes and annexes, the new EU IIAs follow the trends of modern IIAs. The effects of new standards will be known only when implemented in practice by new EU IIA tribunals but the existing jurisprudence provides some indications about their scope.

#### 8.2.1.1 'Investment' and 'Investor'

New EU IIAs adopt a broad definition of investment, which includes a non-exhaustive list of different forms of investment (tangible and intangible assets), in the categories of both foreign direct investment (FDI) and portfolio investment.[83] Despite its form, investment must have certain non-exhaustive characteristics in order to gain protection, including 'certain duration', which must be always met, and assessment of other characteristics, which are typically part of the assessment, such as 'the commitment of capital or other resources', 'the expectation of gain or profit' or 'the assumption of risk'.[84] This definition does not fully codify the so-called Salini test, which has been developed in the practice of ICSID tribunals, as it does not require 'contribution to the development of the host State', which is the most controversial element of the Salini

[82] The focus of this analysis is placed on the Dutch Model BIT 2019, but where relevant, it will be complemented by BITs of Member States that have entered into force recently (n 27).

[83] Art. 8.1 CETA; Art. 1.2 EUSIPA. European Union IIAs' definition of investment is largely inspired by the definition in the US Model BIT 2012 (see Art. 1). As a point of difference, CETA's definition includes a detailed and closed list of intellectual property rights (IPR). Comprehensive Economic and Trade Agreement explicitly excludes claims to money arising solely from commercial contracts for the sale of goods or services and includes a specific sectoral carve-out from the application of investment protections: see Arts. 8.2.2 and 8.2.3 CETA.

[84] In the jurisprudence, intended duration should be between two and five years and contributions of US$1.5 to 3.8 million were considered minor but sufficient (again, intended rather than actual contribution should be taken into account; amount actually invested is likely to be a lower sum than the intended capital but the investor still needs to establish their intentions on the basis of evidence): see analysis of J. A. Bischoff and M. Wühler, 'The Notion of Investment' in M. M. Mbengue and S. Schacherer (eds), *Foreign Investment under the Comprehensive Economic and Trade Agreement (CETA)* (Springer 2019) 25–26, who also consider that this practice would be likely followed in CETA. For more elaborate discussion on the applicability of these criteria in arbitral practice, see also A. Dimopoulos, *EU Foreign Investment Law* (OUP 2011) 21–32.

test. Instead, the EU definition lists 'the expectation of gain or profit', which clearly excludes non-profit activities from the scope of IIAs.[85]

In light of Opinion 1/17, the interpretation of the characteristics of investment must allow for protections of investments made by small and medium size enterprise (SMEs), which usually involves lower commitments of capital and resources compared to multinational enterprises (MNEs).[86] Despite a detailed and extensive definition of investment, adjudicators retain considerable discretion.

In addition to satisfying characteristics and form, an investment must be owned or controlled, directly or indirectly, by an investor.[87] An investor can be a natural person or an enterprise or juridical person, in which case the corporate nationality is established with reference to a combination of criteria (incorporation, seat, control, substantial business activity).[88] The EU–Singapore Investment Protection Agreement (EUSIPA) incorporates the language of Article 54 TFEU, clarifying that an 'effective and continuous link', related to EU freedom of establishment under Treaty law, is equivalent to the concept of 'substantive business operations' in EUSIPA.[89] The same intention, albeit not the same Treaty language, is adopted in CETA.[90] Accordingly, a Canadian corporation not owned by a Canadian investor (but, for example, an US investor) could bring a claim only if it could establish that it has a substantive business operation in Canada. Such a US investor's activities in Canada would be required to have an effective and continuous link with the Canadian economy in accordance with the concept of establishment

[85] Claims submitted under the ICSID Convention, should also fulfil its criteria regarding the investment and investor, regardless of the BIT under which they have been submitted: see Section 1.3.1 in Chapter 1.

[86] See Opinion 1/17 (n 37) paras. 205–222. While access to justice primarily relates to the financial cost of the proceedings (high financial costs of investment arbitration), it would make no sense if the threshold for the 'commitment of capital and resources' in the definition of investment is interpreted in a way that sets commitment thresholds too high for SMEs' investments.

[87] Art. 8.1 CETA; Art. 1.2 EUSIPA.

[88] For explanation of these criteria, see Section 1.3.1 in Chapter 1.

[89] Moreover, the EUSIPA defines establishment in Art. 1.2.9 in light of EU law, referring to the establishment of a juridical person or a branch or representative office, with a view to 'establishing or maintaining lasting economic links' with the host State 'for the purpose of performing an economic activity'. For freedom of establishment, see Section 4.5.1 in Chapter 4. The concept of 'substantive business operations' is used in WTO law in relation to the establishment of services (Arts. V(6) and XXVIII(m) GATS).

[90] To that effect, see Council of the EU, 'CETA – Statements to the Council Minutes' (27 October 2016) 13463/1/16, Statement No. 31.

under EU law.[91] Accordingly, the EU concept of investor should disable 'mailbox' companies from utilising EU IIAs.[92]

Comprehensive Economic and Trade Agreement does not specify the relationship of the ownership or control requirement between the investor and the investment.[93] Arguably, since these requirements are not cumulative, both owner and controller could have a claim. Further, there could be several layers of control over the investment through intermediary companies, increasing the risk of numerous shareholders' claims, including those for reflective loss, otherwise excluded under customary international law (CIL)[94] and domestic law.[95] Comprehensive Economic and Trade Agreement, similarly to North America Free Trade Agreement (NAFTA) and the US Model BIT 2012, expands the availability of recovery to the company which can eliminate the need for shareholders' reflective loss recovery, but CETA adopts less restrictive language.[96] In order to limit multiple claims over the same breach

91 However, CETA does not contain a denial of benefits clause, unlike the US Model BIT 2012: see Art. 17.

92 However, EU law is rather generous in extending freedom of establishment to 'mailbox' companies that do not have a fixed establishment or permanent presence in their home Member State: see, for example, Case C-212/97 *Centros* [1999] ECR I-1459, para. 17; Case C-106/16 *POLBUD – WYKONAWSTWO* ECLI:EU:C:2017:804, para. 62.

93 Cf. Arts. 3.1 and 3.2(c) EUSIPA.

94 *Barcelona Traction Case, Light and Power Company Limited, Case concerning (New Application, 1962)* (Belgium v Spain) (Second Phase) [1970] ICJ Rep 3.

95 See discussion in Bischoff and Wühler (n 84) 27–29. The authors note that CETA does not explicitly require 'overall control' of the investor in cases when investment is held through multiple layers of intermediation. In the absence of 'overall control', interpretation of investment could be limitless, for which reason it is more likely that an investor would need to exercise some form of *de facto* or *de iure* control over intermediary companies in order to avail themselves of the CETA protections. On investors' treaty shopping, see Section 1.3.2 in Chapter 1.

96 In Art. 8.23 CETA prescribes that a claim may be submitted by an investor on his behalf or 'on behalf of a locally established enterprise which it owns or controls directly or indirectly', in which case the claim must satisfy the requirements of Art. 25(1) of the ICSID Convention: see Art. 8.23.5 CETA. Similarly, Art. 3.2(b) EUSIPA. Art. 25(2)(b) ICSID allows certain domestic companies access to ISDS, with the consent of the host State. However, in such cases shareholders' ISDS claims for reflective loss should be prohibited although investment tribunals have generally rejected such a proposition: see D. Gaukrodger, 'Investment Treaties as Corporate Law: Shareholder Claims and Issues of Consistency' (OECD Publishing 2013) 56–58; and 'Investment Treaties and Shareholder Claims: Analysis of Treaty Practice' (OECD Publishing 2014). In CETA, the claim may be submitted for 'loss or damage to a locally established enterprise *or* to an interest in a locally established enterprise that the investor owns or controls directly or indirectly': Art. 8.22.2 CETA. Cf. In the NAFTA context, the division between an investor's claims 'on its own behalf' and 'on behalf of an enterprise', in Arts. 1116 and 1117 respectively,

and avoid overlapping compensation, CETA incorporates an elaborate joinder of overlapping claims.[97] Further, any award of monetary damages or restitution of property must be made to the locally established enterprise rather than to the shareholders,[98] and such damages 'shall not be greater than the loss suffered by the investor or locally established company and will be reduced by any prior damages or compensation already paid'. This measure is aimed at protecting the company and all its shareholders, having a similar rationale as domestic law mechanisms. The CJEU thus found that it is not in breach of EU competition rules nor that it breaches the requirements of equality under EU law.[99] Finally, provisions aimed at avoidance of parallel claims apply both to the investor and a locally established enterprise.[100] These provisions together should limit, if not eliminate, the State's exposure to overlapping claims and double recovery by multiple shareholders.

New extra-EU BITs mostly follow the main features of the definitions of investment and investor in EU IIAs, with a number of variations on the theme (regarding forms and characteristics of 'investment' and the criteria for corporate nationality). Some BITs follow the list of characteristics of investment in EU IIAs, while some add additional characteristics, notably contribution to the economy of the host State.[101] Some exclude portfolio investment and provide a list of other forms of investment excluded from protection.[102] The Dutch Model BIT 2019 adopts the

has been used to argue that only direct shareholder claims and shareholder derivative suits are permitted, implicitly excluding shareholders' claims for reflective loss: see J. Arato and others, 'Reforming Shareholders Claims in ISDS', Academic Forum on ISDS Concept Paper 2019/9, Version 2 (17 September 2019) 9–10. NAFTA practice is mostly followed in the US Model BIT 2012: see Arts. 24(1)(a) and (b); 26(2)(b)(ii).

97 Art. 8.43 CETA. Similarly, Art. 3.24 EUSIPA.

98 Art. 8.39.2 CETA. However, EUSIPA clarifies that only where a claim is submitted on behalf of a locally established company will the award be made to the locally established company: Art. 3.18.3.

99 Opinion 1/17 (n 37) paras. 183–186. See Section 9.3.1 in Chapter 9. AG Bot equated the locally established company and the investor: Opinion 1/17, Opinion of AG Bot (n 37) para. 194.

100 Art. 8.22.2 CETA. EUSIPA in Art. 3.7.2 explicitly states that for the purposes of withdrawal of pending claims, the term 'claimant' includes 'all persons who directly or indirectly have an ownership interest in, or who are controlled by the investor, or where applicable, the locally established company'.

101 See Art. 1(2) Slovakia–UAE BIT and Art. 1(2) Slovakia–Iran BIT for nuances in drafting the clause.

102 Art. 1(2) Slovakia–Iran BIT; however, portfolio investment is not excluded in the Slovakia–UAE BIT.

definition of investor from CETA and additionally provides the non-exhaustive list of indications for 'substantive business activity'.[103] Unlike CETA, the new Dutch Model BIT also includes specific limitations on public debt restructuring.[104]

European Union IIAs and new extra-EU BITs additionally include provisions that serve to impose jurisdictional limitations on access to ISDS by implementing the clean hands doctrine. Comprehensive Economic and Trade Agreement prescribes that an investor may not submit a claim if the investment has been made through fraudulent misrepresentation, concealment, corruption or conduct amounting to an abuse of process.[105] However, it is not further specified with reference to which applicable law this behaviour will be established.[106] Some other extra-EU BITs explicitly refer to investors' illegal conduct through the violations of host States' laws.[107] In such cases, it seems that tribunals would need to assess domestic law as a matter of *law*, which could pose a problem if EU law is to be taken into account as part of Member States' domestic laws.[108] European Union IIAs and new extra-EU BITs contain an applicable law clause stating that 'in determining the consistency of a *measure* with the agreement', the tribunal may consider domestic law 'as

[103] See Art. 1(a)-(c) Dutch Model BIT 2019. This is important given that the Netherlands has been notorious for the number of 'mailbox' companies established for ISDS purposes.

[104] See Protocol on public debt Dutch Model BIT 2019, which follows similar provisions on public debt in Annex 4 EUSIPA.

[105] Art. 8.18.3 CETA; Art. 16 Dutch Model BIT 2019. The EUSIPA in Art. 3.7.5 clarifies that a tribunal must decline jurisdiction in cases of restructuring of investment for the 'main purpose' of submitting the claim under the treaty.

[106] Comprehensive Economic and Trade Agreement requires that investment is made in accordance with the applicable law at the time the investment is made, however such requirement is not mentioned in the EUSIPA's definition of investment.

[107] See, for example, Art. 14 Slovakia–Iran BIT. An investor's claim will be dismissed in cases of 'sufficiently serious or material' violations of the host State law, whereby fraud, tax evasion, corruption or bribery, or investment made through fraudulent misrepresentation, concealment, corruption, or conduct amounting to an abuse of process, are always considered as such violations: Art. 14(2). In the alternative, they will be taken into account if raised by the host State as a defence, counterclaim, right of set off: Art. 14 (3). See similarly (but with explicit reference only to fraud and investment made through an abuse of process under the Host State's laws and regulations) Art. 17(2) Slovakia–UAE BIT. In arbitral practice some tribunals have already been declining their jurisdiction when the investor failed to comply with domestic laws: see, for example, *Cortec Mining Kenya Limited, Cortec (Pty) Limited and Stirling Capital Limited v Republic of Kenya*, ICSID Case No. ARB/15/29, Award (22 October 2018).

[108] See discussion under Section 8.1.1.2.

a matter of fact'.[109] This formulation would, however, indicate that the limitation of the applicability of domestic law as a fact relates only to a host State's measures (intending to protect the State's right to regulate) but not investors' illegal conduct (whereby domestic law serves as a reference point for determining the scope and content of the obligation). The provisions relating to host State law are in some cases at odds with the governing law provisions, which specify treaty provisions and applicable rules of international law (with no reference to domestic law) as applicable law, thus likely excluding a possibility of State counterclaims.[110]

Accordingly, and more generally, the inclusion of investors' obligations with reference to domestic law as a matter of law would pose a problem for EU IIAs and to a lesser extent also for extra-EU BITs. This might explain the general exclusion of mandatory investors' obligations and instead the inclusion of reference to international soft law instruments (voluntary CSR) in EU and Member States' IIAs.[111] In any case, liability of investors is not envisaged under IIAs. In the absence of liability under international law, investors are still subject to liability under general domestic laws and procedures, or, in cases of some BITs, they might be liable under their home State's laws.[112]

#### 8.2.1.2 Expropriation

The definition of expropriation in EU IIAs largely follows the established definition in IIL.[113] It covers both direct and indirect expropriation, which are subject to the same criteria of legality found in any BIT.[114] The clarification of criteria for establishing indirect expropriation is provided in the Annexes.[115] While the definition of expropriation mostly

[109] See, for example, Art. 18 Slovakia–Iran BIT; Art. 20(12) Dutch Model BIT 2019. The identical clause is found in EU IIAs (see, for example, Arts. 8.31.2 CETA; 3.13.2 EUSIPA). However, no reference to domestic law as a matter of fact is made in Art. 19 (applicable law clause) of the Slovakia–UAE BIT. For the application of EU law as a matter of fact in light of Opinion 1/17, see Section 9.2.1 in Chapter 9.

[110] See, for example, Art. 14, in combination with Arts. 17 and 19 of Slovakia–Iran BIT. See also Section 3.2.1 in Chapter 3.

[111] See Section 8.2.1.3.

[112] Art. 6(4) Dutch Model BIT 2019, which envisages liability for acts or decisions made in relation to the investment where such acts or decisions lead to significant damage, personal injuries or loss of life in the host State.

[113] See Arts. 8.12 CETA; 2.6 EUSIPA.

[114] Arts. 8.12.1 CETA; 2.6.1 EUSIPA. See Section 1.2.1 in Chapter 1.

[115] Annex 8-A CETA, Annexes 1–3 EUSIPA.

codifies past case law of investment tribunals, it arguably also provides more clarity on the differentiation between indirect expropriation and regulatory activity that does not require the payment of compensation.[116]

The determination of indirect expropriation requires 'a case-by-case, fact-based inquiry', and focuses on the impact of the measure on investment, which must result in substantive deprivation of the 'fundamental attributes' of property.[117] A number of non-exhaustive factors are to be taken into consideration in assessing whether indirect expropriation occurred: the economic impact of the measure;[118] its duration;[119] its interference with 'distinct, reasonable investment-backed expectations';[120] and the character of the measure (its object, context and intent).[121] It is also clarified that non-discriminatory measures that are designed and applied to protect legitimate public welfare objectives (a non-exhaustive list includes health, safety and the environment) do not constitute indirect expropriation, except 'in the rare circumstances' when the impact of the measure is 'so severe in light of its purpose that it appears manifestly excessive'. This provision codifies an exception to the

[116] See A. de Nanteuil, 'Expropriation' in Mbengue and Schacherer (n 84) 127–158. Cf. Y. Radi, '"Much Ado about Nothing?" An Appraisal of CETA's Investment Chapter' (2017) 6 *ESIL Reflection* 1.

[117] See CETA Annex 8-A para. 1(b). The same is required in the arbitral practice: see, for example, *CMS Gas Transmission Co. v Argentine Republic* ICSID Case No. ARB/01/8, Award (12 May 2005) para. 262.

[118] The provision clarifies that 'the sole fact' that the measure has 'an adverse effect on the economic value of the investment' does not establish indirect expropriation. This, however, does not exclude the sole effect doctrine: see Section 1.2.1 in Chapter 1.

[119] It is, however, not specified whether duration must be permanent or temporary, and, if the latter, how long it has to last to amount to expropriation.

[120] It is open to interpretation what legitimate expectations mean in this context. Tribunals have taken into account all circumstances when assessing the existence of legitimate expectations – including special commitment or representation, the investors' economic expectations and whether the investment is made in a highly regulated sector (in assessing the reasonableness of the investors' expectations). Moreover, the concept of 'distinct-investment-backed expectation' originates from the United States, not the European legal practice: see Y. Radi, 'Realizing Human Rights in Investment Treaty Arbitration: A Perspective from within the International Investment Law Toolbox' (2011) 37 *North Carolina Journal of International Law and Commercial Regulation* 1107, 1145–1160.

[121] The reference to 'among other factors' indicates the non-exhaustive nature of the list. See CETA Annex 8-A para. 2, and similarly, EUSIPA Annex 1 para. 2. However, unlike CETA, EUSIPA does not have reference to the duration of the measure and investment-backed expectations.

police powers doctrine in the arbitral practice, which is otherwise itself an exception in IIL.[122]

These criteria have been adopted from the US Model BIT 2012 and arbitral practice.[123] While not including substantially new criteria, the codification avoids the risk of tribunals departing from this practice in the future.[124] It has also been suggested that an explicit reference to the intent of the measure is an important improvement as it removes the focus from the effect of the measure on the investor's property to the general objective of the State measure and its overall context.[125] However, pursuing a public interest objective is a requirement of lawfulness of expropriation.[126] Therefore, a measure that serves a public interest can still result in lawful expropriation, whether direct or indirect, which gives rise to liability for the payment of compensation. Any proportionality analysis takes place after it has been established that

[122] Radi (n 116). For the recent application of the police powers doctrine, which reiterates this CETA provision, see *Philip Morris v Uruguay*, ICSID Case No. ARB/10/7, Award (8 July 2016) para. 300. Codifying the police powers doctrine without an exception would have been a more revolutionary approach in CETA.

[123] See Annex B US Model BIT 2012. The Annex does not refer to the duration of the measure as an explicit factor to be taken into account in determining indirect expropriation. There is also an explicit reference to both tangible or intangible property rights or property interests in investment, which is missing from the CETA Annex, but it can nevertheless be inferred from the CETA definition of investment. The exceptions are IPR. Comprehensive Economic and Trade Agreement prescribes that its expropriation clause does not apply to the issuance of compulsory licences consistent with the TRIPS agreements: Art. 8.10.5 (again, this provision has been inspired by the US Model BIT 2012: see Art. 6(5)). The same provision is included in Art. 2.6.3 EUSIPA. Comprehensive Economic and Trade Agreement (but not EUSIPA) further clarifies that a determination of revocation, limitation or creation of IPR that is inconsistent with the TRIPS Agreement or CETA's IP chapter does not constitute an expropriation: Art. 8.10.6 CETA. Compulsory licences could qualify as indirect expropriation under IIL as they can allow beneficiaries (e.g. pharmaceutical laboratories) to access patented innovations (e.g. patented medicines) without the consent of the holder of the patent. They can therefore be an important public health policy tool.

[124] According to Radi, CETA codifies the proportionality approach already adopted by some investment tribunals (most notably, *Técnicas Medioambientales Tecmed, S.A. v The United Mexican States*, ICSID Case No. ARB (AF)/00/2, Award (29 May 2003) para. 122) and does not bring anything new: see Radi (n 116). Similarly, De Nanteuil (n 116) 141–142. However, such an approach to proportionality is only a middle way between the sole effect and police powers doctrines and thus is different to the proportionality analysis applied in European legal practice: see Section 4.5.2.1 in Chapter 4.

[125] De Nanteuil (n 116) 138–139.

[126] Art. 8.12.1 CETA; Art. 2.6.1 EUSIPA.

lawful expropriation occurred, and not in the course of determining the lawfulness of expropriation.

European Union IIAs specify that the payment of compensation in case of any lawful expropriation must be 'prompt, adequate and effective', adopting the Hull formula. Such compensation should amount to the fair market value of the investment.[127] However, since these provisions do not specify any particular calculation method, they give tribunals a margin of appreciation and do not exclude compensation for future profits.[128] Accordingly, compensation under EU IIAs will likely continue to result in higher payments than compensation available under domestic remedies. New EU IIAs in this sense do not bring substantive change compared to the current arbitral practice.

A similar standard of expropriation and compensation is endorsed in new Member States' extra-EU BITs.[129] Apart from nuances in wording across different Member States' BITs, some BITs also adopt a different standard of compensation. For example, the Slovakia–Iran BIT refers to the payment of 'prompt, effective and *appropriate*' compensation, which excludes losses that are not actually incurred and merely probable or unreal profits.[130] In practice this should result in a lower payment of compensation compared to the Hull formula. Accordingly, while generally coherent with EU IIAs, and equally adopting the middle way between the sole effect and police powers doctrines, extra-EU BITs allow

[127] Fair market value is assessed at the time immediately before the expropriation or before the impending expropriation became known, whichever is earlier. Valuation criteria include going concern value, asset value (declared tax value) and other appropriate criteria: Arts. 8.12.2 CETA; 2.6.3 EUSIPA.

[128] De Nanteuil (n 116) 146–147.

[129] The Dutch Model BIT 2019 follows the CETA provision and its Annex 8-A but excludes reference to 'distinct, reasonable investment-backed expectations' (Art. 12(4)) while includes a broader non-exhaustive list of legitimate public interests in the clause on a State's police powers (Art. 12(8)). Arguably, this does not substantively change the practical effects of the expropriation clause but clarifies the areas of relevant public interest in the relations between particular States. For example, Art. 7(8) of the Slovakia–UAE BIT includes health, safety, defence and the environment in this list.

[130] Art. 6(1)(d) Slovakia–Iran BIT (emphasis added). This approach could be explained by Iran's negative experience of the US–Iran tribunal practice: see, for example, *AIG v Islamic Republic of Iran* (1983) 4 Iran–USCTR 96, paras. 109–110, where the tribunal included lost profits despite expropriation being lawful. Cf. Slovakia–UAE BIT refers to the payment of 'prompt, effective and *just* compensation' (Art. 7(1)(d)), whereby the justness of the compensation is determined in accordance with 'internationally recognised principles of valuation': Art. 7(4). While in the latter case referring to 'profit and loss forecast', their effect can be diminished in consideration of the other factors.

for variations adjusted to a particular bilateral situation, which can result in a higher or lower level of investment protection in each particular case.

#### 8.2.1.3 Fair and Equitable Treatment

Pre-Lisbon extra EU BITs do not specify the fair and equitable treatment (FET) standard. With a more precise FET definition, EU IIAs introduce an improvement. Unlike the US Model BIT 2012 which endorses the minimum standard of treatment (MST) under CIL, EU IIAs introduce a standard independent of CIL but inspired by the NAFTA case law.[131] The codified NAFTA FET jurisprudence in the CETA FET clause was a compromise between Canada's MST position[132] and the EU's unqualified FET stance.[133] This approach in some way also reflects a continued inconclusiveness about what the content of the MST under CIL is and to what extent it is different to a broader concept of the FET standard.[134]

The definition of FET in the EU IIAs contains a closed list of State actions which can lead to a FET breach, indicating Contracting Parties' intentions for a narrow application of this standard.[135] The list includes denial of justice; fundamental breach of due process; manifest arbitrariness; targeted discrimination on manifestly wrongful grounds; and abusive treatment; however, it is not specified what each of these terms includes.[136] While the NAFTA case law, from which these concepts have

[131] North America Free Trade Agreement parties have clarified that NAFTA prescribes MST under CIL: see Section 1.2.2 in Chapter 1.

[132] Canada's experience with ISDS has been mostly negative. It was subject to more claims under NAFTA than the United States and Mexico, while Canadian investors have not been particularly successful in utilising investment treaty arbitration in NAFTA: D. Garcia-Barragan, A. Mitretodis and A. Tuck, 'The New NAFTA: Scaled-Back Arbitration in the USMCA' (2019) 6 *Journal of International Arbitration* 739, 742.

[133] In particular, the EC believed that reference to the MST would significantly reduce the level of protection under the FET standard: see P. Dumberry, 'Fair and Equitable Treatment' in Mbengue and Schacherer (n 84) 98–100. The EC's initial minimalist FET clause approach also reflects the initial Member States' preferences for broad investment protection standards: see Section 7.2.3 in Chapter 7.

[134] Dumberry argues that CETA includes all the elements of the umbrella concept of the MST, ultimately reflecting Canada's willingness to link the FET standard in CETA to the one under the MST: see ibid 103. See also G. Ünüvar, 'Is CETA the Promised Breakthrough? Interpretation and Evaluation of Fair and Equitable Treatment and (Indirect) Expropriation Provisions' (June 2017) iCourts Working Paper Series No. 97.

[135] Art. 8.10 CETA; Art. 2.4 EUSIPA.

[136] There are some nuances in the way these provisions have been drafted. For example, CETA refers to the 'fundamental breach of due process, including a fundamental breach of transparency, in judicial and administrative proceedings' (Art. 8.10.2(b)), while

been adopted,[137] arguably implements the MST under CIL, it is difficult to define with precision what the MST includes.[138] It does, however, include a broader meaning of the denial of justice, which entails all types of wrongful acts committed by the State's executive, legislative or judicial branches, and it is not limited to denial of access to a State's judicial system.[139]

The most important difference between the FET standard under NAFTA and other BITs seems to be in the application of the legitimate expectations element of the FET standard. European Union IIAs include a reference to the concept of legitimate expectations, which in the interpretation of the FET standard has been considered the core element. Importantly, in many cases, an assessment of legitimate expectations is independent from the evaluation of a State measure's objectives, the conduct of the State in implementing these objectives and the legality of the measure under domestic law.[140] However, following the NAFTA jurisprudence, legitimate expectations of investors in EU IIAs are to be taken into account only as *one of the factors* when assessing whether the FET standard has been breached, and not as a stand-alone factor, which was the approach of tribunals outside the NAFTA context.[141] The effects of this concept are further limited to 'a specific representation' made to an investor, which created a legitimate expectations 'upon which the investor relied in deciding to make or maintain the covered investment' but which was subsequently frustrated.[142] Nevertheless, this drafting provides tribunals with 'a significant margin of appreciation' in assessing

EUSIPA's drafting refers to 'a fundamental breach of due process', without further specifying it (Art. 2.4.4(b)).

137 See, for example, *Waste Management, Inc. v United Mexican States ("Number 2")*, ICSID Case No. ARB(AF)/00/3, Award (30 April 2004) para. 98.

138 See Section 1.2.2 in Chapter 1.

139 See analysis in S. Matiation, 'Arbitration with Two Twists: Loewen v United States and Free Trade Commission Intervention in NAFTA Chapter 11 Disputes' (2003) 24 *University of Pennsylvania Journal of Economic Law* 451. However, NAFTA tribunals have required proof of a high threshold of severity and gravity in order to conclude the breach of any of the elements of the FET standard: Dumberry (n 133) 117–118.

140 See Y. Levashova, *The Right of States to Regulate in International Investment Law* (Kluwer 2019) 107–111.

141 The notable exception from this NAFTA practice is the approach of the tribunal in *Bilcon v Canada* PCA Case No. 2009-04. For this view, see Dumberry (n 133) 107.

142 Arts. 8.10.4 CETA; 2.6.3 EUSIPA.

legitimate expectations.[143] Specific representations can be made in any form, including legislation, with case law indicating the criteria to be fulfilled, depending on jurisprudential interpretations.[144] The wording of the provision also leaves open to interpretation whether the representation so made must have been objectively reasonable or reasonable only subjectively from the investor's point of view.[145] Changes made to the general regulatory framework of the host State, however, should not suffice to breach the FET standard. For example, CETA specifies that the 'mere fact that a Party regulates', including through the legislative changes, 'in a manner which negatively affects an investment or interferes with an investor's expectations, including its expectations of profits' does not amount to a breach of investment protection standards under CETA.[146] Equally, a host State measure that breaches domestic law does not *per se* result in breach of the FET obligation.[147] The new FET standard further clarifies that 'full protection and security' does not

[143] U. Kriebaum, 'FET and Expropriation in the Comprehensive Economic Trade Agreement between the European Union and Canada (CETA)' (2016) 13 *Transnational Dispute Management*; Levashova (n 140) 62.

[144] A *specific representation* must fulfil three criteria: it must be provided by a competent State authority; it must have legal force (which is assessed with reference to the legal form, the content and the wording of the representation); and it must be designated for the investor: Levashova (n 140) 262–263. This nevertheless leaves tribunals with sufficient discretion (e.g. when determining who is the competent authority of the host State, or deciding on the legal form of the representation – which can be a law, letter, political statement, a licence, etc.). See the analysis of these criteria in the arbitral tribunals' practice by Levashova in ibid 123–139.

[145] Dumberry (n 133) 108. However, in EUSIPA, it is required that the investor must have 'reasonably relied upon' the representation made. In the case law, reasonableness of investor expectations depends on the special circumstances in the host State and investor's due diligence but this jurisprudence is inconsistent: see Levashova (n 140) 152–166. In some recent awards, tribunals have considered that due diligence is a prerequisite for the reasonableness of an investor's legitimate expectations (objective standard): see, for example, *Stadtwerke München GmbH, RWE Innogy GmbH, and others v Kingdom of Spain*, ICSID Case No. ARB/15/1, Award (2 December 2019) para. 264.

[146] Similarly, Art. 2.2.2 EUSIPA. However, in combination with other factors (e.g. targeted discrimination, manifest arbitrariness), a change to the regulatory framework can play a role in assessing the breach of the FET standard: Levashova (n 140) 264–265. See also Dumberry (n 133) 108–109.

[147] Art. 8.10.7 CETA. In the case of a breach of domestic law, the tribunal would still need to consider whether the host State acted inconsistently with other factors (e.g. manifest arbitrariness, etc.). In EUSIPA, the reference is made to the breaches of another provision of the EUSIPA, or of a separate international agreement, the breach of which does not establish a breach of the FET standard (Art. 2.4.7). A reference to domestic laws is made with respect to a contractual written obligation through the exercise of

include legal stability but is exclusively limited to 'physical security of investors and covered investments'.[148]

On the other hand, the EU IIAs' FET clause does not specify any obligations on the side of the investor. In particular, no reference is made to an investor's duty of due diligence in the assessment of the breaches of the FET clause.[149] Including investors' due diligence in EU IIAs as a requirement with reference to a higher standard would also bring the concept of legitimate expectations closer to the standard of EU law.[150] Further, EU IIAs do not include any other specific obligations of investors. Rather, the emphasis is placed on explicitly guaranteeing the States' right to regulate and balancing investors' rights against the legitimate objectives of the States' regulatory activity. A specific clause on 'investment and regulatory measures', explains the meaning of the right to regulate and providing examples of legitimate policy objectives for the purposes of that right.[151] Arguably, these provisions provide more clarity about the intentions of Contracting States that legitimate policy objectives must be taken into account when assessing the host State's conduct.[152] However, given the general nature of these clauses, a State's right

*governmental authority* (the authority of a State as a sovereign and not as a commercial party): see Art. 2.4.6 EUSIPA.

148 Arts. 8.10.5 CETA; 2.4.5 EUSIPA. The standard was unclear in arbitral practice. Some tribunals understood it in the same sense as the CETA provision: *Saluka Investments B.V. v The Czech Republic*, UNCITRAL, Partial Award (17 March 2006) para. 484. However, other tribunals adopted a broader scope of the standard, extending it to legislative amendments and administrative actions: see *Compañiá de Aguas del Aconquija S.A. and Vivendi Universal S.A. v Argentine Republic*, ICSID Case No. ARB/97/3 Award (20 August 2007) para. 7.4.15 and case law cited in para. 7.4.16.

149 Tribunals have employed different standards of due diligence, allowing for different levels of investors' lenience when exercising due diligence and taking into consideration broader socio-political and economic circumstances in the host State. For example, the tribunal in *Masdar v Spain* held an investor must be familiarised with the existing laws: *Masdar Solar & Wind Cooperatief U.A. v Kingdom of Spain*, ICSID Case No. ARB/14/1, Award (16 May 2018) para. 494. In *Charanne v Spain*, 'regulatory measures must not have been reasonably foreseeable at the time of the investment': *Charanne B.V. v Spain*, SCC Arb. No. 062/2012, Final Award (21 January 2016) para. 505. Recently, tribunals employed an even higher standard, determining the threshold on the basis of whether the new regulatory changes were not foreseeable by a 'prudent' investor: see Levashova (n 140) 163–166. Different standards eventually have different impacts on State's responsibility.

150 See Section 4.5.2.2 in Chapter 4.

151 See Art. 8.9.1 CETA and Art. 2.2.1 of the EUSIPA, with some nuances between the two provisions in the list of legitimate public policy objectives.

152 See Levashova (n 140) 270.

to regulate remains subordinate (an exception) to more specific investor rights guaranteed under EU IIAs (the rule).[153]

The FET standard in post-Lisbon extra-EU Member States' BITs differs across the treaties. Some BITs follow the path of the FET standard in EU IIAs, with some variations and improvements. For example, the 2019 Dutch Model BIT contains a more elaborate closed list of illegal State behaviour that could lead to breach of the FET.[154] At the same time, the framing of investors' obligations is looser but still more elaborate than in EU IIAs. In addition to including a reference to voluntary CSR soft law instruments,[155] the importance of conducting a due diligence process by investors is 'reaffirmed' by the Contracting Parties.[156] While these provisions can have some interpretative value, their normative value is inconclusive.[157] Some other BITs simply refer to the MST under CIL.[158] The practical effects of these BITs should not significantly differ in practice if CETA codifies the NAFTA case law. Differing from this practice, however, some post-Lisbon extra-EU BITs still include broad wording of the FET standard of pre-Lisbon BITs.[159]

[153] For further discussion of the right to regulate, see Section 8.2.2.

[154] See Art. 9(2) Dutch Model BIT 2019. For example, wrongful grounds of direct or targeted indirect discrimination are also nationality and sexual orientation: Art. 9.2(d). Examples of abusive treatment are also abuse of power, corrupt practices or similar bad faith: Art. 9.2(e). In the general provision on the scope of application it is also specified that 'the mere fact' that the State regulates in a way that 'negatively affects an investment or interferes with investor's expectations, including its expectation of profits' does not constitute a breach of obligation under the BIT: Art. 2(2).

[155] For example, the OECD Guidelines for Multinational Enterprises, the UN Guiding Principles on Business and Human Rights, and the Recommendation CM/REC(2016) of the Committee of Ministers to Member States on human rights and business: Art. 7(2) Dutch Model BIT 2019. See also Slovakia–UAE BIT, which refers to 'national and international standards of corporate governance for the sector involved', in particular for transparency and accounting practices (Art. 12(3)) and OECD Guidelines, which should be promoted to the extent of their compatibility with domestic law: Art. 12(4).

[156] See Art. 7 Dutch Model BIT 2019.

[157] Only the investors' obligation to comply with domestic laws and regulations is expressed in normative terms ('shall'): Art. 7(1) Dutch Model BIT 2019. Investor conduct, in particular its non-compliance with CSR voluntary codes can be taken into account when deciding on compensation: Art. 23 Dutch Model BIT 2019. Some tribunals have taken investor conduct into account to reduce the amount of compensation: see, for example, *Biwater Gauff v Tanzania*, ICSID Case No. ARB/05/22, Award (24 July 2008).

[158] See, for example, Art. 4 Slovakia–Iran BIT. Contrary to that, the FET in the Slovakia–UAE BIT largely follows the expression found in CETA: see Art. 3.

[159] 'Fair and equitable treatment and full and constant protection and security'. See, for example, Art. 3 Austria–Kyrgyzstan BIT; Art. 2 Hungary–Cambodia BIT.

Taking into consideration all these developments, it could be said that, overall, the new EU FET provisions codify a higher regulatory threshold for States and clearly indicate the intention of States to take control from implementing bodies over the scope and content of the FET standard. Such intention can in particular be seen in the FET provisions of EU IIAs, which envisage regular reviews of the content of the FET obligation by the Contracting Parties and recommendations about the content of the FET standard in accordance with the prescribed IIAs procedure through joint committees.[160] However, some margin of appreciation is still left to investment tribunals. It is likely that it will be easier to exert interpretative control over a permanent body (in EU IIAs) than over many *ad hoc* tribunals (in extra-EU BITs).[161] In the latter case, and in light of the NAFTA case law, the success will still largely depend on the argumentative skills of the respondent States.[162] In the context of a permanent tribunal, it might also be easier to rely on the principle *iura novit curia*, which has rarely been applied in the context of *ad hoc* tribunals.[163]

#### 8.2.1.4 Non-discrimination

In addition to FET, investors are protected against discrimination through the national treatment (NT) and most-favoured-nation (MFN) treatment clauses.[164] European Union IIAs follow the general trend of

[160] See Arts. 8.10.3 CETA and 2.4.4 EUSIPA.

[161] In this context, some prominent arbitrators have already offered their views on the matter: see S. Myron Schwabel, as cited in N. Angelet, 'CETA and the Debate on the Reform of the Investment Regime' in Mbengue and Schacherer (n 84) 6.

[162] North America Free Trade Agreement States have had mixed success when arguing the FET standard, with the United States being more successful than the others. See remarks by US trade negotiators: UK Government Department for International Trade, 'UK–US Trade & Investment Working Group' (2–7 November 2018) 32–33. In the same context, US negotiators questioned the EU theory of having a closed list and wondered whether it was providing *greater* rights to investors. The US view was that 'the concepts contained in the closed list are subject to a great amount of subjectivity, which could provide investors with wider protections and lead to increased claims than originally envisaged': ibid.

[163] Generally speaking, in international arbitration, arbitrators can only in limited circumstances raise ex *officio* legal issues not discussed by parties due to the risk of the award possibly being set aside in the enforcement stage. See the overview by A. P. Mantakou, 'The Misadventures of the Principle of Jura Novit Curia in International Arbitration: A Practitioner's Approach' in N. Vivliothiki (ed), *Essays in Honour of Professor Emeritus Spyridon Vrellis* (2014), referring to the practice of French and Swiss Courts in the enforcement of arbitral awards where this principle has been applied by tribunals.

[164] See Section 1.2.3 in Chapter 1.

recent IIAs, expressly specifying that these relative obligations depend on the level of treatment provided to nationals and other foreign investors in 'like situations'.[165] Under CETA, NT and MFN standards apply to all levels, sub-federal in Canada, and the EU Member States' and sub-EU Member State levels in the EU.[166] Potentially, this could also result in a more advantageous treatment of Canadian investors than domestic investors in a particular EU Member State. Due to the broader scope of non-discriminatory treatment, the EU legal order can require that Member States accord investors from other EU Member States more favourable treatment than they would accord to their own investors, which would then have to be extended to Canadian investors.[167]

Generally, NT and MFN in both EU IIAs and extra-EU BITs apply only to the post-establishment phases of investment and the breaches of these provisions are usually subject to ISDS.[168] Comprehensive Economic and Trade Agreement is an exception given that NT and MFN apply to pre- and post-entry situations,[169] but with the exclusion of ISDS for breaches of these obligations regarding the establishment of investment.[170] This can be explained by CETA's free trade agreement

[165] Arts. 8.6.1 (NT) and 8.7.1 (MFN) CETA; Arts. 2.3.1 (NT) and 2.4.1 (MFN) EUVIPA; Art. 2.3.1 EUSIPA (NT only). Reference is made to treatment 'no less favourable' than the treatment that each Party accords 'in like situations' to its own investments and investors (NT), or to investors of a third country and their investments (MFN). Cf. pre-Lisbon Member States' extra-EU BITs mostly have unqualified NT and MFN clauses. Post-Lisbon extra-EU BITs follow the trend of EU IIAs and include a qualifier 'in like circumstances' (see, for example, Art. 5(1) Slovakia–Iran BIT) or 'in like situations' (Art. 8(1) and (2) Dutch Model BIT 2019).

[166] See Arts. 8.6.2 and 8.7.2 CETA.

[167] Notably, this could be the case in regard to fundamental freedoms of establishment and capital movements under EU law. See EP, DG for External Policies, 'The Investment Chapters of the EU's International Trade and Investment Agreements in a Comparative Perspective' (September 2015) EP/EXPO/B/INTA/2015/01, 117. See Chapter 4 for further discussion on the EU internal market.

[168] See, for example, Arts. 2.3.1 (NT) and 2.4.1 (MFN) EUVIPA respectively referring to 'operation of the covered investments'; Art. 5(1) of the Slovakia–UAE BIT (NT and MFN in the same clause) referring 'only to management, conduct, operation, maintenance, use, enjoyment and sale or other disposition of investments' and the almost identical clause in Art. 4(1) of the Slovakia–Iran BIT. Identical to these are also NT and MFN clauses in Arts. 8(1) and (2) of the Dutch Model BIT 2019. The NT and MFN clause of the Slovakia–Iran BIT provides further instructions for tribunals how to assess comparable situations: see Art. 4(3).

[169] Arts. 8.6.1 and 8.7.1 CETA specify that NT and MFN respectively shall also be accorded with respect to the establishment, acquisition and expansion.

[170] See Arts. 8.18.1(a) and 8.18.2 CETA.

(FTA) character aimed at trade and investment liberalisation, which is different to the orientation of stand-alone EU IIAs towards protecting investments after their establishment in the host State. In this regard, it could generally be said that EU IIAs and extra-EU BITs continue to follow the old European BIT type, rather than North American IIAs.[171] Further, EU IIAs and extra-EU BITs contain a number of other different exceptions, which limit the application of NT and MFN treatment, in the specific[172] or more general treaty clauses.[173] Importantly, in order to limit 'treaty shopping',[174] MFN clauses specifically exclude from their application substantive and procedural obligations provided under other international agreements.[175]

### *8.2.2 The Right to Regulate in the EU*

As a preliminary remark, it should be emphasised that the right to regulate is the basic right of every State, stemming from sovereignty. As international law aims to achieve a minimum harmonisation of laws through treaties and other mechanisms of cooperation, a State's sovereignty and the right to regulate are inevitably limited. The extent of these limitations depends on the provisions of each individual international treaty at hand. The exercise of the right to regulate, even when guaranteed in a specific provision, depends on all the terms and conditions of the treaty in question. To that effect, for example, parties in CETA

[171] See Section 2.1.2 in Chapter 2.

[172] For example, the NT clause of EUSIPA allows measures that could provide less favourable treatment to foreign investors compared to domestic investors in cases when State measures are taken towards achieving defined legitimate public policy goals (listed under (a) to (f) in Art. 2.3.3), but such measures still must not be applied in a manner which would 'constitute a means of arbitrary or unjustifiable discrimination': Art. 2.3.3 EUSIPA. In EU IPAs exceptions can also relate to market access NT and MFN clauses in related EU FTAs with the same parties. See, for example, Art. 2.3.2 EUSIPA. For exceptions in extra-EU BITs, see, for example, Art. 4(4) and (6) of the Slovakia–Iran BIT.

[173] See, for example, Arts. 8.2.2 and 8.2.3 (sectoral exemptions), 8.15 (non-conforming measures), 28.3 CETA (general exception clause with reference to GATT Article XX) and others; however, these provisions in CETA are also due to its comprehensive FTA character, which is different to more specific EU IPAs.

[174] See Section 1.3.2 in Chapter 1.

[175] Art. 8.7.4 CETA; EUSIPA generally excludes an MFN clause; Art. 2.4.3 EUVIPA. Extra-EU BITs largely follow these trends. See, for example, Art. 4(5) Slovakia–Iran BIT; Art. 8 (3) Dutch Model BIT 2019. For more detailed analysis of MFN clauses in CETA and other EU FTAs, see C. Crépet Daigremont, 'Most Favoured Nation Treatment' in Mbengue and Schacherer (n 84) 71–93.

'*reaffirm* their right to regulate within their territories to achieve legitimate policy objectives'.[176] Accordingly, the right to regulate in IIL has a narrow meaning, according to which the State retains its right to regulate within its borders but is liable for the payment of compensation stemming from the exercise of that right.[177] The State's right to regulate is thus an expression of the prevalent contemporary neoliberal approach to the regulation of the economy.[178]

In accordance with the EU external action objectives, in developing trade and investment policy, the EU needs to balance investment objectives and non-trade goals in ways that reflects the EU's approach in the internal market. Accordingly, the right to regulate in the EU must be guaranteed. In its Opinion 1/17 the CJEU established that the right to regulate is a *substantive* criterion of the autonomy of EU law, according to which decisions of investment tribunals cannot undermine the capacity of EU institutions to carry out their duties under EU Treaties.[179] These duties include regulatory activity, although the CJEU framed this criterion in accordance with the prevalent liberal understanding of it as 'a right' rather than a duty.

Accordingly, the right to regulate is not a subjective right that amounts to a duty of EU authorities to protect directly defined individual legal situations. A failure by a public authority to perform the so defined duty (e.g. duty to protect the environment) does not result in liability of the relevant public authority. Rather, the right to regulate serves to protect the higher regulatory standards already achieved in the EU.[180] With respect to its normative nature, the right to regulate could be considered a meta-principle, which encompasses the existing CFR principles but cannot be reviewed in the same manner as CFR principles that are implemented in EU legislation under EU law.[181] Moreover, its applicability as a substantive criterion of EU autonomy is limited to the acts of EU institutions.

[176] Art. 8.9.1 (emphasis added).

[177] C. Titi, 'The Right to Regulate' in Mbengue and Schacherer (n 84) 162.

[178] See Section 3.2.1 in Chapter 3.

[179] Similarly, see reasoning of the CJEU in *Kadi*, Joint Cases C-402/05 P and C-415/05 P, para. 285.

[180] See, for example, Arts. 35, 37 and 38 CFR, which guarantee a high level of environmental, health and consumer protection under EU policies.

[181] See I. Damjanovic and N. de Sadeleer, 'Values and Objectives of the EU in Light of Opinion 1/17: "Trade for All", above All' (2020) 4(1) *Europe and the World: A Law Review* [25].

Early in the development of the EU IIP, the EC contemplated the right to regulate as 'a basic underlying principle', to be considered by tribunals when assessing any dispute settlement case.[182] In Opinion 1/17, when assessing the effects of the ICS on the EU constitutional order, the Court first examined the effects of CETA Tribunal decisions on the validity of EU measures, and, second, the effects of the ICS on the capacity of EU institutions to legislate in the public interest. With respect to both issues, the CJEU concluded that the ICS does not affect the operation of EU institutions within the EU constitutional framework and consequently does not adversely affect the autonomy of the EU legal order. Accordingly, the CJEU concluded that the right to regulate in the EU is guaranteed under CETA.

#### 8.2.2.1 Validity of EU Measures Protected

The CJEU found that CETA Tribunals cannot call into question the validity of EU measures contested before them, and thus will not have a negative effect on the acts or practices of the EU.[183] In other words, CETA Tribunals do not have the power to annul or to change a challenged EU measure,[184] and accordingly cannot undermine the operation of EU institutions which undertake such measures in accordance with EU law. The only power that tribunals have is to award damages to a private investor.

On one hand, CETA can be distinguished from the unacceptable EU Patent Court in Opinion 1/09, and on the other, from the acceptable World Trade Organization (WTO) regime. The Patent Court was unacceptable because it might have been called upon to examine the validity of an EU act,[185] which is the jurisdiction of the CJEU.[186] On the contrary, ICS tribunals can order only a payment of damages.[187] On the other hand, compared to the ICS, the WTO regime offers more flexibility: apart from paying damages, the EU has a range of different options for enforcing WTO rulings, depending on the success of negotiations

182 See 'Online public consultation on investment protection and investor-to-State dispute settlement (ISDS) in the Transatlantic Trade and Investment Partnership Agreement (TTIP)', SDW (2015) 3 final, 72.

183 Opinion 1/17 (n 37) paras. 142–145.

184 See Art. 8.39.1 CETA

185 Opinion 1/17 (n 37) para. 124.

186 Art. 267(1)(b) TFEU.

187 Indeed, the EU will have to pay any such sum if so ordered in a final award of the ICS tribunal: Opinion 1/17 (n 37) para. 145.

with States that are parties to a particular dispute.[188] Therefore, in the spectrum of different powers, the ICS is somewhere between the failed EU patent system and a more flexible and thus also more political WTO system.

In the current ISDS system, investment tribunals cannot question the *validity* of sovereign acts of State parties to IIAs. States can be deterred from adopting measures that might negatively affect investors by a tribunal making a large award of monetary compensation to the investors. How can then the CJEU be certain that ICS awards would not lead to this (in)famous 'regulatory chill'? The answer lies in the CJEU's analysis of EU regulatory autonomy, as an aspect of the substantive autonomy of the EU legal order.

#### 8.2.2.2 Public Interest Protected in the EU

The CJEU was adamant that investors' claims cannot lead to changes of legislation that the EU has made in the public interest.[189] A contrary outcome in which the right to regulate was undermined by the ICS would run counter to the principles of democracy, the guarantee of the level playing field in the EU and the objectives of the EU.

First, EU legislation aims to introduce restrictions in the internal market that apply to *all* operators who invest in a particular commercial or industrial sector to which such legislation applies.[190] Therefore, if investors' claims had an effect on EU legislation, this would run counter to the principles of democracy.[191] In such cases, the interest of the majority – the public – would be superseded by the interest of a specific category of a few (foreign) investors from third countries that have concluded an IIA with the EU.

Second, an adverse effect of the ICS on EU legislation would run counter to the principles of equality in the EU, allowing the minority of foreign investors to escape restrictions introduced by general legislation intended to apply to all investors in a particular sector. The CJEU's rationale for the protection of 'public interest' is thus also based on the rationale of protecting the level playing field between foreign and other investors in the EU. Nevertheless, while not affecting EU legislation, it could be argued that the

[188] ibid para. 146.
[189] ibid para. 152.
[190] ibid para. 148 (emphasis added).
[191] Art. 2 TEU.

special right to compensation available to particular foreign investors can still disturb the level playing field in the EU.

In particular, the CJEU considered a scenario in which a Canadian investor alleged a breach of CETA on the basis of a fine imposed by the EC or a competition authority of a Member State for breaches of Articles 101 or 102 TFEU.[192] The CJEU reached a conclusion that, in light of Article 17.2 CETA which acknowledges the importance of competition for trade liberalisation, the CETA Tribunal would only issue an award if the TFEU competition rules have not been correctly applied by the competent authority.[193] While not affecting EU legislation, the special right to compensation available to particular foreign investors could still in *exceptional circumstances* somewhat affect the level playing field in the EU but would not be such to create a situation of an unequal treatment to the disadvantage of EU investors.[194]

Third, if the right to regulate was not guaranteed, the lawmaking process in the EU and its legitimate objectives would also be undermined. Every piece of EU legislation is based on the conferral of powers, subsidiarity and proportionality, and it is both appropriate and necessary to achieve a legitimate objective of the EU for which that legislation is being created. Under the treaties, the authority to review the validity of EU legislation made in the public interest for its compliance with EU Treaties belongs only to those courts that are situated within the EU judicial system.[195] The ICS is situated outside the EU judicial system. Accordingly, changing EU public interest legislation in reaction to ICS decisions would undermine the prescribed role of EU institutions under the founding treaties. Ultimately, as EU legislation serves to achieve different EU objectives, legislative changes in response to foreign investors' claims would weaken the achievement of EU objectives and would run counter to the EU project more generally.

In assessing the autonomy of EU institutions to operate within the EU constitutional framework, the CJEU paid particular attention to the guarantees of the State 'right to regulate' in CETA and its interpretative instrument.[196] Additionally, the Court noted the exceptionality of

[192] Opinion 1/17 (n 37) para. 184.

[193] ibid para. 185.

[194] ibid para. 186 (emphasis added).

[195] ibid para. 151.

[196] In particular, these are CETA Arts. 28.3.2; 8.9.1; 8.9.2, Point 3 of Annex 8-A CETA and Point 2 of the Joint Interpretative Instrument.

situations in which CETA Tribunals could condemn States for indirect expropriation due to public interest measures and the exhaustive nature of the FET standard in Article 8.10.2 CETA.[197] The CJEU thus found that the manner in which these provisions have been drafted offers sufficient limitations on the discretionary powers of CETA Tribunals. Accordingly, these tribunals will have *no jurisdiction* to question public interest choices made following a democratic process in areas relating to: the level of protection of public order or public safety, public morals, health and life of humans and animals, food safety, plants and the environment, welfare at work, product safety, consumer protection or fundamental rights.[198] This list appears to be non-exhaustive.

However, what in practical terms means that CETA Tribunals have '*no* jurisdiction' to 'call into question the level of protection of public interest determined by the Union following a democratic process'?[199] Does it mean that CETA Tribunals cannot ever review any public interest measure since they should decline jurisdiction every time when a question related to public interest choices of States appears in claims before them? Or does it mean that tribunals can examine the effects of a public interest measure but cannot mandate that it be changed, although they can order the payment of damages if the measure breaches investors' substantive rights? If the former were the case, CETA Tribunals' jurisdiction would be significantly limited to review exclusively the breaches of procedural justice and due process.[200] In the case of the latter, CETA Tribunals would still have the jurisdiction to review a public interest measure, albeit indirectly – when examining the effects of the measure on the investor. Accordingly, they could condemn the State to pay the compensation to the investor. *De facto*, the latter scenario could still lead to controversial 'regulatory chill'.

Therefore, the crucial question is whether the CETA substantive provisions are sufficiently 'expressly restricting' in their scope that they can limit the tribunals' jurisdiction to the award of compensation without producing the 'regulatory chill' on the level of regulatory standards and protection of public interest in the EU. In answering this question, the CJEU employed the same logic that the Court applies when assessing the compliance of the Member States' measures with EU law.

[197] Opinion 1/17 (n 37) paras. 157–158.
[198] ibid para. 160.
[199] ibid paras. 160 (emphasis added), 156.
[200] The analysis of CETA provisions in Section 8.2.1 does not support this conclusion.

The role of the CJEU in the EU system is to assess which of the Member States' measures made in the public interest are justified under EU law and which are hidden obstacles to the four EU freedoms in the internal market. When the CJEU finds that a national measure is incompatible with EU law, the measure must be annulled. The annulment of the measure does not automatically nor necessarily mean compensation for the injured party. The non-contractual liability of the Member State to make reparation for loss or damage caused to individuals as a result of EU law breaches will be established only if three conditions are met: the infringed rule of EU law must be intended to confer rights on the individual; the breach of that rule must be sufficiently serious; and there must be a direct causal link between that breach and the loss or damage sustained by the individual.[201] While the annulment of a national measure can happen in any case of an EU law breach, compensation for individuals stemming from such a breach is awarded only if the breach is sufficiently serious. As the breach must be sufficiently serious, the standard for determining compensation is high.[202]

*Mutatis mutandi*, these conditions apply to measures of EU institutions that breach EU law. Non-contractual liability of the EU is prescribed in Article 340(2) TFEU, which provides that the EU will 'make good any damage caused by its institutions or by its servants in the performance of their duties', in accordance with the 'general principles common to the laws of the Member States'. For example, in cases when an EU legislative measure restricts the right to property or the right to pursue a trade or profession, the EU will be held liable under EU law if the restriction imposed impairs 'the very substance of those rights in a

[201] Joined Cases C-46/93 and C-48/93 *Brasserie du Pêcheur and Factorame III* [1996] ECR I-1029, para. 51; Case C-224/01 *Köbler* [2003] ECR I-10239, para. 51; Case C-420/11 *Leth* ECLI:EU:C:2013:166, para. 41.

[202] Among the factors which can be taken into consideration in determining whether there is a sufficiently serious breach of EU law are, in particular: the degree of clarity and precision of the rule infringed; the scope of room for assessment that the infringed rule allows for national authorities; whether the infringement and the damage caused were *intentional* or involuntary; whether any error of law was excusable or *inexcusable*; and the fact that the position taken by an EU institution may have contributed to the adoption or maintenance of national measures or practices contrary to EU law, and non-compliance by the national court in question with its obligation to make a reference for a preliminary ruling under the third para of Art. 267 TFEU: *Brasserie du Pêcheur* and *Factortame*, para. 56; *Köbler*, paras. 54–55; Case C-446/04 *Test Claimants in the FII Group Litigation* ECLI:EU:C:2006:774, para. 213.

*disproportionate* and *intolerable* manner', even if the legislation was made in the pursuit of the objectives of general interest of the EU.[203]

Reasoning by analogy, ICS tribunals do not have the power to annul domestic or EU measures that breach foreign investors' rights under CETA. Investment Court System tribunals can only award compensation to foreign investors. In light of the restrictive CETA provisions, such compensation will be awarded only in cases of *sufficiently serious* breaches of CETA investment chapter provisions. As the goal of the ICS is not to assess the compatibility of State public interest measures with the EU founding treaties, the ICS is limited to awarding compensation for the impact of these measures on investors, and only in such cases when measures constitute targeted discrimination, manifest arbitrariness or abusive treatment. In the case of indirect expropriation, the impact of a measure must be 'so severe in light of its purpose that it appears manifestly excessive'.[204] In the case of FET breaches, the possible breaches are exhaustively listed and include denial of justice, fundamental breaches of due process, manifest arbitrariness, targeted discrimination and abusive treatment.[205]

Accordingly, it could be argued that if the compensation conditions include a high standard, the 'chilling' effect of ICS awards on the EU regulatory activity will be significantly reduced. Moreover, the effects could even be positive. Sufficiently serious breaches reasonably justify compensation for a foreign investor that was genuinely mistreated by the host State. If such compensation can deter States from abusive, manifestly arbitrary and discriminatory legislation and measures, the overall outcome is a win-win situation: compensation for genuinely mistreated foreign investors and the elimination of genuinely inequitable legislation. In any case, 'the required level of protection of a public interest' would not be negatively affected.[206]

The CJEU assessed CETA's investment chapter as a breakthrough from the old ISDS regime that has been subject to public interest criticism. The 'old' system was based on broadly undefined standards; the 'new' ICS system is based on restrictive provisions which limit the discretion of ICS tribunals. However, the CJEU assessed the investment chapter provisions through the lenses of EU law, while CETA provisions

[203] Case C-120/06 *FIAMM v Council and Commission* [2008] ECR I-6513, paras. 183–184.
[204] Annex 8-A point 3 CETA; Opinion 1/17 (n 37) para. 157.
[205] Art. 8.10.2 CETA; Opinion 1/17 (n 37) para. 158.
[206] Opinion 1/17 (n 37) paras. 159–160.

to a great extent codify the existing case law of investment tribunals. Additionally, the impact of national public interest measures on foreign investors is assessed differently to the usual proportionality analysis of the CJEU. As a consequence, compensation can be awarded even in cases where measures have been justified by legitimate public interest goals and are proportionate under EU law.[207]

Further, the Court did not discuss the effects of investors' legitimate expectations on the breach of the FET standard.[208] As discussed, this concept produces different effects in EU law and international law.[209] Investors' legitimate expectations are important for determining compensation in international law, unlike in EU law, which gives more weight to public interest.[210] In practice, it is also likely that legitimate expectations of investors will be more often assessed in the context of Member States' national measures rather than EU measures. In light of the investment case law, ICS tribunals might embrace the concept of legitimate expectations as developed and applied in IIL rather than EU law. Consequently, this could lead to investors' challenges of measures made in the public interest.

While it is difficult to predict what standards and interpretative approaches will be adopted by the ICS tribunals, CETA Contracting Parties have additional tools in CETA through which they can ensure the correct interpretation of the investment chapter of CETA. For example, CETA envisages that parties will regularly review the content of the FET obligation and may develop recommendations for the CETA Joint Committee.[211] This Joint Committee may adopt interpretations of CETA which will be binding on the ICS tribunals.[212] In the system of *ad hoc* tribunals similar interpretative statements have had limited effects (e.g. in the NAFTA context). However, the permanent character of ICS tribunals could ensure a more effective application of the interpretative statements in the CETA context. Therefore, in legal terms, parties can

[207] See Section 8.2.1.2.

[208] Art. 8.10.4 CETA. On the FET standard, see Section 1.1.2 in Chapter 1. In EU law, legitimate expectations are a general principle of EU law, the breach of which incurs non-contractual Member State or EU liability.

[209] See Section 8.2.1.3 and Section 4.5.2.2 in Chapter 4.

[210] Strik (n 13) 206–207.

[211] Art. 8.10.3 CETA.

[212] Art. 8.31.3 CETA. The CJEU explicitly placed two safeguards on such interpretations: they cannot have retroactive effect or direct effect on pending cases: Opinion 1/17 (n 37) para. 237.

correct any ICS' interpretation that strays from the right to regulate as envisaged by the Contracting Parties. Politically, it might be more difficult to agree on the content of the correct standard. In any case, the available mechanisms allow for some level of EU control over the compliance of CETA standards with EU law, which was sufficient for the CJEU to conclude that the right to regulate in the EU would be guaranteed.

#### 8.2.2.3 The Right to Regulate and Extra-EU BITs

The right to regulate is a new substantive criterion of the autonomy of EU law, as declared in Opinion 1/17. However, does this CJEU's finding have any consequences for Member States' extra-EU BITs? Importantly, pre-Lisbon BITs do not include the right-to-regulate clause found in CETA. The question is therefore whether Opinion 1/17 renders Member States' pre-Lisbon BITs incompatible with EU law and whether these IIAs should be changed to incorporate the right-to-regulate clause.

In light of the CJEU's reasoning in Opinion 1/17, it is likely that its effects are limited to EU agreements. The CJEU focused on the effects of CETA awards on acts of EU institutions and the public interest, which is in the EU guaranteed under EU legislation and within the EU constitutional framework.[213] Since extra-EU BITs do not bind the EU, they cannot affect the powers of EU institutions under the founding treaties in the same way that EU agreements can. The impact of extra-EU BITs on the autonomy of the EU legal order is not inconceivable but it is remote.[214]

On the other hand, expansive extra-EU BITs could still have negative effects on the protection of public interest in individual Member States. In the majority of cases, such effects are limited to the challenged Member States' measures which might or more often might not concern EU law. Nevertheless, the effects of extra-EU arbitral awards on EU legislation cannot be fully excluded. They could be more prominent in cases when a number of Member States are exposed to claims stemming from the same EU legislation. Numerous claims across Member States could create political pressure on the EU to abandon its legislation in order to exculpate Member States from paying damages for implementing EU law. On the other hand, in the absence of such a scenario, an individual Member State will be required to choose whether to comply

[213] See Opinion 1/17 (n 37) paras. 137–161.
[214] See Section 8.1.1.2(iii).

with its obligations under EU law or under IIL, and ultimately bear the cost of this choice.

The other issue is whether adding the right-to-regulate clause, without more substantive changes to investment protection standards in pre-Lisbon extra-EU BITs, would have a desired practical impact which would guarantee the Member States' regulatory autonomy. In light of Opinion 1/17, it seems that a more substantially restrictive drafting of these standards, *in addition to* the right-to-regulate clause, would be required to guarantee protection of the public interest in the Member States.[215]

Post-Lisbon extra-EU BITs follow the pathway of EU IIAs and include the right-to-regulate clauses.[216] Some include more specific provisions on regulating anti-competitive practices,[217] labour,[218] environmental standards and/or sustainable development.[219] The objective of many of these BITs is to prevent a race-to-the-bottom in the developing third States rather than enabling the implementation of higher standards.[220] The effectiveness of these clauses will be known only after their implementation in the arbitral practice.

### 8.2.3 *Dispute Settlement and Procedural Provisions*

Different to investment standards, EU IIAs and Member States' post-Lisbon extra-EU BITs more substantially differentiate with respect to the

[215] See M. Fanou, 'The CETA ICS and the Autonomy of the EU Legal Order in Opinion 1/17 – A Compass for the Future' (2020) 22 *Cambridge Yearbook of European Legal Studies* 106.

[216] See Art. 2(2) Dutch Model BIT 2019; Art. 3 Hungary–Cabo Verde BIT. Cf. Slovakia–Iran BIT and Slovakia–UAE BIT, which do not have such general clauses.

[217] See Art. 2(3) Dutch Model BIT 2019, which reserves the right of Contracting Parties to 'introduce or maintain non-discriminatory, appropriate and necessary measures for the purpose of preventing investors who, alone or together, have the ability to affect materially the terms of participation in the relevant market as a result of their position in the market, from engaging in or continuing anti-competitive practices'.

[218] Art. 5 Austria–Kyrgyzstan BIT. The standard of labour laws refers to 'internationally recognised labour rights', in line with similar labour provisions in EU FTAs: see Chapter 7.

[219] See a very elaborate provision in Art. 6 Dutch Model BIT 2019, which, *inter alia*, aims to ensure that States provide for and encourage high levels of environmental and labour protection (Art. 6(2)) and do not lower the existing standards in order to attract investment (Art. 6(4)); Cf. Art. 4 Austria–Kyrgyzstan BIT, which focuses only on the latter.

[220] See Art. 2(3) Hungary–Cambodia BIT. However, some BITs include both objectives (discouraging the relaxation of standards and establishing their own level of environmental and sustainable development policies): see Art. 12(1) and (2) Slovakia–UAE BIT.

dispute settlement mechanism. While EU IIAs incorporate quasi-permanent ICS,[221] post-Lisbon extra-EU BITs continue implementing *ad hoc* ITA.[222] The reasons for this divergent approach are mainly pragmatic and should persist only until the establishment of a Multilateral Investment Court (MIC).

The two key differences between the ICS and ITA are the permanency of the appointment of the ICS tribunal members and the availability of an appellate mechanism. The ICS tribunal members are, at both the first and the appellate instances, appointed for a fixed period of time by the EU and the Contracting Party to the respective EU IIA. Their number and terms of tenure vary on the basis of the bilateral IIA.[223] This mechanism aims at ensuring independence of adjudicators from the parties and addressing the perception of bias which exists in traditional ITA. In addition, cases are randomly allocated and decided by the divisions consisting of three members and chaired by a non-national, both at first and appellate level.[224] The appellate instance is an additional procedural instance between the issuance of the provisional award and the final award, to which, *mutatis mutandi,* a number of rules applicable in the first instance apply.[225] The appeal is limited in its grounds and time. The award can be appealed on the basis of: (i) errors in the interpretation or application of the applicable *law*; (ii) manifest errors of facts, including the appreciation of domestic law as a matter of fact; and (iii) the grounds

[221] See Section 9.3.2 in Chapter 9.

[222] See Section 1.3.3 in Chapter 1 and Section 3.2.2 in Chapter 3.

[223] For example, CETA envisages a First Instance Tribunal of fifteen members (five nationals of EU Member States, five nationals of Canada and five nationals of third countries) appointed for a five-year term, renewable once: Art. 8.27.2 and 8.27.5 CETA; the EUSIPA envisages six members (two *appointed* by the EU, two by Singapore and two jointly by the EU and Singapore, who will be nationals of third States): Art. 3.9.2 EUSIPA. Their term is longer than in CETA (eight years) and 'may be renewed' by the decision of the Joint Committee: Art. 3.9.5 EUSIPA. The numbers of tribunal members can be increased or decreased, depending on the caseload. *Mutatis mutandi* provisions for the appointment apply to the Appeal Tribunal in EUSIPA: see Art. 3.10; The Appellate Tribunal members in CETA are appointed for a nine-year non-renewable term: see Art. 2, Decision 001/2021 of the CETA JC of 29 January 2021 setting out the administrative and organisational matters regarding the functioning of the Appellate Tribunal.

[224] Art. 8.27.6 and 8.27.7 CETA; Art. 3.9.7 and 3.9.8 EUSIPA. However, parties may agree to have their case heard by a sole Member: Arts. 8.27.9 CETA and 3.9.9 EUSIPA.

[225] For example, composition of the tribunal, transparency, non-disputing party submissions, third party funding, costs. See Arts. 8.28 CETA and 3.19 EUSIPA.

listed in Article 52 ICSID Convention.[226] The final award should be issued on average within twenty-four months from the submission of the claim to the First Instance Tribunal.[227]

The significance of the permanency of adjudicators and the appellate mechanism must be understood in the context of consistency and predictability, which are important objectives of the EU IIP.[228] Apart from these two ICS features, other key elements of arbitration (submission of the claim, consent, procedural rules and enforcement of awards) remain unchanged in the ICS framework. A claim can be submitted under the ICSID or the United Nations Commission on International Trade Law (UNCITRAL) Rules,[229] which consequently determine the requirements for the consent,[230] the procedure and the enforcement.[231] While double-hatting should be disallowed,[232] the ethics rules,[233] the code of conduct and the remuneration of tribunal members are nevertheless developed from the existing arbitration rules.[234] The code of conduct is based on the rules in the IBA Guidelines on Conflict of Interest in International Arbitration.[235] Tribunal members are paid a monthly retainer fee and a

226 Arts. 8.28 CETA and 3.19 EUSIPA. EUSIPA rules on appellate proceedings are more elaborate than CETA's. For example, the EUSIPA in Art. 3.19.3 prescribes that the Appeal Tribunal may modify or reverse the legal findings and conclusions in the provisional award in whole or in part and refer the matter back to the First Instance Tribunal, which is bound by the conclusions of the Appeal Tribunal. A new hearing seems to be possible 'if appropriate'.

227 Art. 8.39.7 CETA. In the EUSIPA the provisional award should be issued within eighteen months: Art. 3.18.4. As a general rule, the appeals proceedings should be finalised within 180 days and in any case should not exceed 270 days from the date a disputing party notifies its decision to appeal the provisional award: Art. 3.19.4.

228 See Section 7.2.3 in Chapter 7.

229 Arts. 8.23.2 and 8.23.7 CETA; 3.6.1 EUSIPA.

230 Arts. 8.25.2 CETA; 3.6.2 EUSIPA.

231 Arts. 8.41.3, 8.41.5 and 8.41.6 CETA; Arts. 3.22.5 and 3.22.6 EUSIPA.

232 Art. 8.30.1 CETA; Art. 3.11.1 EUSIPA. However, the formulation of this rule ('shall refrain from acting as counsel or as party-appointed expert or witness in any pending or new investment dispute' under CETA or any other IIA) leaves the possibility for tribunal members to engage in other outside activities.

233 However, the ethics rule in CETA in Art. 8.30.2 envisages that the President of the ICJ would make a decision regarding conflicts of interest by tribunal members. In the EUSIPA, the challenge is resolved through internal procedures with the involvement of the President of the First Instance or the Appeal Tribunal respectively: see Art. 3.11.2 EUSIPA.

234 The Secretariat of ICSID acts as Secretariat for EU IIAs First Instance tribunals and provides appropriate support: Arts. 8.27.16 CETA and 3.9.16 EUSIPA.

235 See Art. 8.30.1 CETA. See also Art. 3.11 and Annex 7 of the EUSIPA. See Section 9.3.2.2 in Chapter 9, for further discussion on conflict of interest issues in CETA.

daily fee for days actually worked, the latter being determined pursuant to the ICSID financial rules, which eventually might transform into a regular salary.[236] Although extra-EU BITs retain *ad hoc* ITA, some include innovations in the appointment of arbitrators. For example, the Dutch Model BIT 2019 envisages that all tribunal members will be appointed by an appointing authority.[237] However, this will be done in consultation with disputing parties. The requirements of qualifications are similar to those in EU IIAs and double-hatting is also disallowed.[238] The ethics provisions generally follow those in CETA.[239]

European Union IIAs and extra-EU BITs include a number of procedural improvements commonly found in modern IIAs, which are aimed at enhancing transparency, openness and effectiveness of the process. Transparency is ensured by reference to the UNCITRAL Rules on Transparency in Treaty-based Investor–State Arbitration.[240] Given the court-like features of the ICS, EU IIAs envisage a more open and inclusive process than Member States' BITs. For example, CETA envisages that hearings would be open to the public, apart from issues concerning confidential and protected information, and allows interested third parties to make submissions to the Tribunal under certain conditions.[241] Further rules are aimed at improving the effectiveness of

[236] Arts. 8.27.12, 8.27.14 CETA and 8.27.15 CETA; see also Arts. 3.9.12–15 EUSIPA.

[237] By the Secretary General of ICSID if the claim has been submitted according to the ICSID Convention or the Additional Facility Rules – however, the appointment does not have to be from the ICSID Panel of Arbitrators, or the Secretary General of the PCA if the claim has been submitted under the UNCITRAL Rules: Art. 20(1).

[238] Arts. 20(2) and (5).

[239] Reference is made to IBA Guidelines on the Conflict of Interest in International Arbitration or any agreed supplemental rules: see Art. 20(6) to (8).

[240] Art. 8.36.1 CETA. In some respects CETA goes even further by allowing the publication of a number of otherwise publicly unavailable documents: see Art. 8.36.2–4 CETA; see Annex 8 of the EUSIPA for separate procedures on transparency in the context of that agreement. Extra-EU BITs also refer to the UNCITRAL Transparency Rules: see, for example, Art. 20(13) Dutch Model BIT 2019; Art. 11 Hungary–Cabo Verde BIT; Art. 24 Slovakia–UAE BIT and Art. 14(4) Slovakia–Iran BIT (but both UAE and Iran respectively reserve the right not to apply UNCITRAL Transparency Rules to any proceedings initiated against them).

[241] See Arts. 8.36.5 and 8.38 CETA. Similarly, see Art. 3.17 EUSIPA. However, EU IIAs are not bringing any revolutionary novelties, given that these options are available as part of the UNCITRAL Transparency Rules or the reformed ICSID Rules. See also Art. 20(13) Dutch Model BIT 2019. Other extra-EU BITs are mostly silent on these issues but their inclusion is possible also through the relevant arbitration procedural rules.

the system by imposing procedural timelines,[242] encouraging mediation[243] and facilitating the access of SMEs to the ICS tribunals.[244] The access to the ICS as the access to justice requirement under EU law (Art. 47 CFR) has been particularly emphasised by the CJEU in Opinion 1/17.[245] Some extra-EU BITs also have provisions aimed at enabling SMEs' access to arbitration,[246] although reference to SMEs in extra-EU BITs is the exception rather than the rule.

Finally, a number of procedural tools are envisaged to prevent undue uses of the system.[247] For example, an expeditious procedure is envisaged for the dismissal of frivolous claims,[248] based on the existing practice in IIL.[249] The cost provisions are additionally aimed at discouraging unfounded claims. European Union IIAs as a general rule incorporate the 'loser pays principle', whereby the costs of the proceedings are borne by the unsuccessful party.[250] European Union IIAs also include disclosure obligations for third-party funding.[251] All these procedural improvements

242 For example, discontinuance of the proceedings (Art. 8.35 CETA); the timeline for the appeal process (Art. 3.19.4 EUSIPA) and for the issuance of the final/provisional awards (Arts. 8.39.7 CETA; 3.18.4 EUSIPA; similarly, Art. 22(1) Dutch Model BIT 2019.

243 See Art. 8.20 CETA; Art. 3.4 and Annex 6 EUSIPA.

244 Art. 8.39(6) CETA. Similarly, see Art. 3.21.5 EUSIPA. Several other procedural provisions of EU IIAs are also aimed at facilitating access by SMEs to the ICS: see, for example, Arts. 8.27.9 CETA and 3.9.9 EUSIPA; Arts. 8.19.3 CETA and 3.3.7 EUSIPA.

245 See Section 9.3.3 in Chapter 9.

246 See, for example, Arts. 20(3) and 22(5) Dutch Model BIT 2019.

247 See also jurisdictional limitations discussed in Section 8.2.1.1.

248 'Claims manifestly without legal merit' (Arts. 8.32 CETA; 3.14 EUSIPA) and 'claims unfounded as a matter of law' (Arts. 8.33 CETA; 3.15 EUSIPA), both concerning non-existent legal rights (for example, sale and purchase contracts which are not subject to protections under IIAs) and a similar legal test but with objections submitted as preliminary objections at different times in the proceedings.

249 Similar provisions are found in other modern IIAs (see, for example, Art. 28(4) US Model BIT 2012). For extra-EU BITs practice, see Art. 21(2) Dutch model BIT 2019. The rule on the claims that are manifestly without legal merits is found in ICSID Rule 41(5), where it is considered a residual rule. See M. Potestá and M. Sobat, 'Frivolous Claims in International Adjudication: A Study of ICSID Rule 41(5) and of Procedures of Other Courts and Tribunals to Dismiss Claims Summarily' (2012) 3 *Journal of International Dispute Settlement* 137.

250 See Arts. 8.39.5 CETA and 3.21 EUSIPA. In the practice of post-Lisbon extra-EU BITs, similar provision is found in Art. 22(8) Slovakia–UAE BIT (but cf. Art. 21(4) Slovakia–Iran BIT which is silent on the issue). In the Dutch Model BIT 2019, only reasonable costs incurred by the successful disputing party will be borne by the unsuccessful party, at the discretion of the tribunal: see Art. 22(5).

251 See Arts. 8.26 CETA and 3.8 EUSIPA. However, the obligation includes only the notification to the other disputing party and to the tribunal of 'the name and the address of the third party funder', without further more specific details (e.g. terms of the funding

take into account different outcomes of the arbitral practice and follow the current trends in IIL. Importantly, they are subject to the ISDS reform in UNCITRAL so any outcomes of that reform could be incorporated into the existing treaties through a future multilateral instrument.[252]

A new MIC should replace both the ICS in EU IIAs as well as ITA in Member States' extra-EU BITs. European Union IIAs are used as a mechanism to build support for establishment of an MIC, envisaging that the Parties 'shall pursue' with (each other and) other (interested) trading partners 'the establishment of a multilateral investment tribunal and appellate mechanism'.[253] The replacement of a bilateral ICS with an MIC should not pose a problem for the EU if and once the MIC has been established, although the third States' commitment regarding the future multilateral mechanism varies across treaties.[254] Similar expressions are found in post-Lisbon extra-EU BITs.[255] However, the replacement of ISDS in these agreements with an MIC will require the accession of both Contracting Parties to a multilateral instrument establishing an MIC,[256] which should not be taken for granted, in particular in the case of the Member States' post-Lisbon BITs.[257]

## 8.3 The Energy Charter Treaty as an Extra-EU IIA of the EU and the Member States

The ECT is a notable exception among EU IIAs. It is an 'old-style' pre-Lisbon IIA and the only EU agreement with traditional ISDS

agreement), which could limit speculative funding. New extra-EU BITs do not have provisions for third-party funding. Cf. Amended ICSID Arbitration Rule 14.

252 See Chapter 10.

253 See Arts. 8.29 CETA and 3.12 EUSIPA.

254 Comprehensive Economic and Trade Agreement is rather categorical (the CETA Joint Committee 'shall adopt a decision' providing for the replacement of the ICS with MIC and any appropriate transitional arrangement); the EUSIPA less so (the Committee 'shall *consider* adopting a decision'), while the EUVIPA is least certain about the form of the new mechanism and its applicability in the bilateral context: see Art. 3.41.

255 See Art. 15 Dutch Model BIT 2019; Art. 24(4) Slovakia–Iran BIT; Art. 9(11) Hungary–Cabo Verde BIT. But no such provision is found in the Hungary–Cambodia BIT or Austria–Kyrgyzstan BIT.

256 In the EU's proposal to UNCITRAL, this would involve a combination of (1) an instrument for the accession to the MIC, and (2) a multilateral instrument which would allow that a particular existing or future agreement would be subject to the jurisdiction of an MIC: see UNCITRAL, 'Possible reform of ISDS, Submission from the EU and its Member States' (24 January 2019) UN Doc A/CN.9/WG.III/WP.159/Add.1, paras. 35–36. For further discussion on MIC, see Chapter 10.

257 See, for example, Art. 26(4) of the Slovakia–UAE BIT.

clauses.[258] It has both intra- and extra-EU dimensions.[259] It is also an extra-EU IIA of the Member States. In its *Komstroy* judgment, the CJEU explained its jurisdiction to interpret the ECT, providing insights into normative relations between the ECT and EU law. As the ECT is undergoing the modernisation process, its compatibility with EU law and ongoing participation of the EU and its Member States in the ECT, remain under scrutiny.

### *8.3.1 Jurisdiction of the CJEU to Interpret the ECT*

In the *Komstroy* judgment, made in the preliminary ruling procedure concerning the enforcement of an ECT award before French courts, the CJEU was asked to interpret the notion of investment in Article 1(6) of the ECT and accordingly the Ukrainian investor's eligibility to access ISDS under Article 26(1) of the ECT in the proceedings against Moldova. The judgment is of interest in the EU external context as it extends the CJEU's jurisdiction to cases falling within the scope of the ECT which involve *non-EU* investors and States, as long as such cases also 'fall within the EU legal order'.[260]

The CJEU provided several reasons to explain how the interpretation of the ECT concerns the EU legal order and thus provides grounds for the jurisdiction of the CJEU. First, its jurisdiction stems from the nature of the ECT as an international agreement to which the EU is a party and which thus forms part of EU law.[261] Second, the jurisdiction to interpret questions regarding 'investment' within the meaning of the ECT further stems from EU post-Lisbon competence in the field of foreign investment.[262] Third, the CJEU has jurisdiction to ensure *uniform* application of *EU* law whenever an international agreement can apply to both situations falling directly within the scope of EU law *and* situations that are not covered by EU law.[263] A dispute between a non-EU investor and a non-EU State falls in the latter category, and in principle the CJEU does not have a jurisdiction to interpret an international agreement in such situations.[264] However, the establishment of the seat of arbitration in the

[258] For more on the ECT and its status under EU law, see Section 5.1.3 in Chapter 5.
[259] For intra-EU issues, see Section 5.2 in Chapter 5.
[260] Case C-741/19 *Republic of Moldova v Komstroy* ECLI:EU:C:2021:655, para. 37.
[261] ibid para. 23. See Section 5.2.2(iii) in Chapter 5.
[262] Art. 207 TFEU; Opinion 2/15 ECLI:EU:C:2017:376; *Komstroy* (n 260) para. 26.
[263] *Komstroy* (n 260) para. 29. See Section 5.3.3 in Chapter 5, particularly the discussion on direct effect of the ECT.
[264] ibid para. 28.

territory of a Member State entails the application of the Member State law – and thus EU law – in the enforcement stage, and consequently the obligation of the Member State court to ensure compliance with EU law in accordance with Article 19 TEU.[265]

Accordingly, three set of situations can be distinguished: (i) intra-EU ECT disputes, for which the CJEU has sole jurisdiction in all cases;[266] (ii) extra-EU ECT disputes (between a third country investor and a Member State), which can take place either before an ECT arbitral tribunal or a domestic court of the respondent Member State,[267] subject to the CJEU's assessment of compatibility of the ECT with EU law;[268] and (iii) non-EU ECT disputes (between a non-EU investor and a non-EU State), which are subject to the jurisdiction of the CJEU whenever they choose the seat of their arbitration in the EU *and* when the domestic court finds it necessary to direct to the CJEU preliminary ruling questions concerning the ECT interpretation in the enforcement of the arbitral award. While such cases would be rare, they are nevertheless possible, as demonstrated in *Komstroy*.[269]

With a broad assertion of the CJEU's jurisdiction to interpret the ECT, issues regarding the relationship and compatibility between the ECT and EU law in the extra-EU dimension could also become more prominent. This is compounded with the prospect that a number of extra-EU investment disputes against the EU and Member States is likely to rise.[270] Investors will likely be advised to avoid the intra-EU controversy by (re) structuring their investments through a non-EU ECT jurisdiction (e.g.

[265] ibid para. 34.

[266] ibid paras. 41–64. See Sections 5.2.2 and 5.3.3 in Chapter 5.

[267] ibid para. 31.

[268] ibid para. 65.

[269] In practice, there would be no significant difference in effects between situations involving arbitration under (ii) and (iii), with the assessment of compatibility taking place in the enforcement of the award, except for the obligations of the Member States to challenge any awards contrary to EU law in extra-EU cases (ii). If cases under (ii) take place before the domestic courts, questions for preliminary ruling can be directed to the CJEU at any stage of the proceedings.

[270] The first case involving a claim against the EU under the ECT was made by a subsidiary of Russian Gazprom incorporated in Switzerland, challenging the measures of the new EU Directive 2019/692 of 17 April 2019, which amends the earlier EU Gas Directive 2009/73/EC: *Nord Stream 2 AG v the European Union*, PCA Case No. 2020-07. Following the Russian invasion of Ukraine, the case has been suspended due to the claimant's inability to access its bank accounts and thus finance the arbitration proceedings: see Procedural Order No. 7 (16 March 2022).

Switzerland or the United Kingdom).[271] All this could replace intra-EU arbitration with more extra-EU investment disputes. Following *Komstroy*, *all* investors will likely be advised to avoid the seat of arbitration in the EU to escape the reach of EU law.

In order to protect EU autonomy, following Opinion 1/17 the EU submitted to the ECT Secretariat a statement ensuring that the ECT awards do not affect the allocation of powers between the EU and the Member States fixed by the EU Treaties. The statement clarified the apportionment of financial responsibility for measures challenged before the ECT tribunals. It explained that the EU (and not an investment tribunal) will determine the respondent in the arbitration proceedings in extra-EU claims that concern the implementation of measures under EU law.[272] The statement therefore serves to preserve the exclusive jurisdiction of the CJEU to give rulings on the division of powers between the EU and its Member States, and thus serves to protect the autonomy of the EU legal order.[273]

With the CJEU's jurisdiction to interpret the ECT, the issue of divergent interpretations of the ECT will also become more prominent. *Komstroy* demonstrates the CJEU's narrower vision of 'investment'[274] and insistence on a 'clear distinction' between notions of trade and investment under the ECT. Accordingly, investment involves the immobilisation of resources abroad which generally cannot easily be repatriated in the event of a dispute.[275] More broadly, the CJEU's more restrictive approach also augurs the diversions between the EU and other ECT States regarding the modernisation of the ECT.[276]

[271] See for example, S. Collins, 'Moldova v Komstroy: A Moment of Reckoning for Intra-EU Investment Arbitration under The ECT? Considering Its Impact on Tribunals, Investors and EU Member States' (*EFILA Blog* November 2021).

[272] Statement submitted to the Energy Charter Treaty (ECT) Secretariat pursuant to Art. 26 (3)(b)(ii) of the ECT replacing the statement made on 17 November 1997 on behalf of the European Communities [2019] OJ L115/1.

[273] See Opinion 1/17 (n 37) para. 132.

[274] The CJEU considers the types of assets listed in ECT Art. 1(6) as exhaustive rather than indicative as interpreted by previous decisions of investment tribunals: see *Komstroy* (n 260) paras. 67–69.

[275] ibid paras. 80–82. Therefore, a claim arising from a contract for the supply of electricity, which is not connected to an investment, is not in the scope of investment but trade under the ECT.

[276] The definition of investment in the modernised ECT nevertheless protects claims to money and credit arising solely from commercial transactions for the sale of goods and services: see ECT Secretariat, Decision of the Energy Charter Conference, CCDEC 2022 (24 June 2022) and Section 8.3.2.

In the general interest of legal certainty and coherence in international law, two judicial authorities – ECT tribunals and the CJEU – should refrain from encroaching into their respective competences. The autonomy of the EU legal order will be protected if EU law is treated as a matter of fact and its interpretations by the CJEU taken as authoritative interpretations in investment arbitration. As a step in this direction, the modernised ECT clarifies that the domestic law of the Contracting Party will not be part of the applicable law and can only be considered as a matter of fact.[277] On the other hand, the CJEU should take into account the ECT interpretations of arbitral tribunals made in accordance with the VCLT and the rules and principles of international law. In light of Opinion 1/17, the ECT in its extra-EU dimension should continue to operate in the sphere of international law and separately from EU law, although their conflicts cannot be entirely excluded. Some parallels could be drawn with CETA, which forms part of EU law as an agreement to which the EU is a Party, but where tribunals are called upon to interpret CETA as an international agreement in accordance with the rules of international law.[278] However, and unlike in CETA, the ECT arbitral system is not fully separated from the EU judicial system, as confirmed by the CJEU in *Komstroy*.

### *8.3.2 The Compatibility of the ECT with EU Law and the ECT Reform*

The ECT is currently undergoing modernisation.[279] In June 2022, after fifteen rounds of negotiations, the ECT Parties reached an agreement in principle on the ECT amendments. As part of this politically challenging process, the EU, as the original 'mastermind' behind the ECT, has sought to achieve a more substantial reform, which would align the ECT with EU law and its IIP.[280] The main achievements of the negotiations offer some indications about the modernised ECT,[281] while noting that the devil is likely to be in the detail of the legal text, interpreted by future

277 ibid point 2.
278 See Opinion 1/17 (n 37) para. 122.
279 See ECT Secretariat, 'Decision of the Energy Charter Conference: Adoption by Correspondence – Policy Options for Modernisation of the ECT' (6 October 2019) CCDEC 2019.
280 See Council of the EU, 'Negotiating Directives for the Modernisation of the Energy Charter Treaty – Adoption' (2 July 2019) 10745/19.
281 Decision of the ECT Conference (n 276).

ECT arbitral tribunals. In the meantime, the compliance of the current ECT with EU law remains an open issue.[282]

The focus of the ECT modernisation process was placed on substantive issues rather than the dispute settlement mechanism. Despite its assumed leading role in the negotiations, the EU did not succeed to place the structural aspects of ISDS on the negotiating table, due to Japan's veto.[283] Therefore, there is no reference to a possible future MIC in the negotiation outcomes, despite such proposal from the EU.[284] Unlike in its other IIAs, the EU did not propose to introduce a bilateral ICS first, which would be replaced by a MIC, if and when established. Instead, the reference was made directly to an MIC, which would apply to the exclusion of arbitration, also allowing submission of claims by investors from non-Contracting Parties to an MIC.[285] Traditional ITA will thus remain the ECT's core ISDS mechanism, with promised improvements regarding frivolous claims, security for costs, third-party funding, valuation of damages and transparency.[286] The inclusion of the UNCITRAL Rules on Transparency in Treaty-based arbitration of 1 April 2014 to arbitral proceedings under the modernised ECT has been emphasised as the greatest achievement with respect to ISDS.

Sustainable development and climate change have been the EU's main normative objectives for the modernised ECT.[287] The EU envisaged that the modernised ECT should facilitate clean energy transition 'in line with the Paris Agreement and recently concluded EU agreements and EU

[282] Scholarly opinions early emphasised a number of problems between EU law and the ECT, in both intra- and extra-EU dimensions. See J. Kleinheisterkamp, 'The Next 10 Year ECT Investment Arbitration: A Vision for the Future – From a European Law Perspective' (Report for the SCC/ECT/ICSID Conference, 9–10 June 2011). See also Opinion 1/20.

[283] Japan was the main obstacle for the EU in the ECT negotiations, opposing the MIC, while proposing further liberalisation, by extending protections to investments in the pre-establishment phase: see Japan's comments in the ECT Secretariat, Policy options for modernisation (n 279) 5.

[284] See EU's ECT Negotiating Directives (n 280) 3, and general comments of the EU in the ECT Secretariat, Policy options for modernisation (n 279) 2–3.

[285] See EU proposal for the modernisation of the ECT, tabled for discussion with the ECT Contracting Parties, 15–16. The EU has also proposed a new article, which would oblige the ECT Contracting Parties 'to pursue' the establishment of a multilateral investment tribunal and an appellate mechanism. Both proposals are not mentioned in the outcomes of the negotiations.

[286] See Decision of the ECT Conference (n 276) point 4.

[287] EU's ECT Negotiating Directives (n 280) 3.

positions in ongoing negotiations'.[288] Given the divergencies among the ECT Parties regarding climate policies, the modernised ECT includes a compromise in flexibility and review mechanisms. On the one hand, the flexibility mechanism would allow carve-outs for fossil fuel related investments; and on the other, the regular five-year revisions of carve-outs and energy materials and products covered by the ECT investment protection regime would provide means to respond to new technological and political developments.[289] This was intended to give the EU and its Member States more leeway in bringing the ECT closer to their own climate goals, which nevertheless remains doubtful.[290]

The modernised ECT also provisions on sustainable development and corporate social responsibility – however not as obligations of investors but obligations of the Contracting Parties – reaffirming their obligations in multilateral environmental and labour agreements, as non-regression clauses, and as best effort obligations to 'promote adherence to international standards and principles of responsible business conduct among the investors operating within their areas'. It was intended that these new provisions would give States more leeway in applying their own laws and regulations to environmental impact assessments of energy investment projects to ensure higher level of environmental protection.[291]

Regarding investment protection, the aim was to align the ECT with new IIAs of the EU and Member States. This includes 'appropriate' standards of protection, consistent with EU law and the EU's reformed approach to investment protection.[292] In particular, the current ECT contains broad substantive provisions and no specific 'right to regulate' clause. This was to be corrected in the modernised ECT.[293] A new article

[288] ibid 5.

[289] See Decision of the ECT Conference (n 276) point 1. The new energy materials and products include hydrogen, anhydrous ammonia, biomass, biogas and synthetic fuels. It is unclear whether the review mechanism could also provide more flexibility for the Contracting Parties to withdraw from the ECT if necessary adjustments do not suffice in meeting their climate objectives.

[290] The EU envisaged to introduce a carve-out for fossil fuel related investments, including for existing investments after ten years from the entry into force of the modernised ECT and for new investments made after 15 August 2023, with some exceptions. For comment see A. Van den Berghe, L. Schaugg and H. de Anzizu, 'The New Energy Charter Treaty in Light of the Climate Emergency' (*Jus Mundi* 6 July 2022).

[291] See Decision of the ECT Conference (n 276) point 5.

[292] EU's ECT Negotiating Directives (n 280) 4–5.

[293] See Decision of the ECT Conference (n 276) point 2.

on the FET introduces a closed list of measures that constitute a violation of the FET and conditions under which legitimate expectations may be considered. In a similar manner, the modernised ECT includes a more specific definition of indirect expropriation, with a list of factors relevant for the determination (economic impact, character of the measure). The right to regulate is reiterated in a new stand-alone article, listing legitimate public policy objectives (environment, climate change mitigation and adoption, public health, safety and public morals). In contrast, under the current ECT, some clauses allow for the integration of environmental aspects[294] and envisage public interest exceptions in the case of measures which are 'necessary to protect human, animal or plant life or health'[295] or 'safety'.[296] However, the latter exceptions do not apply to all clauses.[297] The substantive incompatibilities between the ECT and Treaty law regarding the unqualified capital transfer guarantees were also to be brought in line with the unqualified EU law in the modernised ECT.

It is likely that the new approach in the ECT would not be very different from the approach in CETA and other EU IIAs, with a view to limit compensation to investors to cases of sufficiently serious breaches.[298] However, given that the new standards would be interpreted by 'old' tribunals, it would remain to be seen whether these clauses offer sufficient limitations on the discretionary powers of the ECT tribunals in the manner envisaged by the CJEU in Opinion 1/17. Would the modernised ECT leave 'no jurisdiction' to ECT arbitral tribunals to question public interest choices made following the democratic process in the EU, when assessing their effects on investors' rights under the ECT?[299] If not, how would the right to regulate in the EU, as a substantive requirement of the EU law autonomy,[300] be guaranteed under the ECT, which is an agreement to which the EU is a party?

In light of Opinion 1/17, a further issue is whether ITA under the ECT complies with the requirements of Article 47 CFR. The CJEU's assessment in Opinion 1/17 suggests that the EU's ICS is a *minimum* standard that an international tribunal must fulfil to comply with the right of

[294] Art. 19 ECT.
[295] Art. 24(2) ECT.
[296] Art. 24(3) ECT.
[297] Importantly, the much-invoked Art. 13 (expropriation) is excluded from the scope of public interest exceptions: Art. 24(1) ECT.
[298] See analysis in Section 8.2.2.
[299] Opinion 1/17 (n 37) para. 160.
[300] See Section 8.2.2.2.

access to an independent tribunal under Article 47 CFR.[301] In its reasoning the CJEU particularly emphasised the importance of the rules on the composition of ICS tribunals (on a rotational and random basis) and on dealings with cases before these tribunals, to support the assertion about CETA's break from traditional ISDS mechanism – based on arbitration as a private justice mechanism – towards the public judicial system.[302] While procedural rules of the ICS build upon the rules of ISDS, it remains debatable whether an ISDS tribunal would pass the compliance test in light of the CJEU's overall assessment of the ICS.[303] This issue would arguably be less important for extra-EU BITs since they mostly concern Member States' national measures, but it would be relevant in cases when measures made by the EU have been challenged before the ECT tribunals.[304]

The completion of the ECT modernisation is politically complex and very uncertain. The amendments require unanimity and the treaty must be ratified by three-fourths of the Contracting Parties to enter into force.[305] Not all ECT States have considered that the reform of the ECT was necessary, including some EU 'like-minded' partners (Japan). Given the opposition in a number of Member States and the EP's stance, the EU's and Member States' participation in the ECT remains very uncertain and politically sensitive.[306] For the Commission, the modernised ECT has turned into a choice of a 'lesser evil' – a unilateral

[301] Opinion 1/17 (n 37) paras. 190–192. See also analysis in Chapter 9.

[302] ibid para. 194–195.

[303] Cf. Remarks by AG Wathelet on the compliance of ISDS tribunals with requirements of independence and accessibility in his Opinion (ECLI:EU:C:2017:699) in *Achmea* (n 29) paras. 124–125. For normative analysis of the compatibility of ISDS arbitration with the rule of law requirements, see Section 3.3.2 in Chapter 3. For the ICS and the rule of law, see Section 9.3 in Chapter 9.

[304] See also comments already made regarding Member States' extra-EU BITs in Section 8.1.1.2(iii).

[305] Arts. 36(1)(a) and 42(4) ECT respectively, thus requiring ratification by thirty-nine Parties. Provisional application is possible under Art. 45 ECT.

[306] The ECT is a mixed agreement, and the Member States are Contracting Parties to this treaty in their own right: see Chapter 6. A number of Member States have announced their decision to withdraw from the ECT. The EP has called for a coordinated withdrawal of the EU and Member States from the ECT: see EP Resolution of 23 November 2022 on the outcome of the modernisation of the Energy Charter Treaty, 2022/2934 (RSP). See also 'Statement on the modernisation of the Energy Charter Treaty' (3 November 2020), signed by 139 members of the European and national parliaments.

withdrawal from the current ECT would trigger a sunset clause and likely longer application of the unreformed ECT investment protections and ISDS to existing investments (over twenty years).[307] The ECT is a good example of tensions between the EU's external objectives: on one hand, the EU's attempts to strengthen its geopolitical position by influencing the governance of international energy markets;[308] and on the other, the EU's aspiration to lead and achieve an ambitious climate change reform.

## 8.4 How Coherent Is EU External Investment Framework?

In light of the above analysis, a decade following the introduction of the EU IIP, its external investment regulatory framework remains fragmented between IIAs of the EU and Member States. The largest segment remain the 'old' pre-Lisbon Member States' BITs, which are largely inconsistent with the new EU IIP, with respect to both broadly defined substantive standards and the traditional ISDS as the dispute settlement mechanism.

The most important segment of the external EU investment regulatory framework are the new EU IIAs. These agreements introduce more specified substantive standards balanced against the right to regulate, and the ICS, which is largely adopting the procedural elements of arbitration, with two major differences: the permanency of tribunal members and the appellate mechanism. European Union IIAs incorporate the EU IIP but have not yet been ratified nor implemented. However, among EU IIAs, the ECT remains an exception. Even the reformed ECT would retain ISDS, as a significant element likely to undermine substantive changes to the ECT. Any new standards would be interpreted by arbitral tribunals, likely to retain the legacy of the old system. The interpretations by arbitral tribunals are likely to set the direction of any jurisprudence stemming from new standards.[309]

[307] Art. 47(3) ECT. It remains unclear whether the modernised ECT retains a sunset clause.

[308] The modernised ECT was to include a reference to the 2015 International Energy Charter: see Decision of the ECT Conference (n 276) point 1. For its relevance in the context of international energy governance, see P. Aalto, 'The New International Energy Charter: Instrumental or Incremental Progress of Governance?' (2016) 11 *Energy Research and Social Science* 92.

[309] See W. Alschner, *Investment Arbitration and State-Driven Reform* (OUP 2022). However, the author seeks solutions not in new dispute settlement bodies but in the

In addition to the ECT, the most surprising segment of the EU investment framework is its approach to post-Lisbon Member States' extra-EU BITs. Investment protection standards in these agreements are mostly consistent albeit not the same to those found in EU IIAs, and with different variations across BITs. The Dutch Model BIT 2019 stands out from the other Member States' BITs because it more comprehensively embraces, and in some elements even further develops, the standards of EU IIAs. However, new extra-EU BITs retain ITA as a dispute settlement mechanism. Accordingly, in this part they are inconsistent with the EU IIP. While the EU declared ISDS 'dead',[310] it continues to approve new Member States' BITs that implement ISDS, and the compatibility of which with EU law remains questionable following Opinion 1/17. The reasons are primarily pragmatic and political.[311]

Ultimately, an MIC is the only viable EU solution for coherent EU external investment regulation framework. A single standing dispute settlement mechanism would primarily encompass all investment treaties of the EU and its Member States, but would be open to third States if they wish so – thus giving the global ISDS reform much needed flexibility.[312] The assumption is that this new court would accordingly – through interpretation of EU IIAs and post-Lisbon Member States' extra-EU BITs – provide coherent interpretations of new *EU* standards across different treaties, ensuring the right of States to regulate.[313] However, there are several open questions, including very fundamental ones – whether coherent standards are possible if the regulatory framework remains fragmented across many IIAs. The significant limitation of the

modernisation of old treaties, including through the completion of incomplete old treaties through renegotiation, with the ECT as a case in point: ibid ch. 8.

310 See Part III introductory quote.

311 Different policy options and their costs are outlined in the EC's impact assessment of the MIC. The document notes that the option of including the ICS at the bilateral Member States level is 'overly burdensome in terms of time and resources' and accordingly 'not feasible': EC, 'Multilateral Reform of Investment Dispute Resolution, Impact Assessment', SWD (2017) 302 final, 27. The EC further notes that 'multiple ICSs trigger high costs and a significant administrative burden (in terms of workforce, time and financial resources) for the Commission': ibid 18. See further calculations of these ICS costs (about €800,000 per bilateral ICS per year, on the basis of one case before each instance): ibid 21–22 and Annex 4.

312 See Chapter 10.

313 See analysis in Section 8.2.2.

Table 8.1 *Coherence of EU external investment regulatory framework*

| Coherence with EU IIP | Investment protection | Dispute settlement |
|---|---|---|
| **Pre-Lisbon extra-EU BITs** | • Broadly drafted investment protections<br>• Capital transfer clauses inconsistent with EU law | • Traditional ISDS (ITA)<br>• Procedural standards of ICSID/UNCITRAL |
| **New EU IIAs** | • Clearly drafted investment protection clauses<br>- Largely based on NAFTA case law<br>• The right to regulate guaranteed (Opinion 1/17) | • New ICS:<br>- permanency<br>- appellate mechanism<br>• Improved procedural standards<br>- jurisdictional limitations for abusive investors<br>- transparency and openness<br>- largely based on the existing standards<br>• MIC in the long-term |
| **Post-Lisbon extra-EU BITs** | • More detailed investment protections with variations across treaties | • Traditional ISDS (ITA)<br>• Improved procedural standards with variations across treaties<br>• MIC in the long-term |

UNCITRAL's reform and thus also the MIC in the global context remains the focus on only procedural (dispute settlement) and not substantive (investment standards) issues.

The coherence between key elements of different IIAs represented in the regulatory framework of the EU external investment is presented in Table 8.1.

In the interim, the coherence of the EU external investment regulatory framework will depend on the interpretation of standards by adjudicative bodies – the ICS if and once established under EU IIAs, and arbitral tribunals in case of the ECT and Member States' post-Lisbon extra-EU BITs. Early in the development of the EU IIP, the EC noted that investment standards are 'subject to a common understanding among experts in the field (lawyers, academics, arbitrators, judges)' regarding their meaning and thus are not 'absolute rules'.[314] In that sense, they are objectively defined by the legislator, but their meaning is determined by the adjudicator, depending on the case-specific circumstances. In light of different dispute settlement bodies across many different treaties, these different meanings given to investment standards undermine consistency and thus also compound the fragmentation of the EU foreign investment regulatory framework.

Finally, a large number of different IIAs offer to strategic investors an opportunity to circumvent the EU IIP through 'treaty shopping', by restructuring investments in ways in which more favourable IIAs and arbitration can be utilised. Since the MIC still faces a number of political and legal obstacles, the realisation of a coherent EU international investment regulatory framework might be feasible only as a long-term goal.

## 8.5 Conclusion

European Union IIAs endorse the established standards of protection in IIL. While largely codifying the jurisprudence of arbitral tribunals, new EU IIAs provide more clarity about the content of these standards. At the same time, they missed the opportunity to introduce more precision in defining limitations between State legal and illegal regulatory activity, leaving sufficient scope for jurisprudential interpretations of new standards. The scope of investors' obligations, including their due diligence, under new EU IIAs remains limited. The risk of States' regulatory measures breaching investors' rights is accordingly higher under new EU IIAs than under EU law.

Regardless, the EU provisions of IIAs should sufficiently guarantee the right to regulate in the EU and therefore the public interest should be protected. This conclusion of the CJEU was reached in the bilateral context of CETA and its specific features played a role: clearly drafted investment provisions with high thresholds, permanent tribunals and more control by the Contracting Parties over the interpretation of standards through the joint interpretative mechanism. While the right to regulate has been the exception and the compensation for State regulatory measures the rule, the CJEU is striving to bring IIL back closer to a public international law notion of regulatory sovereignty.

[314] EC, 'Follow up to the European Parliament Resolution on the Future European International Investment Policy' (5 July 2011) 2.

The investment and regulatory standards of EU IIAs, except for a few rare exceptions, do not endorse or promote EU standards. The inclusion of regulatory standards stemming from the NAFTA jurisprudence rather than the more expansive Member States' BITs has to be understood in the context of the early development of the EU IIP and the negotiations for TTIP.[315] The new standards endorse higher thresholds for breaches of investors' rights and reflect positive IIL developments when balancing private and public rights. The EU's approach in its IIP accordingly confirms its commitment to observance and development of international law.[316]

In the meantime, the reliance on extra-EU BITs remains a valid Plan B for EU investors. It could turn into a viable Plan A in case the EU IIP fails; for example, if neither of the EU IIAs complete the process of ratification in the Member States, or if the EU proposal for an MIC does not succeed in UNCITRAL. The retention of ITA in the modernised ECT is indicative of difficulties that the EU continues to face in introducing an MIC. While new extra-EU BITs are largely coherent with EU IIAs in regard to substantive standards, they substantially differ regarding the ISDS mechanism. A system of *ad hoc* tribunals could ultimately undermine the coherence of new substantive standards in their implementation. Without reforming the ISDS mechanism, the EU efforts will eventually achieve more or less substantial improvements of bilateral Member States' BITs – something that all other States have been doing for some time. While still worthwhile, the reform in that case would be reduced to a shadow of its envisaged potential.

In light of nearly 1,300 Member States' extra-EU BITs in force, and the ECT with ITA as the ISDS mechanism, and not a single EU IIA yet in force, fragmentation remains a dominant feature of the EU external investment regulation framework. Consistency between these many agreements and thus the coherence of the EU IIP depends on effective implementation of the available coordination mechanisms and the Member States' compliance with their duty of sincere cooperation in the short term, and the overall success of the EU's ISDS reform in the longer term. With ITA as still the dominant ISDS mechanism, traditional ISDS remains practically relevant in the EU and the EU external regulation of investment, at least for the time being, remains as (in)coherent as the entire field of IIL.

[315] See Chapter 7.

[316] Art. 3(5) TEU.

# 9

# The Investment Court System

## Integrating the Rule of (EU) Law

The Investment Court System (ICS) is the core feature of the EU international investment policy (IIP). In its Opinion 1/17, the Court of Justice of the European Union (CJEU) confirmed the legality of the new ICS in Comprehensive Economic and Trade Agreement (CETA) under EU law, providing important legal and policy implications for the future co-existence of EU law and international investment law (IIL). This chapter offers a critical assessment of the ICS, examined through the CJEU's reasoning in Opinion 1/17. First, we discuss the nature of the ICS in relation to the EU judicial system. Second, we consider the effects of the ICS on the autonomy of the CJEU and the interpretation of EU law. Finally, we focus on the main features of the ICS in light of the rule-of-law criteria, as the core EU value. Where relevant, the CJEU's Opinion is supplemented by remarks of late Advocate General (AG) Bot, which uncover a number of relevant political considerations.[1] The design and functioning of the ICS thus provide important insights into the EU's understanding of the rule of law in IIL, which is ultimately envisaged to be implemented through a Multilateral Investment Court (MIC).

### 9.1 The Nature of the ICS

In Opinion 1/17,[2] the CJEU mostly agreed with the reasoning of late AG Bot,[3] establishing the compatibility of the ICS with primary EU law. However, they characterised the nature of the new ICS with subtle differences. Advocate General Bot emphasised the 'hybrid' or

[1] Parts of this chapter have been published in I. Damjanovic and N. de Sadeleer, 'Values and Objectives of the EU in Light of Opinion 1/17: "Trade for All", above All' (2020) 4(1) *Europe and the World: A Law Review* [25].

[2] Opinion 1/17 ECLI:EU:C:2019:341.

[3] Opinion 1/17, Opinion of AG Bot ECLI:EU:C:2019:72.

'quasi-judicial'[4] nature of the ICS, which would 'gradually acquire characteristics of a genuine court'.[5] The CJEU found that the ICS is 'primarily judicial in nature' while implicitly confirming its 'work-in-progress' nature. This rather pedantic differentiation enabled the Court to nuance the political background of the AG's argumentation and eventually justify the legitimacy of the ICS under international law, although the mechanism falls short of the rule-of-law standard of a 'genuine' court under EU law.

### *9.1.1 Political Background Does (Not) Matter*

Advocate General Bot in his Opinion provided the context in which the request for an opinion was made,[6] *inter alia* referring to criticism of investor-State dispute settlement (ISDS) and challenges that the European Commission (EC) had to face and address in developing a new ICS model. On the political side, these challenges relate to 'the functioning of arbitration tribunals' and the 'legitimacy of an arbitration scheme between investors and States'.[7] At the same time, AG Bot correctly noted the reality of IIL, where arbitration clauses continue to be 'regarded as a key component of the protection of foreign investments in the host State'.[8] In that context, and bearing in mind the EU's urge to develop bilateral free trade relations with third States,[9] the Commission's space for manoeuvre was limited. The choice was to be made between abandoning investment dispute settlement, which seemed unrealistic, and improving the traditional arbitration model to address the criticism.[10]

In opting for the second option, the EU developed a 'hybrid' model, which not only depicts a '*compromise* between an arbitration tribunal and an international court', but also epitomises the EU's leading role in this 'experiment', which could well determine the future of the whole

[4] ibid para. 165.
[5] ibid paras. 33, 242, 260–261.
[6] ibid Section II (paras. 10–33).
[7] Opinion 1/17, Opinion of AG Bot (n 3) paras. 15–17. NB. All ISDS elements to which AG Bot referred as being subject to criticism are, according to the Commission, being addressed through the ICS and the EU's proposal for an MIC: see European Commission Factsheet, 'Investment Provisions in the EU-Canada Free Trade Agreement (CETA)' (February 2016)
[8] ibid para. 14.
[9] ibid para. 16.
[10] ibid para. 17.

system.[11] According to AG Bot, the approach that the EU adopted is '*pragmatic*'. It balances the needs of EU negotiating partners (third States), which see arbitration as 'an essential component in the protection of investors',[12] with the needs of the public in the EU, expressed in the 'spirited debate' of the consultation process.[13] The AG's task was to examine whether this pragmatic hybrid compromise, which adopts the practice of investment arbitration 'with a view to *moving towards* a judicial model', is compatible with primary EU law.[14]

The CJEU in its Opinion adopted a more cunning approach by avoiding a reference to the political background and indeed any reference to ISDS or ICS criticism, beyond what was presented before the Court in the submissions made by the parties (mostly the Kingdom of Belgium that made the request). While the CJEU could have been equally impressed with the Commission's ability to compromise and seek pragmatic solutions, the Court saw no value in emphasising the political dimension of the Opinion. The Court thus seemingly avoided criticism for political bias in the solution that, reading the AG's Opinion, seemed realistic for saving the EU IIP.

### 9.1.2 *Judicial Albeit Hybrid*

In the AG's Opinion the hybrid nature of the ICS is put forward as a solution to address political challenges but it poses a legal challenge because 'the main principles' governing the ICS must be consistent with the EU legal order, in particular the founding treaties and the EU constitutional principles.[15] As a judicial body, the ICS must comply with Article 47 Charter of Fundamental Rights (CFR), which guarantees effective access to justice and a remedy before an independent and impartial tribunal previously established by law.

However, referring to the Belgian assessment of the ICS as falling short of the criterion of independence for courts, the AG found the justification in the hybrid model, noting: 'Although the term "tribunal" has been chosen in the agreement envisaged, *which could suggest that it is a*

[11] ibid para. 18 (emphasis added).
[12] ibid para. 19 (emphasis added).
[13] ibid para. 20.
[14] ibid para. 33 (emphasis added).
[15] Opinion 1/17 (n 2) para. 165; Opinion 1/15 ECLI:EU:C:2017:592, para. 67; Case C-266/16 *Western Sahara Campaign UK* ECLI:EU:C:2018:118, para. 46.

*genuine court*, it is, however, a mechanism which remains greatly inspired by the rules of arbitration.'[16] The AG then listed provisions of the CETA ICS which were 'explicitly' inspired by the arbitration rules: the submission of a claim to the Tribunal,[17] the consent to the settlement of the dispute by the Tribunal,[18] the transparency of proceedings[19] and the enforcement of awards.[20] Moreover, with respect to the remuneration of members of the Tribunals[21] and the question of ethics[22] the AG noted that the CETA text makes reference to the rules applicable in the field of arbitration. As a final point, the AG observed that 'the CETA Tribunal does not give judgments but rather issues awards'.[23]

While the system is characterised by a number of arbitration-like features, it is nevertheless 'an expression of the *wish*' of the EU and Canada in this particular case to 'move towards a new system *inspired by* the judicial systems of [the EU and Canada]'.[24] In that sense, the mechanism is only a step towards the creation of an MIC,[25] and it offers room for improvement with respect to procedural safeguards that could not have all been clarified in the CETA text.[26] Importantly, the mechanism is an expression of the political wish of the two State entities, which provides necessary legitimacy for continuing their pursuit of legal improvements.

The new mechanism should not be equated with a genuine court and it should rather be assessed in the context of its '*experimental* and *dynamic* nature'.[27] First, the CJEU should take into account the improvements that have been made in the ICS compared to the traditional investment treaty arbitration (ITA) and assess the new model against what has been done rather than what could have been done.[28] Therefore, the

16 Opinion 1/17, Opinion of AG Bot (n 3) para. 242 (emphasis added).
17 Art. 8.23 CETA.
18 ibid Art. 8.25.
19 ibid Art. 8.36.
20 ibid Art. 8.41.
21 ibid Art. 8.27.14 CETA.
22 ibid Art. 8.30.1.
23 Opinion 1/17, Opinion of AG Bot (n 3) para. 242.
24 ibid para. 243 (emphasis added).
25 ibid para. 246.
26 ibid para. 247. In particular, the AG refers to additional rules regarding the Appellate Tribunal, mandatory code of conduct, which will further strengthen the guarantees of impartiality and independence, and the rules on mediation.
27 ibid para. 246 (emphasis added).
28 ibid para. 245.

mechanism does not need to perfectly satisfy the conditions of a genuine court, as suggested by the Kingdom of Belgium, but only ensure a '*sufficient* level' of safeguards and protection of the right of access to an independent and impartial tribunal under Article 47 CFR.[29] Second, the ICS is still, in layman's language, a 'work in progress' and the CJEU should appreciate its potential to become a genuine court. The emphasis placed on the CETA parties' wishes to adopt an imperfect court model reflects the *political* essence of international negotiations and thus also serves to justify the noted imperfections.

The CJEU came to a more nuanced conclusion about the ICS: while largely inspired by the traditional ISDS mechanism, it is nevertheless 'primarily judicial in nature'.[30] Regardless of whether ICS tribunals are formally classified as 'judicial bodies' and their members as 'judges', they will 'in essence' be judicial bodies with judicial functions. This is because these bodies are: permanent and established by law (CETA); follow an adversarial procedure; apply rules of law; exercise their functions autonomously; and issue final and binding decisions.[31] The CJEU, while not denying the hybrid nature of the new ICS,[32] diverts the focus from impliedly *political* issues associated with 'hybrid' bodies towards *legal* issues related to the compliance of judicial bodies with the basic legal principles. In particular, judicial bodies must ensure procedural justice, which encompasses the right to a fair hearing (*audi alteram partem*) and the rule against bias (*nemo iudex in causa sua*).[33] Accordingly, the Court particularly emphasised the difference between the ICS and ISDS with respect to 'the rules on the composition of the [CETA] Tribunal and on dealing with cases [before that Tribunal]'.[34]

If hybrid bodies are impliedly political and judicial bodies independent from politics, the differentiation was not only canny but also necessary. If the ICS tribunals are 'experimental', 'dynamic', 'hybrid' and a 'compromise', it is valid to ask how they could comply with legal principles for judicial bodies, in particular those outlined in Article 47 CFR. On the other hand, if ICS tribunals are, despite their other characteristics, essentially judicial, their compliance with essential judicial principles can be

[29] ibid paras. 245, 251 (emphasis added).
[30] Opinion 1/17 (n 2) para. 190.
[31] ibid para. 197.
[32] ibid para. 193.
[33] See Section 3.2.2 in Chapter 3.
[34] Opinion 1/17 (n 2) paras. 193–194.

justified. This ultimately changes the impliedly political character of the ICS into, in essence and primarily, a legal body that complies with essential requirements of EU law for judicial bodies. In any case, this characterisation also transforms the ICS' political discourse into a legal one, at least in the context of its compliance with EU law. If law could be translated to poetry,[35] that which we call the ICS by any other name would perform its duties as a court would – independently and in accordance with the law.

### 9.1.3 *Outside the EU Judicial System*

The CJEU and the AG both placed the ICS outside the EU judicial system. The Court thus followed its earlier observations about ISDS, expressed in Opinion 2/15 and *Achmea*. The CJEU also reiterated that an international dispute settlement mechanism is in principle compatible with EU law.[36] However, for the first time the CJEU explained how such a mechanism can co-exist with EU law. The Court provided a list of procedural and substantive criteria for the preservation of the autonomy of EU law.[37] The emphasis of the CJEU's analysis was placed on the separation of the ICS from the EU legal order. Since the ICS tribunals remain outside the EU judicial system, the CJEU could frame the ICS as, in principle, a world apart from the EU legal order. However, in those aspects where the two worlds meet, the Court found sufficient reasons to justify that ICS tribunals would not erode its authority on EU law.

## 9.2 Autonomy of the CJEU to Interpret EU Law

In examining the effects of the ICS on the EU legal order, the CJEU had to determine whether CETA Tribunals could undermine the CJEU's authority to interpret EU law. The Court found that a number of procedural safeguards serve to protect its autonomy and that ICS tribunals would not interpret EU law *other than CETA*. These procedural safeguards relate to the CETA provisions on (1) the status of domestic law in the ICS proceedings, (2) the applicable law in the ICS proceedings

[35] 'That which we call a rose by any other name would smell as sweet', William Shakespeare, *Romeo and Juliet*, Act II, Scene II.

[36] Opinion 1/17 (n 2) paras. 106–107.

[37] For the substantive element – the right to regulate – see Section 8.2.2 in Chapter 8.

and (3) the apportionment of responsibility between the EU and the Member States for the measures challenged before the ICS.

### 9.2.1 Interpretation versus Examination of Law

Comprehensive Economic and Trade Agreement prescribes that domestic law, and thus also EU law, is to be treated as a matter of fact in the proceedings before the ICS tribunals.[38] Since the application of foreign law as a matter of fact in ITA is more prevalent in the tradition of common law courts and applied less in the civil law tradition that the CJEU follows,[39] many commentators were sceptical about the effectiveness of this provision. The CJEU provided its own view on what it means to apply EU law as a matter of fact. The Court distinguished between the interpretation of domestic law and the *examination* of the effect of a measure. The latter refers to assessing domestic law as a matter of fact, which includes the obligation of a tribunal to follow the prevailing interpretation of domestic law by domestic courts or authorities. In turn, domestic courts and authorities are not bound by the *meaning* given to their domestic law by the tribunal.[40]

It follows then that interpretation refers to assessing domestic law as a matter of law. In this scenario the ICS tribunal would determine the *meaning* of the domestic legal rule according to its own understanding, without following the prevalent interpretation given by domestic courts. Such a tribunal's determination of the meaning of the domestic legal rule would bind domestic courts. In essence, therefore, interpretation includes determining the meaning of a legal rule *in abstracto*, and it is akin to lawmaking. In accordance with the EU founding treaties, interpretation of EU law is exclusively the prerogative of the CJEU.[41]

[38] Art. 8.31.2 CETA.

[39] This is, *inter alia*, due to the application of the doctrine *iura novit curia*, which is not accepted in common law systems. German legal doctrine also significantly influenced the continental courts' *ex officio* treatment of foreign law: see analysis by S. L. Sass, 'Foreign Law in Civil Litigation: A Comparative Survey' (1968) 16 *The American Journal of Comparative Law* 332. Such application of foreign law by courts, whereby the courts ascertain on their own, in cooperation with the parties, the content of foreign law (rather than parties proving the content through their own experts) blurs the dividing line between law as a matter of fact and law as a matter of law. The court participates actively in framing both the factual and legal issues of the case, and, with such a role of the court, it is more difficult to ascertain foreign law as a matter of fact or as a matter of law.

[40] Opinion 1/17 (n 2) para. 131. See also Art. 8.31.2 CETA (emphasis added).

[41] Arts. 267 and 344 TFEU.

Interpretation is therefore not the prerogative of investment arbitral tribunals since their decisions are not binding *erga omnes*. Arbitral tribunals only interpret international investment agreements (IIAs) in accordance with the criteria set out in Article 31 Vienna Convention on the Law of Treaties (VCLT) and their decisions apply only to a particular case in point. Therefore, standard arbitration agreements do not vest in investment tribunals lawmaking powers analogous to those vested in the CJEU by the EU Treaties.[42] Accordingly, in Opinion 1/17, the CJEU clarified that the ICS would not have any lawmaking powers with respect to EU law, confirming also that the ICS will not have such powers with respect to CETA either.[43]

It would have been clearer if the CJEU had explained the distinction between the application (rather than interpretation) of law and examination of the effects of law. Interpretation refers to determining the meaning of a legal rule more generally and regardless of particular facts. Contrary to that, the application of law entails the determination of the consequences of a legal rule with respect to facts specific to each particular case.[44] In the EU legal order, the role of the CJEU is to interpret an EU legal rule, while the role of the national courts is to apply that EU rule, as interpreted by the CJEU, to the particular facts of a particular case before the national court.

Instead, when explaining the difference between interpretation and examination, the Court made a reference to Opinion 1/09 and distinguished the ICS in CETA from the EU Patent Court on the basis of the applicable law in the proceedings before these courts. The EU Patent Court was incompatible with EU law because the applicable law clause in the draft international agreement allowed the proposed Patent Court to *interpret and apply* EU secondary law and to determine the dispute in light of the fundamental rights and principles of EU law.[45] It can accordingly be reasoned that, unlike the EU Patent Court, ICS tribunals will have the competence only to examine the effects of law, which does not include the competence either to interpret (determine the meaning of

[42] F. Rosenfeld, 'Abstract Interpretations in International Investment Law' in P. Pazartzis and others (eds), *Reconceptualising the Rule of Law in Global Governance, Resources, Investment and Trade* (Hart 2016) 339–342. However, as discussed in Chapter 3, tribunals have effectively assumed such a role due to broadly worded provisions of early BITs.

[43] Opinion 1/17 (n 2) para. 234. In accordance with Art. 8.31.3 CETA such power lies with the CETA Joint Committee, which is empowered to issue binding interpretations.

[44] Rosenfeld (n 42) 332–333.

[45] Opinion 1/09 ECLI:EU:C:2011:123, para. 78. See Opinion 1/17 (n 2) para. 124.

the rule *in abstracto*), or to apply EU law (determine the meaning of the rule *in concreto*). The CJEU's approach clearly distinguishes the ICS from domestic courts and reaffirms its conclusion that the ICS stands outside the EU judicial system.

Accordingly, the CJEU was satisfied that the ICS, unlike the proposed EU Patent Court, would not endanger its position as the highest authority for the interpretation of EU law, although EU law could appear as an issue before ICS tribunals and despite the fact that ICS tribunals might not correctly appreciate EU law in the *examination* of its effects. The CJEU was satisfied that the appellate mechanism[46] would correct all errors made in the first instance and concluded that the CETA Appellate Tribunal, equally as the First Instance Tribunal, is not called upon to interpret or apply domestic law.[47]

### 9.2.2 *Domestic versus International Law*

The only EU law that CETA Tribunals may interpret is the CETA, which is an international agreement to which the EU is a party. In the hierarchy of legal norms in the EU legal order, the CETA must be compatible with primary EU law but prevails over secondary EU law and national legislation of Member States. Secondary EU legislation must be interpreted harmoniously with the international agreements of the Union.[48] Accordingly, insofar as possible, national courts of the Member States and EU courts must apply EU secondary legislation in a manner that is consistent with the CETA. The CETA therefore binds the EU and Member States as a matter of EU law *and* as a matter of international law.

National courts and EU courts could be called upon to interpret the CETA when respectively assessing the compatibility of national and EU secondary legislation with the CETA. For example, a national court of an EU Member State, in assessing an intellectual property rights matter appearing before the court, would need to assess whether the relevant national Member State legislation on the matter complies with the relevant EU secondary law and the CETA requirements.[49] In doing so,

[46] The Appellate Tribunal is conferred with the power to identify manifest errors in the appreciation of the facts, and thus also the manifest errors in the appreciation of domestic law: Art. 8.28.2 CETA.

[47] Opinion 1/17 (n 2) para. 133.

[48] Case C-61/94 *Commission v Germany* [1996] ECR I-3989, para. 52.

[49] While the IPR chapter of CETA does not fall within the jurisdiction of CETA investment tribunals, IPR rights are nevertheless included in the definition of 'investment' in Art. 8.1

the national court may request from the CJEU the interpretation of the CETA provisions through the preliminary ruling procedure.

The CJEU's practice has recorded cases in which national courts had referred questions for preliminary ruling on the interpretation of mixed agreements.[50] While this jurisprudence is far from clear, the CJEU retained its jurisdiction for the interpretation of provisions of mixed agreements falling both within the EU's exclusive and non-exclusive competence.[51] In the case on non-exclusive competence, the Court held that its jurisdiction applies if the EU has already legislated in the area or, if the EU has not yet exercised its competence, when the provision in question could also be applied in an area in which the EU has legislated.[52] The CJEU retains its jurisdiction to interpret a mixed agreement regardless of whether the interpretation of the provision is needed for the application of national or EU law.[53]

In this exercise, it is likely that the national court would apply national and EU law, including the CETA, in accordance with the domestic and EU constitutional principles. The CJEU's intervention in issues of mixed treaties like CETA is justified on the grounds of consistent interpretation of EU law.[54] In particular, the CJEU has held that the uniform interpretation of mixed treaty provisions is 'clearly in the Community interest', whatever the circumstances in which such a provision is to be applied, 'in order to forestall future differences of interpretation'.[55] Moreover, in cases of mixed agreement provisions that can fall both within the scope of national law and EU law, the CJEU has emphasised the obligation of close cooperation in fulfilling the commitments undertaken under the joint competence. This cooperation 'requires the judicial bodies of the Member States and the Community, for practical and *legal* reasons, to give it a uniform interpretation'.[56] While the denial of the CETA's direct

(g) so IPR might appear as a legal issue both before CETA Tribunals and national courts, albeit in the context of separate and/or different type of legal actions.

50 For shared competence and mixed agreements, see Chapter 6.

51 See for example, Case C-741/19 *Republic of Moldova v Komstroy* ECLI:EU:C:2021:655, para. 29 and Section 8.3.1 in Chapter 8.

52 M. Broberg and N. Fenger, *Preliminary References to the European Court of Justice* (OUP 2010) 125–130.

53 Case C-53/96 *Hermès* [1998] ECR I-3603, para. 32.

54 The principle of consistent interpretation stems from the overarching principle of primacy of EU law: see Chapter 4.

55 *Hermès* (n 53) paras. 32–33, and case law therein cited.

56 Joined Cases C-300/98 and C-392/98 *Dior* [2000] ECR I-11307, paras. 36–37 (emphasis added).

effect limits the involvement of domestic courts and the CJEU in the matters of the CETA, this involvement cannot be fully avoided. The CJEU's jurisdiction to make preliminary rulings does not depend on the direct effect of the legal act in question.[57] Interestingly, and maybe exactly for this reason, the CJEU did not discuss the absence of direct effect in its Opinion as an important element for safeguarding the procedural autonomy of EU law.[58]

On the other hand, the CETA Tribunals must interpret the CETA as an international agreement, in accordance with the VCLT and the rules and principles of international law.[59] Such interpretation would not be the same as the interpretation of the CETA in accordance with the rules and principles of EU law accorded by national or EU courts. For this reason, the CJEU highlighted in its Opinion that CETA Tribunals stand outside the EU judicial system. Accordingly, any intervention of the CJEU or domestic courts into the decision-making and rulings of CETA Tribunals in any given particular case should be correctly and consistently avoided. This is the case in the pre-award stage as no reference for preliminary ruling can be made, but also post-award since no procedure for the re-examination of the rendered award before the domestic courts is envisaged.[60] This reasoning can be contrasted with the CJEU's ruling in *Achmea*, where the absence of the CJEU's and the domestic courts' pre- and post-award control was an important consideration which led the CJEU to conclude that ISDS is incompatible with the EU legal order in an intra-EU setting.[61] The main differences between the two methods of dispute settlement are outlined in Table 9.1.

[57] See Case 111/75 *Mazzalai v Ferrovia del Renon* [1976] ECR 657, paras. 6–7 and Case C-373/95 *Maso* [1997] ECR I-4051, para. 28.

[58] The provision of Art. 30.6.1 CETA is mentioned in Opinion 1/17 (n 2) para. 40, and the Court refers to the observations made by the parties in para. 77. However, the Court does not discuss the absence of direct effect in support of the separation of the ICS from the EU legal order. The CJEU also does not anywhere in the Opinion support the argument made by the parties in the same paragraph that the CETA Tribunal and the CJEU operate within legal orders that are '*wholly* separate' (emphasis added).

[59] Opinion 1/17 (n 2) para. 122.

[60] ibid paras. 134–135. Aligned with this finding of the CJEU is also the EU's proposal for an MIC, which excludes the need for review of awards at the domestic level; instead, the review of the future MIC's awards would take place through its second tier (the appellate mechanism): see UNCITRAL, 'Possible Reform of ISDS, Submission from the EU and Its Member States' (24 January 2019) UN Doc A/CN.9/WG.III/WP.159/Add.1, paras. 30–31.

[61] See Case C-284/16 *Achmea* ECLI:EU:C:2018:158, para. 43. For consideration of the CJEU's jurisdiction regarding the ECT, see Section 8.3.1 in Chapter 8.

Table 9.1 *Comparison of investment dispute settlement according to* Achmea *and Opinion 1/17*

| | Settlement of investment disputes in accordance with *Achmea* | Settlement of investment disputes in accordance with Opinion 1/17 |
|---|---|---|
| **Applicability** | Intra-EU<br>▪ Between investors from EU Member States and Member States | Extra-EU<br>▪ Between investors from the EU/Member States and third non-EU Member States, and *vice versa* |
| **Status of EU Law** | ▪ EU law as applicable law = as part of applicable domestic law<br>▪ Exclusive jurisdiction of the CJEU to interpret EU law | ▪ EU law is treated as a matter of fact = prevailing interpretation of EU law by the CJEU to be followed by ICS tribunals<br>▪ No role for the CJEU |
| **Adjudicator** | Domestic courts in the EU + the CJEU through the preliminary ruling procedure = *within* the EU judicial system | Bilateral ICS tribunals (such as CETA Tribunals) or a Multilateral Investment Court = *outside* the EU judicial system |
| **Remedies** | ▪ Right to effective remedy before an independent tribunal (Art. 47 CFR)<br>▪ Substantive protections under primary and secondary EU law<br>▪ Legal remedies under Member States' domestic law available to both domestic and foreign investors | ▪ Right to effective remedy before an independent tribunal (Art. 47 CFR)<br>▪ Substantive protections under EU-third States IIAs<br>▪ Specific legal remedies under EU-third States IIAs available to foreign investors only |
| **Principles** | Mutual trust and sincere cooperation within the EU | Reciprocity in relations between the EU and third non-EU States |
| **Rationale** | Integration of the internal market ⟹EU integration<br>▪ Elimination of discrimination between investors from different Member States and exclusive CJEU jurisdiction to interpret EU law serve to achieve these objectives | Protection of EU investors in third States ⟹Free and fair trade<br>▪ Independence of ICS tribunals from the host State and the access of foreign investors to these tribunals serve to achieve these objectives |

The CJEU's distinction between interpretation and examination of law should be understood in this context. The rights of foreign investors, in this case Canadian investors, and the obligations of the EU and the Member States towards these investors are prescribed in the CETA. Although it forms part of the EU legal order, CETA is also an international agreement. Interpreting CETA in accordance with international law will determine the *content* of rights and obligations regarding foreign investors. If EU law appears as relevant in the proceedings – for example, if a Member State breached an obligation under CETA in order to comply with an EU law obligation – the CETA Tribunal will not engage in interpreting what was the *content* of the Member State's obligation under EU law.[62]

Instead, the Tribunal will only examine the *effect* of the Member State's compliance with that EU law obligation on the foreign investor and whether it amounts to a breach of the Member State's obligation under the CETA and international law. In doing so, the content of the Member State's EU law obligation will be determined through expert opinion provided by both parties to the proceedings. Experts on EU law will provide their opinion about the scope of the Member State's obligation and the tribunal will, in accordance with the opinion that it finds more convincing, assess the effect of the measure on the investor and whether the measure could have been avoided. A more convincing opinion does not necessarily mean the most correct and certainly not the same opinion in each and every case; however, the limited applicability of the opinion and the Tribunal's assessment in a particular case (*inter partes, res judicata*) avoids the applicability *erga omnes*, which would endanger the position of the CJEU in the EU legal order.

In light of the above discussion, the differences between the proceedings concerning investment issues before the ICS and the CJEU are summarised in Table 9.2.

[62] Moreover, whether the EU or the Member State is the respondent in such a case will be decided by the EU in accordance with Art. 8.21 CETA, while the division of financial responsibility between the EU and the Member States will be determined in accordance with Regulation (EU) 912/2014 of the EP and of the Council of 23 July 2014 establishing a framework for managing financial responsibility linked to investor-to-State dispute settlement tribunals established by international agreements to which the European Union is party [2014] OJ L257/121.

Table 9.2 *Comparison between investment proceedings before the CETA Tribunals and the CJEU*

| | CETA Tribunals | CJEU |
|---|---|---|
| **Applicable Law** | CETA + international public law: Art. 8.31.1 | EU law + international law that binds the EU: Opinion 1/17, para. 117<br>• Includes CETA provisions as part of the EU legal order: principle of consistent interpretation<br>• Excludes direct effect of CETA provisions: investors cannot invoke CETA before domestic courts (Art. 30.6) |
| **Applicability** | *Inter partes*: Art. 8.41 | *Erga omnes* |
| **Scope of the proceedings** | Examination of the effects of the EU's or the Member State's measure:<br>• Has the investor suffered damage due to the measure?<br>• What compensation should be provided to the investor (monetary damages or restitution of property)?<br>• EU law as a fact: Arts. 8.31.2; 8.28.2(b) | Examination of the legality and the effects of the EU measure:<br>• Is the measure valid under EU law?<br>• If the measure is invalid, have the conditions for non-contractual liability been fulfilled to compensate the investor?<br>• EU law as applicable law |
| **Objectives** | Non-discriminatory treatment and protection of foreign investments: Opinion 1/17, paras. 199–200 | Protection of four freedoms, in particular free movement of services and capital, and freedom of establishment |

### 9.2.3 *The Respondent before the ICS Tribunals*

As an additional safeguard of procedural autonomy, CETA provisions ensure that the Union retains the power to determine whether the challenged measure before the CETA Tribunal is an EU or a Member State measure. Accordingly, the CETA allows the EU to determine the respondent in the proceedings.[63] This is an important consideration which preserves the exclusive jurisdiction of the CJEU to give rulings on the division of powers between the EU and its Member States.[64]

In practical terms, the apportionment of responsibility entails the obligation of an investor to deliver to the EU a notice requesting a determination of the respondent prior to submitting their claim to the ICS tribunal.[65] The EU will make a determination and inform the investor as to whether the EU or the Member State is to be the respondent in the proceedings.[66] The determination will be made in accordance with the apportionment criteria and procedural requirements set out in the 2014 EU Regulation establishing a framework for managing financial responsibility arising from investment claims under international agreements to which the EU is a party.[67] As a general rule, the EU will fully bear the responsibility arising from the treatment of the EU institutions and bodies. The Member State will equally bear the responsibility arising from the treatment of its own institutions. However, if such a Member State's treatment was required by EU law, financial responsibility will be borne by the EU,[68] subject to conditions prescribed in the Regulation.

Given the sheer complexity of interactions between domestic law and EU law in a number of policy areas of shared competence and the difficulty of determining to what extent something is 'required' or not required by Union law, internal conflicts between the EU and the Member States are likely. The situations where the EU will bear the full

63 Art. 8.21 CETA.

64 Opinion 1/17 (n 2) para. 132. Cf. Opinion 2/13 ECLI:EU:C:2014:2454, paras. 224–235, where the CJEU ruled that the EU's accession to the ECHR would be contrary to EU law because, *inter alia*, the ECtHR would be deciding on the apportionment of responsibility between the EU and its Member States.

65 Art. 8.21.1 CETA. Consultations are guided by Art. 8.19 CETA, according to which the investor is to submit a request for consultation to the EU, regardless of whether the alleged breach concerns an EU or a Member State measure: Art. 8.19.7 CETA. In the internal aspect, these consultations are guided by Art. 7 of the Regulation 912/2014.

66 Art. 8.21.3 CETA.

67 Regulation 912/2014.

68 ibid Art. 3(1).

responsibility are limited to acts or measures undertaken exclusively by EU institutions. In practice, only a small number of such cases would concern foreign investors; for example, EC decisions regarding infringements of EU competition law.[69] The vast majority of cases will concern the area of shared EU and Member State competence; for example, in the area of the internal market, environmental and labour law. In these cases, what is 'required by EU law' refers only to those measures which leave no discretion or margin of appreciation for the Member States,[70] effectively excluding all directives and possibly a number of regulations too.[71] The cases of partial, if not full, Member States' financial responsibility will be more common in practice, ultimately placing the financial burden of litigation on the Member States.

Importantly for investors, EU internal disputes about financial responsibility will not have an impact on the proceedings before the ICS nor on the promptness of the final award payments. Externally, in all such cases, the EU will act as a respondent[72] and will pay any award.[73] Internally, the Commission will apportion the financial responsibility of the Member State and this decision may always be reviewed by the CJEU.[74] Therefore, the EU and effectively the CJEU have the final say in determining the responsibility for the measure challenged by the foreign investor. In the EU internal dimension, the Commission and the Member States are required to cooperate in carrying out the ICS proceedings, in accordance with the principle of sincere cooperation.[75]

### 9.2.4 *Interim Conclusion*

In light of the CETA provisions on the applicable law and the apportionment of responsibility between the EU and the Member States, the CJEU concluded that ICS tribunals would be sufficiently separated from the EU legal order. The Court accordingly found that the procedural safeguards

[69] This example is mentioned as a possibility in the Opinion 1/17 (n 2), but in the context of the effectiveness of EU law: see paras. 184–186.

[70] Art. 2(l) Regulation 912/2014.

[71] Although regulations have direct applicability, Member States might be required to introduce specific arrangements regarding fees, control, penalties and setting up of enforcement bodies, which all leave a certain amount of discretion to Member States.

[72] Art. 9(1) Regulation 912/2014.

[73] ibid Art. 18.

[74] ibid Art. 19.

[75] See in particular Arts. 6, 9, 10 and 11 Regulation 912/2014.

inserted in the CETA[76] sufficiently protect the autonomy of the CJEU from the influence of the ICS. The EU procedural autonomy protects the role of the CJEU as the highest authority for interpreting EU law and determining the meaning of EU norms. Given the *erga omnes* applicability of the CJEU's rulings, its authority is not only limited to interpretation of rules in a typical civil law setting but it is akin to the lawmaking authority of common law courts.

Comprehensive Economic and Trade Agreement Tribunals are to be fully internationalised tribunals.[77] They will operate in the sphere of the international legal order and apply international law – both CETA as an international treaty and general principles of international law. They will not be subject to any control mechanism of domestic law, either in the pre- or post-award stage, and will be insulated from domestic law. Their awards will be final and binding on the EU and Canada. The lack of control from domestic courts is to be substituted by the appellate mechanism of the CETA, which will review first instance awards on the basis of errors of law and manifest errors of fact. Applicable law in the appeal process is also international law, while any domestic law issues must be examined as facts, rendering the appeals separated from domestic law. State parties can exercise control over the ICS tribunals only through binding interpretations by the CETA Joint Committee (hereafter CETA JC); however, this is the usual mechanism of State control in international law.[78] Importantly, any decisions rendered by the CETA JC can never have retroactive effect nor direct effect on pending cases,[79] thus insulating closed and pending cases from any undue interventions. These ICS attributes indicate that CETA drafters have been inspired by the International Centre for the Settlement of Investment Disputes (ICSID) system, whose tribunals can also be characterised as fully internationalised tribunals.

[76] For substantive safeguards, see Chapter 8 on the right to regulate.

[77] For the discussion about internationalised tribunals, see H. E. Kjos, *Applicable Law in Investor–State Arbitration: The Interplay between National and International Law* (OUP 2013) 44–46, 54–56.

[78] Art. 31(3)(a) VCLT. See D. Gaukrodger, 'The Legal Framework Applicable to Joint Interpretative Agreements of Investment Treaties' (OECD Publishing 2016). See also Opinion 1/17 (n 2) para. 233.

[79] Opinion 1/17 (n 2) para. 237.

## 9.3 The Compatibility of the ICS with the Rule of Law

The CETA system, since it is established under an EU international agreement, must be compatible with the EU founding treaties and its values, objectives and principles.[80] Given its court-like nature, the compatibility of the ICS with the rule of law as one of the EU's core constitutional values is of particular importance. In its policy documents the EC has emphasised the aspiration to strengthen the rule of law in IIL as an important rationale for the ICS and a prerequisite of its legitimacy. In particular, the rule of law is linked to the public law nature of the ICS, where disputes are decided by judges appointed on a permanent basis 'without any role for the disputing parties'.[81]

The key components of the rule of law are encapsulated in the principles of equality before the law and judicial protection.[82] Unlike Articles 18 Treaty on the Functioning of the European Union (TFEU) and 21(2) CFR, which apply to internal discrimination based on the grounds of nationality, Article 20 CFR is applicable in the EU external dimension.[83] The general principle of judicial protection is embodied in Articles 6 and 13 of the European Convention on Human Rights (ECHR) and Article 47 CFR. The judiciary component of the rule of law in the EU law has been recently clarified in a number of the CJEU's judgments.[84] Article 19 Treaty on European Union (TEU) 'gives concrete expression to the value of the rule of law' by entrusting both the CJEU and domestic courts to apply EU law.[85] The essence of the rule of law includes the right of individual parties 'to challenge before the courts the legality of any decision or other national measure relating to the application to them of an EU act'.[86]

80 See Section 7.1 in Chapter 7.

81 See EC, 'Multilateral Reform of Investment Dispute Resolution, Impact Assessment', SWD (2017) 302 final, 38.

82 On the notion of the rule of law and its applicability in IIL, see Section 3.2.2 in Chapter 3.

83 To that effect, see Case C-617/10 *Åkerberg Fransson* ECLI:EU:C:2013:105, paras. 19–21; Case C-418/11 *Texdata Softwarer* ECLI:EU:C:2013:588, para. 72; Case C-682/15 *Berlioz Investment Fund* ECLI:EU:C:2017:313, para. 49; Opinion 1/17 (n 2) para. 176.

84 Case C-625/18 *AK (Independence of the Disciplinary Chamber of the Supreme Court)* ECLI:EU:C:2019:982; Case C-487/19 *WZ* ECLI:EU:C:2021:798; Joined Cases C-748/19 to C-754/19 *Prokuratura Rejonowa w Minsku Mazowieckim* ECLI:EU:C:2021:931; Case C-64/16 *Associação Sindical dos Juízes Portugueses* ECLI:EU:C:2018:117. The rule of law was first affirmed by the CJEU in 1986: Case C-294/83 *Parti écologiste "Les Verts" v European Parliament* [1986] ECR 1339.

85 *Associação Sindical dos Juízes Portugueses* (n 84) para. 32.

86 ibid para. 31.

In Opinion 1/17 the CJEU assessed the new ICS in light of Articles 20 and 47 CFR. First, the Court ascertained that differentiated investment regimes under EU law and international law do not undermine the principle of equality in the EU. Second, the CJEU established that the ICS complies with the requirements of Article 47 CFR, which guarantees effective access to justice and a remedy before an independent and impartial tribunal previously established by law.[87] Effectively thus, the CJEU concluded that the ICS complies with the-rule-of-law requirements.

### 9.3.1 *Equality before the Law in the EU*

The CJEU confirmed that the ICS complies with the requirements of equality in Article 20 CFR. In coming to this conclusion, the CJEU compared the position of third States' investors in the EU with the position of EU investors in third States. Importantly thus, the CJEU found that the situations of domestic and foreign investors in the EU are not comparable as the EU legal order offers sufficient protections for *all* investors incorporated in the EU.

The CJEU thus reaffirmed its position that intra-EU investors enjoy equal protections across the internal market, as expressed in *Achmea.* The principle of mutual trust in the EU requires that Member States comply with the right to an effective remedy before an independent tribunal guaranteed in Article 47 CFR to ensure effective judicial protection.[88] The principle of mutual trust ensures the equal level of justice across the EU. In this internal aspect, in Opinion 1/17 the CJEU reiterates its integrationist view of EU law.

However, the principle of mutual trust is not applicable in relations between the EU and non-EU States.[89] Accordingly, effective remedies before an independent tribunal and thus effective judicial protection are *not* guaranteed in third States. The status of a State as a respondent in investment proceedings raises the question 'whether its courts are effectively in a position to settle the dispute impartially, without political influence or interference or indeed the *appearance* of such influence or interference'. In third States where separation of powers and the rule of law 'may not apply consistently and reliably in practice', the lack of trust

[87] In that sense, the Belgian request asked the CJEU to ascertain whether the CETA Investment chapter was compatible with Art. 47 CFR.

[88] Opinion 1/17 (n 2) para. 128.

[89] ibid para. 129.

in the judicial system 'may discourage EU foreign investment and thus undermine the Union's objective of contributing to free and fair trade, set out in Article 3(5) TEU'.[90] For this reason, the CJEU reached the conclusion that the two categories of investors – domestic and foreign – do not find themselves in a comparable situation, and consequently cannot be treated in the same way. Only EU investors in Canada and *vice versa* find themselves in a comparable situation and, therefore, must be treated in the same way.[91]

This differentiated treatment, as an exception to the principle of the equality before the law, is permissible whenever the situations are not comparable but must be objectively justified.[92] Advocate General Bot in his Opinion explained that third States' investors in the EU would not be placed in a preferential situation compared to EU domestic investors since access to the ICS compensates for the absence of direct effect of EU IIAs.[93] On the other hand, since EU internal investors enjoy better protections under the EU legal order compared to EU investors incorporated in third non-EU States, it is important to ensure effective remedies and protection for EU investors in third States. As noted by the CJEU, the purpose of the CETA 'is to give complete confidence' to EU investors investing in Canada, and *vice versa*.[94]

When assessing equality the CJEU has given preference to some EU values and objectives, prioritising the need to protect EU investors abroad.[95] The Court was not focused on substantively more favourable treatment of external investors in the EU compared to internal EU investors, but on the judicial protection for EU investors abroad. In assuming that EU investors would not be equally protected abroad due to the absence of mutual trust in external relations, the CJEU has in effect endorsed the traditional ISDS narrative. The CJEU's immediate concern is not the protection of EU investors in countries with effective judicial system such as Canada, but the desirability of the ICS in relations with third States more generally.

[90] K. Lenaerts, 'Modernising Trade whilst Safeguarding the EU Constitutional Framework: An Insight into the Balanced Approach of Opinion 1/17' (Seminar on Opinion 1/17, Belgian Ministry of Foreign Affairs, 6 September 2019) (emphasis added).

[91] Opinion 1/17 (n 2) paras. 180–181; Opinion of AG Bot (n 3) paras. 201–203.

[92] Case C-101/12 *Schaible* ECLI:EU:C:2013:661, para. 76; Case C-540/16 *Spika and Others* ECLI:EU:C:2018:565, para. 35.

[93] Opinion 1/17, Opinion of AG Bot (n 3) para. 205.

[94] Opinion 1/17 (n 2) para. 199.

[95] Art. 3(5) TEU.

The CJEU also emphasised the necessity of the ICS in fostering trade with third States and, more generally, in achieving the objective of free and fair trade.[96] The ICS is needed to ensure a fair treatment of EU investors in third countries and accordingly their confidence to invest.[97] The justification of a new system is thus found through the endorsement of a traditional economic paradigm in international trade and investment relations.

### *9.3.2 Independence of the ICS Tribunals*

According to the CJEU, judicial independence is an 'essential' element of the rule of law, as emphasised in judgments regarding domestic courts.[98] Since the judicial nature of the ICS was acknowledged in Opinion 1/17, the first issue is whether the ICS complies with the criteria for judicial independence under EU law. Second, given that the ICS stands outside the EU judicial system, the question is whether the standard of independence that applies to domestic courts in the EU should equally apply to international courts formed under an international treaty to which the EU is a party, such as the CETA.

In Opinion 1/17, the CJEU implied that the rule-of-law standards for external courts might be lower than standards for EU courts but are sufficient as long as they satisfy the minimum standards of Article 47 CFR. The right to an effective remedy before an independent and impartial tribunal prescribed in Article 47 CFR constitutes 'a reaffirmation of the principle of effective judicial protection'[99] and a general principle of EU law.[100] In virtue of Article 52(3) CFR, Article 47 must be interpreted in light of Article 6 ECHR, while the provisions of the Charter must be interpreted in light of the case law of the European Court of Human Rights (ECtHR). Accordingly, the ECtHR case law is relevant for assessing the requirements of independence and impartiality of Article 47 CFR. Further, as a general principle, the scope of the right to effective judicial protection in Article 47 CFR is broader than the scope of Article 6 ECHR, which is restricted to 'civil rights and obligations' and criminal

[96] Opinion 1/17, Opinion of AG Bot (n 3) paras. 173–178; Opinion 1/17 (n 2) paras. 199–200.

[97] Opinion 1/17 (n 2) para. 200.

[98] *Associação Sindical dos Juízes Portugueses* (n 84).

[99] See, to that effect, judgments in Case 432/05 *Unibet* [2007] ECR I-2271, para. 37; Case C-93/12 *Agrokonsulting-04* ECLI:EU:C:2013:432, para. 59; Case C-562/13 *Centre Public d'Action Sociale d'Ottignies-Louvain-la-Neuve v Abdida* ECLI:EU:C:2014:2453, para. 45.

[100] Case C-97/91 *Borelli* [1992] ECR-I 6313.

proceedings.[101] In contrast to Article 6 ECHR, Article 47 CFR imposes obligations and restrictions on the EU both internally and externally. This is confirmed in Opinion 1/17 where the CJEU for the first time applied Article 47 CFR to a court outside the EU judicial system.

The ECtHR case law highlights four elements of judicial independence that are either external or internal: the method of judicial appointment; the term of office; the existence of guarantees against outside pressures – including in budgetary matters; and whether the judiciary *appears* independent and impartial.[102] Similarly, the notion of independence in the CJEU's case law encompasses both external and internal dimensions. The rationale of these two dimensions is related to the public perception of independence of courts. The aim is 'to dispel any reasonable doubt in the minds of individuals as to the imperviousness of that body to external factors and its neutrality with respect to the interests before it'.[103] Accordingly, 'justice must not only be done, it must also be seen to be done'.[104] The rule is strictly applied to any appearance of a bias, even when there is none. This principle[105] has been embraced in the EU's ISDS reform and emphasised by other States in United Nations Commission on International Trade Law (UNCITRAL).[106]

#### 9.3.2.1 The External Dimension of Independence

According to the settled case law of the CJEU, the concept of independence in its external dimension presupposes

> that the body concerned exercises its judicial functions wholly autonomously, without being subjected to any hierarchical constraint or subordinated to any other body and without taking orders or instructions *from any source whatsoever*, and that it is thus protected against external interventions or pressure liable to impair the independent judgment of its members and to influence their decisions.[107]

101 D. Shelton, 'Article 47' in S. Peers and others (eds), *The EU Charter of Fundamental Rights: A Commentary* (Hart 2014) 1210 (para. 47.44).

102 *Campbell and Fell v the UK* App nos 7819/77 and 7878/77 (ECtHR, 28 June 2014) para. 78 (emphasis added).

103 Case C-222/13 *TDC* ECLI:EU:C:2014:2265, para. 32 and the case law cited.

104 See, for example, *De Cubber v Belgium* App no 9186/80 (ECtHR, 26 October 1984) para. 26; *Micallef v Malta* App no 17056/06 (ECtHR, 15 October 2009) para. 98; *Oleksandr Volkov v Ukraine* App no 21722/11 (ECtHR, 9 January 2013) para. 106.

105 *R v Sussex Justices, Ex Parte McCarty* [1924] 1 KB 256, [1923] All ER Rep 233.

106 See for example, UNCITRAL, 'Possible Reform of ISDS, Submission from the EU' (12 December 2017) UN Doc A/CN.9/WG.III/WP.145, para. 27.

107 See, to that effect Case C-506/04 *Wilson* ECLI:EU:C:2006:587, para. 51, and Case C-503/15 *Margarit Panicello* ECLI:EU:C:2017:126, para. 37 and the case law cited (emphasis

Accordingly, the ICS should be fully immune from the external influence. However, the ICS is subject to the control of the CETA JC in a number of ways: through binding interpretations; the appointment and removal of tribunal members; and their remuneration. The issue is whether this influence could adversely impact the autonomy of the ICS. The CJEU concluded that it would not.

First, the CETA JC can adopt interpretations of the CETA provisions that would be binding on the ICS tribunal.[108] One of the Belgian observations was that the CETA JC can be qualified as an executive body exerting a significant influence on the ICS' adjudication and is thus likely to undermine the autonomy of the ICS. The argument of Belgium has to be placed in the context of the rule-of-law standard, which presupposes the separation of powers as the cornerstone of the independent judiciary. There lies a paradox: the separation of powers is engrained in domestic legal systems, not in the international realm, part of which is CETA. The challenge is to safeguard the independence of the new court in a regime that is ill-tailored for full independence from political influence.

In Opinion 1/17 the CJEU resolved this paradox by touting the middle ground. It embraced an international law standard of binding interpretations issued by States, while subjecting these interpretative instruments to a basic rule-of-law standard: the binding interpretations cannot have retroactive effect nor direct effect on pending cases.[109] The Court particularly noted that it is 'neither illegitimate nor unusual under international law' for the *joint wishes* of the parties to be expressed in such binding statements.[110] In other words, the Court expressly distinguished the rule of law in a domestic context where any political interference should be absolutely excluded from the international context in which such interference – as long as it is expressed through the wishes of the State Parties to an international agreement – is acceptable.[111]

added). See also Principle 12 of the Magna Carta of Judges: Council of Europe, Recommendation CM/Rec (2010)12 of the Committee of Ministers to member States on judges: independence, efficiency and responsibilities (adopted by the Committee of Ministers on 17 November 2010 at the 1098th meeting of the Ministers' Deputies).

[108] Art. 8.31.3 CETA.

[109] Opinion 1/17 (n 2) para. 237.

[110] ibid para. 233 (emphasis added).

[111] See Decision No. 2/2021 of the CETA JC of 29 January 2021 adopting a procedure for the adoption of interpretations in accordance with Articles 8.31.3 and 8.44.3(a) of CETA as an Annex to its Rules of Procedure (2021/265), Art. 5 of the Annex, which specifies that the JC may decide that an interpretation shall have binding effect from a specific date.

With respect to the correct application of EU law, the Court has set forth a safeguard: the binding interpretations are governed by Article 218 (9) TFEU. Nevertheless, such a safeguard has its limitation. The CETA JC decisions cannot be challenged *per se*, only the consent of the EU to such decisions can be subject to judicial review by the CJEU. The standing for this judicial review is restricted to the Member States, the European Parliament and the Council.[112] In practice, only a few Member States have initiated proceedings. It is rather the Council that challenges the positions adopted by the EC, and *vice versa*. While judicial control exists as a matter of principle, it remains to be seen whether review of the consistency of the CETA JC decisions with primary EU law would be effective. Further, if the ICS is under the control of the CETA JC, under which control is the CETA JC? How can a flawed interpretation of the Appellate Tribunal be corrected if a disagreement about the interpretation persists at the CETA JC level? Under these circumstances, a breach of EU law principles (for instance, compliance with the right to regulate) could not be corrected.[113] Ultimately, a potential judicial review of the EU's consent to the CETA JC decisions also compounds the risk of a disagreement between the EU and Canada in issuing binding interpretations.

Second, the CETA JC exerts other powers over the ICS, in particular regarding the appointment and the removal of its members. According to a non-binding statement by the Commission and the Council,[114] the members nominated by the EU must comply with the standards for candidates to the CJEU pursuant to Article 253(1) TFEU. However, this statement does not guarantee that Canada would comply with similar standards. Further, there is no independent judicial council intervening in the assessment of the quality of the candidates that could offset the politicisation of the appointment regime.[115] Given the significant impact that investment awards have on communities and decision-makers, a degree of democratic control in the appointment of the ICS members, in some form of parliamentary involvement, would be a welcome

[112] Art. 263 TFEU; Case C-687/15 *Commission v Council* ECLI:EU:C:2017:803.

[113] See Section 8.2.2 in Chapter 8.

[114] Council of the EU, 'CETA between Canada, of the One Part, and the EU and Its Member States, of the Other Part – Statements to the Council Minutes' (27 October 2016) 13463/1/16.

[115] Commission of Venice, *The Rule of Law Checklist* (Council of Europe 2016) para. 2.

development towards a more legitimate system.[116] *Mutatis mutandis*, these arguments about the appointment of the ICS members could be made with respect to their removal. The CJEU nevertheless noted that decisions of the CETA JC would be made by mutual consent, which is in the Court's reasoning a sufficient guarantee that both the appointment and the removal of the ICS members would not be subject to any other conditions but those laid down in CETA.[117] Bipartite and equal composition of the CETA JC is to serve as such a guarantee.[118]

Third, in its request Belgium stressed, referring to Article 6 of the European Charter on the Statute for Judges, that the remuneration of members must be fixed 'so as to shield them from pressures aimed at influencing their decisions'.[119] The German Magistrates Association also questioned whether the criteria for the financial independence of judges have been met.[120] The AG noted that the remuneration of Members of the Tribunals in CETA makes reference to the rules applicable in the field of arbitration[121] and that these rules have not yet been fully developed.[122] The Court follows that reasoning, noting that the remuneration rules permit 'the gradual establishment of a court composed of members who will be employed full time'.[123] In the long run, full-time employment, as opposed to an *ad hoc* engagement currently present in the arbitration regime, and the determination of arbitral tribunals' remuneration by the States through the CETA JC, should be sufficient to guarantee financial independence of the ICS members.

In its impact assessment, the EC has expressed the adjudicators' full-time employment with a fixed salary as a preferred, albeit more expensive, option for an MIC, which would contribute to a higher level of adjudicator independence and impartiality and thus would be more consistent with the right to an effective remedy before an independent tribunal under EU law.[124] However, the EC does not exclude the option

[116] However, there is no requirement of that sort even in the TFEU for the appointment of EU judges: Art. 253(1) TFEU. The involvement of national parliaments in the appointment of constitutional court judges is a practice adopted in several Member States.
[117] Opinion 1/17 (n 2) para. 228.
[118] Opinion 1/17, Opinion of AG Bot (n 3) para. 267.
[119] Opinion 1/17 (n 2) para. 61.
[120] German Magistrates Association, 'Opinion No 04/16 on the Establishment of an Investment Tribunal in TTIP' (February 2016).
[121] Art. 8.27.14 CETA.
[122] Opinion 1/17, Opinion of AG Bot (n 3) paras. 260–261.
[123] Opinion 1/17 (n 2) para. 231.
[124] EC, MIC Impact Assessment (n 81) 42–43.

of adjudicators commencing part-time before becoming full-time. In the interim, it is claimed that their independence would be 'effectively managed' through the code of conduct.[125] While this would be a more pragmatic option, it might also have negative consequences for the new system's legitimacy. Ultimately, if the remuneration of new adjudicators depends on the frequency of cases, stimulating the industry by increasing the caseload could be perceived as an ulterior motive of the adjudicators, similar to such public perception in the current system.[126]

#### 9.3.2.2 The Internal Dimension of Independence

The internal dimension in the CJEU's case law 'is linked to impartiality and seeks to ensure that an equal distance is maintained from the parties to the proceedings and their respective interests with regard to the subject matter of those proceedings'. It requires 'objectivity and the absence of any interest in the outcome of the proceedings apart from the strict application of the rule of law'.[127] In the context of the ICS, there are two relevant issues regarding the internal dimension: first, whether the rules of ethics ensure the equal distance of the ICS members from the interests at stake (prevention of conflicts of interest), and second, whether the composition requirements ensure the objectivity of the ICS members in balancing different interests involved in the investment disputes (the lack of disciplinary bias).

According to the ECtHR, the judiciary must be and *appear* to be independent and impartial. The impartiality should be examined from a subjective as well as an objective perspective since bias can be either manifest or apparent.[128] The subjective approach relates to 'the personal conviction of a given judge in a given case', while the objective approach determines whether they 'offered guarantees sufficient to exclude any legitimate doubt'. In this respect, any judge 'of whom there is a legitimate reason to fear a lack of impartiality must withdraw. At stake is the confidence which the courts must inspire in the public in a democratic

[125] ibid 43. For the CETA Code of Conduct, see Section 9.3.2.2.

[126] For empirical studies on this issue, see Section 3.2.2 in Chapter 3.

[127] *Wilson* (n 107) para. 52.

[128] See also International Commission of Jurists, 'International Principles on the Independence and Accountability of Judges, Lawyers and Prosecutors' (2007) Practitioner Guide No. 1, 28. If this standard is applied to the sphere of arbitration, for instance, a manifest bias would be in the case of identity between a disputing party and the arbitrator. In contrast, an apparent bias would be if the arbitrator previously advised a disputing party.

society'.[129] Accordingly, a trial is unfair not only if the judge is not impartial but also if they are not *perceived* as impartial.

The CETA endorses a narrow approach to the requirement of impartiality.[130] First, it limits the scope of potential conflict of interests to those related to the dispute at stake, mandating that tribunal members shall not take instruction from any organisation or government, or participate in the consideration of any dispute that would create a direct or indirect conflict of interest. Given that the terms 'direct or indirect conflict of interest' are not defined, Article 8.30 CETA further refers to the International Bar Association (IBA) Guidelines on Conflict of Interest in International Arbitration – a soft law instrument created for traditional ISDS.[131] The IBA Guidelines classify arbitrators' direct or indirect interest in the dispute under the 'Waivable Red List' referring to only three situations (holding shares, close family members having significant interest in the outcome, close relationship with a non-party who may be liable on the part of the unsuccessful party).[132] These situations mirror only manifest biases. The prohibition of double-hatting in CETA is also loosely worded; the text requires members of the tribunal only to '*refrain* from' acting as counsel or a party appointed expert or witness in any pending or new investments disputes under the CETA or any other international agreement.[133]

In addition to these rules, the CETA Code of Conduct envisages a duty of disclosure of any conflicting activities, whether real or apparent, in at least five years preceding the candidature.[134] While these disclosure obligations serve to indicate situations which 'could reasonably be seen as creating a direct or indirect conflict of interest, or that create or might reasonably be seen as creating an appearance of impropriety or bias', the

[129] *Piersack v Belgium* App no 8692/79 (ECtHR, 1 October 1982) para. 30. Similarly, see Art. 3.2 Council of Europe, European Charter on the Statute for Judges (1998).

[130] See Art. 8.30 CETA.

[131] Approved on 22 May 2004 by the IBA Council.

[132] See IBA Guidelines on Conflict of Interest in International Arbitration, Part II, Practical Application of the General Standards, Waivable Red List, 20 (point 2.2).

[133] Art. 8.30 CETA (emphasis added). While the provision prescribes that members of the tribunal 'shall not participate' in disputes creating a direct or indirect conflict of interest, double-hatting is worded with reference to 'shall refrain'.

[134] Art. 3(1) Code of Conduct, Decision No. 1/2021 of the Committee on Services and Investment of 29 January 2021 adopting a code of conduct for Members of the Tribunal, Members of the Appellate Tribunal and mediators.

Code does not further specify situations of such conflict or bias.[135] The reference in the main text of CETA to the IBA Guidelines, which are more specific regarding the conflict of interest, thus remains relevant. The Code also prescribes obligations for former members, requiring from them not to act as representatives of any of the disputing parties appearing before the CETA Tribunals.[136] It thus appears that they could act before ICS tribunals established under other EU agreements, which would render this provision only narrowly effective.

Additionally, and more generally, the concept of impartiality has been defined as creating a correlative duty for a judge to withdraw from a case in which they are unable to decide the matter impartially or in which it may appear to a reasonable observer that the judge is unable to decide the matter impartially.[137] This duty relates both to cases of manifest and apparent bias. In IBA Guidelines the concept of conflict of interest does include a 'reasonable third person' but limits the justifiable doubt to a very narrow list of situations which would amount to a serious conflict of interest and thus a manifest bias.[138] The IBA Guidelines also enumerate, albeit not exclusively, different situations which do not mandate a duty for an arbitrator to step down.[139] The IBA's list of situations referring to 'specific situations where no appearance and no actual conflict of interest exist from an objective point of view' would create an apparent bias in the eyes of the public if such a standard were applied to judges.[140] The CETA and the Code of Conduct are silent on the duty of withdrawal.

The IBA Guidelines adopt the traditional ISDS dichotomy between subjective test for disclosure as assessed from the perspective of disputing parties, and objective third party knowledge of the relevant facts and

[135] However, see Arts. 4(1), (2) and (3) Code of Conduct. The latter refers to 'any' obligation, benefit, relationship or financial interest – directly or indirectly that is likely to affect or *appear to affect* their independence and impartiality (emphasis added).

[136] ibid Art. 5(2).

[137] UNDOC, 'The Bangalore Principles of Judicial Conduct' (2018) ECOSOC 2006/23, Principle 2.5. A similar duty is recognised as part of the rule against bias (*nemo iudex in causa sua*) in domestic administrative law practice. See, for example, *AWG Group Ltd. & Anor v Morrison & Anor* [2006] EWCA Civ 6; *Howell & Ors v Lees Millais & Ors* [2007] EWCA Civ 720.

[138] See IBA Guidelines on Conflict of Interest in International Arbitration, Part II, Non Waivable Red List, 20.

[139] See ibid Waivable Red List, Orange List, and Green List.

[140] See the Green List, ibid 25–26. This list includes, among others, 'the arbitrator and counsel for one of the parties have previously served together as arbitrators' (4.3.2). 'The arbitrator holds an insignificant amount of shares in one of the parties or an affiliate of one of the parties which is publicly listed' (4.4.2).

circumstances for disqualification, whereby all issues that are subject of disclosure are not also grounds for disqualification.[141] In effect, from the perspective of judicial impartiality, they endorse only a narrow subjective standard of impartiality as a ground for disqualification. This is not surprising given that the IBA Guidelines have been conceived for arbitrators and not judges. They were intended to be applied in a private law dispute resolution framework, relying on the consent of the parties. The CJEU thus recognised that the rules of the IBA Guidelines must be 'adapted' to the 'realities of an investment tribunal that is primarily judicial in nature'.[142] The CETA Code of Conduct does adopt a stricter test as it refers to both actual and apparent effects on independence or impartiality; however, it is not sufficiently clear whether all issues for disclosure are also to serve as grounds for disqualification.

Finally, the CETA prescribes that tribunal members 'shall possess the qualifications required in their respective countries for the appointment to judicial office or to be jurist of recognised competence', with demonstrated expertise in public international law.[143] This requirement repositions the ICS towards the judicial sphere and public law. Nevertheless, it remains 'desirable' that future members have particular expertise in IIL, in international trade law and the resolution of disputes arising under international investment or international trade agreements.[144] The criteria set forth under the CETA therefore narrow down the general level of competence of the ICS members.[145] Given that the newly appointed members would shape the ICS case law, specialisation in trade and investment law could likely retain the disciplinary bias of the current system. Judicial techniques appropriate for adjudicating disputes involving conflicts between private and public interests are also less likely in a system that requires a narrow competence gained through arbitration.

In light of the preceding discussion, Table 9.3 summarises and compares the core features of the rule-of-law standard, as applied externally (in CETA) and internally (in the EU).

[141] See Explanation to General Standard 3, IBA Guidelines. Similar approach is also adopted in UNCITRAL's proposal of the Code of Conduct: see Art. 10(5) Draft Code of Conduct (15 September 2021) UN Doc A/CN.9/WG.III/WP.209.

[142] Opinion 1/17 (n 2) para. 243.

[143] Art. 8.27.4 CETA.

[144] ibid.

[145] German Magistrates Association (n 120).

Table 9.3 *Comparison of the rule-of-law standards in CETA and in the EU*

| Rule of Law | CETA | EU |
|---|---|---|
| **Equality before the law** | ▪ Art. 20 CFR<br>▪ Equality of treatment for foreign investments only | ▪ Art. 18 TFEU and Art. 21 (2) CFR<br>▪ No discrimination on grounds of nationality |
| **Effective legal remedy** | Specific legal remedy for foreign investors | Complete system of judicial remedies for all EU citizens |
| **Judicial review** | All EU measures against foreign investors are subject to review by ICS tribunals for their compliance with the CETA and public international law | All acts of EU institutions are subject to review by the CJEU for their compliance with the founding treaties, general principles of law and fundamental rights |
| **Independence of tribunals** | ICS tribunals are subject to an indirect control and directions by the CETA Joint Committee | EU courts are not subject to executive control nor receive directions from other EU institutions |
| **Compliance with the rule of law standard** | Complies with the rule of law in international law (compliance and implementation of international rules) | Complies with the rule of law in robust constitutional systems (full independence of judiciary that ensures compliance and implementation of EU rules) |

### 9.3.3 *Access to Justice*

The Belgian request for an opinion gave the CJEU its first opportunity to consider in detail whether an international jurisdiction established by the EU complies with the right to effective judicial protection. The CJEU confirmed that the ICS complies with the requirements of Article 47 CFR, albeit imperfectly. As discussed, throughout its Opinion the CJEU emphasised different restrictions on the rule of law imposed by CETA: the indeterminacy of the remuneration of the tribunal members; the incomplete rules on the conflict of interest of the tribunal members; the financial burden of proceedings for small and medium size enterprises (SMEs).[146]

While it is legitimate to expect that the standards for an external EU jurisdiction could be lower than the standards expected for an EU domestic court, of relevance is whether such a different standard of the rule of law is justified under EU law. It is settled case law that EU fundamental rights do not 'constitute [an] unfettered prerogative'; they may be restricted provided the restrictions 'correspond to objectives of general interest'.[147] The question is thus whether the limitations accepted by the CJEU in its Opinion 1/17 'touch the essence of the right or only one element at the periphery of the scope of protection'.[148] In other words, whether limitations placed on the rule of law in the ICS context affect the core of the rule of law or whether they are peripheral. The limitations touching the periphery are permissible if they pursue a legitimate public policy objective and are proportionate.[149]

Given that the CJEU found the ICS compatible with EU law, it considered the mentioned limitations peripheral and permissible. However, proportionality was not at the core of the Court's concern when assessing the rule of law restrictions in the CETA. The CJEU mentions proportionality only in relation to access to justice.[150] In this sense, a reference is made to the financial aspects of access to ICS tribunals rather than formally guaranteed access to the court system structured by rules of standing or procedure.[151]

It follows that if the ICS cannot entirely comply with Article 47 CFR, EU institutions must demonstrate that the rule of law restrictions are proportionate, which entails a test of suitability and necessity. The objectives to protect EU investors abroad and free and fair trade are legitimate and the establishment of the ICS is appropriate for achieving

[146] Opinion 1/17 (n 2) paras. 208–213.
[147] Joined Cases C-317/08 to C-320/08 *Alassini* [2010] ECR I-2213, para. 63.
[148] HCH Hoffman, 'Article 47' in S. Peers and others (eds), *The EU Charter of Fundamental Rights: A Commentary* (Hart 2014) 1225 (para. 47.83).
[149] ibid.
[150] Opinion 1/17 (n 2) para. 201.
[151] For example, in formal terms, access to justice would be limited if the definition of 'investment' in CETA were interpreted in a way that would make an investment made by an SME ineligible to qualify for CETA protections. On the definition of investment in CETA and EU IIAs, see Section 8.2.1.1 in Chapter 8.

these objectives, satisfying the test of suitability.[152] Further, it is settled case law that the restrictions affecting a protected interest (the rule of law) or a fundamental right (effective judicial protection) must prove to be necessary in achieving the purpose being pursued (free and fair trade; protection of EU investors abroad). If it appears that an alternative, less burdensome measure would achieve the same goal in a less restrictive manner, the contested measure does not appear to be necessary.[153] Accordingly, it must be demonstrated that the restrictions of the rule of law are not entirely unreasonable and could not be replaced by less burdensome measures.

In contrast to its case law on economic freedoms, the CJEU does not compare the restrictions placed by CETA on Article 47 CFR with measures that could appear less burdensome. The CJEU only stressed the evolving character of the mechanism under CETA.[154] Thus, the focus is placed on 'the work in progress' in order to conclude that at this stage the measures are sufficient not to impair the rule of law.[155] However, the CJEU has taken for granted that the ICS would be improved, endorsing AG Bot's position on the 'gradual establishment of a court'.[156] Finally, in the CJEU's assessment the benefits of the ICS (protection of EU investors abroad; free and fair trade) outweigh its costs (the limitations placed on the right of access to an independent and impartial tribunal). However, the CJEU did not assess how protected interests of investors may be directly or indirectly affected by such restrictions.[157] Such analysis would have addressed the concerns that the investment business community has expressed in regard to the ICS.

[152] The test of suitability concerns the appropriateness of the measure for attaining the legitimate objective, requiring a causal relationship between the measure and the objective pursued.

[153] In such case the institution must refrain from action or replace the contested restriction by a less-burdensome measure if the latter one allows the institution to achieve the same goal: X. Groussot, *General Principles of Community Law* (Europa Law Publishing 2006) 147.

[154] See, for example, Opinion 1/17 (n 2) para. 231.

[155] The CJEU has endorsed this pragmatic approach before and held that whenever EU regulatory schemes are new and complex, the EU lawmaker may lawfully make use of a step-by-step approach that at the outset imperfectly applies the principle of equal treatment: Case C-127/07 *Arcelor* [2008] ECR I-9895, paras. 60–62.

[156] See Opinion 1/17 (n 2) para. 231; Opinion of AG Bot (n 3) para. 242; see Section 9.1.1.

[157] In EU law proportionality requires the assessment of whether some legally recognised right has been unacceptably infringed: G. de Búrca, 'The Principle of Proportionality and Its Application in EC Law' (1993) *Yearbook on European Law* 125.

The CJEU's Opinion 1/17 leaves the impression that the ICS was 'saved' thanks to the promises of financial assistance for SMEs in accessing the new system.[158] In particular, it is envisaged that the CETA JC 'shall consider supplemental rules aimed at reducing the financial burden on claimants who are natural persons or SMEs'.[159] The all-inclusive character of the ICS for all foreign investors has been emphasised as an important improvement of the ICS compared to ISDS. At the same time, the ICS excludes other categories of potential litigants, such as affected local communities. This has been one of the main criticisms of ISDS by NGOs and human rights activists.[160] The approach endorsed in the CETA demonstrates a lack of ambition for the reform of the ISDS system, which is not likely to be eradicated by an MIC.[161]

## 9.4 Conclusion

The CJEU's Opinion 1/17 offers fresh perspectives on the EU constitutional order and its values and objectives in EU external trade and investment relations. First, by placing the ICS outside the EU judicial system and separating it fully from the EU legal order, the CJEU endorses a dualist approach to international law.[162] While adverse effects of the ICS' jurisdiction are 'not inconceivable' in 'exceptional circumstances', such effects are highly unlikely.[163] In any event, they were sufficiently unlikely to convince the CJEU that the ICS would not have negative effects on the autonomy of the EU legal order.

Second, the CJEU confirmed that EU trade relations with third States are subject to a new set of constitutional values underpinning the EU legal order, including the CFR. However, compared to its earlier case law,[164]

[158] Opinion 1/17 (n 2) para. 201.

[159] Art. 8.39(6) CETA. See also the commitment made by the EU in the Statement No. 36 (n 114) to take the appropriate measures to ensure the accessibility of the ICS to SMEs (co-financing SMEs' actions and technical assistance).

[160] See Section 2.2 in Chapter 2.

[161] The EU proposal envisages that the jurisdiction of the new MIC would be defined by the existing IIAs rather than by the statute of the new court: UNCITRAL, Submission from the EU and Its Member States (n 60) para. 37.

[162] See Section 4.1 in Chapter 4.

[163] Opinion 1/17 (n 2) para. 186.

[164] See Joined cases C-402/05 P and C-415/05 P *Kadi* [2008] ECR I-6381. For discussion of *Kadi* in the IIL context, see I. Damjanovic and N. de Sadeleer, 'I Would Rather Be a Respondent State before a Domestic Court in the EU than before an International Investment Tribunal' (2019) 4 *European Papers* 19, 24–28.

conditions that primarily-in-nature international law instruments must fulfil seem to be relaxed, depending on specific circumstances. In view of free and fair trade, which is conditioned upon an effective mechanism for protection of EU investors in third States, the Court concluded that the ICS in CETA complies with the general EU principle of equal treatment and the right to an independent tribunal, guaranteed under Articles 20 and 47 CFR, respectively.

Third, considering all aspects, the standard of autonomy and compliance with EU law is not the same for the courts in the EU and the ICS. While a higher standard of independence is required for domestic courts in the EU, as exemplified by the CJEU in a number of cases against Poland, the ICS must comply only with the minimum rule-of-law requirements under the CFR. On the one hand, this approach is justified by the necessity of the protection of EU investors abroad, whereby the *independence* of ICS tribunals *from the host State* is the core element for assessing independence. However, this approach confirms the primarily political nature of EU objectives, in particular free and fair trade. On the other hand, the CJEU's approach in requiring a lower rule-of-law standard is justified by the 'work-in-progress' premise of the ICS. The CJEU has accepted the restrictions on the rule of law as long as they would be attenuated in the future, including in the new MIC.

Finally, Opinion 1/17 elucidates the significance that the CJEU attaches to different EU values and objectives in external relations. The protection of EU investors abroad has the highest importance, being the *conditio sine qua non* of another priority – free and fair trade. The rule of law, while endorsed by the CJEU, evolves around 'strict observance and development of international law'.[165] The rule-of-law standard could have been taken to a new level in IIL if the vision of the EU's domestic rule-of-law standard of independence had been promoted in the ICS framework. Instead, by placing the emphasis on the protection of EU investors abroad, the CJEU has embraced a traditional ISDS narrative while nevertheless framing the new mechanism as 'judicial in nature' – albeit also 'primarily'.

Ultimately, in light of the ICS' political dimension, the CJEU has adjusted its own standards of the rule of law to the given international trade and investment context with a view to 'promote an international

[165] Art. 3(5) TEU.

system based on stronger multilateral cooperation and good global governance'.[166] This approach, which favours the promotion of EU commercial objectives over other values, has allowed the EU to maintain its assumed leadership role in the ISDS reform, but also to miss the opportunity to lead a genuine change of IIL.

[166] Art. 21(5) TEU.

# 10

# The EU and UNCITRAL

## A Multilateral Investment Court

The future of investor-State dispute settlement (ISDS) is at its historic crossroads. In this final chapter we provide an overview of the ISDS reform process in the United Nations Commission on International Trade Law (UNCITRAL) and discuss the EU proposal for a Multilateral Investment Court (MIC) in the context of this reform. First, we contextualise the current ISDS reform against earlier attempts to negotiate multilateral international investment agreements (IIAs) to explain how the current reform is different. Second, we discuss the scope of the reform and its process in the framework of UNCITRAL, particularly focusing on the identified ISDS concerns. Third, we outline the reform options that have emerged in the discussion and explain their correlation to the EU's MIC proposal. In the final part of this chapter, we consider the potential contributions that an MIC could make to the rule of law and the legitimacy of international investment law (IIL). While the negotiations are expected to be concluded by 2026, the aim of this chapter is to place the EU's proposal in the broader ISDS reform context and reflect on its external challenges in this reform process.

### 10.1 A History of Failed Multilateralism in International Investment Law, or Not?

The UNCITRAL reform is not the first attempt at multilateral reform in IIL. Some of the early multilateral attempts have been successful, but others failed.

In the IIL literature, the International Centre for the Settlement of Investment Disputes (ICSID) and its Convention are considered a 'success story'.[1] The system was conceived to address the perceived political and non-commercial risks in developing countries, which were seen as

[1] C. Baltag (ed), *ICSID Convention after 50 Years: Unsettled Issues* (Kluwer 2017).

major impediments to private investment.[2] At the time, a number of initiatives were undertaken with a view to establishing a multilateral framework for the protection of foreign investment, most notably the Abs–Shawcross Draft Convention on Investments Abroad[3] and the 1962 OECD Draft Convention on the Protection of Foreign Property.[4] Both proposals envisaged arbitration as a dispute settlement mechanism and a possibility of direct claims against host States, albeit with differences.[5] Both proposals also had substantive provisions on the treatment of investment.

Additionally, and at the same time, in the framework of the UN, the emphasis was placed on the development of different arbitral mechanisms, such as the 1958 UN Convention on the Recognition and Enforcement of Arbitral Awards and UN's International Law Commission Model Rules on Arbitral Procedure, and on accommodating the existing arbitral institutions, notably, the Permanent Court of Arbitration (PCA) and the International Chamber of Commerce (ICC), to adjudicate investment claims. However, the ICSID was also established because the commercial arbitration mechanisms were, in light of their private nature, seen as inadequate for claims against States.[6] Ultimately, both the Abs–Shawcross and OECD Draft Conventions failed; however, their substantive provisions survived through bilateral treaties, adopted first by Germany and the United States respectively.[7] On the other hand, ICSID and UNCITRAL rules, as multilateral procedural mechanisms, continued.

Globalisation sparked the idea to make another attempt to conclude an agreement that would regulate investment comprehensively. The

[2] UN ECOSOC, 'The Promotion of International Flow of Private Capital: Progress Report by the Secretary General' (26 February 1960) E/3325. See also Chapter 1.

[3] The International Convention for the Mutual Protection of Private Property Rights in Foreign Countries was prepared by the Society to Advance the Protection of Foreign Investments under the guidance of Herman Abs in 1957 and it was combined with a draft prepared under the guidance of Lord Shawcross in 1959.

[4] Draft Convention on the Protection of Foreign Property, Text with Notes and Comments (OECD Publication No. 15637, December 1962).

[5] See A. R. Parra, *The History of ICSID* (2nd ed., OUP 2018) 14–15.

[6] See ICSID, 'History of the ICSID Convention, Documents Concerning the Origin and the Formulation of the Convention on the Settlement of Investment Disputes between States and Nationals of Other States' (1968).

[7] See G. W. Haight, 'International Organisations O.E.C.D. Resolution on the Protection of Foreign Property' (1968) 2 *The International Lawyer* 326. The Abs–Shawcross Draft Convention principles were incorporated in German BITs.

Organization for Economic Cooperation and Development's (OECD's) negotiations on an (in)famous Multilateral Agreement on Investment (MAI) envisaged a very ambitious capital liberalisation agenda combining investment protection with investment liberalisation, both subjected to ISDS.[8] These negotiations ultimately collapsed in 1998 due to the French opposition and the pressure from the global citizens' movement.[9] A similar attempt was made in 2003 when a WTO-led Multilateral Investment Agreement (MIA) was proposed as part of the WTO's 'Singapore issues' agenda.[10] As the 'deep' trade multilateral agenda, it failed due to the opposition from the developing States.[11] If the multilateralisation of IIL could not succeed at the peak of globalisation, how it can succeed post-GFC?[12]

Multilateral initiatives which attempted to institutionalise substantive protections in a multilateral agreement failed. On the contrary, initiatives which focused on procedural mechanisms succeeded, except for attempts to create a court.[13] This was an important lesson for the UNCITRAL process, which is limited to procedural aspects of ISDS as more 'feasible' to be reformed.[14]

## 10.2 The ISDS Concerns and the UNCITRAL Process

The choice of the forum for deliberation about the proposed reforms was another important factor in the initiation of the global ISDS reform. The OECD was to be avoided as a forum of developed States. The United

[8] Negotiations included twenty-five OECD countries, with the participation of the EU, but the agreement would be open to accession by non-OECD countries: see W. H. Witherell, 'Developing International Rules for Foreign Investment: OECD's Multilateral Agreement on Investment' (1997) 32 *Business Economics* 38.

[9] See UNCTAD, 'Lessons from the MAI' (1999) UNCTAD/ITE/IIT/Misc.22.

[10] See J. Kurtz, 'A General Investment Agreement in the WTO? Lessons from Chapter 11 of NAFTA and the OECD Multilateral Agreement on Investment' (2002) 23 *University of Pennsylvania Journal of Economic Law* 713.

[11] See Section 2.1.1 in Chapter 2 and Section 7.2.1 in Chapter 7.

[12] Cf. S. W. Schill, *The Multilateralisation of International Investment Law* (CUP 2009), who argued that despite the lack of a formal multilateral agreement on investment, *de facto* multilateralisation has been achieved through specific clauses of bilateral IIAs.

[13] Attempts in the Hague and Paris Conferences (1899–1919) failed, *inter alia*, because States could not agree on the composition of the court: see J. M. Alvarez Zárate, 'Legitimacy Concerns of the Proposed Multilateral Investment Court: Is Democracy Possible?' (2019) South Centre Investment Policy Brief 4–6.

[14] UNGA, 'Report of the United Nations Commission on International Trade Law Fiftieth Session' (July 2017) UN Doc A/72/17, para. 257.

Nations Conference on Trade and Development (UNCTAD), as a forum considered overly sympathetic to the interests of developing States, would not be appropriate either. The Solomon's solution was found in the UNCITRAL, the UN's technical body on private aspects of international law on trade, which had recently successfully concluded the reform on transparency in investment treaty arbitration (ITA).[15]

There were several reasons why UNCITRAL was also the best possible choice for the EU's policy agenda. First, UNCITRAL allows non-Member States to participate in debates in the same manner as its full-fledged Members.[16] Accordingly, the EU may participate as an observer and propose solutions that contribute to shaping the reform debate. Second, this UNCITRAL *modus operandi* allows wide participation by other observers – NGOs, professional organisations of investors and lawyers, arbitral organisations, etc. – to raise their voice in the debate. Ultimately, inclusiveness in combination with transparency[17] should provide the required legitimacy.[18] Third, legislative work by UNCITRAL is based on consensus which does not require unanimity. The consensus is based on a widely prevailing majority and the absence of a formal objection.[19] This approach allows for broader flexibility in considering different reform options. Finally, given its legally technical orientation, UNCITRAL is the ideal forum for watering down the heated politicisation of the ISDS debate.

[15] UNCITRAL was established under the UN umbrella in 1966, as a subsidiary body of the UN General Assembly, to play an active role in reducing barriers to trade through harmonisation of national laws on international trade. In international commercial arbitration, UNCITRAL's biggest achievement are its Arbitration Rules.

[16] UNCITRAL is composed of seventy Members but non-Members are invited to participate in different UNCITRAL working groups as observers. The mandate of the Members is six years, and half of Members are elected every three years by the UN General Assembly.

[17] Transparency has been fully embraced with all official information publicly available through the UNCITRAL's website: UNCITRAL, 'Working Group III: ISDS Reform'.

[18] This was one of the important lessons from the MAI experience: see UNCTAD (n 9) 29. See also the remark of the UNCITRAL Commission noting suitability of the UNCITRAL as a multilateral, inclusive and transparent forum: UNGA Report 2017 (n 14) para. 258.

[19] In the case of a formal objection, a vote is triggered. While extremely rare, the vote took place for the election of the WG III chairperson Shane Spelliscy from Canada, demonstrating highly politicised context of the ISDS reform. See UNCITRAL, 'Report of Working Group III (ISDS Reform) on the Work of Its Thirty-Fourth Session (Vienna, 27 November – 1 December 2017)' (19 December 2017) UN Doc A/CN.9/930/Rev.1, paras. 11–14. Observers cannot object and have no voting rights.

The UNCITRAL's Secretariat has played an important role in setting the reform's agenda and direction even before the official start of the reform.[20]

In July 2017, the UNCITRAL agreed by consensus that work on the possible ISDS reform should take place. The Commission gave a broad mandate to its Working Group (WG) III to undertake this work in three phases, with distinct tasks: to identify issues and concerns (Phase I); to consider accordingly whether the reform is desirable (Phase II) and in the affirmative; to develop recommendations (Phase III). Given the connection of the ISDS to a number of policy issues, it was made clear that the reform would be State-led.[21] This was also to indicate that these negotiations would be different to usually apolitical and technical discussions led by experts in UNCITRAL.

Working Group III relatively quickly identified major concerns to be addressed by the reform:[22] (1) concerns pertaining to consistency, coherence, predictability and correctness of arbitral awards;[23] (2) concerns pertaining to arbitrators and decision makers;[24] (3) cost and duration of ISDS proceedings;[25] and (4) third-party funding.[26] It was reiterated that the mandate of WG III requires focus on procedural aspects of ISDS while 'taking due note of the interaction with underlying substantive standards' and concerns, such as means other than arbitration to resolve investment disputes and dispute prevention; exhaustion of local remedies; third-party participation; counterclaims; regulatory chill; and

[20] The Secretariat conducted a study on whether the Mauritius Convention on Transparency could provide a useful model for ISDS reforms, following which the UNITRAL's Commission requested from the Secretariat a broad consultation with States and regional economic integration organisations: see UNGA, 'Report of the United Nations Commission on International Trade Law Forty-Eighth Session' (July 2015) UN Doc A/70/17, para. 268, and UNCITRAL Secretariat, 'Possible Future Work in the Field of Dispute Settlement: Reforms of ISDS' (20 April 2017) UN Doc A/CN.9/917.

[21] UNGA Report 2017 (n 14) paras. 250, 264.

[22] See UNCITRAL Secretariat, 'Possible Reform of ISDS' (30 July 2019) UN Doc A/CN.9/WG.III/WP.166, paras. 4–8.

[23] UNCITRAL Secretariat, 'Possible Reform of ISDS: Consistency and Related Matters' (28 August 2018) UN Doc A/CN.9/WG.III/WP.150.

[24] UNCITRAL Secretariat, 'Possible Reform of ISDS, Ensuring Independence and Impartiality on the Part of Arbitrators and Decision Makers in ISDS' (30 August 2018) UN Doc A/CN.9/WG.III/WP.151, and 'Possible Reform of ISDS, Arbitrators and Decision Makers: Appointment Mechanisms and Related Issues' (30 August 2018) UN Doc A/CN.9/WG.III/WP.152.

[25] UNCITRAL Secretariat, 'Possible Reform of ISDS: Cost and Duration' (31 August 2018) A/CN.9/WG.III/WP.153.

[26] UNCITRAL Secretariat, 'Possible Reform of ISDS, Third-Party Funding' (24 January 2019) A/CN.9/WG.III/WP.157.

calculation of damages. While these cross-cutting issues have not been framed as specific additional concerns, it was agreed that any solutions developed by WG III should be flexible enough to incorporate them.[27]

In light of the broad discretion given to the WG III in discharging its mandate, the chairperson and the Secretariat have had an important role in framing the issues and setting the direction of the deliberations. From the very start, the emphasis has been placed on separation of 'facts' (legal, objective) from 'perceptions' (political, subjective), in which facts have been supported by 'constructive contributions' from the experts in the field.[28] However, input from informal Academic Forum and Practitioners' Group has been particularly criticised by public interest groups given the inherent interest of these stakeholders in retaining the ISDS' status quo.[29]

The reform entered into Phase III in April 2019, with a number of reform options in consideration. The debate was highly politicised in its early stage; however, the focus has been shifting from 'big questions' (e.g. do we need a structural reform/a new court?) to more technical non-structural questions (code of conduct, selection procedures for adjudicators, the scope of appeal, etc.).[30] With a range of technical issues and online/hybrid negotiations during the Covid-19 pandemic, the process has been structured through the main WG sessions every six months and more regular intersessional work (meetings, drafting groups and other initiatives), challenging both the inclusiveness and transparency of the process.[31] Additionally, the cross-cutting issues have been absent or only marginally addressed in the Secretariat's working papers, deliberations and intersessional work. The already limited initial potential of the reform has thus been further reduced to largely technical improvements and codification within the existing regime.

The work plan to implement the ISDS reform project envisages the conclusion of the process by the end of 2025. In the meantime, the process will move forward with different reform options, which are to be presented to the Commission for the 'approval in principle' in a

[27] See UNCITRAL, 'Report of Working Group III (ISDS Reform) on the Work of Its Thirty-Seventh Session (New York, 1–5 April 2019)' (9 April 2019) A/CN.9/970, paras. 26–40.

[28] See ibid para. 42.

[29] See, for example, A. Beunder and J. Mast, 'As the World Meets to Discuss ISDS, Many Fear Meaningless Reforms' (*Transnational Institute* 4 April 2019).

[30] See, for example, UNCITRAL, 'Report of Working Group III (ISDS Reform) on the Work of Its Thirty-Eighth Session' (28 January 2020) UN Doc A/CN.9/1004, and its addendums.

[31] See CCSI, IIED and IISD Workplan Submission (1 March 2021).

staggered manner.[32] The feasibility of the proposed plan, meaningful debates on a large number of issues and impactful reform outcomes within the proposed time framework, albeit aspirational remain rather uncertain.

## 10.3 The MIC and the Main Reform Options

In the preparation for the reform, the consultation process of the UNCITRAL Secretariat indicated three core possible options for the reform: (1) adjustments to the current ISDS regime; (2) the establishment of a stand-alone appellate body; and (3) the establishment of an international investment court.[33] At the time of the UNCITRAL's decision to undertake the reform, the report noted that 'a significant number of references' about a possible permanent MIC were made. It was said that this option 'should be given due consideration' and that such a court 'might be a built-in appellate mechanism'. The report also mentioned suggestions to establish regional courts.[34]

The UNCITRAL's mandate to WG III indicated that reform solutions would be designed by taking into account the ongoing work of relevant international organisations and 'with a view to allowing each State the choice of whether and to what extent it wished to adopt the relevant solution(s)'.[35] Already then, doubts were expressed about the feasibility of the reform, which does not tackle substantive investment protections, and the need for diversified approaches, which would allow States to adopt those that best suit their particular legal, political and economic circumstances.[36] In light of these remarks, *flexibility* and *consensus* have

[32] UNCITRAL Secretariat, 'Workplan to Implement ISDS Reform and Resource Requirements' (17 March 2021), UN Doc A/CN.9/WG.III/WP.206.

[33] The Secretariat's note in fact indicates two main options for the reform: (1) adjustments to the current ISDS regime, which could include a stand-alone appellate body as a sub-option; and (2) setting up an international investment court, with two sub-options – either as a two-tier adjudicative system, or a one-tier court without an appeal. See UNCITRAL Secretariat, Possible future work in the field of dispute settlement (n 20) 5–14. In the later discussion, the Secretariat's first option crystallised as two separate options since not all States who support the improvements of the current regime also support the establishment of a stand-alone appellate body: see, for example, UNCITRAL Secretariat, 'Possible Reform of Investor-State Dispute Settlement (ISDS), Submission from the Governments of Chile, Israel, Japan, Mexico and Peru' (2 October 2019) UN Doc A/CN.9/WG.III/WP.182.

[34] UNGA Report 2017 (n 14) para. 255.

[35] ibid para. 264.

[36] ibid para. 244.

been the guiding principles of the reform. In addition, work on all reform options in parallel was also adopted as a middle-ground solution.[37]

In these negotiations the interests of the EU are represented by the European Commission (EC), which has received a mandate from the EU Member States to negotiate the establishment of an MIC. In accordance with the principle of sincere cooperation, the EU and its Member States should speak with a coordinated voice throughout the negotiations, and their vision also echoes the UNCITRAL's principles for conducting negotiations (inclusiveness of States, international organisations and civil society; government-led; consensus based; transparent).[38] In the event of a vote, Member States which are Members of the UNCITRAL should vote in accordance with the agreed EU positions. The EU's strategy to create one court for all its external agreements has thus been carefully designed to take advantage of the UNCITRAL as a negotiating forum for this reform.

The proposal for a 'standing mechanism' submitted by the EU to UNCITRAL provides a 'systemic response' to the UNCITRAL's concerns and accommodates the demand for flexibility. It is envisaged that an MIC would combine *judicial independence* with an *appellate mechanism.*[39] It should further ensure the integration of other mechanisms, such as amicable dispute resolution, and avenues for a '*dialogue*' between the treaty parties, which should guarantee long-term State control over the interpretation of IIAs.[40] The 'systemic' and 'alternative' lenses approach to the concerns identified by UNCITRAL should appease those States whose vision of ISDS reform goes beyond the UNCITRAL's mandate. In particular, some strong players of the South have emphasised the need for a genuine systemic reform, which would not 'divorce' procedural from substantive concerns, thus supporting a sustainable-development oriented reform.[41]

[37] See UNCITRAL Secretariat, 'Possible Reform of ISDS' (30 July 2019) UN Doc A/CN.9/WG.III/WP.166.

[38] Council of the EU, 'Negotiating Directives for a Convention Establishing a Multilateral Court for the Settlement of Investment Disputes' (20 March 2018) 12981/17 ADD 1 DCL 1, paras. 1–4. The same principles are reflected in the 'Possible work plan for Working Group III', proposed as part of the EU submission: see UNCITRAL, 'Possible Reform of ISDS, Submission from the EU and Its Member States' (24 January 2019) UN Doc A/CN.9/WG.III/WP.159/Add.1.

[39] See the EU submission to UNCITRAL paras. 40–56; EU Negotiating Mandate, paras. 10–11; 13–15.

[40] EU Negotiating Mandate, para. 9; EU submission to UNCITRAL, para. 26.

[41] See UNCITRAL, 'Possible Reform of ISDS, Submission from the Government of South Africa' (17 July 2019) UN Doc A/CN.9/WG.III/WP.176. Further, Brazil has continuously

Since States have different preferences, the jurisdiction of the MIC would be open to all existing IIAs, allow opt-ins for future agreements[42] and accommodate more progressive bilateral reforms of IIAs.[43] This is particularly important for the EU in the context of numerous Member States' extra-EU bilateral investment treaties (BITs) and new EU IIAs. Flexibility should be ensured by exploring whether the MIC could be utilised in cases when only the respondent State is a party to it.[44] Moreover, given its standing nature, the 'open architecture' of a future MIC would provide flexibility even for those countries that only support the establishment of an appellate mechanism.[45] Importantly, in this category is China, who supports a permanent appellate mechanism but wishes to retain party autonomy in the appointment of adjudicators engrained in the current arbitration mechanism.[46] In the big picture, the MIC would be part of a multilateral convention that will reform ISDS. This arrangement should thus offer sufficient flexibility to those States that support the ISDS reform within the existing arbitration framework and through a less ambitious 'suite approach'. They envisage a Multilateral Investment Reform Agreement with different opt-in options, which could be adopted individually, in combination or in their entirety as a package. According to the States that advocate it, the 'suite' approach would offer 'maximum flexibility'.[47] Figure 10.1 contextualises the EU's proposal vis-à-vis the core aspects of the broader UNCITRAL reform debate.

The EU internal negotiating mandate for an MIC corresponds to the demands of the UNCITRAL's mandate for the ISDS reform. In the same

promoted ADR (through an Ombudsperson and State-to-State consultations) as their preferrable option: See UNCITRAL, 'Possible Reform of ISDS, Submission from the Government of Brazil' (11 June 2019) UN Doc A/CN.9/WG.III/WP.171. For a more detailed analysis on the polarisation between the States in UNCITRAL, see A. Roberts, 'Incremental, Systemic and Paradigmatic Reform of Investor–State Arbitration' (2018) 112 *American Journal of International Law* 410.

42 EU Negotiating Mandate (n 38) paras. 6–7; EU submission to UNCITRAL (n 38) paras. 35–36.

43 EU Negotiating Mandate (n 38) para. 12; EU submission to UNCITRAL (n 38) para. 37.

44 EU Negotiating Mandate (n 38) para. 8; EU submission to UNCITRAL (n 38) para. 35.

45 EU submission to UNCITRAL (n 38) para. 39.

46 See UNCITRAL, 'Possible Reform of ISDS, Submission from the Government of China' (19 July 2019) UN Doc A/CN.9/WG.III/WP.177. This arrangement should also allow China to utilise its new network of arbitral institutions: see Section 2.1.1 in Chapter 2.

47 See UNCITRAL, 'Submission from the Governments of Chile, Israel and Japan' (15 March 2019) UN Doc A/CN.9/WG.III/WP.163, and 'Possible Reform of ISDS, Submission from the Governments of Chile, Israel, Japan, Mexico and Peru' (2 October 2019) A/CN.9/WG.III/WP.182.

**Figure 10.1** The EU proposal for a Multilateral Investment Court in perspective with other core reform proposals in UNCITRAL

manner, the EU solution corresponds to the identified UNCITRAL concerns. The EU proposal for an MIC has been promoted as the only solution that addresses all concerns identified in the UNCITRAL.[48] Moreover, following the Court of Justice of the European Union's (CJEU's) Opinion 1/17, the EU has been promoting its MIC not only as a solution that would address all procedural concerns but that would also have positive effects on ensuring the right to regulate as a substantive standard.[49] As the reform has moved towards more specific deliberations on particular issues, the EU proposal for an MIC has also been establishing itself as distinct from other options, in particular regarding independence of judges with full-time office in a permanent body, as opposed to *ad hoc* arbitrators.[50]

At the same time, the EU proposal for an open architecture would ensure flexibility, the continuation of arbitration and fulfilment of the

[48] EU submission to UNCITRAL (n 38) para. 57.

[49] See Section 8.2.2 in Chapter 8.

[50] See UNCITRAL Secretariat, 'Draft Codes of Conduct and Commentary' (23 November 2022) UN Doc A/CN.9/WG.III/WP.223, with a separate Code for Judges and specific provisions. See in particular Arts. 4, 7, 9 and 12 of the proposed Codes.

mandate of WG III in a multilateral instrument on ISDS reform.[51] Such instrument would provide a framework for the implementation of various reform options, in the form of a Framework Convention on ISDS reform with core provisions binding upon all States Parties, and specific provisions in *optional* annexes and/or protocols, one of which would be an MIC. The scope of application of any new legal instruments regarding the existing and future investment agreements would be carefully considered to ensure consistency between many overlapping instruments. Alternatively, a multilateral institution for investment dispute settlement could be set up as an umbrella institution, allowing States to choose between different modes of dispute settlement, which would be administered by that institution (e.g. reformed arbitration, State-to-State arbitration, MIC with an appellate mechanism, domestic remedies), although it would remain to be clarified how this new institution would relate to the existing institutions in the field (e.g. ICSID and PCA). Inspiration for the solutions could be found in the United Nations Convention on the Law of the Sea (UNCLOS), while a possible model for the application of an MIC (and other reform options) to the existing IIAs could be the Mauritius Convention on Transparency or the OECD Multilateral Convention to Implement Tax Treaty Related Measures to Prevent Base Erosion and Profit Sharing (MLI). Despite many yet unresolved questions and ongoing deliberations, this marriage of convenience between the EU and UNCITRAL continues as seemingly flawless, with flexibility in mind on both sides.

## 10.4 MIC between a Unilateral Approach and a Multilateral Forum

The EU proposal for an MIC is an expression of the EU's aspiration to promote multilateral solutions to common IIL problems through the ISDS reform in UNCITRAL. It is proposed to third States with care not to undermine the success of either the EU's own policy agenda or the ongoing multilateral reform. The establishment of an MIC would require the preparation and adoption of a Statute, detailed rules on procedural matters and a commitment of financial resources. Various models are only under initial consideration and subject to negotiations in

[51] See UNCITRAL Secretariat, 'Possible Reform of ISDS, Multilateral Instrument on ISDS Reform' (16 January 2020) UN Doc A/CN.9/WG.III/WP.194 and (22 July 2022) UN Doc A/CN.9/WG.III/WP.221.

UNCITRAL.[52] While details remain unknown, what at this stage could be concluded about the realities of establishing a new court that mirrors the EU vision of modernised IIL and its contribution to the development of international law?

### *10.4.1 MIC and the Procedural Rule of Law*

The EU proposal for the establishment of an international court for the settlement of investment disputes is a contribution to the international rule of law, despite its main procedural focus. From the EU perspective, it is the most comprehensive and coherent solution for its external regulation (the EU's IIAs and many Member States' extra-EU BITs), likely to increase the consistency, coherence and predictability of the case law stemming from these agreements. In light of this, the EU has suggested that the court should have the widest possible jurisdiction – adjudicating over many international investment instruments – both investor-to-State and State-to-State, focusing on the consent to the jurisdiction of an MIC, rather than its form. Further, its members should be appointed for 'long and staggered terms', which should contribute to the creation of 'continuous collegiality and institutional memory necessary to retain expertise and develop a more consistent case law'.[53]

This EU proposal subjects international investment dispute settlement to a set of constitutional rights and principles. In particular, the EU must guarantee to its investors the right of access to an independent court in accordance with the EU Charter of Fundamental Rights (CFR). By subjecting the EU to this obligation, a new MIC must be independent and allow equal access to all potential claimants as long as the EU is a party to the MIC. Through the establishment of an MIC, the EU will expand the reach of its constitutional rights and obligations into international law.

[52] See for example, UNCITRAL, 'Cost and Financing of a Permanent Multilateral Body', Outline of the working paper, draft for comments only (December 2021), which is based on the assumptions that a permanent multilateral body with a first and an appellate instance would be established under the auspices of the UN without links to an existing body. The calculation assumes a scenario in which this body would be established by a treaty conference in 2027, and become operational as of 2028, with expected workload of ten cases at first instance and three appellate cases per year in the initial period (2028–2032), employing seven full-time appellate body members and fifteen part-time first instance court members.

[53] See Initial draft on standing multilateral mechanism: the selection and appointment of ISDS tribunal members and related matters, Comments from the EU and Its Member States (November 2021) comments on draft provisions 2 and 9(a).

The EU reform of IIL thus places the issues of independence and access to justice into the limelight of the global IIL reform. Access to justice should be ensured by removing financial barriers to accessing the current ISDS system and making justice before the new court affordable to *all* foreign investors.[54] This should make the investment dispute settlement system fairer for the category of foreign investors as a whole – regardless of their corporate power. Further, the EU vision of independence reduces the autonomy of private parties as the core element of the traditional ISDS system while seeking to guarantee the independence of the new MIC *from the host State*, in line with the established ISDS narrative. For example, the EU has emphasised its approach to independence by advocating for longer, non-renewable terms, and full-time employment of judges, even if that means starting by a smaller number of tribunal members and their gradual increase.[55] Their nomination should come not only from the State Parties to the MIC but also through open and transparent calls for direct applications, to discourage politicisation.[56] Candidates should be vetted through an independent selection panel and appointed by a Committee of the Parties establishing the MIC, with separate processes for the first instance and appellate level members.[57] In such a system, reminiscences of party autonomy through *ad hoc* judges would also not have a place.[58]

In limiting party autonomy, this EU vision of the rule of law in the form of a court goes to the heart of arbitration as the defining element of ISDS. It shifts the private law character of ITA towards a public law paradigm in IIL. Courts must be independent from the parties and their independence is a precondition for delivering natural justice. The work of the court should be further subject to more public scrutiny. The EU model changes the narrative of ISDS from a secretive transnational private justice system into an international court specialised for investment disputes. No other reform option goes as far in an attempt to embrace the transparency and independence of proceedings.

[54] This will likely depend on the modes of financing the future court and contributions from constituting member States. For different options, see UNCITRAL, 'Cost and financing of a permanent multilateral body' (n 52) paras. 35–52.

[55] Comments from the EU and Its Member States (n 53), comments on draft provision 4(1) and 9(a).

[56] ibid, comments on draft provision 6.

[57] ibid, comments on draft provisions 3, 7 and 8.

[58] ibid, comments on draft provision 5.

### *10.4.2 MIC and Substantive Law*

However, this attempt of a metamorphosis is not as systemic as it has been presented by the EU. The new MIC would rely on the underlying substantive rules of the existing IIAs. How will the new court interpret these rules? Will it adopt the interpretative approach of the tribunals and interpretations of standards currently existent in IIL? How will it strike the balance between private and public interests? In doing so, will it be more inclined to adopt judicial principles and methods of interpretation of the CJEU and standards of EU law? Will it continue making large awards of compensation, taking into account speculative future profits? How will it treat other international agreements – in line with the dominant interpretative approaches of the specialised international courts (labour, environmental, human rights, the UNCLOS, the CJEU), or would it continue to interpret international law through the paradigm of the law of contracts rather than public international law?

The difficulty of the continuous application of the existing substantive rules by the new court is the underlying private law paradigm of IIAs. The arbitration agreement, which is concluded on the basis of the offer to arbitrate extended by States to investors in IIAs, would remain the basis of claims submitted to a new international court. How will these underlying arbitration agreements restrain the performance of the functions of the new MIC? Will the MIC adopt the principle *iura novit curia*? If so, how will that principle interact with the limitations of the mandate defined in the arbitration agreement? Will the procedures before the court substantially differ from the adversarial type of procedures currently adopted in arbitration? If that is not the case, what is the added value for the States?

While the EU proposes a new multilateral institutional framework, the normative attributes of that new framework are 'relegated' to a bilateral level of IIAs. It is left to individual States and bilateral negotiations to determine the substantive rules that would be applied by the new MIC, such as: what are the specific rights and duties of investors? When the access to ISDS would be granted to investors, what kinds of defences could States use against investors' claims? Would counterclaims be possible? Would local communities adversely affected by foreign investment also have some kind of access to dispute resolution? The EU proposal for an MIC thus avoids the core difficult issues and 'devolves' their resolution from the multilateral to a bilateral level of IIAs.

However, a number of normative issues could still be addressed in defining the scope of jurisdiction and the relevant procedures before the

MIC. For example, the Statute could adopt *sui generis* definitions of 'investor' and 'investment' which could address controversial issues of reflective loss, corporate restructuring and the abuse of process.[59] The ICSID Convention adopts such definitions, and these conditions must be fulfilled alongside the underlying IIA requirements. A number of precisely defined public interest carve-outs could also be prescribed in order to better protect States' right to regulate. Further, procedures before the new MIC could be inspired by the International Court of Justice (ICJ) rather than the arbitration approach in order to reduce the complexity and thus also cost and duration.

In light of the cross-cutting nature of investment, it would be important that the new court provides a sufficient margin of appreciation for domestic public policy decisions. This approach could assist in distinguishing between good faith practices of States and bad faith conduct of investors, and *vice versa*. It could further ensure that international law does not amount to a race to the top in determining the appropriate investment standards, compared to those standards in developed legal systems. Additionally, insufficient regard for domestic public policy can produce invasive effects of international law on domestic legal systems and thus undermine the legitimacy of international institutions. Ultimately, a different approach to domestic public policy would change the 'parallel justice' nature of the current ISDS. In response to the challenges of climate change, the regulatory activity of States has intensified, and this trend is likely to continue. Accordingly, an MIC should be able to correctly balance obligations of States towards investors with their other obligations under international law, in particular those concerning sustainable development.

An MIC should embrace a wide spectrum of values and cultures represented in domestic law and other areas of international law, especially given the complex regulatory context in which investment takes place. The composition of the new court could address this issue in a way similar to that in which the composition of domestic constitutional courts is addressed – by a careful balance between different political beliefs and values that can ensure the long-term prevalence of law over politics. This should involve the appointment of specialists from different fields that interact with investment – international law generalists,

[59] However, the EU does not envisage a separate investment test, and a MIC would thus apply a definition of investment in the applicable BIT in any given case: see Comments from the EU and Its Member States (n 53), comments on draft provision 2.

environmentalists, human rights experts, constitutional lawyers, alongside the trade and investment law specialists. A new court staffed only by judges with the same investment and trade background as the legal professionals in the current ISDS system cannot bring a substantive change.

While a new MIC would be a contribution to the international rule of law, the exact extent of its normative contribution will depend on the Statute of the new court, its members and its procedures. The Committee of the Parties establishing the MIC will likely be responsible for carrying out different functions, including the adoption of procedures, amendments to the Statute and the appointment of adjudicators.[60] The EU has proposed that its decisions should be adopted by qualified majority, and that only those States that accept the court's jurisdiction should have a possibility to select its members.[61] Given the EU's leading role in the creation of the court, this could likely give the EU and its Member States more power in acting as a bloc and thus also more leeway in setting the direction for the functioning of a new court, even if the court is eventually established under the auspices of the UN.

### *10.4.3 MIC and Legitimacy*

By enhancing procedural rule of law, the new court could likely enhance throughput legitimacy. With increased coherence and predictability, at least in the EU external relations field, more legally sound norms in MIC judgments could also achieve more output legitimacy. Internally, greater involvement of civil society and Member States' parliaments in the discussions of EU IIAs could increase input legitimacy. Figure 10.2 depicts the possible effects of the new MIC on legitimacy and the rule of law in the EU context.

However, will this theoretical normative approach be sufficient for the acceptance of the system by a variety of stakeholders? Despite the technicality of legitimacy criteria, the more a system reflects a society's

[60] UNCITRAL Secretariat, 'Possible Reform of ISDS, Standing Multilateral Mechanism: Selection and Appointment of ISDS Tribunal Members and Related Matters', initial draft (November 2021) draft provision 3.

[61] Comments from the EU and its Member States (n 53), comments on the draft provision 3; and last sentence of para. 26. While diversity has been emphasised as the main principle, the EU does not see nationality as an important element: ibid, comments on the draft provision 4(1). This approach does favour competence and independence but it could also be more favourable to the EU.

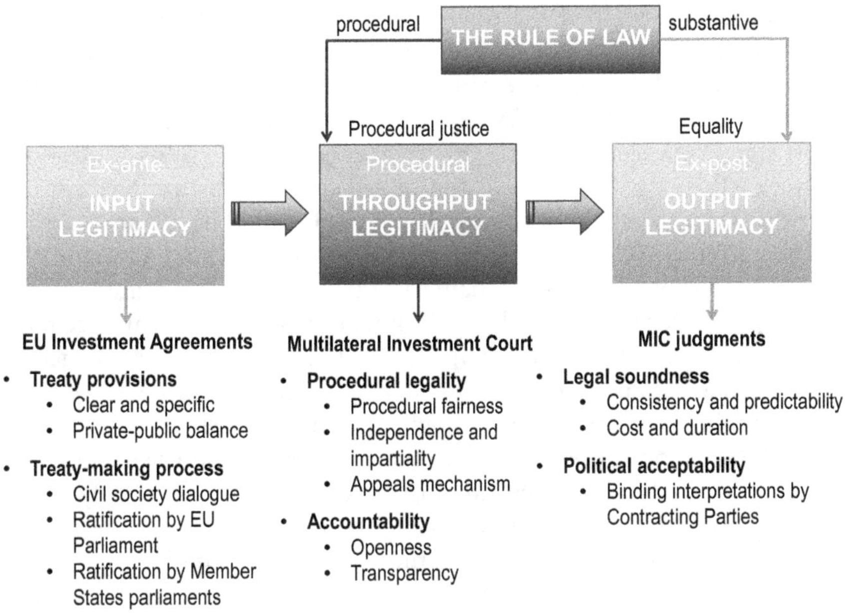


**Figure 10.2** The Multilateral Investment Court in the framework of legitimacy and the rule of law in the EU context

values the more likely it is that such a system would be accepted as authoritative.[62] For the time being, and for different reasons, the MIC largely remains 'an unwanted court' for the majority of the different stakeholders, both within and outside the EU.

The EU's main trump card for increasing legitimacy is the promise of independence for an MIC and greater access to justice. A new MIC should be a court that will deliver 'justice for all'. The financial openness of the new court to all foreign investors is aimed at ensuring the support of the small business sector that has been excluded from the benefits of ISDS.[63] This argument should also attract the support of the political centre and it can be used as leverage in opposing the radical left, which detests the power of big capital and has expressed the strongest opposition to ISDS.

[62] See Section 3.1 in Chapter 3.

[63] In particular, the EU Negotiating Mandate for a MIC (n 38) emphasises the need for provisions that will ensure the access of small and medium-sized enterprises and natural persons to the MIC: para. 17.

However, the logic of the rule of law in the form of an independent court, which should restore the legitimacy of ISDS,[64] has not convinced the sceptical public. The core concern for the general public remains the legacy of the current ISDS system in any new ISDS arrangement. The most significant element of the EU reform is the removal of arbitration; however, this could be futile if the new court only institutionalises the current system's rules and culture. If it does, it would be a worse version of the current ISDS. With increased public focus on climate change, the misalignment between the outdated *values* of the ISDS regime – which *inter alia* protects fossil fuels, and climate objectives – which require accelerated phase-out of fossil fuels, has become the central concern. A court that does not address climate justice will not be seen as working in the public interest, no matter how independent it is.

At the same time, the EU must convince investors that its court model, eliminating party appointed adjudicators, would be sufficiently independent from the States' politics (including on issues concerning public interest) and that it would deliver enforceable judgments.[65] The success of the future court will depend on investor confidence. Due to the underlying arbitration agreement in an investment instrument, without investors' claims, the court as a business model could fail. As long as investors have recourse to arbitration through restructuring, it is unlikely that they would favour a court.[66]

Externally, the very typically EU style of thinking about a court as a solution is unlikely to be shared by those with a more pragmatic mindset in other legal systems; in particular, those in the common law family that have in many ways moved towards privatisation of justice in domestic commercial disputes. For the United States, international institutions, and courts in particular, have always been met with scepticism. Similar

[64] See, for example, the submission from the EU emphasising the perception of justice dependant on the perception of independence of the adjudicators: UNCITRAL, 'Possible Reform of ISDS, Submission from the EU' (12 December 2017) UN Doc A/CN.9/WG.III/WP.145, para. 27.

[65] Indeed, enforcement of future MIC judgments could pose a difficulty and it remains to be considered whether the possible MIC would establish its own specific enforcement regime under its founding mechanism, and, if so, how decisions would be enforced with respect to non-participating States of such a mechanism: see UNCITRAL, Report of Working Group III, January 2020 (n 30) Addendum IV.

[66] See Section 3.3.3 in Chapter 3. See also survey by Queen Mary University of London, finding that on balance, respondent investors do not favour the creation of a MIC, and believe that the MIC would negatively affect the confidence of investors in the ISDS system: '2020 QMUL-CCIAG Survey: Investors' Perceptions of ISDS' (May 2020).

sentiment can be found among all great powers that are reluctant to submit themselves to the power of international law. The unusual alliances in the UNCITRAL are a testament to this – with the United States, Russia, Iran and Israel united in opposition to the 'EU court'. The success of the EU project will largely depend on its ability to convince the developing States, which have so far been on the 'losing' side of ISDS, about the salience of the new EU vision.[67]

### *10.4.4 MIC and Fragmentation*

As contradictory as it sounds, fragmentation is, and is likely to remain for some time, the only common denominator in IIL. Since IIL has not been redesigned in its substance, fragmentation will continue due to numerous IIAs. The procedural reform in UNCITRAL, however, aims at some level of harmonisation. The proposed MIC could possibly incorporate into its own framework other procedural reforms envisaged in UNCITRAL, including means to address frivolous claims, multiple proceedings, reflective loss, counterclaims, security for costs, third-party funding and transparency rules.[68] At the same time, the EU has been putting forward proposals that reflect its practice in bilateral EU IIAs, either with respect to the assignment of cases, appointment of members or conditions of their service.[69] However, fragmentation could be further increased if the new court develops its own set of standards through the interpretation of new EU IIAs. On the other hand, if the MIC does not develop its own standards, one might ask (just as China did albeit for different reasons), what would be the added value of the court of first instance? An appellate body could more practically resolve the issues of correctness, consistency and predictability if the new system only embraces the dominant investment law paradigm of the current ISDS system.

The EU has proposed an MIC as one of the options for ISDS reform. This flexible approach is in contradiction to the aspiration for a

67 Accordingly, in the EU's proposal, the emphasis is placed on establishing 'an assistance mechanism', which could 'aid least developed and developing countries in litigation in international investment disputes and possibly in other aspects of the application of international investment law': EU submission to UNCITRAL (n 38) para. 38. An identical aspiration has been included in the EU Negotiating Mandate for a MIC (n 38): see para. 16.

68 Comments from the EU and Its Member States (n 53), comments on para. 67.

69 See for example, ibid, comments on draft provision 10 (limitations on outside activities for permanent adjudicators) and 11.

multilateral solution to common ISDS problems. However, more flexibility provides more chances for the establishment of a new court. Importantly, an MIC is the EU solution for its own external fragmentation. One single court should ensure consistency among many extra-EU Member States' BITs and EU IIAs. For the EU and its Member States collectively the court would also be more affordable than the expensive ITA. The EU's 'open architecture' approach is thus a pragmatic strategy with a view to primarily establish a framework for an MIC, which will allow the adjustment of the details regarding its functioning at a later stage. Given the proportion of the BITs of EU Member States in the total number of IIAs, coherence of dispute settlement among extra-EU BITs could in the long-term have a positive integrating spill-over effect on the coherence of IIL.

As seen so far, multilateralism in the context of IIL reform does not mean one single solution but an opportunity for developing 'like-minded' partnerships tailored to specific investment contexts. It includes convincing as many 'smaller' players to join as possible. The EU has a challenging task to persuade 'the others' that its reform of IIL is not a self-centred expression of multilateralism on EU terms but a savvy pragmatic solution with 'better' outcomes for States. This strategy goes hand-in-hand with the EU's pragmatic-lateralism in trade. In the multilateral rules-based order that is currently under different threats, having rules, albeit imperfect rules, is still better than having no rules.

# Conclusion to Part III

## EU External Investment Regulatory Framework between International and EU Law

The constitutional character of the Lisbon Treaty signalled a new phase of EU engagement with 'the wider world'. With the foreign direct investment (FDI) competence, EU institutions have assumed the leading role in designing the EU international investment policy (IIP) and the EU has emerged as a new actor in the field of international investment regulation (IIR). The EU IIP and its improved investment standards are implemented in EU international investment agreements (IIAs), post-Lisbon Member States' bilateral investment treaties (BITs) and the EU proposal for a new Multilateral Investment Court (MIC) in the United Nations Commission on International Trade Law (UNCITRAL). In line with its other key decisions (Opinion 2/15, *Achmea*), the Court of Justice of the European Union (CJEU) has played a key role in defining the policy scope and legitimising the EU IIP. In Opinion 1/17 the CJEU has dismissed the fears of Belgium and reinforced the European Commission's (EC's) decision to move forward with the establishment of an MIC.

Opinion 1/17 clarified the compatibility of the new EU IIP, particularly the compatibility of the Investment Court System (ICS) as its core element, with EU law. Unlike its international adjudicative predecessors – the EU Patent Court in Opinion 1/09, the European Court of Human Rights (ECtHR) in Opinion 2/13 and intra-EU investment tribunals in *Achmea* – the ICS confirms that the CJEU and a dispute settlement mechanism outside the EU judicial system can co-exist in their own separate universes. While it is 'not inconceivable' that Comprehensive Economic and Trade Agreement (CETA) awards could, in exceptional cases, undermine the effectiveness of EU law,[1] it is sufficiently improbable that this scenario will adversely affect the autonomy of EU law.

The treatment of EU law in proceedings before the ICS seems to be the core argument for the CJEU's conclusion that the autonomy of EU law is

[1] See Opinion 1/17 ECLI:EU:C:2019:341, para. 186.

sufficiently preserved in the CETA. European Union law (other than the CETA) is to be treated as a matter of fact and the ICS tribunals are not to interpret EU law but to examine its effects on foreign investors. Nevertheless, in the absence of a less abstract distinction between interpretation and examination, the impression is that the CETA restricts ICS tribunals from interpreting and applying EU law on rather formalistic grounds. Opinion 1/17 thus confines the autonomy of EU law to the interpretative autonomy of the CJEU. Since the CJEU's autonomy is sufficiently preserved, the right to regulate in the EU is also guaranteed. And while the new ICS does not embrace the same rule-of-law standard which is required for EU courts, the restrictions placed on the rule of law by the CETA are not such to render the ICS incompatible with EU law (Articles 20 and 47 CFR).

Against this background, it is legitimate to ask, in what ways has the EU IIP improved IIL? EU IIAs are built upon and developed from the existing IIL. They largely follow the trends of modern IIAs and codify the existing arbitral tribunals' case law, thus providing more clarity about the content of investment standards. The core departure from IIL relates to the permanency of ICS tribunal members and the appellate mechanism. Accordingly, the scope and content of EU standards will depend on their interpretation by the new court(s). In the short-term, the EU remains primarily focused on concluding comprehensive free trade agreements (FTAs) with trading partners and on establishing an MIC.

Given the long-term feasibility of the EU IIP, the CJEU's approach in Opinion 1/17 was pragmatic as it allows the EC to move forward with its implementation, both bilaterally and multilaterally. With the vision of an MIC as a 'work-in-progress', the CJEU gave the ICS a 'bare pass'. At this stage, it is important for the EU to establish an international investment court, while the identified issues can be improved through further negotiations. However, the CJEU's review of the ICS' validity involves a dynamic approach. The establishment of an MIC will entail a multilateral agreement to which the EU will also be a party. With respect to that and all future EU IIAs, a new opinion on the compatibility of the new arrangements with the rule of law could be requested under Article 218 (11) Treaty on the Functioning of the European Union (TFEU). Accordingly, the standards laid down by the CJEU in its Opinion 1/17 are the minimal standards that must be improved.

Opinion 1/17 confirms the CJEU's vision of constitutionalism in international law,[2] endorsed in the earlier *Kadi* judgment. Any international law mechanism that enters the EU legal order – in this case the ICS in CETA – must meet a set of criteria determined by EU law. However, the CJEU's approach in assessing these criteria has been adjusted to the specific context of IIL. The CJEU has recognised the importance of a future MIC in providing an effective remedy to foreign investors while ensuring the compliance of States with international law. The criteria of 'independence' and 'accessibility' in Article 47 Charter of Fundamental Rights (CFR) must primarily be seen in these specific circumstances. Independence of ICS tribunals prioritises independence *from the host State* and the *access* to these tribunals *for foreign investors*, whereby both serve the *objective* of *free and fair trade*.[3]

The CJEU has recognised the practical realities of international trade; however, the EU's aspiration to export its own vision of the rule of law into IIL for now remains mainly an aspiration. The EU has declared old investor-State dispute settlement (ISDS) 'dead',[4] but kept 'reviving' it through post-Lisbon Member States' extra-EU BITs and the modernised Energy Charter Treaty (ECT). The future of a more coherent EU investment regulatory framework thus ultimately depends on the outcome of the multilateral negotiations for an MIC, which will make or break the EU IIP.

[2] See M. Koskenniemi, *The Politics of International Law* (Hart 2011) 345-350.

[3] Opinion 1/17, paras. 199-200 (emphasis added).

[4] See the quote at the beginning of Part III.

# General Conclusion

## The EU Reform: Between Aspirations and Reality

The legitimacy crisis of investor-State dispute settlement (ISDS) in Europe has prompted the EU – an emerging actor in international investment law – to reform this field. In particular, the EU reform was designed to enhance the rule of law in international investment law, as a means of legitimising the field. However, the reform of international investment law has ultimately exposed the clash of different visions of the rule of law in international law and the multifaceted nature of this concept. The purpose of this book was to evaluate the EU's vision and its contribution to the development of international law in the field of investment. In particular, the book sought to assess whether the EU reform addresses the key international investment law problems and in doing so contributes to the achievement of the rule of law and legitimacy. To answer this question, a substantial analysis was undertaken of EU investment law and policy in both its internal dimension (Part II) and external relations (Part III), and placed in the broader context of international investment law and its reform (Part I). As many scholars have written about international investment law, what value does this book add? The following observations encapsulate the findings of this research and attest to its relevance and contribution to the international investment law reform debate.

*First*, this book has sought to explore the complexities of the interaction between EU law and international investment law, as two distinct systems of law within international law, and the manner in which the EU legal order has impacted this branch of international law. Scholars have mainly focused on selected issues arising from the interplay between EU law and international investment law; this book provides a comprehensive legal analysis of this relationship and of different regulatory trends in international investment law. While this book aimed to demonstrate how the two legal systems share the same paradigm (the protection of foreign investors abroad), it has also striven to explain how the differences between these two systems stem from their fundamentally different visions of the rule of law in international law. The assumed anti-ISDS discourse of the EU must be placed in the broader context of international law, the place of the EU legal order within international law and the general objectives of EU integration.

International law aims to ensure the compliance of domestic law with international legal standards, while the rule of law guarantees supremacy of law over politics. In the EU these goals are set in place by EU law and the founding treaties, which are ultimately instruments of international law. The success of the EU lies in its ability to integrate international law into domestic law, while subjecting Member States to the control of international law through the EU judicial system. In addition to socio-political domestic opposition, the core ISDS philosophy, which mistrusts domestic courts, directly contradicts the core principle of mutual trust in domestic courts under EU law. The elimination of ISDS in the intra-EU dimension thus serves to achieve the objectives of closer EU integration and to enhance the rule of law in the EU through the implementation of EU law via domestic courts. By enhancing the rule of law in twenty-seven Member States of the EU, the EU is also contributing to the international rule of law.

This is the core aspect of the EU and its legal order that has been somewhat absent from the debate. 'Legalism' in this thinking might not be convincing for the 'realists' among international investment lawyers, who mistrust the assumption that is made by EU law of equal justice in the Member States. However, should international investment law be about the race to the top in protecting investors or about ensuring the compliance by States with the minimum standards of treatment under international law? Does EU law and its enforcement mechanisms fall so far short of these standards when protecting EU investors who invest in other Member States? The realist perspective is in its essence also an issue of institutional hegemony in international law.

In the internal EU dimension the focus has been placed on the clash between the two legal orders, however the *cross-fertilisation* of norms in the external dimension is another important aspect of this research. By examining the normative leverage of the EU in reforming international investment law, this book has shed light on the ways in which the EU attempts to influence developments in international investment law and also on the extent to which the EU's own reform solutions have been influenced by international investment law.

New standards in post-Lisbon investment agreements concluded by the EU and by the Member States embrace the standards the EU has sought to establish in international investment law. In line with the constitutional aspiration of the EU to contribute to the development of international law, the later EU agreements integrate the best practice of modern investment treaties. At the same time, they incorporate EU law by ensuring that international investment law standards do not conflict with the fundamental principles of EU law and the right of the EU to regulate.

The aspirational coherence between the internal and external EU dimensions is not to be ensured through substantive standards of protection but through the requirement for independence of the dispute settlement body. The new Multilateral Investment Court will have to comply with the criteria of independence and access to justice enshrined in the EU Charter of Fundamental Rights (CFR), just as the Court of Justice of the European Union (CJEU) and all domestic courts in the EU are obliged to do, in order to ensure effective judicial protection. In reality these criteria are not identical to the EU internal criteria but emanate from the same principles; primarily the independence of the new court from the host State and effective judicial protection for EU investors abroad.

As demonstrated, the control of law over power (aka the rule of law) in the EU context ultimately also means the control of EU law and its highest court over intersections and boundaries of the two regimes, both internally and externally. In defining these boundaries, the CJEU has been guided by different objectives. In the internal context, the CJEU has focused on enhancing the rule of law through the implementation of EU law (EU integration). In the external context, emphasis has been placed on the EU's geo-economic interests, which have found their expression in the rule of law. Indeed, a specific protection regime for EU investors should ensure a sufficient level of protection for EU investors in third countries (legal protection of EU citizens and their investments abroad). It should provide guarantees that EU investors are placed on a par with the United States, Chinese and other third country investors, that they compete with the rest of the world on an *equal* footing (another aspect of the rule of law). This should not only encourage their investments abroad but ultimately result in fair competition and consequently *free(r) and fair (er)* trade, with these benefits extending beyond the internal market (an EU contribution to the world).

*Second*, this book has shed light on questions about *the rule of law* in international law more broadly and in the autonomous legal discipline of international investment law more specifically. The questions about the rule of law are primarily questions of control of law over power. International investment law shifts the judicial (public domestic) control over States' legislative and executive action in issues of public importance – from States to international arbitration tribunals. By eschewing domestic courts in favour of a private law dispute settlement mechanism, ISDS disturbs the domestic democratic process of checks and balances in the creation and domestic implementation of public policy. It touches upon the core of State regulatory processes.

For the EU, the reform of international investment law should return control over international investment law back to States. In the EU context, the control is returned to national and EU courts. In the international context, the EU reform thus contemplates a new shift – from internationalised tribunals controlled by disputing parties to an internationalised court controlled by States. By transforming quasi-private arbitration to a public court process, the EU vision of a Multilateral Investment Court should take international investment law away from the special interests of transnational elites and the 'managerial world' of narrowly specialised investment lawyers and place it in a domain of more traditional State-controlled public international law. However, this shift will not eliminate the power game in international investment law; it will rather recalibrate the power balance between States and tribunals and shift the power to where it was at the time when the system was created. The financial arrangements of the new court should make the new system more attractive to developing States that have been on the receiving end of investors' claims.

As States contemplate change of the dispute resolution paradigm, perhaps the core question for them to consider is what this change entails for the international rule of law and whether it gives States more control over this autonomous legal discipline that so significantly affects their domestic policy processes. Will the new court allow more influence by the States – the actual masters of international treaties – in setting the standards in international investment law? For the EU, the answer to this question is in the affirmative.

*Third*, this book has shed light on the extent to which the EU is caught between internal and external limitations in achieving its investment strategy. The *limited EU sovereignty* to conclude international investment agreements (shared competence) affects EU external action because it disallows conclusion by the EU of modern comprehensive free trade agreements. These limitations on EU sovereignty stem from the internal factors – the EU constitutional framework – and ultimately pose a challenge for both deepening (internally) and widening (externally) of the EU investment policy.

*Fourth*, and stemming also from these reasons, this book has exposed the complexity and contradictions of EU reform. On the one hand, 'old' ISDS is fully abolished internally, to the extent that it is to be removed from the EU legal order, while externally declared 'dead'. On the other hand, traditional ISDS continues at the level of Member States' pre- and post-Lisbon extra-EU investment treaties, and even in the (modernised) Energy Charter Treaty (ECT) – an agreement to which the EU is also a party. In effect, the EU approach is as pragmatic as it can be, with fragmentation into many investment treaties of the EU and the Member States, and flexibility, seen in the new court's 'open architecture', for example, as dominant features. The multiplicity of treaties and tribunals at the global level is thus mirrored at the EU level.

Further, because the ratification of mixed EU international investment agreements is a lengthy and politically complex process domestically, the EU is engaged in bilateral and multilateral agendas in parallel. The critical mass of support, expressed through the conclusion of bilateral investment agreements, should give the EU important political leverage in the United Nations Commission on International Trade Law (UNCITRAL) negotiations. The aspiration is to establish a new multilateral court as quickly as possible, however it need only be plurilateral in reality. At the same time, this new adjudication mechanism should eventually enhance coherence between the investment agreements initiated by all Member States and by the EU by integrating one single court instead of many tribunals. Ultimately, a new court would also develop new interpretations of substantive rights, through improved, if not new, standards in EU and Member States' agreements. In essence, it is a unilateral EU solution to advance its own investment policy. However, the reality is that only five EU bilateral agreements encapsulate a new Investment Court System (ICS), none of which are in force (Canada, Singapore, Vietnam, Mexico and Chile). The new approach to establish the court has not found its way into the modernised ECT, thus drawing into question the prospects of a multilateral solution, which could not have been implemented even at the plurilateral level.

*Fifth*, this book has shed light on the relationship between the *legitimacy*, primarily a political concept, and the rule of law as a legal concept. Legitimacy is essentially a matter of perception, despite its important normative dimension. It is difficult to draw a line between its objective and subjective criteria. Ultimately, legitimacy depends on the perspective from which the system in question is examined – and the perception of it differs between States, investors and society as a whole. It also entails different visions of the rule of law in international law. For civil society, it means endorsing better dissemination of domestic rule of law, including the right to regulate. For investors, it is about party autonomy and effective enforcement of the awards. For States, it is a choice between the visions of the rule of law of the big powers (the United States, China and the EU). As a contribution to this debate, this book has striven to analyse possible malfunctions of the current system of international investment law on one hand, and the advantages and drawbacks of the envisaged reform on the other.

*Finally*, and beyond the EU, this book has questioned the effectiveness of a procedural approach to reform in an autonomous area of international law, which functions in accordance with its established standards, methods and culture. Can the procedural reform, which avoids the issues of substance, achieve consensus on the desired normative goals? As the reform process continues, it might be years before a conclusive answer about its outcomes can be given. At this stage, it is too early to say whether a new Multilateral Investment Court will be established, let alone the kind of legacy it will create.

In light of the historical context of international investment law, procedural reform is politically more salient, or in realistic terms it has more potential to succeed. Procedural reform could also be a first step towards a more substantive reform. It could enhance the rule of law by implementing more prominently the procedural requirements of the rule of law. These requirements are also institutional in character: a court with judges who are independent from political influence; the access to this court guaranteed to all investors; its procedures, reasoning and decisions open to public scrutiny; and legal methods that could achieve more equilibrium between different interests, especially between the investors' rights and public policy goals. It is an assumption of many lawyers, in particular those in the common law world, that proper procedure expressed in the concept of the procedural rule of law eventually leads to a fair outcome. More rule of law could also foster more legitimacy – a system with independent judges could also be *seen* as more just. On the other hand, not everyone is convinced that an approach focused on the procedure would eventually lead to substantive justice, in the same way that the formalism enshrined in the rule of law is not convincing for everyone, and indeed can create substantive inequalities.

Despite the attempts to transform difficult political issues into a technical sphere of the law's objectivity through the ISDS reform, the core unanswered substantial and ultimately existential questions of international investment law keep returning. Despite the attempts to neutralise law, its values remain its very core. Every system that calls itself a rule of law system must eventually be able to answer the difficult questions about its values through its domestic democratic processes. But what are the values of international investment law? Is that the rule of law? And if it is the rule of law, what is its meaning in international law? The movements for reform of international investment law avoid answering these core existential questions. Since the core questions have not yet been properly framed, they have not been answered, and regardless of the outcome of this reform they are likely to return.

Flexibility, fragmentation and complexity in international investment law are likely to remain, as 'a trap and a display' – the question is what each of us makes of it.[1] The EU has aspired to bring the system of international investment law closer into line with the rule of law, which would make it more acceptable; however, the practical effects of its reform have not (yet) been achieved. Indeed, the reform process is ongoing and long-term. However, the post-COVID world and climate change will only further expose the deeper existential questions. The system of international investment governance is ill-tailored for State measures that are required to address current and impending situations of crisis.

The EU solution for the reform of international investment law seems like a Belgian solution,[2] with no likely 'Brussels effect'. As in trade, the EU approach to investment is a trade-off between the aspiration for multilateralism and the reality of pragmatic-lateralism. However, and more optimistically, not every solution must be an answer to *every* problem.[3] Albeit insufficient, the establishment of a Multilateral Investment Court would be an important first step for the EU.

[1] 'Everything is a trap and a display; the secret reality of the object is what the Other makes of it': J. P. Sartre, *Critique of Dialectical Reason* (Alan Sheridan-Smith tr, Verso 2004) vol. 1, 135.

[2] A 'Belgian compromise' implies the resolution of social and political problems in Belgium through a process of negotiation and adaptation. Complicated issues are settled through a complex and ambiguous compromise, which is usually insufficient to resolve the issues but is sufficient to stop the existing conflict and allow life to continue without obstructions. See F. Heylingen, 'Belgium: Society, Character and Culture: An Essay on the Belgian Identity' (*Principia Cybernetica Web* 1998).

[3] 'Not every solution is an answer to a problem': D. Helbich, *Belgian Solutions* (2016) vol. 1.

# BIBLIOGRAPHY

## General Works


Aalto P, 'The New International Energy Charter: Instrumental or Incremental Progress of Governance?' (2016) 11 *Energy Research and Social Science* 92

Abdelal R and Meunier S, 'Managed Globalisation: Doctrine, Practice and Promise' (2010) 17 *Journal of European Public Policy* 350

Akhtar SI and Weiss AW, 'U.S. International Investment Agreements: Issues for Congress' (2013) Congressional Research Service

Ali AH and others, *The International Arbitration Rulebook: A Guide to Arbitral Regimes* (Kluwer 2019)

Alschner W, *Investment Arbitration and State-Driven Reform* (OUP 2022)

Alter KJ, 'The European Court's Political Power' (1996) 19 *West European Politics* 458

*Establishing the Supremacy of European Law: The Making of an International Rule of Law in Europe* (OUP 2001)

Alvarez JE, 'The Return of the State' (2011) 20 *Minnesota Journal of International Law* 223

Alvarez JE and Khamsi K, 'The Argentine Crisis and Foreign Investors: A Glimpse into the Heart of the Investment Regime' in Karl P Sauvant (ed), *The Yearbook on International Investment Law and Policy 2008/2009* (OUP 2009)

Angelet N, 'CETA and the Debate on the Reform of the Investment Regime' in MM Mbengue and S Schacherer (eds), *Foreign Investment Under the Comprehensive Economic and Trade Agreement (CETA)* (Springer 2019)

Ankersmit L, '*Achmea*: The Beginning of the End for ISDS in and with Europe?' (*Investment Treaty News*, 24 April 2018) <https://www.iisd.org/itn/2018/04/24/achmea-the-beginning-of-the-end-for-isds-in-and-with-europe-laurens-ankersmit/#_edn11>

Arato J, 'The Logic of Contract in the World of Investment Treaties' (2016) 58 *William & Mary Law Review* 351

Arato J and others, 'Reforming Shareholders Claims in ISDS' Academic Forum on ISDS Concept Paper 2019/9, Version 2 (17 September 2019) <https://www.jus.uio.no/pluricourts/english/projects/leginvest/academic-forum/papers/papers/arato-reforming-shareholder-claims-isds-af-9-2019.pdf>

Araujo BAM, *The EU Deep Trade Agenda* (OUP 2016)

Baltag C (ed), *ICSID Convention after 50 Years: Unsettled Issues* (Kluwer 2017)

'The ICSID Convention: A Successful Story – The Origins and History of the ICSID' in C Baltag (ed), *ICSID Convention after 50 Years: Unsettled Issues* (Kluwer 2017)

Barbiere C, 'France and Germany to Form United Front against ISDS' (*Euractiv*, 15 January 2015) <https://www.euractiv.com/section/trade-society/news/france-and-germany-to-form-united-front-against-isds/>

'Mathias Fekl: The EU Should Have Its Own Arbitration Court' (*Euractiv*, 3 June 2015) <https://www.euractiv.com/section/trade-society/interview/matthias-fekl-the-eu-should-have-its-own-arbitration-court/>

Barents R, 'The Internal Market Unlimited: Some Observations on the Legal Basis of EU Legislation' (1993) 30 *Common Market Law Review* 85

Barnard C, *The Substantive Law of the EU: The Four Freedoms* (6th edn, OUP 2019)

Barragan DG, Mitretodis A and Tuck A, 'The New NAFTA: Scaled-Back Arbitration in the USMCA' (2019) 6 *Journal of International Arbitration* 739

Basedow R, 'The EU's International Investment Policy Ten Years On: The Policy-Making Implications of Unintended Competence Transfers' (2021) 59(3) *Journal of Common Market Studies* 643

Bauer M, 'Campaign-Triggered Mass Collaboration in the EU's Online Consultations: The ISDS-in-TTIP Case' (2015) 14 *European View* 121

Bellak C, 'Economic Impact of Investment Agreements' (2015) Vienna University Department of Economics Working Paper Series 200 <https://epub.wu.ac.at/4625/1/wp200.pdf>

Bermann GA, 'The Prospects of Eco Swiss v Benetton for International Commercial Arbitration: A Comment on *Eco Swiss v Benetton*' in P Wautelet and others (eds), *The Practice of Arbitration: Essays in Honour of Hans van Houtte* (Hart 2012)

Beunder A and Mast J, 'As the World Meets to Discuss ISDS, Many Fear Meaningless Reforms' (*Transnational Institute*, 4 April 2019) <https://longreads.tni.org/isds-many-fear-meaningless-reforms/>

Bischoff JA and Wühler M, 'The Notion of Investment' in MM Mbengue and S Schacherer (eds), *Foreign Investment Under the Comprehensive Economic and Trade Agreement (CETA)* (Springer 2019)

Bjorklund A, 'Investment Treaty Arbitral Decisions as Jurisprudence Constante' (2008) UC Davis Legal Studies Research Paper No. 158

Bodansky D, 'Legitimacy in International Law and International Relations' (2011) APSA 2011 Annual Meeting Paper, 11–12 <https://papers.ssrn.com/sol3/papers.cfm?abstract_id=1900289>

'Legitimacy in International Law and International Relations' in J Dunoff and MA Pollack (eds), *Interdisciplinary Perspectives on International Law and International Relations: The State of the Art* (CUP 2013)

Bonnitcha J, *Substantive Protection under Investment Treaties: A Legal and Economic Analysis* (CUP 2014)

Bradford A, *The Brussels Effect: How the European Union Rules the World* (OUP 2020)

Bremmer I, 'The New Rules of Globalization' (2014) 92 *Harvard Business Review* 103

Broberg M and Fenger N, *Preliminary References to the European Court of Justice* (OUP 2010)

Bromund TR, Roberts JM and Dasgupta R, 'The U.S. Should Reject the European Commission's Proposed Investment Court' (The Heritage Foundation, 13 November 2015) 4485 <https://www.heritage.org/trade/report/the-us-should-reject-the-european-commissions-proposed-investment-court>

Brower CN and Schill SW, 'Is Arbitration a Threat or a Boon to the Legitimacy of International Investment Law' (2009) 9 *Chicago Journal of International Law* 471

Brown CM, 'Changes in the Common Commercial Policy of the European Union after the Entry into Force of the Treaty of Lisbon: A Practitioner's Perspective' in M Bungenberg and C Herrmann (eds), *Common Commercial Policy after Lisbon* (Springer 2013)

Bungenberg B, 'A History of Investment Arbitration and Investor-State Dispute Settlement in Germany' (2016) Centre for International Governance Innovation, Investor-State Arbitration Series Paper No. 12

Burley AM and Mattli W, 'Europe before the Court: A Political Theory of Legal Integration' in M Eilstrup-Sangiovanni (ed), *Debates on European Integration* (Palgrave 2006)

Bush G, 41st President of the USA, 'Address before a Joint Session of the Congress of the State of the Union' (Washington, DC, 29 January 1991) <https://www.presidency.ucsb.edu/documents/address-before-joint-session-the-congress-the-state-the-union-1>

Calamita NJ, 'The Principle of Proportionality and the Problem of Indeterminacy in International Investment Treaties' in *Yearbook on International Investment Law and Policy 2013–2014* (OUP 2014) 157–200

Campbell TD, *The Legal Theory of Ethical Positivism* (Routledge 1996)

Caplan LM and Sharpe JK, 'United States' in Chester Brown (ed), *Commentaries on Selected Model Investment Treaties* (OUP 2013)

Chaisse J (ed), *China–European Union Investment Relationships: Towards a New Leadership in Global Investment Governance?* (Edward Elgar 2018)

Chaisse J and Renouf Y, 'Investor–State Dispute Settlement' in J Drake-Brockman and P Messerlin (eds), *Potential Benefits of an Australia–EU Free Trade Agreement: Key Issues and Options* (Adelaide University Press 2018)

Chalmers D, Davies G and Monti G, *European Union Law* (2nd edn, CUP 2010)

Chase P, 'TTIP, Investor–State Dispute Settlement and the Rule of Law' (2015) 14 *European View* 217

Chase P and Heather S, 'Investment Protection: If It Isn't Broken, Why "Fix" It?' (*US Chamber of Commerce*, 1 October 2015) <https://www.uschamber.com/issue-brief/investment-protection-if-it-ain-t-broke-why-fix-it>

Chen H, 'China's Innovative ISDS Mechanisms and Their Implications' (2018) 112 *American Journal of International Law* 207

Claes M, 'The Validity and Primacy of EU Law and the "Cooperative Relationship" between National Constitutional Courts and the Court of the Justice of the European Union' (2016) 23 *Maastricht Journal of European and Comparative Law* 151

Cohen A, 'Constitutionalism without Constitution: Transnational Elites between Political Mobilisation and Legal Expertise in the Making of a Constitution for Europe (1940s–1960s)' (2007) 32 *Law and Social Inquiry* 109

'The European Court of Justice in the Emergent European Filed of Power: Transnational Judicial Institutions and National Career Paths' in Y Dezaley and B Garth (eds), *Lawyers and the Construction of Transnational Justice* (Routledge 2012)

Cohen HG and others, 'Legitimacy and International Courts – A Framework' in N Grossman and others (eds), *Legitimacy and International Courts* (CUP 2018)

Collins S, 'Moldova v Komstroy: A Moment of Reckoning for Intra-EU Investment Arbitration under The ECT? Considering Its impact on Tribunals, Investors and EU Member States' (EFILA Blog, November 2021)

Commission JP, 'Precedent in Investment Treaty Arbitration: A Citation Analysis of a Developing Jurisprudence' (2007) 24 *Journal of International Arbitration* 129

Costa JAF, 'Comparing WTO Panelists and ICSID Arbitrators: The Creation of International Legal Fields' (2011) 4 *Oñati Socio-Legal Series* 1

Côté C, 'Is Chilling Out There? International Investment Agreements and Government Regulatory Autonomy' (2016) 16 *Academy of International Business Insights* 14

Craig P and De Búrca G, *EU Law, Text, Cases and Materials* (6th edn, OUP 2015)

Crema L, 'Testing *Amici Curiae* in International Law: Rules and Practice' (2012) 22 *The Italian Yearbook of International Law* 91

Cremona M, 'Disconnection Clauses in EU Law and Practice' in C Hillion and P Koutrakos, *Mixed Agreements Revisited, The EU and its Member States in the World* (Hart 2010)

Crépet Daigremont C, 'Most Favoured Nation Treatment' in MM Mbengue and S Schacherer (eds), *Foreign Investment under the Comprehensive Economic and Trade Agreement (CETA)* (Springer 2019)

Cullen H and Charlesworth H, 'Diplomacy by Other Means: The Use of Legal Basis Litigation as a Political Strategy by the European Parliament and Member States' (1999) 36 *Common Market Law Review* 1243

D'Argent P, 'Sources and the Legality and Validity of International Law: What Makes Law "International"?' in Samantha Besson and Jean d'Aspremont, *The Oxford Handbook on the Sources of International Law* (OUP 2017)

Dahl RA, 'Can International Organisations Be Democratic? A Sceptic's View' in I Shapiro and C Hacker-Cordon (eds), *Democracy's Edges* (CUP 2009)

Dai AC, 'The International Investment Agreement Network under the "Belt and Road" Initiative' in J Chaisse and J Gorski (eds), *The Belt and Road Initiative: Law, Economics and Politics* (Brill 2018)

Damjanovic I, 'Investment and EU International Agreements' in X Groussot and others (eds), *The EU Law of Investment: Past, Present and Future* (Hart 2023)

Damjanovic I and de Sadeleer N, 'I Would Rather Be a Respondent State before a Domestic Court in the EU than before an International Investment Tribunal' (2019) 4 *European Papers* 19

'Values and Objectives of the EU in Light of Opinion 1/17: "Trade for All", above All' (2020) 4(1) *Europe and the World: A Law Review* [25]

Damjanovic I and Quirico O, 'Intra-EU Investment Dispute Settlement in Light of *Vattenfall* and *Achmea*: A Matter of Priority' (2019) 26 *Columbia Journal of European Law* 102

Dammann J and Hansmann H, 'Globalising Commercial Litigation' (2008) 94 *Cornell Law Review* 1

De Búrca G, 'The Principle of Proportionality and Its Application in EC Law' (1993) *Yearbook on European Law* 125

Decleve Q, '*Achmea*: Consequences on Applicable Law and ISDS Clauses in Extra-EU BITs and Future EU Trade and Investment Agreements' (2019) 4 *European Papers* 99

De Nanteuil A, 'Expropriation' in Makane Moïse Mbengue and Stefanie Schacherer (eds), *Foreign Investment under the Comprehensive Economic and Trade Agreement (CETA)* (Springer 2019)

De Sadeleer N, *EU Environmental Law and the Internal Market* (OUP 2014)

'The End of the Game: The Autonomy of the EU Legal Order Opposes Arbitral Tribunals under Bilateral Investment Treaties Concluded between Two Member States' (2018) 9 *European Journal of Risk Regulation* 355

De Souza Fleury PP, 'Umbrella Clauses: A Trend towards Its Elimination' (2015) 31 *Arbitration International* 679

De Witte B, 'Direct Effect, Primacy and the Nature of the Legal Order' in P Craig and G de Búrca, *The Evolution of EU Law* (2nd edn, OUP 2011)

'Variable Geometry and Differentiation as Structural Features of the EU Legal Order' in B de Witte, A Ott and E Vos (eds), *Between Flexibility and Disintegration: The Trajectory of Differentiation in EU Law* (Edward Elgar 2017)

Dezalay Y and Garth BG, *Dealing in Virtue* (University of Chicago Press 1996)

Dikova D and others, 'Immediate Responses to Financial Crises: A Focus on U.S. MNE Subsidiaries' (2013) 22 *International Business Review* 202

DiMascio N and Pauwelyn J, 'Nondiscrimination in Trade and Investment Treaties: Worlds Apart or Two Sides of the Same Coin?' (2008) 102 *The American Journal of International Law* 48

Dimopoulos A, *EU Foreign Investment Law* (OUP 2011)

Di Pietro D, 'Applicable Law under Article 42 of the ICSID Convention' (*Transnational Notes*, 19 November 2011) <https://blogs.law.nyu.edu/transnational/2011/10/applicable-law-under-article-42-of-the-icsid-convention/>

Dolzer R and Yun-I K, 'Germany' in C Brown (ed), *Commentaries on Selected Model Investment Treaties* (OUP 2013)

Douglas Z, 'Nothing If Not Critical for Investment Treaty Arbitration: Occidental, Eureko and Methanex' (2006) 22 *Arbitration International* 27

Drieghe L, Orbie J, Potjomkina D and Shahin J, 'Participation of Civil Society in EU Trade Policy Making: How Inclusive Is Inclusion' (2021) 27(4) *New Political Economy* 581

Dumberry P, 'Fair and Equitable Treatment' in MM Mbengue and S Schacherer (eds), *Foreign Investment under the Comprehensive Economic and Trade Agreement (CETA)* (Springer 2019)

Eeckhout P, *External Relations of the European Union, Legal and Constitutional Foundations* (OUP 2004)

Elsing SH and Townsend JM, 'Bridging the Common Law Civil Law Divide in Arbitration' (2002) 18 *Arbitration International* 1

Fanou M, 'The CETA ICS and the Autonomy of the EU Legal Order in Opinion 1/17 – A Compass for the Future' (2020) 22 *Cambridge Yearbook of European Legal Studies* 106

Fauchald OK, 'The Legal Reasoning of ICSID Tribunals – An Empirical Analysis' (2008) 19 *European Journal of International Law* 301

Fiezzoni SK, 'The Challenge of UNASUR Member Countries to Replace ICSID Arbitration' (2011) 2 *Beijing Law Review* 134

Franck SD, 'The Legitimacy Crisis in Investment Treaty Arbitration: Privatizing Public International Law through Inconsistent Decisions' (2005) 73 *Fordham Law Review* 1521

Franck SD and Wylie LE, 'Predicting Outcomes in Investment Treaty Arbitration' (2015) 65 *Duke Law Journal* 459

Franck TM, *The Power of Legitimacy Among Nations* (OUP 1990)

Frantescu D, 'How Will EU Parliamentarians Vote on TTIP?' (*VoteWatch Europe*, 9 June 2015) <https://www.votewatch.eu/blog/what-will-eu-parliamentarians-vote-on-ttip/>

Fukuyama F, 'The End of History?' (1989) 16 *The National Interest* 3

Fuller LL, *The Morality of Law* (Yale University Press 1969)

Gaillard E and Penushliski IM, 'State Compliance with Investment Awards' (2020) 35(3) *ICSID Review* 540

Galanter M, 'Why the "Haves" Come Out Ahead: Speculations on the Limits of Social Change' (1974) 9 *Law and Society Review* 95

Gaukrodger D, 'Investment Treaties as Corporate Law: Shareholder Claims and Issues of Consistency' (OECD 2013)

'The Legal Framework Applicable to Joint Interpretative Agreements of Investment Treaties' (OECD 2016)

Gaukrodger D and Gordon K, 'Investor–State Dispute Settlement: A Scoping Paper for the Investment Policy Community' (OECD 2012)

Ghouri AA, 'Resolving Incompatibilities of Bilateral Investment Treaties of the EU Member States with the EC Treaty: Individual and Collective Options' (2010) 16 *European Law Journal* 806

Ginsburg T, 'The Culture of Arbitration' (2003) 36 *Vanderbilt Journal of Transnational Law* 1335

Grossman N, 'Legitimacy and International Adjudicative Bodies' (2009) 14 *The George Washington International Law Review* 107

Groussot X, *General Principles of Community Law* (Europa Law Publishing 2006)

Gustafson D, Jimenez E and Linn JF, 'Developing the Private Sector: A Challenge for the World Bank Group' (World Bank Group 1989)

Guthrie BK, 'Beyond Investment Protection: An Examination of the Potential Influence of Investment Treaties on Domestic Rule of Law' (2013) 45 *New York University Journal of International Law and Politics* 1151

Guzman AT, 'Why LDCs Sign Treaties That Hurt Them: Explaining the Popularity of Bilateral Investment Treaties' (1998) 38 *Virginia Journal of International Law* 639

Haight GW, 'International Organisations O.E.C.D. Resolution on the Protection of Foreign Property' (1968) 2 *The International Lawyer* 326

Haltern U, 'Integration through Law' in A Wiener and T Diez (eds), *European Integration Theory* (OUP 2005)

Hancher L and Larouche P, 'The Coming of Age of EU Regulation of Network Industries and Services of General Economic Interest' in P Craig and G de Búrca (eds), *The Evolution of EU Law* (2nd edn, OUP 2011)

Hayek F, *The Road to Serfdom* (first published 1944, University of Chicago Press 1994)

Heiskanen V, 'Forbidding dépeçage: Law Governing Investment Treaty Arbitration' (2009) 32 *Suffolk Transnational Law Review* 367

Henckels C, 'Balancing Investment Protection and the Public Interest: The Role of the Standard of Review and the Importance of Deference in Investor–State Arbitration' (2013) 4 *Journal of International Dispute Settlement* 197

Hindelang S, *The Free Movement of Capital and Foreign Direct Investment* (OUP 2009)

'Conceptualisation and Application of the Principle of Autonomy of EU Law – The CJEU's Judgement in *Achmea* Put in Perspective' (2019) 44 *European Law Review* 6

Hoffman HCH, 'Article 47' in S Peers and others (eds), *The EU Charter of Fundamental Rights: A Commentary* (Hart 2014)

Houde MF and Yannaca-Small K, 'Relationships between International Investment Agreements' (OECD 2004)

Howarth R, 'Lex Mercatoria: Can General Principles of Law Govern International Commercial Contracts?' (2004) 10 *Canterbury Law Review* 36

Humphreys S, *Theatre of the Rule of Law: Transnational Legal Intervention in Theory and Practice* (CUP 2010)

Juergen M, 'German Association of Judges on the TTIP Proposal of the European Commission' (*Global Arbitration News*, 21 March 2016) <https://globalarbitrationnews.com/german-association-judges-proposal-european-commission-introduction-investment-court-system-settle-investor-state-disputes-transatlantic-trade-investmen/>

Kaufmann-Kohler G, 'Arbitral Precedent: Dream, Necessity or Excuse?' (2007) 23 *Arbitration International* 357

Kaufmann-Kohler G and Potestà M, 'Can the Mauritius Convention Serve as a Model for the Reform of Investor–State Arbitration in Connection with the Introduction of a Permanent Investment Tribunal or an Appeal Mechanism? – Analysis and Roadmap' (3 June 2016) CIDS-Geneva Center for International Dispute Settlement

'The Composition of a Multilateral Investment Court and of an Appeal Mechanism for Investment Awards' (15 November 2017) CIDS Supplemental Report

Kelemen RD, 'The Court of Justice of the European Union in the Twenty First Century' (2016) 79 *Law and Contemporary Problems* 117

Kennedy DW, 'Some Caution about Property Rights as a Recipe for Economic Development' (2011) 1 *Accounting Economics and Law* 1

Keohane RO, 'Global Governance and Legitimacy' (2011) 18 *Review of International Political Economy* 99

Kidane VL, *The Culture of International Arbitration* (OUP 2017)

Kinkartz S, 'German Social Democrats Fear Free Trade' (*Deutsche Welle*, 23 February 2015) <https://www.dw.com/en/german-social-democrats-fear-free-trade/a-18275595>

Kirchner S and Geler-Noch K, 'Compensation under the European Convention on Human Rights for Expropriations Enforced Prior to the Applicability of the Convention' (2012) 19 *Jurisprudence* 21

Kjos HE, *Applicable Law in Investor–State Arbitration: The Interplay between National and International Law* (OUP 2013)

Kleinheisterkamp J, 'The Next 10 Year ECT Investment Arbitration: A Vision for the Future – From a European Law Perspective' (Report for the SCC/ECT/ICSID Conference on '10 Years of Energy Charter Treaty Arbitration', 9–10 June 2011) <https://sccinstitute.com/media/61991/jan_kleinheisterkamp_report-ect-eu-law.pdf>

'Investment Protection and EU Law: The Intra- and Extra-EU Dimension of the Energy Charter Treaty' (2012) 15 *Journal of International Economic Law* 85

'Investment Treaty Law and the Fear for Sovereignty: Transnational Challenges and Solutions' (2015) 78 *The Modern Law Review* 793

Kline JM and Ludema RD, 'Building a Multilateral Framework for Investment: Comparing the Development of Trade and Investment Accords' (1997) 6 *Transnational Corporations* 1

Koskenniemi M, *The Politics of International Law* (Hart 2011)

Koutrakos P, 'Legal Basis and Delimitation of Competence in EU External Relations' in Marise Cremona (ed), *EU Foreign Relations Law* (Hart 2008)

Krajewski M, 'New Functions and New Powers for the European Parliament: Assessing the Changes of the Common Commercial Policy from the Perspective of Democratic Legitimacy' in M Bungenberg and C Herrmann (eds), *Common Commercial Policy after Lisbon* (Springer 2013)

Kramer MH, *Objectivity and the Rule of Law* (CUP 2007)

Kriebaum U, 'Regulatory Takings: Balancing the Interests of the Investor and the State' (2007) 8 *The Journal of World Investment and Trade* 717

'FET and Expropriation in the Comprehensive Economic Trade Agreement between the European Union and Canada (CETA)' TDM 1 (2016) < www.transnational-dispute-management.com/article.asp?key=2320>

Kurtz J, 'A General Investment Agreement in the WTO? Lessons from Chapter 11 of NAFTA and the OECD Multilateral Agreement on Investment' (2002) 23 *University of Pennsylvania Journal of Economic Law* 713

Langford M, Behn D and Lie RH, 'The Revolving Door in International Investment Arbitration' (2017) 20 *Journal of International Economic Law* 301

Leblond P and Viju-Miljusevic C, 'EU Trade Policy in the Twenty-First Century: Change, Continuity and Challenges' (2019) 26 *Journal of European Public Policy* 1836

Lenaerts K, 'How the ECJ Thinks: A Study on Judicial Legitimacy' (2013) 36 *Fordham International Law Journal* 1302

'Modernising Trade Whilst Safeguarding the EU Constitutional Framework: An Insight into the Balanced Approach of Opinion 1/17' (Seminar on Opinion 1/17, Belgian Ministry of Foreign Affairs, 6 September 2019)

Levashova Y, *The Right of States to Regulate in International Investment Law* (Kluwer 2019)

Lewis DJ and Moise D, 'One Belt One Road ("OBOR") Roadmaps: The Legal and Policy Frameworks' in J Chaisse and J Gorski (eds), *The Belt and Road Initiative: Law, Economics and Politics* (Brill 2018)

Mantakou AP, 'The Misadventures of the Principle of Jura Novit Curia in International Arbitration: A Practitioner's Approach' in Nomiki Vivliothiki (ed), *Essays in Honour of Professor Emeritus Spyridon Vrellis* (Nomiki Bibliothiki 2014) 487–498

Martines F, 'Direct Effect of International Agreements of the European Union' (2014) 25 *European Journal of International Law* 129

Matiation S, 'Arbitration with Two Twists: Loewen v United States and Free Trade Commission Intervention in NAFTA Chapter 11 Disputes' (2003) 24 *University of Pennsylvania Journal of Economic Law* 451

Matic AA, 'Transatlantic Trade and the Case for Investment Protection' (2017) The German Marshall Fund of the United States, No. 20/2017

McDeod I, *Legal Theory* (2nd edn, Palgrave 2003)

McDonagh T, 'Unfair, Unsustainable, and Under the Radar: How Corporations Use Global Investment Rules to Undermine a Sustainable Future' (*The Democracy Center*, 2013) 8 <https://www.democracyctr.org/unfair-unstable-and-under-the-radar>

Moldenhauer O and Schmidt N, 'ECT Data Analysis: Results and Methods' (*Investigate Europe*, 23 February 2021)

Nassar N, 'Internalization of State Contracts: ICSID, The Last Citadel' (1997) 14 *Journal of International Arbitration* 185

Newcombe A and Paradell L, *Law and Practice of Investment Treaties: Standards of Treatment* (Kluwer 2009)

Parra AR, *The History of ICSID* (2nd edn, OUP 2018)

Parish M, *Mirages of International Justice* (Edward Elgar 2011)

Patomaki H, 'Neoliberalism and Global Financial Crisis' (2009) 31 *New Political Science* 431

Pattison JE, 'The United States-Egypt Bilateral Investment Treaty: A Prototype for Future Negotiation' (1983) 16 *Cornell International Law Journal* 305

Paulsson J, 'Arbitration without Privity' (1995) 10 *ICSID Review – Foreign Investment Law Journal* 232

'Avoiding Unintended Consequences' in KP Sauvant and M Chiswick-Patterson (eds), *Appeals Mechanism in International Investment Disputes* (OUP 2008)

Pauwelyn J, 'The Rule of Law without the Rule of Lawyers? Why Investment Arbitrators Are from Mars, Trade Adjudicators from Venus' (2015) 109 *American Journal of International Law* 761

Perrone NM and Schneiderman D, 'International Economic Law's Wreckage: Depolitization, Inequality, Precarity' in E Christodoulidis, R Dukes and M

Goldoni (eds), *Research Handbook on Critical Legal Theory* (Edward Elgar 2019)

Pohl J, Mashigo K and Nohen A, 'Dispute Settlement Provisions in International Investment Agreements: A Large Sample Survey' (OECD 2012)

Pollack MA, 'The Legitimacy of the European Court of Justice' in N Grossman and others (eds), *Legitimacy and International Courts* (CUP 2018)

Potestá M and Sobat M, 'Frivolous Claims in International Adjudication: A Study of ICSID Rule 41(5) and of Procedures of Other Courts and Tribunals to Dismiss Claims Summarily' (2012) 3 *Journal of International Dispute Settlement* 137

Poulsen LNS, 'The Importance of BITs for Foreign Direct Investment and Political Risk Insurance' in Karl Sauvant (ed), *Yearbook on International Investment Law and Policy 2009–2010* (OUP 2010)

Poulsen LNS and Aisbett E, 'When the Claim Hits: Bilateral Investment Treaties and Bounded Rational Learning' (2013) 65 *World Politics* 273

Puig S, 'Social Capital in the Arbitration Market' (2014) 25 *The European Journal of International Law* 387

Radi Y, 'Realizing Human Rights in Investment Treaty Arbitration: A Perspective from within the International Investment Law Toolbox' (2011) 37 *North Carolina Journal of International Law and Commercial Regulation* 1107

'"Much Ado About Nothing?" An Appraisal of CETA's Investment Chapter' (2017) 6 *ESIL Reflection* 1

Raff M, *Private Property and Environmental Responsibility: A Comparative Study of German Real Property Law* (Kluwer 2003)

Raz J, *The Authority of Law: Essays on Law and Morality* (Oxford Scholarship Online 2012)

Reisman M, 'The Breakdown of the Control Mechanism in ICSID Arbitration' (1989) 4 *Duke Law Journal* 739

Reisman M and Sloane RD, 'Indirect Expropriation and Its Valuation in the BIT' (2004) Yale Law School Faculty Scholarship Series, Paper 1002

Rimmer M, 'Trojan Horse Clauses: Investor-State Dispute Settlement', Trade and Foreign Investment (Protecting the Public Interest) Bill 2014, Submission 104 – Supplementary Submission to the Australian Parliament

Roberts A, 'Power and Persuasion in Investment Treaty Arbitration: The Dual Role of States' (2010) 104 *American Journal of International Law* 179

'Clash of Paradigms; Actors and Analogies Shaping the Investment Treaty System' (2013) 107 *American Journal of International Law* 45

'Incremental, Systemic and Paradigmatic Reform of Investor–State Arbitration' (2018) 112 *American Journal of International Law* 410

Rogers CA, 'The Politics of International Investment Arbitrators' (2013) 12 *Santa Clara International Law Review* 223

Rosas A and Armati L, *EU Constitutional Law: An Introduction* (Hart 2010)

Rosenfeld F, 'Abstract Interpretations in International Investment Law' in P Pazartzis and others (eds), *Reconceptualising the Rule of Law in Global Governance, Resources, Investment and Trade* (Hart 2016)

Roth BR, *Governmental Illegitimacy in International Law* (OUP 2000)

Rubins N, '*Loewen v United States*: The Burial of an Investor–State Arbitration Claim' (2005) 21 *Arbitration International* 1

Rusche TM, 'Available Actions in the German Courts against the Abuse of Intra-EU Investor-State Arbitration Proceedings' (2021) 6 *IPRax* 494

Sacerdoti G, 'Investment Arbitration under ICSID and UNCITRAL Rules: Prerequisites, Applicable Law, Review of Awards' (2004) 19 *ICSID Review – Foreign Investment Law Journal* 1

Sadowski W, 'Protection of the Rule of Law in the European Union through Investment Treaty Arbitration: Is Judicial Monopolism the Right Response to Illiberal Tendencies in Europe?' (2018) 55 *Common Market Law Review* 1025

Sartre JP, *Critique of Dialectical Reason* (Alan Sheridan-Smith tr, Verso 2004) vol 1

Sass SL, 'Foreign Law in Civil Litigation: A Comparative Survey' (1968) 16 *The American Journal of Comparative Law* 332

Scharpf F, 'Economic Integration, Democracy and the Welfare State' (1997) 4 *Journal of European Policy* 18

'Problem-Solving Effectiveness and Democratic Accountability in the EU' (2003) Max Planck Institute for the Study of Societies Working Paper 03/1 <http://apps.eui.eu/Personal/Researchers/pblokker/Week%206_Scharpf.pdf>

Scheuerman WE, 'Economic Globalization and the Rule of Law' (1999) 6 *Constellations* 3

Schiemann K, 'From Common Law Judge to European Judge' (2005) 13 *Zeitschrift für Europäisches Privatrecht* 741

Schill SW, *The Multilateralisation of International Investment Law* (CUP 2009)

'Enhancing International Investment Law's Legitimacy: Conceptual and Methodological Foundations of a New Public Law Approach' (2011) 52 *Virginia Journal of International Law* 57

Schmidt VA, 'Democracy and Legitimacy in the European Union Revisited: Input, Output and "Throughput"' (2013) 61 *Political Studies* 2

Schneiderman D, 'Global Constitutionalism and Its Legitimacy Problems: Human Rights, Proportionality and International Investment Law' (2017) 12 *Journal of Law and Ethics of Human Rights* 251

Schreuer C, 'Travelling the BIT Route of Waiting Periods, Umbrella Clauses and Forks in the Road' (2004) 5 *The Journal of World Investment and Trade* 231

Shalakany AA, 'Arbitration and the Third World: A Plea for Reassessing Bias under the Specter of Neoliberalism' (2000) 41 *Harvard International Law Review* 419

Shany Y, 'Stronger Together? Legitimacy and Effectiveness of International Courts as Mutually Reinforcing or Undermining Notions' in N Grossman and others (eds), *Legitimacy and International Courts* (CUP 2018)

Shelton D, 'Article 47' in S Peers and others (eds), *The EU Charter of Fundamental Rights: A Commentary* (Hart 2014)

Shihata I, 'The World Bank and Private Sector Development – A Legal Perspective' in F Tschofen and AR Parra (eds), *The World Bank in a Changing World* (Brill 1991) vol 1

Sklair L, 'The Transnational Capitalist Class and the Discourse of Globalisation' (2000) 14 *Cambridge Review of International Affairs* 67

Smit H, 'The Pernicious Institution of the Party-Appointed Arbitrator' (2010) 33 *Columbia FDI Perspectives*

Snell J, 'Non-discriminatory Tax Obstacles in Community Law' (2007) 56 *The International and Comparative Law Quarterly* 339

Spencer ME, 'Weber on Legitimate Norms and Authority' (1970) 21 *The British Journal of Sociology* 123

Stiglitz J, 'The Secret Corporate Takeover' (*Project Syndicate*, 17 May 2015) <https://www.economics.utoronto.ca/gindart/2015-05-13%20-%20The%20secret%20corporate%20takeover.pdf>

Stone Sweet A, *Governing with Judges: Constitutional Politics in Europe* (OUP 2010)

'The European Court of Justice and the Judicialization of EU Governance' (2010) Yale Law School Faculty Scholarship Series Paper No. 70

'Arbitration and Judicialisation' (2011) 1 *Oñati Socio-Legal Series* 1

Strik P, *Shaping the Single European Market in the Field of Foreign Direct Investment* (CUP 2014)

Suse A and Wouters J, 'The Provisional Application of the EU's Mixed Trade and Investment Agreements' (2018) Working Paper No. 201

Szilágyi SG, 'It Is Not Just About Investor-State Arbitration: A Look at Case C-284/16, Achmea BV' (2018) 3 *European Papers* 357

Thurow LC, *The Future of Capitalism: How the Today's Economic Forces Will Shape Tomorrow's World* (William Morrow and Company 1996)

Titi C, 'The Right to Regulate' in MM Mbengue and S Schacherer (eds), *Foreign Investment under the Comprehensive Economic and Trade Agreement (CETA)* (Springer 2019)

Tropper J and Reinisch A, 'The 2020 Termination Agreement of Intra-EU BITs and Its Effect on Investment Arbitration in the EU' (2022) 16 *The Austrian Yearbook on International Arbitration* 301

Ünüvar G, 'Is CETA the Promised Breakthrough? Interpretation and Evaluation of Fair and Equitable Treatment and (Indirect) Expropriation Provisions' (June 2017) iCourts Working Paper Series No. 97 <https://papers.ssrn.com/sol3/papers.cfm?abstract_id=2986049%20>

Van den Berghe A, Schaugg L and de Anzizu H, 'The New Energy Charter Treaty in Light of the Climate Emergency' (*Jus Mundi*, 6 July 2022)

Van Der Loo G and Wessel RA, 'The Non-ratification of Mixed Agreements: Legal Consequences and Solutions' (2017) 54(3) *Common Market Law Review* 735

Vandevelde KJ, 'The Political Economy of a Bilateral Investment Treaty' (1998) 92 *The American Journal of International Law* 621

'A Brief History of International Investment Agreements' (2005) 12 *UC Davis Journal of International Law and Policy* 157

Van Harten HHA, 'The Emerging System of International Investment Arbitration' (DPhil thesis, London School of Economics 2005)

'Pro-Investor or Pro-State Bias in Investment-Treaty Arbitration? Forthcoming Study Gives Cause for Concern' (2012) *Editorials and Commentaries* 136

'Arbitrator Behaviour in Asymmetrical Adjudication: An Empirical Study of Investment Treaty Arbitration' (2012) 50 *Osgoode Hall Law Journal* 211

'Leaders in the Expansive and Restrictive Interpretation of Investment Treaties: A Descriptive Study of ISDS Awards to 2010' (2018) 29 *European Journal of International Law* 507

Van Harten HHA and Loughlin M, 'Investment Treaty Arbitration as a Species of Global Administrative Law' (2006) 17 *European Journal of International Law* 121

Waibel M and Wu Y, 'Are Arbitrators Political? Evidence from International Investment Arbitration' (2017) <https://pdfs.semanticscholar.org/0be8/b7c939d4943917b9879ebd4183afe98b8c55.pdf>

Wälde TW, 'Interpreting Investment Treaties: Experiences and Examples' in *International Investment Law for 21st Century: Essays in Honour of Christoph Schreuer* (OUP 2009)

Weiler JHH, 'The Transformation of Europe' (1991) 100 *Yale Law Journal* 2403

'Europe in Crisis – On "Political Messianism", "Legitimacy" and "the Rule of Law"' (2012) *Singapore Journal of Legal Studies* 248

Witherell WH, 'Developing International Rules for Foreign Investment: OECD's Multilateral Agreement on Investment' (1997) 32 *Business Economics* 38

Wöss H and San Román A, 'Full Compensation, Full Reparation and the But-For Premise' (*Global Arbitration Review*, 29 November 2018) <https://globalarbitrationreview.com/chapter/1177419/full-compensation-full-reparation-and-the-but-for-premise>

Yackee JW, 'Conceptual Differences in the Empirical Study of Bilateral Investment Treaties' (2008) 33 *Brooklyn Journal of International Law* 405

Young AR, 'European Trade Policy in Interesting Times' (2017) 39 *Journal of European Integration* 909

Zárate JMA, 'Legitimacy Concerns of the Proposed Multilateral Investment Court: Is Democracy Possible?' (2019) South Centre Investment Policy Brief

Zhu W, 'Some Considerations on the Civil, Commercial and Investment Dispute Settlement Mechanism between China and the Other Belt and Road Countries' in J Chaisse and J Gorski (eds), *The Belt and Road Initiative: Law, Economics and Politics* (Brill 2018)

## EU Documents, Reports and Other Sources

Cecilia Malmström, EU Commissioner for Trade, 'Discussion on Investment in TTIP at the Meeting of the International Trade Committee of the European Parliament' (Speech/15/4624, 18 March 2015) <https://ec.europa.eu/commission/presscorner/detail/en/SPEECH_15_4624>

Committee on Constitutional Affairs of the European Parliament, 'Opinion of the Committee on Constitutional Affairs for the Committee on International Trade on Recommendations to the Commission on the Negotiations for the Transatlantic Trade and Investment Partnership (TTIP)' (16 May 2015) 2014/2228(INI)

Committee on Foreign Affairs of European Parliament, 'Opinion of the Committee on Foreign Affairs for the Committee on International Trade on Recommendations to the Commission on the Negotiations for the Transatlantic Trade and Investment Partnership (TTIP)' (1 April 2015) 2014/2228(INI)

Committee on Legal Affairs of the European Parliament, 'Opinion of the Committee on Legal Affairs for the Committee on International Trade on Recommendations to the Commission on the Negotiations for the Transatlantic Trade and Investment Partnership (TTIP)' (4 May 2015) 2014/2228(INI)

Communication of 4 October 2006 from the Commission to the Council, the European Parliament, the European Economic and Social Committee and the Committee of the Regions, 'Global Europe: Competing in the World – Contribution to the EU's Growth and Jobs Strategy', COM (2006) 567 final

Communication of 19 July 2018 from the Commission to the European Parliament and the Council, 'Protection of Intra-EU Investment', COM (2018) 547 final

Communication of 18 February 2021 from the Commission to the Council, the European Parliament, the European Economic and Social Committee and the Committee of the Regions, 'Trade Policy Review – An Open, Sustainable and Assertive Trade Policy', COM (2021) 66/2 final

Communication of 22 June 2022 from the Commission to the Council, the European Parliament, the European Economic and Social Committee and the Committee of the Regions, 'The Power of Trade Partnerships: Together for Green and Just Economic Growth', COM (2022) 409 final

Council of the European Union, 'Comprehensive Economic and Trade Agreement (CETA) between Canada, of the One Part, and the European Union and Its

Member States, of the Other Part – Statements to the Council Minutes' (27 October 2016) 13463/1/16

'Conclusions on a Comprehensive European International Investment Policy', 3041st Foreign Affairs Council Meeting (25 October 2010)

'Directives for the Negotiation on the Transatlantic Trade and Investment Partnership between the European Union and the United States of America' (17 June 2013) 11103/13 DCL 1 (declassified)

'Draft Council Conclusions on the Negotiation and Conclusion of EU Trade Agreements' (8 May 2018) 8622/18

'Negotiating Directives for a Convention Establishing a Multilateral Court for the Settlement of Investment Disputes' (20 March 2018) 12981/17 ADD 1 DCL 1

'Negotiating Directives for the Modernisation of the Energy Charter Treaty – Adoption' (2 July 2019) 10745/19

'Negotiating Directives for the Negotiation of an Agreement on Investment Facilitation with the Republic of Angola' (10 May 2021) 8441/21

Declaration of the Representatives of the Governments of the Member States of 15 January 2019 on the Legal Consequences of the Judgment of the Court of Justice in *Achmea* and on Investment Protection in the European Union

Declaration of the Representatives of the Governments of the Member States of 16 January 2019 on the Enforcement of the Judgment of the Court of Justice in *Achmea* and on Investment Protection in the European Union (signed by Sweden, Luxembourg, Malta, Finland, and Slovenia)

Declaration of the Representative of the Government of Hungary of 16 January 2019 on the Legal Consequences of the Judgment of the Court of Justice in *Achmea* and on Investment Protection in the European Union

Directorate-General for External Policies of the European Parliament, 'Comparing International Trade Policies: The EU, United States, EFTA and Japanese PTA Strategies, European Parliament' (February 2014) EXPO/B/INTA/FWC/2009-01/Lot7/36

Directorate-General for External Policies of the European Parliament, 'Investor–State Dispute Settlement Provisions in the EU's International Investment Agreements: Volume 2-Studies' (September 2014) EXPO/B/INTA/2014/08-09-10

Directorate General for External Policies of the European Parliament, 'The Investment Chapters of the EU's International Trade and Investment Agreements in a Comparative Perspective' (September 2015) EP/EXPO/B/INTA/2015/01

Economic and Financial Committee, '2007 EFC Report to the Commission and the Council on the Movement of Capital and the Freedom of Payments' (8 January 2008) 5123/08

Economic and Financial Committee, '2008 EFC Report to the Commission and the Council on the Movement of Capital and the Freedom of Payments' (17 December 2008) 17363/08

Economic and Financial Committee, '2009 EFC Report to the Commission and the Council on the Movement of Capital and the Freedom of Payments' (10 December 2009) 17446/09

European Commission, 'Energy Charter Treaty, Background Note' (16 December 1994) MEMO/94/75 <https://ec.europa.eu/commission/presscorner/detail/en/MEMO_94_75>

European Commission Staff Working Document – Annex to the Communication from the Commission to the Council, the European Parliament, the European Economic and Social Committee and the Committee of the Regions – Global Europe: Competing in the World – Contribution to the EU's Growth and Jobs Strategy (2006) SEC/2006/1230

European Commission, 'Towards a Comprehensive European International Investment Policy', COM (2010) 343

European Commission, 'Trade, Growth and World Affairs: Trade Policy as a Core Component of the EU's 2020 Strategy', COM (2010) 612

European Commission, 'Follow up to the European Parliament Resolution on the Future European International Investment Policy' (5 July 2011)

European Commission, 'Decision Requesting an Opinion of the Court of Justice Pursuant to Article 218(11) TFEU on the Competence of the Union to Sign and Conclude a Free Trade Agreement with Singapore', COM (2014) 8218 final

European Commission, 'Online Public Consultation on Investment Protection and Investor-to-State Dispute Settlement (ISDS) in the Transatlantic Trade and Investment Partnership Agreement (TTIP)', SDW (2015) 3 final

European Commission, 'Trade for All: Towards a More Responsible Trade and Investment Policy', COM (2015) 497

European Commission, 'Investment in TTIP and beyond – The Path for Reform. Enhancing the Right to Regulate and Moving from Current Ad Hoc Arbitration towards an Investment Court' (5 May 2015)

European Commission Press Release, 'Commission Proposes New Investment Court System for TTIP and Other EU Trade and Investment Negotiations' (16 September 2015) <https://ec.europa.eu/commission/presscorner/detail/en/IP_15_5651>

European Commission Press Release, 'EU Finalises Proposal for Investment Protection and Court System for TTIP' (12 November 2015) <http://trade.ec.europa.eu/doclib/press/index.cfm?id=1396>

European Commission, 'A Balanced and Progressive Trade Policy to Harness Globalisation', COM (2017) 492

European Commission, 'Reflection Paper on Harnessing Globalisation', COM (2017) 240

European Commission, 'Multilateral Reform of Investment Dispute Resolution, Impact Assessment', SWD (2017) 302 final

European Commission, 'A New EU Trade Agreement with Japan', Factsheet (July 2018) <http://trade.ec.europa.eu/doclib/docs/2017/july/tradoc_155684.pdf>

European Commission, 'Report from the Commission to the European Parliament and the Council on the Application of Regulation (EU) No 1219/2012 Establishing Transitional Arrangements for Bilateral Investment Agreements between Member States and Third Countries', COM (2020) 134 final

European Commission, 'EU–Mexico Agreement in Principle' (*European Commission*, 6 May 2020) <http://trade.ec.europa.eu/doclib/press/index.cfm?id=1833>

European Commission, 'October Infringements Package: Key Decisions' (30 October 2020)

European Commission, 'December Infringements Package: Key Decisions' (2 December 2021)

European Commission, 'Cross-border Investment within the EU – Clarifying and Supplementing EU Rules' (26 May 2020) <https://ec.europa.eu/info/law/better-regulation/have-your-say/initiatives/12403-Investment-protection-and-facilitation-framework/public-consultation>

European Commission, Inception Impact Assessment, Ares(2020)2716046

European Commission, *A European Green Deal* (2019)

European Commission, 'EU-New Zealand: Text of the agreement' (2022) https://policy.trade.ec.europa.eu/eu-trade-relationships-country-and-region/countries-and-regions/new-zealand/eu-new-zealand-agreement/text-agreement_en

European Commission, *Overview of FTA and Other Trade Negotiations* (2022)

European Parliament, 'Report Containing the European Parliament's Recommendations to the European Commission on the Negotiations for the Transatlantic Trade and Investment Partnership (TTIP)' (1 June 2015) 2014/2228(INI)

European Parliament, 'Resolution of 23 November 2022 on the Outcome of the Modernisation of the Energy Charter Treaty' 2022/2934(RSP)

European Parliamentary Research Service, 'EU Competence in Private Law' (2015)

'Joint Statement: Canada–EU Comprehensive Economic and Trade Agreement (CETA)' (26 February 2016) <https://ec.europa.eu/commission/presscorner/detail/en/STATEMENT_16_446>

'Proposal for a Directive of the European Parliament and of the Council on Corporate Sustainability Due Diligence and amending Directive (EU) 2019/1937,' COM (2022) 71

'Proposal for a Regulation of the European Parliament and of the Council Establishing a Carbon Border Adjustment Mechanism', COM (2021) 564

'Proposal for a Regulation of the European Parliament and of the Council on Applying a Generalised Scheme of Tariff Preferences and Repealing Regulation (EU) No 978/2012 of the European Parliament and of the Council', COM (2021) 579 final

'Report from the Commission to the EP, the Council, the European Economic and Social Committee and the Committee of the Regions on Implementation and Enforcement of EU Trade Agreements', COM (2021) 654 final

## UN Documents, Reports and Sources

Declaration on the Establishment of a New International Economic Order, UNGA Res 3201 (S-VI) (1 May 1974) UN Doc A/RES/320 (S-VI)

Havana Charter for an International Trade Organisation (1948) UN Doc E/CONF.2/78

ILC, 'Draft Articles on the Law of Treaties with Commentaries' (1966)

ILC, 'Report of the International Law Commission to the General Assembly on the Work of Its Thirtieth Session' (1978) UN Doc A/33/10

ILC, 'Fragmentation of International Law: Difficulties Arising From the Diversification and Expansion of International Law' (2006) Report of the Study Group, UN Doc A/CN.4/L682

UNGA, 'Report of the United Nations Commission on International Trade Law Forty-Eighth Session' (July 2015) UN Doc A/70/17

UNGA, 'Report of the United Nations Commission on International Trade Law Fiftieth Session' (July 2017) UN Doc A/72/17

UNCITRAL, 'Arbitration Rules' (2010) <http://www.uncitral.org/pdf/english/texts/arbitration/arb-rules-revised/arb-rules-revised-2010-e.pdf>

UNCITRAL, 'Rules on Transparency in Treaty-Based Investor–State Arbitration' (2014) <https://uncitral.un.org/sites/uncitral.un.org/files/media-documents/uncitral/en/rules-on-transparency-e.pdf>

UNCITRAL, 'Possible Future Work in the Field of Dispute Settlement: Reforms of Investor–State Dispute Settlement (ISDS)' Note by the Secretariat (20 April 2017) UN Doc A/CN.9/917

UNCITRAL, 'Possible Reform of Investor–State Dispute Settlement (ISDS)' Note by the Secretariat (30 July 2019) UN Doc A/CN.9/WG.III/WP.166

UNCITRAL, 'Possible Reform of Investor–State Dispute Settlement (ISDS): Submissions from International Organisations' (13 October 2017) UN Doc A/CN.9/WG.III/WP.143

UNCITRAL, 'Possible Reform of Investor–State Dispute Settlement (ISDS), Submission from the European Union' (12 December 2017) UN Doc A/CN.9/WG.III/WP.145

UNCITRAL, 'Report of Working Group III (Investor–State Dispute Settlement Reform) on the Work of Its Thirty-Fourth Session (Vienna, 27 November – 1 December 2017)' (19 December 2017) UN Doc A/CN.9/930/Rev.1

UNCITRAL, 'Report of Working Group III (Investor–State Dispute Settlement Reform) on the Work of Its Thirty-Fifth Session (New York, 23–27 April 2018)' (14 May 2018) UN Doc A/CN.9/935

UNCITRAL, 'Possible Reform of Investor-State Dispute Settlement (ISDS): Consistency and Related Matters' Note by the Secretariat (28 August 2018) UN Doc A/CN.9/WG.III/WP.150

UNCITRAL, 'Possible Reform of Investor–State Dispute Settlement (ISDS), Ensuring Independence and Impartiality on the Part of Arbitrators and Decision Makers in ISDS' Note by the Secretariat (30 August 2018) UN Doc A/CN.9/WG.III/WP.151

UNCITRAL, 'Possible Reform of Investor–State Dispute Settlement (ISDS), Arbitrators and Decision Makers: Appointment Mechanisms and Related Issues' Note by the Secretariat (30 August 2018) UN Doc A/CN.9/WG.III/WP.152

UNCITRAL, 'Possible Reform of Investor–State Dispute Settlement (ISDS): Cost and Duration' (31 August 2018) UN Doc A/CN.9/WG.III/WP.153

UNCITRAL, 'Possible Reform of Investor–State Dispute Settlement (ISDS), Third-Party Funding' Note by the Secretariat (24 January 2019) A/CN.9/WG.III/WP.157

UNCITRAL, 'Possible Reform of Investor–State Dispute Settlement (ISDS), Submission from the European Union and Its Member States' (24 January 2019) UN Doc A/CN.9/WG.III/WP.159/Add.1

UNCITRAL, 'Submission from the Governments of Chile, Israel and Japan' (15 March 2019) UN Doc A/CN.9/WG.III/WP.163

UNCITRAL, 'Report of Working Group III (Investor–State Dispute Settlement Reform) on the Work of Its Thirty-Seventh Session (New York, 1–5 April 2019)' (9 April 2019) A/CN.9/970

UNCITRAL, 'Possible Reform of Investor–State Dispute settlement (ISDS), Submission from the Government of Brazil' (11 June 2019) UN Doc A/CN.9/WG.III/WP.171

UNCITRAL, 'Possible Reform of Investor–State Dispute Settlement (ISDS), Submission from the Government of South Africa' (17 July 2019) UN Doc A/CN.9/WG.III/WP.176

UNCITRAL, 'Possible Reform of Investor–State Dispute Settlement (ISDS), Submission from the Government of China' (19 July 2019) UN Doc A/CN.9/WG.III/WP.177

UNCITRAL, 'Possible Reform of Investor–State Dispute Settlement (ISDS)' Note by the Secretariat (30 July 2019) UN Doc A/CN.9/WG.III/WP.166

UNCITRAL, 'Possible Reform of Investor–State Dispute Settlement (ISDS): Advisory Centre' (25 July 2019) UN Doc A/CN.9/WG.III/WP.168

UNCITRAL, 'Possible Reform of Investor-State Dispute Settlement (ISDS), Submission from the Governments of Chile, Israel, Japan, Mexico and Peru' Note by the Secretariat (2 October 2019) UN Doc A/CN.9/WG.III/WP.182

UNCITRAL, 'Possible Reform of Investor–State Dispute Settlement (ISDS), Multilateral Instrument on ISDS Reform' Note by the Secretariat (16 January 2020) UN Doc A/CN.9/WG.III/WP.194

UNCITRAL, 'Report of Working Group III (Investor–State Dispute Settlement Reform) on the Work of Its Thirty-Eighth Session' (28 January 2020) UN Doc A/CN.9/1004

UNCITRAL, 'Report of Working Group III (Investor–State Dispute Settlement Reform) on the Work of Its Resumed Thirty-Eighth Session' (28 January 2020) UN Doc A/CN/9/1004/Add.1

UNCITRAL, 'Workplan to Implement ISDS Reform and Resource Requirements' (17 March 2021) UN Doc A/CN.9/WG.III/WP.206

UNCITRAL, 'Initial Draft on Standing Multilateral Mechanism: The Selection and Appointment of ISDS Tribunal Members and Related Matters, Comments from the EU and Its Member States' (November 2021)

UNCITRAL, 'Cost and Financing of a Permanent Multilateral Body', Outline of the Working Paper, Draft for Comments Only (December 2021)

UNCITRAL, 'Expedited Arbitration Rules' (2021)

UNCITRAL, 'Possible Reform of Investor–State Dispute Settlement (ISDS), Multilateral Instrument on ISDS Reform' Note by the Secretariat (22 July 2022) UN Doc A/CN.9/WG.III/WP.221

UNCITRAL, 'Possible Reform of Investor–State Dispute Settlement (ISDS), Draft Codes of Conduct and Commentary' Note by the Secretariat (23 November 2022) UN Doc A/CN.9/WG.III/WP.223

UNCITRAL, 'Working Group III: Investor–State Dispute Settlement Reform' <https://uncitral.un.org/en/working_groups/3/investor-state>

UNCITRAL, 'Investor–State Dispute Settlement Reform: On-Line Resources' Working Group III: Investor–State Dispute Settlement Reform <https://uncitral.un.org/en/library/online_resources/investor-state_dispute>

UNCTAD, 'Lessons from the MAI' (1999) UNCTAD/ITE/IIT/Misc.22

UNCTAD, 'International Investment Agreements: Key Issues' (2004) UNCTAD/ITE/IIT/2004/10 (Vol. I)

UNCTAD, 'Recent Developments in International Investment Agreements' (2005) IIA Monitor No. 2, UNCTAD/WEB/ITE/IIT/2005/1

UNCTAD, 'Scope and Definition (A Sequel) – UNCTAD Series on Issues in International Investment Agreements II' (2011) UNCTAD/DIAE/IA/2010/2

UNCTAD, 'Fair and Equitable Treatment' (2012) Issues in International Investment Agreements (Second series) UNCTAD/DIAE/IA/2011/5

UNCTAD, 'Bilateral Investment Treaties 1959–1999' (2000) UNCTAD/ITE/IIA/2

UNCTAD, 'Trade and Development Report 2014: Global Governance and Policy Space for Development' (2014) UNCTAD/TDR/2014

UNCTAD, 'UNCTAD's Reform Package for the International Investment Regime (2018 edition)' (2018) <https://investmentpolicy.unctad.org/publications/1190/unctad-s-reform-package-for-the-international-investment-regime-2018-edition->

UNCTAD, *Investment Policy Hub* <https://investmentpolicy.unctad.org>

UNDOC, 'The Bangalore Principles of Judicial Conduct' (2018) ECOSOC 2006/23

United Nations Economic and Social Council (ECOSOC), 'The Promotion of International Flow of Private Capital: Progress Report by the Secretary General' (26 February 1960) E/3325

## Other Documents, Reports and Online Sources

'300+ Civil Society Organisations from 73 Countries Urge Real Reform at United Nations Discussions on Corporate Investor Rights' (Center for International Environmental Law, 30 October 2018) <https://www.ciel.org/news/300-civil-society-organizations-from-73-countries-urge-real-reform-at-united-nations-discussions-on-corporate-investor-rights/>

American Chamber of Commerce to the European Union, 'AmCham EU's Response to the European Commission's Public Consultation on Modalities for Investment Protection and ISDS in TTIP' Consultation Response (11 July 2014) <https://www.amchameu.eu/sites/default/files/position_papers/file_20140717_105720_LFEcSE_0.pdf>

'An Open Letter to the Chair of UNCITRAL Working Group III and to all Participating States Concerning the Reform of the Investor–State Dispute Settlement: Addressing the Asymmetry of ISDS' (Erasmus University Rotterdam, 13 February 2019) <https://www.eur.nl/en/news/erasmus-institute-public-knowledge>

Client Earth, 'Potential Solutions for Phase 3: Aligning the Objectives of UNCITRAL Working Group III with States' International Obligations to Combat Climate Change' <https://uncitral.un.org/sites/uncitral.un.org/files/media-documents/uncitral/en/wgiii_clientearth.pdf>

Columbia Center on Sustainable Development (CCSI), International Institute for Environment and Development (IIED) and International Institute for Sustainable Development (IISD) Joint Submission to UNCITRAL, 'UNCITRAL Working Group III on ISDS Reform: How Cross-Cutting Issues Reshape Reform Options' (15 July 2019)

Columbia Center on Sustainable Development (CCSI), International Institute for Environment and Development (IIED) and International Institute for Sustainable Development (IISD) Workplan Submission (1 March 2021)

Commission of Venice, 'The Rule of Law Checklist' (Council of Europe 2016)

Corporate Counsel International Arbitration Group, 'Investor–State Dispute Settlement (ISDS) Reform, Submission by the Corporate Counsel International Arbitration Group (CCIAG) to UNCITRAL Working Group III' (18 December 2019)

Council of Europe, European Charter on the Statute for Judges (1998)

Recommendation CM/Rec (2010)12 of the Committee of Ministers to Member States on Judges: Independence, Efficiency and Responsibilities (adopted by the Committee of Ministers on 17 November 2010 at the 1098th meeting of the Ministers' Deputies)

Draft Convention on the Protection of Foreign Property, Text with Notes and Comments (OECD Publication No. 15637, December 1962)

Energy Charter Secretariat, 'Decision of the Energy Charter Conference: Adoption by Correspondence – Policy Options for Modernisation of the ECT' (6 October 2019) CCDEC 2019

'Decision of the Energy Charter Conference' (24 June 2022) CCDEC 2022

European Federation for Investment Law and Arbitration, 'EFILA's Written Comments Made at the UNCITRAL Working Group on ISDS Reform' (June 2018)

German Magistrates Association, 'Opinion No 04/16 on the Establishment of an Investment Tribunal in TTIP' (February 2016)

German Model Bilateral Investment Treaty (2008) <https://investmentpolicy.unctad.org/international-investment-agreements/treaty-files/2865/download>

Government of the Republic of Croatia, Answer to the Written Question Posed by MP Goran Aleksic in Relation to a Proceeding before ICSID in Washington (October 2017) (in Croatian) <https://vlada.gov.hr/UserDocsImages//2016/Sjednice/2017/10%20listopad/64%20sjednica%20Vlade%20Republike%20Hrvatske//64%20-%2024.3.pdf>

Government of the Netherlands, Ministry of Economic Affairs and Climate of the Netherlands, Letter to the Parliament (17 May 2021)

Group of the Progressive Alliance of Socialists & Democrats in the European Parliament, 'S&D Position Paper on Investor–State Dispute Settlement Mechanisms in Ongoing Trade Negotiations' (4 March 2015) <https://www.socialistsanddemocrats.eu/sites/default/files/position_paper/ISDS_mechanisms_ongoing_trade_negotiations_en_150304.pdf>

International Bar Association Guidelines on Conflict of Interest in International Arbitration <https://www.ibanet.org/Publications/publications_IBA_guides_and_free_materials.aspx>

ICSID, 'History of the ICSID Convention, Documents Concerning the Origin and the Formulation of the Convention on the Settlement of Investment Disputes between States and Nationals of Other States' (1968)

The ICSID Rules of Procedure for Arbitration Proceedings (April 2006) <https://icsid.worldbank.org/en/Documents/icsiddocs/ICSID%20Convention%20English.pdf>

ICSID, Amended Rules (July 2022)

International Commission of Jurists, 'International Principles on the Independence and Accountability of Judges, Lawyers and Prosecutors' (2007) Practitioner Guide No. 1

IPCC, 'Climate Change 2022, Mitigation of Climate Change', Working Group III Contribution to the IPCC Sixth Assessment Report (4 April 2022)

Jaap-Verbeek B, 'A Social Mapping of the UNCITRAL Process on ISDS Reform' (2020) <https://kumu.io/bjverbeek/uncitral#uncitral>

Model Text for the Indian Bilateral Investment Treaty <https://dea.gov.in/sites/default/files/ModelBIT_Annex_0.pdf>

NAFTA Free Trade Commission, 'Notes of Interpretation of Certain Chapter 11 Provisions' (31 July 2001) <http://www.sice.oas.org/tpd/nafta/Commission/CH11understanding_e.asp>

Netherlands Model Investment Agreement (2019)

<https://investmentpolicy.unctad.org/international-investment-agreements/treaty-files/5832/download>

OECD, 'OECD Guidelines for Multinational Enterprises' (OECD 2018) <https://mneguidelines.oecd.org>

'Investment Treaties and Climate Change', Public Consultation, Compilation of Submissions (13 April 2022)

Pew Research Center and Bertelsmann Foundation, 'Support in Principle for US–EU Trade Deal, But Some Americans and Germans Wary of TTIP Details' (*Pew Research Center*, 9 April 2014) <https://www.pewresearch.org/global/2014/04/09/support-in-principle-for-u-s-eu-trade-pact/>

Polish Government, 'White Paper on the Reform of Polish Judiciary' (7 March 2018) <https://www.premier.gov.pl/files/files/white_paper_en_full.pdf>

Public Citizen, 'Recommendations for UNCITRAL ISDS Discussions' (15 July 2019)

SADC Model Bilateral Investment Treaty Template with Commentary (July 2012) <https://www.iisd.org/itn/wp-content/uploads/2012/10/sadc-model-bit-template-final.pdf>

'Statement on the Modernisation of the Energy Charter Treaty' (3 November 2020)

'Trading Together – For Strong and Democratically Legitimized EU International Agreements' (25 January 2017) <https://www.trading-together-declaration.org>

Tweede Kamer der Staten-Generaal, 'The Role of National Parliaments in Free Trade Agreements' (17 June 2014) <https://www.parlament.mt/media/89931/81.pdf>

'Improvements to CETA and beyond' (6 March 2015)

The Secretariat of the ECT, 'Statistics of the ECT Cases' (10 January 2023) <https://www.energychartertreaty.org/fileadmin/DocumentsMedia/Statistics/All_statistics_-_10_January_2023.pdf>

UK Government Department for International Trade, 'UK–US Trade & Investment Working Group' (2–7 November 2018) 32–33 (*Global Justice Now*, 27 November 2019) <https://www.globaljustice.org.uk/news/2019/nov/27/explosive-leaked-trade-papers-show-nhs-chlorinated-chicken-already-table-us-trade>

US Model Bilateral Investment Treaty (2012) <https://ustr.gov/sites/default/files/BIT%20text%20for%20ACIEP%20Meeting.pdf>

Queen Mary University, '2020 QMUL-CCIAG Survey: Investors' Perceptions of ISDS' (May 2020)

World Bank, 'Disputes over Defaults on External Debt, Expropriation, and Breach of Contract' (July 2001) Operational Manual OP 7.40

World Trade Organization, 'World Trade Report 2011, The WTO and Preferential Trade Agreements: From Co-existence to Coherence' (2011)

# INDEX

For EU product safety concerns, contact us at Calle de José Abascal, 56–1°, 28003 Madrid, Spain or eugpsr@cambridge.org.

www.ingramcontent.com/pod-product-compliance
Lightning Source LLC
LaVergne TN
LVHW011659200926
848484LV00004B/992